D0018695

Borneo

Chris Rowthorn

Muhammad Cohen, China Williams

RETIRÉ DE LA COLLECTION UNIVERSELLE

Bibliothèque et Archives nationales du Québec

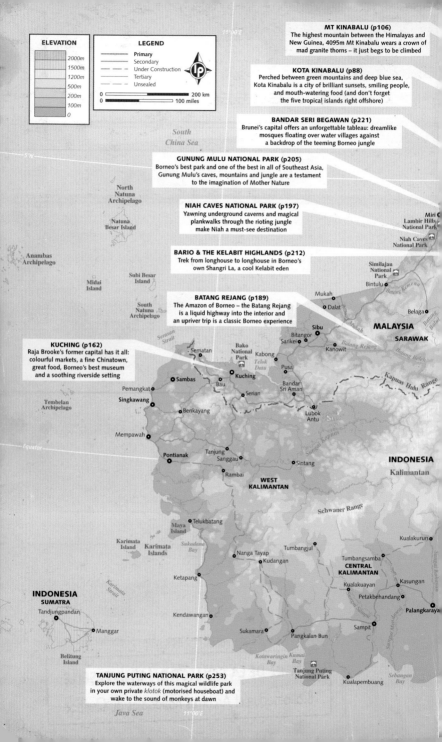

MT KINABALU (p106)
The highest mountain between the Himalayas and New Guinea, 4095m Mt Kinabalu wears a crown of mad granite thorns – it just begs to be climbed

KOTA KINABALU (p88)
Perched between green mountains and deep blue sea, Kota Kinabalu is a city of brilliant sunsets, smiling people, and mouth-watering food (and don't forget the five tropical islands right offshore)

BANDAR SERI BEGAWAN (p221):
Brunei's capital offers an unforgettable tableau: dreamlike mosques floating over water villages against a backdrop of the teeming Borneo jungle

GUNUNG MULU NATIONAL PARK (p205)
Borneo's best park and one of the best in all of Southeast Asia, Gunung Mulu's caves, mountains and jungle are a testament to the imagination of Mother Nature

NIAH CAVES NATIONAL PARK (p197)
Yawning underground caverns and magical plankwalks through the rioting jungle make Niah a must-see destination

BARIO & THE KELABIT HIGHLANDS (p212)
Trek from longhouse to longhouse in Borneo's own Shangri La, a cool Kelabit eden

BATANG REJANG (p189)
The Amazon of Borneo – the Batang Rejang is a liquid highway into the interior and an upriver trip is a classic Borneo experience

KUCHING (p162)
Raja Brooke's former capital has it all: colourful markets, a fine Chinatown, great food, Borneo's best museum and a soothing riverside setting

TANJUNG PUTING NATIONAL PARK (p253)
Explore the waterways of this magical wildlife park in your own private *klotok* (motorised houseboat) and wake to the sound of monkeys at dawn

THE IBAN

Despite their former reputation as head-hunters, the Iban are now more renowned for their great hospitality and this is particularly evident during their harvest festival, Gawai Dayak (1 June). Visitors to their longhouses are feted and are expected to visit every room to sample the food and drink. Expect lots of *tuak,* a potent homemade rice liquor.

Martin Heng, Lonely Planet staff, Australia

4

PETER GUTTMAN/CORBIS

THE NIAH CAVES

Take the boardwalk back through the ages to Homo sapiens' ancient camp site, the Niah Caves (p197). Bring a good torch and explore the caves network; you can't miss the Great Cave or the Moon Cave, nature's cathedrals of light and darkness. It's worth the dimly lit ramble to the Painted Cave, a burial gallery of earthen abstractions, ancient petroglyphs and remnant 'death ships'.

Debra Herrmann, Lonely Planet staff, Australia

GLENN BEANLAND

5

TOM COCKREM

6 **MARKETS**

Don't miss the open market in Kuching (p166) for cheap, tasty food in a vibrant atmosphere. Try *roti canai* (flatbread with chickpeas) and *roti telur* (flatbread with eggs) – perfect with the accompanying curry to dip it in. Whatever you do, try *midin*, a local jungle fern often served stir-fried with *belachan* (shrimp paste).

Leah Schwartz, traveller

RAFFLESIA

Trek through forest at Poring Hot Springs (p116), led by a local village guide, to witness the rare event of a giant rafflesia, the world's largest flower, in bloom. Emitting a stench of rotting meat to attract the flies, this flower takes around nine months to bloom and then only stays in bloom for about five days.

Lisa Vitaris, Bluelist, traveller

8

CHRISTER FREDRIKS

PETER SOLNESS

7

KUCHING

The laid-back locals and scenic views make Kuching (p162) an undeniably relaxing experience. Unhurried and unassuming, this small fishing village cannot fail to charm you. Rainbows of tiny canoes line the water's edge and bob peacefully in the breeze. Fishers and fruit sellers encourage you to sample their tasty goods, knowing you'll be back for more.

footprint2008, Bluelist, traveller

MICHAEL

9

PULAU SIPADAN

Stepping off the beach at Pulau Sipadan (p150) I have no idea of the world I am about to enter. The shallow waters of the beach quickly give way to a sheer 900m vertical wall teeming with the most incredible ocean life. The island is in fact a column of coral rising almost a kilometre from the dark seabed below. Tropical fish and gigantic pacific green sea turtles brush past while moray eels and leopard sharks patrol the murky depths below. Schools of chevron barracuda, thousands in number, surround me.

Eoin Dunlevy, Lonely Planet staff, Australia

Contents

Regional Map Contents

Brunei
p220

Sabah
p88

Sarawak
p160

Kalimantan
p236

Destination Borneo

'Going up the river arms was like traveling back to the earliest beginnings of the world, when vegetation rioted on the earth and the big trees were kings.'

Joseph Conrad wrote about the Congo, but he may as well have been talking about Borneo. When you're deep in the heart of the Borneo jungle, it's easy to imagine that you've slipped back in time to a world where plants and animals went about their business undisturbed by human beings.

First and foremost, Borneo is the result of a grand experiment. It answers the question of what would happen if you put a giant island right on the equator, sprinkled it with a vast amount of genetic material, soaked it with heaping quantities of sunlight and water, and then waited a few million years. The result is an explosion of life in exuberant abundance – Mother Nature's wildest fantasy.

Borneo is 1000 species of orchids with heavenly aromas, and flowers three-feet across that stink like rotting meat. It is towering dipterocarp trees shrouded in a lattice of strangler figs and wide-eyed orangutans peering from the green walls of forest. It is hornbills soaring above canopy like modern-day pterodactyls or iridescent snakes that look like slithering gemstones. It is coral reefs that burst with clouds of tropical fish and mangrove swamps where crocodiles wait with patient eyes.

Not surprisingly, the people who call Borneo home are almost as diverse as the nature that surrounds them. From the dozens of indigenous peoples who've been on the scene for at least 40,000 years, to the more recent immigrants like the Chinese and Indians, walking down a crowded Borneo street is like snorkelling over a particularly healthy coral reef: the eye is drawn here and there by flashes of brilliant colour and beguiling shapes.

With such a rich cultural and natural bounty, it's hardly surprising that Borneo was one of the great prizes of the imperial age, and the modern-day map of the island reflects its varied ancestry. The Indonesian state of Kalimantan occupies almost two-thirds of the island, laying claim to its entire southern region; the Malaysian states of Sabah and Sarawak occupy most of the island's north; while the tiny oil-rich sultanate of Brunei lays claim to two slivers of land between Sabah and Sarawak.

Unfortunately, the riches of the Borneo environment are an irresistible temptation for modern industrial society. The primary tropical rainforest that once blanketed the island almost from coast to coast has been cut right back to the spine of the island and a few pockets in other parts of Sabah and Brunei. A quick look at any recent satellite image of the island only confirms the worst: the network of logging roads expands with each passing day, creating rivers of dirt down which the trees of the rainforest are funnelled to the waiting world.

Despite the damage done by modernity, Borneo is still a place with great attractions. Both above and below the surface of the ocean, the natural environment of Borneo is among the most biodiverse in the world. And if you like to experience nature by getting right among it, this is the place for you – Borneo is a vast natural playground where you can spelunk, jungle trek, scuba dive and snorkel to your heart's content. And with cheap airfares from Jakarta, Kuala Lumpur, Singapore and Bangkok, along with comfortable, modern cities along its coasts, it's easy to see why adventure travellers the world over are making tracks to Borneo.

'Borneo is 1000 species of orchids with heavenly aromas, and flowers three-feet across that stink like rotting meat.'

Getting Started

Despite its image as one of the wildest places on earth, Borneo is an incredibly easy place in which to travel. In the coastal areas of Sabah, Sarawak and Brunei, you will find good infrastructure, excellent transport and a decent range of good accommodation. Kalimantan is generally less developed and more challenging, but it's still within reach of ordinary adventurous travellers. Indeed, perhaps the biggest surprise for most travellers to Borneo is just how 'first world' it all seems.

In terms of cost, the essentials of life – food, lodging and most forms of transport – are quite cheap indeed. It's the luxuries – coastal resorts, independent river-travel and journeys deep into the jungle – that can really add up.

WHEN TO GO

Travel is possible any time in Borneo. It's hot and humid, with ample rain falling throughout the year, usually in the form of afternoon showers. While there's little or no seasonal temperature variation, there is an indistinct rainy season from October to February, but it's not usually enough to interfere with travel. It's sometimes said that the best time to climb Mt Kinabalu is between March and October, but most locals agree that it's pointless to try to determine a 'dry' season on the mountain.

See Climate Charts (p291) for more information

If you're interested in indigenous culture, you might consider visiting at the beginning of June, when the local Dayak peoples of Sarawak hold their Gawai Dayak celebrations. Otherwise, the best time to visit Borneo is whenever you can find the time.

See Climate (p291) for more information on the weather.

DON'T LEAVE HOME WITHOUT...

What you bring to Borneo will depend on what you plan to do there – if you plan to go up Mt Kinabalu, go jungle trekking or diving, you'll have to consider your kit carefully. The most important thing to remember is to travel light – dragging a heavy pack or suitcase around is troublesome in any climate, but in the tropics, it's murder. Keep in mind that even if you forget something, you can buy most things that you need in the bigger cities such as Kota Kinabalu or Kuching. The exceptions are specialised outdoor gear such as leech socks, good backpacks, snorkelling and diving gear, and really large-sized clothing.

Unless you've got business in Borneo, you won't need any formal clothes. Men should keep in mind that most adult males in Borneo don't wear shorts in cities or towns, particularly not in smart restaurants or hotels. Likewise, women should remember that Borneo is largely Muslim and relatively discreet clothing is a good idea – you certainly don't have to cover your hair, but walking around with a tank top or bikini top is a bad idea.

Here are a few things you should definitely consider bringing:

- Leech socks – if you're going jungle trekking, you'll be glad for these when the leeches make their move.
- Fast-drying synthetic clothing – cotton really never dries in the jungle, so bring something that will dry fast and not weigh you down.
- Good books – there are a few good bookstores in Sabah and Sarawak, but if you're picky about what you read, you'll be happy you brought some from home.
- Medicine – you can get most medicines in Borneo but it can take time.
- Gifts – if you plan to visit longhouses, a few trinkets from home will be appreciated.
- A song – after your longhouse hosts treat you to a song, they'll expect you to reciprocate.

SAMPLE DAILY BUDGETS

SABAH & SARAWAK
Budget

Guesthouse accommodation (per person): RM15

Two *kedai kopi* (coffee shop) meals: RM7

One bus trip: RM5

One entry fee: RM3

Snacks, drinks and sundries: RM5

Total: RM35

Midrange

Simple hotel accommodation (per person): RM50

Two typical meals: RM20

One bus trip: RM5

One taxi ride: RM10

One entry fee: RM3

Snacks, drinks and sundries: RM10

Total: RM98

BRUNEI
Budget

Guesthouse accommodation (per person): B$35

Two *kedai kopi* meals: B$6

One bus trip: B$2

Snacks, drinks and sundries: B$5

Total: B$48

Midrange

Simple hotel accommodation (per person): B$60

Two typical meals: B$25

One bus trip: B$2

One taxi ride: B$10

Snacks, drinks and sundries: B$10

Total: B$107

KALIMANTAN
Budget

Guesthouse accommodation (per person): 80,000Rp

Two simple meals: 20,000Rp

One bus trip: 15,000Rp

Snacks, drinks and sundries: 10,000Rp

Total: 125,000Rp

Midrange

Simple hotel accommodation (per person): 250,000Rp

Two typical meals: 35,000Rp

One bus trip: 15,000Rp

One taxi ride: 30,000Rp

Snacks, drinks and sundries: 20,000Rp

Total: 350,000Rp

COSTS & MONEY

Borneo can be a very cheap place in which to travel. Food, in particular, is generally very cheap. Indeed, we know of few places where you can eat so well for so little. Meals in a typical *kedai kopi* (coffee shop) average about US$2. Accommodation costs are roughly what you expect to pay in other parts of Southeast Asia. Public transport is quite cheap and even air travel is within the reach of most budget travellers.

If all you plan to do is see a few of the main sights and relax on a beach somewhere, you will find Borneo competitive with, say, Thailand. It's when you want to experience some of Borneo's famous jungles or coral reefs that things can get expensive. Trips into Sabah's two brilliant conservations areas, Danum Valley and Maliau Basin, will really dent your wallet, as will diving in places such as Pulau Sipadan or Layang Layang. Likewise, if you've read Redmond O'Hanlon's *Into the Heart of Borneo* and want to follow in his footsteps, you'll have to shell out upwards of US$1000.

Fortunately, some of Borneo's greatest highlights, including Gunung Mulu National Park, Mt Kinabalu, Niah Caves and Tunku Abdul Rahman National Park, are all reasonably inexpensive to visit.

HOW MUCH?
SABAH & SARAWAK

Litre of petrol: RM1.90

Street snack (Chinese pork bun): RM1

Cup of tea in *kedai kopi*: 50 sen

T-shirt: RM10

Beer (large bottle of Tiger beer): RM10

Litre of bottled water: RM1.50

TRAVEL LITERATURE

Borneo has occupied the world's imagination for centuries and there is no shortage of books about the island. Easily the best recent title is *Stranger in the Forest* by Eric Hansen, in which the author recounts his 1976 journey across the island in the company of Penan guides. It is not just the difficulty of the feat – Hansen is the only Westerner ever to cross Borneo on foot – it is the author's brilliant and sensitive storytelling that makes the book a classic. One cannot read the book without a sense of real sadness, for the world and the people Hansen describes in his book are now almost completely gone. If you read only one book before going to Borneo, make it this one.

The most popular book about Borneo is Redmond O'Hanlon's *Into the Heart of Borneo*, which is a humourous account of the author's 1983 journey up a river in Sarawak to a mountain on the border with Kalimantan. While O'Hanlon makes a bit much of what was a fairly unremarkable journey, one cannot help but enjoy his colourful narrative.

Espresso with Headhunters: A Journey Through the Jungles of Borneo by John Wassner tells of a more extensive and adventurous recent river/land trip by an Australian traveller (and inveterate caffeine and nicotine addict). Not nearly as famous as O'Hanlon's book, this book actually gives a more realistic account of what life is really like in Sarawak. We only wish he had chosen a different title – it's time to let the whole headhunter thing in Borneo die a quiet death.

Three Came Home by Agnes Newton Keith cannot strictly be called travel literature, but it's one of the most fascinating books on Borneo. Newton Keith spent most of WWII in a Japanese prisoner-of-war camp in Sarawak with her young son. The woman's toughness and hope in the face of appalling conditions makes a great and inspiring read. This book has recently been reprinted and is easy to find online. It's the follow-up to her excellent *Land Below the Wind*, which tells of her life in Borneo before the war.

Another book about Borneo during the war is *Escapes and Incursions* by Kevin Smith. The book covers two main themes: escapes by mostly Australian prisoners of war before and during the famous Sandakan Death March (the escapes section), and secret missions by Allied forces in Borneo during the war (the incursions section). Again, it's not typical travel lit, but if you enjoy wartime history, this is an absolute must.

If you climb Mt Kinabalu, you can't help but notice the gaping chasm of Low's Gully to your right as you climb the final summit pyramid. *Kinabalu Escape: The Soldier's Story* by Rich Mayfield tells of the British Army's ill-fated 1994 attempt to descend the gully. The expedition, which was a textbook case in how not to run an expedition, led to an expensive rescue operation and the near-deaths of several team members. Think of it as a tropical version of *Into Thin Air*.

Finally, if you want to get a sense for what life was like in Borneo during the time of the 'white rajas', you'll do no better than *My Life in Sarawak* by Margaret Brooke, the Ranee of Sarawak (wife of Charles Brooke). This adventurous woman embraced Borneo wholeheartedly and her sympathetic portraits of its people are fascinating.

HOW MUCH? KALIMANTAN

Litre of petrol: 4500Rp

Street snack (a few satay sticks): 4000Rp

Cup of tea in *kedai kopi*: 2,000Rp

T-shirt: 20,000Rp

Beer (large bottle of Bintang beer): 20,000Rp

Litre of bottled water: 3000Rp

HOW MUCH? BRUNEI

Litre of petrol: B$0.72

Street snack (a few satay sticks): B$2.50

Cup of tea in *kedai kopi*: B$1

T-shirt: B$10

Beer: unavailable

Litre of bottled water: B$1

INTERNET RESOURCES

There's no better place to start your web explorations than at lonely planet.com. Here you'll find succinct summaries of travelling to most places on earth, postcards from other travellers and the Thorn Tree bulletin board, where you can ask questions or dispense advice when you get back. You can also find travel news and updates to many of our most popular guidebooks.

Other websites with useful Borneo information are:

Brunei Government (www.brunei.gov.bn) The Brunei government's site has daily news updates, links to all the ministries and a brief background on the country.

Google Earth (http://earth.google.com) This service is one of the best ways to check out exactly where Borneo's forests remain intact and where they've been logged.

Indonesia: Society & Culture (http://coombs.anu.edu.au/WWWVLPages/IndonPages/WWWVL-Indonesia.html) The Australian National University's links site is a good place to do some serious Indonesia/Kalimantan research.

Tourism Malaysia (http://travel.tourism.gov.my) Malaysia's national tourism organisation has some limited information about Sabah and Sarawak on its site.

World Wildlife Fund Heart of Borneo Page (www.wwf.org.uk/heartofborneo) This site has good information on the Heart of Borneo project and an absolutely heartbreaking graphic on forest loss in Borneo.

Itineraries
CLASSIC ROUTES

THE BEST OF BORNEO   Two Weeks

Fly into **Kota Kinabalu** (KK; p88) and spend a day or two in the city getting acclimatised to the tropics. A day trip out to the palm-fringed islands of **Tunku Adbul Rahman National Park** (p102) is highly recommended.

Next, head up to **Kinabalu National Park** (p106) and attempt Mt Kinabalu.

Drag your weary limbs back to KK and then fly to **Miri** (p200) and hit **Niah Caves National Park** (p197). Return to Miri and then fly up to **Gunung Mulu National Park** (p205). You'll want to spend as long as you can here checking out the caves, the canopy walkway and the Pinnacles.

From Gunung Mulu, there are several ways to return to KK: heading overland via the Headhunter's Trail to Limbang and from there back to KK, taking a series of boats down the Sungai Baram to Miri and then on to KK or flying directly from Mulu to KK.

Some of Borneo's best sights are clustered in the northwest part of the island, within easy travelling distance of Borneo's main gateway, the city of Kota Kinabalu. This popular two-week itinerary is convenient and easy – apart from the climb up Mt Kinabalu. It's the best way to see some of Borneo's real highlights in a limited time.

KK TO KUCHING: A COASTAL ODYSSEY   One Month

The northwest coast of Borneo is adventure from north to south. This journey down the coast from KK to Kuching is the best way to take it all in. You'll experience the island's three most important cities, several of its best national parks and you'll have the opportunity to head up the Batang Rejang, the so-called 'Amazon of Borneo'.

Fly into **KK** (p88) and spend a few days settling into the old backpacking life. Wander the night market and take a boat out to the islands of **Tunku Abdul Rahman National Park** (p102).

Then, head up to **Kinabalu National Park** (p106) and do battle with the granite beast. After bagging the summit, you might head to Poring Hot Springs to soak them weary bones or search for the elusive rafflesia.

Next, take the ferry from KK to **Pulau Labuan** (p121) and on to **Muara** (p230) in Brunei, the port of **Bandar Seri Begawan** (BSB; p221). Spend a day or two in BSB checking out the museums and mosques and then take the speedboat ride through the marshes to **Bangar** (p233), which is one of Borneo's best boat rides.

Continue overland to **Miri** (p200) and take your pick: fly up to **Gunung Mulu National Park** (p205) for some caving and climbing or fly up to the **Kelabit Highlands** (p212) for a spot of longhouse trekking. Return to Miri and continue down the coast to **Niah Caves National Park** (p197) to check out the limestone caves there.

From Niah, head onward to **Bintulu** (p194), with a possible sidetrip to **Similajau National Park** (p196), then it's on to **Sibu** (p185), where you can embark on a river journey up the **Batang Rejang** (p189) into the interior, stopping in **Kapit** and **Belaga**.

Head back to Sibu and then dash down to wonderful **Kuching** (p162) and then fly back to KK.

ROADS LESS TRAVELLED

THE FULL MONTY: RIGHT ROUND BORNEO   Two Months

A trip right around the coast of the world's third-largest island is for hardcore travellers. Fly into **KK** (p88) and go down the northwest coast of Borneo to **Kuching** (p162). The usual route is via ferry from KK to **Pulau Labuan** (p121) and on to **Muara** (p230) in Brunei, the port of **Bandar Seri Begawan** (BSB; p221). Be sure to include a side trip to **Bangar** (p233).

From BSB, travel to **Miri** (p200) and consider a side trip into **Gunung Mulu National Park** (p205) or a flight up to **Bario** in the **Kelabit Highlands** (p212). Continue down to **Niah Caves National Park** (p197). From Niah, travel to **Bintulu** (p194) and onward to **Sibu** (p185), where you can catch a boat for the river journey up **Batang Rejang** (p189). Head back to Sibu and then to **Kuching** (p162), Borneo's cultural capital. From Kuching, head overland to **Pontianak** (p237) in Kalimantan. After checking out the city, fly south to **Pangkalan Bun** (p250), from which you can visit **Tanjung Puting National Park** (p253). Then, continue along the coast to **Banjarmasin** (p260), where you can check out the surrounding rivers.

Next, go up to **Balikpapan** (p267), and on to **Samarinda** (p272), the gateway to **Sungai Mahakam** (p277). Head up the river into the interior and then return to Samarinda. The next leg up to **Berau** (Tanjung Redep; p282) is a 16-hour hell ride. After the journey, head out to **Pulau Derawan** (p284) and treat yourself to some relaxing island life. Continue by boat up to **Tarakan** (p287), where you can catch boats onward to **Tawau** (p151). The remaining trip from KK via **Lahad Datu** (p144), **Sandakan** (p133), and **Kinabalu National Park** (p106) will seem like child's play after the wilds of Kalimantan...until you tackle Mt Kinabalu.

For those who want to see it all (or pretty damn much of it) and don't mind some rough travel en route, this is the mother of all Borneo trips – the full circuit right round the outside of the world's third-largest island.

TAILORED TRIPS

SABAH PLUS MULU: THE NATURAL
WONDERS OF THE NORTH
Two to Three Weeks

Fly into **Kota Kinabalu** (p88) and spend a day or two enjoying everything the city has to offer. Next, take the bus up to **Kinabalu National Park** (p106) and make the trek up to the summit to see the sunrise over Borneo. Descend the mountain and treat yourself to a soak in **Poring Hot Springs** (p116) before continuing by bus to the east side of Sabah, where you can visit with our orangutan cousins in **Sepilok Orang-Utan Rehabilitation Centre** (p138).

The next stop is the **Sungai Kinabatangan** (p143), accessed via **Sukau**. After enjoying the wildlife along the river, head down to **Lahad Datu** (p144). If your budget allows, stay at **Borneo Rainforest Lodge** in **Danum Valley** (p145).

If you're a diver, you'll want to tack on a trip down to **Semporna** (p149) and **Pulau Sipadan** (p150), one of the world's great dive sites.

Then, it's a flight back to KK and, if time and budget allow, a flight to Sarawak's **Gunung Mulu National Park** (p205). You'll want to give this as much time as you can, because it's simply spectacular.

ON THE TRAIL OF RAJAS AND SULTANS
Three weeks

Fly into **KK** (p88) and check out the old Jln Gaya area and Australia Place to learn about the city's colonial and wartime history. From here, head inland to **Kinabalu National Park** (p106) and continue just a bit further to **Kundasang** (p115) to check out the Kundasang War Memorial.

Return to KK and head by ferry to **Pulau Labuan** (p121), which is rich in WWII history. Next, continue by boat to Brunei's **Bandar Seri Begawan** (BSB; p221). Spend a few days in and around BSB checking out mosques, museums and palaces.

Next, head down the coast to **Miri** (p200) and take a flight up to **Bario** (p213) in the Kelabit Highlands, where you can immerse yourself in Kelabit culture.

Head back to Miri and continue by bus to **Sibu** (p185), where you can catch a boat up the **Batang Rejang** (p189) to **Kapit** and **Belaga**, where you can check out the historical sites of the so-called 'white rajas'.

Return to Sibu and head down to **Kuching** (p162), which is Borneo's most culturally rich city. From Kuching, it's an easy flight back to KK.

Snapshot

These days, cranky old men at your typical *kedai kopi* (coffee shop) in Borneo will most likely be decrying the current high cost of living, due to the rise in the price of crude oil. The odd optimist among them will likely point out that they've all got more money in their pockets to pay for the high prices of goods, due to the fact that the entire island has been undergoing something of an economic boom, particularly the Malaysian states of Sabah and Sarawak.

It's a sure bet that politics will follow the state of the economy in most *kedai-kopi* conversations. In Malaysia, the current government of Abdullah Ahmad Badawi is going through a difficult period as it has been hit by several scandals in the last year, including charges of corruption and cronyism. Religious freedom in Malaysia is becoming another contentious issue due to several high-profile incidents in the last two years.

In Sarawak, the Bakun Hydroelectric Project is currently in the final stages of construction. When completed, it will be the second-largest dam in Asia outside of China, and aims to provide East Malaysia with a large increase in electrical-generating capacity. Plans are being discussed to lay sub-marine cables from Borneo to Peninsular Malaysia where excess capacity will be sent. The Bakun dam will flood an area the size of Singapore in the Malaysian rainforest.

On the positive side, in 2007 an initiative was announced by the Malaysian, Bruneian and Indonesian governments in cooperation with the World Wildlife Fund and the International Tropical Timber Organization to create the Heart of Borneo conservation area, using conservation areas and sustainable forestry to protect 2 million hectares of rainforest straddling all three countries that share the island of Borneo.

Whatever happens, it is clear that Borneo is one of those places in the world where the forces of conservation and consumption clash. It is, quite literally, a contest between mind-boggling diversity and a creeping monoculture. The island is a place where all those arguments about wilderness preservation versus economic development take on a horrible reality. It is the place where the first-world desire for hardwood furniture takes the form of a chain saw biting into a towering rainforest giant, or, conversely, where enlightened conservation efforts mean an undisturbed night in the jungle canopy for a family of orangutans.

The fact is, Borneo is one of the most important places on earth right now. It is a treasure trove of unbelievable biodiversity and almost all of this biodiversity hangs in the balance. The next two decades or so will determine the fate of hundreds of species unique to Borneo. What the world stands to gain in terms of a few pieces of nice furniture or a few million barrels of palm oil, it will lose in terms of unimaginable and irreplaceable living forms. One of the most important things we can do as travellers is to go to Borneo now and get out there on the front lines and see just what this battle looks like up close – and to see what we all might lose.

FAST FACTS

Population:
Kalimantan – 12,223,300
Sabah – 2,449,389
Sarawak – 2,357,500
Brunei – 374,577

GDP:
Sabah – US$8 billion
Sarawak – US$8.8 billion
Brunei – US$9.5 billion

Borneo is one of only two places in the world where you can see wild orangutans

Mt Kinabalu is the highest mountain in South East Asia

UNESCO World Heritage Sites: Gunung Mulu and Kinabalu National Park

The first season of *Survivor* was shot on Pulau Tiga in Sabah

Plants: Borneo is home to 40% of all palm species in the world

Animals: Borneo is home to 20% of all snake species in the world

There is no record of any human entering Sabah's Maliau Basin until the 1980s

History

Who Borneo belongs to has been a key question for much of the past 1500 years; internal contenders, neighbouring islands and Europeans all staked claims. Far from resolving the question, 20th-century nationhood left the island divided and created new levels of conflict.

SUNDALAND TO SRIVIJAYA

Geologists believe Borneo's land mass was joined to the rest of Southeast Asia 2.5 million years ago, as part of a continent called Sundaland. About 10,000 years ago, seas rose and Borneo became a large, remote island.

Despite separation from the mainland, Borneo retained contact with the outside world. Migrants arrived some 3000 years ago, probably from southern China, mixing with the descendants of the original owner of a 40,000-year-old skull discovered in Niah Caves to form some of Borneo's indigenous groups.

Traders from India and China began visiting Borneo as a sideshow to their bilateral commerce around the 1st century AD. Borneo's forest products including birds nests (which Chinese prized for soup and medicine), black pepper and animal skins were exchanged for textiles, beads and Chinese porcelain. From about 500 AD, Chinese traders began settling along Borneo's coasts.

Traders also introduced Hinduism and Buddhism to Borneo. South Kalimantan's Museum Lambung Mangkurat (see p264) displays artefacts of that influence. Traditional social principles known as *adat* are also a Hindu legacy (see p30).

Sumatra's Hindu-Buddhist kingdom of Srivijaya rose during the 7th century AD, and its influence extended to Borneo. Srivijaya controlled much of Southeast Asia's trade through command of the Strait of Melaka. Merchants from Arabia, Persia and India brought goods to Srivijaya's coastal outposts in exchange for goods from China and local products.

In Srivijaya's time, Brunei emerged as Borneo's centre for China trade. Sumatran pioneers established additional settlements along Borneo's coast, broadening the empire's reach and bringing more traders to the island. When Srivijaya's 600-year run ended, more Malays migrated to Borneo.

> Archaeological finds in western Borneo include glass beads from the Roman Empire.

KINGDOMS COME

The founding of Melaka in 1400 (see p26) refocused regional trade. This harbour on Malay peninsula's west coast is half-way between China and India. In addition to their goods, Indian traders carried Islam to Melaka. These Muslim practices mainly absorbed, rather than erased, prevailing Hindu and animist customs. Muslims in Borneo today predominantly practise

TIMELINE

2.5 million BC	2500–1000 BC	c 1st century AD
Borneo is part of Sundaland, attached to mainland Southeast Asia. The rising seas of a geological separatist movement about 10,000 years ago transformed Borneo into the world's third-largest island.	Migrants from mainland Asia bring Dongson culture techniques for rice farming, metallurgy and buffalo sacrifice to Borneo. With ancestors of the 40,000-year-old Niah Caves skull, they form many of Borneo's indigenous groups.	Chinese and Indian traders detour to Borneo. Egyptian geographer Ptolemey's uncannily accurate descriptions of Borneo likely came from Indian voyagers. By 500 AD, Chinese are settling in coastal present-day West Kalimantan.

this more mild, tolerant form of Islam. Travellers may notice it in Borneo's more pluralistic societies, with fewer women in headscarves and continued adherence to some pre-Islamic traditions (see p36).

Through diplomacy, often cemented by marriage, Borneo's coastal sultanates turned toward Melaka and Islam. Brunei's sultan married a Melaka princess; Sharif Ali, a descendant of the Prophet Mohammed, married a Brunei royal and became sultan, introducing a legal system based on Islamic law.

By the late 15th century, Europeans sought a direct role in the rich Asian trade. Christopher Columbus failed to reach India by sailing west, but Portugal's Vasco da Gama found the way around Africa in 1498. In 1511, Portugal conquered Melaka in its bid to control the lucrative spice trade. Muslim merchants shunned Melaka after Portugal's takeover, moving much of their custom to Borneo's sultanates.

Brunei succeeded Melaka as the regional Islamic trade centre. Under Sultan Bolkiah in the 16th century, Brunei was Borneo's most powerful kingdom. Its influence extended east to Luzon in the modern Philippines and on Borneo as far south as Kuching.

The sultanate let Portugal to establish a Brunei trading post to service its burgeoning spice trade in the Malukus. This link also helped check Spanish ambitions in the Philippines, but Brunei's reach exceeded its grasp. Facing a succession of rebellions, Brunei repeatedly turned to foreigners for help.

For assistance suppressing an uprising in 1701, Brunei ceded Sabah to the Sultan of Sulu (an island between Borneo and Mindanao). That cession is the basis for ongoing Philippine claims to Sabah. In the 19th century, a rebellion against Brunei led to a British foothold in Sarawak (see p24).

Brunei gave Britain a second front in Borneo more obliquely. In 1865, Brunei's ailing sultan leased Sabah to the American consul in Brunei. The rights eventually passed to an Englishman, Alfred Dent, who also received Sulu's blessing. In 1881, with London's support, Dent formed the British North Borneo Company, later called the Chartered Company, to administer the territory.

The prospect of further fragmentation led the nearly ruined sultanate to become a British protectorate in 1888. Ironically, its 19th-century status as a dependent paved Brunei's path to becoming Borneo's only independent state a century later.

> The name Borneo comes from foreigners, and is either a mispronunciation of Brunei or *buah nyior*, Malay for coconut; Malays call the island Kalimantan.

THE EMPIRE(S) STRIKE BACK

Portugal's success in the spice trade and as a coloniser drew European imitators. The British and Dutch began sparring over Borneo in the 17th century, extending a regional rivalry that began in Java and spread to the Strait of Melaka.

To more effectively exploit the Asia trade, the Dutch government amalgamated competing merchant companies into the Vereenigde Oost-Indische

600s–1200s	c 1400	1445
Sumatra's Hindu-Buddhist Srivijaya kingdom dominates Southeast Asia's sea trade. Under Srivijaya, ethnic Malays immigrate to Borneo. Modern social values known as *adat* are a Hindu legacy.	Ibans migrate from West Kalimantan's Kapuas River valley to Sarawak, displacing Bidayuhs. Some Ibans ally with coastal Malays to become 'Sea Dayak' pirates. Ibans will be Sarawak's last group to renounce head-hunting.	Islam becomes the state religion of Melaka, Srivijaya's successor as Southeast Asia's trading power. Merchants spread a predominantly tolerant, mild form of Islam that accommodates existing traditions.

MEANWHILE, BACK IN THE JUNGLE...

While regional kingdoms and Europeans tried to get pieces of Borneo, the island's indigenous people were developing their own societies. In most cases, we know little about this history due to the lack of written records, particularly about forest tribes.

It's known that Iban Dayaks migrated from the mid-Kapuas River area in today's West Kalimantan to Sarawak around 1400. But it's not known why they moved. Tribal wars are believed to have been frequent with some groups, such as Kenyah and Ibans, pitted in traditional rivalries, but details are scarce.

More is known about Borneo's coastal sultanates, such as Brunei, which dominated northern Borneo before the Europeans came. These coastal states were usually established by envoys from kingdoms across the Indonesian archipelago, setting up trading posts, intermarrying with indigenous people, and outlasting or outgrowing their distant sponsors.

In the south, Banjarmasin emerged as the major political power among the Islamicised former Buddhist and Hindu minikingdoms. Ethnically, the Banjars are a mix of Dayak, Sumatran Malay, Javanese and Bugis. Royal intermarriage with Dayaks helped cement good relations. The sultanate adopted Islam under Pangeran Samudera shortly after Portugal's conquest of Melaka. By the 18th century, Banjarmasin's influence stretched coast to coast, from Sambas to Berau.

Today, regional royalty often remains a point of local pride, and residents expect tourists to visit the town's palace, now usually a royal museum. The Kutai dynasty palace-cum-museum in Tenggarong, East Kalimantan, (see p276) is Borneo's best.

Compagnie (VOC; United East India Company). The VOC established a diamond-trading outpost in Sambas on Kalimantan's northwest coast in 1610, but its focus soon shifted to spices. Britain operated through its East India Company (EIC), building a flourishing pepper trade from Borneo that aroused Dutch jealousies.

Joseph Conrad's *Lord Jim* depicts life in Borneo's interior during the 19th century.

The rivals' Anglo-Dutch Treaty of 1824 carved the region into separate spheres of interest that were to become 20th-century national boundaries. The Dutch got what became Indonesia; Britain got the Malay peninsula and Singapore. (A legacy of the split is the more widespread use of English in Sabah and Sarawak than in formerly Dutch Kalimantan.) Britain did not include Borneo in the treaty, preferring its EIC concentrate on the Malay peninsula and Singapore, which it dubbed the Straits Settlements.

THE WHITE RAJAS

The Anglo-Dutch Treaty didn't end British interest in Borneo. Brunei's decline in the late 18th century led Sarawak to assert its independence. The region was emboldened by a flourishing trade in antimony, a metal used in medicines and as an alloying agent; *sarawak* means 'antimony' in Malay. Brunei's sultan dispatched his uncle Raja Muda Hashim, but he

1511	1610	1701
Portugal conquers Melaka in a bid to control the spice trade. Brunei succeeds Melaka as Southeast Asia's leading Islamic kingdom and trading centre, dominating northern Borneo and beyond.	Dutch build a diamond-trading post in Sambas, West Kalimantan, beginning a period of more than 300 years of digging and ignoring the rest of Kalimantan's resources.	Brunei cedes Sabah to the Sultan of Sulu, creating the basis for persistent Philippine claims on the territory. Meanwhile, sneezing mad over the pepper trade, the Dutch eject the British from Kalimantan.

failed to quell the separatists. Seeing a chance to evict Brunei, the rebels looked south for Dutch aid.

In a case of impeccable timing, James Brooke, an independently wealthy, India-born son of a British magistrate, moored his armed schooner in Kuching. Raja Muda offered to make the Englishman the raja of Sungai Sarawak if Brooke helped suppress the worsening revolt. Brooke, confident London would support any move to counter Dutch influence, accepted the deal. Backed by superior fire power, Brooke quashed the rebellion, held a reluctant Raja Muda to his word, and in 1841 became sovereign of the Kuching region. As expected, the British endorsed Brooke's initiative, eventually knighting him, and Sarawak remained Brooke's personal fiefdom.

Perhaps most surprisingly, the white raja line survived Brooke for two more generations. Unlike British colonial administrators, Brooke and his successors included tribal leaders in their ruling council and honoured local customs. The white rajas discouraged European immigration and European companies from destroying native jungle for huge rubber plantations. They encouraged Chinese migration – despite a rebellion by Hakka immigrants in 1857 that Brooke brutally suppressed – and Chinese came to dominate Sarawak's economy.

Brooke's nephew, the less-colourful Charles Johnson – who changed his name to Brooke – took over in 1863. Charles succeeded in areas his uncle had lagged in, expanding Sarawak's economy and slashing government debt. In 1916, the 86-year-old second white raja installed his eldest son, Charles Vyner Brooke. A two-decade veteran of government service, Vyner professionalised Sabah's administration, preparing it for a modern form of rule.

Sarawak's government website (www.sarawak .gov.my) has a balanced history of the state and useful contemporary information.

OUT OF THEIR SHELL

An English ruler in Sarawak spurred the somnolent Dutch to cement their interests in Kalimantan, starting with new coal mines in South and East Kalimantan. Assertiveness bred disputes with indigenous groups, culminating in a four-year war between the Dutch and the Banjarmasin sultanate in 1859. The Dutch retained control but resistance persisted until 1905.

Dutch commercial exploitation of the archipelago reached its peak at the end of the 19th century with thriving rubber, pepper, copra, tin, coal and coffee exports, plus oil drilling in East Kalimantan. In 1907, Britain's Shell Transport & Trading merged with the Royal Dutch Company for the Exploitation of Petroleum Sources in the Netherlands Indies to form Royal Dutch Shell. By 1930, Shell was producing 85% of Indonesia's oil, lubricating Dutch control.

1700s	1824	1841
South Kalimantan's Sultanate of Banjarmasin extends its influence to Borneo's east and west coasts. After initially accommodating Dutch colonists, the Banjar War erupts in 1859, with four years of battles and four more decades of resistance.	The Anglo-Dutch Treaty divides the region into what eventually becomes Malaya and Indonesia. Although the Dutch are granted Kalimantan, they are too preoccupied with fighting in Sumatra and Java to pay much attention to it.	After helping Brunei's local governor suppress an uprising and correctly surmising that Great Britain would welcome his presence to counter the Dutch in Kalimantan, Englishman James Brooke becomes first white raja of Sarawak.

BORNEO'S BUCCANEERS

Rich trade routes around Borneo bred piracy, which helped shape the region. The Srivijaya Empire (AD 600–1200) deployed the Orang Laut (local seafaring people) as antipiracy patrols. Also called Sea Gypsies, the Orang Laut converted to piracy by the 11th century.

One Orang Laut buccaneer, Parameswara, fled to Temasek (Singapore) and, driven from there, founded Melaka. An agreement with China's emperor turned Parameswara from piracy to policing the Strait of Melaka, making Melaka Srivijaya's successor as the region's commercial centre. Indian traders brought Islam to Borneo through Melaka.

In the 19th century, Sarawak's first Raja Brooke energetically battled pirates. He was trying to protect more than the high seas: Brunei loyalists hoping to unseat Brooke teamed with Iban brigands dubbed Sea Dayaks. The white raja had an ally in British Royal Navy Captain Henry Keppel, founder of Singapore's Keppel Shipyard, and they jointly attacked pirate groups. Using British aid and forging his own alliances with indigenous groups allowed Brooke to confirm and expand his rule as well as reduce piracy.

In eastern Borneo, Bajaus from the Philippines and Bugis from South Sulawesi also picked up the nickname Sea Gypsies and occasionally preyed on trading vessels. The term 'boogey man' came from Dutch fear of Bugis pirates.

Tunku, a village near Lahad Datu on Sabah's Celebes Sea coast, was a long standing pirates' nest. Even in modern times, the law's reach remains limited in these waters shared between Malaysia, Indonesia and the Philippines. In 1986 bandits in speedboats with automatic weapons staged a daylight raid on a leading Lahud Datu bank. The 2000 kidnapping of tourists from Sipidan, a world-famous diving destination, brought welcome world-class law-enforcement to the area.

BATTLEGROUND BORNEO

A lack of active volcanoes means Borneo's soils are not as agriculturally rich as neighbouring islands such as Java.

Imperial Japan coveted Borneo's resources to power its war machine. Japan seized Sarawak's Miri oilfields on 16 December 1941, and other targets in the poorly defended region fell rapidly.

In West Kalimantan, Japanese occupiers' brutality united local sultans with Dayak, Chinese and Malay leaders. They met secretly in Pontianak in 1942 to plan resistance but were betrayed from within. With accurate information, the Japanese summoned leaders one by one to Mandor, two hours east of Pontianak, for execution. At the start, victims were sultans and their families, intellectuals and ethnic leaders, but soon the Japanese extended the killings to any potential threat. That definition included most men above the age of 17 plus influential women. In all, 21,037 people were murdered and buried in Mandor, Kalimantan's Killing Fields. Pak Sambad, a resident who pushed for recognition of the site, lives outside the gates and recounts its history for visitors.

Agnes Keith, author of *The Land Below the Wind*, recounted her WWII Japanese prison-camp internment in *Three Came Home*.

In Sabah, an infamous labour camp at Sandakan's Agricultural Experimental Station housed Allied captives from across Southeast Asia. Of 2400 Australian

1881	1888	1905
British North Borneo Company (later the Chartered Company) is established in Sandakan to administer Sabah. It remains Britain's governing authority until Sabah and Sarawak become crown colonies after WWII.	Once Southeast Asia's pre-eminent Islamic trading centre, teetering Brunei slumps into British arms as a protectorate, giving Westminster three proxies north of Kalimantan.	Dutch institute *transmigrasi* policy, moving villagers from overpopulated Java to outer islands. Independent Indonesia continues the policy: during *transmigrasi's* 1984–89 heyday, 3.2 million people are relocated, many to East Kalimantan.

and British POWs, only six survived; today, a quiet park in Sandakan houses an exhibition where prisoners' accounts can be read (see p135). Many Sandakan residents – Chinese, Filipinos and Europeans – aided the captives, smuggling in food, medical supplies and a radio. Those caught assisting the prisoners were tortured, some executed.

In 1944 a primarily Australian force, Z Special Unit, parachuted into Bario (see p213) in the Kelabit Highlands and allied with indigenous Kelabits against the Japanese. Armed with blowpipes and led by Australian commandos, this unlikely army scored several successes. As the tide turned toward Allied victory in the Pacific, bombers targeted occupied Sabah. In 1945, Australian troops landed in East Kalimantan, fighting bloody battles in Tarakan (p287) and Balikpapan (p267), where memorials to Australian and Japanese casualties can be visited. However it wasn't until after the atomic bombings of Japan that its forces surrendered Borneo.

> As part of the resistance to Japan's occupation, Australian commandos encouraged a headhunting revival, offering 'ten bob a nob' for Japanese heads.

MEET THE NEW BOSSES

Japan's occupation unbottled the *merdeka* (freedom) genie throughout Southeast Asia. For Borneo, though, the end of war didn't mean independence, but division along the old colonial lines.

The Japanese occupiers gave Indonesians more responsibility and, for the first time, participation in government. The Japanese also gave prominence to nationalist leaders, such as Soekarno and Mohammed Hatta, and trained *pemuda* (youth militias) to defend the country. As the war ended, Soekarno and Hatta were by far the most popular nationalist leaders. In August 1945 they were kidnapped and pressured by radical *pemuda* to declare independence before the Dutch could return. On 17 August 1945, with tacit Japanese backing, Soekarno proclaimed Indonesia's independence.

Indonesians rejoiced, but the Netherlands still claimed sovereignty over Indonesia. British troops entered Java in October 1945 to accept the surrender of the Japanese. Clashes between British troops and the new Republican army came to a head in the bloody Battle of Surabaya. After a bomb killed a commander, British ground and air forces attacked the city on 10 November 1945. Thousands of Indonesians died, civilians fled to the countryside, and the poorly armed Republican forces fought a three-week pitched battle. The brutal retaliation of the British, and spirited defence by Republicans, galvanised Indonesian support and helped turn world opinion.

The Dutch dream of easy reoccupation was shattered, and 55,000 troops were dispatched as the British withdrew. Several tentative settlements failed to hold. During the four years of fighting, Kalimantan was on the sidelines, though Dutch intriguers sought deals with local leaders there. In 1949, the Netherlands withdrew under international pressure, including the threat

1907	**1941–45**	**1945**
Britain's Shell Transport & Trading merges with the Royal Dutch Company for the Exploitation of Petroleum Sources in the Netherlands Indies to form Royal Dutch Shell.	Imperial Japan captures and occupies Borneo. Early resistance by local Chinese is brutally repressed. Nascent nationalists greet the Japanese as liberators, but cruelty turns opinion against the occupation.	Soekarno and Hatta proclaim independence of the Republic of Indonesia on 17 August. The Dutch send 55,000 troops, attempting to reassert their authority, but give up the fight in 1949.

of losing American reconstruction aid. The new Indonesian government didn't focus on Kalimantan, but events in northern Borneo soon drew its attention.

Postwar rebuilding in Sabah and Sarawak was beyond their private owners' means and the territories became British crown colonies. Sabah's Chartered Company simply ceded authority to Westminster, but Sarawak proved a far more complex matter. On the eve of the Japanese invasion, amid a rising tide for Malay independence on the peninsula, Raja Vyner Brooke had been ready to hand power to a Supreme Council of local representatives. But after the war, Brooke returned briefly under Australian military administration, then gave control to the British.

Cession inspired a bloody anticessionist movement supported chiefly by Anthony Brooke, Vyner Brooke's nephew and would-be heir. The conflict climaxed in late 1949 when a Malay student assassinated the governor of Sarawak. By 1951, however, the movement had lost its momentum, and Brooke urged supporters to abandon his cause.

> Allied bombing raids in 1945 left Sandakan in ruins, and authorities moved Sabah's capital to Jesseltown, now Kota Kinabalu.

KONFRONTASI

While Sabah and Sarawak remained colonies through the 1950s, Kalimantan was part of independent Indonesia, the peninsula's Malaya Federation gained *merdeka*, and Singapore and Brunei achieved internal self-rule under Britain. In 1961 Malaya's ruler Tunku Abdul Rahman proposed a merger with Singapore. To prevent Singapore's Chinese majority from tipping the racial balance away from Malays, his plan required adding British Borneo to the new nation. Malaysia was born in July 1963, fusing Malaya, Singapore, Sabah and Sarawak.

The short-lived federation – Singapore left in 1965 – immediately faced diplomatic crises. The Philippines broke off relations over its claim to Sabah. A UN commission confirmed Malaysian sovereignty, but the Philippines still refuses to recognise it. More seriously, Indonesia's increasingly radicalised, communist-leaning President Soekarno laid claim to all of Borneo. His response to Malaysia's 'annexation' was a military campaign, dubbed Konfrontasi.

> The US government endorsed the Sulu Sultanate's claim to Sabah in 1906 and 1920.

Soviet Union–equipped Indonesian armed forces crossed into Sabah and Sarawak from Kalimantan. Additionally, Soekarno supported communist revolts in Brunei and among Chinese farmers in Sarawak. At the height of the conflict, 50,000 troops from Britain, Australia and New Zealand patrolled Sabah and Sarawak's borders with Kalimantan. The presence of 'imperialist' forces fuelled Soekarno's fiery speeches, but the military campaign fizzled. It was three years before Indonesia officially renounced Konfrontasi, but Malaysian rule of Sabah and Sarawak was never seriously threatened.

1963	1969	1984
Sarawak and Sabah join the short-lived union of Malaya and Singapore to maintain a non-Chinese majority. Indonesia counterclaims all of Borneo and declares Konfrontasi against Malaysia. Sporadic fighting continues into 1966.	Race riots in Peninsular Malaysia result in national New Economic Policy of positive discrimination for Malays. Borneo's indigenous people are granted the same rights as Malay *bumiputra*.	After pulling out of the Malaysia Federation at the last minute two decades earlier, oil-rich (for now) Brunei becomes Borneo's only independent nation under Sultan Hassanal Bolkiah.

A PLACE IN THEIR COUNTRY

Although Borneo's parts are now firmly ensconced in their respective nations, they remain imperfect fits. Malaysia's national New Economic Policy of preference for native Malays sits uneasily over the ethnic quilts of Sarawak and Sabah. Although Kuala Lumpur has promised to respect indigenous rights and traditional claims, the only thing clear-cut have been forests, frequently over local objections. The unbroken rule of the Barisan Nasional (National Front; BN) coalition at the federal level and the seven-term rule of Chief Minister Abdul Taib Mahmud in Sarawak has led to talk of corruption. After joining Malaysia, Sabah was governed for a time by Tun Mustapha, who ran the state almost as a private fiefdom and clashed frequently with the central government. Clashes persisted even after the Kadazan-Dusun–controlled Parti Bersatu Sabah (Sabah United Party; PBS) took power in 1985 and joined BN.

In 1990 PBS dropped its alliance with BN just before the general election. PBS claimed that the federal government was not equitably sharing Sabah's wealth, and banned the export of logs from Sabah to reinforce the point. The federal government overturned the ban. Despite ongoing discussions, little has changed – a mere 5% of the revenue Sabah generates trickles back into state coffers. Sabah remains the poorest of Malaysia's states, despite its rich natural resources. With an unemployment rate of twice the national average, 16% of Sabah's population lives below the poverty line.

eMas Sabah (www .sabah.org.my/biindex .asp), a project of the Sabah State Library, provides historic and contemporary information about the state.

The story is similar in Kalimantan. Soekarno's successor Soeharto ran an autocratic 'kleptocracy' that exploited Kalimantan's resources, disproportionately benefiting Jakarta favourites. Soeharto also expanded transmigration polices initiated under the Dutch, moving millions from overpopulated Java and Bali to more remote areas, with East Kalimantan a particular target. Occasional violent clashes make headlines, but the more insidious effect of this *transmigrasi* is to marginalise Kalimantan's indigenous communities, particularly in the democracy emerging since Soeharto's 1998 ouster. Similarly, extension of local autonomy has mainly expanded the power and payrolls of entrenched politicians, whose loyalties often lie more with Jakarta than their presumed constituents.

Brunei had been planning to become part of Malaysia in 1963 but at the eleventh hour Sultan Sri Muda Omar Ali Saifuddien III had second thoughts. He had inherited a fabulously rich country following the discovery of oil in 1929 and, having wrested control of internal affairs from the British, was determined to use this vast wealth to modernise and develop his nation rather than see Kuala Lumpur take the spoils. Shell Oil undoubtedly sympathised with his position. In 1967 the sultan abdicated in favour of his eldest son and the current ruler, the 29th in the unbroken royal Brunei line, Sultan Hassanal Bolkiah. The scandalous spending of Prince Jefri, revealed in the 1990s, harmed the economy and national confidence. With oil reserves declining, hard decisions loom. The maps have been drawn, but the question of who Borneo belongs to remains open.

The Jakarta Post website, www.thejakaratapostl .com, and Soeharto-banned Tempo, www .tempointeraktif.com, cover Indonesian news.

1991	1998	2007
Sabah's opposition state government prohibits log exports to safeguard rainforests and indigenous lifestyles. Malaysia's central government in Kuala Lumpur rolls back the ban.	Indonesia's President Soeharto is elected to his seventh term in February. May shootings of student *reformasi* demonstrators and mass rioting in Jakarta pave the way to his resignation and towards democracy.	UN Framework Convention on Climate Change on the neighbouring island of Bali draws global attention to Borneo's shrinking rainforests and sprouts new initiatives to encourage their preservation.

The Culture

Borneo's biodiversity extends to its human inhabitants, from rainforest tribespeople living in natural harmony to Western retirees lured by special visas. The world's third-largest island is a multicultural jungle of more than 200 groups, with indigenous peoples, ethnic Malays (from either Malaysia or Indonesia), Chinese and others blossoming and becoming entwined in Borneo's fertile soil.

On the surface, lifestyles throughout Borneo divide sharply along urban and rural lines. But for many urban dwellers – no matter which country they live in – the village remains their true home. Traditional customs and values, based on village traditions known as *adat* (as opposed to *agama*, meaning religion, though one frequently reinforces the other), remain strong.

'The world's third-largest island is a multicultural jungle of more than 200 groups...'

Tracing back to Hindu kingdoms, *adat* places emphasis on collective rather than individual responsibility and maintaining harmony. Many aspects of *adat* are a part of everyday life in the *kampung* (village), and indeed even in urban areas. All villagers are equal, under a community leader *(penghulu* or *ketua kampung* or *kepala desa)*, whose ancestry often traces back to the village founder. Respect for elders is another ingrained value.

Visitors will find hospitality is a pan-Borneo value. The indigenous longhouse culture, which survives even where longhouses no longer do, includes elaborate rituals for greeting and treating visitors, and has become part of Borneo's character. People realise you've gone out of your way to get here, and they appreciate the effort.

POPULATION

When Malaysia commemorated 50 years of independence on 31 August 2007, it celebrated success as a multicultural, multiracial state. Indonesia's motto is *Bhinneka Tunggal Ika* (Unity in Diversity). For both countries, Borneo is the showplace for aspirations of weaving a cohesive social fabric from many different threads.

Group tensions that have plagued both nations are far less pronounced in Borneo. With more than 200 groups, none which have a dominant majority, Borneo is a mix of indigenous peoples, including the forest dwellers often called Dayaks, ethnic Malays (from Indonesia or Malaysia), and Chinese. Unlike the rest of Malaysia (and to a lesser extent Indonesia), there's no significant Indian population in Borneo.

People from different backgrounds intermingle more easily in Borneo than in their national heartlands. Tensions can erupt, most spectacularly when they involve Dayak groups that practised head-hunting before it became a synonym for executive search.

Brunei's small scale (not to mention great wealth) has allowed all its citizens, some 30% of whom are not Muslim, to find common goals and live together harmoniously in a state run according to Islamic laws. Out in the longhouses of the country's tiny interior, life is practically indistinguishable from that across the border in Sarawak.

Borneo beyond Brunei has experienced increased population growth since 1980, with its population doubling to 18 million people today. Sabah has ballooned from less than a million residents in 1980 to an estimated 2.5 million today. Immigrants from the southern Philippines, with its long running conflict with Muslim separatists, have poured in, legally and otherwise.

Chinese

Comprising about 10% of Borneo's population, Chinese have traditionally been urban traders and businesspeople. That role dates back to Chinese traders visiting Borneo and settling here some 1500 years ago. It has been reinforced through institutionalised discrimination at the national level in Indonesia and Malaysia that restricts Chinese opportunities in the public sector.

Sarawak has Borneo's largest proportion of Chinese, at nearly 30%. In addition to traders, many came as farmers, encouraged to migrate during the rule of the white rajas in the 19th century. Hakka Chinese poured into West Kalimantan after an early 18th-century gold strike. Today, there's a high concentration of Chinese around Pontianak, where they make up more than a third of the population, and Singkawang, where they're a majority. Singkawang's tourist trade staples include Chinese men, particularly from Taiwan, shopping for brides.

Half a century ago, Chinese traditionally lived above their shops in urban business districts. Today many have moved to the suburbs, often leaving town centres desolate after dark.

Malays

As empires ruling the Malay peninsula and Indonesian archipelago expanded to Borneo, Malay migrants followed. Many Malays came from the Sumatran heartland of the Srivijaya kingdom during its heyday in the 11th and 12th centuries, settling in coastal areas to farm and fish. More recently, Malays have come as government and national commerce have expanded in Borneo.

Today, Malays (including Indonesians) account for about 30% of Borneo's population, but the numbers and composition vary significantly across the island. In Brunei, Malays make up 70% of the population, including the dynasty that's ruled the sultanate since the 14th century. In Sabah, Malays are 12% of the population, and in Sarawak 21%.

Kalimantan has a higher proportion of Indonesians from elsewhere in the archipelago. East and South Kalimantan have sizable minorities of Bugis, seafarers from neighbouring South Sulawesi who established settlements throughout Southeast Asia. But most of the migration from within Indonesia has resulted from national policies and national circumstances.

Dutch colonial authorities initiated *transmigrasi* (transmigration) programs in 1905 to relieve overpopulated areas, mainly in Java, through relocation to remote areas. During the peak period, 1984 to 1989, 3.2 million people were moved, many of them to East Kalimantan. Conflicts have arisen, repeatedly in Sampit between Madurese transmigrants and native Dayaks, with hundreds killed and thousands displaced. Success stories exist, but many transmigrants and their granted land were unsuited to the government-mandated farming life. The program has been curtailed.

Today, Kalimantan is Indonesia's frontier, the land of opportunity. With the nation slow to recover from the Asian economic crisis of 1997 and the upheavals that followed, good opportunities are hard to find.

Indigenous Peoples

Borneo's indigenous people include descendants of traditional Islamic kingdoms as well as rural groups often categorised under the blanket term 'Dayak'. Particularly in Sarawak and Sabah, individual group names are used more often. Dayak cultures have taken a beating at the hands of the 20th and 21st centuries, but they remain a distinctive feature of Borneo, well worth experiencing with a longhouse visit.

The term 'Dayak' was first used by colonial authorities: it means upriver or interior in some local languages, human being in others.

THE BORNEO LONGHOUSE

Longhouses are the traditional dwellings of the indigenous peoples of Borneo. These communal dwellings are raised above the ground and may contain up to a hundred individual family 'apartments' under one long roof. The most important area of a longhouse is the common veranda, which serves as a social area and sometimes as sleeping space.

It's fair to say that there are two types of longhouse: 'tourist longhouses' and 'residential longhouses'. The former, as you can guess, are set up for tourists and are often built using traditional materials and construction techniques. They look like you might imagine (or hope) a longhouse should look, but they're pretty much just for display purposes.

In contrast, residential longhouses are where people actually live. If you're expecting these longhouses to look like something out of the Raja Brooke–era, you might be disappointed: most residential longhouses these days are quite modern in construction, with electronic appliances in all the apartments and parking lots out the front. Still, this is where real life happens, and if you want to see how Borneo's modern-day indigenous peoples live, a visit to one is a must.

When visiting a longhouse, it is polite to wait outside until someone from the longhouse invites you in. Bringing a few gifts is always appreciated. Usually, if you are travelling upriver with a guide, your guide will take you to a longhouse where he or she has relatives or friends.

KALIMANTAN

Banjarese dominate South Kalimantan and are also the largest distinct group in Central Kalimantan (which was split from South Kalimantan in 1957). Banjarese (or Banjars) trace their roots to Sumatra more than 1500 years ago and settled along the Martapura River, mixing with Dayaks, adopting Islam, and eventually establishing a sultanate in Banjarmasin.

Ngaju people instigated the creation of Dayak-majority Central Kalimantan from part of South Kalimantan. Ngaju are the largest of dozens of Central Kalimantan Dayak groups. Barito Dayaks, like Barito River, are in both Central and South Kalimantan. Baritos' Hill Dayak subgroups inhabit the scenic Meratus mountain range.

Along East Kalimantan's Mahakam River, the Kutai are the main indigenous group in the lower reaches, hosting the annual Erau Festival for Dayaks at their capital Tenggarong. Dayak villages begin midriver, featuring Benuaqs around Tanjung Isuy.

Kayan and closely related Kenyah Dayaks are found in the Apokayan Highlands, branching throughout Kalimantan and into Sarawak and Brunei. They share many characteristics with other Dayak groups, including living in longhouses, growing rice and rivalry with the Iban. Kayan stand out for their use of ironwood (*ulin*) for longhouses and boats, and for an elaborate social hierarchy based on class. Unlike most other groups, Kayan men as well as women sport elongated ear lobes.

The unique Punan cave dwellers live between the headwaters of the Mahakam and Kapuas rivers, spanning East and West Kalimantan. Today, most Punan have moved out of caves. Opinion differs as to whether these Punan are related to Sarawak's Punan and Punan Bah groups.

The Borneo Project's documentary film *Rumah Nor*, highlighting a landmark 2001 court-victory to protect Punan Dayak forest rights, can be viewed online at http://borneoproject.org/article.php?id=628.

SABAH

More than 30 indigenous groups make Sabah a medley of traditions and cultures. There's no majority group, and immigration complicates the picture.

Kadazan-Dusun are the largest ethnic group in Sabah, at about 18% of the population. Kadazan and Dusun share a common language and customs, and are traditionally rice farmers and rice-wine brewers. Kadazan originally lived mainly in Sabah's western coastal areas and river deltas, while Dusun inhabited the interior highlands. Mainly Roman Catholic, Kadazan and

Dusun rarely intermarry with Muslims but Kadazan and Dusun-Chinese couples are not unusual.

Living along Sabah's coasts, Bajau trace their roots to the Islamic sultanate on the Philippine island of Sulu, which once ruled eastern Sabah. According to legend, Bajau were once sea nomads who came ashore only to bury their dead. East-coast Bajau (and those in neighbouring East Kalimantan – see p284) remain seafarers, living in coastal stilt homes or aboard their boats. West-coast Bajau have become farmers, growing rice and raising livestock. Nicknamed 'Cowboys of the East', they show off their equestrian skills at an annual Tamu Besar in Kota Belud.

Murut, Sabah's third-largest indigenous group, originated in the southwestern hills bordering Kalimantan and Brunei, and were soldiers for Brunei's sultans. Murut grow hill-rice and hunt with spears and blowpipes that have poison darts. They were Sabah's last group to abandon head-hunting.

Based in Kuching, the *Borneo Post* offers print and online editions (www.theborneopost .com) and specialises in reporting on Sarawak's indigenous communities.

SARAWAK & BRUNEI

Indigenous people make up about half of the population of Sarawak. Dayak culture and lifestyles are probably easiest to observe and experience here. The Penan Dayaks, highly idealised for living in harmony with the forest, inhabit Sarawak and Brunei (see below).

The Iban, comprising about 30% of Sarawak's population, migrated from West Kalimantan's Kapuas River starting in the 16th century. Iban are rice-growers and longhouse dwellers, but they became known as Sea Dayaks for their exploits as pirates. Reluctance to renounce head-hunting, which they practised on Japanese occupation forces during WWII, enhanced Ibans' ferocious reputation.

Also migrants from West Kalimantan, Bidayuh are concentrated in the hills west of Kuching, near the Kalimantan border. Dubbed 'Land Dayaks', Bidayuh were displaced by other Dayak settlers entering their territories and victimised by Brunei's governors. The Brooke dynasty's efforts to assist the Bidayuh – and make war on their enemies – helped preserve the group's identity.

Several Dayak groups are known collectively as the Orang Ulu (Upriver People) in Sarawak, including Penan, Kayan and Kenyah. Kelabit, living in the highland headwaters of the Baram River, are related to Sabah's Murut people. Living in a cool climate, they're Borneo's most prolific vegetable-farmers.

In Brunei, indigenous non-Malays, mainly Iban and Kelabit, account for less than 10% of the population.

DAYAK LIFESTYLES

Anthropologists generally agree Dayaks share roots with Malays and are analogous to the Orang Asli (original people) of the Malay Peninsula. Dayak's

---

PENAN: 'MOLONG' LIFE

The rightly romanticised hunter-gatherers of the forest, Penan were originally nomads in Sarawak and Brunei. Most have settled in longhouses in northern Sarawak's Baram and Bukit Mas districts, though several hundred remain pure nomads. Nomadic or not, they practise *molong*, never taking more than they require from the forest. Settled Penan may plant rice, but they still rely on the jungle for most of their food – including sago from palm trees and game, hunted with poisoned darts from blowpipes – as well as medicine and clothing.

With their lifestyle under severe threat from timber cutting in their traditional areas, Penan have joined campaigns to block logging roads. While many sympathisers want to protect the Penan way of life, Malaysian authorities say the Penan should be assimilated into mainstream society, whether they like it or not.

ancestors arrived in Borneo about 3000 years ago. They brought influences of the Dongson culture from Vietnam and southern China including irrigated rice-cultivation, buffalo-sacrifice rituals, and ikat (fabric patterned by tie-dying the yarn before weaving) weaving. These migrants mixed with ancestors of Niah cave-dwellers, developing into more than 200 groups with distinct languages and cultures. Dayaks adapted imported skills to their particular environments and became self-reliant tribal units; outsiders introduced the concept of trading centuries later.

Traditional clothing includes ikat worn as sarongs and loin clothes with beadwork for ceremonial dress, and Dayaks use rattan and bamboo for a variety of needs. Woodcarving is a key craft both for decoration and ceremonial purposes. Many groups erect totems to commemorate buffalo-sacrifices or other milestones. Dayaks are also renowned for forging *mandau* (machetes), suited for brush-clearing as well as combat.

Up the Notched-Log Ladder is Sydwell Mouw Flynn's memoir of her parent's missionary work among Sarawak's Dayaks from 1933 to 1950, and her return to the land where she was raised half a century later.

Head-hunting, the most notorious aspect of Dayak culture, was largely eliminated by the end of the 19th century, though it makes sporadic comebacks. Severed heads were roasted and skulls preserved as tribal trophies.

The most striking feature of many older Dayak women is their elongated pierced ear lobes, stretched by the weight of heavy gold or brass rings. This custom is increasingly rare among the young. Older Dayaks may trim their ear lobes as a sign of conversion to Christianity.

Women once tattooed their forearms and calves with bird and spirit designs. Tattooing of young women has almost disappeared, except deep in the interior. Men still do it, although in many Dayak cultures, men were expected to earn their tattoos by taking heads.

Dayak men also practised penis adornment by surgically inserting beads and bell into the foreskin. The most extreme practice involved placing a *palang* (a metal rod or bone) horizontally through the penis. The result is believed to emulate the natural endowment of the Sumatran rhino. (It's worth noting that species is nearly extinct and notoriously hard to breed.) Traditional insertion methods employ a bamboo vice and a cold river.

Dayak community life still centres on the longhouse (*rumah betang, rumah panjai,* or *balai*), a dwelling for dozens of families, sometimes hundreds of metres in length. Longhouses take a variety of shapes and styles, but most are built off the ground, accessible by a log carved into steps, and have individual quarters for each family plus communal areas.

These days longhouses can be divided into two categories, tourist longhouses and residential longhouses. The former have been preserved (or reconstructed) for tourists, often using traditional materials and construction methods. They look the way you'd expect a longhouse to look, but village residents usually live nearby in individual houses.

Residential longhouses, where people actually live, may disappoint if you're expecting something out of the Rajah Brooke era. Longhouses often use modern materials, have electricity and even parking lots in front. But a longhouse is a way of life. It embodies a communal lifestyle of mutual reliance and responsibility, and it is this spirit rather than the building that makes it significant.

An elder (*tuai rumah* or *ketua rumah*), is leader of the longhouse. Depending on the tribe, the leader may be appointed by his predecessor or elected. Either way, heredity often plays a key role in selection. Ceremonies feature a variety of dances and often entail consumption of *tuak*, a wine of fermented rice or a variety of other plants. It's potent. If you attend a ceremony, you'll be expected to drink. Accepting an invitation to join the dance and making a fool of yourself are sure crowd-pleasers.

GIFT TIPS

It's traditional to give gifts when you visit a longhouse. Some say the tradition began with guided tours. Standard suggestions for gifts – cigarettes and candy – appal many visitors. So we asked guides and Dayaks themselves for alternatives.

First, ask your host (if you've been invited) or your tour guide what the longhouse needs. Useful items such as fishing line are hard to find in the jungle. Some hosts are reluctant to make suggestions (and it's difficult to get answers to any direct question throughout Asia), so ask, 'What am I going to miss out there?' Fruits or spices common in the city may be longhouse luxuries.

Communal gifts are presented to the longhouse leader, who then parcels them out as he (invariably, it's a man) sees fit. Individually packaged, pre-portioned items work best. A couple dozen envelopes of powered milk may be welcome in some areas. Toothbrushes and/or toothpaste can help combat rampant tooth decay. Notebooks and pencils for school children seem ideal, but beware that logging for paper production is a major issue among many Sarawak Dayaks.

If you've been invited by a family, present a gift to them (again, seek advice) and benefit the community by hiring a guide or taking a canoe trip.

Most Dayaks today do not live in longhouse communities, but in towns and cities, visiting their villages only for family events and festivals. Deforestation and the success of Christian missionaries over the last century has resulted in fragmented communities and the slow disappearance of traditional identity.

Many politicians contend Dayaks are better off being brought into the modern world. Indeed, Dayaks often go to school, get modern jobs, and live in towns. Today's Dayaks welcome these options, but increasingly find they have no other choice.

ECONOMY

Two truisms hold regarding Borneo's economy outside Brunei. First, Chinese generally control business, with Malays' political power giving them a cut. Second, primary commodities dominate.

The traditional export is timber, with Sarawak among the world leaders in log shipments. Not surprisingly, Borneo also has Asia's highest deforestation rates; a UN report estimates that 98% of its primary forest will be logged by 2022. Much of the logging in Kalimantan is believed to be illegal, so be careful about snapping photos.

Palm-oil plantations often replace logged forests and are an excuse for more cutting (see p53). Many areas in Kalimantan granted permits for palm-oil plantations have been cleared of timber but never planted. Malaysia and Indonesia together produce 86% of the world's latest miracle juice. Indonesia is poised to overtake Malaysia as the top palm-oil producer sometime this decade, with much of its new production from Kalimantan.

Traditional crops such as rubber, cacao, sago, rattan and pepper in addition to seafood, remain important. Borneo is also a famed source of swiftlet nests, the key ingredient in the Chinese favourite, birds-nest soup. The nests also has medicinal and cosmetic uses. Kalimantan still produces gold and diamonds.

Since steamship times, coal miners have been digging into Kalimantan. Output has increased dramatically in the past decade with demand from China in particular. Coal carriers now compete with logging barges as flagships for environmental challenges along the Mahakam River.

Oil and natural-gas production from mainly offshore fields thrives throughout Borneo. Industry centres are Seria in Brunei, Miri in Sarawak, and Balikpapan in East Kalimantan.

The Malaysian Palm Oil Council chronicles 'Malaysia's quest to be a responsible and efficient supplier of palm oil in the global market' at www .malaysiapalmoil.org.

BruDirect.com (www .BruDirect.com) presents a mix of fresh news, business information and visitor tips about Brunei.

Industry analysts project Brunei's oil and gas reserves will be exhausted between 2015 and 2030. Production is capped to try to stretch the supply, and extensive new deep-sea explorations are planned. Government initiatives to diversify the economy, which focused on agriculture, technology and banking, have gained some traction but attracting foreign investment necessary for large projects remains difficult. Foreign labour is limited to protect the domestic workforce, 60% of which works in either the civil service or armed forces.

RELIGION

Liberal Islam Network (http://islamlib .com/en/page.php) offers a Southeast Asian counterpoint to Muslim fundamentalism.

In Borneo, as in Indonesia and Malaysia, religion blends with traditional beliefs. Malaysia and Brunei have declared Islam the state religion, while Indonesia is the country with the world's largest Muslim population without being an 'Islamic state'. In all three nations, religious freedom is constitutionally guaranteed. Except in Brunei and South Kalimantan, no religion has an overwhelming majority in any jurisdiction; most urban areas have prominent mosques, churches and Chinese temples.

Islam

Islam came to the region with South Indian traders and didn't follow orthodox Arabian tradition. It was adopted peacefully by coastal trading ports, absorbing rather than conquering existing beliefs, and remains tolerant and moderate. Many ceremonies and beliefs include pre-Islamic traditions.

Brunei's Sultan has steered his nation towards Muslim fundamentalism, adopting a national ideology known as Melayu Islam Beraja (MIB), stressing Islam, Malay culture and the monarchy.

Dayak Religions

Dayak religion is called Kaharingan, a form of animism focused on spirits associated with virtually all places and things. Its practice differs between tribes, though there are many commonalities.

Carvings, totems, tattoos, and other objects (including severed heads in earlier times) are used to repel bad spirits, attract good spirits and soothe spirits that may be upset. Totems at entrances to villages and longhouses are markers for spirits. The hornbill is considered a powerful spirit, and is honoured in dance and ceremony, its feathers treasured. Black is widely considered a godly colour, so it features in traditional outfits.

Ancestor worship plays a large part in Kaharingan. After death, Dayaks join their ancestors in the spirit world. For some groups, spirits may reside in a particular mountain or other natural shrine. Burial customs include elaborately carved mausoleums, memorial monoliths, or internment in ceramic jars.

Even when Dayaks convert (mainly to Christianity but also to Islam) remnants of old religious practices remain. These include festivities such as the harvest ceremony, known broadly as Gawai Dayak, and they're usually considered tradition rather than religion.

Christianity

Missionaries have converted many Dayaks to Christianity, and their work continues in remote areas. Roman Catholic, traditional Protestant, and evangelical sects all have Dayak followers. Some of the evangelicals insist on purging all vestiges of previous beliefs, but usually Christianity overlays traditional practices.

Chinese Religions

Chinese in the region generally follow a mix of Buddhism, Confucianism and Taoism. At one level Chinese religion is animistic, with a belief in the innate vital energy in rocks, trees, rivers and springs. At another level, figures from the distant past, both real and mythological, are worshipped as gods.

Day-to-day, most Chinese are less concerned with the high-minded philosophies and asceticism of the Buddha, Confucius or Lao Zi than with pursuing worldly success, appeasing the dead and the spirits, and seeking knowledge about the future. Chinese religion includes what Westerners might call 'superstition' – to get your fortune told, for instance, go to a temple.

As with other groups, there's no bright line where tradition ends and religion begins. Chinese who adopt Christianity or Islam may carry out some Chinese religious practices under the banner of tradition.

WOMEN IN BORNEO

In Borneo, women face the same issues as in their national societies. Whatever their group, their challenge is balancing customary duties with responsibilities of the modern era. Women still undertake traditional roles but are also well educated and gainfully employed. Two-income households are increasingly common and often a necessity, with women widely represented in government and industry.

Dayaks track lineage through both father and mother, and gender roles are strictly prescribed. In some tribes, women have special roles. A female priestess, called a *bobohizan,* presides over many key Kadazan-Dusun traditional rituals. Dayak traditions include penis adornments to enhance partner pleasure (see p33).

Islamic society is male-oriented but regional customs regarding women are more relaxed than in many other Muslim societies. Gender politics rarely top the agenda, but many organisations promote women's rights. The region's most outspoken critic of women's roles has been Marina Mahathir, daughter of Malaysia's former prime minister, Mahathir Mohamad. In 2006, she compared the lot of Malaysia's Muslim women to that of blacks under South African apartheid, held back by rules that don't apply to more liberated Chinese women and other non-Muslims.

The *tudong* (headscarf) is a recent sticking-point as Muslim women in Malaysia and Indonesia feel increasing pressure to cover their hair. Wearing a *tudong* doesn't make a woman subservient or docile, but when it becomes a mandate, it also becomes a sign of gender inequality.

In Islamic Brunei more women wear the *tudong,* yet many work. There are even female politicians. Since 2002, female Bruneians have been able to legally transfer their nationality to their children if the father is not Bruneian. Indonesia passed a similar law in 2006.

It's not just Islamic society that fosters gender inequality. A thriving bride-market centres on Sinkawang in West Kalimantan, with men from Taiwan the primary buyers.

Trafficking of young women is a serious problem in Kalimantan. The long, mainly unguarded border makes it simple to move people into Malaysia, as a destination or a transshipment point. Sometimes relatives sell women to traffickers. In other cases, women are duped into accepting overseas work that turns out to be forced prostitution.

Even legitimate contracts as household workers can go bad. Rape and abuse of Indonesian maids – favoured in Muslim countries for their Islamic background – is reportedly rampant. In 2007, an Indonesian domestic made headlines when she tried to escape her employer's high-rise apartment in Kuala Lumpur by climbing down a bed sheet.

In Borneo hotels, 'satellite TV' often doesn't mean CNN, HBO and ESPN; picking up faraway national broadcast channels often requires a dish.

ARTS

Punan people painted on their cave walls in ancient times, but traditional crafts trump fine arts throughout Borneo.

The woven baskets of the Iban, Kayan, Kenyah and Penan are among the most highly regarded in Borneo. The most memorable craftwork for many travellers is the Kadazan-Dusun tall backpack of rattan, bamboo and bark seen at Mt Kinabalu. The most common weaving material is rattan, but bamboo, swamp nipah grass and pandanus palms are also used for baskets, sleeping mats, seats and materials for shelters.

In Brunei, too, crafts (especially *jong sarat* weaving, silverwork and basketware) have traditionally been more important than fine arts. While each ethnic group has certain distinctive patterns, hundreds or even thousands of years of trade and interaction has led to intermixing.

Ikat, or cloth weaving, is another pan-Borneo craft. West Kalimantan's Kapuas region is renowned for its ikat, and the provincial government supports efforts to preserve it in longhouse communities around Sintang. Sambas and Sarawak are well-known for *songket*, fine cloth with threads of gold or silver woven in. *Doyo*, beaten tree bark, is used mainly in East Kalimantan's Mahakam River region for both clothing and decorations.

Pua kumbu is a colourful weaving technique attributed to the Iban, and used to produce both everyday and ceremonial items decorated with a wide range of patterns. A special dyeing process creates the colours for *pua kumbu*. Ikat dyeing is performed while the threads of the pattern are already in place on the loom, giving rise to its English name, 'warp tie-dyeing'. Banjarmasin is known for *kain sasirangan* (tie-dyed batik).

Kenyah and Kayan are the most skilled carvers of Borneo. They create *kelirieng* (burial columns), up to 2m in diameter and 10m in height, and entirely covered with detailed carvings, to bury the remains of headmen. Decaying remnants of *kelirieng* are still uncovered in Sarawak, and an example can be seen in Kuching Municipal Park.

Singing and dancing, often accompanied by copious consumption of *tuak*, play big parts in Borneo's indigenous cultures. All Dayak groups have some variation of the graceful hornbill dance. Many also have various *mandau* dances performed in battle regalia as a prelude or conclusion to hunting or fighting.

Gongs and drums accompany dancing. Ensembles often include the *sape*, a four-string guitar with wooden body and rattan strings. Other Dayak musical instruments include bamboo flutes and the *engkerurai* or *keluri*, a kind of bagpipe with bamboo pipes and a gourd as its wind sack.

Food & Drink

Borneo's food mirrors national standard dishes, with local specialities spicing up the mix. Both Indonesian and Malaysian food are heavily influenced by traders that frequented their shores and by the immigrants that settled in the region.

Generally, Indonesian cuisine is simpler and has less of an Indian influence compared to Malaysian food. Malay cuisine tends to blend flavours while Indonesia keeps them distinct. Malay food also has more borrowed names from the Chinese dialects (the array of Malay noodle dishes are bewildering). Bruneian cookery is almost identical to Malaysian.

Fork and spoon, in the left and right hand respectively, are the usual utensils, though, especially in Kalimantan or Dayak communities, it's common to eat with your right hand (only).

STAPLES & SPECIALTIES

Throughout Borneo, *nasi* (rice) and *mee/mie* (noodles) are staples. Rice is eaten steamed; as *nasi goreng* (fried with other ingredients); as *bubur* (boiled into sweet or savoury porridge, often eaten for breakfast); or in glutinous varieties, steamed and moulded into tubes or cubes. Noodles can be made from wheat, wheat and egg, rice, or mung beans, and are served fried or boiled in soups (*soto*) or dry as a main or side dish.

Fresh fish, usually cooked whole, *goreng* (fried) or *bakar* (grilled), is a regional favourite. *Pepes ikan* (spiced fish cooked in banana leaves with tamarind

---

BREAKFAST IN BORNEO

Breakfast is a toughie in Borneo. Unless you stay in international-class resorts or hotels, you can forget about a nice 'full English'. More than likely, you'll have to make do with some plain factory-bread and instant coffee in a guesthouse. Or, if you're more adventurous, you may wander down to a Chinese *kopitiam* (coffee shop) and see what the locals are eating. You'll be disappointed to find that most people there will be slurping on noodles. If you're like us, you like your noodles, just not for breakfast. So what else is there to eat when you need to fill up before a day of sightseeing?

One option is finding an Indian or Malay/Indonesian *kedai kopi* (coffee shop), where you can order a *roti*, a type of unleavened flatbread cooked on a griddle. This is often the closest you can come to toast and it's usually served with a curry to dip it in (okay, it's not exactly strawberry jam).

If you demand toast and eggs, you may be surprised that this is actually fairly easy to get at most Chinese *kopitiam*. The drinks stall at these places usually serve toast and the fried-noodle stall will usually have some eggs that they can fry in their wok – just stress the fact that you don't want soy sauce or ketchup on your eggs. These items will be delivered separately for you to put together at your table.

If eggs aren't on offer, there is another option: most 'toastmasters' also stock *kaya*, which is a sweet coconut-based spread that they will slather on your buttered toast. You may find yourself developing a taste for this wonderful stuff as you travel around Borneo.

Buying a *Pao* (Chinese steamed dumpling) is another option at a *kopitiam*, and you will usually see these steamed out the front of the shop in a pile of wooden steamers, along with various forms of dim sum.

Finally, keep in mind that many towns in Borneo have morning markets where you can pick up some fresh fruit and perhaps a bit of sticky rice.

For information on drinks available at coffee shops in Borneo, see p44.

and lemon grass) is also popular. Seafood is also popular where available. *Terasi* (fish paste) and *belacan* (shrimp paste) are common spices.

Chicken is the next choice for carnivores, also often prepared *goreng* or *bakar*. Chicken and fish are often served *lalapan* style with aromatic raw *kemangi* (basil) leaves and fresh *sambal* (spicy chilli sauce). Beef is relatively rare and found mainly in upmarket establishments.

Satay (skewered meat cooked over a flame) has become a pan-Asian favourite. *Satay* is usually made from *ayam* (chicken), *kambing* (goat, but the word is also used for lamb and mutton), and occasionally *ikan* (fish), *cumi* (squid) or *udang* (shrimp). It's served with peanut sauce. *Satay kambing* can be accompanied by *gule*, a spicy soup from goat stock.

Protein-rich soya bean (*dao* or *tau*) is present in many dishes, whether in the form of *tauhu* (bean curd), *tempe* (fermented whole beans) or cooked with *kicap* or *kecap* (soy sauce). Soy sauce comes in salty, sweet, and other varieties.

Pork is *haram* (forbidden for Muslims). It's available in some Chinese restaurants, though many boast they are 100% *halal* (compliant with Muslim dietary laws). Alcohol is also *haram*, but it's available everywhere in Sabah and Sarawak, less widely in Kalimantan. Resident expats in Brunei can purchase tipples at special shops but visitors are limited to what they can carry in (12 cans of beer or two bottles of spirits).

The neighbourhood *warung*, *kedai kopi* or *kopitiam* (the Bahasa Indonesian, Malay and Hokkien terms are commonly used; the latter two translate as coffee shop) is a no-frills café where neighbours may stop for a *kopi* (coffee) or *teh* (tea) and a meal. Kalimantan has many Padang restaurants where the food is cooked in advance and displayed in the window. Put aside concerns about refrigeration – Padang's Minang people cook once a week, and the tradition predates refrigerators. Variety includes spicy *rendang* (coconut curries) also popular in Malaysia. The food is room temperature, served over hot rice, either to eat in or take away as *nasi bungkus*, usually wrapped in banana leaf.

The hawker meal is central to the experience of eating in the region. In Kalimantan, they are known as *kaki lima* (five legs: two for the proprietor, three for the cart). Different carts specialise in specific dishes.

Fruits are plentiful everywhere but Central Kalimantan. In addition to oranges, bananas and pineapples, Borneo is famous for growing durian, the spiky, smelly king of fruits that people either love or hate. Rambutan are bright red with soft spikes (its name means hairy) and similar to lychee.

> *Udang galah* is a giant river prawn found throughout the region that grows to more than 30cm and is great fried or grilled with garlic.

BORNEO SPECIALITIES

Different parts of Borneo have their own food specialities, often riffs on national dishes.

Dayak food varies, but you may sample *sayur asem rembang* (sour vegetable soup). Sago palm is the main starch component of some tribal meals. Sago-based dishes include *linut*, a thick translucent paste eaten hot with *sambal*. As an honoured guest, you'll likely be served meat on any longhouse visit, pig among non-Muslims, deer or chicken in other hunting communities. It's polite to at least appear to eat some of it.

Fish dishes are popular, including Sabah's *hinava* (raw fish marinated with lime juice and herbs) and *ketupat Kandangan* (fish and pressed rice with lime-infused coconut sauce) in Kandangan, South Kalimantan. Banteng is a popular river-fish this is bony but very tasty. Wild boar and deer are Sarawak favourites, and vegetable dishes made with jungle ferns and *paku* (fern shoots) are not to be missed. In Kalimantan, *kijang* (deer) *satay* is popular.

The one Borneo cuisine worthy of the term is Banjar, which thrives in South Kalimantan's capital Banjarmasin. For breakfast, try *kue* (cakes) or deep-fried breads with various fillings, sticky banana rice cakes, *bingka barandum* or *bingka kentang* (baked pancakes from rice or potato respectively), all cheap and tasty options at tea stalls. *Nasi kuning* (saffron rice served with chicken or fish and vegetables), a breakfast speciality elsewhere in Indonesia, is served anytime here and is topped with a zesty tomato sauce.

People here often enjoy fish and seafood, especially *udang galah* (giant river-prawn), barbecued or fried with an array of marinades and sauces. Other Banjar specialities include *ayam panggang* and *ayam goreng* (chicken barbecued or fried, served in sweet soy sauce) plus *ayam masak habang* (chicken with large, red chillies). Don't miss *soto banjar*, fragrant chicken soup packed with rice noodles, herbs and topped with a piece of barbecued chicken – order with *lontong*, rice cooked in pandanus leaves . Food stalls and *warungs* serve delicious versions of these specialities.

Sugar freaks will love many little Banjar sweets, known as *ampar tatak* (literally meaning 'cut plate'). Banjarmasin's Pasar Wadai cake market is renowned throughout Indonesia for breaking the fast during Ramadan.

VEGETARIANS & VEGANS

If you're vegetarian, say: *Saya hanya makan sayuran* (I only eat vegetables). If you're a vegan, you may want to take it a step further: *Saya tidak makan yang di perbuat dari susu, telur, ikan atau daging* (I don't eat dairy products, eggs, fish or meat).

Vegetarians will be pleased to know that *tempe* and *tauhu* are common. Finding fresh veggies requires more effort. Look for Chinese establishments; they can whip up *cap cai* (mixed vegetables). Vegetarian fried rice or noodles can be found at other eateries.

Padang and other *warungs* offer *nasi campur* (rice with a choice of side dishes). Load up on tofu, *tempe*, *nangka* (jackfruit), egg dishes and leafy vegetables (ask for *daun/doun ubi*, cassava leaves). If meat is in a dish it's usually pretty obvious, but ask about hidden things such as fish paste, often used in *sambal*, or for bones lurking in the soup stock.

> 'Britain may have its chip shops, New York its delis, but in Borneo, the *kedai kopi* reigns. '

KEDAI KOPI: WHERE BORNEO EATS   By Jeremy Tan

Britain may have its chip shops, New York its delis, but in Borneo, the *kedai kopi* reigns. Literally meaning 'coffee shop' in Malay, *kedai kopi* serve much more than coffee. They are the precursors to the famous hawker centres found in Singapore, and run the gamut from small holes-in-the-wall dating back to colonial days selling only a single type of food, to newer, larger establishments with a larger choice of food stalls. A few things are standard though: the food is good, cheap, and the atmosphere is loud and boisterous during meal times (not the best place to bring a date perhaps). A good majority of the local population will stop into a *kedai kopi* at least once a day for one of the six daily meals (breakfast, morning tea, lunch, afternoon tea, dinner, supper).

Depending on the town and neighbourhood you're in, you will run into Malay *kedai kopi*, Chinese *kopitiam*, or Indian *gerai mamak*. In Indoneasia, these places are referred to as *warung*. The food on offer at each will differ greatly but the operating principle is the same. Usually, the shop owners will rent out space for food stalls while they operate the drinks concession themselves. Occasionally, the shop owner will also serve up rice with a selection of meat and vegetable dishes which are kept warm in heated buffet servers. In larger establishments, there may also be short-order food available. Individual stalls usually sell one dish or a group of related dishes and most of them will have signs in English displaying what they are serving; the trick for the traveller is to figure out what that is.

When you walk into a *kedai kopi*, especially a busy one, you may be a little confused as to etiquette of sitting at a table and ordering. There is rarely any orderly system for table appropriation; the rule is whoever plonks themself down first after the table is vacated will get the spoils. If you are with a small group and there is a large table free, sharing the table with others is a common practice. As for ordering, the general guideline is that in the older-style places where there is only one single stall, grab a table and someone will come and take your order for drinks and food. In such places, the stall is usually owned by the shop owner as well, so the bill will be tallied up at the end of your meal and you pay when you leave. In a newer establishment, where there are multiple food stalls, after securing a table, look around for what looks appetising, and order food directly from the stall owner. Don't worry, they'll magically figure out where you're sitting, no matter how large the place is. Drinks, however, are not ordered at the drinks station; someone will come to your table instead. In such places, food and drink is paid for immediately upon serving, and not after your meal.

Stalls at most places will have English or at the least phonetic translations in the Roman alphabet on their signs, so you'll be able to figure out what they have on offer.

'Malay *kedai kopi* will usually have *nasi campur* which is rice with a selection of Malay dishes.'

Malay Kedai Kopi

Malay *kedai kopi* will usually have *nasi campur* which is rice with a selection of Malay dishes. At some places, this is called *nasi padang*, which is the Indonesian equivalent. The price varies on what you select from the buffet to accompany your rice. Some special dishes one can generally expect to find in the *nasi campur* buffet:

Cangkok Manis – A dark leafy vegetable, usually stir-fried with egg.

Kangkong Belacan – Water spinach stir-fried with *belacan* (shrimp paste).

Midin Belacan – Local wild fiddlehead fern fried with *belacan*.

Rendang – A spicy dry coconut-based curry usually made with beef, sometimes with chicken.

Sambal – An assortment of spicy dishes made from ground chillis and *belacan,* usually cooked with calamari (*sambal sotong*) or dried anchovies (*sambal ikan pusu*).

Sometimes, the restaurant may also prepare fried rice or noodles, called *nasi goreng* and *meei goreng* respectively, done in a variety of styles. Generally there will be one or two stalls selling other Malay food which you can order from in lieu of *nasi campur*. There are several dishes common to these places:

Nasi Lemak – Rice cooked in coconut milk, served with salted fish, egg, and *sambal* – a common Malaysian breakfast.

Mee Jawa – Javanese-style thick yellow noodles with chicken and bean sprouts in a rich sauce.

Mee Sapi – Noodles with beef, either served in a hearty broth or with a light gravy.

Satay – Grilled meat skewers, served with the peanut sauce.

Sup Ekor – Oxtail soup.

Sup Tulang – Stew made from beef bones.

East Malaysians tend to have their food less spicy then Malays from Peninsular Malaysia. Also, the choice of Malay food is somewhat limited when compared to the heartlands of Kelantan and Terengganu, but what is available in Borneo is still very good. Recently, Malay food from the Peninsula has slowly started coming into Sarawak and Sabah, and so it is starting to become common to see traditional Kelantanese dishes such as *nasi dagang* (rice and glutinous rice cooked in coconut milk, served with side dishes) becoming available.

Chinese Kopitiam

The venerable Chinese *kopitiam* can be found in abundance all over East Malaysia, especially in the Chinese-dominated downtowns of the major cities. Some have been operating within the same family for a few generations, only specialising in a single dish, while many of the newer ones have multiple stalls featuring a smorgasbord of food to choose from. Chinese hawker food in Malaysia is the most varied by region compared with Malay and Indian food. There are many regional specialities, owing to successive waves of immigrants from different provinces in China. Chinese cuisine has also intermingled with Malay to form a distinct *peranakan* or *nonya* cuisine in older areas of Chinese settlement such as in Melaka. This style has grown beyond its original borders and influences much of what constitutes Chinese hawker fare today. Regional differences in Chinese stall food is still quite pronounced and it has become quite common to see regional specialities being sold in another locale (labelled proudly with its provenance, naturally). Furthermore, new dishes are being devised every day.

Chicken Rice – Chicken served with rice that has been cooked in chicken stock. This dish can also be found with roast chicken or pork instead of the standard boiled chicken.

Fish ball soup – Fish balls and stuffed tofu in a pork broth, usually with *tang hoon* (mungbean noodles).

Foochow Meesua – Wheat vermicelli, chicken and mushrooms in a large bowl of broth laced with Chinese wine; found in Foochow areas such as Sibu.

Kampua Mee – Another Foochow specialty, similar to Kuching-style *kolo mee* but tossed with lard.

Kolo Mee – A speciality of the Kuching area but found throughout the country, this is *mee* (wheat noodles) tossed in a mixture of oil and light soya sauce, garnished with barbecued pork and vegetables. Variations of this exist with different types of noodles such as *bee hoon* (rice vermicelli) or *kueh teow* (flat rice noodles), or served in different sauces, such as Chinese barbecue sauce.

Kueh Chap – For the adventurous, a tasty soup dish with various pork spare parts.

Laksa – Not to be confused with *laksa* from other parts of Malaysia, Sarawak *laksa* has a taste of its own. Rice vermicelli is served in a rich coconut-based broth with strips of chicken, egg and bean sprouts.

Lok-lok – Various deep-fried snacks which are ordered by the skewer.

Lui Char – A traditional Hakka soup, bitter in taste, made of ground-up herbs and vegetables, served with rice and crushed peanuts.

Porridge – Rice porridge with mince pork, usually eaten for breakfast.

Rojak – A salad of pineapple, turnip and other vegetables tossed in a shrimp sauce.

Tomato Kueh Teow – Fried *kueh teow* with a sweet-and-sour tomato sauce: a Kuching speciality.

'The venerable Chinese *kopitiam* can be found in abundance all over East Malaysia...'

The Chinese also have their own version of *nasi campur*, inexplicably called 'Economy Fast Food.'

Most of the older *kopitiam* will open only for breakfast and lunch, and generally stop selling when they run out of their day's allocation of ingredients. A few stay open in the afternoons, but you will only be able to get drinks and a few snack items such as toast with *kaya* (coconut jam), soft-boiled eggs or Chinese buns. Newer *kopitiam* will generally stay open the whole day, with some of the stalls closing in the afternoons for a few hours.

Indian Gerai Mamak

In local slang, *mamak* means a Muslim of Indian descent, and *gerai mamak* describes a Muslim Indian restaurant descended from the humble *mamak* roadside stalls selling *roti* (flatbread cooked on a griddle) and *teh tarik* ('pulled' tea). While these are less common in East Malaysia than in Peninsular Malaysia owing to the lower concentration of Indian Malaysians there, they are very popular wherever you can find them. Usually there will be an Indian-style *nasi campur* buffet comprising a large selection of curries. *Nasi biryani,* a rice dish prepared with a mixture of spices and served with a curry of your choice, and *mee* or *nasi goreng* will generally also be available. The most popular items at these places though, are their wide variety of flatbreads, which are prepared in spectacular fashion on a large iron skillet located at the front of the shop. *Roti* is usually served with curry gravy. Depending on the shop, there may be metal containers at the tables ready-filled from which you will spoon out your choice of gravy yourself, or someone will ask you which gravy you want. Usual choices are chicken, vegetable, or *dahl* (lentil) gravy.

Chapati – Flatbread made from whole wheat flour.

Murtabak – *Canai*-style flatbread stuffed with a variety of fillings such as meat (*murtabak daging*) or canned sardines (*murtabak sardin*).

Roti Bawang – A *roti canai* with onions.

Roti Canai – Fried flatbread made from white flour.

Roti Telur – A roti canai with egg.

Thosai – Thin, slightly crispy flatbread made from lentils and rice flour.

Thosai Masala – Spicy potato and onion mix wrapped in a *thosai*.

Various new variations of *roti canai* include *roti bom* (smaller but thicker *roti*) and *roti tisu* (paper-thin *roti*), both of which are worth trying. Some *gerai mamak* serve what is known as *banana leaf*, which is rice with a set selection of curries and chutneys traditionally served on a piece of banana leaf.

Hindu restaurants, while common in Peninsular Malaysia, are much rarer in Sarawak and Sabah. They are good bets for vegetarians, however.

Drinks

Malaysia has a long-standing history of coffee drinking quite distinct from other coffee cultures. However global chains such as Starbucks are making inroads into the country. Coffee in a *kopitiam* is traditionally made by repeatedly pouring hot water over coffee grounds filtered through a cloth bag, similar in shape to a sports sock. Tea is also made in a similar fashion using powdered tea instead of tea bags or loose-leaf.

Ordering coffee or tea in a *kopitiam* can be a confusing experience for a newcomer. *Kopitiam* will rarely, if ever, keep fresh milk or cream on hand. The two kinds of dairy available are condensed milk, which is thickened heavily sweetened milk, and evaporated milk, which is thickened but unsweetened. The default is condensed milk. Because of this, it is quite common for a tourist to order 'coffee with milk' and end up getting served a very sweet coffee, leading thereafter to a bungling conversation with the staff. Rarely does anyone leave that conversation any wiser. The following is a guide for ordering coffee or tea in a *kopitiam*:

Kopi/Teh (pronounced 'tay') – Coffee/tea with sweetened condensed milk.

Kopi/Teh 'C' – Coffee/tea with evaporated milk and sugar.

Kopi/Teh 'C' Kosong – Coffee/tea with evaporated milk but sans sugar.

Kopi/Teh 'O' – Coffee/tea with sugar.

Kopi/Teh 'O' Kosong – Coffee/tea sans sugar.

Malaysians tend to drink their coffee or tea with enough sugar in it to rot the tusks off an elephant. If you'd prefer to keep your teeth healthy, you can add the '*kurang manis*' suffix to your order (it means 'less sweet' in Malay). If you want it without sugar, say you want it *pahit* in Indonesia, *tidak gula* in Malaysia. *Susu* (milk), often condensed milk, is frequently included in Malaysia; *tidak susu* or *hitam* (black) is the way to opt out.

Try *teh tarik* at Indian tea stalls. The tea is poured from one cup at a height to another lower one. The tea has a head of froth when served *Teh alia* is the same tea but with ginger added for bite.

A regional speciality tea preparation known as *teh tarik* (literally 'pulled tea') can be ordered from Indian stalls or restaurants. The tea is poured back and forth between two containers, one held high and the other low, to work air into it and to mix in the condensed milk (it is only ever served with condensed milk). The pouring action creates the optical illusion that a 'rope' of tea is being pulled from the lower container to the upper one. The result is a creamy, frothy brew, and is a very popular breakfast drink. Do not try to order this in a Chinese *kopitiam* as you'll just get funny looks.

Apart from Western soft drinks, freshly made traditional Asian drinks can usually be ordered as well. Some of the local drinks are traditional soy milk, *air limau* (limeade made from key limes), *air tebu* (sugar-cane juice), *air kelapa* (coconut juice) usually served in the young coconut (*kelapa muda*) – spoon out the inside after drinking for maximum delight.

Check to see that they are made on-the-spot rather than served from a can, especially for sugar-cane juice. Additionally, you may spot pastel-coloured posters plastered randomly on the walls of the shop. These are advertisements for other drinks that are available.

Other favourite drinks include soursop, a dark green, prickly fruit with a slightly acidic, tropical-flavoured pulp; and *kalamansi* – a tiny lime. Juices come in two varieties, *air* (water) or *es* or *ais* (ice, a blended concoction). *Air* normally includes sugar unless you stipulate you want just juice (*hanya air* or *air saja*). *Es* drinks habitually include condensed milk and sugar.

Look out for *air kelapa*, coconut juice served in its shell. The top of the coconut is usually hacked off and a straw is inserted. A spoon is provided to dig out the tasty white flesh once you've drained the juice..

Environment

You might think that an island has a fairly simple environment, but Borneo is one of the most geologically complex and biologically diverse places in the world. Situated where three great plates of the earth's crust join, and composed of fragments from old continents, Borneo is an intricate mosaic of rocks, plants and animals derived from both Asian and Australian sources. Now an island, Borneo owes much of its astounding biological diversity to the fact that as recently as 10,000 years ago it was joined with the Asian mainland, providing a corridor over which plants and animals migrated to the otherwise isolated island.

The world-famous forests of Borneo are critically imperiled by logging and the northern third of the island administered by Malaysia is one of the few places in the world where tropical rainforests can be found in a soon-to-be-fully developed nation. Thus, Borneo will be an important test-case for conservation policies in developing countries.

THE LAND

At 740,000 sq km, Borneo is the third largest island in the world after Greenland and New Guinea. Straddling the equator between Vietnam and Java, the island lies in an evergreen climate characterised by abundant amounts of year-round rain. While rain supports lush rainforests, it also erodes the landscape and leaches nutrients out of the soil, thus defining Borneo more than any other factor. Ironically, rainforests cloak the land so densely that Borneo has one of the most poorly understood geologic landscapes in the world.

For an excellent, colourful introduction to Borneo's environment check out *Wild Borneo* by Nick Garbutt.

Also hidden from sight is one of Borneo's most important geologic features – a continental shelf that extends underwater from Peninsular Malaysia to Sumatra, Borneo and Java. Western Borneo is actually the southeasternmost tip of the Eurasian continental plate, even though above water it seems to be a separate island. Sticking out into the South China Sea by itself, Borneo is being rammed from the east by the Pacific plate and from the south by the Indo-Australian plate.

It is thought that over the course of at least 100 million years, Borneo took shape as parts of six different continental fragments (terranes) collided at the tip of the Eurasian plate, squeezing together ancient ocean-basins and scrapping up seafloor sediments in the process.

Western Borneo exhibits what is called a 'basement block', so named because it is part of the original continental shelf; while rocks in the rest of Borneo show evidence of originating in shallow- to deep-water seas at the edge of ancient continental landmasses. Compressed and altered by time, these ancient sand and mud sediments now show up as rocks such as sandstone and shale.

Borneo is a remarkably flat island, with over 50% of the landscape less than 150m in elevation and covered in lush rainforest and swamp forest drained by large, slow-moving rivers. There are mountains in the interior of Borneo, but unlike the rest of the Indonesian and Philippine islands there are no active volcanoes because Borneo itself is part of a very stable continental shelf.

Rather than being created by volcanoes, the island's mountain chains resulted from forces that lifted sea bottoms out of the water and often crumpled them into jagged hills. Uplift began just north of Sarawak's Lupar River about 40 million years ago, and progressively moved north until it culminated in Sabah about 17 million years ago. Now exposed to abundant rainfall, these uplifted mountains have since eroded vast quantities of sediment into adjacent lowlands and coastal areas.

Extensive pockets of limestone in northern Borneo show where ancient coral reefs were buried under thousands of metres of sediment, then subsequently uplifted to form mountain ranges. Gunung Mulu National Park in Sarawak is one of the world's premier limestone landscapes, including sheer 45m limestone pinnacles and the world's largest cave chamber (large enough to park eight 747 jets end to end).

Mountains include 4095m Mt Kinabalu in Sabah, the highest mountain between the Himalayas and New Guinea and arguably the epicentre of Borneo's fabulous biodiversity. This colossal dome of granite forced through the earth's crust as molten rock 10 to 15 million years ago and continues to rise about 5mm a year. Despite its location just north of the equator, Kinabalu was high enough to be exquisitely sculpted by glaciers during the ice ages, and is today one of Borneo's premier destinations.

WILDLIFE

From breathtaking coral reef to mind-boggling rainforest, Borneo is one of the greatest showcases of life on the entire planet. It's hard to comprehend how so many species have come to live in one place, but part of the reason lies in the complex origin of the island. Formed from the collision of different continental fragments, each acting much like an ark carrying groups of ancient species, Borneo sits at the junction of Asian and Australian biomes and shows elements of both.

Borneo's strongest affinity is with the Asian mainland because Borneo becomes connected to Peninsular Malaysia when sea levels drop. This has happened on at least several occasions, once about 50 million years ago, and more recently during the ice ages that lasted from 2 million years ago until 10,000 years ago. Each time, plants and animals travelled across the land bridge and colonised Borneo, bringing new species and gene pools to the island.

In one measure of how rich the wildlife of Borneo is, it has been reported that 361 new plants and animals have been discovered since 1996, with an additional 52 new species discovered between July 2005 and December 2006.

Despite the superficial abundance of life, one of the unfortunate ironies is that tropical soils are usually of poor quality because heavy rainfalls leach out nutrients. As soon as forests are logged or farmed they revert into the highly degraded *padang* (field or grassy area) wastelands that now cover vast swathes of the island. Sadly, the loss of Borneo's forests and wildlife is occurring on a staggering scale and without immediate action the end is in sight (see below).

'From breathtaking coral reef to mind-boggling rainforest, Borneo is one of the greatest showcases of life on the entire planet.'

Habitats

Borneo has a number of distinctive habitats, and knowledge of these habitats will help you find specific plants and animals. In some cases, the best remaining examples of these habitats are easily viewed in national parks.

CORAL REEF

Borneo's coral reefs are part of the so-called 'Coral Triangle', a fantastically rich portion of the South China Sea that is home to 75% of the world's coral species and over 3000 types of marine fish. Reefs are in the best shape along the northeast coast of Borneo where the water is clear and free of sediment. Sipadan Island in Sabah and the Derawan Archipelago in East Kalimantan have the greatest concentrations of reefs, while protected areas include Tun Sakaran Marine Park in Sabah and Talang-Satang National Park in Sarawak.

DIPTEROCARP FOREST

Most of the lowland forest in Borneo is dominated by one family of trees called dipterocarps. More than 250 species of these magnificent, towering trees are found on the island, where they form the tallest and most diverse rainforests on earth – a single hectare of dipterocarp forest may have over 200 species of trees! Of the countless animals found in a dipterocarp forest, none are as interesting as the many types of gliding animals. In addition to birds and bats, there are frogs, lizards, snakes, squirrels and lemurs, which 'fly' between trees. Excellent viewing opportunities can be found at Danum Valley Conservation Area in Sabah, but remnants of dipterocarp-forest habitats are found in many other parks.

FRESHWATER SWAMP FOREST

Low-lying floodplains in coastal areas support a rich forest of tall trees. Home to the Borneon pygmy elephant, orangutan and proboscis monkey, these vital forests have been extensively converted to oil plantations. On sites where the soil is more acidic, decaying material accumulates and creates a specialised forest known as peat swamp that covers vast swathes of coastal Sarawak, and West and Central Kalimantan. Swamp forests play a crucial role by acting as sponges that absorb rainwater and release it slowly to a wider environment during the dry months. These forests are found in many coastal parks such as Tanjung Puting National Park in Central Kalimantan or Kutai National Park in East Kalimantan.

HEATH FOREST

Acidic sandy soils that lack nutrients are home to a very important and highly specialised habitat known in Borneo as *kerangas* (heath forest). Found in both coastal and montane areas, heath forest is increasingly restricted to protected coastal areas like Bako National Park or incredibly remote mountain tops like the Maliau Basin in Sabah. This forest type is composed of small, densely packed trees that seldom top 20m in height. Due to lack of nutrients, plants of the heath forest have unique adaptations to help them protect their leaves and acquire nutrients. For example, many plants obtain food by providing homes to ants. Heath forest also has the world's greatest diversity of pitcher plants that eat insects trapped in chambers full of enzyme-rich fluids.

MANGROVE

The watery, tidal world where land meets sea is one of the most biologically productive habitats on earth. Growing precariously in this odd mix of salt and fresh water, mangrove plants stand on stiltlike roots that keep them out of the suffocating mud. Uncounted marine organisms and nearly every commercially important seafood species find sanctuary and nursery sites among these roots. Charismatic wildlife species include the bizarre proboscis monkey and the mudskipper, a fish that spends much of its time out of the water. Mangroves once ringed virtually the entire island, especially around river mouths, but increasingly they are limited to places like Bako National Park near Kuching.

MONTANE FOREST

On mountains over 900m, dipterocarp forest gives way to a magical world of stunted oaks, myrtle and laurel trees. This dripping, cloud-drenched

'On mountains over 900m, dipterocarp forest gives way to a magical world of stunted oaks, myrtle and laurel trees.'

montane forest is chock-full of ferns, rhododendrons, lichens and moss. It is also the site for a stunning wealth of orchids. More than 3000 species of orchids are found in Borneo, and Mt Kinabalu alone has over a thousand species! Visitors from around the world sojourn to the lower edges of Borneo's montane forest with hopes of seeing the legendary rafflesia flower (see p51) at places like Gunung Gading National Park in Sarawak.

Animals

If Borneo has one symbolic animal it would be the orangutan, or 'man of the forest'. At the top of every visitor's wish list, this majestic great ape is a wonder to behold in its native environment, and even the most seasoned traveller will feel a rush of awe if they cross paths with a wild orangutan. It is almost impossible to deny the appeal of a 100kg animal whose facial expressions and obvious intelligence come eerily close to our own.

Ranging over large areas of native forest in search of fruiting trees, the orangutan has suffered greatly due to hunting and logging pressure, and in fact some scientists speculate it may go extinct in the wild without increased protection. Wild orangutans are now difficult to find except in places like Danum Valley Conservation Area or the Lower Kinabatangan Wildlife Sanctuary; but many visitors are content to observe rehabilitated animals at the Sepilok Orang-Utan Rehabilitation Centre in Sabah, or Semenggoh Rehabilitation Centre in Sarawak.

Equally thrilling may be the experience of hearing the loud, whooping songs of gibbons ringing through the rainforest at sunrise. These primates move through the forest canopy with such speed and agility that it seems as if they are falling sideways as they swing effortlessly from branch to branch. One species occurs in southwestern Borneo and can be observed at Gunung Palung National Park; another species is found throughout northern Borneo.

Very little is known about Borneo's two largest land mammals, the pygmy elephant and the rhinoceros. In fact, a Bornean rhinoceros was briefly caught on film for the first time ever in June 2007 and only a few hundred are thought to remain in the wildest parts of Sabah. Borneo's elephants have likewise been a mystery, but new genetic evidence puts to rest the theory that humans introduced them to the island relatively recently. It turns out that they have been on the island possibly as long as 300,000 years and have evolved into a unique pygmy race (adult females are only 2m tall!). Of the 1000 estimated to live in northeastern Borneo, the largest elephant population is thought to roam the Lower Kinabatangan Wildlife Sanctuary where they've come into increasing conflict with the owners of vast oil palm plantations.

If any one animal ties the habitats of Borneo together, it would be the bearded pigs that are encountered in nearly every forested area. Following well-worn paths, these 100kg animals sometimes gather into large herds and migrate incredible distances in search of nuts and seeds. Although they are an extremely popular game animal, they are one creature that hunters and predators truly fear. Be wary of these unpredictable animals and their sharp tusks – they are capable of eviscerating a human in a split second.

At the small end of the scale, few animals are more surprising than the 2kg lesser mouse deer, a rabbit-sized creature that looks like a miniature deer with long protruding canines instead of antlers. Skittish and generally nocturnal, they can sometimes be seen during the day by quiet hikers.

It would be hard to miss the fantastic assortment of birds that fill the forests of Borneo with their ethereal calls. At the top of the list are the eight boldly marked hornbill species. With loud whooping calls, the 105cm-long rhinoceros hornbill is the most obvious hornbill, but when the 125cm-long helmeted hornbill swoops across the sky you might think you're seeing a

Gibbons swing by their hands, a unique mode of travel called brachiation that isn't entirely perfect: most gibbons have bone fractures from falling.

pterodactyl instead. Hornbills play an extremely important ecological role by travelling great distances and dispersing seeds of rainforest fruits that they eat. Revered and hunted by Borneo's indigenous peoples, hornbills are highly threatened by ongoing logging practices.

Although Borneo has one of the most fabulous displays of wildlife in the world, you may find your attention riveted instead on the smallest of organisms. Consider the leech, one rainforest creature that every visitor soon comes to know and dread. They come at you from every direction in the forest, humping along the ground in eager quest for your blood. Slimy and hard to pick off, they slip under your clothes and take up residence in uncomfortable places. They cause no great harm, but do inject anticoagulant juices that keep their bites bleeding for hours afterwards.

And if that wasn't enough, you may encounter night-time swarms of raiding fire ants that sweep down trails and through houses like a living blanket. Steer clear of these fierce ants or you might get some stings you won't soon forget.

Plants

Borneo is a world centre of plant diversity – in fact it has as many plants (about 15,000 species of flowering plants) as the entire continent of Africa, which is 40 times larger than the island. So diverse are Borneo's forests that virtually every tree you encounter on a hike might be a different species and you could hike for days to find two examples of one tree. It would take a lifetime to learn the 3000 different species of trees alone, not to mention the thousands of orchids, or the other numerous groups of fascinating plants.

When trees are this spread out they must evolve special ways to disperse their pollen and seeds, and in Borneo this task is accomplished by animals. Orangutans and hornbills, for instance, travel great distances in search of absolutely scrumptious fruits – including durian, longsat and rambutan – offered as temptations by trees. You may even see trees attracting the attention of passing animals by sprouting fruits directly on their trunks, a very odd adaptation called cauliflory.

At the other end of the scale, there may be so many seed-eaters that trees have to find ways to avoid having all their seeds eaten. The world-famous dipterocarp trees solve this problem through a strategy called masting, whereby every dipterocarp tree in the forest produces vast quantities of seeds once every six years or so and no seeds in the intervening years. The sheer numbers of seeds produced completely overwhelm the seed-eaters and ensure that a few seeds survive. Because dipterocarp seeds are winged and spin gracefully as they fall, the dispersal of millions of dipterocarp seeds during a masting event is one of the greatest spectacles that you can see on planet Earth.

The rainforests of Borneo are exposed to twice as much sunlight as a temperate forest, but nearly all this energy is trapped in the canopy, so few animals live on the forest floor.

Plants typically struggle to survive on the thin, nutrient-poor soils of Borneo. In response, trees may hold themselves upright with wide flaring buttresses rather than deep root systems. Although smaller flowering plants don't have to worry about growing tall they still require hard-to-find nutrients that they may obtain by eating insects (pitcher plants) or by creating shelters for ant colonies that bring food to the plant.

It's a strange world of plants in Borneo and some of the most famous ones are strangler figs. Starting life as tiny seeds, which are are defecated by birds in the rainforest canopy, strangler figs then send down spindly roots in search of the ground. Eventually, the fig grows large enough to embrace its host tree in a death-grip. Once the host tree rots away the giant fig stands upright on a fantastic hollow latticework of its own woven roots. It may seem that figs are all bad, but in fact they are one of the most important fruiting

THE EXTRAORDINARY RAFFLESIA

People revert to words like bizarre, awe-inspiring or enigmatic upon viewing the rafflesia flower. One of the greatest wonders of the plant world, the 1m-wide flower can elicit both astonishment at its incredible size, or revulsion at its smell, which has been likened to the smell of a rotting carcass. Even more amazing is the fact that this oddity erupts directly from the forest floor, with no visible stems or leaves.

The rafflesia plant is actually a parasite that lives entirely on the roots of a grapelike vine in the genus *Tetrastigma*. The parasite does not produce any food of its own, but instead forms a network of microscopic filaments that penetrate the vine's roots and steal water and nutrients.

In preparation for flowering the parasitic rafflesia sends up a cabbage-like bud that grows on the forest floor for a year or more before blossoming. The flower itself is a giant succulent crea-tion with red colour and white splotches. After two or three days the flower begins to deteriorate and within two weeks it is reduced to a blob of black slime.

Seeing a rafflesia is a very special treat. Not only are the flowers themselves fleeting and rarely encountered, but poaching and habitat loss has greatly reduced their numbers. Of the nine spe-cies thought to occur in Borneo, three have not been seen in the past 60 years.

The odds of finding a rafflesia on your own are close to nil, but don't despair. Numerous private plots around Poring Hot Springs on Mt Kinabalu are closely monitored for flowers, with owners advertising prominently along the main road whenever one of their plants is in bloom. Likewise, rangers at Tanbunan Rafflesia Reserve, just southeast of Kota Kinabalu, monitor the forest closely and admit visitors to view flowers if you call in advance. In Sarawak try Gunung Gading National Park.

plants in the entire rainforest ecosystem and everything from orangutans to pigs and birds relies on fig crops for their survival.

NATIONAL PARKS

Despite the fantastic natural wealth of Borneo there are few examples of well-managed parks and preserves, and very little land is strictly protected (see below). Furthermore, access to many parks is difficult and limited, and travel within the rainforest is extremely challenging, making these destina-tions better suited for adventurous hardy travellers. And, while it's possible to list the amazing animals found in these parks, the reality is that in most cases these animals are rarely observed. Fortunately, a handful of parks have well-established access, lodging, and recreation opportunities for a broad range of visitors. For more on national parks in Borneo, see p57.

ENVIRONMENTAL ISSUES

If left intact, the vast forests of Borneo would provide a limitless supply of valuable resources for countless generations. In fact, the true wealth of rain-forest ecosystems is a closed loop to the extent that once the forest is logged and fragmented the entire system falls apart. Soils become degraded, waters become silted, plants and animals go extinct, and native human communities suffer grave ills. Perhaps more terrifying is the fact that rainforest ecosystems may not be recoverable once they are lost, and even limited logging appears to greatly diminish the reproductive capacity of the remaining trees.

Unfortunately, the governing bodies of Borneo have a terrible environmen-tal legacy despite the best efforts of local and international environmental groups. Far too frequently, rainforests are viewed as an impediment to 'progress' or as political spoils for those in power, with a handful of political elites profiting massively from the cutting of the forests.

In February 2007 Sabah, Sarawak, and Kalimantan jointly signed a 'Heart of Borneo' agreement spearheaded by the WWF. However, this forward-thinking

Visiting Sarawak? You'll love the details found in *National Parks of Sarawak* by Hans Hazebroek and Abang Kashim bin Abang Morshidi.

plan to protect 240,000 sq km of forest fell under immediate assault by international companies bent on profiting from Borneo's valuable resources. By May 2007 a prominent group of 1500 scientists from 70 countries labelled the situation in Borneo a 'crisis' and called for urgent action. New satellite images are revealing that over 50% of Borneo's forests have already been cut. And at current rates of logging, it is estimated that 98% of orangutan habitat will be gone by 2022. You would think that national-park status would protect an area but it is now estimated that about 35 of Borneo's 41 national parks have been logged in some way, much of it occurring during a period of political upheaval in the late 1990s.

From 60% to 80% of Borneo's tourism revenue leaks out of the country into the hands of foreign investors, while nearly all of the remaining money goes as profit to local business elites.

Ironically the most serious current threat comes from the European Union decision to replace 10% of its transport fuel with biodiesel. As a consequence, palm oil prices have risen dramatically since 2006 and vast tracts of Borneo rainforest have been cleared to make way for new oil plantations (one project alone is slated to clear 1.8 million hectares). So lucrative are these operations that social and environmental issues are being sweep aside with hardly a thought.

Advocacy groups make the claim that companies are illegally setting fire to pristine rainforest then buying the degraded land at a greatly reduced price after the fire, an all-too-common strategy in Borneo. In 1982, fires set by slash-and-burn farmers and logging companies ended up destroying more than 4 million hectares of rainforest, including half of the newly established Kutai National Park, making it the largest fire ever recorded on Earth.

Not only are many of these rainforest trees ecologically valuable, but these high-quality hardwoods are also treasured for their beautiful woods. It is tragically ironic that the majority of trees logged in Borneo are instead

---

WHAT YOU CAN DO

What can you do on an island where grave injustices have been and continue to be perpetrated against its native peoples, where corrupt businesses strip away resources under the protection of local police and top politicians, and where even the most powerful international aid agencies flounder? The environmental situation in Borneo is a crisis of staggering global ramifications and action is urgently needed.

It may be that some of the best work being done in Borneo is by WWF Malaysia (www.wwf malaysia.org), including forest and species protection, education and international advocacy. Recent WWF achievements include obtaining the first-ever video of a wild rhinoceros in Borneo and gaining support for a vast 'Heart of Borneo' preserve.

Travellers might check out the Wild Asia website (www.wildasia.net) to learn more about responsible tourism in the region. They suggest trying to give your business to operators that follow guidelines established by an internationally established body like Green Globe 21. However, you may find responsible tourism options limited on the island of Borneo so Wild Asia recommends being active in giving feedback to local operators, telling them what you like and what's important to you.

Even though a few sustainable forestry efforts are starting up in Sabah, you can be almost certainly assured that most wood products come from highly degraded forests or illegal logging operations. Please be conscious of all wood products you buy, whether you are travelling or back at home. Wood products made in China or sold in import stores nearly always come from tropical hardwoods. Even widely available plywoods are likely made from trees logged in Borneo (an estimated 80% of the plywood sold in the United States for instance), and sold in home-improvement stores as 'red oak'. Wood dowels (also found in broom handles, mops, toilet bowl plungers and paintbrush handles) are nearly all made from an endangered tree found in Borneo. Rayon fabric is made from wood pulp that often comes from rainforest trees.

BIOFUELLING FOREST DESTRUCTION *Muhammad Cohen*

The fad for biofuels – using crops as a substitute for fossil fuels – is the latest accelerator of Borneo's deforestation. Record prices for palm oil are driving increased acreage for palm-oil plantations that spark destruction of forests and their inhabitants.

For starters, creating a plantation means logging the plantation area. Because oil palms take five years to produce a crop, timber sales subsidise the preproduction phase. In some cases, unscrupulous operators get a plantation concession – more easily obtained than timber concessions – log, then leave the land denuded. Setting a fire may complete land clearing.

While palm oil is an extraordinarily versatile food product, it's a remarkably lousy fuel. Studies show that more carbon is released from the conversion of forests to palm plantations than saved through replacement of fossils fuels with the palm oil produced. The equation is especially unbalanced when the plantation is located on peat swamp forest, increasingly the case in Kalimantan, and off the charts when burning is the final step in clearing.

Substituting oil palms for forest isn't an environmental plus. Plantation monocropping robs local wildlife of native food-sources, increases conflicts between wildlife and humans – plantations consider orangutans pests – and pushes Dayak shifting cultivators toward peat swamps, where slash and burn methods release vast quantities of carbon, often triggering massive fires. Many orangutan advocates now recommend boycotting palm oil products and discouraging new plantations as the best steps to help Asia's great ape survive.

Biofuel presents a new irony: honest people can help destroy the rainforest by trying to save it.

converted into low-grade plywood to feed the insatiable building boom in places like Japan, the European Union and the United States.

It is hard to be optimistic about the fate of Borneo's incredible forests and animals, especially in the relatively lawless provinces of Kalimantan where well-intentioned plans are sabotaged by local officials and virtual lack of oversight from national institutions. The World Bank estimates that $3 billion worth of timber is illegally exported from Borneo each year, but even World Bank agents have been ushered off the island by police so little is known about the true scale of these operations.

The situation is somewhat better in Sabah and Brunei, although it doesn't mean that forests aren't still logged at an unsustainable rate. WWF reported in August 2007, for instance, that more than 40% of Sabah's forests have already been lost to logging and oil plantations. Visit the United Nations Environment Programme site (www.grida.no) and search 'Borneo deforestation' and you will be directed to an excellent map of the current situation in the region. Much is said and promised about protecting the resources of Borneo, but it remains to be seen how much is enacted before it's too late.

Borneo Outdoors

Borneo is Southeast Asia's premier adventure-sports destination. If you're one of those people who like to experience a place by climbing it, diving it, paddling it or trekking it, then you're bound to love the island of Borneo.

For starters, Borneo has some of the best jungle-trekking of anywhere in the world. While forests are disappearing at an alarming rate, vast swathes of intact tropical rainforest remain in the middle of island. If you've never walked through primary tropical jungle, the experience is likely to be a revelation – you simply won't believe the biodiversity (or the leeches, for that matter).

Towering above the forests of Borneo are some brilliant mountains. Even nonclimbers know about 4095m Mt Kinabalu, the highest mountain between the Himalayas and the island of New Guinea. If you're a hiker or climber, one look at a picture of the craggy peaks of this mountain and you're sold – you're not going to be happy until you've set foot on the summit.

But the story doesn't end there: Borneo is capped by a mountain range that runs from north to south almost the entire length of the island. For adventurous climbers, there are interesting and challenging peaks to climb in Sabah, Sarawak and Kalimantan.

Borneo's mountains are literally porous with caves, including some of the world's largest. Sarawak's Gunung Mulu National Park holds the world's largest single cave passage and it's a great place to get a taste for the delights of caving. Sarawak is also home to Niah Caves, a couple of awesome caverns that have to be seen to be believed.

The mountains and jungles of Borneo are drained by some of Southeast Asia's longest rivers. Whether it's tearing up one of these rivers in a speedboat, rafting down one of them in a rubber raft, or paddling down one of the upper tributaries in a kayak, you'll find that these watery highways are perhaps the best way to experience the island of Borneo.

Finally, there is the undersea world. Borneo has some of the richest and most varied coral reefs in the world. On either side of Sabah, you'll find world-class dive sites: Layang Layang, a ring of coral 300km offshore in the South China Sea, and Pulau Sipadan, a coral pinnacle rising from the floor of the Sulu Sea. Even if you don't make it to one of these sites, you'll find excellent snorkelling around the offshore islands all around Borneo.

MOUNTAIN CLIMBING

Sabah's Mt Kinabalu (p106) dominates northern Sabah the way it dominates the mind of most adventurous travellers headed to Borneo. This 4095m peak simply begs to be climbed and there is something magical about starting a climb in humid tropical jungle and arriving in a bare rocky alpine zone so cold that snow has been known to fall. It's not just the transition from hot to cold that makes it so interesting; it's the weird world of Kinabalu's summit plateau that makes it among the world's most interesting peaks. It's got a dash of Yosemite and a pinch of Torres del Paine, but at the end of the day, it's all Kinabalu. Be warned that an ascent of Kinabalu is no joke, but if you're reasonably fit and well prepared, it may well be the highlight of your trip to Borneo.

A little further down Sabah's Crocker Range, you'll find 2642m Mt Trus Madi (p125), which attracts climbers who like their mountains without the crowds. Like Kinabalu, it's generally a two-day climb, but unlike Kinabalu, you'll usually have the summit to yourself. The highlight of the climb is the relatively intact forest that you trek through for much of the way. For those

Mt Kinabalu was first climbed in 1888 by Briton John Whitehead.

BORNEO: NATURE'S PLAYGROUND

Just what is it that makes Borneo an outdoor paradise?

First, Borneo sits right on the equator, in the heart of maritime southeast Asia. Over the course of millions of years, Borneo has been connected to the rest of southeast Asia by a series of land bridges. These bridges, while they lasted, allowed vast amounts of genetic material to flow onto the island, making it a kind of steamy tropical Noah's Ark. When the seas covered over the bridges, the life on the islands was allowed to evolve into fantastic new forms. The result is an island that is one of the world's great biodiversity hot spots.

Second, most of Borneo is located inside the so-called 'Coral Triangle'. Bounded by the Philippines, Borneo, Indonesia and the island of New Guinea, this region of the far-western Pacific is the centre of the world's marine biodiversity and is home to the world's richest coral reefs and most vibrant and varied fish populations.

Third, the island is blessed with some truly peculiar geological features, including some incredible limestone caves and some impressive mountain ranges. Towering above them all is 4095m Mt Kinabalu, the highest mountain between the Himalayas and the island of New Guinea.

Thus, both above and below the sea, Borneo is a kind of vast natural theme park for adrenalin junkies and nature lovers.

---

who have a little time and patience to make the arrangements, this is a very rewarding and seldom-climbed peak.

Down in Sarawak, you'll find more brilliant climbing, starting with the famous 2377m Gunung Mulu (Mt Mulu; p205). If you're a real glutton for punishment, you'll probably find the five-day return trek to the summit of this peak to your liking. Those who make the journey experience a variety of pristine natural environments starting with lowland dipterocarp forest and ending with rhododendron and montane forest.

A much more popular trek in the park is the one-day return trek up to the Pinnacles (p205), on the shoulder of 1750m Gunung Api. These freakish limestone arrowheads that jut up out of the forest on this mountain are among the strangest sights in all of Borneo and they're well worth the brutal slog up to get there (not to mention the equally brutal hike down). If you're fit and keen, you'll probably love the Pinnacles.

Also in Sarawak, the Kelabit Highlands (p212) have several peaks in addition to great longhouse treks (see p56). The most popular trek is the six-day return trip up 2623m Gunung Murud (p215), which will test anyone's endurance. Also popular is the three-day return trip up 2046m Batu Lawi (p215), which allows a good view of the stunning spire of the 'male peak' of Batu Lawi. Standing like a sentinel over the highlands, this lovely peak is sometimes visible on the flight into Bario.

Kalimantan has several notable parklands and while most areas are best suited to trekking, there are a few good climbs. In the area around Sintang (p242) hikers can climb to the peak of Gunung Kelam, seeing butterflies, waterfalls and great vistas along the way. South of Sintang lies the Bukit Baka-Bukit Raya National Park, and while tourism infrastructure is sparse, the broad rivers, forested panoramas and giant rafflesia (the world's largest flower; see p51 for more information) are worth the exertion.

If tracking down a blooming rafflesia is your quest, Gunung Poteng (p246) is 12km east of Singkawang and only takes two hours to climb. While each massive flower blooms only once a year, there are multiple blooming periods that afford a good chance to spot one.

A holy day-hike, Gunung Bondang (p260), of religious significance to some Dayaks, is in the mountains north east of Muara Teweh and features waterfalls, stone carvings and orchids.

Mountains of Malaysia, by John Briggs, though difficult to find, is the best book on climbing routes in Sabah and Sarawak.

Finally, the Apokayan Highlands (p285), sheltered by white-water rapids from the boats of loggers, have some fine trekking and climbing. The Kayan Mentarang National Park traces the border with Sarawak and mixes natural and cultural attractions in a great selection of guided expeditions. Highlights include a trail to the high pass at Apo Napu, routes through pristine forests to Dayak longhouses, waterfalls and burial caves.

TREKKING

Parks of Malaysia, by John Briggs, is a useful resource for those planning a thorough exploration of the parks of Sabah and Sarawak.

The island of Borneo is one of the best places in the world to experience one of the world's fast-disappearing treasures: old growth (primary) tropical rainforest. A look down on the island with Google Earth reveals a swathe of intact jungle around the northern end of the Sarawak–Kalimantan border, as well as several intact areas in central Sabah and Brunei. For nature-lovers, a hike through this forest is an opportunity not to be missed.

Sabah's Danum Valley Conservation Area (p145) is one of the few places on earth where you can experience intact rainforest while staying in an international-class resort. It's also one of the best places on earth to see wild orangutans in their natural habitat. The treks here are all very short and easily managed by most people.

At the opposite end of the spectrum is Sabah's Maliau Basin Conservation Area (p154), which is only really accessible to fit and adventurous hikers. Those who make the slog up over the basin wall and down into the basin itself find themselves rewarded with a Jurassic Park–like hidden world of truly awesome biodiversity. If you don't mind working up a sweat and making a few donations to the leeches, this place should rank high on your list.

Sabah's Kinabalu National Park (p106) also has some great trekking, which is often overlooked by hikers who make a beeline for the summit of Mt Kinabalu. The 6km Liwagu Trail (p110) is one of the finer walks in Sabah and it would be swarming with people if it weren't for the fact that it's located below Borneo's most popular hike of all, the Kinabalu Summit Trail. It's a good introduction to a dipterocarp forest and it can be undertaken by anyone of moderate fitness, especially if you walk it top down.

Of course, Borneo's real trekking paradise is to be found in Sarawak's Kelabit Highlands (p212), which offer the closest thing to Himalayan teahouse treks in Borneo. The Kelabit Highlands are a hanging valley in northern Sarawak, right up against the border with one of the wilder parts of Indonesian Kalimantan. With relatively cool temperatures, a network of winding rivers and fairly intact primary- and secondary-growth forest, the Highlands are a natural trekking destination. Best of all, the area is home to the incredibly hospitable Kelabit people, many of whom live in longhouses scattered about the Highlands. It's possible to do multiday treks here, stopping each night at a different longhouse, where you dine on the fruits (and, most likely, animals) of the surrounding jungle.

The Kinabalu giant red leech can grow up to 30cm in length. Luckily, it doesn't feed on humans.

Not far away, Sarawak's Gunung Mulu National Park (p205) also offers some fine jungle trekking. Around park headquarters, there are several plankwalks through the jungle that allow the timid and leech-averse to experience Borneo's incredible rainforest. More adventurous trekkers can undertake the famous Headhunters Trail (p209), which involves two days of jungle trekking and a night in an Iban longhouse, with the possibility of a side trip up to see the bizarre Pinnacles (see p208).

Down at the other end of Sarawak, Bako National Park (p172), just north of Kuching, offers trekking through a variety of coastal forest and brush environments and a good chance of spotting Borneo's famous proboscis monkeys. An easy overnight trip out of Kuching, this park has the best hiking in western Sarawak.

(Continued on page 65)

NATIONAL PARKS

Borneo's national parks hold some of the world's most spectacular sights and rarest wildlife. Remarkable pinnacles, jagged mountain ranges, mangrove forests, waterfalls and pristine beaches grace the island's precious protected areas. No visitor to Borneo will want to leave without a glimpse of the parks' increasingly endangered and often elusive wildlife: turtles, elephants, the bulbous-nosed proboscis monkey and, of course, the great orange man, orangutan. Look out for, but don't stop to smell the massive rafflesia flower, with the unfortunate scent of rotten flesh.

Sabah

Mountainous rainforests replete with endangered primates and birdlife complement tropical islands in the Malaysian region of Sabah. Many visitors make the trek up Borneo's highest peak, Mt Kinabalu, for the stunning views, while others seek out orangutans and proboscis monkeys. There's even fantastic diving to be had in marine national parks.

❶ Kinabalu National Park

Mt Kinabalu (p106; 4095m), home to a stupendous range of plants and animals, is Borneo's premier natural destination. Most come to climb the magnificent peak capped by soaring granite spikes. Soak at Poring Hot Springs after your ascent.

❷ Danum Valley Conservation Area

Get right into diverse primary tropical rainforest at Danum (p145; 438 sq km), home to rhinoceros and orangutans. Sightings of gibbons, red-leaf monkeys, wild boar, Asian elephants and deer are common. Comfortable lodging and 50km of trails.

❸ Maliau Basin Conservation Area

Scarcely visited, the spectacular and diverse Maliau Basin (p154; 588 sq km) comprises primary rainforest, towering cliffs and tiered waterfalls. Plant species number 1800, bird 230, and rhinoceros, elephants, leopards, orangutans and gibbons have all been spotted. A mere 25% is mapped.

❹ Tunku Abdul Rahman National Park

The five islands of Tunku Abdul Rahman National Park (p102) have some of the most beautiful beaches in Borneo. Highlights include the clear water and a collection of coral enlivened with tropical fish.

❺ Pulau Tiga National Park

A setting for the reality TV show *Survivor*, the three islands of Pulau Tiga (p119) have become popular tourist attractions, with their beaches, bush walks and bubbling mud (caused by volcanic activity).

❻ Turtle Islands National Park

Endangered green and hawksbill turtles lay eggs year-round on the three islands of Turtle Island National Park (p141). It's part of a successful conservation effort, though some nights tourists outnumber turtles.

❼ Tun Sakaran Marine Park

Sabah's largest marine park, also known as Semporna Islands Marine Park (p150), covers 325 sq km of tropical waters, including dive sites widely classed among the top 10 in the world. Pulau Sipadan, an oceanic island atop a volcanic atoll, is a dream come true for any diver – the sides of this island abruptly drop down over 600ft into the sea.

3

Sarawak

Cave systems with ancient rock art, mangrove swamps and breeding grounds for Borneo's endangered turtles are among the unique offerings in Sarawak. Accessible walking trails cut through many of the area's parks, while others can be visited by boat. Other highlights include inviting beaches and diving opportunities.

1

❶ Bako National Park

Easily accessed from Kuching, Bako (p172; 27 sq km) showcases brilliant mangrove swamps, *kerangas* (distinctive vegetation zone of Borneo, usually found on sandstone, containing pitcher plants and other unusual flora) forest, rocky cliffs and secret beach coves. Tame proboscis monkeys, bearded pigs and silvered-leaf monkeys can be seen along the park's 17 well-maintained trails.

❷ Niah Caves National Park

Niah (p197; 31 sq km) has an incredible limestone cave complex containing prehistoric cave paintings, 40,000-year-old human remains and ancient canoe-shaped coffins. Excellent walkways access all major points of interest.

❸ Gunung Mulu National Park

Packed with scenic marvels, Gunung Mulu (p205; 544 sq km) has 45m limestone peaks, mountains, rainforest, a vast underground cave system and evening flights of several million bats. Expect canopy walks, adventure caving boat trips and hikes.

❹ Kubah National Park

Kubah National Park (p178; 22 sq km) is a natural retreat located a mere 15km from downtown Kuching. Shaded trails cut through the forested sandstone hills and offer lookouts, waterfalls and a wide variety of palms and orchids.

❺ Gunung Gading National Park

The massive *rafflesia tuanmudae* flower, blessed with the aroma of rotting flesh, can be sought out year-round at Gunung Gading National Park (p182) from a wooden boardwalk. Steeper day treks are also on offer.

❻ Tanjung Datu National Park

Endangered turtles lay their eggs on a fenced-off beach area in this 14-sq-km park (p183). Rainforest and rivers comprise the inland section, and snorkelling and scuba diving are allowed in selected ocean areas between April and September.

❼ Talang-Satang National Park

Talang-Satang National Park (p183) consists of two pairs of islands and protects turtle egg-laying grounds. If you're lucky you might witness baby turtles being released into the wild. Guided diving is permitted in some areas.

❽ Similajau National Park

A coastal park with attractive white beaches, Similajau National Park (p196) has good walking trails, 230 bird species, including hornbills, and is home to gibbons and macaques. It's perfect for relaxing as you pick your way through Borneo...just take care to avoid the saltwater crocodiles.

❾ Lambir Hills National Park

Lambir Hills National Park (p199; 69 sq km) has waterfalls and a natural swimming pool. Walking trails wind through its rainforest, where a good range of wildlife, including gibbons, pangolins and barking deer, reside.

Kalimantan

Despite reports of widespread illegal logging and agriculture, Kalimantan's national parks are still a refuge for spectacular flora and fauna. Facilities and accessibility vary wildly. Many park staff moonlight as guides, but office staff may know little about field conditions.

❶ Tanjung Puting National Park
Spot orangutans at Tanjung Puting (p253; 3000 sq km), a rehabilitation centre with daily feedings of the hairy primate. Take a houseboat trip through swampy forests which hide proboscis monkeys, sun bears and 200-plus bird species.

❷ Gunung Palung National Park
Seaside Gunung Palung (p249; 90 sq km) has a diversity of habitats and flora that rivals any in Borneo, with three dozen species of mammals, nearly 200 bird species, and wild orangutans. Access is more difficult here than at other parks.

❸ Betung Kerihun National Park
With hundreds of rivers and 180 peaks in the Kalimantan section alone, the truly adventurous can trek, cave and raft this 8000-sq-km park (p245). Wildlife thrives here, including orangutans and other primates, and 300-plus species of birds.

❹ Bukit Baka-Bukit Raya National Park
The forested mountains of this park (p243; 1810 sq km) create a terrain studded with waterfalls and meandering rivers where the giant rafflesia blooms every March. Tourist facilities are scarce.

❺ Danau Sentarum National Park
This wetland rainforest area (p244; 1320 sq km) alternates seasonally between deep lakes and isolated pools. Trophy aquarium fish, crocodiles, storks, orangutans and proboscis monkeys inhabit the waterways and forests. There are Dayak longhouses here and, for visitors, basic accommodation.

❻ Sebangau National Park
This peat swamp forest area (p259; 5687 sq km) is home to a large population of orangutans, which guides will help you find. More than 100 bird species and 35 mammal species inhabit the varied forest.

❼ Kutai National Park
Track wild orangutans by motorised canoe at Kutai National Park (p275; 1980 sq km), where coastal mangroves and ironwood forests house a half-dozen primate species, sun bear, deer, abundant bird life and huge tiger-striped beetles. Accommodation is basic.

❽ Sebuku Sembakung National Park
The plains of Sebuku Sembakung (p286; 4000 sq km) are the preferred haunt of Kalimantan's only elephant population. Other areas are characterised by swampland and green hills with limestone outcrops. Arrange visits ahead as no tourist facilities exist.

❾ Kayan Mentarang National Park
Southeast Asia's largest forest, Kayan Mentrang (p286; 13,600 sq km) features Apokayan Highlands and expanding ecotourism. Diversity abounds and new species are often discovered within the national park. Dayak longhouses can be visited on guided tours.

❿ Pegunungan Meratus
This South Kalimantan range (p267; 2500 sq km), spreading from Loksado to the Makassar Strait, features forest treks through the hills and valleys of limestone mountainsides to farming villages.

Brunei

Despite being one of the smallest countries in the world, Brunei is home to the 500 sq km Ulu Temburong National Park, a swath of virgin rainforest wedged like a dagger in the heart of Sarawak's Limbang Division. Getting there involves navigating a maze of mangrove-lined waterways – an adventure unto itself.

❶ Ulu Temburong National Park

Although 75% of Brunei's forests remain intact, the country has only recently begun to develop parks and tap into its ecotourism potential. Ulu Temburong (p234; 500 sq km) protects a lowland dipterocarp forest with giant trees and has a canopy tower and walkway suspended 50m above the forest floor.

(Continued from page 56)

Most people associate Brunei with oil rigs and sultans, but few realise that it's also home to some of Borneo's best-preserved rainforest. Ulu Temburong National Park (p234), in Brunei's Temburong District, is right in the middle of one of Borneo's largest stands of intact dipterocarp rainforest and the trails and canopy walkway here allow you to experience it 'up close and personal'.

CONSIDERATIONS FOR JUNGLE TREKKING

Jungle trekking can be one of the true highlights of a trip to Borneo. However, to the uninitiated, jungle trekking can be something of a shock – like marching all day in a sauna with a heavy pack strapped to your back. As a general rule, distances and climbs in the tropics feel about double what they do in temperate regions. To make the experience as painless as possible, it's necessary to make some crucial adaptations including the following:

- On overnight trips, bring two sets of clothing, one for hiking and one to wear at the end of the day (keep your night kit in a plastic bag so that it stays dry). Within minutes of starting out, your hiking kit will be drenched and will stay that way throughout your trip. Never blur the distinction between your day kit and your night kit; if you do, you'll simply find that you have two sets of wet clothes.
- If you'll be travelling through dense vegetation, wear long trousers and a long-sleeved shirt. Otherwise, shorts and a T-shirt will suffice. Whatever you wear, make sure that it's loose fitting.
- Bring fast-drying synthetic clothes. Once cotton gets wet, it won't dry out until you bring it to the laundry shop back in town after your trip (and let's not even mention what it will smell like).
- It can be cool in the evening in Borneo, so bring a polypro top to keep warm.
- Unless you like a lot of support, consider hiking in running shoes. It's hard enough hiking in the tropics as it is; clomping around with heavy mountaineering boots is just masochism.
- Buy a pair of light-coloured leech socks that fit your feet. You won't find these in Borneo, so buy them online before coming. For more on leeches, see the 'Leeches Suck…Blood' boxed text in this chapter (p67).
- Drink plenty of water. If you're going long distances, you'll have to bring either a water filter or a water purification agent like iodine (most people opt for the latter to keep weight down).
- Get in shape long before coming to Borneo and start slowly – try a day hike before setting out on a longer trek.
- Always go with a guide unless you're on a well-marked, commonly travelled trail. Navigating in the jungle is extremely difficult.
- Bring talcum powder to cope with the chafing caused by wet undergarments. Wearing loose underwear, or better yet, no underwear at all, will also help prevent chafing.
- If you wear glasses, be sure to treat them with an antifog solution (ask at the shop where you buy your glasses), otherwise, you may find yourself blinded by fog within minutes of setting out.
- Your sweat will soak through the back of your backpack. Consider putting something waterproof over the back padding of your pack to keep the sweat out of your pack. Otherwise, consider a waterproof stuff sack.
- Consider bringing a small pair of binoculars that you can keep on your pack's shoulder strap. You'll be happy you have these when your guide points out wildlife in the treetops.
- Keep your camera in a Tupperware or similar container with a pouch of silica gel or other dessicant in there.

Kalimantan's joint ecotourism organisation, KOMPAKH (p245), is based out of Putussibau, and offers a wide variety of services. It can organise visits to longhouses or Danau Sentarum and Betung Kerihun National Parks; its scope ranges from short treks to expeditions all the way across Borneo by boat and foot, with the assurance that you won't be beheaded like George Muller, the first European to try it.

Life in the Forests of the Far East, by Spencer St John, is a fascinating account of early attempts on Mt Kinabalu and exploration of the interior.

The Kura Kura Resort south of Singkawang (p246) can arrange treks among beautiful beach and forest settings and provide cold beers for when you are done.

Elsewhere, Gunung Palung National Park (p249) is a priceless biodiversity reserve and holds perhaps 10% of the world's remaining wild orangutans. The huge variety of creatures brings international researchers and, unfortunately, poachers. Sights include views of nearby Gunung Palung (1116m) and Gunung Panti (1050m), crystal-clear waterfalls and swimming holes, and distinctive Balinese temples.

In South Kalimantan, the remote Pegunungan Meratus (p266) region features limestone mountains, tropical jungles and rivers that make the strenuous trails worth while. There are trails complimented by exciting bamboo suspension bridges along rivers and waterfalls, caverns, and another path that leads to the sea via Gunung Besar (1892m), the region's highest mountain.

Finally, East Kalimantan has a few gems in addition to the Apokayan Highlands (see p56). The Samboja Lodge (p271), run by the Borneo Orangutan Survival Foundation, organises treks into orangutan release areas where, at a careful distance, visitors can spot orangutans in their natural habitat. Kutai National Park (p275) is also home to a large number of primates and huge insects. Treks or boat tours can be organised at the visitor centre.

CAVING

Sarawak's Gunung Mulu National Park (p205) is a place of spelunking superlatives. It's got the world's largest cave passage (Deer Cave, 2km in length and 174m in height), the world's largest cave chamber (the Sarawak Chamber, 2km in length and 174m in height), and Asia's longest cave (Clearwater Cave, 107km in length). And the best part is that several of the park's caves are accessible to nonspelunkers: you can walk through them on well-maintained walkways.

Butterflies of Borneo and Southeast Asia by Kazuhisa Otsuka is an essential guide for butterfly lovers.

Of course, if you're a real adventure-sport junkie, a gentle journey into one of the so-called 'Show Caves' of Mulu will likely whet your appetite for something more substantial. If so, you'll find that Mulu is a great place to give adventure caving a try. The park offers guided adventure cave-tours ranging from 45 minutes to 10-plus hours, and you can visit the gaping maw of the aforementioned Sarawak·Chamber.

Also in Sarawak, Niah Caves National Park (p197) has some brilliant caves that should rank high on any Borneo itinerary. Indeed, were it not for the gaping wonders of Mulu so close by, we reckon that Niah would be world famous. The main chambers here are accessible by a wonderful plankwalk through intact swampy rainforest (a great way to see the jungle without suffering from leech bites). Once inside, you'll find an underground fantasy world that will almost certainly rank high on your Borneo highlights list.

DIVING & SNORKELLING

Sabah's Pulau Sipadan (Sipidan Island; p150), located in Tun Sakaran Marine Park off Semporna in east Sabah, is widely considered one of the world's greatest dive-sites. Few travellers are aware that the same marine park is also home to two more brilliant dive-sites: Pulau Mabul and Pulau Kapali (p150). While Sipadan is famous for coral walls, large pelagic spe-

LEECHES SUCK...BLOOD

There's just no getting around it: if you want to experience Borneo's magnificent tropical rainforests, you're going to encounter leeches. If it's been dry or you happen to visit a relatively leech-free area, you may come to the conclusion that all this talk of leeches is just a way to scare off the greenhorns. But, it's likely that, at some point, you're going to encounter leeches, perhaps lots of them.

There are two types of leech in Borneo: the common ground-dwelling brown leech and the striped yellow-reddish tiger leech, which often dwells higher up on foliage (meaning that you might discover them on your upper legs, torso, arms or even on your head and neck). You cannot feel the bite of the brown leech; you'll only realise you've been bitten when you actually see the leech on you or when you notice blood seeping through your clothing from the leech or the bleeding bite. You can actually feel the bite of a tiger leech, but it's usually so faint that you ignore it until you later discover the leech feeding on you.

Make no mistake: leeches are horrible, vulgar creatures. But they are almost completely harmless. They do not generally carry parasites, bacteria or viruses that can infect human beings. If a leech has managed to get a good bite of you, the bite may itch and bleed rather profusely for a few hours due to the anticoagulant that the leech injects. The bite may itch slightly for a few days and then it will scab over and resolve into a small dark spot that completely disappears after several weeks. The only danger is that the bite may get infected in damp tropical conditions, for which reason it is important to clean the bite and keep it dry.

Like hangover cures, everyone has a tried and true method of keeping the leeches off. Problem is, most don't work. Putting tobacco in your socks or on your shoes is a favourite method. We tried this one – literally soaking our shoes in tobacco juice – and it only seemed to encourage the little bastards. Many Kelabit people swear that spraying your shoes with a powerful insecticide works (that's insecticide, not insect repellent). We didn't try this one for fear of 'complications'. There is only one really effective method of keeping leeches off: buy yourself a pair of leech socks before coming to Borneo. These are socks made from tightly-knit fabric that reach to your knees. The best ones are light coloured so that you can see the leeches ascending your legs and pick them off. You can find these online from speciality shops.

If you do discover a leech on yourself, the first thing to remember is: don't panic! If you slide your fingernail along your skin at the point where the leech is biting, this will break the suction, at which point you can flick it off. Pulling it off can leave part of the leech's jaws in the wound, while burning it off can cause it to regurgitate its stomach contents into the wound – a horrible prospect indeed!

With a decent pair of leech socks and occasional checks of your legs and torso, you can walk for a full day in leech-infested forest with only a few odd bites. If you find these annoying, console yourself with thoughts of what others have encountered in the Borneo forest:

'We woke periodically throughout the night to peel off leeches. In the light of the head torch, the ground was a sea of leeches – black, slithering, standing up on one end to sniff the air and heading inexorably our way to feed. Our exposed faces were the main problem, with leeches feeding off our cheeks and becoming entangled in our hair. I developed a fear of finding one feeding in my ear, and that it would become too large to slither out, causing permanent damage.'

From Richard Mayfield's Kinabalu Escape: The Soldiers' Story.

If that doesn't put your suffering into perspective, then you can console yourself with the thought that you're playing an active role in the Borneo ecosystem!

cies and deep wall dives, Mabul and Kapali are muck dives, where the emphasis is more on small colourful creatures.

A full 300km out into the South China Sea, northwest of Kota Kinabalu, you'll find another world-class dive-site: the brilliant coral ring of Layang Layang (p130). This remote dive-site is basically a runway, a reef and a purpose-built dive-resort. If you like wall dives, pristine coral and want a real adventure, this place is a must!

Also in Sabah, Pulau Labuan (p121) has a few notable wrecks in the waters surrounding the island.

Pulau Derawan and Sangalaki Archipelago in East Kalimantan (p284) have world-renown underwater worlds that should not be missed by serious divers. Marine life abounds and once you peel off the flippers, the island of Derawan has a small, friendly population that easily makes you feel at home in their laid-back pace of life.

Pasir Panjang and Tanjung Gundul (p246), hidden away by the forests south of Singkawang, have great beaches, opportunities to see (but not disturb) turtles, and snorkelling trips to Pulau Randayan.

Finally, if snorkelling is more your thing, you'll really enjoy the snorkelling off of the five islands of Sabah's Tunku Abdul Rahman National Park (p102), just offshore from Kota Kinabalu. A little further north, the pristine white beaches, awesome visibility and intact coral gardens of Pulau Mantanani (p129) make the island a snorkeller's paradise.

The Sarawak Chamber, in Sarawak's Gunung Mulu National Park, is the world's largest cave chamber.

MOUNTAIN BIKING

There is scope for adventurous mountain-biking in various parts of Borneo, including the Kelabit Highlands (p212) and on the trails around Mt Kinabalu (p106). One operator that can arrange mountain bike tours is Field Skills (www.fieldskills.com), a Sabah-based company that also arranges treks and jungle training.

RIVER RAFTING & KAYAKING

The rivers of Borneo offer scope for exciting river-trips, whether by kayak or raft. Keep in mind that water levels vary significantly throughout the year. Setting out to descend an unknown river in an isolated part of Borneo is a serious and dangerous undertaking indeed. Make sure you know what you are getting into and, ideally, bring a local along with experience on the river in question. More than a few would-be first-descenders have come to grief on the rivers of Borneo.

The 'Coral Triangle', in which Borneo is located, holds 600 species of coral and more than 3000 species of fish.

Rafting is popular through the Padas Gorge south of Beaufort, in southwest coastal Sabah, and is at its best between April and July, when water levels on Sungai Padas create Grade 2 to 4 conditions. The calmer **Sungai Kiulu** nearby is also commonly used for first-time rafters. For more details, see p117().

While not exactly kayaking, in **Tanjung Puting National Park** (p253) visitors can rent wooden canoes to explore the park's rivers and try to see the rehabilitated orangutans.

Near the headwaters of Sungai Kapuas in **Betung Kerihun National Park** (p245) is a great place for water adventure. KOMPAKH offers, in addition to its treks (see p243), kayaking, canoeing and white-water rafting.

Gateway Kuala Lumpur

After years as a regional runner-up, modest Malaysia's capital has found its niche. Kuala Lumpur (KL) is easier to negotiate than Bangkok, grittier than Singapore, and masters an engaging multicultural landscape of Indian, Malay and Chinese enclaves. Best of all, KL is an easy layover for one- or two-night stays: transport into town from the airport is effortless, scams are minimal, and the queen of budget carriers, Air Asia, whisks travels to Borneo for a small wad of ringgit.

See Lonely Planet's *Malaysia, Singapore & Brunei* guidebook for more information.

INFORMATION
Bookshops
Kinokuniya (☎ 2164 8133; 4th fl, Suria KLCC Shopping Complex)
MPH Bookstores (☎ 2142 8231; ground fl, BB Plaza, Jln Bukit Bintang)

Emergency
Fire (☎ 994)
Police & ambulance (☎ 999)

Immigration Offices
Immigration Office – City Centre Branch (Kompleks Wilayah, cnr Jln Dang Wangi & Jln TAR)
Main Immigration Office (☎ 2095 5077; Block I, Pusat Bandar Damansara) Visa extension; 1km west of Lake Gardens.

Internet Access
Internet shops turn over frequently but are usually replaced by another nearby. Try Jln Sultan or the streets surrounding Kota Raya shopping centre in Chinatown. Rates per hour start at RM2.

Medical Services
Kuala Lumpur General Hospital (☎ 2615 5555; Jln Pahang)
Twin Towers Medical Centre (☎ 2382 3500; Lot 401 F&G, 4th fl, Suria KLCC Shopping Complex)

Money
Banks and ATMs are concentrated around Jln Silang at the northern edge of Chinatown. Moneychangers are located in shopping malls, along Lebuh Ampang and near Klang bus station on Jln Sultan.

Post
Main post office (Jln Raja Laut; ☯ 8.30am-6pm Mon-Sat) The office is closed on the first Saturday of the month.

Tourist Information
Malaysian Tourist Information Complex (Matic; ☎ 2164 3929; 109 Jln Ampang; ☯ 9am-midnight) KL's most useful tourist office. It also hosts cultural performances.

Travel Agencies
For discount airline tickets, long-running and reliable student-travel agencies include:
MSL Travel (☎ 4042 4722; 66 Jln Putra)
STA Travel (☎ 2143 9800; Lot 506, 5th fl, Plaza Magnum, 128 Jln Pudu)

SIGHTS
Colonial District
Kuala Lumpur's colonial district hugs Sungai Klang between Jln Tun Perak and Jln Kinabalu The symbolic heart is **Merdeka Square** (Jln Raja Laut), a formal parade ground with dutifully posing architectural legacies of Malaysia's successive conquerors, both Islamic and European. Fittingly, the nation's independence was proclaimed here in 1957. Further

---

FAST FACTS

- Telephone code: ☎ 60 country, ☎ 03 city
- Population: 1.8 million
- Time: GMT+8
- Visas: most nationalities get a 30-day tourist visa on arrival

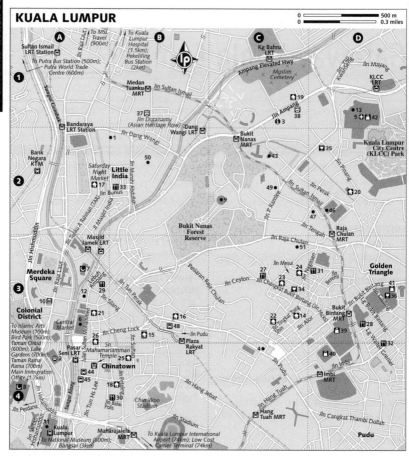

KUALA LUMPUR

south is the **Old Railroad Station** (Jln Hishamuddin), a fanciful castle of Islamic arches and spires.

The **National History Museum** (☎ 2694 4590; 29 Jln Raja Laut; admission free; ☼ 9am-6pm) will instil a sense of Malaysian pride in a new arrival, plus the 2nd-floor view of Merdeka Sq is stunning. Take the Putra LRT to Pasar Seni station.

A tranquil creation built in 1907, **Masjid Jamek** (Jln Tun Perak; admission free; ☼ 8.30am-12.30pm & 2.30-4pm) is set in a grove of palm trees; headscarves and robes are provided at the gate. It's closed during Friday prayers (11am to 2.30pm). Take the Star or Putra LRT to Masjid Jamek station.

The **Masjid Negara** (National Mosque; Jln Perdana; admission free; ☼ 9am-12.30pm, 2-3.30pm & 5-6.30pm) is one of Southeast Asia's largest mosques. The main dome is an 18-pointed star, symbolising

the 13 states of Malaysia and the five pillars of Islam. Remove shoes and dress conservatively. Take the Putra LRT to Pasar Seni station.

Chinatown

Circuitous streets and cramped chaos create a pressure-cooker of sights and sounds. **Jln Petaling** is a bustling street market selling things such as 'authentic' Paul Frank, Birkenstocks and Levis. Chinatown is accessed on the Putra LRT to Pasar Seni station or on the KL Monorail to Maharajalela station.

Chinese **coffee shops** are along Jln Penggong and Jln Balai Polis. You'll spot temples and shops in the side streets – check out KL's principal Hindu temple, **Sri Mahamariamman Temple** (Jln HS Lee).

The **Central Market** (Jln Cheng Lock; 10am-10pm) is a refurbished Art Deco building with stalls selling Malay crafts and art.

Little India

Little India has all the feel of a bazaar. The sari shops and the shopping women along **Jln Masjid India**, the district's main street, are swathed in vibrant sherbets, turquoise and vermilions. Meanwhile Indian pop blasts through tinny speakers, and musky incense and delicious spices flavour the air. The district swings into full spectacle during the Saturday *pasar malam* (night market). Take the Star or Putra LRT to Masjid Jamek station.

Golden Triangle

The Golden Triangle is central KL's business, shopping and entertainment district. Sitting on a forested hill, **Menara Kuala Lumpur** (Kuala Lumpur Tower; 2020 5448; Jln Punchak; adult/child RM20/10; 9am-10pm, last tickets 9.30pm) is the fourth-highest telecommunications tower in the world. Visitors can ride the lift right up to the viewing deck (276m) for panoramic views, superior to those from the Petronas Towers. Take the KL Monorail to Bukit Nanas station.

The twin **Petronas Towers** (Jln Ampang; admission free; 9am-1pm & 2.30-4.45pm Tue-Sun) were once the world's tallest skyscrapers until Taipei 101 swiped the title in 2004. Even so, the towers are still an elegant monument. This is the headquarters of the national petroleum company; visitors are allowed access to the 41st-floor skybridge that connects the towers. First-come, first-serve tickets are issued from 8.30am and 15-minute visits start at 10am. Arrive around 8am if you're particular about the time you want to go up, but tickets are often available until around 11am. Take the Putra LRT to KLCC station.

Lake Gardens & Around

Escape from the heat and concrete to this inner-city garden at the western edge of central KL. Intrakota bus 21C from the Jln Sultan Mohammed bus stop, or buses 21B, 22, 48C and F3 from Chinatown will take you there. It is also a 20-minute walk from Masjid Jamek LRT.

The gardens contain a host of attractions such as the **Bird Park** (2273 5423; adult/child RM28/17; 9am-7.30pm) and **Taman Rama Rama** (Butterfly Park; adult/child RM15/8; 9am-6pm). You can take a stroll or catch the shuttle bus (adult RM1; 9am to 6pm Thursday to Saturday, noon to 3pm Friday) that does a loop of the area.

At the edge of the Lake Gardens, the **National Museum** (Muzium Negara; 2282 6255; Jln Damansara; adult/child RM2/free; 9am-6pm) boasts colourful displays on Malaysia's history, arts and culture.

The **Islamic Arts Museum** (Muzium Kesenian Islam Malaysia; 2274 2020; Jln Lembah Perdana; adult/child RM12/6; 10am-6pm Tue-Sun) has scale models of the world's most famous mosques and a full-scale interior reproduction of a typical Muslim room of the Ottoman Empire.

SLEEPING

Chinatown is your best hunting ground for cheap crash pads. The Golden Triangle has more upscale options as well as pricier but cleaner budget options.

Chinatown & Little India

Accommodation here can be reached by the Star LRT to Plaza Rakyat, Putra LRT to Pasar Seni or the KL Monorail to Maharajalela station.

Le Village (☎ 2026 6737; 99A Jln Tun HS Lee; dm/d RM10/30) A relaxed bohemian air hangs over this shabby, yet charming, guesthouse set in a colonial building decorated with local art.

Wheeler's Guest House (☎ 2070 1386; 131-133 Jln Tun HS Lee; dm/d RM12/30) The entrance is squalid but rooms are clean and well-ventilated. Character comes from potted plants, fish and murals and there's even a roof-top garden.

Anuja Backpackers Inn (☎ 2026 6479; 1st-3rd fl, 28 Jln Pudu; d RM25-40; 🖳) There's hardly room to change your mind, but this reliably clean and friendly place is convenient for inconveniently timed trips from Puduraya bus station.

Coliseum Hotel (☎ 2692 6270; 100 Jln TAR; s/d RM28/38; 🖳) With its famous old planters' restaurant and bar downstairs, the Coliseum is an aging relic. Rooms are huge, without bathrooms (some have sinks) and come with heritage-style furnishings.

Hotel Lok Ann (☎ 2078 9544; 113A Jln Petaling; s/d RM60/70; 🖳) Best value of the cheap hotels in the area. Despite facing noisy Jln Sultan, this neat and clean place has spacious rooms with such luxuries as windows.

Ancasa Hotel (☎ 2026 6060; Jln Cheng Lock; d from RM185; 🖳 🖳) Helpful staff make this Chinatown's best midrange option. All rooms are comfortable and feature satellite TV should you choose to be a couch potato.

our pick Swiss-Inn (☎ 2072 3333; www.swissgarden .com; 62 Jln Sultan; d with breakfast from RM200; 🖳 🖳 🖳) A professional hotel for jet-lag recovery. Silent crypts and cable TV.

Golden Triangle

These places can be reached via the KL Monorail to Bukit Bintang station.

Pondok Lodge (☎ 2142 8449; 3rd fl, 20 Jln Changkat Bukit Bintang; dm/s/d RM20/45/55; 🖳) A spacious, mellow retreat, Pondok has airy common lounges, a rooftop sitting area and a real 'home' feel. The price includes a basic breakfast.

Number Eight Guesthouse (☎ 2144 2050; www .numbereight.com.my; 8-10 Tingkat Tong Shin; dm RM30-85, d RM95-135; 🖳 🖳) Above and beyond the competition, this guesthouse is gussied up with photos of KL, a plaster wall map of Asia and flickering candles on the open porch. The en-suite rooms are boutique quality and rates include breakfast.

Rainforest Bed & Breakfast (☎ 2145 1466; 27 Jln Mesui; d with breakfast RM70-90; 🖳 🖳) Lush greenery tumbles off the façade of this pretty guesthouse. You'll still find the usual cheap windowless rooms visually expanded with wall mirrors. But the rooftop breakfast area is certainly appetising.

Allson Genesis (☎ 2141 2000; www.allson-genesis .com; 45 Tengkat Tong Shin; r from RM150; 🖳 🖳) You get a lot of ring for your ringgit here. The rooms are spacious with furnishings verging on boutique territory. The deluxe rooms at the front peep at the Petronas Towers.

Impiana (☎ 2141 6233; www.impiana.com; 13 Jln Pinang; r from RM380; 🖳 🖳 🖳) This sleek hotel offers chic, spacious rooms with parquet floors and lots of seductive amenities. Another plus is an infinity pool with a view across to the Petronas Towers

Hotel Maya (☎ 2711 8866; www.hotelmaya.com.my; 138 Jln Ampang; r with breakfast from RM600; 🖳 🖳 🖳) It hardly gets trendier than this design darling: timber flooring, picture windows and contemporary furnishings. Rates include transfers to/from KL Sentral and a host of other goodies.

EATING

All the food groups – Indian, Chinese, Malay and Western fast food – abound in KL.

Chinatown & Little India

In the morning, go for a jolt of joe in one of the neighbourhood's *kedai kopi* (coffee shops). Noodle stalls line Jln Sultan at midday and Chinese restaurants dominate Jln Petaling market in the evenings.

Little India's **Saturday night market** (Jln TAR) has sensational tucker, including Indian curry sopped up with flaky *roti canai* (Indian-style flaky flatbread, also known as 'flying dough').

Restoran Yasin (☎ 2698 2710; 141 Jln Bunus; meals RM3.50-7; 🕓 breakfast, lunch & dinner) A locals' institution serving tasty South- and North-Indian fare.

Fatt Yan Vegetarian Restaurant (☎ 2070 6561; cnr Jln Tun HS Lee & Jln Silang; meals RM18; 🕓 lunch & dinner) Herbivores will approve of this Buddhist Chinese restaurant that eschews meat but cooks up some awfully good substitutes.

Old China Café (☎ 20725915; 11 Jln Balai Polis; meals RM25-40; ☻ dinner) Granted it's a tourist spot, but one that nails the 1920s Sino fantasy of shadow-casting ceiling fans, time-worn antiques and a soundtrack of sparrow sopranos. Spicy Baba Nonya (descendants of Chinese Straits settlers who intermarried with Malays) dishes are the speciality.

Golden Triangle

Head to central KL's shopping centres for international and local food. Jln Nagasari, off Jln Changkat Bukit Bintang, is lined with Malay food stalls and open-air restaurants. Jln Alor, one street northwest of Jln Changkat Bukit Bintang, has a carnival-like night market of Chinese hawker stalls. Take the KL Monorail to Bukit Bintang.

Lemon Food Court (basement, Low Yat Plaza; meals RM4-8; ☻ lunch & dinner) Lemon Food Court has sizzling hot plates, mouth-watering aromas and a proletariat ambience.

Crystal Jade La Mian Xiao Long Bao (☎ 2148 2338; Annex Block, Lot 10, 50 Jln Sultan Ismail; meals RM20-40; ☻ 11am-10.30pm Mon-Fri, 10.30am-10.30pm Sat & Sun) Confounded by dim sum? Let the pictorial menu be your guide; come early to beat the lunch crowd.

Restoran Oversea (☎ 2144 0808; 84-88 Jln Imbi; meals RM50) Part of citywide empire, this banquet-style restaurant does melt-in-the-mouth pork belly and hot-pot bacon.

Restoran Nagasari Curry House (Jln Nagasari; meals RM5-10; ☻ 7am-midnight) This simple place gets thumbs up for its authentic banana-leaf meals.

Bijan (☎ 2031 3575; www.bijanrestaurant.com; 3 Jln Ceylon; meals RM60-80; ☻ lunch & dinner Mon-Sat, dinner Sun) Sample traditional Malay dishes in a setting that is urban chic rather than rustic *kampung*. Try *tempeh* with anchovies, tomato rice, fried eggplant in spicy chilli sauce and the surprisingly pleasant durian cheesecake.

DRINKING & ENTERTAINMENT

Drinking in KL is no budget activity (around RM10 per bottle of beer) and drinks at 'proper' bars are nearly double in price. The cheapest places to imbibe are Chinese eateries or open-air hawker stalls.

Green Man (☎ 2141 9924; 40 Jln Changkat Bukit Bintang) Eternally popular, unstuffy expat hangout,

with pool table and quieter reaches upstairs; there's simple food and outside seating.

Rum Jungle (☎ 2148 0282; cnr Jln P Ramlee & Jln Pinang) Take a trip on the wild side with the other party animals who roam this sprawling complex of thatched huts.

Village Bar (☎ 2782 3852; Feast Village, Starhill Gallery, 181 Jln Bukit Bintang; ☻ noon-1am) Like Ali Baba's Bazaar this enticing bar is hung with coloured-glass lampshades and is a fine place to start or finish an evening of grazing at the trendy Starhill Gallery mall.

Cynna (☎ 2694 2888; www.loftkl.com; unit 28-40 Asian Heritage Row, Jln Doraisamy) Dress smart to make it past the clipboard nazis at the most stylish of Asian Heritage Row's clubs. Inside join a lively crowd knocking back cocktails and writhing to seductive sounds.

Zouk (☎ 2171 1997; www.zoukclub.com.my; 113 Jln Ampang) There's a theme for everyone here from the small and edgy Loft Bar, to a plastic palm fringed main venue and sophisticated Velvet Underground (including entry to Zouk RM45).

GETTING THERE & AROUND

For information on getting to specific regions in Borneo, see Sabah (p87), Sarawak (p161), Brunei (p220) and Kalimantan (p237).

The city of Johor Bahru (JB) often has cheap flights to Borneo. To reach JB from Kuala Lumpur, take a bus from KL's Puduraya bus station; the journey costs RM24 and takes four hours. These daily buses leave frequently.

Air

The **Kuala Lumpur International Airport** (KLIA; ☎ 8777 8888; www.klia.com.my; Pengrus Besar) is 75km south of the city centre at Sepang. Airlines serving cities in Malaysian Borneo include Malaysia Airlines and Air Asia. Do note that Air Asia flights arrive and depart from the nearby **Low Cost Carrier Terminal** (LCC-T; ☎ 1300 889 933). Airline companies serving KLIA include:

Air Asia (☎ 08775 4000; www.airasia.com; KLIA)

Cathay Pacific Airways (☎ 2035 2788; www.cathaypacific.com; Suite 22.01, 22nd fl, Menara IMC, 8 Jln Sultan Ismail)

China Airlines (☎ 2142 7344; www.china-airlines.com; Amoda Bldg, 22 Jln Imbi)

Lufthansa (☎ 2161 4666; www.lufthansa.com; 18th fl, Kenanga International Bldg, Jln Sultan Ismail)

Malaysia Airlines (☎ 1300 883 000, 2161 0555; www.malaysiaairlines.com); Bangunan MAS (☎ 7846 3000; Jln Sultan Ismail); KL Sentral Station (☎ 2272 4260)

Royal Brunei Airlines (☎ 2070 7166; www.bruneiair
.com; Menara UBN, 10 Jln P Ramlee)
Singapore Airlines (☎ 2692 3122; www.singaporeair
.com; Menara Multi-Purpose, 8 Jln Munshi Abdullah)
Thai Airways International (☎ 2031 2900; www
.thaiairways.com; 30 Wisma Goldhill, 67 Jln Raja Chulan)

Bus

The primary long-distance bus station in KL
is **Puduraya** (Jln Pudu). For inner-city transport,
local buses leave from Puduraya as well as
Klang bus station (Jln Sultan Mohammed) near the
Pasar Seni LRT station. The maximum fare
is usually RM1 for destinations within the
city limits.

Taxi

Taxis in KL have meters but drivers refuse
to use them so you have to bargain. Ask at
your hotel about fares before heading to a
taxi stand, since the price skyrockets when
a tourist approaches. Trips around town are
about RM5 to RM10.

Train & Light Rail

The easiest way into town from the airport
is via KLIA Ekspres (RM35/65 one way/re-
turn, 30 minutes, every 15 to 20 minutes
from 5am to midnight), which terminates at
KL Sentral train station, about a kilometre
south of the historic Old Railway Station.
KL Sentral is the transit station for all train-
based travel in Kuala Lumpur. From here
you can catch LRT and KL Monorail trains

to Chinatown, Golden Triangle and other
parts of Kuala Lumpur.

Transport within central KL is handled by
a three line system. The most convenient lines
for short-term visitors are the Star and Putra
lines of the **Light Rail Transit** (LRT; ☎ 1800 388 288;
www.rapidkl.com.my) system. Fares range from
RM1 to RM2.80 and trains run every six to
10 minutes from 6am to 11:50pm (11:30pm
Sunday and holidays). **KL Monorail** (☎ 2273 1888)
is convenient for hops between Chinatown and
the northern areas of Bukit Bintang and Chow
Kit. Fares are RM1.20 to RM2.50 and trains
run every 15 minutes from 6am to midnight.

Interchange stations between the different
lines include the following: KL Sentral, transfer between all lines; Masjid Jamek, transfer
between Star and Putra LRT; Hang Tuah and
Titiwangsa, transfer between KL Monorail and
Star LRT; Bukit Nanas, transfer between KL
Monorail and Putra LRT; Tasik Selatan, transfer between KTM Komuter and Star LRT.

Another rail system, the **KTM Komuter**
(☎ 2272 2828) links Kuala Lumpur with outlying suburbs and the historic train station.

For long-distance departures to other parts
of the Malay peninsula, KL is the hub of the **KTM**
(☎ 2267 1200; www.ktmb.com.my) national railway
system. The long-distance trains depart from
KL Sentral. The **KTM information office** (☒ 10am-
7pm) in the main hall of the station can advise on
schedules and check seat availability. There are
daily departures for Butterworth (the closest
station to Penang), Thailand and Singapore.

Gateway Singapore

Tidy and efficient, Singapore is a modern marvel in a region full of anachronisms. It's a perfect intersection of Western-style order in an Asian setting and intelligently cultivates culture, history and, most importantly, cuisine on a tiny spit of land. The island can be tackled in a few days thanks to the slick MRT train system, which delivers city explorers to glitzy Orchard Rd malls, colonnaded antique buildings in the Colonial District, or the pungent lanes of Little India. It's affluent, high-tech and occasionally a little snobbish, but also a great food city with ubiquitous and raucous hawker centres.

See Lonely Planet's *Malaysia, Singapore & Brunei* guidebook for more information.

INFORMATION
Bookshops
Borders (☎ 6235 7146; 01-00 Wheelock Pl, 501 Orchard Rd)
Kinokuniya (☎ 6737 5021; www.kinokuniya.com.sg; 03-10/15 Ngee Ann City, 391 Orchard Rd)

Emergency
Ambulance (☎ 995)
Fire (☎ 995)
Police (☎ 999)

Internet Access
Every backpacker hostel now offers internet – the majority of them for free, some for a nominal charge. There are numerous free wi-fi hotspots throughout the city.

Medical Services
Raffles SurgiCentre (☎ 6334 3337; www.raffleshospital.com; 585 North Bridge Rd)
Singapore General Hospital (☎ 6321 4311; Block 1, Outram Rd)

Money
Moneychangers can be found in every shopping centre and most do not charge fees on foreign money or travellers' cheques. Many shops accept foreign cash and travellers' cheques at lower rates than you'd get from a moneychanger.

Post
Changi Airport (024-39, Terminal 2)
Comcentre (31 Exeter Rd)
Lucky Plaza (02-09 Lucky Plaza, Orchard Rd)
Ngee Ann City (04-15 Takashimaya, 391 Orchard Rd)

Tourist Information
Most Singapore Tourism Board (STB) offices provide a wide range of services, including tour bookings and event ticketing.
STB head office (Tourism Court; ☎ 1800-736 2000; 1 Orchard Spring Lane; ☽ 8.30am-5pm Mon-Fri, 8.30am-1pm Sat)
STB branches Orchard Road (☎ 6336 7184; cnr Orchard/Cairnhill Rds; ☽ 9.30am-10.30pm); Little India (☎ 6296 9169; Inn Crowd, 73 Dunlop St; ☽ 10am-10pm)

Travel Agencies
Jetabout Holidays (☎ 6822 2288, 6734 1818; 06-05 Cairnhill Pl; 15 Cairnhill Rd)
Misa Travel (☎ 6538 0318; 03-106 Hong Lim Complex, 531A Upper Cross St)
STA Travel (☎ 6737 7188; www.statravel.com.sg; 07-02 Orchard Towers, 400 Orchard Rd)

SIGHTS
Colonial District
Architectural remnants of British rule are neatly arranged around the Padang, an old cricket pitch. The state-of-the-art **Asian Civilisations Museum** (☎ 6332 7789; www.acm.org.sg;

FAST FACTS

- Country code: ☎ 65
- Population: 4.6 million
- Time: GMT + 7
- Visas: most nationalities get a 30-day tourist visa on arrival

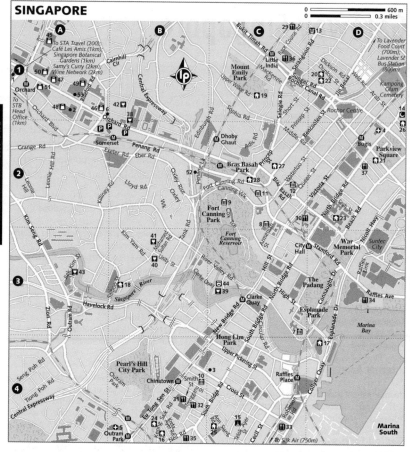

SINGAPORE

GATEWAY SINGAPORE

1 Empress Pl; adult/child & concession S$5/2.50; ⏰ 1-7pm Mon, 9am-7pm Tue-Thu, Sat & Sun, 9am-9pm Fri) has 10 thematic galleries dealing with Asian culture, from the Islamic world to Japanese anime. At the **Armenian St branch** (☎ 6332 3015; 39 Armenian St; adult/child & concession S$3/1.50; ⏰ 1-7pm Mon, 9am-7pm Tue-Thu, Sat & Sun, 9am-9pm Fri) permanent displays include Peranakan culture, Chinese ceramics and Buddhist artefacts. To visit both, buy a combined ticket (adult/child & concession S$6/3); there is also discounted admission between 7pm and 9pm on Fridays.

The architecturally stunning **National Museum of Singapore** (☎ 6332 3659; www.national museum.sg; 93 Stamford Rd; adult/child $10/5; ⏰ 10am-9pm daily) includes a Singapore history gallery.

The **Singapore Art Museum** (☎ 6332 3222; www .museum.org.sg/sam; 71 Bras Basah Rd; adult/child S$3/1.50; ⏰ noon-6pm Mon, 9am-6pm Tue-Thu, Sat & Sun, 9am-9pm Fri) is housed in the former St Joseph's Institution, once a Catholic boys' school, and hosts world-class exhibitions.

Fort Canning Park offers a peaceful and leafy retreat. The **Battle Box** (☎ 6333 0510; 51 Canning Rise; adult/child S$8/5; ⏰ 10am-6pm Tue-Sun) is an underground warren that once served as a British base during WWII.

Chinatown

Bustling Chinatown is crammed with small shops, eateries and tradition, though the latter is being renovated into extinction. One highlight is the **Thian Hock Keng Temple**

GATEWAY SINGAPORE

(☎ 6423 4626; 158 Telok Ayer St; ☻ 7.30am-5.30pm), Singapore's oldest Hokkien building. For a peek into the past, **Chinatown Heritage Centre** (☎ 6325 2878; www.chinatownheritage.com.sg; 48 Pagoda St; adult/child S$8/4.80; ☻ 10am-7pm) is crammed with interactive, imaginative displays.

Orchard Rd

The city's mall corridor, Orchard Rd ranks among Singapore's retail attractions. **Far East Plaza** is the best spot for cheap clothes and shoes, **Tangs** was Singapore's first department store and **Wisma Atria Shopping Centre** has mainstream fashions. Next door is **Ngee Ann City**, packed with high-end brands. **Lucky Plaza** sells electronics and **Paragon's** shops maxes out credit cards. **Heeren** specialises in hip looks for teens. Rest from retail at the serene **Singapore Botanic Gardens** (☎ 6471 7361; www.sbg.org.sg; 1 Cluny Rd; admission free; ☻ 5am- midnight).

Little India & Kampung Glam

Disorderly and pungent, Little India is an incongruous appendage. The area is a sight in itself and one of its pleasures is wandering the little side streets and soaking it all in. For temple hounds there is the **Sri Veeramakaliamman Temple** (☎ 6293 4634; 141 Serangoon Rd; ☻ 8am-12.30pm & 4-8.30pm), dedicated to the goddess Kali.

Southeast of Little India is Kampong Glam, Singapore's Muslim quarter. Here, you'll find the golden-domed **Sultan Mosque** (☎ 6293 4405; 3 Muscat St; ☻ 5am-8.30pm), the biggest mosque in Singapore.

Elsewhere

Nestled among the forest, the **Singapore Zoological Gardens** (☎ 6269 3411; www.zoo.com.sg; 80 Mandai Lake Rd; adult/child S$15/7.50; ☻ 8.30am-6pm), has an open layout for free-ranging orangutans and lemurs. Next door is the **Night Safari** (☎ 6269 3411; www.nightsafari.com.sg; adult/child S$15.45/10.30; ☻ 7.30pm-midnight), a 40-hectare forested park where you view nocturnal animals in their habitats. To get to the zoo, go to Ang Mo Kio MRT station, then catch bus 138; or Choa Chu Kang MRT, then bus 927. After the Night Safari catch a return bus by 10.45pm to ensure you make the last train from Ang Mo Kio (11.30pm) or Choa Chu Kang (midnight).

Sentosa Island (☎ 1800-736 8672; www.sentosa.com.sg; admission S$3; ☻ 7am-midnight) is a theme-park resort filled with such attractions as **luge rides** (luge & chairlift $9, 3 rides for $16; ☻ 10am-9.30pm) and the aquariums of **Underwater World** (☎ 6275 0030; www.underwaterworld.com.sg; adult/child S$19.50/12.50; ☻ 9am-9pm). Take the Sentosa Express light rail (7am and 11.45pm) from the VivoCity shopping centre next to the MRT station. For a more spectacular ride, take the cable car (adult/child $10.90/5.50 return) from World Trade Centre.

SLEEPING

Singapore has some excellent hostels and guesthouses, even in the more expensive parts of the city. For a little comfort upgrade to a sleek boutique.

Colonial District & the Quays

New 7th Storey Hotel (☎ 6337 0251; www.nsshotel
.com; 229 Rochor Rd; dm S$17, d S$53-80; 🖳 🖳) This
well-run hotel has four-bed dorms and double
rooms with shared or private bathroom.

YMCA International House (☎ 6336 6000; www.ymca
.org.sg; 1 Orchard Rd; dm S$30; 🖳 🖳 🖳) Even after
you add on the $3.15 temporary membership,
the Y's spacious dorms are a steal, with a pool,
free breakfast and central location.

Strand Hotel (☎ 6338 1866; www.strandhotel.com.
sg; 25 Bencoolen St; d S$85-95; 🖳 🖳) An above-
average midranger, the Strand is decorated
with earthy colours and jungle-print fabrics.

our pick **Gallery Hotel** (☎ 6849 8686; www.gallery
hotel.com.sg; 76 Robertson Quay; d from S$295; 🖳 🖳 🖳)
Singapore's first boutique hotel is still totally
hip. Rooms go retro with zanily coloured
linen, frosted-glass bathroom walls and room
numbers branded into the floorboards.

Fullerton Hotel (☎ 6733 8388; www.fullerton
hotel.com; 1 Fullerton Sq; d from S$400; 🖳 🖳 🖳)
Named after Robert Fullerton, the first
Straits Settlements' Governor, this converted
1928 post office is one of *the* places to stay
in Singapore.

Raffles Hotel (☎ 6337 1886; www.raffleshotel.com;
1 Beach Rd; ste from S$750; 🖳 🖳 🖳) Is it worth
coughing up the cash to stay at Raffles? The
rooms aren't as bright as modern hotels,
but wooden floors, high ceilings, leafy verandas, unwavering colonial ambience more
than compensate.

Chinatown

A Travellers Rest-stop (☎ 6225 4812; www.atravel
lersreststop.com.sg; 5 Teck Lim Rd; dm/s/d/tw S$20/40/65/70;
🖳 🖳) Brightly painted and extremely
friendly, this well-appointed hostel is the best
budget spot in Chinatown.

Royal Peacock Hotel (☎ 6223 3522; www.royal
peacockhotel.com; 55 Keong Saik Rd; s from S$105, d from
S$145; 🖳) Beautiful lobby, beautiful staff, and
peacock-palette rooms with character by the
bucket-load. Cheaper rooms are windowless
and cramped.

Scarlet (☎ 6511 3333; www.thescarlethotel.com; 33
Erskine Rd; d/ste from S$210/500; 🖳 🖳) Sexy Scarlet
has seduced Singapore's boutique-hotel market with a string of gorgeous 1924 shophouses
and bordello-decorated rooms.

Little India & Kampung Glam

Most hostels in this area include free internet
and breakfast.

Inn Crowd (☎ 6296 9169; www.the-inncrowd.com; 73
Dunlop St; dm/d S$18/48; 🖳 🖳) Extremely popular
for its location, atmosphere and very cheap
dorm, as well as its self-endowed title as a
backpacker party spot.

Sleepy Sam's Guesthouse (☎ 9277 4988; www
.sleepysams.com; 55 Bussorah Rd; dm/s/d S$25/45/69; 🖳)
By far the most peaceful of the area's hostels,
Sam's dorms and rooms are a bit cramped, but
the location on this strip of restored heritage
shophouses more than makes up for it.

Hangout@Mount Emily (☎ 6438 5588; www
.hangouthotels.com; 10a Upper Wilkie Rd; dm S$35, d & tw
S$88; 🖳 🖳) For state-of-the-art hostelling you
can't beat the Hangout. Modern rooms with
dorm beds (not bunks).

Perak Hotel (☎ 6299 7733; www.peraklodge.net; 12
Perak Rd; d with breakfast S$128-188; 🖳 🖳) The reno-
vated Peranakan-style Perak Hotel (formerly
Perak Lodge) is deservedly popular. Staff are
helpful, interiors feature lashings of natural
timber and ceramics. Cheaper rooms don't
have windows.

EATING

You'll eat well in Singapore from a buffet
of ethnic traditions: Malay, South Indian,
Cantonese, Hokkien, Teochew and Indonesian
among others.

Colonial District & the Quays

A former convent, **CHIJMES** (30 Victoria St) has been
converted into a den of worldly pleasure housing more than 20 bars, restaurants and clubs.

Yu Kee (☎ 6337 7525; cnr Liang Seah St & North Bridge
Rd; mains S$3-7; ✌ 7am-11pm Sun-Thu, 7am-2pm Fri &
Sat) Usually packed, Yu Kee does great duck
rice. Friday and Saturday nights see a devoted
crowd slurping down the Katong laksa.

My Humble House (☎ 6423 1881; 02-27/29 Esplanade
Mall; mains S$20-25; ✌ lunch & dinner) With décor
that's Alice in Wonderland–meets–Phillipe
Starck, this place is anything but humble.
Business groups dine from an elaborate
Sichuan menu filled with delicacies. Dress
snazzy; reservations essential.

Chinatown

Chinatown Complex Food Centre (Smith St; ✌ 9am-
11pm) As you'd expect, the large, eternally busy
hawker centre here has some fantastic Chinese
food, appropriately unkempt atmosphere and
wallet-friendly prices.

Da Dong (☎ 6221 3822; 39 Smith St; mains S$12-20,
yum cha items S$2.80-4.80; ✌ 7am-11pm) Grab a serve

GATEWAY SINGAPORE

of the celebrated dim sum from the steamer trolleys that are wheeled to your table.

Lau Pa Sat (18 Raffles Quay; ⏰ 10am-10pm) Famous for its renovated Victorian market building, this place can be so bewildering it even has street numbers. Try the steamed dim sum from stalls on Street 8.

Qun Zhong Eating House (☎ 6221 3060; 21 Neil Rd; mains S$8-10; ⏰ lunch & dinner Thu-Tue) Lunchtime queues conga onto the street for seafood, pork and vegetable dumplings.

Little India & Kampung Glam

Banana Leaf Apolo (☎ 6293 8682; 54-58 Race Course Rd; meals from S$6; ⏰ 10am-10pm) The runaway winner among Singapore's many fish-head curry joints, this place will make you a fan of dishes that sound disgusting.

our pick Tekka Centre (cnr Bukit Timah & Serangoon Rds; ⏰ 10am-late) Indian-Muslim stalls excel in prawn *vadai* (deep-fried prawn dumplings served with savoury lentil sauce or yogurt) or a spicy cup of Indian tea.

Lavender Food Court (cnr Jln Besar & Foch Rd; ⏰ 11-3am) Much less touristed than most food centres, and stays open until the wee hours. The wonton noodles and dim sum are worth queuing for.

Orchard Rd Area

Samy's Curry Restaurant (☎ 6472 2080; Civil Service Clubhouse, Dempsey Rd; dishes from S$3) A Singaporean institution, this banana-leaf curry joint is a culinary pilgrimage and housed in an old wooden army mess hall,

Café Les Amis (☎ 6467 7326; Singapore Botanic Gardens, 1 Cluny Rd; meals S$7-14; ⏰ breakfast, lunch & afternoon tea daily, dinner Sat & Sun) The mild-mannered all-day menu here covers all the luncheon bases and meals are served on an outdoor fountain terrace.

Din Tai Fung (☎ 6836 8336; B1-03/06 Paragon Bldg, 290 Orchard Rd; mains S$8-17; ⏰ 10am-10pm) Famous for its dumplings, but its wonton noodle soups are also excellent.

DRINKING & ENTERTAINMENT

The main party places include Mohamed Sultan Rd, Clarke and Boat Quays, and Emerald Hill Rd off Orchard Rd. Most bars open from 5pm daily until at least midnight Sunday to Thursday, and till 2am on Friday and Saturday. Cover charges at clubs range from S$15 to S$25. For frugal imbibers, the cheapest way to drink is in a hawker centre.

Long Bar (Raffles Hotel; ☎ 6337 1886; 1 Beach Rd; ⏰ 11-12.30am) It's a compulsory cliché to sink a Singapore Sling (S$16, or S$25 with a souvenir glass) in the Long Bar, but for a less touristy experience head for the snooker tables at the Bar & Billiard Room.

Crazy Elephant (☎ 6337 1990; 01-07 Clarke Quay) One of Clarke Quay's oldest and best bars, the grungy Elephant has been bashing out live blues and rock forever.

Zouk (☎ 6738 2988; www.zoukclub.com.sg; 17 Jiak Kim St) The stayer of the Singapore scene still nabs top-name DJs. It's actually three clubs in one (Zouk, Phuture and Velvet Underground), plus a wine bar, so go the whole hog and pay the full entrance charge.

Ministry of Sound (☎ 6235 2292; www.ministryof sound.com.sg; 01-02 Clarke Quay; cover charge S$15-25) Its international credentials made it an instant success, attracting big name DJs and huge weekend crowds.

Wine Network (☎ 6479 5739; Block 13 Dempsey Rd) A rustic bar nestled among the trees and old army barracks of Dempsey Rd.

Emerald Hill has a collection of bars in renovated shophouses including the cool **Alley Bar** (☎ 6738 8818; 2 Emerald Hill Rd) and even cooler **No. 5** (☎ 6732 0818; 5 Emerald Hill Rd). Longtime haunts in the Mohamed Sultan Rd area include **Next Page** (☎ 6238 7826; 17/18 Mohamed Sultan Rd) and **dbl0** (☎ 6735 2008; 01-24, 11 Unity St).

GETTING THERE & AWAY

For information on getting to specific regions in Borneo, see these chapters: Sabah (p87), Sarawak (p171), Brunei (p220) and Kalimantan (p237).

Air

The **Changi International Airport** (☎ 6541 2267; www .changi.airport.com.sg) is about 20km east of the city centre. SilkAir flies daily from Singapore to Balikpapan in Indonesia's Kalimantan province. Here are a few airlines that fly in and out of Changi:

Jetstar Asia (☎ 6822 2288; www.jetstarasia.com) Australia, Cambodia, Hong Kong, Indonesia, Myanmar, Philippines, Taiwan, Thailand and Vietnam.

Malaysia Airlines (☎ 6336 6777; www.sg.malay siaairlines.com; 02-09 Singapore Shopping Centre, 190 Clemenceau Ave)

SilkAir (☎ 6223 8888 www.silkair.com; 77 Robinson Rd, SIA Bldg)

Singapore Airlines (☎ 6223 8888; www.singaporeair .com; Level 2, Paragon Bldg, 290 Orchard Rd)

Tiger Airways (☎ 1800-388 8888; www.tigerairways
.com) Australia, China, Indonesia, Macau, Philippines,
Thailand and Vietnam.

If you plan to fly to Malaysian Borneo,
Johor Bahru's airport in Malaysia often has
cheaper flights on Air Asia and Malaysia
Airlines. Passengers of Malaysia Airlines can
take a connecting bus service (S$12) from
Singapore's **Copthorne Orchid Hotel** (☎ 6250 3333;
214 Dunearn Rd), leaving at 9am, 12.20pm and
3.50pm every day.

Boat

Ferries connect Singapore to Indonesia's
Riau archipelago. There are two departure
points: the HarbourFront Centre (next to
HarbourFront MRT station) for Pulau Batam,
Tanjung Balai and Tanjung Batu; and Tanah
Merah ferry terminal for Pulau Bintan and
Batam. To reach Tanah Merah, take the MRT
to Bedok and then take bus 35. A taxi from
the city is around S$15. Expect to pay around
S$16 for a one-way ticket to Batam, S$24 to
S$36 to Bintan, Balai or Batu.

Bus

If travelling across the Causeway from Singapore
to Johor Bahru in Malaysia, take bus 160 from
Kranji MRT station (S$1.10). The buses stop
at the border for immigration formalities and
to pick-up passengers on the other side. Keep
your ticket so that you can reboard.

You can also catch long-distance buses to
other peninsular Malaysian destinations. The
following agents at the Golden Mile Complex
and Golden Mile Tower on Beach Rd sell tickets: **Grassland Express** (☎ 6293 1166; www.grassland
.com.sg; 01-26 Golden Mile Complex) and **Konsortium**
(☎ 6392 3911; www.konsortium.com.sg; 01-52 Golden Mile
Tower). These coaches typically use the **Lavender
St bus terminal** (cnr Lavender St & Kallang Bahru), a 500m
walk north from Lavender MRT station, or de-
part from outside the Golden Mile Complex.

Train

Singapore's train station is on Keppel Rd.
The Malaysian company **Keretapi Tanah Melayu
Berhad** (☎ 6222 5165; www.ktmb.com.my) operates
three air-conditioned express trains daily to
Kuala Lumpur (3rd class S$19, 2nd class S$34)
with connections on to Thailand.

GETTING AROUND

Singapore has a fantastic transport system.
For frequent MRT train and/or bus trips, buy
a S$15 EZ-link card from any MRT station
(which includes a refundable S$5 deposit and
S$10 credit). This electronic card can be used
on all public buses and trains and offers reduced fares (from S$0.66 to S$1.75). EZ-link
credit can even be used at food outlets such
as McDonald's.

To/From the Airport

Changi Airport has connections by the Mass
Rapid Transit (MRT) to and from points
within the city. Public bus 36 leaves for the
city approximately every 10 minutes between
6am and midnight, and takes about 45 minutes. Taxis from the airport pay a supplemen-
tary charge (S$3 to S$5 depending on time)
on top of the metered fare, which is around
S$18 to the city centre.

Bus

Public buses are operated by **SBS Transit** (www
.sbstransit.com.sg) and **SMRT** (www.smrt.com.sg). Fares
start from S$0.80 and rise to a maximum
of S$1.70 and most buses run between 6am
and midnight.

The **SIA Hop-On** (☎ 9457 2896; http://siahopon
.asiaone.com.sg/; 1-day ticket for SIA passengers S$3, adult/
child non-passengers S$12/6) tourist bus does 19
loops of the city between 9am and 7.30pm,
stopping at 21 points of interest.

Mass Rapid Transit

The **Mass Rapid Transit** (MRT; www.smrt.com.sg) sub-
way system is the most comfortable way to
get around. It operates from 6am to midnight,
with trains running every three to six minutes.
Single-trip tickets cost from S$0.90 to S$1.90
with a S$1 deposit for every ticket.

Taxi

The major taxi companies are **City Cab** (☎ 6552
2222), **Comfort** (☎ 6552 1111) and **SMRT** (☎ 6555
8888) and **TransCab** (☎ 6553 3333).

Fares start from S$2.80 for the first kilo-
metre, then S$0.20 for each additional 385m.
There are various surcharges: peak-hour,
late-night and public-holiday services, airport
pick-ups and bookings. You can flag down a
taxi any time or use a taxi rank.

Gateway Jakarta

Dubbed the 'Big Durian', Jakarta has a spiny outer shell of freeways, skyscrapers, slums and traffic jams built on a plain that floods (often to biblical proportions) every rainy season. But the sweet, if acrid-smelling, centre is a condensed version of vast Indonesia – Batak taxi drivers, musicians from Maluku, religious radicals from Solo – with all the cultural traits and culinary treats that a nation of 250 million has to offer. From the crumbling colonial buildings to the city's decadent nightclubs, Jakarta is literally stuffed with humanity. It is a tough city to explore, lacking a coherent centre, but it is a real workout for urban adventurers.

See Lonely Planet's *Indonesia* guidebook for more information.

INFORMATION
Bookshops
Periplus (☎ 718-7070; lvl 3, Plaza Senayan, Jln Asia Afrika; ☿ 9am-7pm) Has a wide range of English-language titles, including Lonely Planet guide books and Periplus maps.

Emergency
Tourist Police (☎ 566-000; Jln KH Wahid Hasyim) On the 2nd floor of the Jakarta Theatre.

Internet Access
Internet cafés are scattered all over town, including the Jln Jaksa area, and generally charge around 10,000Rp per hour.

Medical Services
SOS Medika Klinik (☎ 750-6001; Jln Puri Sakti 10, Kemang; ☿ 24hr)

Money
Hundreds of banks and ATMs are spread across town including:
Bank Mandiri (Jln KH Wahid Hasyim)
BII Bank (Plaza Indonesia, Jln Thamrin) With an ATM.
BNI Bank (Jln Kebon Sirih Raya)

Post
Main post office (Jln Gedung Kesenian; ☿ 8am-7pm Mon-Fri, 8am-1pm Sat)

Tourist information
Jakarta Visitor Information (☎ 315-4094; www .jakarta.go.id; Jakarta Theatre Bldg, Jln Wahid Hasyim 9; ☿ 9am-5pm Mon-Fri, 9am-2pm Sat) Offers plenty of leaflets and an excellent colour map that shows the city's busway routes. There's also a desk at the airport.

Travel Agencies
24-Hour Tickets (☎ 3192-3173; Jln Haji Agus Salim 57A)
Robertur (☎ 314-2926; Jln Jaksa 20B)

SIGHTS
Kota & Around
Jakarta's crumbling historic heart is Kota, home to the remnants of the Dutch capital of Batavia. From Jln Jaksa take the northbound train from Gondangdia station to Kota station (2000Rp); or take a Koridor 1 bus from the busway on Jln Thamrin.

The finest way to relive the colonial experience is to kick your feet back and take a drink in the **Café Batavia** (see p84). The old Portuguese cannon **Si Jagur** (Taman Fatahillah), or 'Mr Fertility' was believed to be a cure for barrenness.

Nearby, **Gereja Sion** (Jl Pangeran Jayakarta 1; ☿ dawn-dusk) is the oldest remaining church in Jakarta. It was built in 1695 for the 'black Portuguese' brought to Batavia as slaves and given their freedom if they joined the Dutch Reformed Church.

GATEWAY JAKARTA

FAST FACTS

- Telephone code: ☎ 62 country; ☎ 021 city
- Population: 8.9 million
- Time: GMT+7
- Visas: most nationalities get a 30-day tourist visa on arrival

---

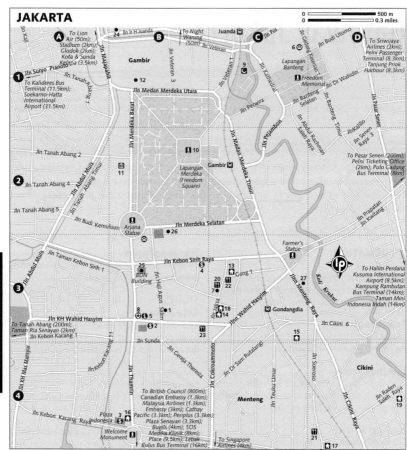

JAKARTA

0 ——— 500 m
0 ——— 0.3 miles

A B C D

To Lion Air (50m);
Stadium (2km);
Glodok (2km);
Kota & Sunda Kelapa (3.5km)

Gambir

Jln Suryo Pranoto
Jln Tanah Abang 1

To Kalideres Bus Terminal (11.5km);
Soekarno-Hatta International Airport (31.5km)

Jln Ir H Juanda   To Night Warung (50m)   Juanda   Jln Pos

24   Jln Veteran   Jln Veteran 3

Jln Majapahit   Jln Veteran 1   9   Lapangan Banteng

12   Jln Medan Merdeka Utara   Freedom Memorial

6

To Sriwijaya Airlines (2km);
Pelni Passenger Terminal (8.3km);
Tanjung Priok Harbour (8.3km)

Jln Budi Utomo

Jln Cideng Kasiran   Jln Dr Wahidin

Jln Petwira   Jln Banteng Selatan   Jln Banteng Timur

Jln Tanah Abang 2

Jln Merdeka Barat

10

Jln Tanah Abang 4

Jln Abdul Muis   Jln Tanah Abang Timur

11

Lapangan Merdeka (Freedom Square)

Gambir

Jln Medan Merdeka Timur

Jln Pejambon   Jln Abdul Rachman Saleh Raya

Jln Kalilio   Jln Senen Raya 3

To Pasar Senen (200m);
Pelni Ticketing Office (2km); Pulo Gadung Bus Terminal (8km)

Jln Tanah Abang 5

Jln Budi Kemuliaan

Arjuna Statue

Jln Merdeka Selatan   26

Jln Prapatan   Jln Kwitang

Jln Abdul Muis   Jln Taman Kebon Sirih 1

25   BDN Building

Jln Kebon Sirih Raya   Jln Haji Agus Salim

4   13   Gang 1

20   22   7

Farmer's Statue

27   Jln Menteng Raya   Kali Kratut

To Halim Perdana Kusuma International Airport (8.5km);
Kampung Rambutan Bus Terminal (14km);
Taman Mini Indonesia Indah (14km)

Jln KH Wahid Hasyim

To Tanah Abang (200m);
Taman Ria Senayan (2km)

Jln Kebon Kacang 1

8   5   1

2   23   18   14   Jln Wahid Hasyim   Gondangdia

Jln Cikini 6

Jln Sunda

Jln Kebon Kacang 1   Jln Thamrin   Jln Cereja Theresia   Jln Cokroaminoto   Jln Dr Sam Ratulangi

15

Jln Soeroso   Jln Cikini Raya   Cikini

Jln KH Mat Mansur

To British Council (800m);
Canadian Embassy (1.3km);
Malaysia Airlines (1.3km);
Embassy (3km); Cathay Pacific (3.3km); Periplus (3.3km);
Plaza Senayan (3.3km);
Bugils (4km); SOS Medika Klinik (8km);
Place (9.5km); Lebak Bulus Bus Terminal (16km)

Jln Kebon Kacang Raya   Plaza Indonesia   3   16

Welcome Monument

Menteng   Jln Teuku Umar

To Singapore Airlines (4km)

21

Jln Raden Saleh Raya   19

17

More fine Dutch architecture lines the grotty Kali Besar canal, including the **Toko Merah** (Jln Kali Besar Barat), formerly the home of Governor-General van Imhoff. Further north is the last remaining Dutch drawbridge, the **Chicken Market Bridge**.

Among the hubbub, **Sunda Kelapa** (admission 1000Rp) is the old Dutch port that is still used by colourful Buginese schooners. It's a 1km walk from Taman Fatahillah, or take an *ojek sepeda* (push-bike taxi; 2500Rp).

Central & Southern Jakarta

Soekarno attempted to tame Jakarta by giving it a central space, **Lapangan Merdeka** (Freedom Square), and topping it with a gigantic **National Monument** (Monas; ☎ 384-0451; admission 6000Rp;

8.30am-5pm Mon-Fri, 8.30am-7pm Sat & Sun). The 132m-high column, capped with a gilded flame, has been dubbed 'Soekarno's last erection' – whiz up the shaft for a shot of the city. The **National History Museum** (8.30am-5pm Mon-Fri, 8.30am-7pm Sat & Sun), in the base, tells the story of Indonesia's independence struggle.

The **National Museum** (☎ 386-8171; Jln Merdeka Barat 12; admission 750Rp; 8.30am-2.30pm Tue-Thu & Sun, 8.30-11.30am Fri, 8.30am-1.30pm Sat) is something of an oddity in that it is genuinely worth visiting. There are excellent displays of Han ceramics and ancient Hindu statuary and bejewelled kris handles. The **Indonesian Heritage Society** (☎ 572-5870) conducts free tours of the museum in English every Tuesday and Thursday at 9.30am.

INFORMATION		National Museum.....................**11** B2		EATING 🍴	
24-Hour Tickets..........................**1** B3		Presidential Palace................**12** B1		Jasa Bundo..............................**20** C3	
Bank Mandiri................................**2** B3				Lara Djonggrang.....................**21** D4	
BII Bank.......................................**3** B4		SLEEPING 🛏		Margot Café...........................**22** C3	
BNI Bank......................................**4** B3		Bloem Steen Homestay.............**13** C3		Paprika......................................**23** B3	
Jakarta Visitor Information.........**5** B3		Djody Hotel..............................**14** C3			
Main Post Office.........................**6** C1		Gondia International		TRANSPORT	
Robertur......................................**7** C3		Guesthouse........................**15** C3		Batavia Air................................**24** B1	
Tourist Police.............................**8** B3		Grand Hyatt Jakarta.................**16** B4		Continental..............................**25** B3	
		Hotel Marcopolo.....................**17** D4		Garuda Indonesia....................**26** B2	
SIGHTS & ACTIVITIES		Hotel Tator...............................**18** C3		Menara Buana Surya...............**27** C3	
Mesjid Istiqlal..............................**9** C1		Yannie International		Qantas....................................(see 25)	
National History Museum.......(see 10)		Guesthouse........................**19** D4		Thai Airways International......(see 25)	
National Monument (Monas)....**10** B2					

Built to celebrate the nation, **Taman Mini Indonesia Indah** (☎ 545-4545; www.jakweb.com/tmii; TMII Pintu 1; admission 6000Rp; ☙ 8am-5pm) includes traditional houses from (most) Indonesian provinces set around a lagoon. There's also an assortment of museums, including an insect house and bird park, and, best of all, displays of gifts given to Soeharto. To get here take the Koridor 7 bus to Kampung Rambutan bus station and then hop on a T15 metro-mini; it's about an hour from central Jakarta.

North of Lapangan Merdeka is the gleaming white **Presidential Palace** (Jl Medan Merdeka Utara) and to the northeast is the vast **Mesjid Istiqlal** (Jl Veteran 1; ☙ dawn-dusk), one of the grandest mosques in Southeast Asia.

SLEEPING
Jln Jaksa & Cikini Area

Jakarta's guesthouse ghetto is a short stroll from the main drag, Jln Thamrin, and close to Gambir train station. The Cikini area is east of Jln Jaksa and has a few pricier guesthouses.

Bloem Steen Homestay (☎ 3192-5389; Gang I 173; s/d with shared mandi 25,000/40,000Rp) On a quiet lane, this place has sparse rooms with ancient mattresses (but clean sheets). There's a tiny garden out the front.

Djody Hotel (☎ 390-5976; Jln Jaksa 27; r 55,000-135,000Rp; ❄) Get past the Jaksa minimalist look and this place has plain but clean, tiled rooms that are fair value. There's a safety deposit box at reception.

Hotel Tator (☎ 3192-3941; Jln Jaksa 37; r 75,000-120,000Rp; ❄) Cleanliness standards are high here, where the rooms come with bleach-fresh aromas and there's a front patio where you can munch your breakfast.

Yannie International Guesthouse (☎ 314-0012; Jln Raden Saleh Raya 35; s/d 125,000/140,000Rp; ❄) Yannie has well-kept rooms with hot-water bathrooms. There is no sign, just a 'Y' out front.

Gondia International Guesthouse (☎ 390-9221l; Jln Gondangdia Kecil 22; d from 160,000Rp; ❄) Pleasantly old-fashioned place with cosy, neat rooms that all have hot-water bathrooms, phones and reading lights. There's a small garden area too.

Hotel Marcopolo (☎ 230-1777; Jln Teuku Cik Ditiro 19; r from 240,000Rp plus 21% tax; ❄ 🖳) In the heart of suburbia, Marcopolo is great value for money. This high-rise offers a range of enormous rooms (all of which are kept in top condition), with baths and balconies.

Grand Hyatt Jakarta (☎ 390-1234; http://jakarta .grand.hyatt.com; Jln Thamrin; r from US$175; ❄ 🖳 🖳) The Hyatt is the city centre's most salubrious hotel, rising above Plaza Indonesia. It attracts the grand and the beautiful to its top-notch bars and restaurants.

Elsewhere

Quality Hotel Aspac (☎ 559-0008; fax 559-0018; r from US$80; ❄ 🖳) For transit visitors, Aspac is handily located right in the international terminal at the airport, upstairs in the departure area. It has a small bar and restaurant, but no other facilities.

Batavia Hotel (☎ 690-4118; www.batavia-hotel .com; Jln Kali Besar Barat 44-46; r from 365,000Rp; ❄) The rooms at Batavia are surprisingly plush and it's also a lot closer to the airport than most hotels. Discounts are available for 12-hour stays.

EATING
Jln jaksa area

Jln Jaksa's fine for no-nonsense Indonesian and Western grub. Also head to the night hawker stalls around the southern end of Jln Haji Agus Salim (also known as Jln Sabang).

Margot Café (☎ 391-3830; Jln Jaksa 15; mains 15,000Rp; ☙ breakfast, lunch & dinner) Classic Jaksa hangout with bamboo walls, wood floors, TV soaps, and cheap grub.

Jasa Bundo (☎ 390-5607; Jln Jaksa 20A; mains 12,000Rp; ☺ breakfast, lunch & dinner) Agreeable, inexpensive *masakan padang* (a spread of dishes) where all the usual favourites are piled up on the counter.

Paprika (☎ 314-4113; Jln KH Wahid Hasyim; mains 40,000Rp; ☺ lunch & dinner Mon-Sat) This hip, classy restaurant-cum-lounge bar has slick service and serves fusion food; it even starred in the film *Arisan*.

Elsewhere

The upmarket suburb of Kemang has plenty of stylish nightlife. Street food can be picked up at the **night warung** (market, Jln Pecenongan), about 1km north of the National Monument.

Place (Jln Kemang Raya; ☺ dinner) Highly sociable 'food bazaar' serving up everything from Indo regulars, teppanyaki steaks to gelato.

Pasar Pagi (Jln Mangga Dua; ☺ dinner) A great food bazaar next to the Mangga Dua mall. Half of the stalls serve Indonesian and halal cuisine.

Lara Djonggrang (☎ 315-3252; Jln Teuku Cik Ditiro 4; mains 45,000-150,000Rp; ☺ lunch & dinner) An attractive selection of dishes from around the archipelago fill the tables of this stylish restaurant mixing traditional Indonesian flair with North African charm.

DRINKING & CLUBBING

Jakarta nights are some of the most hedonistic in Asia with expat pubs and 'beautiful people' lounge bars. The bar zone on Jln Falatehan near Blok M is a good all round bet. Jakarta has an extraordinary clubbing scene centred in Glodok and Kota. In the south of the city the scene revolves around a richer crowd. Most places don't get going until 11pm, and rarely close before 4am.

Bugils (☎ 574-7650; ☎ 574 7650; www.batavia cafe.com; Taman Ria Senayan, Jln Jenderal Gatot Subroto; ☺ 11am-late; ⌘) Jakarta's prime expat watering hole in the *Cheers* mould is ideal for a pint and a game of pool.

ourpick **Cafe Batavia** (☎ 691-5531; Jln Pintu Besar Utara 14; mains from 50,000Rp; ☺ 24hr) This refined bar-restaurant, dating from 1805, is a Kota landmark. Revel in the colonial surrounds as you sip your tropical cocktails.

Embassy (☎ 574-2047; Taman Ria Senayan, East Bldg. 704, Senayan) Upmarket club where Jakarta's rich and beautiful gather to groove.

Stadium (☎ 626-3323; www.stadiumjakarta.com; Jln Hayum Waruk 111 FF-JJ) An all-weekend party at this hardcore club, with a capacity of 4000, that opens on a Thursday and closes Monday morning. Be warned that alcohol is not the drug of choice here and take care outside as this is not Jakarta's safest area.

GETTING THERE & AWAY

Jakarta is the main travel hub for Indonesia, with flights and ships to destinations all over the archipelago. Buses depart for cities across Java, Bali and Sumatra, while trains travel across Java. For information on getting to specific regions in Borneo, see these chapters: Sabah (p87), Sarawak (p161), Brunei (p220) and Kalimantan (p237)

Air

The **Soekarno-Hatta International Airport** is 35km northwest of the city. **Garuda** (www.garuda-indo nesia.com) and its Citilink subsidiary connect from international destinations to Jakarta and on to Balikpapan, Kalimantan on the island of Borneo. Batavia, Adam Air, Lion Air and Sriwijaya Air also serve Balikpapan.

Domestic and international airlines serving Jakarta include:

Adam Air (☎ 550-7505, 690-9999; www.adamair.co.id; Soekarno-Hatta airport)

Air Asia (☎ 0804-133-3333; www.airasia.com; Soekarno-Hatta airport)

Batavia Air (☎ 384-0888; www.batavia-air.co.id; Jln Ir H Juanda 15)

Cathay Pacific (☎ 515-1747; www.cathaypacific.com; Tower 1, Jakarta Stock Exchange Bldg, Jln Sudirman 26-F)

Continental (☎ 3193-4417; www.continental.com; ground fl, BDN Bldg, Jln Thamrin 5)

Garuda Indonesia (24-hr booking line ☎ 0807-1-427832; www.garuda-indonesia.com; Garuda Bldg, Jln Merdeka Selatan 13)

Lion Air (☎ 632-6039; www.lionair.co.id; Jln Gajah Mada 7)

Malaysia Airlines (☎ 522-9685; www.malaysiaairlines .com; ground fl, World Trade Center, Jln Jend Sudirman Kav 29-31)

Qantas (☎ 230-0655; www.qantas.com; 11th fl, BDN Bldg, Jln Thamrin 5)

Singapore Airlines (☎ 5790-3747; www.singaporeair lines.com; 8th fl, Menara Kadin Indonesia, Jln HR Kasuna Said, Blok X15 2-3)

Thai Airways International (☎ 230-2552; www .thaiairways.com; ground fl, BDN Bldg, Jln Thamrin 5)

Boat

The **Pelni ticket office** (☎ 421-2893; www.pelni .co.id; Jln Angkasa 18; ☺ 8am-4pm Mon-Fri, 8am-noon Sat) is 13km northeast of the city centre in

Kemayoran. Tickets (plus commission) can be bought through Pelni agents including **Menara Buana Surya** (☎ 314-2464; Jln Menteng Raya 29), in the Tedja Buana building, 500m east of Jln Jaksa. To Kalimantan, the *Lawit* goes via Tanjung Pandan to Pontianak.

Pelni ships arrive at and depart from Pelabuhan Satu (Dock 1) at Tanjung Priok, 13km northeast of the city centre. Koridor 10 Transjakarta buses should start serving the terminal from 2008, or you can take bus 10 from Jln Haji Agus Salim (allow at least an hour). The bus terminal is at the old Tanjung Priok train station from where it is a 1km walk to the dock.

Bus

Kalideres (☎ 541-4996) is 15km northwest of the city centre and has frequent buses to destinations west of Jakarta. Take a Koridor 3 Transjakarta bus to get here. **Kampung Rambutan** (☎ 840-0062) is 18km south of the city and primarily handles buses to destinations south and southeast of Jakarta. Koridor 7 Transjakarta buses serve this terminal. **Pulo Gadung** (☎ 489-3742), 8km east of the centre, serves central and eastern Java, Sumatra and Bali. Take Koridor 4 or 2 Transjakarta buses. **Lebak Bulu** is 16km southwest of the city and handles some deluxe buses to Yogyakarta, Surabaya and Bali.

Train

Jakarta's four main train stations are the easiest way out of the city to points elsewhere on the island of Java. **Gambir** (☎ 386-2361), on the eastern side of Lapangan Merdeka, is a convenient 15-minute walk from Jln Jaksa. Gambir handles express trains to Bogor, Bandung, Yogyakarta, Solo, Semarang and Surabaya. Some Gambir trains also stop at **Kota** (☎ 692-9083), the train station in the old city. **Pasar Senen** (☎ 421-0164), to the east, has mostly *ekonomi* trains to eastern destinations. **Tanah Abang** (☎ 314-9872) has trains west to Merak.

Smaller, but useful if you are staying in Jln Jaksa is **Gondangdia**, 500m east of most of the area's guesthouses. From here, there are trains to Bogor and Kota.

GETTING AROUND
To/From the Airport

Soekarno-Hatta International Airport is 35km northwest of the city. It's about an hour away via a toll road (up to two hours during rush hour).

There's a Damri bus service (15,000Rp) every 30 minutes from 3am to 7pm between the airport and Gambir train station.

Alternatively, a metered taxi costs about 130,000Rp, including the airport service charge and toll road charges. These should be organised through the official booths in the arrival terminal. Avoid the freelance drivers outside for safety reasons.

Bus

Jakarta has a comprehensive city bus network. Big, regular city buses charge a fixed 2000Rp fare. The big express *patas* buses also charge 2000Rp to 2500Rp and the air-con *transjakarta* buses cost 3500Rp. Supplementing these services are *mikrolet* and other minibuses (1000Rp to 2500Rp).

Taxi

Metered taxis cost 5000Rp for the first kilometre and 250Rp for each subsequent 100m. Make sure the *argo* (meter) is used. **Bluebird cabs** (☎ 794-1234; www.bluebirdgroup.com) can be booked ahead and have the best reputation; do *not* risk travelling with the less reputable firms. Typical taxi fares from Jln Thamrin: to Kota (20,000Rp) or Blok M (30,000Rp). Any toll-road charges are extra and are paid by the passengers.

Sabah

Topped by the wild granite spires of Mt Kinabalu, Sabah rolls like an undulating green wave from the South China Sea to the Sulu Sea. It offers pristine tropical rainforest, incredible animal and plant life, challenging trekking and mountain climbing, wild jungle rivers, and some of the world's best diving.

The west coast of Sabah is one long beach from north to south, with several beautiful islands offshore, including the islands of Tunku Abdul Rahman National Park and Pulau Mantanani, a tiny gem of a tropical island with blinding white sands. Central Sabah has Maliau Basin, a mountain-fringed sanctuary that was only properly explored in the late 1980s. It's a world of such incredible biodiversity that you may feel like you're walking through some sort of vast open-air zoo. Eastern Sabah offers more natural wonders, including the Sungai Kinabatangan, a river that winds through a corridor of primary jungle. For those who want an even more up-close-and-personal orangutan experience, there's the Sepilok Orang-Utan Rehabilitation Centre.

Of course, some of Sabah's most incredible attractions lie beneath the waves. If you're a diver, you already know about Pulau Sipadan, off the east coast of Sabah in Tun Sakaran Marine Park. This coral-fringed pinnacle rises 600m from the floor of the Celebes Sea and offers some fantastic wall-diving and plenty of large pelagic species. Lesser known are the nearby dive sites of Mabul and Kapalai, both of which offer great muck diving. On the other side of Sabah, some 300 kilometres northwest of Kota Kinabalu, is Layang Layang, which offers seemingly endless wall-diving, gin-clear water and occasional hammerhead sightings.

HIGHLIGHTS

- Enjoy the most attractively-located city in Southeast Asia, **Kota Kinabalu** (p88), which also happens to be the perfect gateway to Borneo

- Climb Borneo's highest mountain, **Mt Kinabalu** (Gunung Kinabalu, p106), and watch the sunrise over Borneo – an unforgettable experience for the adventurous and fit

- Trek into a hidden world of incredible biodiversity – a world unknown to science until the 1980s – at the **Maliau Basin Conservation Area** (p154)

- Spend a little quality time with our red-haired cousins, the orangutans, and do some great jungle walking at **Danum Valley Conservation Area** (p145)

- Descend the walls of the fantastic coral pinnacle that rises from the floor of the Celebes Sea at one of the world's best dive sites, **Tun Sakaran Marine Park** (p150)

★ Mt Kinabalu

★ Kota Kinabalu

★ Danum Valley Conservation Area

★ Maliau Basin Conservation Area

★ Tun Sakaran Marine Park

- POPULATION: 3 MILLION
- AREA: 73,619 SQ KM

HISTORY

After centuries as a pawn in various Indonesian and Southeast Asian power games, Sabah was neatly carved up by enterprising British business in the late 19th century, when it was known as North Borneo and administered by the British North Borneo Company. After WWII Sabah and Sarawak were handed over to the British government, and both decided to merge with the peninsular states to form the new nation of Malaysia in 1963.

However, Sabah's natural wealth attracted other prospectors and its existence as a state was disputed by two powerful neighbours – Indonesia and the Philippines. There are still close cultural ties between the people of Sabah and the Filipinos of the nearby Sulu Archipelago and Mindanao, through not always manifested positively: several small islands to the north of Sabah are disputed by the Philippines, there's a busy smuggling trade, Muslim rebels often retreat down towards Sabah when pursued by government forces, and pirates based in the Sulu Sea continue to raid parts of Sabah's coast.

After independence, Sabah was governed for a time by Tun Mustapha, who ran the state almost as a private fiefdom and was often at odds with the federal government in Kuala Lumpur (KL). Even when the Kadazan-controlled Sabah United Party (Parti Bersatu Sabah; PBS) came into power in 1985 and joined Barisan National (National Front), Malaysia's ruling coalition party, tensions with the federal government were rife. In 1990 the PBS pulled out of the alliance with the National Front just days before the general election. The PBS claimed that the federal government was not equitably returning the wealth that the state generated, and in 1993 it banned the export of logs from Sabah, largely to reinforce this point. The federal government used its powers to overturn the ban, and despite ongoing discussions, to this day nothing has changed – a mere 5% of revenue trickles back into state coffers.

As a result of this imbalance and its bad relations with the federal government, Sabah is the poorest of Malaysia's states, with an unemployment rate that's twice the national average. Although it's rich in natural resources, 16% of the population lives below the poverty line. Part of the problem is a bizarre rotation system that forces a change of political administration every two years.

Just to compound the economic difficulties, Sabah has experienced an extraordinary population boom over the last couple of decades – in 1970 the total number of inhabitants was under 650,000, whereas today it's a staggering 2.8 million. The government puts the blame squarely on illegal immigrants, claiming there are around 1.5 million foreigners in the state, but whatever the truth, a solution will need to be found in the next few years for Sabah's stretched resources.

CLIMATE

For information on the climate of Sabah, see p13 and p291.

GETTING THERE & AWAY

For more information on visas to the region, please see p300.

Air

There are flights between Kota Kinabalu and the following cities: Cebu and Manila (Philippines); Guangzhou, Hong Kong and Macau (China); Kaohsiung and Taipei (Taiwan); Seoul/Incheon (Korea); Singapore; and Tokyo (Japan). There are also flights to/from the following cities in West Malaysia: Kuala Lumpur, Kuala Terengganu, Kuantan, Penang and Johor Bahru (note that it's usually much cheaper to fly to/from Johor Bahru than Kuala Lumpur, so consider taking a bus to/from Johor Bahru). There are also flights to/from the following cities in Borneo: Bandar Seri Begawan (Brunei), Bintulu, Kuching, Miri, and Sibu (all in Sarawak). For details, see p100.

Boat

There are boat connections between Kota Kinabalu and Pulau Labuan, where you can get easy connections onward to Muara, the port of Bandar Seri Begawan (Brunei), as well as speedboat connections to/from Lawas and Limbang, both in Sarawak's northern Limbang Division. For details, see p121. There are boats between Tawau, in east Sabah, and Nunukan/Tarakan in Kalimantan (Indonesia). For details, see p153. Finally, there are boats between Sandakan, in east Sabah, and the city of Zamboanga, in the southern Philippines. For details see p138.

SABAH

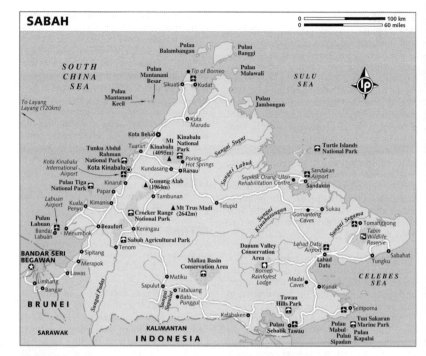

Road

There are road connections between Sipitang, in far southwest Sabah, and Lawas, in Sarawak's Limbang Division. For details, see p121.

GETTING AROUND

The west coast of Sabah is traversed by a good network of mostly paved roads, this network extends east over the Crocker Range in three places and one good paved road goes all the way to the east coast, which also has a good road network. Beyond this, most of the roads in the state are logging roads. The main highways in Sabah are serviced by regular bus, minivans and taxi services.

Sabah also has a good air network, serving both major cities and some smaller towns. River travel is possible in a few places, but not nearly to the extent of Sarawak or Kalimantan. Finally, the best way to explore Sabah is on foot and the trekking here is as good as anywhere in Borneo.

For details on getting around Sabah, see the Getting There & Away sections in this chapter and the Transport chapter (p302).

KOTA KINABALU

☎ 088 / pop 300,000

Sandwiched between the Crocker Range and the clear waters of the South China Sea, Sabah's capital city of Kota Kinabalu lays claim to one of the best locations of any city in Southeast Asia. With convenient flights from several nearby Asian countries KK (as the city is universally known) is the logical entry point for most travellers to Borneo.

Those expecting to step off the plane and find some languid tropical backwater are in for a real surprise. Sure, you'll spot a few picturesque 'water villages' on the ride from the airport, but once you get downtown you'll find yourself in a world of crowded shopping malls, big hotels and rising office blocks.

This bustling boomtown is the perfect place to catch your bearings and acclimatise to the tropical heat. The city's most notable feature is its pleasantly varied ethnic mix: Chinese, Malay, Indian and Filipino residents share the sidewalk with crowds of Asian holidaymakers and an increasing population of Western expats. With a population like this, it's no surprise that KK is a good eating city, and as you plan your Borneo adventure, you can feast on excellent Chinese, Malay, Filipino, Western and Indian food.

If you need to cool off or just want a break from city life, catch a taxi boat to the islands of Tunku Adbul Rahman National Park. You can easily make a half-day trip for some snorkelling or sunbathing and be back in town sipping a cool drink by midafternoon. On the way to the islands, you may catch a glimpse of the mad spires of Mt Kinabalu rising above the clouds behind the city. Even if you don't intend to climb it, you'll probably find yourself drawn to the mountain, and KK is the natural access point to Kinabalu National Park.

Above all, KK is remarkable for its sunsets: the city faces straight west across the South China Sea and each night the low clouds of the tropics come alive with brilliant reds, oranges and purples. In fact, we don't know of any city in the world that enjoys more regular and more spectacular sunsets than KK. All told, it's the perfect gateway to the island of Borneo.

HISTORY

In 1882, the British North Borneo Chartered Company established a base of Pulau Gaya (p102), offshore from Kota Kinabalu. The city was originally knows as Jesselton, after Sir Charles Jessel, a chairman of the company. Jesselton grew rich on rubber exports, which were facilitated by the completion of the North Borneo Railway, which reached all the way down to Beaufort (p117). The city was occupied by the Japanese for three years in WWII and was heavily bombed during the later stages of the way. The city was officially named Kota Kinabalu in 1967. At present, KK is undergoing a serious development boom and money is rushing into the city from mainland China, Singapore and Korea.

ORIENTATION

Geography dictates that KK is an easy city to navigate – it's squeezed by the mountains and sea into a fairly narrow corridor that runs southwest to northeast. The airport is on the coast about 5km southwest of town, and it's an easy trip by minivan or taxi (for details on getting to/from the airport, see p101).

Jln Kemajuan marks the southern boundary of the central area and one main street runs right through the centre of town, from the old Kampung Air ('Water Village') section, through the Sinsuran district, up to Kota Kinabalu Lama ('Old Kota Kinabalu'). Like many streets in Malaysia, this street changes names as it goes, with no fewer than four names in the downtown area alone: Lebuh Raya, Jln Pasar Baru, Jln Tun Razak, and Jln Haji Saman. The all-important ferry terminal/jetty (for trips to the offshore islands and Pulau Labuan) is on the foreshore at the northeast end of town.

While there are plenty of shops, restaurants and hotels in Kampung Air, travellers tend to gravitate to Sinsuran and Kota Kinabalu Lama, which are somewhat more atmospheric and within easy walking distance of the jetty and the Night Market, as well as many of the city's best restaurants and shops.

While there are several minivan and taxi stands in the downtown area, the Inanam long-distance bus station is about 8km north of town and is accessible by minivan and taxi from downtown (for more on transport, see the Getting There & Away section p99 and the Getting Around section p101).

Maps

The free *Traveller's Map Sabah*, available at the airport and the Tourism Malaysia office (p91) has a good map of Kota Kinabalu, as well as Tunka Abdul Rahman National Park, Labuan, Tawau and Sandakan. The free *Kota Kinabalu Street Map*, available at the same places, is a decent map of the city centre and outskirts. For something better, pick up a copy of the Periplus *Sabah & Kota Kinabalu* map at any of the bookstores in town (below). It costs around RM20.

INFORMATION
Bookshops

Borneo Books I (☎ 538-077; ground fl, Phase 1, Wisma Merdeka; www.borneobooks.com ☻ 10am-7pm) This is a smaller branch of the following Borneo Books II.

Borneo Books II (☎ 538-077; ground fl, Phase 1, Wisma Merdeka; www.borneobooks.com ☻ 10am-7pm) A brilliant selection of Borneo-related books, maps and a small used-book section. Free internet on the premises.

Iwase Books (☎ 233-757; ground fl, Phase 1, Wisma Merdeka; ☻ 10am-7pm) Iwase has a great selection of new fiction and nonfiction titles as well as lots of Borneo titles.

Times Books & Magazines (☎ 447-020; ground fl, Warisan Sq, Jln Tun Fuad Stephens; ☻ 10am-10pm) This new bookstore has a good variety of English-language titles, including books on Borneo and travel guides.

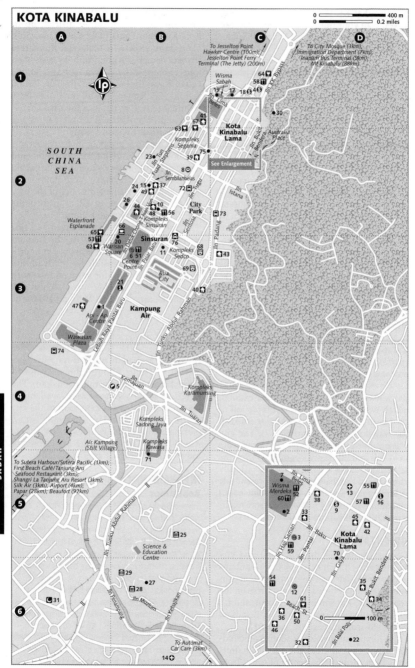

Consulate

Indonesian Consulate (☎ 218-600; Lg Kemajuan, Karamunsing; ⏰ 9am-5pm Mon-Fri)

Emergency

Ambulance (☎ 999 or 218-166)
Fire (☎ 994 or 214-822)
Police (☎ 999, 212-092; Jln Dewan)

Internet Access

Borneo Net (Jln Haji Saman; ⏰ 9am-midnight; per hour RM3) This popular spot has around 20 terminals (all PCs) with fast connections. Just try to ignore the earsplitting heavy metal music they tend to play.

IT Point (2nd fl, Centre Point Jln Pasar Baru; ⏰ 9.30am-9.30pm; per hour RM3) If you need access while in Centre Point, this is a convenient spot.

Net Access (Jln Pantai; ⏰ 9am-2am; per hour RM3) Plenty of connections and less noise than other net places in KK. LAN connections are available for use of your own laptop.

Immigration

Immigration office (☎ 488-700; Kompleks Persekutuan Pentadbiran Kerajaan, Jln UMS; ⏰ 8am-1pm & 2-5pm Mon-Thu, 8-11.30am & 2-5pm Fri)

Laundry

Mega Laundry (Sinsuran ☎ 238-970; Ruang Sinsuran 2; Kampung Air ☎ 231-970; Chinese Chamber of Commerce Building, Jln Laiman Diki; ⏰ 8am-8pm daily; per kilo

RM6) This fast and efficient laundry place is one of the few in KK open on Sunday. Ask them not to write your name on your laundry. The Kampung Air branch is the newer of the two.

Medical Services

Permai Polyclinic (☎ 232-100; 4 Jln Pantai) This is a private outpatient clinic.

Queen Elizabeth Hospital (☎ 218-166; Jln Penampang) This is out past the Sabah Museum.

Money

You'll find numerous moneychangers on the ground floors of Centre Point and Wisma Merdeka.

HSBC (☎ 212-622; 56 Jln Gaya; ⏰ 9am-4.30pm Mon-Thu, 9am-4pm Fri) 24hr ATM.

Maybank (☎ 254-295; 9 Jln Pantai; ⏰ 9am-4.30pm Mon-Thu, 9am-4pm Fri) 24hr ATM.

Standard Chartered Bank (☎ 298-111; 20 Jln Haji Saman; ⏰ 9.15am-3.45pm Mon-Fri) 24hr ATM.

Post

Main Post Office (☎ 210-855; Jln Tun Razak; ⏰ 8am-5pm Mon-Fri) Western Union cheques and money orders can be cashed here.

Tourist Information

Sabah Parks (☎ 211-881; Lot 1-3, ground fl, Block K, Sinsuran Kompleks, Jln Tun Fuad Stephen; ⏰ 8am-1pm & 2-4.30pm Mon-Thu, 8-11.30am & 2-4.30pm Fri, 8am-

SABAH

12.50pm Sat) Good source of information on the state's parks.

Sabah Tourism Board (☎ 212-121; www.sabahtour ism.com; 51 Jln Gaya; ☺ 8am-5pm Mon-Fri, 8am-4pm Sat, 9am-4pm Sun) An excellent source of information on all aspects of Sabah.

Scuba Paradise (☎ 266-695; www.scubaparadisebor neo.com.my; ground fl, Wisma Sabah, Jln Haji Saman; ☺ 9am-5pm Mon-Fri) This office arranges trip out to Pulau Mantanani (see p129).

Sutera Sanctuary Lodges (☎ 243-629; www .suterasanctuarylodges.com; Lot G15, ground fl, Wisma Sabah, Jln Haji Saman; ☺ 9am-6.30pm Mon-Fri, 9am-4.30pm Sat, 9am-3pm Sun) Books accommodation in Kinabalu National Park (including Poring Hot Springs and Mesilau) and on Manukan Island in Tunku Abdul Rahman National Park.

Tourism Malaysia (☎ 248-698; www.tourism.gov.my; ground fl, Api-Api Centre, Jln Pasar Baru; ☺ 8am-4.30pm Mon-Thu, 8am-noon & 1.30-4.30pm Fri) This office is of limited use for travellers and seems to specialise in giving out brochures that are long on pictures and short on practical details. Geared more toward travel in other parts of Malaysia.

Travel Agency

Airworld Travel & Tours (☎ 242-996; airworld@ tm.net.my; ground fl, block 2 Api-Api Centre, Jln Pasar Baru) This efficient travel agency is the place to go for domestic and international air tickets.

SIGHTS

While most travellers use KK as a staging point for journeys elsewhere in Sabah, there are enough attractions in the city to keep you occupied for a few days. Without a doubt, the Night Market is the city's most interesting attraction. The Central Market and the Filipino Market are also worth a look, particularly if you've got souvenir shopping to do. Of course, the best ways to enjoy KK is to just wander aimlessly, stopping in sidewalk café's to watch the world pass by.

Sabah Museum

The **Sabah Museum** (☎ 253-199; Jln Kebajikan; admission RM15; ☺ 9am-5pm Sat-Thu) comprises three museums/galleries and a collection of traditional dwellings on a hill south of the city centre, at the corner of Jln Tunku Abdul Rahman and Jln Penampang. A visit could easily occupy a half day or so and it's a good choice on a rainy day.

The main hall, modelled on a Rungus longhouse, contains a decent collection of tribal

and historical artefacts, including ceramics, and some nicely presented exhibits of flora and fauna. The prehistory gallery even has a replica limestone cave, in case you can't make it to Niah or Mulu.

Down the hill from the main hall, the **Heritage Village** (☺ dawn to dusk) offers the chance to wander round examples of traditional Borneo dwellings, including Kadazan bamboo houses and a Chinese farmhouse, all nicely set on a lily-pad lake. This is probably the highlight of the museum and it shouldn't be missed.

Just north of the main hall, at the end of the parking lot, the **Science & Technology Centre** (☺ 9am-5pm Sat-Thu) has some small exhibits on the petroleum industry. It's quite missable, so head upstairs to the more interesting **Sabah Art Gallery** (☺ 9am-5pm Sat-Thu), which features regular shows and exhibitions by local artists.

A 15-minute walk northeast of the Science & Technology Centre (past a hall used mostly for storage), the **Museum of Islamic Civilisation** (☎ 538-234; admission included in the Sabah Museum ticket; ☺ 9am-5pm Sat-Thu), is devoted to Muslim culture and history. The small collection includes a few illuminated Korans and maps of the spread of Islam throughout the world. Worth a look.

To get to the museum complex, catch a bus (50 sen) along Jln Tunku Abdul Rahman and get off just before the mosque. Bus 1 and 2, among others, stop at the mosque. Bus 13 also goes right round past the hospital and stops near Jln Muzium.

State Mosque

A fine example of contemporary Islamic architecture, the Sabah **State Mosque** (Jln Tunku Abdul Rahman) is set some distance from the heat and noise of central KK. It's south of the city centre past the Kampung Air stilt-village, not far from the Sabah Museum; you'll see the striped minaret and Octopussy-style dome on your way to or from the airport.

Built in 1977, the mosque has since been upstaged by the massive new City Mosque at Likas Bay; nonetheless, it's still an impressive building, accommodating 5000 male worshippers inside and 500 women on the balcony. Non-Muslim visitors are allowed to enter outside of prayer times, but must dress appropriately and remove their shoes before entering.

City Mosque

Heading north out of KK, you can't miss the four minarets and graceful dome of the Kota Kinabalu **City Mosque** (off Jln Tun Fuad Stephens), in Kampung Likas, about 4km north of the city centre. Overlooking the South China Sea, this mosque is more attractive than the State Mosque in terms of setting and design. Completed in 2000, it can hold up to 12,000 worshippers. It can be entered by non-Muslims outside of regular prayer times.

To get there, take bus 5A from Wawasan Plaza going toward UMS (RM1.50). Just ask the conductor to drop you off outside the City Mosque after the Tanjung Lipat round about. Taxis are about RM15 each way.

Central Market

KK's vast **Central Market** (Jln Tun Fuad Stephens; ⏲ 6.30am-6pm daily) occupies a long stretch of primer waterfront real estate in the middle of town. While it's not as interesting as the Night Market (see below), it's fun to wander the aisles and watch as locals transact their daily business. The ground floor handles seafood, fruit and vegetables etc, and the first floor has a decent hawker centre, where you can eat breakfast or lunch after perusing the stalls.

Night Market

KK's brilliant **Night Market** (Jln Tun Fuad Stephens; ⏲ late afternoon-11pm) is the best market in Borneo and one of the best in all of Southeast Asia. It is a place of delicious contrasts: the market huddles beneath the imposing gaze of the ultramodern Le Meridien Kota Kinabalu hotel, yet most of the goods for sale would have been instantly familiar to the residents of the city a hundred years ago. As jets soar overhead bound for Tokyo, Hong Kong and Singapore, you can bargain for sago palm, *belacan* (fermented prawn paste used as a condiment in Chinese, Malay and Indonesian cuisine), jungle honey, an incredible variety of fruit and an astonishing range of fish pulled from the South China Sea. Clouds of smoke from the many stalls barbequing fish and chicken give the place a decidedly primeval air, and the whole market echoes with heart-warming cries of 'dua ringgit, dua ringgit' (it seems as though everything costs a mere RM2). If you've never seen a proper Southeast Asian market, this place will be a revelation.

The market is divided into two main sections: the southwest end is given over mostly to produce (fruit, vegetables, fish, chicken etc) while the northeast end (the area around the main entrance) is a huge hawker centre, where you can eat your way right through the entire Malay gastronomy: *ais kacang* or ABC (the Southeast Asian shaved-ice treat), *nasi* and *mee goreng*, fried chicken and fish, *kueh* (Malay cakes), *pisang goreng* (banana fritters) and incredibly colourful arrays of *nasi campur* (tray after tray of Malay curries, veggie dishes etc). Finally, at the northern end, hidden behind the Filipino Market, is the brilliant Filipino Barbeque area (see the boxed text on p98).

Filipino Market

Sandwiched between the Central Market and the Night Market, the **Filipino Market** (Jln Tun Fuad Stephens; ⏲ 10am-6pm daily) is a good place to shop for inexpensive souvenirs. Offerings include pearls, textiles, seashell crafts, jewellery and bamboo goods, some from the Philippines, some from Malaysia and some from other parts of Asia. Needless to say, bargaining is possible here and you should be wary of fake pearls etc. Next door, there is a fruit market that stays open until late.

Other Attractions

You can wander up to the UFO-like **Signal Hill Observation Pavilion** (free admission; ⏲ dawn to dusk), at the eastern edge of the city centre, to escape the traffic and to get another take on the squatters' stilt village at Pulau Gaya. The view is best as the sun sets over the islands. From the top, it's also possible to hike down to the bird sanctuary on the other side.

The modest timepiece at the foot of the hill is the **Atkinson Clock Tower** (Jln Bukit Bendera), one of the only structures to survive the Allied bombing of Jesselton in 1945. It's a square, 15.7m-high wooden structure that was completed in 1905 and named after the first district officer of the town, FG Atkinson, who died of malaria aged 28. The tower was once visible from the sea, though there's now quite a few buildings in the way!

On Sunday a very lively Chinese street market takes over the entire length of Jln Gaya, with all kinds of food and goods (including some great pancakes) on offer. On Chinese New Year it goes completely crazy – you'll hear the gongs and dances starting around 7am!

SABAH

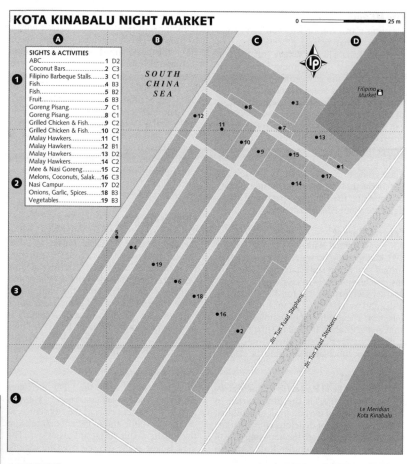

KOTA KINABALU NIGHT MARKET

0 ————————————— 25 m

SIGHTS & ACTIVITIES

SOUTH
CHINA
SEA

Filipino
Market

Jln Tun Fuad Stephens

Jln Tun Fuad Stephens

Le Meridian
Kota Kinabalu

SABAH

ACTIVITIES

Japanese Shiatsu & Reflexology (☎ 258-829; 2nd Floor, Wisma Merdeka, Phase 1; one-hour full-body massage RM50) Nothing feels better than a massage after a climb up Kinabalu or a trek through Maliau Basin. This cramped massage parlour in the Wisma Merdeka shopping mall doesn't look very encouraging at first glance, but the masseuses here are very good indeed.

SLEEPING

Kota Kinabalu has Borneo's best selection of accommodation in all price brackets. For budget travellers there are actually too many choices – the city is currently experiencing a glut of backpacker accommodation, most of it clustered in Sinsuran and Kota Kinabalu

Lama. Midrange choices also abound, with a good variety of clean Chinese cheapies scattered all through the town. Finally, there are several international-class hotels in the city itself and three resort hotels on the coast south of town.

Budget

North Borneo Cabin (☎ 272-800, www.northborneocabin .com; 74 Jln Gaya; d with fan/ac 18/20, private room with fan/ac 50/56; 🖳) Right downtown, the Cabin offers large, light-filled rooms, clean showers and toilets and a spacious common area. It also offers free internet and luggage storage for while you're away in the jungle.

Backpacker's Lodge/Lucy's Homestay (☎ 261-495; backpackerkk@yahoo.com; Lot 25 Lg Dewan; dm RM18, r from

RM42) The eponymous Lucy runs a friendly and homey backpacker joint that is fairly unique in offering cooking facilities. It's a little lived-in, but clean enough and has a veranda for chilling out in the evening.

Summer Lodge (☎ 244-499; www.summerlodge .my; Lot 120 Jln Gaya; dm RM18, r from RM55; ✶ ☐) The Summer is a large new hostel right on one of the main pedestrian malls of KK. It's got a spacious and pleasant common area and free internet. You can't miss its bright yellow façade as you approach.

Borneo Backpackers (☎ 234-009; www.borneoback packers.com; 24 Lg Dewan, Australia Pl; dm fan/ac RM20/25; ✶ ☐) This long-running backpackers is a little cramped but still popular. There's free internet but no cooking facilities. It's fairly clean and the location is good.

Akinabalu Youth Hostel (☎ 272-188; akinabaluyh@ yahoo.com; Lot 133 Jln Gaya; dm with fan/ac RM20/23, r from RM50) With a big common area, clean showers and friendly staff, the Akinabalu Youth Hostel (it's actually a backpackers), is another decent choice for budget travellers, although there are no cooking facilities.

our pick Step-In Lodge (☎ 233-519; Block L Kompleks Sinsuran; www.stepinlodge.com; dm with fan/ac RM25/35, r with fan/ac from RM60/80; ✶ ☐) The best backpacker place in town, the Step-In, has a large and airy common area, clean rooms and bathrooms and very informative staff. It's a great place to meet other travellers and exchange information.

Midrange

Ang's Hotel (☎ 234-999; 28 Jln Bakau; s/d from RM60/65; ✶) We've got a fondness for clean, well-maintained, simple Chinese hotels and Ang's is a perfect example. The deluxe rooms are light and spacious, if a little spare. The standard windowless rooms are similar but not as appealing. This is a good value midrange choice.

City Park Lodge (☎ 257-752; cplodge@streamyx.com; 49 Jln Pantai, tw/d from RM60; ✶) The brand new City Park Lodge tries hard to please and it does a good job. It's clean and well taken care of. The deluxe doubles (actually twins) are a good value, and if you don't mind being up on the 4th floor or not having a window, you'll get the same type of room for RM5 less.

Pantai Inn (☎ 217-095; 57 Jln Pantai; s/tw/family from RM67/73/88; ✶) There's a lot of competition in this price bracket in KK, but the Pantai still manages to rank near the top. With hot-water

showers, neat and sunny rooms, it's a great value in a convenient spot.

Hotel Holiday (☎ 213-116; www.hotelholiday.com .my; Block F Kompleks Segama; s/d from RM70/80; ✶) The Holiday is a very friendly spot right downtown in the Segama Complex. It's showing its age, and hot water here is an on-again-off-again affair, but the folks at the front desk will make you feel at home.

Seri Borneo Hotel (☎ 280-777; Kompleks Sinsuran; s from RM80, tw/d/tr from RM 90/90/115; ✶) This clean, new hotel has everything you need without frills or fuss. It's an excellent choice in this price range.

King Park Hotel (☎ 270-500; fax 270-600; kpkk@ streamyx.com; Jln Masjid Lama; r from 108; ✶) The King Park is a good choice if you want something nicer than a bare-bones midrange room but don't want to top-end prices. It's got large, clean, new rooms with TVs and fridges. There are no bathtubs, but the showers are good and the bathrooms are clean. It's a little far from the centre of town, but still within walking range.

Hotel Capital (☎ 231-999; capitalh@streamyx.com; 23 Jln Haji Saman; s/tw from RM140; ✶) The Capital is a little long in the tooth, but it is well maintained and decent value. There is little to distinguish it from others in this class except its convenient downtown location. Oh, and let's not forget Little Italy, the great Italian restaurant downstairs.

our pick D'Borneo Hotel (☎ 266-999; www.dbor neohotel.com; Block L Kompleks Sinsuran; r from RM145; ✶) The pleasant spacious rooms here have TVs, fridges, hot showers and the rate includes breakfast. The deluxe rooms are larger than the standards. Free wi-fi and a good location are bonuses.

Top End

Hotel Shangri La (☎ 212-000; fax 212-078; www.kkshang .com.my; 75 Jln Tunku Abdul Rahman; s/tw/d including break fast from RM161/184/184; ✶) The Shangri La (not part of the famous worldwide chain) is a good business hotel for those who want a bit of comfort but don't want to pay international rates. The deluxe rooms (which are actually standard) are spacious and well-appointed and have bathtubs for soaking in after, say, a climb up Kinabalu.

Jesselton Hotel (☎ 223-333; www.jesseltonhotel .com; 69 Jln Gaya; s/d from RM 198/215; ✶) This long-running hotel has a lot to recommend it: clean rooms, nice bathrooms, a great location, a good Italian restaurant downstairs, and a bit of history. However, even smokers will probably find the smoking rooms too 'fragrant'.

Hyatt Regency Kinabalu (☎ 822-1234; fax 821-8909; http://kinabalu.regency.hyatt.com; Jln Datuk Saleh Sulong; r from RM270; 🕸 🕸 🕸) Perfectly located on the foreshore, the Hyatt Regency is a big international-class hotel with an outdoor swimming pool, several on-site restaurants and comfortable rooms (some with ocean views). A few travellers feel that it's getting a little long in the tooth, but we find it perfectly adequate.

Le Meridien Kota Kinabalu (☎ 322-250; fax 322-223; www.kotakinabalu.lemeridien.com; Jln Tun Fuad Stephens; r from RM290; 🕸 🕸 🕸) The Meridien has some of the nicest and best-appointed rooms in KK. There are two restaurants on site, and KK's brilliant Night Market is right out the front door. The deluxe rooms offer ocean views, as does the executive lounge. The pool has a great ocean view and the gym has enough machines to keep you in decent trim. There's in-room LAN access and wi-fi in the lobby. On the downside, the service gets mixed reviews.

Promenade Hotel (☎ 265-555; fax 253-9804; reservations@promenade.com.my; Lg Api Api 3; superior/deluxe r from RM345/379; 🕸 🕸) Very popular with international tour groups and Malaysian business travellers, this mammoth hotel near the south of the city is right on the foreshore and commands great ocean views. The rooms are fairly spacious, with fridges, TVs, bathtubs, etc. Deluxe rooms have ocean views and superior (read: standard) rooms have city views. There's a small pool and a gym. Promo rates are usually available.

our pick **Shangri La Tanjung Aru Resort** (☎ 225-8000; fax 217-155; www.shangri-la.com; Tanjung Aru; r from 700; 🕸 🕸 🕸) The Shangri La is the perfect choice for those who want to combine the attractions of Kota Kinabalu with the features of a tropical resort. It's a sprawling complex which occupies most of the Tanjung Aru point about 3km south of the city centre. The superior rooms here have city/mountain views, while deluxe rooms have ocean views, and all rooms have private balconies. There are seven on-site restaurants and bars; hourly boat service to Manukan Island, two large swimming pools and one small beach. Parents will appreciate the kids club, which has minders who will watch kids all day free of charge. Finally, they're building a new spa on the beach where

you can get massages while peering over the South China Sea.

Sutera Harbour (☎ 318-888; fax 317-777; www.suteraharbour.com; 1 Sutera Harbour Blvd; deluxe garden-view r from RM810, deluxe sea-view r from RM910, packages and discounts available; 🕸 🕸 🕸) On a point about 1km south of the city centre, this complex with a vast reception hall has well-appointed deluxe rooms with private balconies and sea views (the upper floors have particularly nice views, as you would expect). Rooms have nice bathrooms but the tubs are a little small, two pools (one Olympic-size), three restaurants and kids club (not free minding) make this better than the adjoining **Sutera Pacific**. Expect similar features with somewhat more classically decorated rooms and common areas, as well as two restaurants and a golf course. Prices are similar.

EATING

KK is Borneo's best food city and if you only have to visit one of the city's markets to see why: the city's Chinese, Malay and Indian chefs have some of the world's best ingredients to work with, including an incredible variety of fresh seafood and the full range of tropical fruits, vegetables and spices from the nearby plantations and jungle. You'll be spoilt for choice in KK, so to help you narrow things down a bit, we can recommend the following culinary highlights: 1) a seafood feast in one of the city's giant Chinese dining halls and 2) a stroll through the Night Market followed by dinner at one of the stalls. And for breakfast and lunch, you won't go too far wrong at any of the city's *kedai kopi* (Malaysia's ubiquitous coffee shop/restaurants).

Food Courts & Hawker Centres

our pick **Night Market** (off Jln Tun Fuad Stephens; meals from RM2; 🕃 dinner; 🕑) The night market is the best, cheapest and most interesting place in KK for dinner. For details on the Night Market see the Filipino Barbeque Paradise box p98.

Centre Point Basement Food Court (Basement fl, Centre Point Shopping Centre, Jln Pasar Baru; meals RM2-10; 🕃 lunch & dinner; 🕑) Your ringgit will go a long way at this popular and varied basement food-court at Centre Point mall. There are Malay, Chinese and Indian places, as well as drink and dessert specialists.

Wisma Merdeka Food Court (6th fl, Jln Haji Saman, Wisma Merdeka; meals RM3; 🕃 lunch & dinner) Not as

SABAH

KAREN CHIN ON SABAH FOOD

Sabah, with immigrants from neighbouring countries such as the Philippines and Indonesia, has its own kind of food which is a blend of foreign food with local tastes, thus it is very different cuisine from other states of Malaysia. For example, the barbeque seafood at the Night Market in Sinsuran area is cooked in local Filippino style and served with other condiments such as freshly pickled seaweed.

The typical native dish which is more popular among the locals is *hinava*. *Hinava*, raw fish slices pickled with lime juice, chilli padi, sliced shallot, and grated ginger to get rid of the fishy smell, is usually eaten as an appetiser.

Roti canai, flaky pancakes made from flatbread fried on a skillet, is served from the morning till late night at any Indian Muslim *kedai kopi* (coffee shop). A good *roti canai* requires a cook to skilfully flip the dough over and over again before cooking in order to achieve its flaky texture. The flipping of the *roti* is a sight in itself. This dish is served with sauce, usually *dhal* (lentil curry) or another curry made from either fish or chicken. From this simple dough comes variations of *roti* such as *roti tissue, roti planta, roti telur, roti bom, murtabak* etc. These choices are as mind-boggling as they are tasty.

Locals often have their *roti* with different types of *teh* (tea). One favourite is *teh tarik*, a foamy tea prepared with condensed milk and poured from a higher mug to a lower mug in order to generate a foamy head. Other variations include *teh tarik halia* (tea with ginger) and *teh tarik Madras* (Madras-style tea).

One should not miss the famous *sayur manis*, a 'Sabah Vegie' which has been grown in Sabah since the early days. This vegetable can be stir-fried with *sambal*, a spicy shrimp paste, or with garlic or dried shrimp.

Another innovative dish is *fish noodle* (*udon*-like noodles made from fish) and is often served in soup or fried with seafood.

Even Tom Yam noodle soup has its own Sabah spin, with a rich flavour that comes from the addition of evaporated milk. And one can't miss chicken cooked with *lihing* (a sweet local yellow rice wine).

Dumplings filled with minced pork and served fried or steamed are also an all-time favourite among the non-Muslim locals here. They are served with red-wine vinegar and chopped garlic.

Beside common tropical fruits found in other states, Sabah is also home to rare fruits such as *tarap, sukun* and *Luzon* mangoes, but these are seasonal. *Tarap* has fleshy fruit encased in a bristly skin. It has a strong aroma but it's not nearly as pungent as durian. *Sukun* are used for making fritters and taste like sweet potatoes. *Luzon* mangoes are similar to regular mangoes but the skin is green even when ripe.

Finally, there are *kuih cincin*, literally translated as 'ring cookies'. These are made from flour and *gula Melaka* (Melaka sugar), moulded into the shape of blossom flower and then deep-fried. This biscuit is only available in Sabah so take some when you leave the region.

Karen Chin is one of the directors of Step-In Lodge in Kota Kinabalu.

SABAH

large as the one in Centre Point mall, this simple food court is still a good option for a cheap meal up at the northern end of town.

Jesselton Point Hawker Centre (Jesselton Point Jetty; meals from RM3; ☺ breakfast, lunch & dinner) This is a great spot to eat and drink while enjoying one of KK's famous beautiful sunsets. There's a variety of Chinese and Malay stalls here with shared outdoor seating and a couple of proper sit-down air-con restaurants, including Benito's which does a great lunch set including a good Aussie steak for RM17 on weekdays.

Restaurants

Restoran Sempelang (☎ 013-856-9777; Kompleks Sinsuran; ☺ 24hr) Eating outside is a Kota Kinabalu tradition and Restoran Sempelang is a great place to do it – right smack in the middle of the colourful Kompleks Sinsuran. There's a lot to like about this bustling Malay eatery: giant fresh fruit-juices (RM4), English menu, good seafood barbeque (from 6pm nightly), a canopy to keep off the rain, and friendly staff. As with other restaurants in the complex, your meal will be accompanied by the ubiquitous pro-wrestling videos.

Viet Café (Jln Haji Saman; meals RM5; ☪ lunch & dinner) This clean and bright Vietnamese place serves decent *pho* (noodles in soup), good fresh fruit juices, and tasty fried spring rolls.

Kedai Kopi Fatt Kee (28 Jln Bakau; dinner from RM15 per person; ☪ lunch & dinner, closed Sun) The woks are always busy at this popular semi outdoor Chinese place next to Ang's Hotel. Unless you show up early or late for mealtimes, you may have to wait for a table, and even after you order, you may wind up waiting a while for your food – but it's always worth it. *Midin* (jungle fern) cooked in *belacan* (fermented shrimp paste) is a Borneo classic, and salt and pepper prawns are great.

Nishiki (☎ 230-582; 59 Jln Gaya; set meals RM16; ☪ lunch & dinner) Operated by a Japanese expat, this authentic Japanese restaurant takes full advantage of the city's excellent fish markets.

When we were there, the master served up some thick slices of tender yellowjack tuna that were as good as any we've had in Japan. The atmosphere is pleasantly traditional, right down to the sushi counter. There are good-value set meals, sushi sets, and plenty of à la carte choices. You won't find authentic Japanese food for this price anywhere else outside of Japan.

Little Italy (☎ 232-231; Jln Haji Saman; dinner from RM20; ☪ lunch & dinner; Ⓥ) After an ascent of Kinabalu or a long jungle trek, why not reward yourself with a feed at this popular, casual Italian specialist? Choices include surprisingly good salads (RM10) pizzas (small/large RM18/24), and pasta from RM12.

Kohinoor (☎ 235-160; Lot 4 Waterfront Esplanade; dinner about RM50; ☪ 11.30am-2.30pm, 5.30pm-11pm; Ⓥ) There are several excellent restaurants in the

---

FILIPINO BARBEQUE HEAVEN

The best place to eat dinner in KK has no roof, no cutlery, no menu, no cash register and no dress code. They don't serve coffee or dessert and you can forget about a wine list. What they do serve is some of the best grilled seafood in Southeast Asia, along with a few exotic nibbles such as seaweed and sago palm. If you're up for a little culinary adventure and don't mind getting your hands dirty, the Filipino Barbeque Market is *the* place for dinner in KK.

It's located at the north end of the KK Night Market, behind the Filipino Market. Enter the Night Market through the main entrance opposite the north end of Le Meridien Kota Kinabalu. Walk though the first ABC/*nasi campur* stalls and turn right when you reach the stalls selling *goreng pisang* (banana fritters). You'll come to several rows of long tables, each sporting an impressive selection of grilled seafood at its end: giant shrimp, crab, tuna steaks, whole small tuna, squid, skate, rows of crispy baby shrimp of skewers etc.

Each table will be staffed by at least one Filipina server who will likely speak a smattering of English, but even if she doesn't you'll have no communication problems: just point at what you want and take a seat. Your server will send your selections away for one more turn on the grill. She'll also ask if you want rice to go with your meal (she may use the Malay word 'nasi'). She'll then bring you a small plate and a cup, as well as a small basin. The cup is for water, which is found in plastic pitchers on the tables. We've drunk this water several times with no ill effects – if you're worried, you can bring in any drink you want except alcohol (this market is operated by Muslims from the Sulu Archipelago and Mindanao in the Philippines). The basin is for washing your hands; use a bit of the drinking water from the pitchers.

The small plate is for preparing your dipping sauce. You'll find a small pitcher on the table containing red chilli sauce; pour some of this into the plate, then, grab the plastic tray of condiments and doctor the chilli sauce with soy sauce, salt etc. Finally grab some of the fresh *limau* (little limes) and squeeze them into the sauce. If you have any questions about how to create the sauce, your neighbours will be more than happy to help. The result will be a truly sublime dipping sauce (just writing about it makes us want to hop the next plane back to Borneo).

By the time you finish making your sauce, your seafood will be ready and it will usually arrive with your rice. Choose a small plate of *agar-agar* (seaweed) or a salad from the prepared dishes in front of you and dig in with your bare hands. A full meal here, including something nice like a tuna steak and some shrimp will usually run around RM15 to RM20. When you're done, stroll back to the main market for a refreshing bowl of ABC, or head to the coconut bars for a fresh coconut. This is the life, KK style.

Waterfront Esplanade, including this Indian place, which offers comfortable indoor seating and breezy outdoor seating. Take advantage of their authentic tandoori oven and order fish tikka or a tasty pile of garlic naan or sample one of their curries such as lamb rogan josh.

Port View Seafood Village (☎ 221-753; Lot 18 Waterfront Esplanade; dinner from RM50; ☺ lunch & dinner) This cavernous Chinese seafood specialist is like an aquarium where you can eat the displays – we've never seen such an extravagant array of live fish to choose from. Even if you don't eat here, it's worth walking into the foyer to check out the tanks.

First Beach Café (☎ 245-158; Aru Drive, Tanjung Aru; beer RM8; ☺ 9am-2am) This restaurant boasts the best sunsets in KK and it's hard to argue: it's right on the beach at Tanjung Aru and you can literally step down from your table onto the sand. This is a good spot for nibbles and beer in the evening. After a few drinks to put you in the mood, you can step to the following spot for a bang-up seafood feast.

Tanjung Aru Seafood Restaurant (☎ 245-158; Aru Drive, Tanjung Aru; dinner from RM50; ☺ 11am-2pm, 5pm-10pm) This giant seaside eatery does great fresh seafood, which they'll prepare for you any number of tempting ways. The wok-baked lobster in butter and milk sauce sounded horrible when the waiter recommended it, but we were pleasantly surprised. There's a good dinner show here on Friday, Saturday and Sunday evenings starting at 7pm and lasting about an hour. We particularly liked the dance over the bamboo sticks. How many bruised ankles went into learning this?

Cafés & Coffee Shops

Coffee Bean & Tea Leaf (ground fl, Wisma Merdeka, Jln Haji Saman; coffee from RM3; ☺ breakfast, lunch & dinner) Free wi-fi and proper coffee is the draw at this popular chain. In addition to this branch, there's another in the Waterfront Esplanade complex off of Jalan Tun Fuad Stephens.

Snack (Jln Gaya; drinks from RM3; ☺ 8am-6.30 Mon-Fri, 8am-3pm Sat, closed Sun) This hole-in-the-wall joint offers a tempting line-up of real espresso, fresh fruit juice, simple sandwiches – perfect for a break while exploring this part of KK.

Self-Catering

Self-catering choices include:
7-Eleven (Jln Haji Saman; ☺ 24hrs)
Milimewa Superstore (Jln Haji Saman)
Tong Hing Supermarket (Jln Gaya)

DRINKING

KK has a surprisingly lively nightlife scene. There are two main centres for nightlife: the somewhat upscale Waterfront Esplanade complex, which has a variety of good restaurants and Western-style pubs, and the more backpacker-oriented Beach St, which has at least one good bar with indoor/outdoor seating. Count on spending between RM3 and RM10 per drink. Many places sell 'buckets' of beer on ice. These usually cost around RM22 for a bucket containing four bottles. Needless to say, when it comes to drinking, chic places like Cocoon cost a good bit more than the corner *kedai kopi*. Some of the more reliable venues:

BB Café (Beach St) Pool tables, outdoor seating and a convenient location near many of KK's backpacker lodges make this an obvious place to start your evening.

Bed (Jln Tun Fuad Stephens) This cavernous club has live music most nights of the week. It can be pretty dead early in the evening.

Cocoon (Jln Tun Fuad Stephens) Three separate zones, all of them quite stylish, make this an interesting, if somewhat pricey, spot for a drink or three.

Q Bar (Jln KK Bypass) We like the style and the tunes at this gay-friendly bar at the north end of town.

Shenanigan's (Waterfront Esplanade, Jln Tun Fuad Stephens) This is one of several Western-style pubs in this complex. It's got sports on the tube, imported draft and occasional live music. If it doesn't suit, just walk to the next one.

Starbucks (Jln Tun Fuad Stephens; drinks from RM3; ☺ breakfast, lunch & dinner) We assume you've heard of this place – it's the one with the green sign.

Upperstar (Jln Datuk Saleh Sulong) On the 1st floor opposite the Hilton, this pleasant semi outdoor bar has a good menu of bar food and a cheap beer deal: a bucket with two large bottles of beer for 18RM (it's not on the menu, so you have to ask for it).

ENTERTAINMENT

Cathay Ciniplex (☎ 313-777; Jln Sapuluh; from RM7 per person)
Golden Screen Cinemas (☎ 212-322; Jln Sapuluh; from RM6 per person)

GETTING THERE & AWAY

KK has convenient flights to/from several Asian cities including Kuala Lumpur, Singapore, Taipei, Hong Kong, Seoul and Tokyo. There are also two boats a day between KK and Pulau Labuan, which has easy ferry connections with nearby Bandar Seri Begawan in Brunei. This is by far the easiest

SABAH

KOTA KINABALU INTERNATIONAL AIRPORT

Kota Kinabalu International Airport or KKIA (airport code: BKI) is the first stop for most visitors to Borneo. It's an incredibly casual and laid-back place with some of the friendliest immigration officers anywhere. Since the airport's two terminals are some distance apart, it's important to know which airline flies from which terminal when you're departing (see below). Terminal 1 is currently undergoing a massive renovation and it's a bit chaotic. Terminal 2 was recently refurbished and is a clean, well-organised place. There are no good restaurants in either terminal so eat before leaving town or bring food and drinks with you.

Airlines Operating from Terminal 1

- Asiana
- Dragon Air
- Korean Air
- Malaysia Airlines
- Royal Brunei Airlines
- Silk Air

Airlines Operating from Terminal 2

- Air Asia
- Fly Asian Express

For information on getting to/from the airport, see the Getting Around section (opposite).

---

way to travel between Sabah and Brunei and on to Sarawak, since the land journey is time consuming, expensive and fiddly.

Air

Malaysia Airlines (MAS; ☎ 1-300-883-000, 515-555; www.malaysiaairlines.com; 1st fl, Departure Hall, KKIA; ☺ 5.30am-7.30pm Mon-Sun) Has flights to/from the following international destinations: Bandar Seri Begawan (Brunei); Cebu and Manila (Philippines); Guangzhou and Hong Kong (China); Seoul/Incheon (Korea); and Tokyo (Japan). MAS flies to/from the following cities in West Malaysia: Kuala Lumpur, Kuala Terengganu, Kuantan, Penang and Johor Bahru (note that it's usually much cheaper to fly to/from Johor Bahru than Kuala Lumpur, so consider taking a bus to/from Johor Bahru). MAS flies to/from the following cities in Borneo: Bintulu, Kuching, Labuan, Miri, Sibu, Pulau Labuan, Sandakan, and Tawau.

Air Asia (☎ 03-8775-4000 within Malaysia, ☎ 60-3-8660-4343 outside Malaysia; www.airasia.com; Ground fl, Wisma Sabah, Jln Gaya) Flies the following international routes to/from KK: Clark (Manila, Philippines) and Macau (China). Within Malaysia they fly to/from Johor Bahru, Kuala Lumpur and Penang in West Malaysia and Kuching, Miri, Sandakan and Tawau within Borneo. The Air Asia counter at Terminal

2 of KKIA handles all bookings less than 24 hours prior to departure. It's open 8am to 7pm.

Silk Air (☎ 265-770 in KK, ☎ 6223-8888 in Singapore; www.silkair.com; Unit B, 1-2, 1st fl, Block B, Plaza Tanjung Aru, Jln Mat Salleh) Has flights to/from Singapore. Run by Singapore Airlines.

Korean Air (☎ 251-152 in KK, ☎ 1588-2001 in Korea; www.koreanair.com; Lot 2B, Level 2, KKIA) Has flights to/from Seoul (Incheon).

Asiana (☎ 268-677 in KK, ☎ 2669-8000 in Korea; http://flyasiana.com; KKIA) Has flights to/from Seoul (Incheon).

Dragonair (☎ 254-733 in KK, ☎ 3193-3888 in Hong Kong; www.dragonair.com; Lot CG01-05, ground fl, Block C, Bangunan KWSP, Jln Karamunsing; ☺ 8.30am-12.30pm, 2-5pm Mon-Fri, ☺ 8.30am-12.30pm Sat) Has flights to/from Hong Kong

Royal Brunei Airlines (☎ 242-193 in KK, ☎ 221-2222 in Brunei; www.bruneiair.com; Lot BG-3B, ground fl, Block B, Bangunan KWSP, Jln Karamunsing) Has flights to/from Bandar Seri Begawan.

Boat

All ferries, including taxi boats out to Tunku Abdul Rahman National Park, operate from the Jesselton Point Ferry Terminal, commonly referred to as 'the jetty' by locals and taxi drivers.

Passenger ferries (RM31, 3 hours) depart KK for Pulau Labuan (Sabah) Monday to Saturday at 8am and 1.30pm. On Sunday they sail at 8am and 3pm. In the opposite direction, they depart Labuan for KK Monday to Saturday 8am and 1pm, while on Sunday they depart at 10.30am and 3pm. From Labuan there are onward services to Brunei (see p124).

For information on boats to Tunku Abdul Rahman National Park, see p104.

Note, all passengers must pay an RM3 terminal fee for ferries departing from Kota Kinabalu.

Bus & Minivan

Buses serving eastern Sabah destinations operate from the Inanam long distance bus terminal 9km north of the city. Destinations, times and fares include: Sandakan (7am, 8am, 10am, 12.30pm, 2pm & 8pm, RM40 including a meal, six hours), Tawau (7am & 8am, RM40 including a meal, nine hours), Lahad Datu (7am, 9am & 8pm, RM50 including a meal, 6½ hours) and Semporna (7.30am & 7.30pm, RM50, including a meal, 10 hours).

Buses, minivans and private taxis serving destinations on the west coast and northern Sabah as well as the Inanam long distance bus terminal operate from Merdeka Field Bus Station on Jln Padang (often referred to as the 'old bus station'). Destinations served from this terminal include Ranau (bus 8am, RM10; minivan 7am to 5pm on demand, RM12), Tenom (minivan RM16), Keningau (minivan RM13). Buses and minivans to Ranau will drop passengers at Kinabalu National Park. If you're going to Poring Hot Springs, take a minivan to Ranau and switch to a Poring-bound minivan.

Taxi

Share taxis operate from the Merdeka Field Bus Station on Jln Padang. Several share taxis do a daily run between KK and Ranau, passing the entrance road to the Kinabalu National Park office. The fare to Ranau or Kinabalu National Park is RM20 or you can charter a taxi for RM80 per car (note that a normal city taxi will charge RM150 for a charter).

Train

The section of the North Borneo rail line serving KK was under reconstruction at the time of writing and it's unclear when or if it will reopen.

GETTING AROUND

To/from the Airport

Kota Kinabalu International Airport (KKIA) is 7km southwest of the centre. City Bus 1 travels between the city and Terminal 1, while City Bus 2 travels between the city and Terminal 2. Both cost RM1 each way. Minivans cost RM2 for the journey between the city and the airport. Taxis heading from the terminal into town operate on a system of vouchers (RM20), sold at a taxi desk on the terminal's ground floor. In practice, you can usually just board a taxi and pay RM20 in cash.

Minivan

Minivans operate from several stops in KK, including the Merdeka Field Bus Station and the parking lot outside Milimewa Superstore. They also circulate the town looking for passengers. Since most destinations within the city are within walking distance, it's unlikely that you'll need to catch a minivan. If you do catch one, most destinations within the city cost RM1.

Car

The major car rental agencies have counters at KKIA. In addition, there are several rental agencies in town, several of which are located in the Wisma Sabah building.

Automat Car Care (☎ 012-833-6663; www.kkauto mat.com; Lot 1, Lg Pelanduk) This company has some of the lowest rates in town and offers 4WD rental and airport transfer in luxury cars. Some of the fleet is a little wonky – inspect carefully on pick-up.

KMT Global Rent a Car (☎ 223-022; www.kmtglobal rentacar.com; ground fl, Wisma Sabah, Jln Lima Belas) This is a reliable and conveniently located agency.

Taxi

Most of KK's numerous taxis have meters, but few drivers will agree to use them. Luckily, most drivers are pretty honest and the rates they quote are pretty close to what you'd get if you forced them to use the meter (Manila this is not). Nonetheless, to avoid any unpleasant surprises, you should negotiate a fare before heading off. There are several hubs where taxis congregate, including outside the Milimewa Superstore in the centre of town. Most trips around town cost RM5 to RM8.

SABAH

AROUND KOTA KINABALU

TUNKU ABDUL RAHMAN NATIONAL PARK

☎ 088

How many cities in the world have a beautiful tropical island less than half an hour from downtown? How many have five of them? KK is blessed with **Tunku Abdul Rahman National Park** (admission RM10), a collection of five islands that lie a stone's throw from the waterfront. The islands have some of Borneo's best beaches, clear water and some fairly healthy coral and tropical fish. Any of the islands – Manukan, Mamutik, Sapi, Gaya and Sulug – can easily be visited as a day trip from KK. The admission fee covers all the islands, so if you plan to visit more than one, save your receipt.

The three most interesting islands for travellers are Manukan, Mamutik and Sapi. Manukan has, arguably, the best beach of the lot, while Mamutik has the best snorkelling, hands down. Tiny Sapi has a good beach and fairly good snorkelling. Note that all three islands are very popular with day-trippers on weekends. At other times, you'll find the islands very quiet and peaceful. You can rent snorkels on Sapi, Manukan and Mamutik or at the KK ferry terminal, but you'll want to bring your own equipment if you're a serious snorkeller.

There are simple resorts on Manukan and Gaya, and camping is possible on Sapi, Mamutik and at Teluk Malohom. Of course, due to their proximity to KK, you can use your hotel room in the city as your base for exploring the islands, although you may look a little funny striding through the lobby with arm floaties and swim fins on.

Pulau Manukan

With a good resort and a long white-sand beach, claw-shaped Manukan is the most popular island in the group. The entire south coast of the island is one long beach and you can work your way down the full 1.5km length of it at low tide. Most of the interior of the island is covered by forest cover, which you can enter via a jogging track that leads to a viewpoint at the west end of the island. The best snorkelling is off the southwest end of the island, though

it's no match for the snorkelling over on Mamutik (see below). The rocky north coast of the island drops sharply into the sea, with minimal coral (don't bother making the long swim around the island to snorkel here).

Manukan Island Resort, managed by **Sutera Sanctuary Lodges** (☎ 088-243-629; www.suterasanctuarylodges.com; Lot G15, Wisma Sabah, Jln Haji Saman, Kota Kinabalu; ☺ 8.30am-4.30pm Mon-Sat, 8.30am-12.30pm Sun), has the only accommodation on the island, comprising 20 units, a restaurant, swimming pool and tennis courts.

The resort has both beach and hillside units. The beach units include detached **family units** (RM380) that sleep four people in two bedrooms and semidetached **couples units** (RM320) that sleep two people in one bedroom. All have air-con, hot showers and verandas. These are very pleasant and comfortable retreats.

The hillside units include **family units** (RM380) that sleep four people in two bedrooms and also some **couples units** (RM320) that sleep two people in one bedroom. All have air-con, hot showers and verandas. These are somewhat less appealing than the beach units, but some do actually offer good views. Two of these are designated honeymoon suites and have separate showers as well as bathtubs (you should ask when you reserve if they're available).

Pulau Mamutik

A mere 300m from end to end, tiny Mamutik offers the best snorkelling in the group and a nice beach that runs up and down the east coast of the island. There's no resort here, but camping (RM5 per person, payable on arrival) is possible . There's also a small store/restaurant/snorkel rental place, although it's a good idea to bring your own supplies from the mainland.

There's a decent coral garden just beyond the pier on the southeast side of the island, but the best coral gardens are to be found around the back of the island (off the southwest coast of the island). To get there, take the trail that starts just past the toilet block at the south end of the beach, walk to the south end of the island and take a right up the trail that heads uphill away from the point. You'll soon come to a turn-off on the left that heads down to a small shelter. You can climb into the water off the rocks here, but be very careful, as they are pretty treacherous.

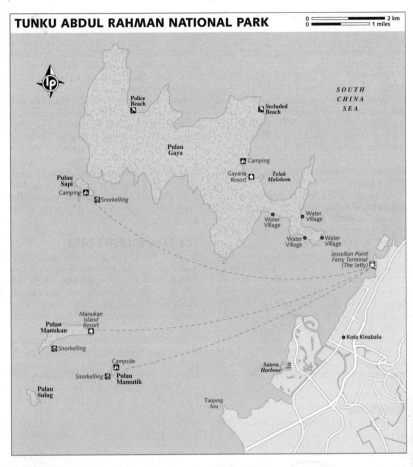

TUNKU ABDUL RAHMAN NATIONAL PARK

Pulau Sapi

Dwarfed by nearby Pulau Gaya, humble Pulau Sapi (Cow Island) is another popular and attractive little island that offers snorkelling and good beaches. The island is separated from Gaya by a very shallow 200m channel that you can swim across if you feel up to it. Otherwise, the main activities here include wading, relaxing on the beach around the jetty or exploring the trails through the forest. There's a decent coral garden around the southeast point of the island, but it's no match for the coral garden off Mamutik. There are changing rooms, toilets, barbecue pits and a small snack kiosk. There is also a campsite (RM5 per person) here but you'll need to bring over most of your supplies from the mainland.

Pulau Gaya

With an area of about 15 sq km, Pulau Gaya is by far the largest island in the park, rising to an elevation of 300m in places. It's also the closest to KK and is covered in virtually undisturbed tropical forest. The bays on the east end of the island are filled with bustling water villages, inhabited by Filipino immigrants (legal and otherwise), who live in cramped houses built on stilts in the shallow water, interspersed with mosques, schools and simple shops, also built on stilts. Residents of KK strongly warn against exploring these water villages, saying that incidents of theft and other crimes have occurred.

The other bays of the island are mostly deserted, with the exception of **Teluk Malohom**, which is home to Gayana Resort. There's also a simple campground (RM5 per person) here but there are no shops or restaurants, so you'll have to bring over all your own supplies.

Police Beach, in a bay on the north coast of the island, is the most popular beach on the island. It's a nice stretch of sand, but the snorkelling offshore is poor. A resort was under construction here at the time of writing. If you are intent on visiting a beach on Gaya, we recommend chartering a boat to take you to one of the secluded private beaches that lie between Teluk Malohom and Police Beach.

Accommodation here is provided by the **Gayana Island Resort** (☎ 301-131; www.gayana-resort .com; units from RM500; 🛰), a luxury development where thatched bungalows sit on stilts over the water. The bungalows here are pleasant, but the resort feels strangely abandoned and it's hard to imagine that the service would be up to much, considering the few guests who visit. Perhaps the lack of a proper beach here is what keeps the resort from catching on. All told, if you want to stay in a resort in these islands, we think you'll do much better at Manukan Island Resort.

Note that the only way to visit Gaya is by chartering a boat (see Getting There & Away on below), as the normal boats don't stop here.

Pulau Sulug

Shaped like a cartoon speech bubble, Sulug has an area of 8.1 hectares and is the least visited of the group, probably because it's the furthest away from KK. It has only one beach, on a spit of land extending from its eastern shore. Unfortunately, the snorkelling is pretty poor around this island. If you want a quiet getaway, Sulug is a decent choice, but you'll have to charter a boat to get here (see Getting There & Away on below), as the normal boats don't stop here. If you want a secluded beach and don't want to lay out for a charter, you'll do better by heading to Manukan and walking down the beach to escape the crowds.

Getting There & Away

Boats to the islands are arranged inside the waiting room at KK's Jesselton Point Ferry Terminal (commonly known as 'the jetty' by locals and taxi drivers). Inquire at the counter

for the next available boat. Sign up for your chosen destination and then take a seat until there are enough passengers (usually eight) to depart. Services run from 7am to 6pm daily but it's best to catch a boat in the morning, as it's much harder to make up boat numbers in the afternoon.

Return fares to Mamutik, Manukan and Sapi are RM17 to RM25, depending on which company you go with. You can also buy two-/three-island passes for RM33/43. The set fee for boat charter to one island is RM204, but you can negotiate a lower price. Try to deal directly with a boatman if you do this – don't deal with the touts who prowl the area. And don't consider paying until you return to the dock. Note that there is an RM3 terminal fee added to all boat journeys.

LOK KAWI WILDLIFE PARK

If you'd like to check out orangutans but won't make it out to Danum or Sepilok, a daytrip from KK out to **Lok Kawi Wildlife Park** (☎ 088-765-710; Jln Penampang, Papar Lama; admission adult/child RM20/10; 🕙 9.30am-5.30pm daily) is highly recommended, especially for those with children in tow.

In addition to the orangutans, whose playful antics make them the star attractions here, the park also plays home to the following: white hornbills, a clouded leopard (in a shamefully small cage), a Malay civet (ditto), tiny rusa deer, barking deer, mouse deer, a Sumatran rhino, a sun bear, an awesome Malayan tiger, proboscis monkeys, otters, gibbons, and some Asian elephants. For kids, there are elephant rides (RM1 per child) and a children's zoo. All animal enclosures have good English explanations, with maps showing the distributions of the animals throughout Borneo and the rest of Asia.

The animal enclosures are laid out along paths that wind through the park. You can easily do a loop of the main path in an hour or two, but be warned that it's hot and sweaty work and you'll be exposed to the tropical sun for most of the way – bring sun hats and sun block.

Don't miss the aviary located at the top of the park. The sign at the entrance to the aviary's main cage is a nice touch: 'Beware of attacking birds'. Also be sure to take a stroll through the botanical garden, which has some great boardwalks through a small section of jungle.

SABAH

Getting There & Away

The park is in Kampung Patoki. A bus service connecting the park and KK is planned (enquire with your lodgings when you arrive) but for now, the only way to get to the park is to take a minibus south from KK to Donggongon Town, then take another minibus serving Jln Papar Lama and ask to be dropped off in Kampung Patoki (RM2.00) and then a taxi onward to the park (RM40) per way, or simply to hire a taxi all the way to the park from KK, which will run around RM100, including a three-hour wait. Your lodgings may be able to get you a better rate than this.

SOUTH OF KOTA KINABALU

There are a few shallow paddling beaches near the highway south of KK. The nearest is at the plush Shangri La Tanjung Aru Resort, but other accommodation is strung out along the coast between the airport and Papar, especially around the nascent resort of Beringgis. The beaches won't win any awards, but you could pleasantly laze away a day or two before catching a plane.

Activities

Kindawan Riding Centre (☎ 088-225-525; www .kindawan.com; Kampung Laut, Jln Papar, Kinarut) Run by a professional Australian riding-coach, this beachside school has a full stable of noble steeds to hire for lessons or pleasure rides. Rates start at RM150 for a 1½-hour ride along the beach and across to a nearby island. Horses have been bred at the centre and are suitable for beginners or experienced riders alike. There is a weight restriction of 90kg. The centre will arrange transfer from your accommodations.

Sleeping

Seaside Travellers Inn (☎ 088-750-555; www.seaside travellersinn.com; Kampung Laut, Km 20 Jln Papar, Kinarut; dm RM25, r with shared bathroom RM30-55, r with private bathroom RM60-99; ❄ ☐ ☎) This small family-run resort is 20km south of KK on the way to Papar and is a reasonable alternative to the more lavish establishments. It offers plenty of facilities (including a TV room with VCD player) and outdoor activities. The view of the sea from the restaurant veranda is brilliant. The rooms are nice, but some are located next to the kitchen or parking lot and can thus be a little noisy. All prices include breakfast, and free airport transfers are available on request.

Beringgis Beach Resort (☎ 088-752-333; www .beringgis.com; Kampung Beringgis, Km 26 Jln Papar, Kinarut; r RM190-300; ❄ ☎) This large midrange resort overlooks a decent stretch of shallow beach. There are a wide variety of rooms and facilities spread over the grounds. It's not on par with the Rasa Ria or Nexus resorts north of KK (below), but it's a decent choice if you want to get out of KK for a few days.

Getting There & Away

To get to the beaches south of KK, take a Papar-bound bus or minivan (RM3) from behind Wawasan Plaza. The hotels and other establishments are signed off the main road.

PAPAR

Mainly consisting of long, low shophouses, this little coastal Kadazan town is 38km south of KK. Local produce includes coconut wine and there's a **tamu** (weekly market) on Sunday. **Pantai Mantis** (Mantis Beach) is about 7km out of town. If you're driving, follow the signs for 'Pantai Mantis' and 'JPSM'. It's nothing special, but if you have reason to be in Papar, it will do for a stroll.

In the centre of town, Restoran Anjung Bistari, a little south of the market, has good fried chicken.

Buses and minivans leave for Papar throughout the day from behind Wawasan Plaza in KK (RM3, one hour).

SHANGRI LA RASA RIA RESORT

The sister resort of the Shangri La Tanjung Aru Resort in KK, the **Shangri La Rasa Ria Resort** (☎ 088-792-888; www.shangri-la.com; Pantai Dalit, Tuaran; standard/deluxe r from RM500/600; ❄ ☐ ☎) occupies a fine stretch of beach about 15km north of the city. It's a sprawling resort complete with its own 18-hole golf course, several good restaurants (including a fantastic Indian one), a great pool, a spa and fitness centre, and a small nature sanctuary with a few resident orangutans. The rooms are fairly spacious and well-appointed and the suites are very nice indeed. The deluxe seaview rooms on the upper floors have unparalleled ocean views. This resort gets consistently good reviews from readers. The resort will arrange airport transfer from KKIA when you book, otherwise, it's an RM80 taxi-ride from KK.

SABAH

NEXUS RESORT KARAMBUNAI

About seven kilometres north of the Rasa Ria Resort, you'll find the **Nexus Resort Karambunai** (☎ 088-411-222; www.nexusresort.com; off Jln Sepangar Bay, Tuaran; r from 500RM; 🔀 🖥 🖭), another international-class beach on Sabah's west coast. Like the Rasa Ria, it's got a great 18-hole golf course, a good stretch of beach, a nice pool, several restaurants and a spa. The standard rooms are getting a little long in the tooth here, so it's better to choose something a step up in price. The resort will arrange airport transfer from KKIA when you book, otherwise, it's an RM80 taxi ride from KK.

KINABALU NATIONAL PARK
☎ 088

Kinabalu National Park is home to Borneo's highest mountain and some of Borneo's best-preserved forest. Most travellers make a beeline for the mountain and the main park headquarters (HQ) area, but there are two other sections of the park worth exploring: Mesilau Nature Resort and Poring Hot Springs. The former offers a less-travelled approach to the mountain and the latter offers a good place to soak your weary bones after an ascent of the peak.

Mt Kinabalu & Park Headquarters Area

Towering 4095m above northern Borneo, **Mt Kinabalu** is the highest mountain between the Himalayas and the island of New Guinea. Known as Gunung Kinabalu in Bahasa Malaysia, the mountain is quite unlike any other on earth, rising almost twice as high as its Crocker Range neighbours and culminating in a crown of wild granite spires. When the summit is visible (usually in the morning, before the clouds close in) the mountain literally demands your attention. It is clearly visible from many parts of Sabah, including Kota Kinabalu and the islands of Tunku Abdul Rahman National Park.

Thousands of people of all ages climb Mt Kinabalu every year, but an ascent of the mountain is not to be taken lightly. It's like spending eight hours climbing a staircase, in gradually thinning air (altitude sickness can strike as low as 3000m or even lower for some people), followed by an equally taxing descent. And it can be close to freezing near the summit.

If the weather is clear on your summit day, you'll be rewarded with an incredible view that starts with the otherworldly summit plateau and extends across all of northern Borneo and the islands of southern Palawan, in the Philippines.

Even if you decide not to do the climb, the park itself is a beautiful spot, and many visitors come just to escape the heat and humidity of the coast. There are several fine walking trails in the rainforest at the base of the mountain, the climate is agreeably cool and accommodation both inside and outside the park is good.

ORIENTATION & INFORMATION

Kinabalu Park HQ is 88km by road northeast of KK and set in gardens with a magnificent view of the mountain. At 1588m the climate is refreshingly cool compared to the coast; the average temperature ranges from 20°C in the day to 13°C at night.

Advance bookings through **Sutera Sanctuary Lodges** (☎ 088-243-629; www.suterasanctuarylodges.com; Lot G15, Wisma Sabah, Jln Haji Saman, Kota Kinabalu; ☽ 8.30am-4.30pm Mon-Sat, 8.30am-12.30pm Sun) in KK or online are strongly recommended for accommodation at park HQ and on the mountain at Laban Rata. You won't usually be allowed to climb Mt Kinabalu without a confirmed spot in one of the huts at Laban Rata (those who intend a day climb are sometimes excepted, but you won't be able to see much if you start for the summit after, say, 7am, due to clouds). It is sometimes possible to turn up at the **Sutera Sanctuary Lodges office** (☽ 7am-7pm) at park HQ and ask if there are any openings, but you may be disappointed. Sutera handles bookings for all accommodation around park HQ and at Laban Rata, Mesilau Nature Resort and Poring Hot Springs.

On arrival, pay your entry fee (adult/child RM15/10) at the park gate and check in at the Sutera Sanctuary Lodges office if you're staying overnight. You'll need to present your reservation slip and you'll be allocated your bed or room. Valuables can be deposited in safety boxes at the office and excess baggage can be stored here (per item RM1) until you return from the mountain. Following this, walk to the adjoining **Sabah Parks office** (☽ 7am-7pm) and arrange your permit and guide (see opposite).

All the hostels and resthouses are within walking distance of the park office. The **Kinabalu Conservation Centre** (admission RM3; ☽ 9am-3pm) is also worth visiting, with good

KINABALU: CLIMBING THE MOUNTAIN IS THE EASY PART

As you trudge through the thin air of Mt Kinabalu on summit day, and you may disagree, but the fact is this: climbing the mountain is the easy part. The hard part is jumping through the bureaucratic hurdles to get there.

The problem is that access to the summit is essentially rationed by access to the huts on the mountain at Laban Rata. In order to have any hope of clear weather when you reach the summit, you must arrive around dawn, and the only way to do this is by spending a night in one of the huts at Laban Rata. Yes, Sabah Parks will let you attempt a one-day ascent, starting around 7am, but by the time you get to the summit in midafternoon, it will almost certainly be clouded over or raining. And, just in case you're thinking about it: A) they won't allow a night climb and B) they will not allow an 'unofficial' climb (permits are carefully checked at several points on the mountain).

Unfortunately, many travellers report extreme frustration with booking huts on the mountain – they complain that the booking system is disorganised and inefficient, the huts are often full, or it's difficult to get a confirmed booking. A private company called Sutera Sanctuary Lodges has an exclusive concession for accommodation at park headquarters, Mesilau Nature Resort and on the mountain at Laban Rata. It may be easier to gain access as part of a tour with one of the large-scale tour companies based in KK.

Sutera Sanctuary Lodges has just instituted a policy whereby climbers must book a three-day/two-night accommodation and meal package tour in order to climb the mountain. It's no longer possible to book just one night in a hut at Laban Rata – you've also got to book accommodation around park HQ.

Assuming you are able to secure a reservation for an accommodation package, you still must pay for an expensive climbing permit and hire a guide to climb the mountain, despite the fact that the mountain is no more dangerous than many commonly climbed mountains in other parts of the world.

There is no doubt who gains from this situation. It's also clear who loses: everyone who wants to climb Mt Kinabalu and everyone in Sabah who stands to benefit from this tourist income.

It is a shame that the Sabah government and Sabah Parks cannot institute a system similar to that on Mt Fuji, in Japan, another mountain that involves a two-day climb with a night on the mountain. On Fuji, there is ample hut space that is allocated on a first-come, first-served basis, with the understanding that, in the event on an overflow of climbers, people will just have to plunk down on the floor in common areas or descend without attempting the summit.

All this said, we want to emphasise one thing: it is definitely worth jumping through the hoops to get to the summit of Kinabalu. Once you see that sun start to come up across Borneo, we're sure you'll agree.

displays on the natural and cultural history of the area.

Permits & Guides

A climbing permit, insurance and guide are *compulsory* if you intend to climb Mt Kinabalu. Permits and guides must be arranged at the **Sabah Parks office** (7am-7pm), which is directly next door to the Sutera Sanctuary Lodges Office, immediately on your right after you pass through the main gate of the park. Pay all fees at park HQ before you climb and don't consider an 'unofficial' climb as permits are scrupulously checked at several points along the climb. Guides are worth the money.

A climbing permit costs RM100 and insurance costs RM7. Guides for the summit trek cost the following: RM70 per group for one to three climbers; RM74 for four to six; and RM80 for seven to eight. Porters can be hired to carry a maximum load of 10kg; for one to three climbers the cost is RM60, for four to six it's RM80, and for seven to eight climbers it's RM90.

You can make a one-day climb, but still need a permit and guide. Sabah Parks has an office adjoining the Sutera Sanctuary Lodges Office where you can make these arrangements. The earliest you can start climbing is 7am. If you have no reservation for a night on the mountain at Laban Rata,

---

FLORA & FAUNA OF MT KINABALU

Mt Kinabalu is a botanical paradise, designated a Centre of Plant Diversity as well as a UNESCO-listed heritage site. The wide range of habitats supports an ever wider range of natural history, and over half the species growing above 900m are unique to the area.

Among the more spectacular flowers are orchids, rhododendrons, and the insectivorous nepenthes (pitcher plants). Around park HQ, there's dipterocarp forest (rainforest); creepers, ferns and orchids festoon the canopy, while fungi grow on the forest floor. Between 900m and 1800m, there are oaks, laurels and chestnuts, while higher up there's dense, rhododendron forest. On the windswept slopes above Laban Rata, vegetation is stunted, with *sayat-sayat* a common shrub. The mountain's uppermost slopes are bare of plant life.

Deer and monkeys are no longer common around park HQ, but you can see squirrels, including the handsome Prevost's squirrel and mountain ground squirrel. Tree shrews can sometimes be seen raiding rubbish bins. Common birds are Bornean treepies, fantails, bulbuls, sunbirds and laughing thrushes, while birds seen only at higher altitudes are the Kinabalu friendly warbler, the mountain black-eye and the mountain blackbird. Other wildlife includes colourful butterflies and the huge green moon moth.

---

go to Sutera office and wait for last-minute cancellation; by 5.30pm you will be informed if there is space in one of the huts.

Your guide will be assigned to you on the morning you begin your hike. If you ask, the park staff can try and attach individual travellers to a group so that guide fees can be shared. Couples can expect to be given their own guide.

A good guide should be able to point out pitcher plants and other interesting sights, but as the trails are pretty straightforward they're more safety supervisors than wayfinders, so will generally position themselves behind the slowest member of their group – don't be surprised if you barely see your guide for the duration of the trek!

Equipment & Clothing

Temperatures can dip close to freezing at the summit and it's usually windy and occasionally rainy. You will need good walking shoes, light gloves, a wool or fleece hat, a fleece top, windproof pants, a shell jacket and a knapsack to carry all this. You will also need a headlamp for the predawn summit climb (don't bring a handheld torch because you'll need your hands free to climb the ropes on the summit massif). A water bottle is also recommended, and you can fill this from tanks en route.

HISTORY

The first recorded ascent of the mountain was made in 1851 by Sir Hugh Low, the British colonial secretary on Pulau Labuan.

Kinabalu's highest peak is named after him, as is the mile-deep 'gully' on the other side of the mountain.

In those days the difficulty of climbing Mt Kinabalu lay not in the ascent, but in getting through the jungle to the mountain's base. Finding willing local porters was another tricky matter – the tribesmen who accompanied Low believed the spirits of their dead inhabited the mountain. Low was therefore obliged to protect the party by supplying a large basket of quartz crystals and teeth, as was the custom of the day. In time, the spirit-appeasement ceremonies performed by the guides upon reaching the summit became more and more elaborate, so that by the 1920s they had come to include loud prayers, gunshots, and the sacrifice of seven eggs and seven white chickens. You have to wonder at what point explorers started thinking the locals might be taking the mickey...

These days getting to the foot of the mountain is a piece of cake, but Low's Gully remains a trickier proposition. In 1994 one of the groups in the first expedition to abseil into the gully got stuck and could not be rescued for three weeks.

GEOLOGY

Many visitors to Borneo assume that Mt Kinabalu is a volcano, but the mountain is actually a huge granite dome that rose from the depths below some nine million years ago. In geological terms, Mt Kinabalu is still very young. Little erosion has occurred on the exposed granite rock faces around the summit, though the effects of glaciers that used to cover much of the mountain can be detected by striations on the rock. There's no longer a snowline and the glaciers have disappeared, but at times ice forms in the rock pools near the summit.

Walks Around Park Headquarters

It's well worth spending a day exploring the marked trails around park HQ; if you have time, it may be better to do it before you climb the mountain, as chances are you won't really feel like it afterwards. The various trails and lookouts are shown on the map, p109.

All the trails link up with others at some stage, so you can spend the whole day, or indeed days, walking at a leisurely pace through the beautiful forest. Some interesting plants, plenty of birds and, if you're lucky, the occasional mammal can be seen. When it rains, watch out for slippery paths and legions of leeches.

At 11am each day a **guided walk** (RM3) starts from the park office and lasts for one to two hours. The knowledgeable guide points out flowers, plants, birds and insects along the way. If you set out from KK early enough, it's possible to arrive at the park in time for the guided walk.

Many of the plants found on the mountain are cultivated in the **Mountain Garden** (admission RM5; ☺ tours 9am, noon & 3pm, garden 9am-5pm) behind the visitors centre.

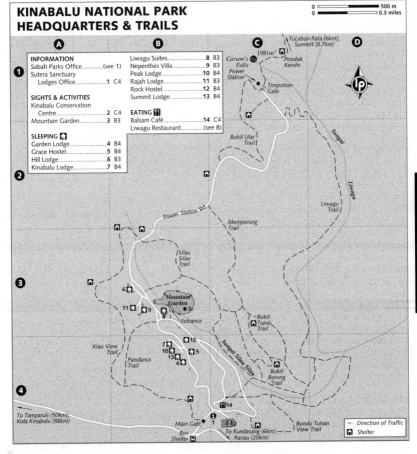

KINABALU NATIONAL PARK HEADQUARTERS & TRAILS

INFORMATION
Sabah Parks Office............(see 1)
Sutera Sanctuary
    Lodges Office.................**1** C4

SIGHTS & ACTIVITIES
Kinabalu Conservation
    Centre.........................**2** C4
Mountain Garden.............**3** B3

SLEEPING
Garden Lodge....................**4** B4
Grace Hostel.....................**5** B4
Hill Lodge........................**6** B3
Kinabalu Lodge.................**7** B4

Liwagu Suites....................**8** B3
Nepenthes Villa.................**9** B3
Peak Lodge......................**10** B4
Rajah Lodge.....................**11** B3
Rock Hostel.....................**12** B4
Summit Lodge..................**13** B4

EATING
Balsam Café.....................**14** C4
Liwagu Restaurant............(see 8)

LIWAGU TRAIL

The 6km **Liwagu Trail**, which follows the Liwagu River, is the most rewarding trail around park HQ, and it's a great option for those who just can't face the trek up Mt Kinabalu. It's a pretty easy walk, but there are few drop-offs which make it unsuitable for children below eight years of age, and those with fear of heights.

The start is 200m before Timpohon Gate (you can catch a minivan from HQ to the starting point). It's very straightforward until the last kilometre or so (just as you get back to the park base area). At one point, you come to a junction where you could go left (downhill) but the trail is closed off. Do not go downhill here. Follow the arrows marked 'Silau Silau Trail' uphill. You will come to some water pipes across the trail after about 100m. Cross these pipes. You will then come to a sign for the Mempening Trail and Silau Silau Trail. Follow the arrow for the Silau Silau Trail.

You'll soon come to a sign for Silau Silau Trail and Liwagu Trail. Go left here, following the arrow for the Liwagu Trail. Then stay on this trail without deviation, ignoring a bridge on your right and the Bundu Tahan trail on your left. It comes out just below park HQ. Don't worry if you take a wrong turn in this area, as almost all routes lead back to park HQ one way or another.

If starting from park HQ, take a right out of the HQ, walk to the end of the parking lot and down the road. You'll pass the start of the Bundu Tahan Trail (ignore this). Continue down and after about 200m you will see the back of the sign for the Liwagu Trail that reads 'Liwagu Trail/Liwagu River 1500m' (note this is the distance to the river, not the full distance of the trail). This is the start of the trail. It's pretty confusing and more difficult to do the trail from this end, so we recommend heading to the top and walking down.

SILAU SILAU TRAIL

The **Silau Silau Trail** is an easy 940m, 30-minute trail through centre of the HQ area, along Silau Silau creek. It's mostly flat and easy to walk, making it suitable for most people, including children. It's makes a nice before- or after-dinner stroll.

KIAU VIEW TRAIL

The **Kiau View Trail** is a more challenging 2.34km, 80-minute trail along a ridge on the west side of the HQ area. There are a few ups and downs on this route. You can combine this with the Silau Silau Trail to make a good loop.

Mt Kinabalu Summit Climb

Climbing Mt Kinabalu is a two-day exercise for most people. The usual routine involves starting around 8am on the first day, taking a minivan to Timpohon Gate and walking four to six hours to reach Laban Rata at 3273m where you spend the night. On the following day you rise at around 3am and climb to the summit in time to catch the sunrise over Borneo.

Do not consider an ascent unless you are in good physical shape. The climb is uphill 99% of the way – an unrelentingly steep path up large dirt steps and overpiled rocks. A couple of sections on the summit massif require that you haul yourself up using thick ropes. Every step can be a struggle as you suck oxygen from the thin air, and it is not unusual for people to give up within sight of the summit. If you are not in excellent shape already, we recommend that you do some climbing, walking or running in the weeks before you come to Sabah. Also, be sure to bring the proper equipment and clothing; see the boxed text on below.

KINABALU PACKING LIST

- hiking or running shorts
- synthetic lightweight T-shirt
- running shoes or hiking boots, depending on preference for climbing
- wool socks
- pack cover
- headlamp with spare batteries
- lightweight fleece gloves
- fleece or wool hat
- polypro thermals top and bottom
- fleece jacket
- wind pants
- lightweight shell jacket or rain jacket
- water bottle
- money
- camera
- earplugs for dorms

SABAH

Your best chance of finding clear weather at the summit is around dawn, but there are plenty of mornings which see the summit wrapped in clouds. If it's raining when you wake at Laban Rata, you should consider abandoning your summit attempt, as the chance of it clearing that day is slim indeed and you'll freeze in the cold, wet weather.

You can also access the trail to Laban Rata from the Mesilau Nature Resort (see p114).

PARK HEADQUARTERS–TIMPOHON GATE (POWER STATION)

The trail officially starts at the Timpohon Gate (1866m), from where it's an 8.72km walk to the summit. Most climbers take a minivan from park HQ to Timpohon Gate (departures approximately every 15 minutes in the morning, RM15 per minivan, 10 minutes). Leave no later than 11am to cover the 6km to Laban Rata (3273m), the first day's stopping point. This section will take between 3½ and six hours depending on your fitness level.

TIMPOHON GATE–LAYANG LAYANG

After a short, deceptive descent, the trail leads up steep stairs through magnificent tall forest. There's a small waterfall, **Carson's Falls**, beside the track shortly after the start, and the forest can be alive with birds and squirrels in the morning. Five *pondok* (shelters) are spaced at intervals of 15 to 35 minutes and it's about three hours to Layang Layang (2621m), where there are staff quarters. Near Pondok Lowii (2286m) the trail follows an open ridge giving great views over the valleys and up to the peaks.

LAYANG LAYANG–PONDOK PAKA

It's about 1¾ hours on to Pondok Paka (3053m), the seventh shelter on the trail and 5.5km from the start. The trail passes through increasingly stunted rhododendron forest, leaving walkers more exposed to the elements. You'll welcome the few flat sections that lie between the seemingly endless steps. This stretch is good for spotting pitcher plants, although you probably won't see any growing by the side of the track – look among the dense vegetation.

PONDOK PAKA–LABAN RATA

This leg takes about 45 minutes to walk. Laban Rata (3273m), right at treeline, is the night's

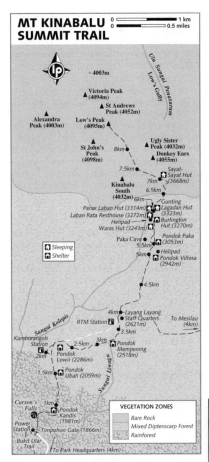

resting spot for most people attempting the summit. The main resthouse has heating, hot water, comfortable beds and a restaurant with fine views – it's perfectly positioned for sunset, which can be just as scenic as sunrise at the top. There's also a flat area sometimes used as a volleyball court if you're feeling overly energetic! There are three other accommodation units, all with basic cooking facilities and hot showers, but no room heaters (see p113).

LABAN RATA–SAYAT-SAYAT

The next morning, hit the trail at around 3.30am and spend the next 2½ to four hours scaling the 2.7km trail to the summit at Low's Peak, ideally in time for sunrise, which happens around 6am in these parts. Then you pick your way back down to park HQ the same day.

The initial one-hour climb to Sayat-Sayat hut (3668m) involves crossing the sheer Panar Laban rock face. There is little vegetation, except where overhangs provide some respite from the wind. It is one of the toughest parts of the climb, especially in the cold and dark of the predawn hours.

Thick ropes are used to haul yourself up the granite sheets; it's hard work in places, but somehow it feels good to be using arm muscles instead of legs! Narrow wooden steps and hand rails help in places, but you'll often find yourself using rocks or bushes for support as you gasp for breath.

SAYAT-SAYAT–SUMMIT

The last stretch of the summit ascent is, of course, the steepest and hardest part of the climb. Past Sayat-Sayat, more desolate rock faces and hoisting await the string of climbers stretched out in the dark, trying to keep warm while holding ropes and torches. In the daylight, thick veins of quartz seem like painted lines on the rock face, and in some precarious spots you'll be glad you couldn't see exactly what you were doing as you climbed up!

The summit looks deceptively close and, though it's just over 1km, the last burst can take up to two hours from Sayat-Sayat. Some people are even reduced to crawling on hands and knees up the last few boulders to the small area that is the top of Borneo. Climbers crowd together, perched over the mysterious abyss of Low's Gully, and huddle against the cold, readying their cameras for a shot of the sunrise and the nearby peaks.

It can get very crowded up there; don't be surprised to be sharing your experience with a

hundred or more people, all jockeying for the essential picture with the summit sign. When the sun has risen and the photos are taken, there's a quick exodus down the mountain to Laban Rata, while the savvy late risers make their relaxed way to a far less crowded summit.

The climb down to Timpohon Gate takes about five hours – don't underestimate the descent, and leave plenty of time to get back before nightfall. While easier than the climb up, it can be a lot more jarring on joints and underused muscles. You'll probably leave the summit around 7am and you should aim to leave Laban Rata no later than noon. The weather can close in very quickly and, although you probably won't get lost, the granite is slippery even when it's dry.

Sleeping

All accommodation in the park is handled by **Sutera Sanctuary Lodges** (☎ 088-243-629; www.sutera sanctuarylodges.com; Lot G15, Wisma Sabah, Jln Haji Saman, Kota Kinabalu; ☉ 8.30am-4.30pm Mon-Sat, 8.30am-12.30pm Sun). Reservations are strongly recommended and are absolutely essential in busy periods.

Park accommodation includes a variety of accommodation around park HQ, five huts on the mountain at Laban Rata, the small Mesilau Nature Resort on the east shoulder of the mountain (see p114), and Poring Hot Springs (see p116). Accommodation is available around park HQ, on the Ranau road between the park turn-off and Kundasang, at Mesilau, at Poring Hot Springs and at Laban Rata on the mountain. Reservations can be made by email, fax or phone, but they will not be confirmed until fully paid for. Note that accommodation at Laban Rata is only available as part of a package (see opposite).

Additional accommodation can be found just on the main road outside park HQ, between the main entrance to the park and the town of Kundasang. These places are handy if the Sutera places are all booked up.

PARK HEADQUARTERS

There is a wide variety of good-value accommodation around park HQ, ranging from simple hostels to deluxe lodges that are perfect for families.

Grace Hostel (20 beds; RM46 per bed) Clean, comfortable 20-bed dorm with fireplace and drink-making area.

Rock Hostel (20 beds; RM46 per bed) Somewhat institutional 20-bed hostel with similar facilities to the Grace Hostel.

SPEED FREAKS

As you limp into Timpohon Gate after a gruelling two-day climb to the summit of Kinabalu, if you really want to add insult to injury, check out the sign that lists the current record times for the Kinabalu International Climbathon. The current men's record is 2 hours and 36 minutes and the women's record is 3 hours and 8 minutes (held by an Italian man and a Czech woman). And, yes, those are the times for the roundtrip – up *and* down.

Hill Lodge (10 two-person units; RM135 per unit) These semidetached cabins are a good choice for those who can't face a night in the hostels. They're clean and comfortable, with private bathrooms.

Liwagu Suite (four four-person rooms; RM255 per room) These hotel like rooms can be found in the Liwagu Building. While they sleep up to four people, they're best for couples, as they contain only one bedroom and one living room.

Peak Lodge (four four-person units; RM300 per unit) These semidetached units have two bedrooms (one with a bunk bed and one with two twin beds), pleasant sitting rooms, fireplaces and nice views from their verandas.

Summit Lodge (one four-person unit, RM360 per unit) This fine one-storey lodge offers a great view, a cosy living room with a fireplace and two bedrooms (one with a double bed, one with two single beds).

Garden Lodge (one six-person unit; RM380) Under renovation at the time of writing, this two-storey private cabin offers brilliant views of the mountain.

Nepenthes Lodge (eight four-person units, RM380 per unit) These attached two-storey units fall somewhere between hotel rooms and private lodges. They have two bedrooms (one with a twin bed, one with a queen) and verandas which offer limited mountain views.

Kinabalu Lodge (one eight-person unit; RM850) With private parking, a private barbeque area, a great living room with a sunken fireplace, three bedrooms (the master bedroom has its own bathroom), and a TV room for the kids, this attractive one-storey cabin would make a wonderful family retreat.

Rajah Lodge (one six-person unit; RM1500) The grand two-storey Rajah Lodge has three bedrooms, a wraparound veranda, a private location and a nice fireplace. Frankly, it's not that much nicer than the Kinabalu Lodge, which can be had for half the price.

LABAN RATA

There are four mountain huts at Laban Rata, the 3273m point on Mt Kinabalu where most climbers spend the night en route to the summit. Bedding is provided in all huts. Accommodation at Laban Rata is only available as part of a three-day/two-night full-board package that includes one night on the mountain at Laban Rata and one night either in lodging at park HQ or in Mesilau Nature Resort. The park HQ package starts at RM488 per person for double occupancy and RM588 per person for single occupancy. The Mesilau package starts at RM413 per person for double occupancy and RM518 per person for single occupancy. For the latest details, check the Sutera website.

Laban Rata Resthouse (52 beds) The main resthouse here, this large building has four- and six-bunk dorm rooms equipped with heaters, and sporadic hot-water showers in common bathrooms, as well as a few private double and quad rooms with similar facilities. The resthouse also has a simple restaurant that serves meals and drinks from 2.30am. You can buy simple snacks at the restaurant.

Gunting Lagadan Hut (60 beds) Simpler than the above, this large hut has unheated dorm rooms and heated showers. There is a cooking area but no restaurant.

Panar Laban Hut (eight beds) This simple unheated hut would be good for small groups. There is a shower and basic cooking area.

Waras Hut (eight beds) Similar to the above, this would also be a good choice for small groups.

OUTSIDE THE PARK

It's generally preferable to stay in the park, mainly because the lodging is reasonable value and it's more convenient for the mountain and walking trails.

However, there are numerous places to stay outside the park, most on the road between the park HQ and Kundasang (6km east of the park's main entrance).

Kinabalu Rose Cabin (☎ 889-233; Km 18, Jln Ranau-Tuaran; r RM70-200) This friendly place has spacious if somewhat rundown rooms with balconies facing Mt Kinabalu. There's a decent on-site restaurant. Rooms usually cost 40% more on weekends. It's about 2km southeast of park HQ; a minivan to/from there will cost RM5.

Kinabalu Pine Resort (☎ 889-388; Kundasang-Ranau Highway; standard/deluxe unit RM105/135) This hillside holiday camp–style place has semidetached units, some of which have nice mountain views. The standard units are rather spartan and it's worth paying extra for the deluxe ones. All units have hot showers. It's about 1km east of Kandasang, on the main road.

D'Villa (☎ 889-282; Km 53, Jln Kinabalu Park; dm RM30, d RM120) Just shy of 1km east of the main entrance to the park on the main road, this is one of the few accommodation options outside the park but within walking distance of the park itself. The dorm is simple and a little grotty. The private rooms are spacious, with verandas that look south over the valley – overpriced but pleasant.

Eating

There are two restaurants at park HQ. Both restaurants are open 6.30am to 11pm daily.

Balsam Café (dishes RM5-10) The cheaper and more popular of the two is this canteen-style spot directly below the park office. The café can little disorganised and chaotic, particularly when busy; they can't quite seem to decide if it's a buffet-style restaurant or a proper sit-down place. It offers basic but decent Malaysian, Chinese and Western dishes at reasonable prices. There is also a small but well-stocked shop in Balsam selling tinned and dried foods, chocolate, beer, spirits, cigarettes, T-shirts, bread, eggs and margarine.

Liwagu Restaurant (dishes RM10-30) In the Liwagu Building about 15 minutes' walk north of the main entrance, this is more expensive and more elegant than the Balsam, with proper waiter service and a wide range of Asian and Western dishes, as well as beer, wine and mixed drinks.

Getting There & Away

A shuttle bus runs from the Pacific Sutera (9am), the Magellan Sutera (9.10am), and Wisma Sabah (9.20am) to Kinabalu Park HQ, arriving at 11.30am (RM40). In the reverse direction, it leaves Kinabalu Park HQ at 3.30pm. There is also a shuttle bus from Kinabalu Park HQ to Poring Hot Springs at noon (RM25) and another at 3.30pm (RM25) to Mesilau Nature Resort.

Express buses and minivans travelling between KK and Ranau and Sandakan pass the park turn-off, from where it's 100m uphill to the park. Air-con express buses (RM15, three hours) leave from KK's Inanam long distance bus terminal seven times daily, starting at 7.30am.

Share taxis operate from terminal at Merdeka Field on Jalan Padang in Kota Kinabalu. Several share-taxis do a daily run between KK and Ranau, passing the entrance road to the Kinabalu National Park office. The fare to Ranau or Kinabalu National Park is RM20 or you can charter a taxi for RM80 per car (note that a normal city taxi will charge RM150 for a charter). Minivans (RM15) depart the same station.

If you're heading back to KK from the park, minivans pass the park HQ until mid-afternoon (stopping on the main road), but the best time to catch one is between 8am and noon. The park also operates three minivans daily to KK (RM40) and one daily to Poring Hot Springs (RM25).

MESILAU NATURE RESORT

Mesilau Nature Resort, which sits on the southeast shoulder of Mt Kinabalu at an altitude of 1951 metres, is the starting point for an alternative approach to Mt Kinabalu. Theis route is favoured by some trekkers as it's more challenging and less crowded than the main route from park HQ. The 5.5km Mesilau route meets up with the main summit trail at Layang Layang (it takes the average climber four hours to walk from Mesilau to Layang Layang). If you intend to climb from here, you can make arrangements for you guide when you book accommodation (see below).

Even if you don't intend to climb the mountain from here, it's worth visiting or staying at Mesilau Nature Resort, as it's a lovely bit of country and the accommodation is quite good. In addition, there are some nice short nature walks in the resort area. The **Kogonon rail** is a quick 30-minute walk through the forest near the resort. It can be done without a permit. It's got a few ups and downs, but it's pretty easy and makes a nice stroll in the early morning or late afternoon. A good warm-up for Kinabalu. The 30-minute **Nepenthes Rajah Trail** takes you past a cave (really a space under a large rock) to an area where you can see a variety of pitcher plants. In order to protect these rare plants, you must buy a permit (RM10) and be accompanied by a guide to do this trail.

The **Sabah Parks office** is on your left as you enter the resort. It's a very casual affair and it is sometimes unmanned. You can get your climbing permit here and must pay an RM10 fee to ascend from here (you will need a guide to proceed beyond the gate). The entrance to the trail up to the summit is barred and they have to unlock it to let you pass.

Sleeping & Eating

Arrange accommodation at Mesilau and on the mountain with **Sutera Sanctuary Lodges** (☎ 088-243-629; www.suterasanctuarylodges .com; Lot G15, Wisma Sabah, Jln Haji Saman, Kota Kinabalu; ⏰ 8.30am-4.30pm Mon-Sat, 8.30am-12.30pm Sun). Accommodation is in the form of lodges and chalets (excellent for families and small groups) and hostels.

Low's Peak Lodge and **St John's Peak Lodge** (RM520 per night) Have six-person chalets with three double bedrooms. They have living rooms, kitchens, room heaters, hot-water showers, decks, barbeque grills and TVs. They are quite nice and comfortable and separated enough from other units for a feeling of privacy. You can do your own cooking in these, so bring supplies from KK if you intend to do so.

Ugly Sister's Peak Lodge and **Donkey's Ear Peak Lodges** (RM450 per night) Four-person chalets with two double bedrooms. They have the same features as the Low's Peak and St John's Peak lodges and are of a similar standard. You can also cook in these.

Witti Range Lodges (RM450 per night) These six-person lodges have three bedrooms, two of which have a pair of single beds in each, and one master bedroom with a queen-size double bed. All have living rooms, room heaters, showers with hot water, but no kitchens. Great for families, but will have to depend on the restaurant for meals. These are very nice and homey. There are four of these.

Crocker Range Lodges (RM450 per night) These six-person lodges are similar to the Witti Range Lodges but one of the bedrooms has a pair of single beds, while other two have queen-size double beds. Otherwise, the features and standard are the same.

Bishops Head Hostels (d RM45) The dorms are what you'd expect; very simple but adequate, with basic kitchens and common areas. They are good enough for a night before or after a climb.

Renanthera Restaurant (dishes RM10-20; ☽ breakfast, lunch & dinner) Serves Malay, Chinese and Western meals, and the Malaxi Café serves breakfast, drinks and snacks.

Getting There & Away

Mesilau is 20km from Mt Kinabalu National Park HQ. To get to the resort, follow the main road past Mt Kinabalu Park headquarters for 6km, heading in the direction of Kandasan and Ranau. In a few minutes you will come to the settlement of Kandasan, which is recognisable by the stalls along the highway selling honey, fruit, baskets etc. You can get nice salak, mangosteen, durian and wild jungle honey here. Turn left (north) just past the stalls, following a sign for the Kundasan War Memorial. Otherwise, drive six km and you will come to some painted tires and a sign for Mesilau Nature Resort. Turn here and drive through the Mt Kinabalu Golf Club. It's a very steep four km to the resort from this turning. We thought our Proton might give up the ghost.

There is a shuttle bus from Kinabalu Park HQ to Poring Hot Springs at noon (RM25). Otherwise, a taxi from Kinabalu Park HQ to Mesilau Nature Resort will cost around RM75.

KUNDASANG WAR MEMORIAL

The turn-off for the Mesilau Nature Resort on the KK–Ranau highway is the site of the **Kundasang War Memorial** (Kundasang; admission RM10; ☽ 8am-5.30pm daily). There are English and Anzac gardens here, commemorating the prisoners from these countries who died on the march. In the Anzac Garden you can see a full list of the dead. At the back of the gardens there is a viewpoint which offers a stunning view of Mt Kinabalu. One can imagine how Mt Kinabalu must have seemed an unobtainable goal as the poor soldiers made their way across the hot middle of northern Borneo.

The memorial is in Kundasang, which is 10km east of Kinabalu Park headquarters. You'll know you're in Kundasang when you see the market stalls on either side of the road. Take the turn on the left for Mesilau Nature Resort. The memorial is on the right 150m after the turnoff. Look for the flags and the stone fort-like structure above the road. A bus from Kinabalu Park HQ will cost RM3 and a taxi will cost RM30.

RANAU

☎ 088 / pop 49,800

Ranau is a collection of concrete shop blocks in on the road between KK and Sandakan, or Kinabalu National Park and Poring Hot Springs. There's a busy Saturday **tamu** (night market). While the surrounding valley is quite lovely, the town itself is uninspiring and it's of most interest to travellers as a transport junction between Mt Kinabalu and Poring Hot Springs or other points in Sabah.

Most of the restaurants, hotels and shops are at the upper end of town, while the mini-van stop is at the bottom of town, and the express stops are out on the main highway. You can easily walk from one end of town to the other in 20 minutes or so.

Bank Simpanan Nasional (Jln Kibarambang) has an ATM.

Sleeping & Eating

Rafflesia Inn (☎ 879-359; 1st fl, Block E, Sedco Bldg; r from RM35; ❄) If you'd prefer a budget place, the same owners of Kinabalu View Lodge run this spartan but well-kept place. It's in the centre of town, above Koktas Restaurant.

Kinabalu View Lodge (☎ 879-111; 1st fl, Tokogaya Bldg, Lg Kibarambang; r RM64-79; ❄) This is the best of an uninspiring lot in Ranau. It's a bit threadbare, but the rooms are clean and there are hot-water showers. If you stand on the back railing, you can catch views of Kinabalu. It's near the top of town – aim for the radio tower.

Restoran Tanjung Putri (Jln Lg Kibarambang; meals from RM3; ☺ breakfast, lunch & dinner) Diagonally opposite Kinabalu View Lodge, this simple Malay place does a great *sup ayam* (chicken soup), which really hits the spot after a climb up the mountain.

Restaurant Double Luck (☎ 879-246; Jln Kibarambang; meals RM6-10; ☺ breakfast, lunch & dinner) This is not the cheapest eatery in town but has the best food, friendly staff and ice-cold beer. Ask for a filled omelette for breakfast or try the tofu claypot for a veggie treat.

Getting There & Away

Minivans operate from the blue-roofed shelter at the bottom of town, 100m in from the main roundabout on the main road. Destinations include KK (RM15), Mt Kinabalu National Park HQ (RM5) and Poring Hot Springs (RM5). You can charter a whole minivan or taxi to the park headquarters or the hot springs for RM30 if you negotiate.

Express buses to Sandakan (RM20, four hours, departures hourly between 9am and 1pm) stop on the main road, in front of the church (roughly opposite the Shell station), 100m uphill from the main roundabout.

PORING HOT SPRINGS

Poring Hot Springs (admission RM15; ☺ visitors centre 9am-4.30pm) lies within Kinabalu National Park some 43km from park HQ and 19km north of Ranau. If you arrive here directly after climbing Mt Kinabalu, you can use your national park entry ticket to gain admission to Poring (and vice versa).

Most visitors come here to soak in the hot springs, especially after an ascent of Mt Kinabalu, but there is also a decent walking trail here, as well as a canopy walkway, a butterfly garden and a tropical garden.

The Hot Springs

At the hot springs, steaming, sulphurous water is channelled into pools and tubs in which visitors relax their tired muscles after a summit of Mt Kinabalu. The outdoor tubs are free to use but are often either occupied or painfully slow to fill (test the taps before choosing one). Consider renting an indoor

tub (per hour RM15); these fill quickly and give you private soaking time.

It's commonly believed that the Japanese discovered Poring Hot Springs during WWII, but accounts written by Japanese residents at the time indicate that they heard about the springs from locals who used to bathe their sick in the pools. Due to their incredible fondness for hot springs, a group of Japanese set off to find the springs, hoping, perhaps, to develop the springs into a commercial *onsen* (hot-spring bath), after the war.

Anyone who's ever been to a real Japanese *onsen* will wish that the Japanese were still in charge of the place. It's very poorly run these days: there are no coin lockers, no buckets for rinsing your body before entering the baths, no towel rental (they are on sale in the store for RM15), no proper changing room. Be sure to bring your own towel and a bathing suit. A pair of flip-flops/thongs will also come in handy.

You fill the tubs yourself, mixing hot-spring water and cold water to get the right balance. If you use only hot water, you'll achieve the right temperature. Put the stopper in yourself. If you get too hot, there's a cold-water swimming pool to cool off in. Parents, note that the tubs are about twice as deep as they should be, which is dangerous for young children – you'll have to keep a close eye on them.

Despite our quibbles with the place, there is a certain magic here in the morning, as steam rises from the tubs and the rainforest comes alive with the call of thousands of tropical birds.

Other Activities

If you've got some time before or after taking a bath (if you're staying the night, for instance), you might like to sample some of Poring's other attractions.

The **butterfly farm** (admission RM4; ☺ 9am-4pm) above the baths is nice, with lots of flowers and several species of butterflies, including the Raja Brooke's birdwing. First, you enter a display area, which has displays of the butterflies and other insects mounted under glass. You walk through this and then enter the butterfly enclosure. Take your time in the enclosure as new butterflies constantly materialize before your eyes. The nearby **tropical garden** (admission RM3; ☺ 9am-4pm) is also worth a quick look.

There's also a 41m-high **canopy walkway** (admission RM5; ☺ 9am-4pm), a short but sweaty walk into the forest above the pools. Unfortunately, the walkway was partially closed at the time of writing and it seems likely to remain so.

You can also walk up to **Kipungit falls** and **bat caves**. The start of the trail is just beyond the entrance to the butterfly farm. It's 400m to the falls and 760m to the bat caves. It's a mostly flat stroll through the forest to the falls and it's well worth the journey. There is a small shelter at the falls and it's a nice place to wade and cool off. It's a fairly sweaty uphill slog to the caves, which are actually crevices between giant rocks. If you're going to see proper caves in the rest of Borneo, don't bother. We recommend doing these hikes before you take your bath, unless you fancy stinking out the minivan on the way home.

Finally rafflesia flowers sometimes bloom in the vicinity of the hot springs. Ask at the shops opposite the hot-spring entrance and if any are in bloom, villagers will lead you to them for RM20.

Sleeping & Eating

Reserve accommodation in advance through **Sutera Sanctuary Lodges** (☎ 088-243-629; www.sutera sanctuarylodges.com.my; Lot G15, ground fl, Wisma Sabah, Jln Haji Saman, Kota Kinabalu). The reception at Poring is on the right as you pass through the building above the parking lot.

The **Serindit Hostel** (dm RM12) is clean enough, with six- and eight-person dorms and cooking facilities for rent (RM100). Otherwise, **Kelicap Lodge** (r RM150) has decent private twin rooms with common bathrooms. A **camping ground** (camp sites RM6) is available for tent-equipped visitors.

The **River Lodge** (per night RM110) sleeps a total of four people in two bedrooms (one with a double bed, the other with two single beds). It's quite nice, with a verandah, and air-con after 5pm, but there are no cooking facilities.

The **Rajawali Lodges** (per night RM380) are similar but sleeps a total of six (in three bedrooms (one with a pair of twin beds, and two with one double bed each). These are good for families, but, again, there are no cooking facilities.

The **Rainforest Restaurant** (meals RM6-20; ☻ breakfast, lunch & dinner) is a proper sit-down restaurant near the baths. There are also inexpensive eating places opposite the spring's entrance.

Getting There & Away

Poring is 19km north of Ranau along a sealed road and can be reached from Ranau by mini-

van (RM7) or hitching. You can also charter a taxi or minivan from Ranau to Poring for RM30.

Kinabalu National Park has minivan that departs park headquarters at noon for Poring (RM25). In the opposite direction, the minivan departs Poring for park headquarters at 2pm (and continues along to KK).

From outside Poring Hot Springs visitors centre, minivans can be chartered for around RM30 to transport you to Ranau, where you can catch minivans onward to Kinabalu National Park or KK.

SOUTHWEST COAST

The southwest coast of Sabah is a long flat shelf of land between the Crocker Range and the South China Sea. There are shallow beaches for most of its length but none can compete with the beaches found on the islands offshore. About 80km south of KK, the Klias Peninsula extends 30km into the South China Sea. Off the northern tip of this Peninsula you'll find Pulau Tiga, forever linked with the American television show *Survivor*, which filmed a series there. Off the southern tip of this peninsula you'll find Pulau Labuan, centre of the region's oil industry and the transfer point for ferries between Brunei and Sabah. The main town in the southwest coastal region is Beaufort, which serves as a transport hub for the region.

BEAUFORT

☎ 087

Despite the rather dandy name, Beaufort is nothing more than a quiet provincial town of a few thousand souls about 90km south of KK. There are a few remaining wooden shophouses on the main street, which have a certain dilapidated charm in the evenings when hundreds of twittering swiftlets pack the telegraph wires like dysfunctional Christmas lights. For most visitors, though, it's little more than a stop-off on the way to Pulau Tiga, Sarawak or Brunei.

There is a **post office** (Jln Masjid) and a branch of **Public Bank** (Jln Lo Chung).

White-water Rafting

White-water rafting is popular through the Padas Gorge south of Beaufort, and is at its best between April and July, when water levels on Sungai Padas create Grade 2 to 4 conditions. The calmer Sungai Kiulu nearby is also commonly used for first-time rafters. Day trips organised out of KK cost RM160 to RM190 per person, including transfers by charter train, and normally require 24 hours' advance notice.

Riverbug (☎ 088-260-501; www.traversetours.com; Wisma Sabah, Jln Haji Saman, Kota Kinabalu) is one of the main specialist outfits operating here.

Sleeping & Eating

There are only two accommodation choices in Beafort and neither is very tempting. If you can get yourself back to KK, then consider this option. Otherwise, head on to Sipitang, where there is at least one better option.

Beaufort Hotel (☎ 211-911; 19-20 Lo Chung Park, Jln Lo Chung; s/d RM36/42; ⌧) Upstairs in the salmon-pink building at the end of its block, the Beaufort is just barely acceptable, with slightly seedy bedrooms and bathrooms.

Mandarin Inn (☎ 211-800; Lg Beaufort Jaya 3; s/d RM35/42; ⌧) The Mandarin Inn, across the river, is of a similar standard with a somewhat inconvenient location (unless you want to eat in the *kedai kopi* downstairs, you'll have to walk across the bridge into town). The rooms here are pretty cramped and worn.

Zulfia Curry House (Jln Chung; meals from RM3; ☯ breakfast, lunch & dinner) Right in the middle of town, this popular local eatery has good *nasi campur* (buffet with rice, RM3.50), *nasi biryani* (RM4) and good rotis.

Brunei Satay House (Jln Chung; meals from RM3; ☯ breakfast, lunch & dinner) Next door, this satay specialist has excellent beef and chicken satay at the bargain price of RM3 for five sticks. We could go for some right about now.

There are two **supermarkets** in town and a good **morning market** for fresh produce.

Getting There & Away

Express buses operate from near the old train station at the south end of Jln Masjid (the ticket booth is opposite the station). There are departures at 9am, 1pm, 2.15pm and 5pm for KK. The fare is RM9 and the journey takes 1½ hours. There are departures at 9.10am, 10.30am, 1.45pm and 6.20pm for Sipitang. The fare to Sipitang is RM4.50, 1½ hours. The KK to Lawas express bus passes through Beaufort at around 3pm; the fare from Beaufort to Lawas is RM13, 1¾ hours.

Minivans operate from a stop across from the mosque, which is at the north end of Jln Masjid. There are frequent departures for Papar (RM7, one hour) and KK (RM9, two hours), and less-frequent departures for Sipitang (RM11, 1½ hours), Lawas (RM15, 1¾ hours) and Kuala Penyu (until around 2.30pm, RM6, one hour). To Menumbok (for Labuan) there are plenty of minivans until early afternoon (RM8, one hour).

Taxis from the stand outside the old train station, at the south end of Jln Masjid. Charter rates include: KK (RM60), Kuala Penyu (RM50), Sipitang (RM32), Menumbok (RM50) and Lawas (RM100).

KLIAS PENINSULA

The Klias Peninsula is a square of dead-flat marshland that serves as the access point to Pulau Tiga and Pulau Labuan (note that it is easier and cheaper to get to Labuan by ferry from KK). The **Sungai Klias** runs through the heart of the Klias Wetlands and it is possible to tour the wetlands by boat along this river. In addition, there are acceptable beaches around the fringes of the peninsula and at least one good place to stay on the coast.

Kuala Penyu

Kuala Penyu, at the northern tip of the peninsula, is the jumping-off point for Pulau Tiga. The town is unremarkable, but there are some good **beaches** nearby. The best is around the headland from the estuary, 8km out of town; there are picnic tables and toilets but no other facilities.

From KK minivans leave from behind Wawasan Plaza (RM10, two hours). From Beaufort minivans to Kuala Penyu (RM5) leave throughout the morning, but return services tail off very early in the afternoon, so you may have to negotiate a taxi or local lift back. A minivan from Kuala Penyu to Menumbok costs RM6. The town itself is bisected by a river; a pontoon ferry shuttles back and forth between 6am and 6pm.

Tempurung Seaside Lodge

The **Tempurung Seaside Lodge** (☎ 088-773-066; 3 Putatan Point; info@borneo-authentic.com; r RM110) is a quiet place to unwind for a couple of days. Prices include breakfast, lunch and dinner. It's set in a nice spot up on a hill overlooking a long stretch of beach and the South China Sea. It's a little lonely and doesn't seem to get many visitors, but the rooms are cosy and homey and it would be a fun place to come with a few friends or for families who want to spend some quality time together. You can walk up into the nearby *kampung* (village) and check out Malay country life.

If you're driving, look for the sign on the right just before Kuala Penyu. The sign says 7km, but that's a conservative estimate, and it will feel like a lot more as you bounce over the gravel/dirt road (just passable in a regular car – keep an eye out for children, piglets and chickens, among other hazards). We suggest you call for direction. A charter taxi from Beaufort will cost about RM50.

Klias River Cruise (Sungai Klias Cruise)

The best way to check out the Klias Wetlands is to join a **Klias River Cruise** (RM75; departs at 5pm, register by 4.30pm). This two-hour cruise includes tea and dinner and takes in a good section of the river/wetlands, where you stand a good chance of seeing proboscis monkeys. The jetty is 20km west of Beaufort. When heading there by driving from Beaufort, look for the sign reading 'Klias Wetland 0.5k', cross the bridge and take an immediate right down the narrow dirt road to the dock (250m). Many tour operators and accommodation owners in KK offer package tours to the wetlands and this is often the easiest and cheapest way to go.

PULAU TIGA NATIONAL PARK

A short distance north of Kuala Penyu on the Klias Peninsula, you will find the three islands of Pulau Tiga (the name means 'Three Islands'), which together form **Pulau Tiga National Park**. **Pulau Tiga** is the largest island; about 1km to the northeast lies tiny **Pulau Kalampunian Damit**; and in between are the remains of the third island, **Pulau Kalampunian Besar**, now only a sandbar eroded by wave action. The islands themselves are recent creations, formed in 1897 by the eruption of mud volcanoes. Continuous volcanic activity has taken place over the last hundred years, and still continues in the form of bubbling mud and escaping methane gas.

In 2001 the main island, Pulau Tiga, was the location for the first season of the US reality TV show *Survivor*, and is heavily marketed now as 'Survivor Island'. It's a little ironic, of course, that the place that those folks struggled just to survive is now a popular tourist destination where families come to spend their vacations.

While Pulau Tiga is fairly attractive, with good walking trails and decent beaches, it's not as nice as the islands of Tunku Abdul Rahman National Park off of KK (p102), let alone the blinding white-sand beaches of Pulau Mantanani (p129; which is, admittedly, much more difficult to visit).

Sights & Activities

In addition to the obvious pastimes in the park – relaxing on the beach, swimming and snorkelling – there are several ways to spend your time, including walking on the island's trail network and visiting nearby 'Snake Island'.

SNAKE ISLAND

Pulau Kalampunian Damit is little more than a large rock covered in dense vegetation but is famous for the sea snakes that come ashore to mate, hence the island's nickname, **Snake Island**. On any one day up to 150 snakes can be present, curled up under boulders, among roots and in tree hollows. It's a fascinating phenomenon, but it's not the writhing mass of snakes that many visitors imagine based on descriptions given tour operators. If you do come out here, beware of the snakes – they are extremely poisonous. Pulau Tiga Resort runs boat trips to the island (RM20 per person or RM100 per boat, two hours), with a stop en route for snorkelling.

WALKING

A walking trail runs right round the outside of Pulau Tiga and a full circuit of the island would take 8 to 10 hours. We don't recommend undertaking this monumental slog. If you decide to try it, arrange a guide, bring several litres of water per person, and let someone reliable know where you are going and when you expect to return.

It is possible to walk from Pulau Tiga Resort to Survivor Resort and at 2km each way, it's a much more reasonable and enjoyable hike. Staring from Pulau Tiga Resort, follow the signs for Tagi Beach. We did the hike alone and disturbed a troop of macaques who showed their displeasure by attempting to drop a coconut on our heads. We wonder if this was one of the challenges faced on *Survivors*. Be sure to bring plenty of water on this hike.

The most popular walk on the island is the 1.2km (one-way) trip to one of the mud 'volcanos' in the forest north of Pulau Tiga Resort/Sabah Parks accommodation.

Sleeping & Eating

All accommodation is on Pulau Tiga.

Sabah Parks Accommodation (☎ 088-211-881; www.sabahparks.org.my; Lot 1-3, Block K, Kompleks Sinsuran, Jln Tun Fuad Stephens, Kota Kinabalu; ☽ 8am-1pm & 2-5pm Mon-Thu, 8-11.30am & 2-5pm Fri) In the middle of the south coast of the island and snug alongside Pulau Tiga Resort, this is the cheapest place to stay on the island. It is either crowded with Malaysian holidaymakers or utterly deserted. It's got nicely tended open grounds here and a good stretch of beach. If you require very little in terms of service and just want a quiet place to stay on the beach, this might suit.

The **Asrama Murai hostel** (d RM30) here has two four-bunk dorms, a simple kitchen with gas ring and fridge, a sitting room, veranda and fresh-water shower. It's simple but acceptable. **Chalet Selangkir** (per night RM120) here is for those who would like a little more privacy. It has a similar kitchen to the hostel and a bedroom with two single beds and air-con. Note that it's not worth paying more for the chalet if you can get the hostel to yourself (and if you don't require air-con).

Sabah Parks can arrange a boat from Kuala Penyu to Pulau Tiga for a hefty RM350, which makes it advisable to see if you can hop a ride of a Pulau Tiga Resort boat (call ahead to ask).

Borneo Survivor Resort (☎ 088-919-686, 088-230-806; www.borneosurvivor.com.my; longhouse/chalet packages from RM238/338; ✷) The more adventurous option on the island; there is one chalet here with two single beds, a shower and veranda. It's nice enough, but it's a little dark due to its location set back in the forest. The longhouse has simple dorm rooms with fan and showers (a little on the grotty side). This place doesn't get many visitors and you might just have it to yourself. Unfortunately, it's not as appealing as the other spots, although the staff were friendly and cheerful when we were there. Packages include meals, accommodation and transport to/from Kuala Penyu.

Pulau Tiga Resort (☎ 087-885-650; http://pulau-tiga.com; per person from RM175-330; ✷) The main player on the island, this place occupies a fair bit of the foreshore on the south side of the island. Grounds are well-tended and grassy.

Superior bungalows here have big double beds, air-con, fridges, hot-water showers, and are clean and spacious. Longhouse rooms have fan, shower, and three single beds per room. Superior family bungalows here have air-con, fridges, hot showers, sitting rooms, one master bedroom with a double bed and one children's room with two single beds. These are nice enough, but set back a bit far from the beach. The two-person standard bungalows are a little tightly grouped together, with cold showers, verandas. These are quite acceptable. We hear from readers that the service here is inflexible.

Getting There & Away

Pulau Tiga is 12km north of Kuala Penyu on the Klias Peninsular. The boat ride takes about 20 minutes and can be pretty bumpy if there's any wind about. Boats leave from the south side of the river in Kuala Penyu. If you take the northern route from KK, you'll have to cross the river via an interesting chain ferry (free). If for some reason you are on foot, there is a tiny passenger ferry that will take you across on demand for 40 sen.

Most visitors to Pulau Tiga come as part of a package with one of the resorts, in which case transport all the way to the island from KK will be included in the price. Otherwise, you could try just showing up in Kuala Penyu and asking if you can board one of the day's boats out to the island (we don't recommend this option as priority is given to resort guests with bookings).

MENUMBOK

The tiny hamlet of **Menumbok** is where you catch the ferry to Pulau Labuan (where you can catch an onward ferry to Brunei or a speedboat to Sarawak). A charter taxi to/from Beaufort costs RM60. Minivans to/from Beaufort cost RM8. The car ferry to Pulau Labuan departs daily at 10.30am and 4.30pm (RM5/person, RM40/car).

SIPITANG

Sipitang is 44km south of Beaufort, 144km from KK and just 18km from the Sarawak border. Located on a wide, shallow bay, Sipitang is pleasant enough, with a pastel mosque and lots of seafront eating, though you'd probably only stop here if you missed a bus.

Maybank at the southern end of town has an ATM.

Sleeping & Eating

Shangsan Hotel (☎ 087-822-2835; Jln Datuk Haji Mohd Yassin; s/d RM40/55) One of the few places to stay in Sipitang, this small hotel is in the second block of businesses as you enter town from the north, about 50m past the Shell station. Although uninspiring at first glance, the rooms are clean and acceptable, with white tile floors typical of Chinese-Malay hotels.

Restoran Selera Asias (Jln Datuk Haji Mohd Yassin; meals from RM3; ☽ breakfast, lunch & dinner) In the centre of town on the foreshore, this fine little Malay restaurant is just north of the morning market. It has an easily understood Bahasa menu with all the standard *kedai kopi* favourites, including a particularly nice plate of *mee goreng*.

Getting There & Away

The bus stop is on the wonderfully named Lg Durian, which starts opposite Restoran Selera Asian in the centre of town. Walk down this street past *Kedai Kopi* Lian Hong to find the stop. There is a bus to Lawas (RM6.50) that leaves at 10.15am. Buses to KK (RM20) leave at 8am, noon, 1.30pm and 4.30pm.

A taxi to/from Beaufort will cost RM8/32 person/car. Taxis leave from outside the morning market in the centre of town near the foreshore.

Speedboats to Labuan leave from the jetty next to the Shell station at the north roundabout. Boats depart at 7.30am and 1pm, cost RM25 and take 40 minutes.

PULAU LABUAN

☎ 087 / pop 76,000

About 115km southwest of KK and only 50km northeast of Bandar Seri Begawan (Brunei) is the small island of Labuan, which serves as the main transit point between Brunei and Sabah. This is the best way to travel between Sabah and Brunei and onward to Sarawak, as the overland journey is time consuming and arduous. There's not much to detain you on Labuan, but if you get stuck between ferry sailings, you'll find it a pleasant spot to spend an evening.

Labuan was once a coal-mining centre and now has major petroleum gas installations. Politically the 92 sq km group of islands is a federal territory governed directly from KL.

The sultan of Brunei ceded Labuan to the British in 1846 and it remained part of the Empire for 115 years. The only interrup-

tion came during WWII, when the Japanese landed and held the island for three years. Significantly, it was on Labuan that the Japanese forces in North Borneo surrendered at the end of the war, and here that the Japanese officers responsible for the death marches from Sandakan were tried. There's a war cemetery and peace park to mark these horrific events.

Bandar Labuan (Labuan Town) is the main town and the transit point for ferries. The population is a mix of Muslim Malays, native groups such as the Kadazan, Dusun, Bugis and Bajau, and large contingents of Chinese, Indians (including a long-standing Sikh presence) and other foreign nationals.

Information

Arcade Moneychanger (☎ 412-545; 168 Jln OKK Awang Besar) Cash and travellers cheques. Inside Labuan Textile shop.

Bertam Mass Money Changer (Jln Bunga Raya) Cash and travellers cheques. Near ferry terminal.

Harrisons Travel (☎ 412-557; 1 Jln Merdeka) Handy and reputable travel agency.

HSBC (☎ 422-610; 189 Jln Merdeka)

Maybank (☎ 443-888; Financial Park)

Labuan Tourism Action Council (☎ 422-622; ground fl, Labuan International Sea Sports Complex; 8am-1pm & 2pm-5pm Mon-Fri, closed Sat & Sun) Located about 1km west of the town centre, this is the most useful information office in town. They stock the excellent *Fly Drive Labuan Island & Town Map of Labuan*.

Tourist Information Centre (☎ 423-445; www .labuantourism.com.my; cnr Jln Dewan & Jln Berjaya; ☽ 8am-5pm Mon-Fri, 9am-3pm Sat) Tourism Malaysia office. Less useful than Labuan Tourism Action Council.

Sights & Activities

BANDAR LABUAN

Labuan's uncharismatic main settlement is light on character but has a couple of passable attractions.

The **Labuan Museum** (☎ 414-135; 364 Jln Dewan; admission free; ☽ 9am-5pm) takes a glossy, if slightly superficial, look at the island's history and culture. The most interesting displays are those on the different ethnic groups here, including a diorama of a traditional Chinese tea ceremony (the participants, however, look strangely Western). There's also an excellent diorama of a water village.

On the coast just east of the centre, the Labuan International Sea Sports Complex houses the **Marine Museum** (☎ 425-927; Jln Tanjung

SABAH

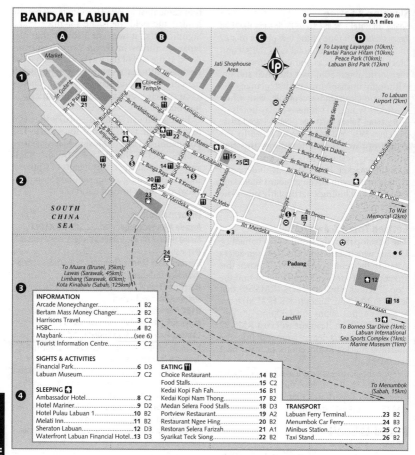

BANDAR LABUAN

INFORMATION	
Arcade Moneychanger	1 B2
Bertam Mass Money Changer	2 B2
Harrisons Travel	3 C2
HSBC	4 B2
Maybank	(see 6)
Tourist Information Centre	5 C2

SIGHTS & ACTIVITIES	
Financial Park	6 D3
Labuan Museum	7 C2

SLEEPING	
Ambassador Hotel	8 C2
Hotel Mariner	9 D2
Hotel Pulau Labuan 1	10 B2
Melati Inn	11 B2
Sheraton Labuan	12 D3
Waterfront Labuan Financial Hotel	13 D3

EATING	
Choice Restaurant	14 B2
Food Stalls	15 C2
Kedai Kopi Fah Fah	16 B1
Kedai Kopi Nam Thong	17 B2
Medan Selera Food Stalls	18 D3
Portview Restaurant	19 A2
Restaurant Ngee Hing	20 B2
Restoran Selera Farizah	21 A1
Syarikat Teck Siong	22 B2

TRANSPORT	
Labuan Ferry Terminal	23 B2
Menumbok Car Ferry	24 B3
Minibus Station	25 C2
Taxi Stand	26 B2

Purun; admission free; 9am-5pm). It's a decent little museum with a good shell collection and displays of marine life to be found in the area. Don't forget to head upstairs where you'll find a 42-foot-long skeleton of an Indian fin whale. The real highlight, however, and a guaranteed hit with the kids is the 'touch pool' opposite reception. This has to be the only shark-petting zoo we've ever seen (readers relax: the sharks are less than a metre long).

Tragically, the modern chrome-and-mirrors **Financial Park** (Jln Merdeka; 10am-10pm) duty-free mall is trumpeted as the town's No 1 'attraction', aiming to seduce shoppers and booze-cruisers into parting with their cash.

AROUND PULAU LABUAN

The **Labuan War Memorial** is an expanse of lawn with row upon row of headstones dedicated to the nearly 4000 Commonwealth servicemen, mostly Australian and British, who lost their lives in Borneo during WWII. The most heartbreaking are the last two rows of memorials on the north end that read merely 'a soldier'. The cemetery is near the golf course, about 2km east of town along Jln Tanjung Purun. A taxi to the memorial will cost around RM10.

A **Peace Park/Surrender Memorial** west of the island at Layang Layangan commemorates the place of Japanese surrender and has a Japanese war memorial. It's in a pleasant garden on the seashore. A taxi here will run around RM25.

Also on the west coast, you'll find **Pantai Pancur Hitam**, a decent shallow beach that has a picnic area for children. Keep your eye out for monitor lizards. Bus 6 runs to the beach from downtown. A taxi from downtown will cost RM25.

Towards the northern tip of the island, **Labuan Bird Park** (☎ 463-544; admission free) offers refuge to a wide range of species in three dome-shaped aviaries connected by tunnels. Some birds are also kept in outlying cages, presumably because they don't play well with others. As you enter, you will be greeted by a pair of hill myna birds who say 'hello' and 'Salaam Aleykum'. When you leave, another pair will bid you goodbye. Bus 6 makes the run to the bird park from downtown. Otherwise, a taxi from downtown will run RM25.

Pulau Kuraman, Pulau Rusukan Kecil and Pulau Rusukan Besar are uninhabited islands lying southwest of Labuan that are now protected as the **Labuan Marine Park**. The beaches are pristine, but dynamite fishing has destroyed much of the coral. There is no regularly scheduled transport to the park.

Labuan has the best **wreck diving** around Borneo, with no fewer than four major wrecks off the coast. The only dive operator in town is **Borneo Star Dive** (☎ 429-279; www.borneostardive.com; ground fl, Labuan International Sea Sports Complex), which offers two-/four-day wreck packages from RM750. They can help arrange transport to Labuan Marine Park.

Sleeping
Budget accommodation in Labuan is of poor quality. Midrange hotels are a better option.

Melati Inn (☎ 416-307; Jln Perpaduan; s/d RM45/50; ☒) This is a peach-coloured place with rooms that are a little worse for wear, but it's the only acceptable budget option. Jln Perpaduan runs inland from the waterfront, close to the wharf.

Ambassador Hotel (☎ 423-233; Lot 0142 Jln Bunga Mawar; r from RM79; ☒) The well-run Ambassador is easily the best-value hotel in town, with clean rooms, comfortable beds, nice bathrooms and wi-fi. Jln Bunga Mawar is in the middle of town – follow Jln Bunga Raya inland from the ferry terminal and turn right at Hotel Pulau Labuan.

Hotel Mariner (☎ 418-822; mhlabuan@tm.net.my; 468 Jln Tanjung Purun; r from RM90; ☒ ☐) With cramped but clean and well-maintained rooms, the Mariner is a good choice in the midrange

category. Rooms come with fridges, laminate floors and neat, spacious bathrooms.

Hotel Pulau Labuan 1 (☎ 417-288; Jln Muhibbah; s/tw from RM95/108; ☒) The Hotel Pulua Labuan 1 is not as good a value as the Mariner or the Ambassador, but it will do in a pinch. Facilities are similar, but it's a little long in the tooth.

Waterfront Labuan Financial Hotel (☎ 418-111; waterfront@streamyx.com; 1 Jln Wawasan; r from RM198; ☒ ☒) Not just for merchant bankers – this is a large, luxurious leisure hotel with full facilities and a small marina attached. The rooms are spacious here and some have great sea views. There's a huge outdoor pool and a restaurant. Wi-fi available. All in all, it's a comfortable place to stay.

Sheraton Labuan (☎ 422-000; www.sheraton.com/labuan; 462 Jln Merdeka; r from RM245; ☒ ☐ ☒) This has everything you would expect from an international hotel, with spacious and well-appointed rooms, a decent pool, a gym and a restaurant. The wi-fi here is a ridiculously overpriced RM60 per day.

Eating
Kedai Kopi Fah Fah (cnr Jln Bunga Raya & Jln Bunga Melati; meals RM3-10; ☾ breakfast, lunch & dinner) With indoor and outdoor seating, an English menu, tasty fresh juice and cheap beer, this simple Chinese restaurant is a good choice. We particularly liked their *kway teow goreng* (fried flat rice noodles).

Other Chinese *kedai kopi* to choose from in town include **Kedai Kopi Nam Thong** (Jln Merdeka; meals from RM3; ☾ breakfast & lunch only), which has chicken rice and fried noodle stalls, and **Restaurant Ngee Hing** (Jln Merdeka; meals from RM3; ☾ breakfast & lunch only), which has a stall that does a good bowl of laksa (it's directly opposite the ferry terminal and serves as a good place to wait for a ferry).

If you prefer a Muslim *kedai kopi*, you could try **Restoran Selera Farizah** (Lg Bunga Tanjung; meals from RM3; ☾ breakfast, lunch & dinner), which serves roti, curries, *nasi campur*, accompanied by the inevitable pro-wrestling videos.

Choice Restaurant (☎ 418-086; 104 Jln OKK Awang Besar; dishes RM1.20-10; ☾ breakfast, lunch & dinner) Forget false modesty, the Choice simply proclaims 'We are the best', and the authentic Indian meals seem corroboratingly popular with the authentic Indian residents who turn out for roti, fishhead curry and sambal.

Portview Restaurant (☎ 422-999; Jln Merdeka; dishes RM15-30; ☾ lunch & dinner) An outpost of the

SABAH

successful Chinese seafood franchise in KK, this waterfront restaurant has air-con indoor seating and outdoor seating that affords a nice view over Labuan's busy harbour. It's one of the few proper sit-down restaurants in town (that is, something nicer than a *kedai kopi*). We liked the baby *kailan* (Chinese vegetable) with crab sauce and butter prawns, which had the unusual addition of sesame to the sauce. Beware of a secret hidden charge in the form of 'special napkin' (tell them at the outset that you don't need it). Service can be a little slow and erratic.

In addition, you'll find outdoor **food stalls** at the east end of Jln Bunga Mawar and in the **Medan Selera Complex** near the Sheraton Labuan. Self-caterers can do their grocery shopping at **Syarikat Teck Siong** (Jln Bunga Mawar).

Getting There & Away

Malaysia Airlines (☎ 1-300-883-000; www.malaysiaair lines.com.my) has flights to/from KK (RM177, 45 minutes) and KL (RM359, 2½ hours).

Passenger ferries (RM31, 3 hours) depart KK for Labuan Monday to Saturday at 8am and 1.30pm. On Sunday they sail at 8am and 3pm. In the opposite direction, they depart Labuan for KK Monday to Saturday 8am and 1pm, while on Sunday they depart at 10.30am and 3pm. Note that the air-con on these ferries is always turned up to 'arctic' – bring a fleece.

Numerous express boats go to Muara port in Brunei daily (economy/1st class RM35/40, one hour) between 9am and 4.30pm, return-ing between 7.30am and 3.30pm. From Brunei the cost is B$15/18 for economy/1st class, with six departures between 7.30am and 4.40pm

There are also daily speedboats from Labuan to Limbang in Sarawak (RM28, 2.30pm, two hours) and Lawas, also in Sarawak (RM33, 12.30pm, two hours). There are also daily speedboats to Sipitang, which cost RM25 and take 40min.

Car ferries go to Menumbok (passenger/car RM5/40, two hours, three times daily) from a separate dock to the east. Speedboats (RM10) do the journey in about 30 minutes and leave roughly every hour between 8am and 4pm.

Getting Around

Labuan has a good minibus network, based on a six-zone system. Minibuses leave regularly from the parking lot off Jln Tun Mustapha. Their numbers are clearly painted on the front,

and fares range from 50 sen for a short trip to RM2 for a trip to the top of the island.

Taxis are plentiful and there's a stand op-posite the local ferry terminal. The base rate is RM6.60 for short journeys, or RM10 to the airport.

SOUTHWEST INTERIOR

The southwest interior of Sabah is dominated by the **Crocker Range**, which rises near Tenom in the south and runs north to Mt Kinabalu. The range forms a formidable barrier to the interior of the state and dominates the eastern skyline from Kota Kinabalu down to Sipitang. Once across the Crocker Range, you descend into the green valley of the Sungai Pegalan that runs from Keningau in the south and up to Ranau in the north. The heart of the **Pegalan Valley** is the small town of **Tambunan**, around which you'll find a few low-key attractions.

While much of the Crocker Range has been gazetted as **Crocker Range National Park**, there are few facilities for visitors. Likewise, the Pegalan Valley has no real must-see attrac-tions. However, the Crocker Range and the Pegalan Valley make a nice jaunt into rural Sabah and are particularly suited for those with rental cars. As you make your way over the range between KK and Tambunan, you'll be treated to brilliant views back to the South China Sea and onward to Mt Trus Madi. The road itself is a lot of fun to drive, and you'll find yourself craving a sports car instead of the Proton rental you're likely to be driving. Of course, with all the trucks on this road, you probably won't have too many opportunities to open it up.

Now that southern road between Keningau and Kimanis is also passable by ordinary cars, a fine loop is possible through the area, star-ing in KK, crossing the Crocker Range via Sinsuron Pass to Tambunan, working your way down the valley to Keningau, then across the Crocker Range again and back to KK via Kimanis.

TAMBUNAN
☎ 087

Right in the heart of the Pegalan Valley, surrounded by the peaks of the Crocker Range, the small town of Tambunan is a scenic 81km drive from KK. The Pegalan Valley region was the last stronghold of Mat Salleh, who became a folk hero for rebelling against the British late in the 19th century. Sadly Salleh later blew his reputation by negotiating a truce, which so outraged his own people that he was forced to flee to the Tambunan plain, where he was eventually besieged and killed.

Around Tambunan you'll find lovely Mahua Falls, 2642m Mt Trus Madi (the second-highest peak in Sabah), and Tambunan Rafflesia Reserve, one of the only developed tourist attractions in the Crocker Range (although Rafflesia are rarely in bloom here).

Sights & Activities

TAMBUNAN RAFFLESIA RESERVE

Near the top of the Crocker Range, next to the main highway 20km from Tambunan, is the **Tambunan Rafflesia Reserve** (admission free; 8am-2pm Mon-Fri, 8am-3.30pm Sat & Sun), devoted to the world's largest flower. The information centre has a few passable displays on the rafflesia. From the centre, eight nature trails lead into the forest where the rafflesias can be found.

Rafflesia bloom irregularly here and the reserve is of limited interest if none are in bloom (unfortunately, there's no reliable phone at the centre, so you can't call in advance to see if any are blooming). A whiteboard out front of the reserve indicates if any are in bloom and staff can give information about their whereabouts.

If you're driving from KK, look out for the reserve about 5km after crossing Sinsuron Pass

MAHUA FALLS

Off the north–south highway that runs between Ranau and Tambunan, you'll find lovely **Mahua Falls** (Air Terjun Mahua), one of the most interesting sights in the valley. When coming from KK, you'll descend into the Pegalan Valley and reach an intersection with the north–south highway where you turn north (you'll see a sign indicating that Mahua Falls are 13km from this intersection). After 7.3km you will come to a sign on the left for Mahua Falls, after which it's 7km down a rough dirt road to the falls.

We really don't recommend that you take an ordinary car down this road (we can still remember the horrible sound of our Proton Wira scraping over the deep ruts and rocks of the road). You'll need either a 4WD vehicle or you can take a regular car some distance down

the road and park it and walk when the going gets too rough (bring plenty of water).

Once at the falls, you'll find a building, from which a trail runs some 500m to the falls. The trail itself is brilliant, leading past several giant dipterocarp trees. The falls themselves are small (about 7m drop) but lovely, falling into a green bowl that might remind you of Hawaii.

There is no public transport to the falls.

MT TRUS MADI

About 20km southeast of Tambunan town is the 2642m peak of **Mt Trus Madi**, Sabah's second-highest peak. It's possible to make an ascent of this peak, but it's more challenging than Mt Kinabalu, and more difficult to arrange. Though Mt Trus Madi is surrounded by logging concessions, the upper slopes and peak are wild and jungle-clad and classified as forest reserve.

The muddy trails to the summit can be treacherous in parts – just the thing for those who find the open expanses of Mt Kinabalu a bit pedestrian. Independent trekkers must be well-equipped and take all their food and water up the mountain. Most climbers take a 4WD vehicle to Kampung Kaingaran then trek for most of the day to arrive at base camp, then summit and descend all the way back to Kampung Kaingaran the next day (often spending that evening in Tambunan before returning to KK).

Before setting off, you are strongly advised to hire a guide or at least get maps and assistance from the **Forestry Department** (Jabatan Perhutanan; ☎ 087-774-691) in Tambunan. The Tambunan Village Resort Centre (see below) can arrange treks; guides cost RM200 per day (up to eight people), and a 4WD will cost RM300 per trip. If you need a porter to carry your gear, it'll cost you another RM150 per day. Tour operators in KK can also arrange trips up the mountain.

Sleeping

Tambunan Village Resort Centre (TVRC; ☎ 774-076; 24 Jln TVRC, Kampung Keranaan; r and chalet RM50-90;) Tambunan's only tourist accommodation is about 2km from the tiny town centre, with several buildings, a small boating lake and grounds that span a river. The bamboo-lined, motel-style rooms above the reception are just acceptable, with fan and outside bath. The regular chalets are a little old, and aren't nearly

SABAH

as good as the more appealing lakeside chalets. The staff at the centre can help arrange trips up Mt Trus Madi. If you're driving here from KK, the centre is just south of the Shell station on the main road.

Eating

There are a few simple restaurants around the minivan shelter in Tambunan town, including the simple but good **Restoran 99** (Tambunan; meals from RM3; ⏲ breakfast, lunch & dinner), which serves a fine *mee goreng ayam* (friend noodles with chicken; RM3.50). You might also consider the wonderfully named **Kedai Kopi Soon Fatt** (Tambunan; meals from RM3; ⏲ breakfast, lunch & dinner), which, despite the name, serves food that is no more caloric than your typical *kedai kopi*.

Getting There & Away

Regular minivans ply the roads between Tambunan and KK (RM10, 1½ hours), Ranau (RM12, two hours), Keningau (RM7, 1 hour) and Tenom (RM12, two hours). KK–Tenom express buses also pass through, though you may have to ask them to stop. The minivan shelter is in the middle of Tambunan town.

Minivans to KK pass the entrance to the rafflesia reserve; you'll usually be charged for the whole trip to KK.

KENINGAU
☎ 087

Keningau is a busy commercial centre in the southern Pegalan Valley. It's of interest to travellers primarily as a place to catch onward transport, do a bit of shopping, or hit an ATM. For locals, though, it's a different matter: attracted by the prospect of well-paid employment, people have flocked here from neighbouring districts, as well as from Indonesia and the Philippines, and the town's population has more than doubled since the 1960s. As you pass through, you may find yourself marvelling how this relatively small city manages to recreate the traffic conditions of Bangkok in the middle of Borneo.

As far as attractions go, you might check out **Taipaek-gung**, a colourful Chinese temple in the middle of town, or the large **tamu** held every Thursday.

Maybank and **Milimewa** supermarket are conveniently located right in the middle of the city, on the west side of the highway.

Sleeping & Eating
Hotel Tai Wah (☎ 332-2092; 24 Jln Besar; s/d RM25/35; ⏹) In the middle of town, visible from the main road, this simple and clean Chinese hotel is a good value, if a little noisy (due to its proximity to the main road).

Hotel Juta (☎ 337-888; www.sabah.com.my/juta; Lg Milimewa 2; standard/superior r from RM85/95; ⏹) The midrange Juta towers over central Keningau, and is convenient to transport, banking and shopping options. The standard rooms here are a little cramped but clean. The superior rooms are slightly more spacious. There is a restaurant on the premises.

Hotel Perkasa (☎ 331-045; Jln Kampung Keningau; s/d RM92/115; ⏹) One kilometre north of town, just west of the northernmost roundabout, you'll find the large pink edifice of the Hotel Perkasa, which is a small step up in comfort from the Hotel Juta (although it's not as conveniently located and only suitable for those with their own cars). The rooms are fairly spacious with decent bathrooms that have actual bathtubs.

Kedai Kopi Wan Hing (meals from RM3; ⏲ breakfast, lunch & dinner) This Chinese *kedai kopi* is a good spot for your morning *char siu pau* (steamed bun filled with barbecue pork) and tea. It's opposite Maybank, which is diagonally opposite Hotel Juta.

Getting There & Away

There are seven express buses daily to/from KK (RM13, 2½ hours) and four to/from Tenom (RM7, 1 hour). These buses stop at the Bumiputra Express stop on the main road across from the Shell station.

Minivans and share-taxis operate from several places in town, including a stop just north of the express bus stop. There are services to/from KK (RM25, 2½ hours), Ranau (RM18, three hours) and Tenom (RM7, one hour).

A road also links Keningau to Kimanis (and KK) on the coast, crossing the Crocker Range en route.

TENOM
☎ 087

This sleepy little town at the southern end of Crocker Range and Pegalan Valley has seen better days but still manages to be more attractive than traffic-choked Keningau. Tenom was closely involved in uprisings against the British in 1915, led by the famous Murut chief Ontoros Antonom, and there's a **memorial** to the tribe's fallen warriors off the main road. The main activity in town is watching the millions of sparrows that gather on the power lines and rooftops downtown each evening. The main reason most people stop in Tenom is to visit the nearby Sabah Agricultural Park (see right).

Sleeping & Eating

There are only three passable hotels here, none of which are up to much. If you demand proper accommodations, you'll have to head north to Keningau.

Hotel Sri Perdana (☎ 734-001; 77 Jln Tun Mustapha; s/d RM30/40; ⚡) Despite the narrow single beds and ineffective electric showers, this hotel is good value for a quick overnight. There's a café underneath, and minivans to Keningau stop right opposite. It's diagonally across from the *padang*.

Hotel Sri Jaya (☎ 735-689; Jln Tun Mustapha; s/d RM30/33; ⚡) The rooms here are monastic spare, but are clean enough to consider for a night. It's on the main street in the centre of town.

Orchid Hotel (☎ 737-600; Jln Tun Mustapha; s/d RM35/44; ⚡) This is arguably the best hotel in town, which isn't saying much. It's got semi-hot showers and reasonably spacious rooms.

Chi Hin Restaurant (off Jln Tun Mustapha; meals from RM3; ⏰ breakfast, lunch & dinner) In one of the shopping streets east of Jln Tun Mustapha you'll find this simple Chinese place that does a nice sweet and sour pork (RM6) or a good *mee goreng* (RM4.50). The ice lemon tea is pretty good, too.

Tenom Superstore (Jln Datuk Yassin; ⏰ 9am-9pm daily) Self-caterers can stock up here. It's a bit east of the main street, in the centre of town.

Getting There & Away

Minivans operate from in front of the Hotel Sri Perdana. Destinations include Keningau (RM6, one hour) and KK (RM20, three to four hours). There are also regular services to Tambunan (RM12, two hours).

An express bus to KK (RM16, 3½ hours) leaves daily from near the train station at 7am, 8am, noon and 4pm.

Taxis congregate at a rank on the west side of the padang. You can charter a whole taxi to Keningau (RM28) or KK (RM120), or, if you show up in the morning, you might be able to wait around and join others going the same way.

SABAH AGRICULTURAL PARK

The **Sabah Agricultural Park** (Taman Pertanian Sabah; ☎ 737-952; www.sabah.net.my/agripark; adult/child RM25/10; ⏰ 9am-4.30pm Tue-Sun), about 15km southeast of Tenom, is run by the Department of Agriculture and covers about 1500 acres (610 hectares). The park is the main tourist attraction in this part of the state, and it's a worthwhile destination for plant lovers, although, like a lot of tourist attractions in Borneo, it seems like more energy was put into starting the place than maintaining it.

The park is laid out around three ponds and all the gardens and facilities are connected by a network of paved or dirt paths. Gardens include an orchid garden (none blooming while we were there), mangosteen orchards, and rambutan orchards.

Due to the size of the place, a fair bit of walking in the hot sun is involved (bring sunscreen, sun hats and sufficient clothing). Exploring by bicycle would be a good idea, but the fleet of rental bikes here has just about rusted to the point of immobility. There is a free 'train' (it's actually more like a bus) that does a 1½ hour loop of the park, leaving from outside the reception hourly from 9.30am to 3.30pm.

The park has an on-again/off-again **hostel** (dm RM25), a restaurant, shop and information centre. It's also possible to camp on one of the lake islands for RM10 per person.

To get here, take a minivan from Tenom heading to Lagud Seberang (RM3). Services run throughout the morning, but dry up in the late afternoon. Tell the driver you're going to Taman Pertanian. The park entrance is about 1km off the main road. A roundtrip in a taxi from Tenom, including a two-hour wait while you visit the park, will cost RM50. If you're driving yourself, the park is well-marked from Tenom.

BATU PUNGGUL

Not far from the Kalimantan border, Batu Punggul is a jungle-topped limestone outcrop riddled with caves, towering nearly 200m above Sungai Sapulut. This is deep in Murut country and Batu Punggul was one of several sites sacred to these people. Batu Punggul and the adjacent Batu Tinahas are even traditionally believed to be longhouses that gradually transformed into stone. It can be difficult and expensive to get here, and you can safely give the area a miss if you intend to visit the caves and longhouses of Sarawak.

Batu Punggul is located a 10-minute motorboat ride upstream along the Sungai Sapulut from the Murut longhouse community of Tataluang. It's possible to get to the top of Batu Punggul, which involves a slippery 20-minute climb up a jungle slope followed by a further hour of climbing along a precarious rock face. Those who dare reach the top are rewarded with wonderful views of the densely forested jungle that surrounds the area. Batu Punggul and the area are also home to several caves, including the 1km-long Tinagas Cave.

The only thing approaching accommodation in the area is the Murut longhouse community of Tataluang. Longhouse headman **Lanter Bakayas** speaks English and can arrange accommodation (RM30/day) and guide and arrange trips to Batu Punggul and nearby areas (starting RM150/day).

Note that due to the cost and difficulty of reaching the area, it probably only makes sense to come here if you have other business in the area (say, if you had your own transport and were heading onto Maliau Basin Conservation Area; p154). If you just want to see some caves, consider a trip to Gunung Mulu National Park (p205) or Niah Caves National Park (p197), both in Sarawak.

Getting There & Away

To reach Batu Punggul/Tataluang, from Kota Kinabalu, take one of seven daily buses to Keningau (RM13, 2½ hours). From Keningau there's no formal transport to Tataluang. Simply ask around in the market area near the Chinese temple where a Land Cruiser/Jeep can be chartered for RM200 to 250 for the three-hour trip to Tataluang.

NORTHWEST SABAH

Heading north from KK, the main road parallels the coast, passing a through a few quiet towns such as Tuaran and Kota Belud. Most of the way, however, the scenery is pastoral, with tiny *kampung* scattered amid rice paddies and palm oil plantations and rice paddies. Eventually, it leads toward the so-called 'Tip of Borneo', at the very end of the Kudat Peninsula, before coming

to rest in the town of Kudat. Those who want to continue north from here can carry on by taking a ferry to the seldom visited island of Pulau Banggi.

The real highlights of northwest Sabah lie offshore: the first is Pulau Mantanani, a perfect tropical island lying about 40km northwest of Kota Belud. The second is Layang Layang, a diving Mecca about 300km northwest of KK. It's basically just an airstrip built on a reef way out in the middle of the South China Sea. Famous for great visibility, seemingly endless wall dives and the occasional school of hammerheads, it is among the best dive sites in Southeast Asia.

TUARAN
☎ 088

Tuaran, 33km from KK, is a bustling little town with tree-lined boulevard-style streets and a distinctive nine-storey **Chinese pagoda**. There's little point stopping in the town itself unless you happen to pass through on Sunday (market day). The main attraction around Tuaran is the Penimbawan Water Village.

Penimbawan Water Village

About 5km north of Tuaran (RM1.5 by mini-van or RM20 by taxi) is the tiny *kampung* of Surusup, which overlooks a lovely estuary. From here you can charter a small boat (RM40 return) to the picturesque water village of **Penimbawan**. The trip up the estuary takes about 15 minutes, and the boat will wait while you wander the plankwalks of the village. Your boat driver may accompany you into the village or he may just wait for you in the boat. Needless to say, don't part with your cash until you arrive back in Surusup (and don't be surprised if a few villagers tag along for a free ride).

Sleeping & Eating

Orchid Hotel (☎ 793-789; 4 Jln Teo Teck Ong; r from RM80; ✷) Given the town's proximity to KK (with heaps of good accommodation options), you probably won't need to stay here. However, if for some reason you need a room, this simple, somewhat overpriced hotel on the main street should suffice. The rooms are clean, if a bit musty.

Tai Fatt Restaurant (7 Jln Teo Teck Ong; meals from RM3.50; ✷ 7am-10pm daily) Next door to the Orchid Hotel, this simple Chinese place does a good plate of *mee goreng* (RM3.50). The owner speaks English.

Getting There & Away
All northbound buses and minivans from KK pass through Tuaran. The minivan station is in the centre of town. Destinations, fares and times include KK (RM4, 30 minutes) and Kota Belud (RM7, 30 minutes).

KOTA BELUD
☎ 088
You might think Kota Belud isn't much to look at, but every Sunday a huge **tamu** takes place on the outskirts of this small, sleepy town. The market is a congested, colourful and dusty melee of vendors, hagglers, browsers, gawpers and hawkers, all brought together by a slew of everyday goods in a bustle that consumes the whole town each and every week. A smaller version takes place on Wednesday.

A *tamu* is not simply a market where villagers gather to sell their farm produce and to buy manufactured goods from traders; it's also a social occasion where news and stories are exchanged. Sadly tourists now often outnumber buffalo, and the fascinating local Bajau horsemen have mostly moved away from the car park, though some do put on a show for visitors.

Visitors looking for tribal handicrafts and traditional clothing will be disappointed, but the market is certainly lively and you can enjoy a good breakfast here after looking around. The hilly views from the *padang* may also tempt you to stay a while and do some walking away from the Sunday crowds.

Sleeping & Eating
Most people visit Kota Belud as a day trip from KK, since you can make it there and back with plenty of time for the market. One reason to stay overnight here is the stunning view of Mt Kinabalu at first light.

Kota Belud Travelers' Lodge (☎ 977-228; 6 Plaza Kong Guan; dm RM25, r RM60-85; ❄) This relatively new guesthouse is clean, simple and well-run. The private rooms have en suite toilets. It's about 200m southwest of the mosque in a shopping block (it's well marked, so finding it shouldn't be a problem).

Bismallah Restaurant (opposite Majlis Daerah Kota Belud; meals from RM3; ☼ breakfast, lunch & dinner) This simple Muslim restaurant does good *roti canai* and curries, as well as good tea to wash it

down with. It's opposite the city offices in the centre of town, halfway along a block of wooden shophouses.

Getting There & Away
Minivans and share-taxis gather in front of Pasar Besar, the main market. Most of these serve the Kota Belud to KK route, (RM5, two hours) or Kudat (RM10, two hours), departing between 7am and 5pm. The bus station is in the south of town, near the Shell station.

PULAU MANTANANI
Pulau Mantanani Besar (Big Mantanani Island) and **Pulau Mantanani Kecil** (Little Mantanani Island) are two little flecks of land about 25km off the coast northwest Sabah (about 40km northwest of Kota Belud). Fringed by blinding white sand and covered with coconut trees, the islands are among the most beautiful in all of Borneo. There are healthy coral gardens around both islands, particularly off the east end of Mantanani Kecil. While there are no bommies or walls here, the excellent visibility and health of the coral will impress all but the most jaded divers and snorkellers. Dugongs used to live around the island, but locals say they haven't been spotted for over a year.

There is a small fishing village in the middle of Mantanani Besar and a simple resort on its west side.

Borneo Sea Resort
The **Borneo Sea Resort** (☎ 088-230-000; www.bornsea .com/mantanani; three-day/two-night all-inclusive dive packages from RM1900; ❄) is the only place to stay on the island. It sits on a nice private beach at the west end of the island. The bungalows here are quite nice, with tile floors, hot-water showers and bathtubs, large double beds, verandas and air-con. Sea kayaks are available for rent and would allow you to explore the area, but be careful as there are strong currents offshore and you could easily get washed out to sea. The management of the place seem a little offhand and the service is probably not up to much, but if you just want a quiet bungalow and don't need much pampering, you'll probably like this spot.

Getting There & Away
If you're not staying at the resort (which will help arrange private transport to the island), the only other way to get to the island is by taking all-inclusive daytrips to the island

SABAH

from KK with **Scuba Paradise** (☎ 088-266-695 www.scubaparadiseborneo.com.my; ground fl, Wisma Sabah, Kota Kinabalu). Rates for snorkelling trips are RM380 per person (minimum four people). Rates for diving are RM560 per person (includes equipment rental, minimum four people).

LAYANG LAYANG

A look at a satellite image of Layang Layang is enough to get any diver's heart racing: it's a brilliant 7km-long ring of coral set amid a vast expanse of dark-blue ocean. You just know those coral walls are going to be pristine and swarming with fish. Zooming in on the image, you notice that, incredibly, a landing strip perches on the only bit of land that reaches rises above sea level on the reef. This airstrip serves **Layang Layang Island Resort**, which holds the sole concession to this brilliant diving destination.

Layang Layang (also known as Swallow Reef) is part of the disputed Spratley Group, which China, Taiwan, the Philippines, Vietnam, Brunei and Malaysia have been tussling over for years, due to their undersea oil reserves and healthy stocks of fish. Malaysia staked its claim by building a naval base on Layang Layang. The base, which shares the tiny bit of land on the reef with the resort, is strictly off limits to resort guests.

Diving

As you would guess from its location, the reef here is healthy and diverse. Although it may not be quite as colourful as the reef at Sipidan, it's likely to be one of the healthiest reefs most divers have seen. And the best part is that it just goes on and on, with new surprises waiting up and down its length. The visibility here is usually excellent, sometimes extending to 30 metres or more. While hammerheads are occasionally sighted, it might be better to consider them windfalls, and to concentrate on the reef fish, which are abundant and varied. There are also plenty of reef sharks in attendance, along with a healthy population of rays (mostly devil rays, diamond rays and the occasional manta).

The resort runs the dive centre here, which is staffed by a friendly crew of mostly Malaysian dive masters. They are fairly serious about safety procedures, which is appreciated, since the nearest decompression chamber is 330km away by plane.

Layang Layang is best for advanced divers, and the morning dive here is often to a depth of 40 metres. The diving consists mostly of excellent wall dives, with a few small cave-like diversions. The schedule also usually includes a few blue-water dives, which are specifically to look for hammerheads and other large pelagics.

Your dives are included in your accommodation package at the resort. Equipment rental and instruction are available. All in all, it's a great adventure and one worth taking for a keen diver.

Other Activities

If you're still hungry to see coral and fish after two or three dives a day, you can always do a bit of snorkelling off the reef on the far side of the runway, but be warned that the rocks are slippery and dangerous – let someone know where you're going and when you expect to return and don't go alone. And don't even think about it when waves are rolling in. Remember: you're 300km away from land here.

There's also a good little sand beach at the southern end of the runway, which you can also snorkel off of. It's also good for sunbathing and swimming.

The resort has a very nice pool and deck area, which is where many guests chill out between meals and dives.

Otherwise, the only other activity here is walking or jogging on the long runway beside the resort.

Sleeping & Eating

Layang Layang Island Resort (☎ 03-2162-2877; www .layanglayang.com/our_story.asp; layang@pop.jaring.my) is the only game in town here. The resort is well-run and efficient. It's really all about diving here. We like the way the room blocks empty right out to the dive area: when dive time rolls around, the divers spring from their rooms like airmen going out on a raid. The five daily meals – that's right, five – are scheduled around the diving schedule. The food is generous and fairly tasty, with at least one veggie option at each meal, as well as salads and fruit.

The standard rooms are very comfortable, with air-con, TV, private verandas, hot-water showers and so on. Those near the pool can be noisy if the present crop of divers are a partying lot. Six-day/five-night all-inclusive packages (accommodation, food, diving and tank usage) start at US$1,260 for single occupancy and US$1,060 for double occupancy (rates are per-person). Rates for nondivers start at US$940/740 single occupancy/double occupancy.

The deluxe (VIP) rooms are available and are very comfortable, but not worth the added price unless you want to be away from the other divers in the main room block.

Getting There & Away
The resort operates its own Antanov 26, which flies every Tuesday, Thursday, Friday and Sunday between KK and Layang Layang. The flight over from KK in this bare bones Russian prop plane is a big part of the adventure: it feels more like a military transport than a commercial airliner, and you feel like you're on some sort of James Bond mission to some secret destination. There are only four windows (grab one on the right side on the outward journey if you want to get a glimpse of Mt Kinabalu). The return flight costs US$256, which is not included in the accommodation/food/dive package.

KUDAT
☎ 088

Kudat is a quiet port town in the very north of Sabah, 190km from KK. The surrounding countryside is home to the friendly Rungus people, tribal cousins of the Kadazan and Duzun, but the town itself displays noticeable Filipino influences, as much of the trade here is with Malaysia's northeastern neighbour.

Kudat itself is fairly unremarkable, but it's got a few good beaches nearby and it serves as the jumping-off point for Pulau Banggi, an island that lies between Borneo and the Philippines.

The town is fairly easy to navigate, with the bus station, jetty, the post office, mosque and colourful Fuk Tek Kung Chinese temple on the west side and the Sedco Shopping Complex on the east side (these are two rows of shophouses). The covered market forms the divide between the two. Everything is in easy walking distance of the bus station.

Information
Maybank (☎ 611-146; Kedai Sedco, Jln Melati) This convenient bank is roughly in the middle of the Sedco Shopping Complex.

Sleeping
Hotel Kinabalu (☎ 613-888; 1243 Jln Melor, Sedco Shopping Complex; s/d RM42/56; ❄) At the west end

of the Sedco Shopping Complex, right next to KFC, you will find this simple and friendly hotel. It's a bit threadbare, but the rooms are good enough for the night.

Hotel Dream Garden (☎ 622-633; Jln Cempaka, Sedco Shopping Complex; s/d RM48/59; ❄) In the middle of the Sedco Shopping Complex, this simple but adequate hotel is similar to the Hotel Kinabalu. It's opposite Maybank.

our pick **Ria Hotel** (☎ 622-794; 3 Jln Marudu; r RM80-98; ❄ 💻) If all hotels were like this, we reckon we'd travel a lot more. The Ria hits all the right notes: clean, spacious, well-appointed rooms, nice bathrooms with hot showers, and little balconies (some with nice views). It's one of the best-value hotels we found in Sabah. We just hope it stays that way. It's a short walk southwest of the bus station.

Upper Deck Hotel (☎ 622-272; Jln Lintas; r RM80-100, ste RM160; ❄) Perched atop the Milimewa Superstore, the well-run and friendly Upper Deck has huge, spartan rooms with air-con and hot-water showers. It's a good hotel, but not quite as nice as the Hotel Ria. It's a short walk southwest of the market.

Eating
Restoran Rakyat (Sedco Shopping Complex; dishes RM1-5; ✕ 24hrs) About halfway along the Sedco Shopping Complex, the Rakyat is a 24-hour Muslim café that serves good rotis and curries.

Restoran Prosperous (Sedco Shopping Complex; meals from RM3; ✕ breakfast, lunch & dinner) Roughly opposite the KFC, Restoran Prosperous is a Chinese place that attracts a good group of locals both wealthy and otherwise. You can get a nice *char siu pau* (steamed bun filled with barbecue pork) and a cup of tea here in the morning for RM2.70.

Getting There & Away
The bus station is in Kudat Plaza, which is in the western part of town, very close to the Ria Hotel. Bus destinations include KK (RM20, 3 hours) and Kota Belud (RM15, 90 minutes). Minivans also operate from this station and other points in town.

AROUND KUDAT
Beaches
You'll find some of Sabah's best beaches around Kudat, where the water is shallow and safe for paddling. **Pantai Bak Bak**, about 5km from Kudat, is the town beach. It's a

SABAH

decent, if slightly rocky, beach. To get there from Kudat (if you have a rental car), take the main coastal road out of Kudat (you must go inland a bit to get around the airport, but otherwise hug the coast), following signs for the Tip of Borneo – Pantai Bak Bak is clearly marked off the main coastal road.

A better beach can be found by continuing along past Pantai Bak Bak for about 4km, then taking a right at the fork and driving about 500m through a mangrove swamp to reach **Pasir Putih** (White Sand Beach).

A taxi from Kudat to either of these beaches will cost about RM10 each way.

Rungus Longhouses

The indigenous people of the Kudat area are known as the Rungus people, a subgroup of the Kadazan-Dusun people who are found across Sabah. The Rungus inhabit the Kudat Peninsula and the Pitas Peninsula, on the other side of Marudu Bay. The Rungus are famous for their basketry, beadwork and fine longhouses, which house one extended family, rather than several unrelated families, as is the case with other groups in Borneo.

These days, as with many other indigenous people in Borneo, most of the Rungus have abandoned their longhouses in favour of Malay-style wooden or concrete-brick houses. However, the Rungus maintain two fine **longhouses** (Bavanggazo Rungus Longhouse; ☎ 088-621-971; per person from RM70 per night) in Kampung Bavanggazo, 44km south of Kudat on the Kudat Peninsula.

Make no mistake, these longhouses are set up for display purposes and to attract tourists, but a night here would still be interesting and provides a good chance to interact with Rungus people and learn about their culture. The rates include dinner and breakfast and simple cultural entertainment. You will sleep in a traditional room in the longhouse with insect netting above your bed.

Kampung Bavanggazo is 44km south of Kudat on the north-south highway (look for the milepost reading 'Kudat 44km'). There is a sign off the highway that reads 'Kg. Bavanggazo 'Rungus Longhouse''. Follow this road (Jln Tinangol) down the hill for about 1.5km, cross a bridge and go uphill to the left. You will quickly come to the first longhouse, and the second one is at the top of the hill 800m further on. There is no public transport right to the longhouses. All KK–Kudat

buses and minivans will stop at Kampung Bavanggazo if you ask the driver. A taxi from Kudat will cost around RM50.

Tip of Borneo

About 13km off the main highway leading to Kudat, a long stretch of mostly dirt road leads to the 'Tip of Borneo' (Tanjung Simpang Mengayu), Sabah's northernmost headland. Sabah Tourism has done everything they can to promote this as a tourist attraction. Everything, that is, except pave the road that leads there.

The view from the cape is quite attractive, but it's not really worth the bumpy drive to get there, especially if you don't have a 4WD vehicle. Once you get there, you'll find a parking lot, a monument and a plaque, as well as some steps that lead down to a viewing area. Much more appealing is the 1km arch of white-sand beach called **Pantai Kalampunian** just before (and southwest of) the cape, where you could probably guerrilla camp if you had to.

There's no public transport, so you'll need to negotiate for a taxi from Kudat (around RM50, including waiting time) or drive yourself (we suggest washing the dust off the car before returning it to the rental agency).

PULAU BANGGI

Travellers who want to fall off the map, or, at least get off the tourist trail for a few days, might want to visit the remote island of Pulau Banggi, which lies some 40km northeast of Kudat. There's not much in the way of developed attractions here, and the island is a bit scruffy, but the people are lovely and the setting is beautiful. You can pay locals to take you by boat to explore the reefs and beaches of Banggi and the nearby islands (bring your snorkel).

Accommodation is provided by a small government **rest house** (r RM40) and the modest **Banggi Resort** (☎ 671-495, 019-587-8078; r fan/air-con RM35/55; ✷), which can arrange boat trips and other activities. In addition to rooms, the resort also has small huts with kitchens and twin beds (RM70). This place can get fully booked on weekends, so reserve in advance.

Kudat Express (☎ 328-118; Kudat) runs a ferry between Kudat and the main settlement on Pulau Banggi. It departs the pier (near the Shell station) in Kudat daily at 9am. In the reverse direction, it departs Pulau Banggi daily at 3pm. The fare is RM15.

SABAH

EAST SABAH

Malaysia's government tourism office touts Sabah as a 'solar-powered theme park'. That makes East Sabah Adventure Land. Behind a veil of palm-oil plantations lurk some of Asia's biggest wild game, oldest, deepest and darkest jungles, flightiest birds (with the priciest nests) and most volatile rivers. Beneath the crystal-clear waters of the east coast are rare turtles, garish reef fish, and sharkskin carpet paths to kaleidoscopic clutches of coral.

As in any good theme park, it's fairly easy to move between the attractions and enjoy them without much special skill or expertise beyond a pair of water-resistant boots or a scuba license. In a week, an independent visitor can see orangutans in Sepilok, seek elephants along Sungai Kinabatangan, spelunk Gomantong or Madai Caves, and survey the depths of Tun Sakaran Marine Park. Sites that require arrangements through specified tour operators – Tabin Reserve, Maliau Basin and Danum Valley – richly merit their special status; investing the time and money to visit usually pays off with an extraordinary experience.

SANDAKAN
☎ 089 / pop 450,000

Once boasting the world's greatest concentration of millionaires (it's claimed), Sandakan still holds its own in the league tables thanks to bird's nest, fish and palm oil. The town has riches for tourists, too. It's the gateway to East Sabah's natural treasures and boasts some stellar attractions between its green hills and picturesque bay.

Downtown Sandakan was once dominated by busy docks by day and shuttered shops at night. But the wharves have moved to the outskirts of town, paving the way for waterfront redevelopment, including a new market and a nascent nightlife hub. The hottest action after dark is still in the nearby suburbs, a bus or taxi ride away.

History

Exotic luxury products such as beeswax, birds' nests and pearls put Sandakan on the map with ancient traders from as far away as China, but timber built the foundation for its settlement and prosperity. Logs from Sandakan are found in Beijing's Temple of Heaven.

Once ruled by the southern Philippines' sultan of Sulu, Scottish gunrunner William Clarke Cowie and the British Resident William Pryer brought Sandakan under the sway of the North Borneo Chartered Company from the 1870s. Declared capital of British North Borneo in 1883, Sandakan enjoyed modern developments such as telegraph service to London and paved streets before Hong Kong or Singapore. Allied bombing and Japanese retaliation in 1945 virtually destroyed the town, and in 1946 the capital was moved to the equally devastated Jesselton, now called Kota Kinabalu.

Orientation

Nature and town planners have conspired to make Sandakan easy for visitors to navigate. The centre of town is couple dozen blocks, most of it landfill squashed between the waterfront and a steep escarpment overlooking the bay.

Leave it to the bureaucrats to throw a spanner into this happy circumstance. Streets are numbered Jln Dua (Second Street) and Lebuh Tiga (Third Avenue), with the occasional Lorong (Lg, lane) tossed in. Simple enough, but addresses are often based on the street lot, which may be identified with a different street than the one the building fronts. Moreover, no one in town distinguishes between the three categories and calls every road Jln. Fortunately, even if you have to look all over town, it's not a long walk.

Like many Malaysian towns, Sandakan has suburbs and outlying areas extending considerable distances down the main highway, denoted by their distance from the centre, eg Batu 1 (Mile 1). Express buses to Kota Kinabalu and other destinations leave from the long-distance bus station at Batu 2½, 4km north of the town centre.

Information

INTERNET ACCESS

Cyber Café (3rd fl, Wisma Sandakan, Lebuh Empat; per hr RM3; ⊙ 9am-9pm)

JazzCyber (1st fl, Centre Point, Jln Pelabuhan Lama; per hr RM4; ⊙ 9am-8pm Mon-Sat, 9am-7pm Sun)

Tadzmera (Jln Elopura cnr Lg Lima) Mediocre Malay restaurant with free wi-fi from 2 to 5pm and 9pm to 6am.

MEDICAL SERVICES

Duchess of Kent Hospital (☎ 219-460; Mile 2, Jln Utara)

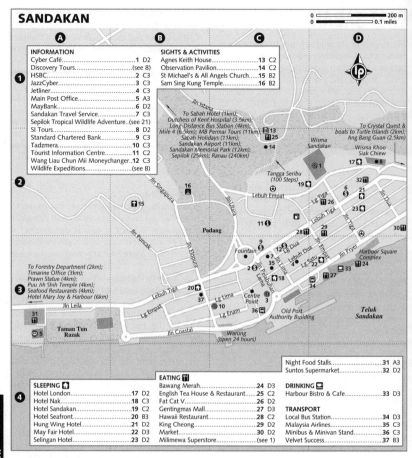

SANDAKAN

To Istana
To Sabah Hotel (1km);
Dutchess of Kent Hospital (3.5km);
Long-Distance Bus Station (4km);
Mile 4 (6.5km); MB Permai Tours (11km);
Sabah Holidays (11km);
Sandakan Airport (11km);
Sandakan Memorial Park (12km);
Sepilok (25km); Ranau (240km)

Wisma Sandakan

To Crystal Quest &
boats to Turtle Islands (2km);
Ang Bang Guan (2.5km)

Wisma Khoo
Siak Chiew

Jln Singapura

Tangga Seribu
(100 Steps)

Lebuh Empat

Jln Utara

Padang

Jln Puncak

Jln Elopura

Lebuh Tiga

Jln Pelita

Jln Dua

Lg Dua

Lg Satu

Jln Pryer

Harbour Square
Complex

To Forestry Department (2km);
Timarine Office (3km);
Prawn Statue (4km);
Puu Jih Shih Temple (4km);
Seafood Restaurants (4km);
Hotel Mary Joy & Harbour (6km)

Fountain

Lebuh Tiga

Lg Lima

Centre
Point

Jln Leila

Lg Empat

Lg Enam

Old Port
Authority Building

Teluk
Sandakan

Taman Tun
Razak

Jln Coastal

Warung
(open 24 hours)

MONEY

HSBC (Lebuh Tiga)

MayBank (Lebuh Tiga) In addition to full-service bank and ATM, a sidewalk currency-exchange window is open 9am to 5pm daily, changing cash and traveller checks.

Standard Chartered Bank (Lebuh Tiga)

Wang Liau Chun Mii Moneychanger (Tung Seng Huat, 23 Lebuh Tiga; ☻ 8.30am-4.30pm) Cash only.

POST

Main post office (☎ 210-594; Jln Leila)

TOURIST INFORMATION

Forestry Department (☎ 213-966; 2nd fl, Jln Leila, next to UMW Toyota, 2km west of main post office) Get permits for the mangrove forest walk to Sepilok Bay (see p140).

Tourist Information Centre (☎ 229-751; pempt. j.mps@sabah.gov.my; Wisma Warisan; ☻ 8am-12.30pm & 1.30-4.30pm Mon-Thu, 8-11.30am & 2-4.30pm Friday) Located opposite the municipal offices (known as MPS) and up the stairs from Lebuh Tiga. Dedicated, garrulous staff are extremely helpful, dispensing advice on everything from regional attractions to local restaurants and can also hook up travellers for group excursions.

TRAVEL AGENCIES

Sandakan Travel Service (☎ 218-112; skantrvl@ steamyx.com; Lebuh Tiga, opposite Standard Chartered Bank) Accommodating, English-speaking help for domestic and overseas flights.

Jetliner (☎ 222-737, Lebuh Dua) Official Air Asia/MAS sales agent.

SABAH

Sight & Activities

The tourist office's *Sandakan Heritage Trail* brochure maps out a waking tour of significant historical sites.

TEMPLES & CHURCH

Puu Jih Shih Temple, 4km west of the town centre, is a large Buddhist temple perched on a steep hill overlooking Teluk Sandakan. Take a bus to Tanah Merah and ask for directions. Closer to the centre of town, the **Sam Sing Kung Temple** dates from 1887 and fronts the municipal *padang*. Granite blocks weighing 64kg each for nearby **St Michael's & All Angels Church** (off Jln Puncak) were delivered by prison labour paid a dollar per cubic metre; no surprise this 1888 church is one of the few stone buildings in Borneo.

AGNES KEITH HOUSE

On a hill overlooking town and Sandakan bay, **Agnes Keith House** (Jln Istana; admission RM15; 9am-5pm) is a trip back to Sandakan's colonial heyday. Keith was an American who came to Sandakan in the 1930s with her British husband, appointed Conservator of Forests (bring him back!), and wrote several books about her experiences, mostly famously *The Land Below the Wind*. The Keiths' two-storey wooden villa was destroyed during World War II and rebuilt identically when they returned in 1946. The house fell into disrepair during the 1990s, but Sabah Museum restored it as a faithful recreation of Keith's original abode.

The villa documents Sandakan in all its colonial splendour, with detailed displays on the lives of the Keiths. Most poignant are mementos of Agnes' imprisonment by the Japanese during WWII, caring for her young son under brutal conditions. Her book, *Three Came Home*, recounts those years. The admission price includes entry to the various branches of the Sabah Museum in KK, so keep hold of your ticket.

During and after museum hours, **English Tea House & Restaurant** (☎ 222-544; www.english teahouse.org; 2002 Jln Istana; mains RM17-33; lunch & dinner) offers recherché colonial atmosphere and elegant food, conveniently ignoring Keith's US background and her complaint that Sandakan was 'too British'. The exquisitely restored restaurant's manicured gardens with rattan furniture and a small croquet lawn overlooking the bay are perfect for afternoon tea (RM17.25) or a gin and tonic sundowner.

To reach the museum, follow Jln Singapura and turn right up the hill, or head up the shady Tangga Seribu (translated as 100 Steps, even though *seribu* means 1000) to Jln Residensi Drive and turn left. Just below the museum garden is an **observation pavilion** built by the local Rotary Club, offering more fine views.

SANDAKAN MEMORIAL PARK

Now just a quiet patch of woods, **Sandakan Memorial Park** (Taman Peringatan; admission free; 9am-5pm) was the site of a Japanese POW camp and starting point for the infamous 'death marches' to Ranau. Of the 1800 Australian and 600 British troops imprisoned here, the only survivors by July 1945 were six Australian escapees. Sandakan accounted for more Australian deaths, one-eighth of Australia's total casualties in the Pacific, than the more infamous building of the Burma Railway.

Large, rusting machines testify to the camp's forced-labour programme, and a pavilion at the centre of park includes accounts from survivors and photographs from personnel, inmates and liberators. In 2006 the original march route was officially reopened as a memorial trail – see www.sandakan-deathmarch .com for details.

To reach the park, take any Batu 8 or higher bus (RM1.50); get off at the 'Taman Rimba' signpost and walk down Jln Rimba. A taxi from downtown runs about RM15.

Tours

Sandakan has many local and regional tour operators offering packages to Sungai Kinabatangan, Gomantong Caves, Turtle Islands National Park and beyond. Hotels in Sandakan and Sepilok can arrange tours, as can agents in KK. Keep in mind that it's possible to visit many attractions independently, and in some cases, such as Sepilok Orang-Utan Rehabilitation Centre, preferable. Also note that tour prices differ massively, sometimes due to dormitory versus room accommodation, sometimes for no good reason at all, so shop around. (If you need more tour operator names, read guides' polo shirts at Sepilok.) For locations that have designated franchisees, such as Turtle Island and Danum Valley, buying direct will mean the lowest price.

Discovery Tours (☎ 274-106; www.discoverytours .com.my; 9th fl, Wisma Khoo Siak Chiew, Lebuh Empat)

SABAH

Book your stay at lonelyplanet.com/hotels

THE SANDAKAN DEATH MARCHES

Sandakan was the site of a Japanese prisoner-of-war camp during WWII, and in September 1944 there were 1800 Australian and 600 British troops interned here. What is probably not widely known is that more Australians died here than during the building of the infamous Burma Railway.

Early in the war, food and conditions were bearable, and the death rate was around three per month. But as the Allies closed in near the end of the war, it became clear to the officers in command that they didn't have enough staff to guard against a rebellion in the camps. They decided to cut the prisoners' rations to weaken them; disease spread and the death rate began to rise.

It was also decided to move the prisoners inland – 250km through the jungle to Ranau. On 28 January 1945, 470 prisoners set off; 313 made it to Ranau. On the second march, 570 started from Sandakan; just 118 reached Ranau. The third march consisted of the last men in the camp and numbered 537. Conditions on the marches were deplorable: many men had no boots, rations were less than minimal and many fell by the wayside; the Japanese disposed of any prisoners who couldn't walk. Once in Ranau, the surviving prisoners were put to work carrying 20kg sacks of rice over hilly country to Paginatan, 40km away. Disease and starvation took a horrendous toll, and by the end of July 1945 there were no prisoners left in Ranau. The only survivors from the 2400 at Sandakan were six Australians who had escaped, either from Ranau or during the marches.

MB Permai Tours (☎ /fax 671-535; 1st fl, Sandakan Airport) Tours and car rental from RM100 per day (4WD from RM350).

Sabah Holidays (☎ 671-718; www.sabahholidays .com; ground fl, Sandakan Airport) Tours, rental cars and minivans, with a branch in KK.

Sepilok Tropical Wildlife Adventure (☎ 271-077; www.stwadventure.com; 13 Lebuh Tiga) Midpriced tour specialist. Owners of Sepilok Jungle Resort and Bilit Adventure Lodge on Sungai Kinabatangan.

SI Tours (☎ 213-502; www.sitoursborneo.com; 10th fl, Wisma Khoo Siak Chiew, Lebuh Empat) This full-service agency opened Abai Jungle Resort in December 2006 as a base for Kinabatangan tours. Also has an airport branch.

Wildlife Expeditions (☎ 219-616; www.wildlife -expeditions.com; 9th fl, Wisma Khoo Siak Chiew, Lebuh Empat) Tour menu includes its Sukau River Lodge on the Kinabatangan. Has a KK office.

Sleeping

BUDGET & MIDRANGE

Sandakan's nascent urban renaissance has prompted a boomlet in hotels straddling the budget–midrange divide around RM60. All rooms quoted have private bathrooms with hot water.

our pick **May Fair Hotel** (☎ 219-855; 24 Jln Pryer; s/d RM40/50; 🛜 🖵) This budget classic's large, tidy rooms include their own big TV and DVD player with a massive library of movies available free in the lobby, and a comfy chair to watch them from. Gruff but helpful owner Mr Lum knows where to find things and how to get virtually anything done around town. Call ahead for bookings to avoid getting shut out.

Selingan Hotel (☎ 227-733; fax 221-001; 14 Lebuh Dua; s/d/f RM50/60/80; 🛜) Best of the other budget choices honeycombed around downtown, Selingan has fresh, well-appointed rooms with attractive bedding. Good alterative if the May Fair is full.

Hotel Mary Joy (☎ 617-788; Jln Pelabuhan; RM50; 🛜) Has small, clean rooms just outside the harbour gate, above a *kedai kopi*. Suitable for travellers who want to wake up near the morning boat.

Hotel London (☎ 219-855; www.hlondon.com.my; 10 Lebuh Empat; s/d/t incl breakfast 55/65/75; 🛜 🖵) Renovated up from its shoestring roots, rooms are bright and comfortable. Guests love the rooftop sitting area overlooking the harbour where breakfast is served.

Hotel Seafront (☎ 222-233; www.seafront.com.my; cnr Lg Empat & Jln Elopura; r RM59-95; 🛜 🖵) Among the newest and absolutely the swishest of budget to midrange options, located west of the Municipal Padang, though some rooms run boxy. There's 24-hour internet in the lobby, and once you're up, a clutch of bars and all-night *warung* (small eating stalls) nearby.

Hung Wing Hotel (☎ 218-855; hungwing@yahoo .com.my; Lot 4, 13 Lebuh Tiga; r incl breakfast RM61-82; 🛜 🖵) Hung Wing has comfortable decor, big shower-heads, and friendly staff as happy to greet tourists as its usual business traveller clientele. Rooms get smaller and cheaper as you climb the stairs, if you'd rather spend calories than money.

Hotel Nak (☎ 272-988; www.nakhotel.com; Jln Pelabuhan Lama; r incl breakfast RM75-125, ste RM150; 🆑 🖳) Behind a 1960s kitschy concrete facade, a 2007 renovation has made this downtown stalwart far less nak-ered. Cheapest rooms run small but the upper ranges include sea view, refrigerator and lots of space.

TOP END

Hotel Sandakan (☎ 221-122; www.hotelsandakan .my; Lebuh Empat; r incl breakfast RM220-240, ste RM280-330; 🆑 🖳) A three-star establishment offering comfortable but characterless Western-style rooms. There's a refreshing lack of attitude among staff and expect frequent discounts.

Sabah Hotel (☎ 213-299; www.sabahhotel.com.my; Km 1, Jln Utara; r RM253-368, ste from 575; 🆑 🖳 🏊) Set in quiet gardens and brimming with facilities, including a playground for kids and a cruisey pub for grownups, Sabah's a favourite with Sepilok tour groups and Malaysia Airlines crew. Rooms meet or exceed international standards. The only knock is a location that's a tad too far for walking downtown but well-short of the more happening suburbs.

Eating

The new **market** on the waterfront at the eastern edge of the town centre is great for cheap breakfast or lunch. Raw food at ground level includes the only unadulterated ground coffee in town. Upstairs find strictly halal food stalls, with a mix of Chinese and Malay on the next level. A couple of ringgit buys a decent meal plus a view of the bay. Most stalls here close by midafternoon. **Night food stalls** set up outside the post office, and there are **Malay warung** operating 24 hours on Jln Coastal.

Sandakan is renowned for authentic southern Chinese food. Most downtown Chinese *kedai kopi* shut down by late afternoon. You can also get a fix day or night at Mile 4, a hub of two-storey shops with restaurants, bars, karaoke lounges and nightclubs.

Appropriate for one of Malaysia's largest fishing ports, seafood is another Sandakan speciality. Ask around for the latest hot tips, or simply take a Pasir Putih minivan from the Centre Point terminal to the giant prawn statue about 4km west of town. Dishes are usually sold by weight, so go in a group. Expect a fish feast to set you back at least RM30.

King Cheong (34 Lebuh Dua; dishes RM2-12; ☯ breakfast, lunch) The clatter of dim-sum carts and chatter of local merchant diners make it seem like Hong Kong. Menus on the wall are in Chinese, but feel free to point at what you see on other plates, and check the daily specials steaming in the back.

Fat Cat V (☎ 216-867; 21 Lebuh Tiga; dishes RM3-10; ☯ lunch & dinner) This local chain flagship has an air-conditioned dining room with a broad menu of Malay, Chinese and Western food. Stop in its bakery to take home breakfast or a late snack. Fat Cat is surrounded by a nightlife node of fast food places open past 9pm.

Bawang Merah (Harbour Sq Complex; dishes RM4.50-5.50; ☯ lunch & dinner) Within weeks of its December 2006 opening, this Malay fast-food joint's tables along the new waterfront promenade were packed. Most of the diners had their backs to the bay, focused on the big-screen TV showing football matches or soap operas, but for Sandakan it's still café society.

Hawaii Restaurant (☎ 273-107; City View Hotel, 23 Lebuh Tiga; dishes RM4.50-25; ☯ breakfast, lunch & dinner) There's nothing Hawaiian about this simple City View Hotel lobby restaurant except its enduring popularity. It packs in Western tourists for its value menu featuring huge Malay and Chinese dishes for RM5, while Asians gravitate towards its pricey steaks and chops.

Ang Bang Guan (☎ 213-854; Jln Buli Sim Sim; mains from RM15; ☯ lunch & dinner) Just east of downtown, next to Sandakan's main mosque, Ang Bang Guan is a tasteful and tasty take on Chinese seafood.

Even tourist business types say **Ocean King Seafood Restaurant** (☎ 618111; Batu 2.5, Jln Batu Sapi; dishes RM10-25; ☯ breakfast, lunch & dinner) has gotten too touristy. **Ban Chuan Lee** (☎ 016-826-7989, Batu 2, Jln Batu Sapi; meals RM45; ☯ dinner) in the big wooden house near the prawn statue is a sophisticated alternative.

Self-caterers have some options:
Gentingmas Mall (☎ 210-010; 26 Jln Pryer)
Milimewa Superstore (☎ 235-021; Centre Point, Jln Pelabuhan Lama)
Suntos Supermarket (cnr Lebuh Tiga & Jln Dua)

Drinking & Entertainment

Sandakan's downtown revival plans include ramping up nightlife. Currently, there are a couple of beer bars along Lebuh Tiga and a few joints off Jln Elopura. The Harbour Sq development is creating a fresh centre for evening activities. In addition to fast-food restaurants, **Harbour Bistro & Cafe** (☎ 235-315; Harbour Sq) offers alfresco dining, coffee and drinks, with an air-conditioned upper-level lodge, open after dark to the wee hours.

Most of the evening action is still out at Bandar Indah, commonly known as Mile 4, 6.5km north of town by taxi. This hub of two-storey shops with restaurants, bars, karaoke lounges and nightclubs attracts expats and locals. Bars generally close around 1am or 2am, music venues slightly later.

Getting There & Away
AIR
Malaysia Airlines (☎ 273-966; cnr Jln Pelabuhan Lama & Lebuh Dua) Has several daily flights to KK, including one connecting to KL.

Air Asia (☎ 222-737; Jetliner, Lebuh Dua) flies daily direct to KL and KK, and three times weekly to Johor Bahru, with frequent promotional fares below RM100.

MASwings (☎ 1-300-883000) serves Tawau and KK daily, plus Kudat three times weekly.

BOAT
Two companies each run twice-weekly passenger ferries between Sandakan and Zamboanga in the Philippines. **Velvet Success** (☎ 212-872; New Sabah Hotel, Jln Elopura) has fast ferries (economy/1st class RM250/265; 13 hours) via Bongao and Jolo, departing at 6am. **Timarine** (☎ 224-009; Batu 1.5, Jln Leila, Bandar Ramai-Ramai) has evening boats (tickets RM250 to 360; 22 hours). Take a Pasir Putih bus (RM1) to its office.

Boats leave from the harbour, about 6km west of town. Take a Batu Sapi minivan from the terminal behind Centre Point (RM3), or pay about RM15 by taxi.

BUS
Buses to KK, Lahad Datu, Semporna and Tawau leave from the long-distance bus station in a large parking lot at Batu 2.5, 4km north of town, not a particularly convenient location. Most buses, and all minivans, leave in the morning. Get the latest schedule from hotels or the tourist office. To reach the bus station, catch a local bus (RM1) from the stand at the waterfront. A taxi from the station to town is around RM10.

Bus companies have booths at the station and touts abound. Most express buses to KK (RM40, six hours) leave between 7.30am and 2pm, with a couple of evening departures.

All pass the turn-off to Kinabalu National Park headquarters (RM30).

Buses depart regularly for Lahad Datu (RM20, 2½ hours) and Tawau (RM30, 5½ hours). There's also a bus to Semporna (RM30, 5½ hours) at 8am. If you miss it, head to Lahad Datu, then catch a frequent minivan to Semporna.

Minivans depart throughout the morning from Batu 2.5 for Ranau (RM24, four hours), and Lahad Datu, some continuing to Tawau. Minivans for Sukau (RM15) leave from a lot behind Centre Point Mall in town.

Getting Around
TO/FROM THE AIRPORT
The airport is about 11km from downtown. The Batu 7 Airport bus (RM1.50) stops on the main road about 500m from the terminal. A coupon taxi from the airport to the town centre costs RM22; going the other way, a taxi should cost around RM20.

BUS & MINIVAN
The local bus terminal is on Jln Pryer, in front of Gentingmas Mall. Buses run 6am to about 6pm on the main road to the north, Jll Utara, designated by how far from town they go, ie Batu 8. Fares range from RM1 to RM4.

Local minivans wait behind Centre Point Mall, fares from RM2. Use them for Pasir Putih seafood restaurants and the harbour area.

TAXI
Taxis cruise the town centre, and park near main hotels. Many hotels will steer you toward a preferred driver, not a bad thing. Short journeys around the town centre should cost RM5, and a trip out to Sepilok is RM35.

SEPILOK ORANG-UTAN REHABILITATION CENTRE
☎ 089
With up to 800 visitors daily, Sepilok Orang-Utan Rehabilitation Centre (SORC) is the most popular place on earth to see Asia's great ape in its native habitat, and second only to Mt Kinabalu as Sabah's favourite tourist attraction. Founded in 1964, SORC occupies a 40 sq km corner of the Kabili-Sepilok rainforest reserve about 25km north of Sandakan.

SABAH

The reason for its popularity is the abundantly endearing orangutan, humankind's closest redheaded cousin. Whether scampering along a rope hand to foot while eating a banana or gazing with moist soulful brown eyes, orangutans are charmers, though humans' affection and interest has proven something of a fatal attraction.

Once ranging across Southeast Asia, orangutans are now found only on the islands of Borneo and Sumatra (see p146). Even here, they are severely endangered due to destruction of their rainforest habitat; the days when an orangutan could swing from tree to tree from one side of Borneo to the other without touching the ground are long gone. They're also coveted as pets and victimised when forests burn. The latest research estimates perhaps as few as 15,000 orangutans are left in the wild, compared with 250,000 a century ago.

Orphaned and injured orangutans, as well as rescued pets, are brought to Sepilok to be rehabilitated for return to forest life. The centre has successfully handled hundreds of apes, and may have about 100 on site at any time in various stages of training. Once they've had medical checks and basic training in climbing and diet in enclosures, the trainees are released into Sepilok's forest.

To keeps tabs on them and supplement their diets as needed, rangers feed the orangutans on a platform in the forest, about 10 minutes' walk from the centre. The number of orangutans turning up for feedings varies from a handful to perhaps a dozen. More trees fruiting in the forest means fewer apes looking for handouts. Females returned to the wild often take advantage of the feedings when they're pregnant or nursing. Macaques show up for scraps.

For some visitors, taking the stroll over a wooden walkway into the jungle and seeing an orangutan's precious antics or simply looking one in the eye just a few metres away is the ultimate wildlife encounter. But you don't have to believe it's not a real adventure unless you're neck-deep in mud and mosquitoes after days of bounding over dirt tracks to find Sepilok too civilised. The ease of the journey and sightings suggest a false alarm about the orangutans' critically endangered status. With visitors often outnumbering apes, the constant click of cameras and camera-phones and the suburban location also contribute to feeling that you're not really seeing orangutans in the wild. But watching these redheaded, soulful acrobats is habit-forming, so let Sepilok be the springboard to further encounters, whether trekking in the reserve (see p140), or travelling to other habitats.

Information

Feedings are usually at 10am and 3pm. Schedules are posted at the **visitor reception centre** (☎ 531-180; soutan@po.jaring.my; admission RM30, camera fee RM10; ◷ 9am-noon & 2-4pm). Tickets are now valid for one day only; in the past, tickets entitled buyers to a pair of feedings, so afternoon arrivals could revisit the next morning on the same ticket. Far more annoying than this (reasonable) change in policy are park staff's angry denials of the change. The feeding platform is short jaunt by over a wooden walkway.

A worthwhile 25-minute video about Sepilok's work is shown five-times daily opposite reception in the **Nature Education Centre** auditorium. The exhibition area there has informative displays on conservation issues threatening Borneo's jungle habitats, orangutans and other wildlife in the reserve including SORC's Sumatran rhino-breeding programme – not open to the public (see www.sosrhino.org). The whole centre closes for lunch from noon (11am on Fridays), though ticket holders can still hike the walking trails.

Use the lockers provided for your valuables – orangutans and macaques have been known to relieve tourists of hats, bags, sunglasses, cameras and even clothing. It's especially important that you don't bring any containers of insect repellent into the reserve, as these are highly toxic to the apes and other wildlife. Spray yourself before entering.

SORC is supported by a UK-based charity, and its orangutan adoption scheme is a particular hit with visitors: for UK£25 a year you can sponsor a ginger bundle of fun and receive updates on its progress. For details, pick up a leaflet or contact **Sepilok Orang-Utan Appeal UK** (www.orangutan-appeal.org.uk). If you're really taken with the place Sepilok has one of the most popular overseas volunteer programmes in Malaysia. Apply through **Travellers Worldwide** (www.travellersworldwide.com).

The **Rainforest Discovery Centre** (RDC; ☎ 533-780; admission RM5; ◷ 8.30am-4.30pm Mon-Fri; ticket window closed 12.30-2pm Mon-Thu, 11.30am-2pm Fri), about 1.5km from SORC, offers an engaging graduate-level education in tropical flora

SABAH

and fauna. Outside the exhibit hall, a botanical garden presents samples of every tropical plant you've heard of and dozens more you haven't, with the accompanying descriptions every bit as vibrant as the foliage, plus a 1km lakeside walking-trail. It's perfect for a lunch break between SORC feedings; for now, the food's strictly BYO.

Walks

Sepilok's **walking trails** (⏱ 9am-4.15pm) are a reminder that, although SORC is on the outskirts of the city, it's at the edge of the rainforest. Trails range from 250m to 4km, and different paths are open at different times of year. Register at the visitor reception centre to use them. Guided night-walks may be arranged through the centre or some lodges.

There's also a 10km trail through mangrove forest to **Sepilok Bay**. A permit from the **Forestry Department** (☎ 213-966; Jln Leila, Sandakan) is required in advance for this route. The department can also arrange basic overnight accommodations at the bay (RM100) or a boat back to Sandakan (RM150). Some travel or tour agencies can assist with the permit and other arrangements.

As circusy as the SORC feeding platform sometimes appears, don't forget it's a jungle out there. Flying squirrel, green snake, gibbon and dozens more species have been spotted beyond the feeding platform. Orangutans are not usually aggressive, but every creature encountered on the trail is a *wild* animal. Food is likely to attract them, and, when it does, few will take no for an answer.

For any walk, carry plenty of water, and cover as much skin as you can bear in the heat to fend off the opportunistic leeches and mosquitoes.

Sleeping & Eating

There's plenty of accommodation in Sepilok, but none that's a great venue with great value (Several places tick one box.) Unless you're already in Sepilok and going to SORC in the morning, there's no reason to stay over, and even then, Sepilok is easy enough to reach from Sandakan. Aside from restoring the 'two feedings' ticket policy to encourage afternoon arrivals to spend the night, Sepilok desperately needs a night-time attraction. Even the store that sells beer closes at 6pm.

Hotels are scattered along Jln Sepilok, the 2.5km access road to the rehabilitation centre, and just off it. Rates include breakfast, there's a restaurant on premises at each, and all can arrange transport, local walks and tours to Sungai Kinabatangan and the Turtle Islands.

Sepilok Jungle Resort (☎ 533-031; www.sepilokjungleresort.com; dm RM20, r RM50-130; 🛏 🖳) Everyone seems to stay here but it's hard to see why. Standard rooms are musty, and staff are indifferent, except to steering guests to better kept, higher-priced digs. Perhaps some find the concrete-swathed gardens or snarls of 50kg unchained guard dogs beguiling.

Sepilok Resthouse (☎ 534-900; sephse@tm.net.my; dm RM20, r RM50-130; 🛏 🖳) Ideally situated right outside the SORC gate, this house is usually full of centre volunteers and staff. Even with vacancies, staff lack enthusiasm for walk-in visitors. If you do stay, you'll get the inside scoop on the centre.

Sepilok B&B (☎ 534-050; www.sepilokbednbreakfast.com; Jln Arboretum; dm RM22, r RM40-85; 🛏) Dorms and budget rooms are recently renovated with pastel decor and bamboo accents at this welcoming inn. The deluxe rooms accommodate up to four people. The drawback is location, about 1km from SORC, but you can rent a bike (per day RM3) and pedal.

Uncle Tan's B&B (☎ 531-639; www.uncletan.com; Mile 16, Jln Gum Gum; dm RM25) Stay in Sepilok or Sandakan? The best answer might just be neither. This Kinabatangan jungle camp operator's simple bed and breakfast, about 5km from SORC, provides transport for feedings and three meals a day. Uncle Tan's family lives here: some visitors relish the collegial, fan-cooled atmosphere while others find it lacks privacy.

Labuk B&B (☎ 533-190; labukbb@tm.net.my; Mile 14, Jln Rambutan; r RM65-78; chalet RM150-500; 🛏) Formerly in a ramshackle house beside the main road, Labuk B&B has been relocated in hillside gardens overlooking a river, repriced and is being rebranded as Sepilok Forest Edge Resort. Rooms – some with shared baths – are ordinary, but all-wood chalets with terraces overlooking greenery and touches such as an antique-style coat rack pack loads of charm.

Sepilok Nature Resort (☎ 535-001; http://sepilok.com; r RM200; 🛏) An oasis of sophistication on the jungle's edge, run by very exclusive Pulau Sipadan Resort and Tours. Rattan-accented chalets are luxuriously furnished and have private verandas overlooking scrumptious gardens. The restaurant boasts Sepilok's finest wine list.

SORC cafeteria (meals from RM4; 7am-4.30pm) Serves breakfast, sandwiches, noodle and rice dishes, snacks and drinks. Runs out of all when busy. Souvenirs sold adjacent to the seating.

Mah Fung Enterprise, a small store opposite the Sepilok B&B turn-off, sells basic provisions, including beer, and closes promptly at 6pm.

Getting There & Away

To get directly to the rehabilitation centre from Sandakan, look for the blue bus marked 'Sepilok Batu 14' (RM3.50, 30 minutes) from the local bus terminus on Jln Pryer. Minivans also make the trip every hour or so from behind Centre Point. Final return bus for Sandakan leaves at 4.30pm.

Regular buses, Batu 14 or higher, drop passengers at the turn-off to Jln Sepilok, 2.5km from the orangutan centre. Taxis wait to take you to a hotel or SORC (or both) for RM2.

Hotels can arrange transport to/from the long distance bus station and the airport. A taxi should cost around RM30 one way.

LABUK BAY PROBOSCIS MONKEY SANCTUARY

Proboscis monkeys (*Nasalis larvatus*) are an even more exclusive attraction than orangutans. After all, you can see orangutans in Sumatra but the proboscis is found only on Borneo. These reddish-brown primates, one of nine totally protected species in Sabah, can grow to 72cm with a tail almost as long, and they can weigh up 24kg. Named for their long bulbous noses, proboscis monkeys are also pot-bellied with white faces, and the males are constantly, unmistakably, aroused. With the arrival of Europeans, Malays nicknamed the proboscis *monyet belanda* (Dutch monkey).

An ecofriendly plantation owner has created a private **proboscis monkey sanctuary** (672-133; www.proboscis.cc; admission RM60, camera fee RM10), serving up sugar-free pancakes at 11.30am and 4.30pm to tempt the local *cognose-centi*. Around 70 proboscis monkeys visit the feeding area regularly. These are divided into two family groups and one bachelor troop. The two family groups never get on the same platform, and rangers find it best to feed each at different times. An estimated 300 completely wild monkeys live in the 600-hectare reserve. Animals in the reserve generally steer clear of human contact,

except for macaques, regular scavengers at feedings, and a house otter.

The sanctuary offers package trips. A half-day visit costs RM160, including transfers from Sandakan (RM150 from Sepilok). Overnight trips with meals and a night walk start at RM250. Food and accommodation are provided at the Nipah Lodge, on the edge of the oil-palm plantations that surround the sanctuary. You can arrange to be dropped at Sepilok after the visit. Independent travel here is difficult; it's 15km down a rough dirt track off the main highway. A taxi from Sandakan costs around RM150 return.

TURTLE ISLANDS NATIONAL PARK

This national park, a trio of island within swimming distance of the Philippines and 40km north of Sandakan, protects nesting areas of two endangered species of sea turtles. The green turtle (*Chelonia mydas*) and the smaller hawksbill (*Eretmochelys imbricata*) lay eggs on the islands year-round. For green turtles, peak season runs July to October on Pulau Selingan and Pulau Bakungan Kecil. For the hawksbill, it's February to April on Pulau Gulisan.

The green turtle can live for more than a century and grow to 160kg and are endangered due to their eggs, which are considered a delicacy. Egg theft has already significantly diminished populations. The hunters say their fathers and grandfathers took eggs and the turtles are still here, without realising that the three generations of humans have been taking eggs from a single generation of turtles and eating the next one. The turtles are also hunted for meat, ironic, since the green turtle is the only sea turtle with a strictly vegetarian diet.

The park is part of the conservation effort, turning three key laying sites into protected hatcheries. After an offshore liaison, females come ashore, dig trenches in the sand and lay dozens of eggs, commonly 50 to 80, but sometimes as many as 200. They bury the golf ball–size eggs and return to the water. In the park, the eggs are uncovered and collected by rangers. They're taken to a hatchery to protect them not just from poachers but monitor lizards and other natural predators. In about 60 days, the hatchlings break out of their shells and are herded to the water. More than 100,000 take the plunge every year, and less than 5 percent reach adulthood, according to experts.

Visiting Turtle Islands is by organised overnight tour only. Many agents sell the tour packages, at a wide range of prices, but **Crystal Quest** (☎ 089-212-711; cquest@tm.net.my; Jln Buli Sim Sim, Sandakan) is the franchise operator and will give the best deal. Packages starting from RM240 per person with shared bathroom and RM265 with private bath include meals, air-con chalet accommodation on Pulau Selingan and speedboat transfers. Those prices exclude the RM10 park fee and RM10 camera fee. Places are strictly are limited and tour companies often make block reservations, so book ahead. Even if tours are fully booked, it can be worthwhile to show up at the Crystal Quest office ahead of the 9.30am departure for last-minute cancellations.

Turtles don't come ashore until around 8pm, so you'll have plenty of time to enjoy the tropical beach. Bring swimming and snorkelling gear, and a book or two. There's a small **information centre** (☸ 6.30-9pm) to help you get up to speed on turtles as arrival time nears.

You may be thrilled or appalled with the wildlife experience. Some nights there may be just a single turtle on the beach with up to 30 people crowding around. Cameras are allowed but flash photography is prohibited (it disorients turtles and hatchlings, who use moonlight to locate the sea). But there's always someone who can't properly disable their camera's flash. The passing of hatchlings around to visitors by park staff seems even more risky than camera mishaps. The good news is that visits here help finance the turtle conservation programme, and experts say it's working.

Transport to the islands is from the wharf on Jln Buli Sim Sim, a 10-minute walk east of Sandakan's centre. The bumpy trip to Selingan takes about an hour, and seas are roughest during the rainy season, October to February.

GOMANTONG CAVES

If you ate birds-nest soup in a Hong Kong restaurant in the 1890s, chances are the nest came for Gomantong Caves. Today, these limestone caves remain Sabah's most famous source of the swiftlet nests used for birds-nest soup, Chinese medicines, and other luxury products. But other caves producing these coveted clumps of swiftlet saliva are far easier for independent travellers to visit.

The most prized white nests of these small birds can sell for as much as RM2000 per kilogram. That explains why villagers shimmy up bamboo poles or climb rickety rattan scaffolding to the cave roofs for their booty. Unlike Kalimantan, urban swiftlet homes (see p249) are rare in Sabah, so harvests come from caves such as Gomantong. Concerns have grown as populations have shrunk in recent years due to the harvesting of nests before swiftlet young are mature.

The caves are 5km south off the road to Sukau, 20km from the main highway, difficult, but not impossible, for visitors to reach without their own transport. The easiest way to see the caves is via tour from Sandakan; most operators include a visit as part of their standard Sungai Kinabatangan package.

The area around the caves is covered in forest and dense vegetation, concealing plenty of wildlife and some good walks. The most accessible of the caves is a 10-minute walk along the trail near the **information centre** (☎ 089-230-189; www.sabah.gov.my/jhl; adult/child RM30/15; ☸ 8am-noon & 2-4.30pm). Head past the living quarters of the nest collectors to get to the main cave, **Simud Hitam** (Black Cave). You can venture in, though it involves wading through ankle-deep guano alive with cockroaches and other insects.

The left-hand trail from the office leads to the top of the mountain. After a few metres the trail forks again. To the right, a 15-minute walk brings you to a top entrance to the cave, while the left-hand trail continues for 30 minutes and leads high up the mountain to **Simud Putih** (White Cave). This cave contains the more valuable white nests. Both trails are steep and require some sweaty rock climbing.

From Sandakan, minivans go directly to Sukau (RM15). Ask to be dropped at the turn-off for the caves. You can also take a minivan for Lahad Datu, get out at the Sukau junction and take another van to the cave turn-off (each leg costs RM10). Either way, you'll have to walk 5km from the turn-off to the ticket office, unless there's a vehicle going down at the same time. Bring your passport (or a photocopy) for the guard at the gatepost.

If you're spending some time in Borneo, note that the great caves of Gunung Mulu and Niah national parks in Sarawak are more spectacular and easier to reach independently than

Gomantong. Even the Madai Caves (p148) near Lahad Datu are more accessible

SUNGAI KINABATANGAN
☎ 089

Sungai Kinabatangan is Sabah's longest river and, as odd as it seems, a man-made natural wonder. Intensive logging and development of oil-palm plantations nearby have left wildlife trapped on the flood plain along the final third of Sungai Kinabatangan's 560km as it approaches the Sulu Sea. The result is an astonishing array of species in a narrow strip of riverine forest, mainly visible while cruising the river's muddy waters.

Big-name wildlife includes orangutans and proboscis monkeys in trees lining river banks, plus flat-headed cats at night along Sungai Menungal, a Kinabatangan tributary. Inside the forest, look for marbled cats, samba deer, and giant squirrels. Long-tailed and pig-tailed macaques are rife. The big prize among mammals is the elephant, rare enough to be a treat but with decent odds of spotting success.

Bird-watchers commonly spot all eight varieties of Borneo's hornbills, plus brightly coloured pittas, kingfishers, and, with elephant luck, Storm's stork or the wacky Oriental darter, also known as the snake bird. Reptiles, including crocodiles, also frequent the Kinabatangan, both in riverine forest areas and mangrove estuaries, so keep any limbs you value inside the boat.

Mammals can be seen anytime of year. They move around the area, and groups will sometimes break up to travel around or through plantations. Birds are more numerous and varied during rainy season, October to March, which coincides with northern-hemisphere migrations. Though friendly for birds, the rainy season isn't very accommodating for humans, or for most lodging in the area. Due to local and global factors, heavy rains now continue deep into March and annual flooding has grown more severe. Most camps are shut down for a time during the wet season. On the flip side, wait too long into the dry season to visit and oxbow lakes go dry.

Your success spotting wildlife depends on the vagaries of migrations, but the location you select and the preparation and skill of guides also matter, especially if you stray from the beaten track. Ask lots of questions and be sceptical of vague answers. With the right help and dollop of luck, you'll enjoy the Kinabatangan for the wonderland it truly is.

Sleeping & Eating

Tour operators in KK or Sandakan can organise a trip, most often nowadays to their own lodges. Alternatively, make arrangements directly with your selected accommodation. Even if you choose to travel independently, lodges often insist on selling you not just their room, but their tour package including wildlife cruises and/or treks, plus transport from Sandakan, which can be convenient. In addition to accommodation details, transport modes can explain package price differences. Boats from Sandakan to camps are more pleasant and offer the bonus of wildlife watching, but usually cost more than riding in a van.

JUNGLE CAMPS

Uncle Tan's Wildlife Camp (☎ 531-639; www.uncletan.com) Its folksy website accurately reflects the welcoming atmosphere at hugely popular Uncle Tan's, run by the deceased founder's family. The standard package costs RM320 for a three-day, two-night stay in the forest, including meals, boat safaris, jungle treks and transport from its office/B&B in Gum Gum (see p140). Accommodation here is very basic; rough huts with no doors or windows and a mosquito net. You'll want plenty of mosquito repellent; fortunately, Uncle Tan's sell its own, highly effective brew at the camp. The location is prone to flooding, but remains open as long as possible in the rains. Book early for peak periods.

Kinabatangan Jungle Camp (☎ 019-804-7756; labukbb@yahoo.com) This camp located on the edge of the Lower Kinabatangan Wildlife Sanctuary is more upmarket than Uncle Tan's with facilities that rival most lodges, including hot showers. Packages from Sandakan start from RM330 for an overnight trip.

LODGES

Sukau is the main village on the lower Kinabatangan, 42km off the main highway between Lahad Datu and Sandakan. Lodges operated by tour companies near Sukau offer wildlife experiences and more, often luxuriously. There's not much difference between them – all have comfortable, mosquito-proof rooms with fan and bathroom, meals and bar (drinks extra), and trained guides.

SABAH

On a twin-share basis, expect to pay RM250 upwards per person per night at a lodge, including transfers and activities. Many tours include Gomantong Caves as part of the package, but you can opt out if you wish. For tours from Sandakan, see p135. Other reliable lodges include:

Sukau Rainforest Lodge (☎ 088-438-300; www .sukau.com) Luxury lodge run by Borneo Eco Tours with overnight packages from RM750.

Nature Lodge Kinabatangan (☎ 088-230-534; www.nasalislarvatustours.com) Located on high ground near Bilit, the owners say flooding is not an issue. Dorm packages from RM300, chalets from RM335.

OTHER ACCOMMODATION

For a taste of village life, as well as wildlife, try bed and breakfast accommodation, mainly around Sukau. Originally established for independent travel, B&Bs now often market packages – meals, tours and transfers – in addition to, or instead of, rooms only. In Sukau, you can hire a local guide for day trips on the river and its tributaries. A three-hour cruise costs around RM100.

Sukau B&B (☎ 230-269; camping RM5, r incl breakfast per person RM20) Built high on stilts over the river, 1km east of the Sukau village, this friendly guesthouse is one of the last places to flood when the river rises. It's also one of the last places to sell accommodation only. It can arrange boats and transfers on request.

Sambil B&B (☎ 019-8420895; overnight package per person RM145) A new entrant with chalet-style rooms including bath and fan, with electricity to turn it. Bilit location minimises flood risk.

Sukau Tomanggong Riverview Lodge (☎ 235-525; nbsafari@streamyx.com; overnight package per person RM230) A convert from selling rooms to tour packages, this pleasant spot by the river features small cabins with attached baths. Its terrace restaurant serves Malay meals and cold beer (not included in your package).

Getting There & Away

Minivans go to Sukau from Sandakan (RM15, two hours), or you can take a minivan to Lahad Datu and get out at the Sukau turn-off. Expect to wait a while for a minivan from here to Sukau (RM10, one to 1½ hours). If you're on a package, transport will be provided. The last 45km to Sukau is along a gravel road that becomes a mud track in rain. Public transport is often suspended when it's wet; 4WD transport is available from

Sandakan or Lahad Datu, or maybe through your accommodation.

If you're heading south from Sukau, ask to be dropped at the highway, where you can catch a minivan to Lahad Datu or possibly a bus to Semporna or Tawau to save repeating the long drive from Sandakan.

LAHAD DATU
☎ 089 / pop156,000

With a small flat area along the bay hemmed in by a large hill, Lahud Datu resembles Sandakan, but its 19th century legacy is pirates, not plutocrats. The nearby village of Tungku was an infamous base for the Lanun brigands, who did a sideline in slave trading. There's still piracy in these waters with speedboats and machines guns rather than schooners and sabres, so stick to land, lubber, and be warned that the waterfront with some ATMs gets deserted after dark.

Modern Lahad Datu is an upstairs-downstairs urban affair. Drivers of boxy Protons honk their horns to offer rides between the two sections for RM3. The lower town has everything tourists need – hotels, restaurants, shopping, buses – except the offices of tour companies, and they're the reason travellers stop in Lahad Datu. Make connections here to Danum Valley and Tabin Wildlife Reserve.

Borneo Nature Tours (☎ 880-207; www.brl.com.my; Block 3, Lot 20, Fajar Centre) and the **Danum Valley Field Centre** (☎ 881-092; Block 3, Fajar Centre) have offices next to each other in the upper part of town.

Around the block, there's the office of **Tabin Wildlife** (☎ 887-620; twrlhd@tm.net.my; Block 2, Lot 17, Fajar Centre), franchisee for Tabin Wildlife Reserve (see p148). If you plan to visit the reserve independently, it's best to contact the **Wildlife Department office** (Pejabat Hidupan Liar; ☎ 884-416), just in case a permit is necessary. It's four blocks south of the Danum Valley Field Centre office. Tour agencies around the Fajar centre service the Sungai Sabahan area between Lahad Datu and Kunak, a getaway mainly for local residents.

Even though travellers come to Lahad Datu to go elsewhere, transport schedules make it difficult not spend a night here at one end of an excursion at least.

Sleeping

Hotels are in lower part of town, and walking from one end to the other is easy.

Tabin Lodge (☎ 889-552; Jln Urus Setia Kecil; r RM20-45; 🔀) The building with the red front diagonal from the bus station has a variety of funky but comfy rooms. Cheapest ones have cold shower and a toilet outside, and none have TVs. There are lounges on each level to share soap operas or soccer broadcasts, and they can get loud if your room is close. Staff are fabulously friendly and cooperative, for instance keeping luggage while you're visiting a reserve.

Mido Hotel (☎ 881-800; fax 881487; r RM52-92; 🔀) A hulking facade, unimpressive lobby and halls hide smart, modern rooms, all including TV, bathtub and hot water. Economy rooms are nearest the first-floor disco, which gets rocking around 10 nightly. It's located at the northwest corner of the lower town's main shopping square.

Executive Hotel (☎ 881-333; 239-240 Jln Teratai; r incl breakfast RM100-150; 🔀) The top business hotel in town has plush, elegant rooms. Discounts run about 30 percent on weekends.

Several hotels, mainly in the budget category, are located around Jln Seroja, near the Chinese temple:

Hotel Unimas (☎ 885-511; fax 881-155; Jln Seroja; r RM55-65; 🔀) Well-equipped rooms with a fresh feel.

Hotel Perdana (☎ 881-166; fax 881-661; Jln Seroja; r 76.50-93.50; 🔀) New business-class contender with wi-fi in its lobby coffee-shop.

Eating

Azura (Jln Tertai; mains RM2-7; 🕑 24hr) This open-air stop on the eastern edge of town has a full range of Malay food plus pick-your-fish barbecue.

Kopi Tiam (Jln Kianbang; mains RM2.50-9; 🕑 24hr) *Kedai kopi* Chinese style, just west of the main shopping block.

Sakura Seafood (☎ 885-623; Block K; Jln Tertai; mains from RM7; 🕑 lunch & dinner) The place in lower town for Chinese food features a big grill outside with fish and shellfish on ice. No menu, bring a group and chow down.

Food stalls for basic Malay food open nightly beside the post office parking lot. Self-catering from **Millemewa Shopping Centre** (Jln Kastam Lama) on the west side of the main shopping square.

Getting There & Away

MASwings (☎ 1800-88-3000, 03-7843-3000) currently operates four daily flights to Lahad Datu. The airport is in the upper part of town.

Express buses on the KK–Tawau route stop at the Shell station near the Danum Valley office in the upper part of town. Other buses and minivans leave from a vacant lot near the waterfront in the lower part of town, with a helpful information kiosk on site. There are frequent departures for Sandakan (RM20, 2½ hours), Sukau (RM12, two hours), Semporna (RM15, two hours) and Tawau (RM18, 2½ hours). All transport to Semporna and Tawau pass the Kunak turn-off for Madai Caves (RM10). There are plenty of services to all these places until around 3pm, and share-taxis are also available. Charter vehicles and 4WDs wait in an adjacent lot.

DANUM VALLEY CONSERVATION AREA & BORNEO RAINFOREST LODGE

The **Danum Valley Conservation Area** (DVCA) is part of the Yayasan Sabah Forestry Management Area, a vast tract of land in southeast Sabah under the control of **Yayasan Sabah** (The Sabah Foundation; www.ysnet.org.my), a semigovernmental organisation tasked with both protecting and utilising the forest resources of Sabah. Yayasan Sabah also manages Maliau Basin Conservation Area (see p154). While Maliau Basin is only really suitable for physically fit people who don't mind roughing it, Danum Valley can be comfortably visited by anyone, and it still offers the chance to get right inside primary tropical rainforest.

The 438-square-kilometre Danum Valley Conservation Area was established in 1981 in recognition of the area's incredible biodiversity. **Danum Valley Field Centre** (www.ysnet .org.my/Maliau/Danum/location.htm) gives preference to researchers, but other travellers can spare its collegial, if spartan atmosphere. A more luxurious way to experience Danum Valley is by staying at **Borneo Rainforest Lodge** (BRL; www.brl .com.my), a comfortable resort overlooking the Sungai Danum in the midst of teeming primary jungle. For those who can afford it, BRL combines a real jungle experience with all the comforts of an international-class resort.

Like Maliau Basin, Danum Valley is one of the world's great storehouses of genetic diversity. It is one of the best places in the world to observe wild orangutans in their natural habitat, and visitors who spend a few days at the lodge have at least even odds of making a sighting. Sightings of gibbons, red-leaf monkeys and wild boar are just about guaranteed, and Asian elephants, mouse deer and

THE ORANGUTANS OF DANUM VALLEY *Tomoko Kanamori*

According to Dr Marc Ancrenaz, who is performing a detailed study of orangutans in the Sungai Kinabatangan area, there are about 11,000 orangutans in Sabah. Of these, about 500 are believed to live in the Danum Valley. Since 2004, Japanese primatologists have been studying the orangutans who live around Borneo Rainforest Lodge (BRL), which is located in the Danum Valley Conservation Area. About 16 orangutans live near BRL, and at any one time visitors to the lodge have a reasonable chance of spotting two or three of them.

Many people glamourise the study of orangutans. The reality is quite different. Here is what one famous primatologist, John McKinnon, had to say about it from *The Ape Within Us* (1978):

'When eventually all the pain and effort pay off and the orang-utan is finally found, is the ardent ape-hunter rewarded by witnessing one of nature's great spectaculars? He is not. He finds a shaggy, surly bundle of complete inactivity. Cousin orang turns out to be the most slothful creature, and only by constantly reminding himself how lucky he is to see such a rare and exotic animal on such intimate terms can the primatologist fight off the urge to head straight back home. He must steel himself to remain in mutual contemplation with his subject for the long tedious hours of observation that are necessary to achieve those rare moments of interest and novelty that the orang offers as the only medals for persistence in this game.'

The great bulk of our work consists of waiting for the orangutans as they rest motionless in the shade of leaves high up in 30-metre rainforest trees. Because this work can be so boring, most primatologists do not want to make orangutans the sole subject of their study.

Walking in the forest with a BRL guide there is a relatively good chance of seeing some orangutans. However, since these are wild animals in a protected zone, it's difficult to get really close to them the way you might at a place like Sepilok Orang-Utan Rehabilitation Centre. Also, unfortunately, it is not possible to accompany primate researchers in the field and we do not seek volunteers to help us. If you would like to help with the study of wild orangutans in the field, I recommend that you visit the following website: www.redapeencounters.com.

Tomoko Kanamori is a researcher from Kyoto University in Kyoto, Japan, working with Dr Noko Kuze to study the orangutans of Danum Valley.

barking deer are fairly common. You'll also see a brilliant variety of tree species, moths, butterflies, fungi and flowers. The lodge is also very popular with bird-watchers.

Leeches are also there in abundance and we strongly recommend that you bring a pair of leech socks and a relaxed attitude to the harmless, if revolting, creatures.

Sights & Activities
JUNGLE WALKS

The main activity at BRL is walking on the trails which surround the lodge. While you are permitted to walk alone and the trails are quite easy to follow and well-marked, the lodge provides guides for all the walks as part of your accommodation. We recommend going with a guide for at least one of your walks each day, since they tend to have incredibly keen eyes, ears and noses and they can spot creatures that you'd miss on your own. They can also explain a lot about what's going on in the forest. The trails are all relatively short and can be done in an hour or two, which makes

it possible to do two routes a day, with a nice lunch break in between.

The **Coffincliff Trail** is a good way to start your exploration of the area and get your bearings. It climbs to a cliff in which the remains of some Dusun coffins can be seen (although the provenance of the coffins is unclear). Above this, you climb to a viewpoint which looks over the Sungai Danum and the lodge. You can either return the way you've come or detour around the back of the peak to descend via scenic **Fairy Falls** and **Serpent Falls**, a pair of 15m falls that are good for a cooling dip. Whichever way you go, you'll want to take a plunge in the Jacuzzi Pool near the base of the trail. The whole circuit can be done in a leisurely two hours.

The **Danum Trail**, **Elephant Trail** and **Segama Trails** all follow various sections of the Sungai Danum and are mostly flat and easy trails which allow good chances for wildlife spotting. All can be done in an hour or two. The **Hornbill Trail** and **East Trail** have a few ups and downs but are still relatively easy, with similarly good chances for wildlife sightings. Finally, if you just need a quick breathe of fresh air after a meal, the **Nature Trail** is a short plankwalk near the lodge that allows you walk into the forest unmolested by leeches.

CANOPY WALKWAY

As you probably know, most of the action in a tropical rainforest happens up in the forest canopy, which can be frustrating for earthbound humans. The lodge's 107m canopy walkway provides a good chance to get up where the action is. It's located on the access road, a 10-minute walk from the lodge. It traverses a nice section of forest, with several fine mengaris and majau trees on either side. Bird-watchers often come here at dawn in hopes of 'bagging' a few species. Even if you're not a keen birder, it's worth rolling out of bed early to see the sun come up over the forest from the canopy walkway – when there's a bit of mist around, the effect is quite magical.

NIGHT DRIVES

The forest around the lodge really comes alive when the 'night shift' comes on. A guided night-walk through the forest is a great way to see the night creatures, but for those who want to do their wildlife spotting in comfort, a night drive is a great way to go. You sit in the back of an open truck with a guide seated above the cab of the truck pointing out animals with a spotlight. Truck leave the lodge after dinner every evening. Sure, it's not the most ecofriendly or aesthetically pleasing way to experience the forest, but it beats walking down a dark trail wondering if that's a log you're stepping over or a hungry python.

You have a decent chance of seeing wild boar, sambar deer, mouse deer and flying squirrels, and if you're really lucky, you might come upon an elephant or two on the road ahead of you. Even more than forest walks, night drives are really hit or miss affairs. Sometimes the truck returns to the lodge with all the passengers chattering excitedly about all the cool creatures they saw. Other times, folks try to make the best of a lone squirrel sighting. The best way to go into it is to think of it as a nice way to take the night air and enjoy the starry sky, with all wildlife sightings mere lucky windfalls.

Things you'll be glad you brought include a light waterproof jacket, camera with flash, binoculars and a powerful torch.

BIRD-WATCHING

Danum Valley is very popular with bird-watchers from around the world, who come here to bag a whole variety of Southeast Asian rainforest species, including the great argus pheasant, crested fireback pheasant, several species of hornbill, blue-headed pitta and Borneo bristlehead, among many others. Some of the guides at the lodge are particularly knowledgeable about birds and attempts are made to match birders up with these guides. The access road and canopy walkway are good for early morning bird sightings and you'll likely make a few worthwhile sightings right from the veranda of your cabin.

Sleeping & Eating

The **Borneo Rainforest Lodge** (BRL; ☎ 088-267-637; www.brl.com.my; standard/deluxe three-day/two-night full-board packages from RM1300/1500) has a total of 31 semidetached and fully-detached cabins connected by wooden walkways with the main building/office/dining room. These cabins contain a mix of standard and deluxe rooms.

Deluxe rooms have nice river/mountain views which you can enjoy from their spacious verandas. These rooms are spacious, comfortable and very pleasant – indeed, you might think you're in an international-class hotel room somewhere else in the world until you look out the window to see the teeming rainforest. Some of the deluxe units have bathtubs and all have hot water and showers. Several of the deluxe cabins are currently under renovation and when they're done, they'll have outdoor bathtubs in which you can soak while enjoying the view of the jungle.

The standard rooms are simpler but perfectly adequate, with hot showers and small porches. Some of these rooms have nice river views, while others have less inspiring views of the nearby forest. Some of these are fully detached, which is nice if you like your privacy. These are very good value indeed.

There is the Royal Chalet, which contains three extradeluxe rooms, although, truth be told, these aren't really much better than the deluxe rooms.

Meals are served in the main dining room in the main building. 'Dining room' is something

SABAH

of a misnomer as it's open to the jungle on two sides and has a fine dining section on a long veranda overlooking the river and mountain. Meals are of a pretty high standard and there is always at least one vegetarian option. Dinners include both Asian and Western dishes, as well as salad, bread, rice and a good dessert spread. Overall, you're unlikely to eat this well in the middle of the rainforest anywhere else in the world. There's also a bar that serves a variety of alcoholic drinks.

Danum Valley Field Centre (☎ 089-881092; d RM66) Scientists and researchers get priority here, and receptivity to tourists varies with management's moods and relations with BRL. But if you can stay here – in separate male and female dormitories with bunk beds and cold-water showers – your naturalist bunkmates are a bonus, sharing findings on research from butterflies to biodiversity. Communal dining and lounge enhance the collegial atmosphere. To make friends fast, bring a case of beer from Lahad Datu. Though much cheaper than DRL, a stay here including RM60 daily for meals and RM40 for transfer each way from Lahad Datu, still runs into money.

Getting There & Away
Borneo Rainforest Lodge is 81km by dirt road from Lahad Datu. Airport pick-up and drop-off is included in accommodation packages.

TABIN WILDLIFE RESERVE
Palm-oil plantations and logged tracts have captured some of Sabah's rarest animals at **Tabin Wildlife Reserve** (☎ 088-264-071; www.tabin wildlife.com.my). The reserve, 48km east of Lahad Datu down a gravel road, is run by the Forestry & Wildlife Department, though visitor facilities are franchised to a private company.

The 1205-square-kilometer reserve consists mainly of lowland dipterocarp forest with mangrove areas at the northern end. Tabin is not entirely primary forest, but that doesn't seem to trouble the wildlife. The stars here are elephants, with primates – orangutans, proboscis monkeys, red-leaf monkey and macaques – running behind the pachyderms. Bird life is abundant, and there's a herd of the endangered Sumatran rhino, though you're unlikely to see any of these incredibly shy creatures.

Several mud volcanoes, similar to those on Pulau Tiga, dot Tabin. Along with salt-water springs, they are important sources of minerals for animals and great spots for viewing wildlife.

Intra Travel Service (☎ 088-261-558; www.intra -travel.com.my; lvl 1, no 5, Airport Terminal 2, Jln Old Airport; Kota Kinabalu) in KK and **Tabin Wildlife** (☎ 887-620; twrlhd@tm.net.my; Block 2, Lot 17, Fajar Centre) in Lahad Datu are agents for the officially franchised visitor accommodation. Day trips cost RM168 per person. Overnight packages in Tabin Wildlife Resort's very comfortable chalets, with air-con and hot showers run RM565 for one night, RM840 for two nights, per person.

The rainy season of 2007 at least temporarily washed away the more economical option of 'eco-tented platforms'. Camping is possible, but bring leech socks and plenty of bug spray, as well as your own tents. If you have transport and plan on visiting Tabin independently, contact the **Wildlife Department office** (Pejabat Hidupan Liar; ☎ 089-884-416) in Lahad Datu for details on permit requirements.

MADAI CAVES
Less renowned than Gomantong Caves to the north, these limestone caves prized for birds' nests are within easier reach for travellers. Exploring Madai Caves independently is not an option, however. The caves shelter ancestral tombs – artefacts date back 15,000 years – and entry requires permission from the local villagers. They keep a careful eye on both ancient bones and savoury bird spit. The eyes of a local guide are also essential to exploring the dark, slippery cave interior. Guides wait at the village entrance, and their fees are subject to negotiation; the going rate is around RM30. For best views, bring your own torch.

A sprawling shanty *kampung* of wooden shacks near the cave entrance serves as temporary accommodation for nest collectors. Harvests take place three times a year and are a spectacle, with collectors setting up a maze of bamboo poles, clambering up to the cave roof to capture their prizes.

The caves are 3km off the Lahad Datu–Tawau road, outside the village of Kunak, 69km south of Lahad Datu. All buses and minivans between Lahad Datu and Semporna or Tawau pass the turn-off; you may be able to get a local minivan from there to take you right to the caves. Many long-distance minivans also stop at the station in Kunak, where minivans as well as private 'taxis' (RM3 to 5) provide transport to the caves.

SEMPORNA

☎ 089 / pop 130,000

The best places to stay in Semporna are about an hour out of town – surrounded by clear waters and some of the world's best coral reefs. The islands of **Tun Sakaran Marine Park** (conservation fee RM40) include dive sites that are the highlight of many scuba fans' underwater dives.

If you forego island accommodation, Semporna makes a pleasant base for diving and snorkelling trips. It's a very simple town for visitors. Buses and minivans drop passengers in the centre of town, all half-dozen blocks of it, between the Shell and Esso petrol stations. There's a **Maybank** (☎ 784-852) on Jln Jakarullah. The market, wharfs, dive operators, plus more hotels and restaurants are reached via the southern road at the traffic circle with a concrete sunfish leaping from it.

Diving

Most operators have offices in the Semporna Ocean Tourism Centre (SOTC), a stilt complex over the water off Jln Kastam or next to the market in shophouse blocks along the docks, known as Semporna Seafront (officially 'New Town Centre'). Some of the dive outfits listed, and others, have offices in Tawau (see p151) or KK (see p91). Check the certification of any operator before signing on.

Arung Hayat Resort (☎ 016-8158197; Pulau Mabul) Very basic budget longhouse homestay on Mabul (per person incl meals RM50) with its own dive operation. Also provides accommodation for day-trip operators from Semporna.

Blue Sea Divers (☎ 781-322; mikealan3068@yahoo .com; Semporna Seafront) Day-trip specialist; request chicken curry for lunch.

Borneo Jungle River Island Tours (Uncle Chang; ☎ 781-789; unclechang99@hotmail.com; SOTC) Offers diving and snorkelling day trips, plus stays at its friendly budget lodge on Mabul (per person RM50) and more aspirational resort on Maiga (per person RM60) with discounted dives for guests. Trips often culminate in a boozy dinner back in Semporna with legendary owner Uncle Chang.

Pulau Sipidan Resort & Tours (☎ 761-899; www .sipidan-resort.com; Jln Kastam) Top-end company with resorts on Kapalai and Lankayan, head office in Tawau. Three-night dive packages are US$590.

Reef (☎ 782-080; www.mataking.com; Jln Kastam) Packages to its resort on Pulau Mataking, one hour from Semporna.

Scuba Junkie (☎ 785-372; www.scuba-junkie.com; 36 Semporna Seafront; s incl breakfast RM60) Very popular operator with international staff, its own hostel (dorm beds for divers incl breakfast RM15) on the wharf, and attached restaurant serving Semporna's best pizza.

Sipidan Mabul Resort (www.sipidan-mabul.com) Range of accommodation from plain bungalows to luxury chalets along Mabul's best stretch of beach. Enjoy sea views from the swimming pool deck and massage tub. Three-night dive packages are US$749.

Sipidan Scuba (☎ 781-788; www.northborneo.net; SOTC) Veteran, very professional operator formerly known as North Borneo Dive & Sea Sports with offices in Tawau and Semporna. Enjoy après-dive cold soft drinks or beer on its waterfront terrace.

Sipidan Water Village (☎ 784-100; www.swvresort .com; Jln Kastam) Mabul resort featuring elegant bungalows on stilts over water with prices to match. Great for diving honeymoons. Three-night dive packages are US$940.

Package prices differ enormously, depending on type of accommodation and whether they include transport to Semporna. Reserving a spot at least a day in advance is required for Pulau Sipidan along with an additional RM40 conservation fee (See p150).

If you reach Semporna on your own, a two-/three-dive day package costs around RM300 per person, including equipment and boat transport (bringing your own gear should earn discounts). Snorkellers pay about half the diver price, and a three-day PADI open-water course costs about RM750. Prices for bookings from KK or abroad may be several times higher. Walk-in rates can be negotiable during low season, and rollercoaster relations between operators can also lead to special deals during periodic feuds.

Sleeping

The advent of budget and midrange accommodation on the islands – at the time of research, several new places were in various stages of development – radically expand options for travellers. But Semporna offers good value at the low end.

Lee's Resthouse & Café (☎ 784-491; suisan@ streamyx.com; Jln Shop Block; r RM40-60; 🔲 🖳) Near the bus drop in the town centre, this friendly hotel gives good value with very modern, comfortable rooms. Its air-con restaurant is a soothing oasis with Western, Chinese and Malay favourites.

Dragon Inn (☎ 781-088; www.dragoninnfloating .com.my; 1 Jln Kastam; dm RM15, r incl breakfast RM66-300;

🔀 🖥) Everyone seems to stay here; as with Sepilok Jungle Resort, it's difficult to suss just why. Dorms are cramped, the all-wood rooms on stilts over the harbour sound better than they perform, and the design of this sprawling harbourside complex makes everything a hike, inside and out.

Seafest Hotel (☎ 782-333; www.seafesthotel.com; Jln Kastam; r incl breakfast RM90-180 plus 10% tax; 🔀) Six storeys of bay-view, business-class comfort past SOTC. Affiliated with Seafest fishery, so check the restaurant's catch of the day.

More options:

Damai Travellers Lodge (☎ 782-011; Jln Masjid, s/d from RM30/45; 🔀) Aging cleanly.

City Inn (☎ 784-733; Jln Bangunan Hing Long; s/d from 40/60; 🔀) Newer, but not all rooms have windows.

Eating

The market has good breakfast options from vendors or in its café area. At night, Malay stalls open alongside the market and behind the Tawau minivan area in the town centre. Several Chinese style *kedai kopi* between Lee's Rest House and the main road offer tasty fish and seafood specialities plus cold beer. Beyond Lee's, find Milemewa Superstore for self-catering.

Anjung Paghalian Café (Jln Kastam, meals RM3-5; 🕙 dinner) Beside the Tun Sarakan Marine Park entrance sign, this indoor/outdoor place on a pier features fish, prawn, chicken, squid, venison sold by portion (for two or more people) and cooked in your choice of up to 12 different styles. It also has standard Malay hawker stalls and even one which serves burgers.

Mabul Steak House (☎ 781-785; Semporna Seafront; meals from RM4.90; 🕙 lunch & dinner) This easygoing, balcony restaurant's large and glacial 'ice-blended juices' are a soothing antidote for sucking bottled air. For further chilling, there's a leather couch and overstuffed chairs around a huge TV showing movies or sports. The RM4.90 and RM7.90 set meals won't leave you cold – or hungry.

Getting There & Away

Minivans to/from Tawau (RM10, 1½ hours) stop at the edge of the town centre near the main road. Lahad Datu (RM20, 2½ hours) and Sandakan (RM35, 5½ hours) minivans are at the other edge, at the corner of Jln Masjid and Jln PG Jaji. All run from early morning until 4pm.

Morning and night buses to Kota Kinabalu (585km, 10½ hours) leave from a lot just north of the Lahad Datu minivan area starting around 7am and 7pm. **Dayana Express** (☎ 784-494; Jln Hospital) has the cleanest air-con buses and most professional operation, with a ticket booth and bright cafeteria open all day. The 7.30am and 7.30pm departures to KK (RM58.50) go via Kunak, Lahad Datu, Sandakan Batu 32, and Ranau.

TUN SAKARAN MARINE PARK

Sabah's newest and largest marine park, gazetted in 2004 and also known as **Semporna Islands Marine Park** (conservation fee RM40), covers 325 sq km of tropical waters, including dive sites widely classed among the top 10 in the world. The best dive seasons run April to July/August, with the first three months outstanding and during November to December, but the marine life is breathtaking year round.

Pulau Sipadan, perhaps the most famous island in Borneo, 36km off the southeast coast is a true volcanic atoll, the tip of a limestone pinnacle that rises 600m from the seabed, and rightly attracts divers from all over the world. Since 2005, overnight stays on Sipadan have been prohibited, and the overall number of divers is limited to 120 per day, with a day's advance registration required.

Many of the other islands in and around the park also offer good diving and have been developed for accommodation as well, including **Mabul**, **Lankayan**, **Mataking**, **Maiga** and **Sibuan**, plus a purpose-built rig resort on the **Kapalai** sandbar. New accommodation, budget backpacker dives to splashy resorts, are springing up fast, with **Pulau Pom Pong** a hotbed

The kidnappings of tourists from Sipadan by gunmen from the nearby Philippines in 2000, plus potential threats from Indonesia, which lost its claim to Sipadan in 2002 World Court decision, guarantee a major military and police presence. The patrols also protect against dynamite fishing and illegal hunting of sea turtles and their eggs. In terms of preserving Tun Sakaran's treasures, crime did pay.

Diving

Dives are conducted from early morning until after dark by all operators (no night dives at Sipadan). Most day trips leave Semporna by 8am and return around 3pm. Qualified dive masters must accompany each group and should brief divers on local conditions. Currents over the reefs can be quite strong.

Sipadan's **near-vertical 'wall'** off its eastern shore is one of the most famous sites in the park, and the world, where colourful tropical fish swim near the surface and huge groupers and wrasse nose about below, green turtles occasionally whizzing by. Throughout the park, there are schools of barracuda and tuna, reef sharks by the dozens on the seabed, occasional whale sharks and friendly hammerheads. Snorkelling is possible at all dive sites, with good visibility and plenty to see.

Boat transfers to your chosen site(s) should be included in any dive package. Hiring a fishing boat for a day trip from Semporna costs around RM250.

TAWAU
☎ 089 / pop 331,000

After seeing its urban core hollow out in recent years, Tawau is making a comeback. This port near Indonesia – with ferry connections across the border to Nunukan and Tarakan – has grown rich shipping timber, rubber, Manila hemp, cocoa, copra, tobacco and palm oil. Now it seems ready to dress the part, with a burgeoning smart restaurant district and a new multiplex cinema (four screens and counting), all designed to lure suburbanites and their money back to the town centre. Website www.etawau.com has a good line on the local buzz.

Despite the progress, desolate pockets remain after dark. Particularly around the local bus terminus, dog packs are big and loud enough to cause distress, and street lighting could use an upgrade. But what's really missing there at night are people.

The lure for travellers is the border: Tawau is the only crossing point with Kalimantan where foreigners can get a visa to enter Indonesia. The (so far) low-profile Indonesian Consulate (see below), about 200m beyond Tawau Hospital, has remained fast and friendly while foreigners have been few. But even the most successful application will likely require staying for at least the night before and after. If you've just come for diving, go directly to Semporna.

Information
Asiatic Travel & Tours (☎ 755-688; myasiatictravel@ yahoo.com; 1st fl, TB 3478, Jln Masjid) Managing director

Wing-Kan Nip has a foot in mainland China, another in San Francisco Bay, and a base in Tawau where he uncovers East Sabah's off-the-beaten track attractions.
City Internet Zone (☎ 760-016; 37 Kompleks Fajar, Jln Perbandaran; per hr RM2-3; ☺ 9am-midnight)
HSBC (Jln Perbandaran)
Indonesian consulate (☎ 772-052; 752-969; Jln Tanjong Batu; ☺ 8am-noon, 1-4pm) Efficient one-day service (usually) for visas.
Maybank (☎ 762-333; Jln Dunlop)
PH Moneychanger (☎ 776-389; Kompleks Kojasa) Changes cash in harbour area.

Diving
Roach Reef, halfway between Tawau and Pulau Sipadan, is mainly used for PADI training. It's better to do training in KK or Tun Sakaran Marine Park to avoid lengthy boat rides, or just to enjoy a more attractive dive site.

Most dive operators offer transport to Samporna.
Pro Divers (☎ 778-128; upper fl, Sabindo Plaza) Dive-equipment retailer also offering courses and trips.
Pulau Sipadan Resort & Tours (☎ 765-200; www .sipadan-resort.com; 1st fl, 484 Bandar Sabindo) Bookings for its dive resorts in Kapalai and Lankayan.
Reef Dive Resort & Tours (☎ 770-022; www.matak ing.com; Heritage Hotel, Jln Bunga) Diving from its resort on Pulau Mataking.
Sipadan Scuba (☎ 942-788; www.northborneo.net; 3rd fl, 581 Jln Haji Karim, Tacoln Complex, Fajar) Formerly known as North Borneo Dive & Sea Sports, offering dive courses as well as trips to Sipadan, Roach Reef and other islands. Office in Samporna.
Sipadan Water Village Resort (☎ 752-996; www .swvresort.com; 1st fl, Jln Bunga) Runs the luxurious stilt resort on Pulau Mabul; entrance just south of Air Asia sales office.

Sleeping
There's good selection of midrange hotels, catering to small business travellers. Except as noted, all rooms have telephone and private bath with hot water.

Hotel Soon Yee (☎ 772-447; 1362 Jln Stephen Tan; r RM22-38; ☻) No prostitutes, no phones, no hot water (except in shared bathrooms), no link to Woody Allen, but lots of value and camaraderie in this guesthouse. Cheaper fan-cooled rooms have shared bathrooms.
Loong Hotel (☎ 778-100; 3868 Jln Abaca; r RM45-60; ☻) Very well-kept place with spacious, occasionally boxy rooms and a homely atmosphere in a quiet area north of the bus station. *Kedai kopi* below has good dim sum and noodles

TAWAU

0 _____ 200 m
0 _____ 0.1 miles

INFORMATION		
Asiatic Travel & Tours	1	B3
City Internet Zone	2	D3
HSBC	3	D3
Maybank	4	C3
PH Moneychanger	5	A4

SIGHTS & ACTIVITIES		
Pro Divers	6	D3
Pulau Sipadan Resort & Tours	7	C4
Reef Dive Resort & Tours	8	C3
Sipadan Scuba	9	C3
Sipadan Water Village Resort	10	C3

SLEEPING		
Belmont Marco Polo	11	B3
First Hotel	12	C3
Hotel Soon Yee	13	B3
Kingston Hotel	14	C3
Loong Hotel	15	A3
North Borneo Hotel	16	B3
North City Hotel	17	A3

EATING		
Good View	18	C4
Kam Ling	19	C4
Milimewa Superstore	20	C3
Milimewa Superstore	21	A4
Restoran Aul Bismillah	22	B4

Restoran Rasa Sayang	23	D2
Sidewalk Café	24	D3
Tia Yuen Supermarket	25	B4

TRANSPORT		
Air Asia/FAX Sales Office	26	C3
Customs Wharf		
(Boats to Indonesia)	27	A4
Express Buses to Kota Kinabalu	28	C4
Land Cruisers to Keningau	29	C4
Local Bus Station	30	A3
Malaysia Airlines	31	D3
Sabindo Sq Minibus Stand,		
Buses to Sandakan	32	D3

for breakfast, but lots of luck getting anyone there to smile.

North Borneo Hotel (☎ 763-060; fax 773-066; 52-53 Jln Dunlop; r RM50-60; ✻) Strategically placed between the Sabindo and Fajar quarters, this older hotel has large rooms, many with terraces overlooking the street, and surprisingly appealing bathrooms, most with bathtubs. Not fancy, but good value.

North City Hotel (☎ 773-100; fax 757-399; 175-176 Jln Belian; r RM50-60; ✻) Sister property to North Borneo Hotel has marginally smarter rooms but except for a *kedai kopi* and a couple of groceries across the street, it's desolate after dark over here.

First Hotel (☎ 778-989; fax 761-296; 208-209 Jln Bunga; r RM65-80; ste 98; ✻) Completed puzzles

hang framed on some room walls, apropos because First Hotel fits the pieces together just right. Budget rates don't buy windows, but every large, bright room has the right furnishings, such as desks and plush chairs, arrayed on spotless marble floors. Amid a clutch of similar and higher priced choices, First is best value.

Kingston Hotel (☎ 702-288; fax 702-688; 4581-4590 Jln Haji Karim cnr Jln Baru; s/d RM66/88; f/ste RM128/166; ✻) In the heart of the Fajar Commercial Centre for daytime business and night-time fun, this new hotel's roomy digs sparkle and shine. Posh but comfortable decor includes hot-water pot and *kain songket* (traditional Malay handwoven fabric with gold threads) bed throws.

Belmont Marco Polo (☎ 777-988; bmph@tm.net
.my; Jln Klinik; r RM180-280; 🕱) Forestry executives
will feel at home with mahogany shutters
and other elegant wooden accents at Tawau's
luxury leader. For work, there's wi-fi, for play
there's transport to the golf course as well as
an airport shuttle.

Eating

The burgeoning restaurant district in Fajar
Commercial Centre is attractive and delight-
fully varied – fine dining to fast food. But
talk to any local about where to eat and they
invariably suggest the longstanding open-air
seafood restaurants between the Sabindo district and shorefront highway. **Good View** (Jln
Chen Fook; meals from RM40; 🕑 dinner) and **Kam Ling** (Jln
Chen Fook; meals from RM40; 🕑 dinner) at two ends are
the two most renowned. Around the corner,
in an open lot nearer the bay, Malay hawker
stalls offer grilled fish meals for RM15.

Between the KK and Sandakan bus stations, several cafeterias serve Malay and/or
Indian food catering to office workers, some
open 24 hours. A plate of rice and two to
three items runs RM3 to 7 with many
vegetarian options.

Restoran Aul Bismillah (☎ 764-675; Jln Bunga
Tanjung; meals RM2.50-6.50; 🕑 breakfast, lunch & dinner) This open-air corner place serves good-
value Malay standards with complimentary
sea breeze.

Restoran Rasa Sayang (☎ 777-042; Jln Haji Karim;
dishes from RM5; 🕑 lunch & dinner) Bright, air-con
Chinese diner in Fajar has the usual menu
with unlisted prices for groups, plus set meals
(lunch RM12, dinner RM15) for singles.

Sidewalk Café (☎ 777-227; TB570 Talcoln Complex,
Jln Haji Karim; mains RM5.50-16; 🕑 lunch & dinner) No
outdoor tables, but a cool, dark-wood interior
and bar that would be at home in New York's
Soho. There's a daily lunch buffet (RM5) and
Friday night crab buffet (RM10), plus menu
featuring Chinese and Western.

For self-caterers, there are two large
branches of **Milimewa Superstore**: near the fish
market and, a bigger one, on Jln Bunga. **Tia
Yuen Supermarket** has the largest selection of
imported foods, albeit mainly from China.

Getting There & Away
AIR
Malaysia Airlines (☎ 761-293; Jln Haji Sahabudin) has
daily flights to both KK and KL. **Air Asia** (☎ 761-
946, 749-162; Jln Bunga) has two daily direct flights

to KL and KK, and flies to Johor Bahru near
Singapore four times weekly. **MASwings** (☎ 1-
300-883000) flies to Sandakan twice daily, the
afternoon flight continuing to KK.

BOAT
Boats for Indonesia leave from the customs
wharf near the fish market. Fast ferry *Tawindo*
or *IndoMaya* to Tarakan (RM75, 3½ hours)
leaves every morning except Sunday. Several
companies run boats daily to Nunukan
(RM40, one hour), an alternative border
crossing. Most sailings continue or connect to Tarakan (from RM35), three hours
from Nunukan.

BUS
Daily express buses for KK (RM45 to RM55,
10 hours) leave from a lot on Jln Chen Fook
in front of the public library. There are frequent departures from 6.45am to 9.30am
and a handful of night buses from 6.30pm to
8pm. Land Cruisers from next to the express-
bus stand leave mornings for rough hauls
to Keningau (RM80, 11 hours) and Sapulut
(RM50, eight hours) to visit Batu Punggul,
and are also available for charter.

Buses to Sandakan (RM30, five hours),
depart hourly 7am to 2pm from the stand in
Sabindo Sq, one block on a diagonal from the
KK terminus, behind the purple Yassin Curry
House sign. That's also the spot for frequent
minivans to Semporna (RM8 to RM10, two
hours) or Kunak (RM8 to RM10, 1½ hours),
Lahad Datu (RM17 to RM20, three hours) and
Sandakan (RM32 to RM35, six hours).

Bus ticket booths and touts line the terminus areas. Book ahead if travelling on holidays
or weekends.

GETTING AROUND
Tawau's airport is 25km from town, almost
halfway to Semporna, on the best stretch of
road in East Sabah, also the route to Sandakan.
A shuttle bus (RM10) to the local bus station
in Tawau's centre leaves six times daily. A
coupon taxi costs RM38.

Many dive operators provide transport
from Tawau or the airport to Semporna. For
travelling independently from the airport to
Semporna, a coupon taxi costs RM95 (one
hour, 20 minutes), hitching a ride with a waiting tour operator can cost RM30 to RM80; or
take the shuttle to Tawau and either get out
at the main road, cross to the other side and

wait for a minivan in the other direction, or ride into Tawau and catch a minivan from Sabindo Sq.

TAWAU HILLS PARK

Located 25km northwest of Tawau, this small reserve's forested hills soaring from the plain cut a dramatic figure on a clear day. Gazetted to preserve water catchment areas in 1979, establishment of the **park** (admission RM10) came too late to save most of the rainforest. What's left clings to 1310m Gunung Magdalena and a host of smaller, steep ridges.

Tawau Hills Park headquarters (Taman Bukit Tawau; ☎ 089-753-564; dm RM20, chalet RM200) has accommodation with steep discounts on weekdays. From park headquarters, a north trail leads to

hot springs and a waterfall three hours away. To the south, there's a 30-minute walk to **Bombalai Hill** (530m). A taxi from Tawau to the park costs about RM35.

MALIAU BASIN CONSERVATION AREA

Looking down on Sabah with Google Earth, the eye is inexorably drawn to what looks like the crater of a giant extinct volcano in the middle of the state, about 45km north of the border with Kalimantan. Zooming in, the heart starts to beat with excitement, for you cannot help but notice one thing: there are no roads here, only winding rivers and lush rainforest. This is **Maliau Basin Conservation Area** (MBCA; www .ysnet.org.my/Maliau/maliau/arial.htm), known very appropriately as 'Sabah's Lost World'.

TREKKING IN MALIAU BASIN

Several treks are possible in the basin, ranging from short nature walks around Agathis Camp to the multiday slog to the rim of the basin via Strike Ridge Camp. The vast majority of visitors to the basin undertake a three-day/two-night loop through the southern section of the basin that we'll call the Maliau Loop. This brilliant route takes in most of the main forest types of the forest and four of the basin's waterfalls: Takob Akob Falls, Giluk Falls, Maliau Falls and Ginseng Falls. Make no mistake: this trek is hard work, with some serious gruelling climbs up forest ridges and out of river valleys above the waterfalls. Do not attempt the trek unless you are in excellent shape (in fact, Borneo Nature Tours will require a letter from a doctor testifying to your ability to undertake the trek). Your tour operator will supply a guide and porters to carry your food. Other than a daypack, camera, leech socks, walking clothes and dry kit for the evening, you don't need to bring any special equipment.

THE MALIAU LOOP

This three-day/two-night loop is the best way to experience Maliau Basin and it's the route favoured by most tour operators.

Day 1: Agathis Camp to Camel Trophy Camp and on to Takob Akob Falls (12.5km)

After spending the night at Agathis Camp, you'll rise early and start with a gruelling 3.2km slog up and over the rim of the basin. There are several stages and false summits before you finally attain the rim, with ladders installed on the really steep bits. Once at the rim, the walk levels out and becomes very enjoyable as you pass through mixed dipterocarp and heath forest. The heath forest here is very atmospheric, with lots of moss and a few boggy sections. Keep an eye out for orchids. After traversing the heath forest, the trail gradually descends for 1.5km to Camel Trophy Camp, where you will eat lunch. The camp here takes its name from an endurance race sponsored by Camel, the participants in which built the camp.

After lunch, make the 2.5km trek onward to Takob Akob falls. The walk to the falls from Camel Trophy Camp starts as a pleasant 2km stroll before plummeting the final 50m down a very tricky valley wall to reach Takob Akob Falls. The falls plunge 30 metres into a natural basin with high jungle-clad walls on either side – this is where you'll really get that 'Lost World' feeling. After making the heartbreaking 500m climb out of the valley, most trekkers stop at the lovely seven-step Giluk Falls, a short detour off the trail on the way back to camp. The view of the falls disappearing over the ledge with the jungle as a backdrop is magical – but be careful on the rocks here as they can be slippery.

The total distance for the day is around 12.5km. If you have any energy left after the day (and no fear of heights), you might try climbing the ladder to the canopy lookout behind the hut.

Maliau Basin is the single best place in Borneo to experience the wonders of a primary tropical rainforest. More than that, it is one of the world's great reserves of biodiversity, a dense knot of almost unbelievable genetic richness. As such, it deserves to rank high on the itinerary of anyone interested in the natural world, as well as the strongest protections afforded by the Malaysian government and world environmental bodies. And a visit to the basin is always a poignant affair, as you'll share the road with a parade of logging trucks hauling trees out of the forest at an astonishing rate.

Unbelievably, there is no known record of human beings entering the basin until the early 1980s (although it is possible that indigenous peoples entered the ba.... time). It is only recently that the ... opened up to a limited number of ... ous travellers, and it's still an expens... time-consuming destination that is pract...lly impossible to visit on your own.

Orientation & Information

Maliau Basin is located in the southern part of central Sabah, just north of the logging road connecting Tawau with Keningau, a minimum of five hours' drive from either of these towns by 4WD vehicle. It is part of the Yayasan Sabah Forest Management Area, a vast swath of forest in southeastern Sabah under the management of **Yayasan Sabah** (www.ysnet.org.my), a semigovernmental body

Day 2: Camel Trophy Camp to Ginseng Camp via Maliau Falls (18km)

After spending the night at Camel Trophy Camp, you'll rise early and backtrack slightly to join the trail across the plateau in the direction of Maliau Falls and Ginseng Camp. Initially, the trail rises gradually as you traverse boggy and mossy heath forest. After about a kilometre, you'll enter the brilliant nepenthes (pitcher plant) garden, which is home to what must be one of the world's best collection of pitcher plants, with a good variety of orchids thrown in for good measure. Next, you will slowly descend and enter a mossy forest, with the trails at time seeming like a moss-lined corridor. You continue to descend and re-enter mixed dipterocarp forest. Finally, after around eight kilometres, you reach a trail junction, where a branch trail heads off in the direction of Maliau Falls. Your porters will likely stash most of their luggage here to pick up on the return.

From the junction, the trail crosses a series of gentle ups and downs for about 2.5km before arriving at an abandoned camp (Lobah Camp) and a high knob that provides a brilliant view over the basin. Take a good look and then plunge down the valley wall, negotiating a series of ropes and ladders to reach a flat area and another abandoned camp before making the final vertiginous 700m descent to the falls, which you can hear roaring in the distance.

Maliau Falls are a great natural wonder of Southeast Asia and if the water level is high, you'll be almost blown away by their grandeur. You observe them from a shelf between the upper falls (20m) and lower falls (15m), which also makes a good spot for your lunch picnic. You can swim in the pool below the upper falls, but be very careful not to get caught in the current. Enjoy your lunch, because the climb out is murder. Drink plenty of water here and bring some for the walk (you'll need a filter or sterilisation agent).

The climb back to Lobah Camp is a real test of endurance and you should not rush it. From there, you return to the main trail and limp the final 1km mostly downhill to Ginseng Camp, which is built near lovely Ginseng Falls. Like Agathis Camp, Ginseng Camp is a bunkhouse with showers and a dining area.

Day 3: Ginseng Camp to Agathis Camp (9km)

After spending the night at Ginseng Camp, you'll start the day with a sweaty 1km climb up a ridge, after which the rest of the day is a cakewalk through mixed dipterocarp forest. There are some gradual ups and downs but the general trend is downward, which is welcome after the exertions of the previous day. Note that some of the distance markers on the trail are reversed, which causes a brief disheartening moment for tired hikers. You'll know you're near Agathis Camp when you start to see obvious signs of human activity, including a bit of litter, some numbers spray-painted on trees and, perhaps, the sound of a generator.

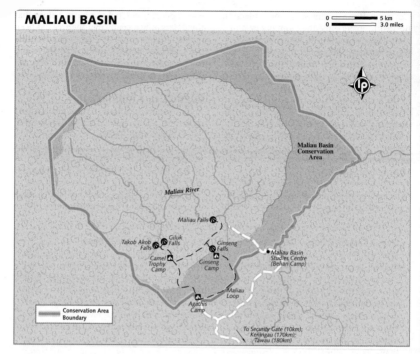

MALIAU BASIN

0 _____ 5 km
0 _____ 3.0 miles

Maliau Basin
Conservation
Area

Maliau River

Maliau Falls

Giluk
Falls
Takob Akob   Ginseng
Falls   Falls
Camel
Trophy   Ginseng
Camp   Camp

Maliau Basin
Studies Centre
(Belian Camp)

Maliau
Loop

Agathis
Camp

To Security Gate (10km);
Keningau (170km);
Tawau (380km)

Conservation Area
Boundary

SABAH

tasked with both developing and protecting the natural resources of Sabah. Innoprise Corporation, the commercial arm of Yayasan Sabah, runs tours to the basin through its subsidiary **Borneo Nature Tours** (☎ 088-267-637; www.borneonaturetours.com; Block D, Lot 10, ground fl, Sadong Jaya Complex, Kota Kinabalu), which also runs Borneo Rainforest Lodge (p147). Other tour operators in Sabah can also arrange tours of the park.

The **MCBA security gate** is just off the Tawau–Keningau Road. From the gate, it's a very rough 25km journey to the **Maliau Basin Studies Centre**, for researchers, and about 20km to **Agathis Camp**, the base camp for most visitors to the basin.

Independent visits to the basin are difficult: proficient 4WD drivers could probably get there under their own steam with private vehicles, and you could arrange for guides and porters at the security gate, if none are out with tours at that time, but the overall expense would likely be similar to an organised tour, once vehicle rental costs are taken into account. It is likely that as the Tawau–Keningau road improves (it is slated to be paved) and

interest in the basin increases, independent travel will become easier. Check online for the latest information when you plan your tour.

Accommodation in Maliau Basin is in the form of simple camps, which range from basic bunkhouses such as Agathis Camp to **Camel Trophy Camp**, a wood-frame two-storey hut with private bedrooms. None of the camps are luxurious, but after a day on the trail fighting leeches, they'll seem like paradise.

Geology

The Maliau Basin is a circular basin ranging in diameter from 20 to 25 km, with a total area of 588 sq km. It is surrounded on all sides by a high rim that reaches an altitude of 1700m along its northern edge. The floor of the basin averages around 800m in height, with some of the deep river valleys dropping as low as 200m. Despite its volcanic appearance, the basin is actually composed of alternating layers of sandstone and mudstone. The unique shape of the basin is thought to be the result of a general upthrust of the entire area, followed by accumulation of water in the centre, which eventually breached the rim along the course of the present day Sungai Maliau. The combination of abundant rainfall and multilayered sedimentary structure of the basin gives rise to an incredible number of distinctive step-like waterfalls along all the watercourses of the basin.

Biology

The lower regions of the basin are mostly covered in lowland dipterocarp forest, the type of rainforest that most people imagine when thinking of tropical jungle. This forest gets its name from the giant dipterocarp trees that tower up to 60 metres over the forest floor. This is among the most diverse forests in the world, with up to 1000 tree species per square kilometre.

As you climb the ridges of the basin, you encounter lower montane rainforest, dominated by conifers such as the agathis tree, interspersed with palms, bamboos and a variety of smaller plants such as pitcher plants. Above 1000m, where the soil is poor and sandy, one encounters heath forest, which is dominated by low trees and mossy areas, as well as an incredible variety of pitcher plants (the plateau that most visitors traverse on the second day of the Maliau Loop traverses several kilometres of this forest). Finally, the upper reaches of the basin rim are covered with montane erinaceous forest (also known as rim forest), characterised by short, twisted trees and an abundance of moss and liverworts.

Researchers estimate that there are at least 1800 plant species in the basin, including over 80 orchid species, at least six types of pitcher plants, and at least two species of rafflesia. Over 230 bird species have been spotted in the basin, including the great argus pheasant, all eight species of hornbill known to occur in Borneo, giant pitta, peregrine falcons, and eight species of kingfishers. As for mammals, over 70 species have been recorded, including the Sumatran rhino, Asian elephants, tembedau (Bornean wild ox), clouded leopards, orangutans, gibbons, several species of monkeys, sun bears, wild boars, barking deer and mouse deer.

Unlike other areas of Borneo, where you will read about incredible wildlife but encounter precious little of it, those who trek into Maliau Basin have an excellent chance of spotting wildlife. Hornbills whoosh overhead at regular intervals, gibbons and other monkeys riot in the treetops, boars, deer and tembedau regularly flee the trail ahead of walkers, and the call of the great argus pheasant are a frequent and magical accompaniment to your trek. And if you're lucky, you might even spot a few elephants as you drive from the security gate to Agathis Camp. In short, if you're interested in trees, birds, mammals, butterflies, moths, fungi or flowers, you'll find it hard to make any progress down the trail as you'll be perpetually stopping to examine a new species. The biodiversity is truly mind-boggling.

Oh, and did we mention the leeches? They're there in force, so bring your leech socks and resign yourself to making a few donations.

Organised Tours

Borneo Nature Tours (☎ 088-267-637; www.borneonaturetours.com; Block D, Lot 10, ground fl, Sadong Jaya Complex, Kota Kinabalu) is the main operator here. They offer five-day/four-night all inclusive tours of Maliau Basin starting at RM3350.

Getting There & Away

There is no public transport to the park and your transport will be arranged by your tour operator. Access is by 4WD vehicle from either Tawau or Keningau. Most organised tours operate from Tawau, from which the ride takes about five hours under good conditions. There are frequent delays en route as logging trucks frequently get bogged down in the mud. Once at the security gate to the park, you'll have to take an even narrower dirt track for the final 20 kilometres or so to Agathis Camp.

SABAH

Sarawak

The east Malaysian state of Sarawak sprawls along the northwest coast of the island of Borneo – a vast expanse of secondary forest and oil palm that gradually gives rise to jungle-clad mountains along the border with Indonesian Kalimantan. Just the name Sarawak is enough to evoke a cascade of romantic images: white rajas presiding over kingdoms of head-hunters and Sea Gypsies; longhouses sitting amid steamy jungle clearings; explorers venturing up nameless jungle rivers in search of undiscovered tribes.

While modern-day Sarawak is considerably more prosaic, you can still catch intriguing flashes of the old magic in various corners of the state. For starters, there's the capital city of Kuching – easily the island's most culturally rich city.

Then, there are the incredible natural attractions of Sarawak, several of which are world-class. Topping the list are Sarawak's incredible caves: the huge chambers of the Niah Caves National Park would be the state's most impressive natural highlight if they weren't overshadowed by those of Mulu National Park. Of course, Mulu is far more than just caves – it's got brilliant primary rainforest to trek though, high mountains to climb, wild geological formations to see and wild rivers to navigate. It is, without a doubt, one of the finest parks in Southeast Asia.

Then there are the rivers: the mighty Batang Rejang is rightly called the Amazon of Borneo, and a trip upriver is the quintessential Borneo experience. Similar trips are possible on Sungai Baram, and this is an interesting way to get to Mulu.

Finally, in northeast Sarawak, right up against the border with Kalimantan you'll find Borneo's very own Shangri La: the Kelabit Highlands, where you can trek through thick jungle, stopping each night in longhouses to savour traditional Kelabit hospitality.

HIGHLIGHTS

- Stroll the riverside promenade of **Kuching** (p162), Borneo's most culturally rich city
- Watch the oil palms and jungle slide by as you make your way into the very heart of Borneo along the **Batang Rejang** (p189)
- Take a Jules Verne–like adventure into the underground world of the **Niah Caves National Park** (p197)
- Climb to the Pinnacles – a forest of giant limestone arrowheads – in Borneo's best nature park, **Gunung Mulu National Park** (p205)
- Get back to the simple life in a longhouse high up in the cool **Kelabit Highlands** (p212)

- POPULATION: 2.01 MILLION
- AREA: 124,449 SQ KM

SARAWAK

HISTORY

Archaeological evidence suggests early man lived in Sarawak as long as 40,000 years ago, 30,000 years earlier than on the Malay peninsula. The Chinese started arriving around the 7th century, along with other Eastern traders, and from the 11th century Sarawak came under the control of various Indonesian factions. Many of today's indigenous tribes migrated from Kalimantan, including the Iban, who came here around the end of the 15th century and now make up around 30% of the state's population.

From the 15th until the early 19th century Sarawak was under the loose control of the sultanate of Brunei. It was only with the arrival of Sir James Brooke, the first of three so-called white raja, that it became a separate political region.

Brooke, invalided from the British East India Company after being wounded in Burma, eschewed an easy retirement and set off on a voyage of discovery, aided by a sizable inheritance and a well-armed ship. He arrived in Sarawak in 1839, just in time to find the local viceroy under siege, providing the perfect opportunity to ingratiate himself with the ruling class. Brooke duly suppressed the rebellion, and by way of reward the sultan of Brunei installed him as raja of Sarawak in 1842.

When James Brooke died in 1868 he was succeeded by his nephew, Charles Brooke. Through a policy of divide and rule and the ruthless punishment of those who challenged his authority, Brooke junior extended his control and the borders of his kingdom during his long reign, which lasted until his death in 1917.

The third and last white raja was Charles Vyner Brooke, the second son of Charles Brooke, whose rule was rudely interrupted by the arrival of the Japanese in WWII. After the Japanese surrender in August 1945, Sarawak was placed under Australian military administration until Brooke, who had fled to Sydney, decided to cede his 'kingdom' to the British in 1946. On 1 July Sarawak officially became a British Crown colony, thus putting Britain in the curious position of acquiring a new colonial possession at a time when it was shedding others.

Cession was followed by a brief but bloody anticessionist movement supported chiefly by Anthony Brooke, Vyner Brooke's nephew and heir apparent. About 300 government officers resigned in protest at being excluded from the political process, and the conflict climaxed in late 1949 when the governor of Sarawak was murdered by a Malay student. By 1951, however, the movement had lost its momentum and Brooke urged supporters to give it up.

Along with Sabah (then North Borneo) and Brunei, Sarawak remained under British control when Malaya gained its independence in 1957. In 1962 the British proposed including the Borneo territories into the Federation of Malaya. At the last minute Brunei pulled out, as the sultan (and, one suspects, Shell Oil) didn't want to see the revenue from its vast oil reserves channelled to the peninsula. At the same time, Malaya also had to convince the UN that Philippine claims to North Borneo were unfounded, as was Indonesia's argument that the formation of Malaysia was a British neocolonialist plot. The agreement was finally hammered out in July 1963, and in September of the same year the Federation of Malaysia was born.

This was also when the Indonesian Konfrontasi (Confrontation) erupted, initiated by then Indonesian president Achmed Soekarno, who hoped to destabilise the fledgling state. Paramilitary raids and army attacks across Kalimantan's border with Sarawak and Sabah continued until 1966. At the conflict's height 50,000 British, Australian and New Zealand troops were deployed in the border area, where some horrific confrontations occurred.

Internally, Sarawak also faced conflict during the early 1960s. The state's large population of impoverished Chinese peasant farmers and labourers were courted by the North Kalimantan Communist Party, which supported guerrilla activity. After the collapse of the Indonesian Communist Party in 1965, however, Indonesians and Malaysians combined forces to drive the rebels out of their bases in Sarawak.

Today Sarawak is the most multicultural state in Malaysia, with no outright ethnic majority. Economically it has avoided the pitfalls of unemployment and federal discord that plague its neighbour, Sabah, but the state budget deficit has grown steadily over the last five years and revenue still depends heavily on the much criticised timber industry. Accusations of corruption and cronyism are virtually a daily occurrence, and most people would be surprised to find out if a major

SARAWAK

SABAH

100 km
60 miles

Merapok
Lawas
Batang Trusan
Long Semado
Ba Kelalan

BRUNEI
Bandar Seri Begawan
Limbang
Sungai Temburong
Bangar
Sungai Limbang
Batang

Gunung Mulu (2377m)
Gunung Mulu National Park
Long Terawan
Long Lama
Sungai

Gunung Murud (2423m)
Bario
Long Seridan
Seridan

Pulong Tau National Park
Long Banga

Kelabit Highlands
Long Lelang
Long Akah
Tama Abu Range
Long Napir
Lio Matoh

Kuala Belait
Seria
Miri Airport
Marudi
Beluru
Long Teru
Long Miri

Bukit Sebunong (1371m)

Bukit Robertson (1710m)

Kuala Baram
Miri
Batu Niah
Niah
Junction
Niah Caves National Park
Lambir Hills National Park

Sungai Tinjar
Baram
Sungai
Dulit Range

Bukit Semalong (1281m)
Bakun Dam

Sungei Linau
Balui

Belaga
Batang
Long Jawi
Hose Range
Baleh

Tubau
Bintulu
Bintulu Airport
Similajau National Park
Batang Kemena
Batang

Batang Tatau
Tutau
Sangan
Murum Range
Baleng Rejang
Interwau
Batang Baleh
Sungai Mujong
Batang Mengiong
Kapit
Batang Rejang

Mukah
Batang Igan
Dalat
Matu
Daro

Sibu
Sibu Airport
Sarikei
Julau
Kanowit
Nibong
Song
Sungai Karibas
Batang Rejang
Batang
Batang Matu

Batang Ai National Park
Batang Ai Reservoir
Lubok Antu

Betong
Sri Aman
Engkilili
Batang Lupar
Batang

SOUTH CHINA SEA

Maludam National Park
Kuching International Airport
Serian
Sadong
Sungai

Tebedu
To Pontianak (275km)

Tanjung Datu National Park
Teluk Melano
Sematan
Lundu National Park
Gunung Gading National Park
Kubah National Park
Bako National Park
Santubong
Kuching
Batu
Siniawan

Pulau Satang Besar
Tanjung-Satang National Park
Pulau Talang-Talang Besar

KALIMANTAN
INDONESIA

VISAS

Sarawak is semiautonomous and treated in some ways like a separate country. If you travel from Peninsular Malaysia or Sabah into Sarawak, your passport will be checked on arrival in Sarawak and a new stay permit issued, either for 30 days or for the same period as your original Malaysia entry visa. If you are travelling directly to Sarawak, you will usually be given a 30-day entry stamp on arrival. When you leave Sarawak, your passport will be checked and a departure stamp put in your passport. When you travel from Sarawak to Peninsular Malaysia or into Sabah, you do not start a new entry period, so your 30-day (or longer) permit from Sarawak remains valid.

company didn't have some link to a government office. Despite the strongest showing for opposition parties since 1987, state elections in mid-2006 once again confirmed the ruling government amid widespread rumours of dubious tactics. Chief Minister Abdul Taib Mahmud (now in his seventh term) has described his unchanged cabinet as 'transitional', but exactly what transitions are involved remains to be seen.

CLIMATE

For information on the climate of Sarawak, see p13 and p291.

GETTING THERE & AWAY

Sarawak can be reached by air from Sabah, Brunei and Kalimantan (all within Borneo) and from Singapore and Peninsula Malaysia. It can be reached by road from Brunei, Sabah and Kalimantan. The Limbang Division of Sarawak can also be reached by boat from Bandar Seri Begawan (Brunei) and Pulau Labuan (Sabah).

Air

Malaysia Airlines (MAS; ☎ 1-300-883-000, 03-7843-3000; www.malaysiaairlines.com) has connections between Kota Kinabalu (KK, Sabah) and Kuching, Sibu, Bintulu and Miri, as well as Gunung Mulu National National Park. They also fly between Kuala Lumpur and Kuching, Sibu, Bintulu and Miri.

Air Asia (☎ within Malaysia 03-8775-4000, outside Malaysia 60-3-8660-4343; www.airasia.com) has flights between Kuala Lumpur, Penang and Johor Bahru (all in Peninsular Malaysia) and Kuching. Within Borneo, they fly between Kuching and Kota Kinabalu.

Silk Air (☎ in KK 265-770, in Singapore 6223-8888; www.silkair.com) has flights between Singapore and Kuching.

Royal Brunei Airlines (☎ in Brunei 221-2222; www.bruneiair.com) has flights between Bandar Seri Begawan (Brunei) and Kuching.

Batavia Air (☎ in Jakarta 386-4308, in Pontianak 721-560, in Kuching 628-166; www.batavia-air.co.id) has flights between Jakarta (Java, Indonesia) and Pontianak (Kalimantan, Indonesia) and Kuching.

For more details, see the Getting There & Away sections of the relevant destinations.

Boat

There are speedboats between Bandar Seri Begawan and Limbang in far northern Sarawak; for details see p227. There are also speedboats between Pulau Labuan (Sabah) and Limbang and Lawas (also in far northern Sarawak); for details see p124.

Bus

There are daily express buses between Kuching and Pontianak in Kalimantan (see p171). There are buses between Miri and Kuala Belait (Brunei), where you can get onward connections to Bandar Seri Begawan (see p232). There are bus connections between Lawas, in far northern Sarawak, and Kota Kinabalu (see p217).

GETTING AROUND

Coastal Sarawak is traversed by a decent network of mostly paved roads, along which you can travel by bus, taxi and private car. A web of logging roads is being built at a furious rate into the interior and you can now reach destinations right up against the Kalimantan border by 4WD vehicle in some parts of the state. Malaysian Airlines flies between the major cities of the coast and also services some of the interior villages. Finally, river boats service some of the major rivers of the state, and this is one of the most interesting ways to get around. For details on getting around Sarawak, see the Getting There & Away sections above and the Transport chapter (p302).

SARAWAK

KUCHING

☎ 082 / pop 496,000

Raja Brooke's former capital city of Kuching is sure to surprise you – for who would expect to find such a stylish, hip and progressive city perched on this corner of Borneo? It's easy to see why Brooke chose this spot for his capital: overlooking the languid Sungai Sarawak, it seems the perfect gateway to both jungle and sea. With a long riverfront esplanade for evening strolls and some refreshing bits of greenery scattered about, the city has a pleasantly relaxed feeling. And hidden among the modern new buildings are some intriguing reminders of the city's past.

Without a doubt, the most attractive part of the city is the old Chinatown area, which stretches the length of Jln Carpenter. This is Borneo's most charming neighbourhood and the lanes are punctuated with excellent little restaurants, craft shops and markets. The east side of the city is more modern, but not without its attractions, including Jln Padungan, a strip of cool restaurants that wouldn't be out of place in Melbourne, London or San Francisco.

Additional attractions include a brilliant weekend market, some fine museums and a couple of well-preserved relics from the time of Brooke. All told, Kuching is one of the more character-filled cities in Southeast Asia and if you find yourself staying a bit longer than expected, you won't be the first.

HISTORY

Built principally on the south bank of the Sungai Sarawak, Kuching was known as Sarawak in the 19th century. Before James Brooke settled here, the capital had been variously at Lidah Tanah and Santubong. Kuching was given its name in 1872 by Charles Brooke.

Unlike some of the other large towns in Malaysian Borneo, Kuching's historic buildings escaped damage during WWII, and many have been tastefully renovated.

ORIENTATION

The main sights – and most of the city – are on the south bank of the Sungai Sarawak. The western end of the city is overlooked by the Kuching Mosque, and is home to markets, local bus stations and museums. The most useful hotels, places to eat, banks and offices are between the mosque and the Great Cat of Kuching, 2km east. The waterfront is a busy thoroughfare between the eastern and western parts of town.

Across the river from the wet market is the Astana (Palace). Nearby, Fort Margherita is on a low hill and visible from most points along the waterfront; the new State Assembly Building is currently rising between the Astana and Fort Margherita and should be just about finished by the time this book is published.

Almost all attractions are within easy walking distance of each other; public buses or taxis are only really needed to reach the airport (about 12km away), the Jalan Penrissen express bus terminal (5km) and the Pending wharf for the boat to Sibu (6km).

Maps

The free *Kuching Tourist Map*, available at the Visitors' Information Centre (opposite), has a good map of Kuching, lots of useful transport info and inset maps of Sarawak, Damai and Matang. The Periplus *Sarawak* map, which you can buy for around RM20 at Mohamed Yahia & Sons (below), has a decent map of Kuching and other parts of Sarawak (for downtown Kuching, the free map is better).

INFORMATION
Bookshops

Mohamed Yahia & Sons (☎ 416-928; Basement, Sarawak Plaza, Jln Tunku Abdul Rahman; ☯ 9am-5pm) Has English-language fiction and books on Borneo, plus Sarawak maps.

Popular Book Co (☎ 411-378; Level 3, Tun Jugah Shopping Centre, 18 Jln Tunku Abdul Rahman; ☯ 9am-7pm) This is a more modern and spacious bookshop with a good selection of international titles but fewer local interest books, however.

Emergency

Ambulance (☎ 999)
Fire (☎ 994)
Police (☎ 999)

Internet Access

Coffee Bean & Tea Leaf in Sarawak Plaza offers free wi-fi to their customers (see p170).

Cyber City (☎ 243-680; off Jln Borneo; per hr RM4; ☯ 10am-11pm Mon-Sat, 11am-11pm Sun) This is easily the best internet café in town.

Laundry

City Laundry (off Jln Borneo; 2kg load RM20; ☒ 7.45am-5pm Mon-Fri, 7.45am-12.30pm Sat, closed Sun) Overpriced compared to Mr Clean.

Mr Clean (Jln Green Hill; per kg RM6; ☒ 8am-6pm Mon-Sat, 8am-4pm Sun) Reliable and economical; next to the Mandarin Hotel.

Medical Services

Normah Medical Specialist Centre (☎ 440-055; www.normah.com.my; Jln Tun Abdul Rahman) A private hospital with good facilities and staff. It's favoured by many residents and expats.

Sarawak General Hospital (☎ 257-555; Jln Ong Kee) For emergencies and major ailments only.

Timberland Medical Centre (☎ 234-991; Mile 3, Jln Rock) Private hospital with highly qualified staff.

Money

Everrise Money Changer (☎ 233-200; 199 Jln Padungan; ☒ 9am-5pm) Cash only.

Majid & Sons (☎ 422-402; 45 Jln India) A licensed moneychanger dealing in cash only.

Maybank (☎ 416-889; Jln Tunku Abdul Rahman; ☒ 9.15am-4.30pm Mon-Thu, 9.15am-4pm Fri, ATM 6am-midnight daily)

Mohamed Yahia & Sons (☎ 416-928; Basement, Sarawak Plaza, Jln Tunku Abdul Rahman; ☒ 9am-5pm) Inside the bookshop here.

Standard Chartered Bank (☎ 252-233; Jln Padungan; ☒ 9.15am-4.30pm Mon-Thu, 9.15am-4pm Fri)

Post

Main post office (Jln Tun Abang Haji Openg; ☒ 8am-4.30pm Mon-Sat)

Tourist Information

Visitors' Information Centre (☎ 410-944; www.sarawaktourism.com; Sarawak Tourism Complex, Jln Tun Abang Haji Openg; ☒ 8am-6pm Mon-Fri, 9am-3pm Sat, Sun & holidays) Located in the old courthouse and with extremely helpful staff. Pick up the free *Kuching Tourist Map*.

Visas

Immigration office (☎ 245-661; 2nd fl, Sultan Iskandar Bldg, Jln Simpang Tiga; ☒ 8am-noon & 2-4.30pm Mon-Fri) Visa extensions 3km south of town centre. From in front of the mosque, take CLL bus 11 or 14A/B/C. Get off at Simpang Tiga.

SIGHTS

Like many cities, Kuching is much more than the sum of its parts. While it's got some great museums and a few historical attractions to keep you occupied, the main attraction of Kuching is the city itself. Leave plenty of time to wander aimlessly and soak up the relaxed vibe and pleasant cityscapes of Chinatown, the waterfront and Jalan Padungan.

Waterfront

Kuching's lovely paved waterfront makes for a fine stroll, especially when a cool evening breeze blows off the river. At night the promenade is ablaze with colourful lights and is busy with people buying cheap dinners or snacks from the permanent food stalls (the best of which can be found in front of the Hilton Hotel). While you're strolling, be sure to have a look at the **Brooke Memorial**, in front of the Visitors' Information Centre.

Chinatown

Kuching's **Chinatown** is centred on Jln Carpenter and runs roughly from Jln Wayang to Jln Tun Abang Haji Openg. It's a collection of beautiful colonial-era shophouses and Chinese temples that is conducive to strolling (if you can take the heat). At the western end you'll find **Harmony Arch**, an ornate arch that marks the official entrance to the district. Continuing east along Jln Carpenter, you'll see **Sang Ti Miao** on your right. Take some time to enter the spotless main hall of this temple to soak up the gaudy brilliance (across the way you'll find a good Chinese hawker centre in case you need to fuel up).

At the very eastern end of Chinatown you'll find the **Hong San Temple**, which is easily Kuching's finest Chinese temple. Thought to date back to around 1840, this Hokkien Chinese temple was fully restored in 2003. The new stone carvings, done by stonemasons brought in from mainland China, are superb, as is the Buddhist altar.

There is a big celebration at this temple in April, with a long procession of floats, lion and dragon dancers and other groups winding their way through town following the altar of Kong Teck Choon Ong (the diety at the temple).

Finally, be sure to have a look at **Tua Pek Kong**, the temple on the red wedding-layer-cake structure on Jln Padungan at the end of Main Bazaar. It's the most popular temple in town for local Chinese residents.

Museums

SARAWAK MUSEUM

Established in 1891, the **Sarawak Museum** (☎ 244-232; www.museum.sarawak.gov.my; Jln Tun Abang

SARAWAK

SARAWAK

KUCHING

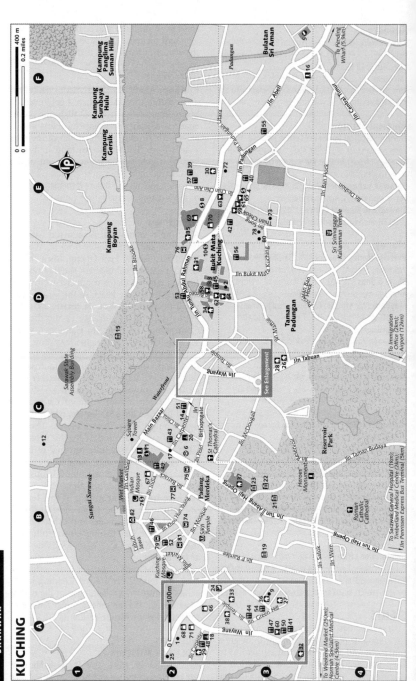

Haji Openg; admission free; 9am-6pm) has a fascinating collection of cultural artefacts and is a must-visit for anyone who wants to learn more about the region's indigenous peoples and natural environment. It consists of two wings connected by an ornate footbridge.

The **Old Wing** houses the main ethnology and natural-history exhibits. There's an excellent Borneo shell collection and a decent stuffed bird collection, including interesting examples of art created with hornbill 'ivory'. The highlight, however, is the reptile area, which has some great stuffed snakes and some giant crocodile skulls. Here, observant visitors will find a display of a hairball taken from the stomach of a man-eating crocodile with the following legend: 'human dental plate found attached to hairball'. It seems the unfortunate victim wore dentures (Redmond O'Hanlon mentions this exhibit in *Into the Heart of Borneo*). And if this isn't enough to put you off from wading in the mangrove swamps, the 'watch found inside stomach' surely will.

Upstairs in the Old Wing you'll find a recreated traditional longhouse display that you can enter and explore. Nearby, there are good wooden models of the different types of longhouse found in Sarawak. In the basketry section you'll find a beautiful Bidayu door charm, which was used to keep evil spirits out of the longhouse.

Across the footbridge, the **New Wing** (Tun Abdul Razak Hall) has temporary exhibits and is of less interest – check what's on before walking over.

While you're at the Sarawak Museum, be sure to have a look at the its **Art Museum** and **Natural Science Museum**, both of which are just down the hill from the museum's Old Wing. The former houses both permanent and temporary exhibits, some of which are very good. The latter was not open at the time of writing, but it is expected to open soon.

ISLAMIC MUSEUM

Over the hill from the Sarawak Museum, the **Islamic Museum** (Muzium Islam Sarawak; ☎ 244-232; Jln P Ramlee; admission free; 9am-6pm) is well worth the walk. It's divided into seven thematically-based rooms: weapons; decorative arts and domestic utensils; Korans; Islamic architecture; science, technology, economy and literature;

SARAWAK

music and costumes; and the coming of Islam to the Malay Archipelago. Of particular note are the fantastic wooden and metal boxes in the decorative-arts section and the fine carved panels in the architecture section.

Astana

Built by Charles Brooke in 1869, the **Astana** (Bahasa Sarawak for 'palace') still serves as the home of the governor of Sarawak. It's not usually open to the public and it's not really worth the trip across the river to see it, since the view is actually better from the south bank of the Sungai Sarawak. If you want a closer look, you can take a *tambang* (river ferry) from the jetty in front of the courthouse for 80 sen.

Fort Margherita

Built by Charles Brooke in 1879 and named after his wife, Rani Margaret, **Fort Margherita** (ad-

mission free; dawn-dusk) guarded Kuching against pirates. Sitting on a knoll opposite the waterfront, this little white fort, complete with battlements, offers fine views along the river. The impressive whitewashed building has been left to rot under the Borneo sun. It seems that the city fathers have decided that there's no point in maintaining the place, which is a shame, considering its historical significance. Now, all you can do is wander the weed-strewn grounds and look at the building from the outside. To get there, take a *tambang* (80 sen) from the pier on the waterfront, opposite the Hilton, walk up through the *kampung* (village), bearing left, past the school, through the parking lot and into the grounds.

COURSES

Bumbu Cooking School (380-050; bumbucooking class@hotmail.com; 57 Jln Carpenter; per person RM70)

WEEKEND MARKET *Jeremy Tan*

The **Weekend Market** (Jln Satok; late afternoon Sat, 5am-noon Sun), locally known in Malay as 'Pasar Minggu', is a Kuching institution that dates back several decades. Every weekend, traders and farmers from around the city and the surrounding villages and longhouses converge on a compact area in the Satok neighbourhood, setting up wooden stalls and colourful tarpaulin rain covers, and sell their products, ranging from fresh fish to wild jungle ferns, power tools to herbal cure-alls. It's a garrulous gathering and a large proportion of the neighbourhood's residents, and some from further away, show up to do their grocery shopping for the week. It is also a boon for self-catering travellers. The market starts on Saturdays at 1pm in the afternoon, rain or shine, and ends on Sunday at the same time. Most stall owners will start closing up on Saturday evening at around 10pm at night, and some of them sleep there, waking up before dawn when everything starts up again on Sunday.

To get to the market from downtown, walk the kilometre or so from downtown along Jln Tun Ahmad Zaidi Adruce, and turn right onto the westbound lanes of Jln Satok after you have crossed under the Satok overpass. The markets are liveliest in the late afternoons and evenings on Saturday, and mid-Sunday morning. If the weekend coincides with a major holiday, however, then some of the stalls will not be open, for instance, the Dayak-owned stalls on Gawai. A good place to start exploring the market is from the pedestrian overpass. The first section, directly south, has stalls selling a wide range of goods from hardware to souvenirs to clothing. This is a good place to pick up a bargain on batiks and cheesy Sarawak T-shirts. From here, head towards the fresh-plants section, where you can stop to admire delicate bonsai, pick up a bunch of local flowers for your dearly beloved, or see what a durian sapling looks like.

Walking south from here, you will enter the general produce section, which sprawls around and takes up space wherever it can, with stalls selling eggs, vegetables and fruits, sprinkled with various others hawking drinks and snacks. The fruits section sells in-season popular tropical fruits such as watermelon and mango, and at the far end is a stall selling *cakoi*, which is deep-fried bread dough, a popular snack item. Going back up, stalls selling *kueh* (small Malaysian cakes) jostle with others selling Malay food and Chinese pastries. Definitely try *apam balik*, a Malaysian pancake folded over and stuffed with butter and peanuts, or *kueh salat*, a small cake made from salty glutinous rice and pandan-flavoured jelly.

Malay rice and noodle staples such as *nasi lemak* and *mee goreng* can also be found here, as well as some imports from the mainland, such as *nasi dagang* and *nasi kerabu* (blue rice!) from

---

Courses here are a great way to learn how to cook some of the dishes you've enjoyed in local restaurants. You start with a shopping trip to a local market, then you cook four dishes and sit down to enjoy them.

Kak Rosnah's Kitchen (kakrosnah@gmail.com; RM100 per person for groups of 2 to 4) Another great way to learn some local Malay and Bidayuh cooking. Classes are held in an old Malay *kampung* so in addition to cooking, you get a look at traditional Malay life. Classes are only held on Sunday.

ACTIVITIES

Y.C.Y. Massage (☎ 013-816-9891; 1st fl, 42 Main Bazaar; one-hour massage RM35; ⊙ 9.30am-9.30pm daily) A nice spot for a massage after a day of sightseeing or hiking. The blind masseurs and masseuses here are a friendly bunch and some are good sources of information about the city.

TOURS

Travel agents and tour operators in Kuching can arrange trips to nearby attractions such as Bako National Park (p172) and the Batang Rejang (p189). A good tour operator is **Borneo Interland Travel** (☎ 413-595; www.bitravel.com.my; 1st fl, 63 Main Bazaar).

FESTIVALS & EVENTS

The three-day **Rainforest World Music Festival** (www.rainforestmusic-borneo.com) unites Borneo's indigenous tribes with international artists for a musical extravaganza in the Sarawak Cultural Village outside Kuching. It's held annually in the middle of July.

SLEEPING

Kuching has a good selection of accommodation in all price brackets, with most of the budget places located in or near Chinatown

Kelantan. Close by is a large aquarium supplies stall selling exotic tropical goldfish. You can pick up *kampung*-style grilled fish just before heading into the fresh seafood section, featuring fresh catch such as pomfret, Spanish mackerel, skate and local shellfish. This section lies next to Pasar Tamu DBKU, the covered market that operates on weekdays when the weekend market is closed. Halal (food prepared according to Muslim dietry laws) beef and lamb is sold by butchers next to the seafood section. From here, the produce in the stalls start giving way to more local vegetables and spices and stall-owners here are more likely to be Bidayuh from the surrounding longhouses. Keep an eye out for local vegetables such as *kangkong* (water spinach) or *paku* (jungle ferns found only in Sarawak), fruits such as *salak* (a sweet and acidic fruit with skin resembling that of a snake's) or *dabai* (an olive-like fruit from the Sibu area). If in doubt, ask the vendor as to the identity of what you are looking at, and how to eat it. Those taking Malaysian cooking lessons will find this a great place to buy some *serai* (lemongrass), *lengkuas* (galangal) or *kunyit* (turmeric) as well as *kerisik* (ground coconut, look for stalls with a grinding machine). Other items of interest to foodies are fresh *tempeh* (Javanese-style fermented soy beans), *belacan* (shrimp paste) and *cincalot* (fermented krill dip) while the more adventurous might want to try live sago grubs, which are available from time to time.

Pasar Tani Mega, which is a farmers' market organisation, is a new addition to the market, and features stalls selling strictly local produce, great for 100-mile foodies.

Finally, Chinese butchers set up their stalls in an isolated section, selling pork and other non-halal meats. If you are here during the durian fruiting season (November to February), check out the durian stalls that are set up at the intersection of Jln Rubber and Jln Rubber Lorong to smell and taste what the fuss is all about. Just don't bring them back to your hotel.

If you are looking for a meal to complement your market shopping experience, you can try Fu Xiang Café, where the laksa, only available in the mornings, is especially good; Kueh Fah Café in spite of its Chinese name, is a popular Malay *kedai kopi* (coffee shop); Buhari, an Indian café, has great *nasi biryani* (saffron rice flavoured with spices and garnished with cashew nuts, almonds and raisins); while Hiong Mon Low is another bustling Chinese *kopitiam* (coffee shop). If you are here on Saturday evenings, by all means head to the Malay hawker's area, which starts at 5pm, and where you can pick up some great *satay* and *nasi goreng*.

Kuching resident Jeremy Tan is a photographer with an interest in Asian culture and development issues. You can visit his website at www.jeremytanphotography.com.

SARAWAK

and the top-end places located right in the centre of town along the river. Midrange places are scattered all about, with several located in the Jln Greenhill area.

Budget

B & B Inn (☎ 237-366; bnbswk@streamyx.com; Jln Tabuan; dm RM16, s/d RM25/35; ✖ ▣) Simple but clean rooms, a rooftop patio and a fairly convenient location make this a very good choice in the budget bracket.

Borneo B&B (☎ 231-200; borneobedbreakfast@yahoo .com; 3 Jln Green Hill; dm RM17, s RM28-32, d RM34-36; ✖ ▣) This homey place is popular with backpackers, although it's a little rundown and can be hot.

our pick Mandarin Hotel (☎ 418-269; 6 Jln Green Hill; r from RM50; ✖) This fine budget hotel is head and shoulders above the similarly priced joints nearby. It's simple, clean and good value.

Carpenter Guesthouse (☎ 256-050; www.carpen terguesthouse.com; 94 Jln Carpenter; dm RM28, r from 60; ✖) Located in an old Chinese shophouse, this brand new guesthouse has a great atmosphere and helpful owners. Rooms are on the small side and quite spartan, but it's clean and well run, and it's got a great location. Wi-fi is available.

Singgahsana Lodge (☎ 429-277; www.singgahsana .com; 1 Jln Temple; dm RM30, r from RM80; ✖ ▣) This stylish and well-run guesthouse has an unbeatable location and nice common areas. It's a bit overpriced, but very popular with Western backpackers.

City Inn Hotel (☎ 414-866; 276 Jln Abell; r RM46-70; ✖) This compact hotel on the east side of town is better than most comparably priced places in Kuching. It's got fairly neat carpeted rooms and reasonably clean bathrooms.

Midrange

Fata Hotel (☎ 248-111; fatahotel@hotmail.com; Jln McDougall; r RM52-80; ✖) A slight step up in comfort from the budget hotels, this simple hotel has cosy rooms, a lift and its own restaurant. Rear-view balconies look out over lovely parkland, rather than the daily traffic-jam views out the front.

Borneo Hotel (☎ 244-122; 30 Jln Tabuan; s/tw/tr RM110/125/145; ✖) With fairly clean and spacious rooms and a convenient restaurant in the lobby, this is one of Kuching's more reasonably priced midrange options. It's just up the street from some of the city's best dining options, and within easy striking distance of the Jln Carpenter Chinatown district.

Harbour View Hotel (☎ 274-666; www.harbour view.com.my; Jln Temple; r from RM115; ✖ ▣) This large hotel is good value, with small but neat rooms, some of which have decent views over the city or river. It's very convenient to Chinatown and the waterfront.

Top End

Merdeka Palace Hotel (☎ 258-000; www.merdekapal ace.com; Jln Tun Abang Haji Openg; standard r from RM180, deluxe r from RM260; ✖ ▣ ☎) The grand marble lobby and the great location overlooking the Padang Merdeka heighten expectations, but the service and rooms here are decidedly underwhelming. Some of the standard rooms here offer inside views of the parking garage and the food odours in the hallways don't improve matters.

Hilton Hotel (☎ 248-200; www.kuching.hilton.com; Jln Tunku Abdul Rahman; r RM200; ✖ ▣ ☎) Dominating the waterfront even from across the street, the Hilton offers spacious, clean rooms, some of which have ripping views over the river (and desks to sit at while you enjoy the view). The rooms are otherwise similar to the other contenders in this price range.

our pick Holiday Inn Kuching (☎ 423-111; www .holiday-inn.com/kuchingmys; Jln Tunku Abdul Rahman; r including 2 breakfasts from RM270; ✖ ☎) Kuching's sprawling Holiday Inn occupies a fine piece of real estate right on the river smack dab in the middle of town. While the service is a little uneven, the rooms are of good quality and well-kept and the pool is welcome after a day of sightseeing. The views from some of the rooms are as good as any in town.

Crowne Plaza Riverside Kuching (☎ 247-777; www .crowneplaza.com; Jln Tunku Abdul Rahman; r from RM325; ✖ ▣ ☎) Not only does the stylish Crowne Plaza have the usual spectrum of eating, business and sports amenities, it's also attached to the Riverside shopping complex, which provides an extra flurry of shopping plus a cinema and bowling alley. The rooms here are slightly nicer than those of the nearby Hilton, though the Riverbank Suites block the view of the river.

EATING

Kuching is a good place to work your way through the entire range of Sarawakian Malay and Chinese cooking. There are plenty of good hawker centres around town where you can pick and choose from a variety of stalls, each specialising in a particular cuisine or dish. For proper sit-down meals with wait-service, you'll find several stylish restaurants near the roundabout at the junction of Jln Tabuan and Jln Wayang. You'll find several more modern choices along Jln Padungan, which is currently undergoing a major restaurant, café and bar boom.

Hawker Centres

Chinese food stalls (Jln Carpenter; meals from RM3; breakfast, lunch & dinner) There are some brilliant Chinese hawker stalls in the small covered courtyard across from Sang Ti Miao. At the front on the right side there is a stall that does a sublime bowl of laksa (RM4, morning until lunchtime only). At the back to the left there is a stall that does a great ginger chicken in the evenings. Note that Chinese locals refer to this hawker centre as Lau Ya Keng in Hokkien.

Hawker Centre (Jln Khoo Hun Yeang; meals from RM3; breakfast, lunch & dinner) One of the best hawker centres in town, with both Malay and Chinese sections, is in the west end of town near Kuching Mosque (locals sometimes refer to this as the 'open-air market'). On the eastern side are stalls selling hawker food; good dishes to try include: beef noodle soup (Chinese-style *mee sapi*) from Ah Mui (evenings until late); red *kolo mee* (noodles with sweet barbecue sauce) at the noodle stall right at the front entrance (this stall has no name but is open all day); shaved ice desserts from Lock Ann (open lunchtime until late; ask for 'ABC' – the Southeast Asian Italian ice); and tomato *kway teow* (another fried rice-noodle dish) from Teck Huat (open all day). This section is usually closed on Sunday. In the other section, on Jln Market, are stalls serving Chinese food. The steamed fish at It Hng is particularly good; other stalls offer steamboat, a Chinese version of the Japanese *shabu shabu* dish.

There's another, less interesting **hawker centre** (off Jln Borneo; meals from RM3; breakfast, lunch & dinner) in the shopping complex opposite the Hilton.

Green Hill Corner (Jln Temple; meals RM3-4; breakfast, lunch & dinner) Several stalls here crank out a variety of noodle and rice dishes, including a brilliant plate of *kway teow goreng* (fried rice noodles). Problem is, the chef who makes this dish only shows up when he damn well feels like it.

Riverside Food & Drink Stalls (Waterfront Promenade, opposite the Hilton Hotel; meals from RM5; dinner) What could be better than an evening constitutional along the river followed by a fresh fruit juice and a few sticks of *satay?*

Top Spot Food Court (Jln Padungan; meals RM4-35; breakfast, lunch & dinner) An excellent rooftop plaza with acres of tables and a good variety of stalls. Order anything from abalone to banana prawns or numerous varieties of fish, and chase it down with a cold bottle of Tiger. To get here, climb the stairs leading from Jln Padungan to Tapanga restaurant, and keep heading upstairs from there.

Restaurants

Oriental Park (off Jln Mosque; noodles RM2.40; 5am-11.30am) Many Kuching Chinese start their day with a bowl of *mee sup* (ramen-style egg noo-dles in soup). This friendly little place does a brilliant version of this dish, complete with sa-voury bits of pork in a wonderfully rich soup. You can order this as *jooi mee* in Hokkien.

Chin Sa Barbeque Specialist (Jln Padungan; chicken rice from RM3; breakfast, lunch & dinner) Eat in or take away at this popular Jln Padungan barbecue joint, where savoury chicken or pork slices over rice are the speciality of the house.

Min Joa (Jln Carpenter; noodles with entrails RM6.50; 7am-noon) The signature dish – noodles with pork entrails – at this cramped, popular Chinatown noodle house won't be to every-one's liking. We tried it and found it surpris-ingly tasty and rich. Just ask for *mee sup*.

Little Lebanon (247-523; Sarawak Tourism Complex; mains from RM8; lunch & dinner, closed Mon) This sim-ple restaurant is a pleasant spot for a drink or a snack while exploring the Chinatown–Little India area.

Zhun San Yen Vegetarian Food Centre (Jln Chan Chin Ann; meals from RM10; lunch & dinner; V) If you find yourself at the east end of town in need of simple vegetarian food, this buffet-style restaurant is a decent choice.

Tao (175 Jln Padungan; meals from RM15; 10am-midnight daily) Tao rivals the following three res-taurants as Kuching's most stylish spot. It serves a variety of Malaysian and pan-Asian fare in a setting that seems more Bali than Borneo.

our pick **Bla Bla Bla** (233-944; 27 Jln Tabuan; mains from RM25; dinner) One of Borneo's most styl-ish restaurants. Expect tasty fusion food in a cool, indoor dining area that you access by traversing stepping stones across a carp pool under the watchful eye of a Buddha.

Junk (259-450; 80 Jln Wayang; mains from RM25; dinner Wed-Mon) Bla Bla Bla's sister restaurant, Junk is like a funky antique store that happens

SARAWAK

to serve whopping portions of Western comfort food. If you're ready for a break from *mee goreng*, this is a fascinating choice.

Living Room (☎ 233-944; Jln Wayang; mains from RM25; ☺ dinner) The same management as Junk also runs the impossibly cool Living Room, where you can drink and dine in outdoor *salas* (living rooms) while soaking up the soothing ambiance. You will no doubt find yourself wondering where you are: is this Borneo, Bali or Barcelona?

Benson Seafood (Jln Chan Chin Ann; meals from RM30; ☺ dinner) Ignore the aircraft hangar ambience and concentrate on the wonderful fresh Chinese seafood at this giant riverside eatery. The oyster omelettes are enough to make us want to hop on the next plane back to Kuching and the *midin* (jungle fern) stir fried with *belacan* (shrimp paste) is a Sarawak classic.

Café's & Coffee Shops

Life Café (Jln Carpenter; drinks from RM2, meals from RM5; ☺ lunch & dinner) This atmospheric little tea house and Chinese eatery offers a wide range of mostly Chinese dishes, including several good vegetarian choices.

Coffee Bean & Tea Leaf (ground fl, Sarawak Plaza; drinks from RM3; ☺ breakfast, lunch & dinner) This popular chain coffee shop offers free wi-fi and air-con surroundings.

Bing (☎ 421-880; 84 Jln Padungan; drinks from RM4; ☺ breakfast, lunch & dinner) Bing is a stylish, dimly lit café in the heart of the Jln Padungan nightlife zone. It's equally good for an afternoon cuppa or an evening tipple. There's wi-fi on premises.

Gallery Café (☎ 232-788; 88 Main Bazaar; drinks from RM4; ☺ 9am-6pm, closed Mon) What's not to like about a place that serves proper coffee in cool air-con surroundings, along with simple sandwiches and a good selection of desserts, with free wi-fi thrown in for good measure?

Sin Mei Café (Jln Green Hill; meals from RM5; ☺ breakfast & lunch) If you're staying in one of the Chinese cheapies nearby, you'll find this friendly little *kedai kopi* to be a great spot for your morning congee, noodles or toast and eggs.

DRINKING

The shopping complex across from the Hilton Hotel on Jln Borneo has a collection of bars and nightclubs that make for an easy pub crawl – if one isn't happening, just walk to the next one along. The bars and clubs along this strip are pretty casual and some can get a little rowdy at times. The main players here are **Cat City**, **Miami** and **Rainforest**.

Jln Padungan is a more upscale and civilised affair, with a selection of cool nightspots that would be equally at home in New York. Some likely spots to check here are **Mojo**, a wine shop and bar where you can buy wine and drink it on the premises; **Grappa**, a chilled-out spot with a long wooden bar under a sky of disco balls; **Ipanema**, a chic, spartan bar that also serves tapas; and **Soho**, a popular club where people dance to DJ-spun international pop on weekends.

Finally, there is an intriguing collection of restaurants-bars on Jln Tabuan, just south of the Jln Tabuan–Jln Wayang roundabout, including Bla, Bla, Bla, Living Room and Junk (see p169). You'll also find **Havana Café** here, which is more of a straight-up bar.

SHOPPING

If it's traditional Borneo arts and crafts you want, you've come to the right place. The aptly named Main Bazaar is one long strip of souvenir shops from Jln Wayang all the way to Jln Tun Abang Haji Openg. There are several standouts:

Fabriko (☎ 422-233; 56 Main Bazaar; ☺ 8.30am-5pm, closed Sun) This fine little shop has a well-chosen selection of traditional and imported fabrics and clothes made from them.

Unika Sarawak (☎ 235-012; 70 Main Bazaar; ☺ 10am-5.30pm) We love the cluttered interior of this handicraft and wood-carving shop. If you're after something in wood, this is a good place to look.

ARTrageously Ramsey Ong (☎ 424-346; 94 Main Bazaar) Moving away from customary handicrafts, this private gallery exhibits and sells mainly contemporary paintings, and champions local artists, including Mr Ramsey Ong himself.

There are two main shopping centres in the downtown area, located almost directly across from one another:

Sarawak Plaza (Jln Tunku Abdul Rahman; ☺ 9am-9pm daily, shops from 10am) A little long in the tooth, but home to a few useful shops.

Tun Jugah Shopping Centre (Jln Tunku Abdul Rahman; ☺ 9am-9pm daily, shops from 10am) A new place with modern shops and a good bookshop.

For camera supplies and repairs, as well as digital services such as CD burning, **Empress**

Studio (☎ 241-009; 1B Jln India) is one of the best all-round photo shops in town.

GETTING THERE & AWAY
Air

Air Asia (☎ within Malaysia 03-8775-4000, outside Malaysia 60-3-8660-4343; www.airasia.com; ground fl, Wisma Ho Ho Lim, 291 Jln Abell) has numerous daily flights to/from Kuala Lumpur at bargain-basement prices. They also fly to/from Penang and Johor Bahru. Within Borneo, they fly to/from Bintulu, Kota Kinabalu, Miri and Sibu. Check for prices as they constantly change.

Batavia Air (☎ in Jakarta 386-4308, in Pontianak 721-560, in Kuching 628-166; www.batavia-air.co.id; no. 1, ground fl, Padungan Arcade Garden, Jln Song Thian Cheok) has flights to/from Jakarta (Java) and Pontianak (Kalimantan) for around US$50 one way.

Malaysia Airlines (MAS; ☎ anywhere in Malaysia 1-300-883-000, 03-7843-3000, in Kuching 220-618; www.malaysiaairlines.com; 215 Jln Song Thian Cheok) offers flights between Kuching and Kuala Lumpur (RM259) and Johor Bahru (RM199). They also fly between Kuching and Hong Kong and Guangzhou. Within Borneo, MAS flies to/from Bintulu (RM139), Kota Kinabalu (RM229), Miri (RM139) and Sibu (RM89).

Silk Air (☎ in Kuching 256-772, in Singapore 6223-8888; www.silkair.com; 7th fl, Gateway Building, Jln Bukit Mata) has flights to/from Singapore.

Finally, **Royal Brunei Airlines** (☎ in Brunei 221-2222; www.bruneiair.com) is reported to be planning to start a Kuching to Bandar Seri Begawan route (check online to see if it's in operation). For information on getting to/from the airport, see the Getting Around section (right).

Boat

Express Bahagia (☎ 410-076) has boats running to and from Sibu (RM36, 4½ hours), departing from the express boat wharf in Pending at 8.30am daily. Note that this is an easier and faster trip to Sibu than the bus, which takes eight hours.

The express-boat wharf is 6.5km east of town in the suburb of Pending. Chin Lian Long (CLL) bus 1 (RM1.50, 40 minutes) connects the wharf with Kuching. It operates from the STC-CLL bus stand near Kuching Mosque and stops on Jln Tunku Abdul Rahman just west of the Holiday Inn. Taxis from town cost RM20.

Finally, note that there is talk that the Pending Wharf may be moved but this is, as yet, unconfirmed. Ask at your lodgings before setting out.

Bus

Long-distance buses depart from the **Express Bus Terminal** (Jln Penrissen), 5km southeast of the centre. There are regular services to Sibu (RM40, eight hours, 10 departures daily between 6.30am and 10pm), Bintulu (RM60, 10 hours, nine departures daily between 6.30am and 10pm), and Miri (RM80, 14 hours, eight departures daily between 6.30am and 10pm).

Numerous Sarawak Transport Co (STC) buses run between the terminal and city for 90 sen. The buses are 3A, 4B and 6 and leave from either in front of the mosque or on Jln Barrack behind the courthouse. A taxi costs RM15.

TO/FROM INDONESIA

From the Express Bus Terminal, there are services to Pontianak (Damri, SJS and BH bus companies; RM45, nine hours, four departures daily between 8am and 1pm) in Kalimantan. Buses cross at the Tebedu–Entikong crossing. You must apply for a visa at the Indonesia Consulate in Kuching before setting out. If you want to travel in a bit more comfort, SJS runs a 'deluxe' bus at 11am, which has nicer seats and costs RM70.

Border Crossings

The closest border crossing from Kuching into the Indonesian state of Kalimantan is located at Tebedu, near Serian. Travellers making land crossings into Kalimantan are required to obtain a visa beforehand from the **Indonesian Consulate** (☎ 421-734; 6th fl, Bangunan Binamas, Jln Padungan; ✆ 9am-1pm Mon-Thu, 9am-noon Fri) as the border posts at the Kalimantan border does not issue visas on arrival. Fees and requirements differ from country to country; contact the consulate for more information.

GETTING AROUND
To/From the Airport

Kuching International Airport (KCH) is 12km south of the city centre. STC's green-and-cream bus 12A does a circuit that takes in the airport (RM1.60), while CLL's blue-and-white bus 8A does a direct airport-to-city run (RM1.40). In Kuching, these services operate from near Kuching Mosque and stop on Jln Tun Abang Haji Openg, near the Padang Merdeka (note that 8A sometimes

SARAWAK

p here). To catch the bus from
t, exit the terminal and turn right.
is also swing by the stop and can
t. ort you to town for about RM3 per
seat or RM20 to charter. A coupon-fare taxi
between Kuching airport and the city centre costs RM17. Buy coupons at the counter
outside the terminal entrance.

Boat
Tambang (small passenger ferries) will ferry
you across Sungai Sarawak for destinations
such as Margherita and the Astana. The fare
is 30 sen, which you pay as you disembark.
You can catch *tambang* at several jetties
along the waterfront. If there isn't one waiting when you arrive, just wait and one will
usually materialise fairly soon.

Car
There are several car rental agencies in
the arrivals hall of Kuching International
Airport. Despite the fact that they have different names, most of them are fronts for
the same company, and it's very difficult to
play one off against another in the hope of
getting a better price.

Taxi
There are taxi ranks at the market and at
the Express Bus Terminal. Most short trips
around town cost between RM6 and RM10.
Taxis in Kuching do not have meters, so be
sure to settle on the fare before setting out.
Luckily, most of the drivers are fairly honest
and you don't have to bargain too hard.

AROUND KUCHING

BAKO NATIONAL PARK
Sarawak's oldest national park, **Bako National
Park** (☎ 011-225-049; admission RM10; ⊙ park office 8am-
5pm) is a 27-sq-km natural sanctuary located on
a jagged peninsula nestled between the mouths
of the Sarawak and Bako Rivers and jutting out
into the South China Sea. Although it's less
than 20km from downtown Kuching as the
crow flies, it feels like worlds and eons away.

The coast of the peninsula consists of
lovely pocket beaches tucked into secret bays
alternating with stretches of brilliant mangrove swamp. The interior plateau of the
park is marked by rainforest and *kerangas*,
the distinctive sandstone habitat that forms

the geological backbone of the plateau.
Hiking trails cross the plateau and connect
with most of the main beaches (which can
also be reached by boat).

First and foremost, the park is notable for
its incredible biodiversity, from pitcher plants
to terrestrial orchids to bearded pigs and long-
tailed macaques. Of course, the stars of the
show are the proboscis monkeys, and Bako
is one of the best places in Borneo to observe
these long-nosed creatures up close.

Bako is an easy day trip from Kuching, but
it would be a shame to rush it – we recommend staying a night or two to really enjoy
the wild beauty of the place.

Orientation & Information
Register for the park (adult/child RM10/5)
upon arrival at the boat dock in Bako Bazaar.
From here it's a choppy 30-minute boat ride
to **park headquarters** (Telok Assam; ☎ 011-225-049),
where you'll find accommodation, a cafeteria and the park office. The office is about
400m along a wooden boardwalk from the
boat dock. Staff will show you to your quarters and can answer any questions you have
about trails. There's a large trail map hanging
outside the office; ask for a free copy. Storage
lockers are available for RM5 per day.

There's a good, if slightly scruffy, information centre here, with photos and displays
on various aspects of the park's ecology. An
entertaining video on the proboscis monkey is
shown at regular times and also on request –
ask at the office.

Sights & Activities
WALKING
Bako has a total of 17 trails ranging from
short walks around park headquarters to
strenuous day treks to the end of the peninsula. Guides are available (RM20 per hour),
but it's easy to find your way around because
all trails are colour-coded and clearly marked
with splashes of paint. You don't have to go
far to see wildlife, and there are walks to suit
all levels of fitness and motivation. Plan your
route before starting out on longer walks, and
aim to be back at Telok Assam before dark
(about 6.45pm). Some trails may be closed
for maintenance after the wet season – check
at the park office before setting out.

If you have only one day in Bako, try to
get here early and attempt the Lintang Trail
(5.25km, four to five hours). It traverses a

AROUND KUCHING

0 ——————— 14 km
0 ——————— 8 miles

SIGHTS & ACTIVITIES
Bidayuh Longhouse
(Kampung Benuk)...........................**1** B5
Bidayuh Longhouse
(Kumpung Annah Rais)................**2** B6
Bidayuh Longhouse
(Kumpung Gayu)...........................**3** B5
Matang Wildlife Centre.................**4** A3

Rock Carvings.....................................**5** D5
Sarawak Cultural Village.................**6** C5
Semenggoh Wildlife Rehabilitation
Centre...**7** B4
Wind Cave...**8** A4

SLEEPING
Borneo Highlands Resort.................**9** A6

Holiday Inn Resort Damai Beach....**10** C5
Nanga Damai Luxury Homestay.....**11** C5
Permai Rainforest Resort................**12** C5
Santubong Kuching Resort.............**13** C5
Sarawak Cultural Village.............(see 6)

EATING
Green Paradise Café.........................**14** C5

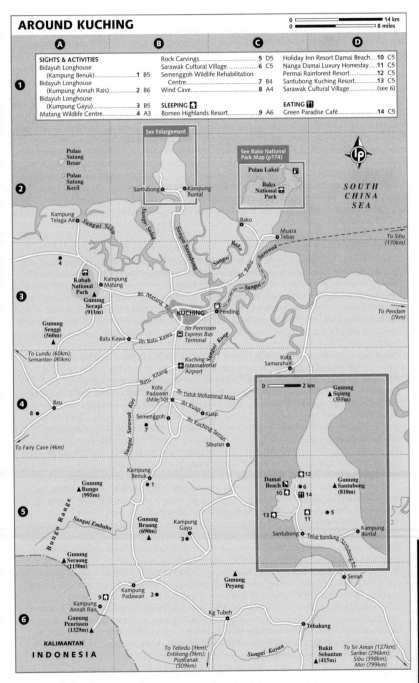

SARAWAK

range of vegetation and climbs the sandstone escarpment up to the *kerangas*, where you'll find many pitcher plants as well as some grand views over the nearby island plateaus.

The longest trail is the Telok Limau, a 12km walk that's impossible to do as a return trip in one day. You will need to carry camping equipment or else arrange to be dropped off by boat in the morning and walk back to park headquarters (expect to be charged about RM200; and be sure to let someone know of your plans). See below for the park's main trails; the times given are those recommended by the national park.

Take adequate water or purification tabs and be prepared for intense sun with sun hats and sunscreen as it gets particularly hot in the *kerangas* and there's no shade for long stretches (sun-sensitive folks might consider lightweight long-sleeve shirts and trousers).

In the evening, park rangers may offer a guided night trek, if there is enough interest from guests. This is an opportunity not to be missed, as the wildlife present at night is entirely different from that seen during the day. The rangers are also particularly good at spotting things that an ordinary traveller would miss. Inquire at the welcome desk to see if there is a trek on that night. The trek lasts between 1½ to two hours and costs about RM10 per person.

WILDLIFE

Bako is a storehouse of incredible natural diversity: biologists estimate that the park is

---

BAKO TREKKING & WALKING TRAILS

The following is a selection of the park's main hiking trails. Note that times are estimates and muddy conditions and fallen trees can increase walking times significantly. And, as usual, keep in mind that hiking in the tropics is much harder than in temperate zones. A good rule of thumb is that one kilometre in the tropics is equivalent to two in temperate zones. A note on trail names: *tanjung* means point, *telok* means bay, *bukit* means hill, and *ulu* means upriver or interior.

Tanjung Sapi Trail (cliffs, viewpoint, 0.8km, 30 minutes) This short, steep trail leads to a point, which affords good views over Telok Assam, Gunung Santubong and the South China Sea. Proboscis monkey sightings are possible in the evening.

Telok Delima Trail (mangroves, 1km, 45 minutes) This walk leads to Telok Delima, the next bay south of Telok Assam. It's a good chance to see mangrove swamp and all the creatures that live there. The last part can only be done at low tide (during low tide, you can walk along the beach all the way to/from Telok Assam).

Telok Paku Trail (Cove Beach, 1.2km, 45 minutes) This trail follows the plank walk and then diverts along rocky cliffs before arriving at rocky Telok Paku beach and bay. More proboscis sightings are possible here.

Telok Pandan Kecil Trail (Cove Beach, 2.5km, 1½ hours) This trail initially follows the Lintang Trail across the plateau before branching off to Pandan Besar and then Pandan Kecil, one of the park's loveliest bays and beaches.

Ulu Serait Trail (park boundary, 4.8km, 1½ hours) This inland route parallels the park boundary and it can be combined with the Bukit Kruing Trail to form one very long (seven hour) and very tiring loop. The trail passes through some fairly open country, so be prepared for intense sun.

Tajor Trail (waterfalls, 3.5km, 2½ hours) This trail takes the Lintang/Pandan Kecil route before continuing east across the plateau to arrive at the Tajor Waterfall, a nice spot for a swim or picnic. A path leads from the stream to Telok Tajor.

Tanjung Rhu Trail (cliffs, viewpoint, 4.2km, 2½ hours) Largely the same as the above Tajor route, this trail branches off shortly before the waterfall and heads north to the Tanjung Rhu promontory.

Lintang Trail (circular path, 5.25km, 4 to 5 hours) This varied and challenging trail provides an excellent sample of the main geological formations and vegetation types in the park. Parts are exposed and can be hot. Steps and plankwalks ease your way through some of the tougher sections. The detour up Bukit Tambi is worth it for the views of Gunung Santubong.

Bukit Kruing/Jln Bukit Gondol Trail (mountain path, 7.7km, 7 hours) This challenging route is only for the fit and adventurous. Bring plenty of water, wear a hat and consider a long-sleeve shirt. There are two variations, one of which involves climbing Bukit Gondol (which is obviously more strenuous).

Ulu Serait/Jln Telok Limau Trail (Pulau Lakei, 12km, up to 10 hours) This marathon trail leads over varied terrain and through various types of vegetation all the way out to Telok Limau, at the northeast end of the park. You'll need to bring a water filter or purification tabs or iodine since carrying sufficient water would be feasible only for lowland sherpas. It's best to arrange to take a boat out to Telok Limau and then walk back, but the reverse is also possible. Make sure someone at the park knows of your plans when attempting this hike.

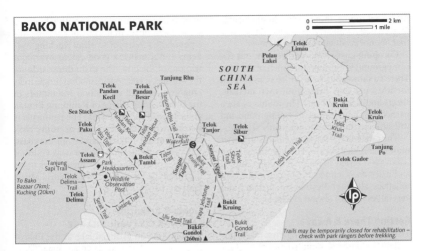

BAKO NATIONAL PARK

Trails may be temporarily closed for rehabilitation – check with park rangers before trekking.

home to 37 species of mammals, 24 reptile species and 184 bird species (some of which are migrant species).

Walking trails pass through peat swamp, rainforest and, on the low sandstone plateau behind Telok Assam, *kerangas*. The latter, especially near the intersection of the Lintang and Ulu Serait trails, is a fascinating ecosystem where pitcher plants are common.

Animals include long-tailed macaques, silver-leaf monkeys, monitor lizards, palm squirrels and, at night, mouse deer, civets and culago (flying lemur). The best place to look for the proboscis monkey are along at the beach at the end of the Telok Paku trail, where they forage around the trees lining the cliff. Walk very quietly and listen for them crashing through the trees – they will see you long before you see them. Telok Delima trail offers a more close-up experience: listen for grunts and crashing vegetation and follow the sound with your eyes. You've also got a good chance of seeing them feeding around the mangrove boardwalk just before the park jetty in the late morning.

Bird-watching is best near the park headquarters, especially in and around the mangroves at Telok Assam.

The large bearded pig that hangs around near the cafeteria is a minor celebrity in the park and a big hit with kids. It often ambles by in the afternoons.

BEACHES

The beach at **Telok Pandan Kecil**, surrounded by spectacular sandstone rock formations, is gorgeous. Around the point is the famous Bako Sea Stack, which you have no doubt already seen on countless postcards; to get close to it for a photo, however, you'll have to hire a boat.

The quiet, attractive beach at **Telok Pandan Besar** is only accessible by boat from the park headquarters as the final descent from the cliff top of the trail is closed. The beach at **Telok Sibur** is accessible by foot but hard to reach as the descent is steep, and you have to negotiate through a mangrove swamp, but it is worthwhile as others rarely make it down here.

If you're thinking of hitching a boat ride to or from a beach, boats to beaches near park headquarters will cost around RM25 (one way or return), but to beaches further away it is quite expensive (eg RM80 to Telok Sibur). **Pulau Lakei**, on the park's northeastern tip, is accessible by boat (RM120).

Sleeping & Eating

There is plenty of accommodation at Bako National Park, including two- and three-room chalets, as well as hostels and a muddy campground. You can book accommodation through the **visitors' information centre** (☎ 082-410-944; www.sarawaktourism.com; Sarawak Tourism Complex, Jln Tun Abang Haji Openg; ☺ 8am-6pm Mon-Fri, 9am-3pm Sat, Sun & holidays) in Kuching. Phone bookings are accepted, but must be confirmed and paid for at least three days before your intended arrival.

The **hostel** (dm/r RM15/40) has four beds with a shared kitchen and bathroom. Variously sized **chalets** (r RM50-100) are also available. Bookings are essential for the chalets and advisable for the hostel rooms, though you should be able to get a bed if you arrive on a weekday. Note that 5% tax is added to all these rates.

Camping costs RM5 per person, but the campground is a swamp for much of the year. There's a shower block and lockers can be hired for RM5 per day. Bring your own utensils, sheets and sleeping bags. The monkeys are a particular nuisance near the campground and will steal anything that is not firmly secured.

The **cafeteria** (✆ 8am-9pm) sells cheap buffet noodle and rice meals. The adjoining shop sells a good variety of reasonably priced tinned and dried food, chocolate, biscuits, film and toiletries, although fresh bread, produce and vegetables are not always available.

Getting There & Away

To get to Bako from Kuching, first take a bus to Bako Bazaar in Kampung Bako, then charter a boat to the park. Petra Jaya bus 6 leaves from near the hawker centre (open-air market) near Kuching Mosque in Kuching every hour (approximately) from 7.20am to 6pm (RM2.50, 45 minutes). The last bus back to Kuching leaves Kampung Bako at 5pm. You can also go by taxi all the way from Kuching (RM35, 30 minutes).

A boat from Bako Bazaar to the park headquarters costs RM40 each way for up to five people, or RM8 per person for larger groups. The chances are that someone on the bus will be looking to share a boat, especially on a weekend; tourists sometimes wait at the boat dock for the same reason.

Take note of the boat's number and be sincere when you agree to a pick-up time. If you do want to share a different boat back, tell park headquarters your boat number – staff are happy to call and cancel your original boat.

It's a pleasant 20-minute boat trip past coastal scenery and fishing boats. From November to February the sea is often rough, adding a real touch of excitement to the ride, and at times it may not be possible for boats to approach or leave Telok Assam. If you're planning a day trip, be aware that boatmen may insist on an early-afternoon return time to beat the tides. Take a waterproof jacket to protect against spray in the open boats.

SANTUBONG PENINSULA
☎ 082

Like Bako National Park, the Santubong Peninsula (also known as Damai) is a spit

of land jutting out into the South China Sea some 20km north of the city of Kuching. It's a popular getaway for wealthy Kuching residents and it makes a good day or overnight trip out of the city. The main drawcards are the beaches, a golf course, modest jungle trekking and a clutch of seafood restaurants in the small fishing village of Kampung Buntal, at the base of the peninsula. The peninsula is also known for a collection of primitive rock carvings about 1.5km inland from the coast. The peninsula also has the Sarawak Cultural Village, a photogenic ethnic theme park that's the site of the annual Rainforest World Music Festival (p167).

Sights & Activities
SARAWAK CULTURAL VILLAGE
Surrounding an artificial lake at the foot of Gunung Santubong, the **Sarawak Cultural Village** (☎ 846-411; www.scv.com.my; adult/child RM60/30; ✆ 9am-5.15pm) is an excellent living museum. It has examples of traditional dwellings built by different peoples of Sarawak – in this case Orang Ulu, Bidayuh, Iban and Melanau – as well as Malay and Chinese houses.

There are six buildings in all, plus a games centre and a shelter of the type used by the nomadic Penan in the jungle. The dwellings are staffed by tribespeople who demonstrate local arts and crafts, including basketry and weaving, blowpipe shooting, sago processing and bird's nest–goods production. Even travellers who have ventured to the Borneo interior are generally impressed by this unique opportunity to see the original styles of the now modernised longhouses. Many of the participants speak English well and can offer a wealth of information about Sarawak.

There's also a twice-daily performance showcasing the traditional dances of the various tribes, which include spectacular physical feats such as the Melanau funeral pole dance. The audience is usually invited onstage to dance at some point, but don't be put off by this breaking of the fourth wall, as dancing with your hosts is considered the thing to do in Malay and Dayak culture. It's all quite touristy, of course, but tastefully done and sincere in intent.

All the tribespeople are paid to take part in the daily activities, and they sell their own products for additional income. Great pains are taken to make the village authentic – just to prove the point, the nomadic Penan occasionally go AWOL.

Hotels and travel agencies in Kuching have packages that include admission, lunch and transport ranging in price from RM80 to RM100. An extra RM30 will net you dinner at a seafood restaurant in Kampung Buntal. If you're planning to get married in Sarawak, you can choose to tie the knot in style here according to Iban, Bidayuh, Orang Ulu or Malay ceremonies.

There's no public transport to the village, but a shuttle bus leaves the Holiday Inn Kuching at 9am and 12.30pm, returning at 1.45pm and 5.30pm (RM10 each way).

JUNGLE WALKING

The Santubong Peninsula offers good jungle walking within easy reach of Kuching, and more adventurous walkers can attempt the ascent of **Gunung Santubong** (810m), a 3.4km trail that takes around five hours one way.

An easy to moderate circular walk (2km, one to two hours) starts near the Holiday Inn Resort and ends near the cultural village, passing a pretty **waterfall** on the way. Both trails start at the **Green Paradise Café**, where you register and pay a RM1 fee. The trails are well marked so you shouldn't get lost. If you really wish to put in the hours, there's a camp site near the café, but if you want to make an overnight trek you'd be better off investigating somewhere more adventurous like Bako National Park.

ROCK CARVINGS

Although they're a little difficult to find, the Santubong rock carvings on Sungai Jaong are worth seeking out, if you have an interest in archaeology. There's said to be nearly 40 of these artefacts, mostly carvings on boulders (including a distinct human figure), though it's unlikely you'll be able to find that many without spending quite a bit of time looking around. An accurate dating of the site hasn't been made yet, but it's thought to be at least a thousand years old. Chinese ceramic pieces from the Tang dynasty and evidence of iron-making have also been found here, making it one of Sarawak's most important archaeological sites.

To reach the petroglyphs, turn into a gravel road south off the main road going into Santubong, about 3km after the turn-off for Kampung Buntal and near the 6km marker on the road to Damai. The gravel road will take you to two houses and a walking trail to

the rock is behind them. You will more than likely need to ask a local for directions. The site is called Batu Gambar in Malay, but don't be surprised if the first local you ask does not know about it – keep trying and you'll find someone who does.

WILDLIFE TOURS

The Santubong area is home to a wide variety of wildlife, and guided wildlife tours are beginning to catch on here. Commonly spotted species include endangered Irrawaddy dolphins, known locally as *pesut*, estuarine monkeys, crocodiles and all manner of birds.

CPH Travel (☎ 242-289; www.cphtravel.com.my; per person RM150, minimum 2 persons), based in Santubong, runs wildlife tours to the area. If you are already in the Santubong-Buntal area, consider going with local Buntal boatman, **Mr Ehwan bin Ibrahim** (☎ 019-826-5680), who offers a selection of tours of the area. Expect to pay around RM450 for a four-person boat for a dolphin-and-mangrove tour, and be sure to book three or four days in advance. **Camp Permai** (☎ 846-847) offers guided kayaking tours for about RM60 per person.

Sleeping & Eating

Sarawak Cultural Village (☎ 846-411; psw@scv.com.my; food & lodging packages per person per night from RM60) Theme village stays can be arranged with packages of varying lengths in the dwelling of your choice. Prices vary according to group size and length of stay.

Permai Rainforest Resort (☎ 846-487; www.permairainforest.com; Damai Beach, Santubong; camp site RM10, longhouses RM120, treehouses RM198, cabins RM208-228; 🈺) This excellent ecofriendly nature retreat offers a choice of longhouse dorms, six- to eight-person cabins and luxury treehouse rooms (which include breakfast and minibar), as well as space for camping. Even better, the adjoining Camp Permai training centre (day entry RM5) is the best spot on the peninsula for leisure and adventure activities, with a high-ropes course, rock climbing, kayaking, boat cruises, obstacle course and abseiling to name but a few. This place is good for those travelling with children.

Nanga Damai Luxury Homestay (☎ 019-887-1017; www.nangadamai.com; Jln Sultan Tengah, Santubong; r RM80-120; 🈺 🈺) If you're expecting a mattress on a longhouse veranda you might be surprised – this lovely family-run guesthouse isn't kidding when it says 'luxury', and the beautiful garden setting makes it easy to meet the two-night minimum stay. Breakfast is included and there's even a private jungle trail, but children under 12 are not permitted.

Santubong Kuching Resort (☎ 846-888; skresort@ po.jaring.my; Jln Sultan Tengah, Santubong; weekend r RM138-380, slightly cheaper on weekdays; ❄ ❂) This home-grown alternative to the big resorts has an equally good range of facilities, plus activities such as tennis, basketball, water sports, golf and mountain biking. The beach is a five-minute walk and discount packages are usually available.

Holiday Inn Resort Damai Beach (☎ 846-999; www .holiday-inn.com/damaibeach; Teluk Bandung, Santubong; r RM460-640; ❄ ▢ ❂) A massive seafront resort with a touch of traditional design in its beach, pool and hillside suites. It's also close to Sarawak Cultural Village and has a nice beach, a spa, a pool and other resort-style amenities.

There are several restaurants around the resorts in the peninsula. Kampung Buntal, a few kilometres away, boasts a large collection of seafood restaurants with attractive patios on stilts over the beach, all very popular with Kuching locals, the favourite being Lim Hok Ann near the end of the restaurant strip.

Getting There & Away

To reach Kampung Buntal from Kuching, take Petra Jaya bus 2D from the intersection of Jln Khoo Hun Yeang and Jln Market (RM2, one hour, leaves every 90 minutes from 6am). For Santubong, take a taxi from Kampung Buntal (around RM10, 15 minutes). The last return bus for Kuching leaves at 6.40pm; if you want to stay for a meal the only option is to take a taxi back to Kuching (around RM25, 45 minutes).

A taxi to the resorts costs RM25 to RM30 from Kuching; if you want to be picked up after dinner, expect to pay RM60 for the return trip. A taxi from Kampung Buntal to any of the resorts should cost around RM10. Taxis can also be hired for a trip from the resorts out to Kampung Buntal and Santubong.

KUBAH NATIONAL PARK

Only 15km from downtown Kuching, **Kubah National Park** (☎ 011-225-003; admission RM10/5 adult/ child) is yet another good natural retreat within easy striking distance of the city. While Bako has the edge for wildlife, Kubah offers good trekking and the trails are more shaded, which is a plus for the sun-averse. The 22-sq-km park consists of a range of forested sandstone hills that rise dramatically from the surrounding plain to a height of 450m. There are waterfalls, walking trails and lookouts, and the beautiful rainforest is home to a wide variety of palms and orchids. Kubah National Park has also played host to two Hollywood productions, *Farewell to the King*, starring Nick Nolte and the more recent *The Sleeping Dictionary*, with Jessica Alba.

Walking trails include the paved entrance road, which runs right up to the summit of Kubah's highest peak, 911m **Gunung Serapi**; it's a two- to three-hour walk. The peak is often shrouded in mist but there are lookouts along the way. You can probably hitch a lift up then walk down. Most of the other trails run off the entrance road. The **Rayu Trail** links Kubah with the Matang Wildlife Centre, 5km from the turn-off, and takes about three hours to walk.

The **Waterfall Trail**, which ends at a natural swimming pool, takes about 1½ hours from the park headquarters, while an alternate starting point from the main summit road takes about 45 minutes from the turn-off.

A moderately easy trail, the **Belian Trail**, showcases its namesake tree, otherwise known as 'ironwood', a tropical hardwood traditionally used in longhouse construction and blow-pipe barrels. Bintangor trees are common in the park as well; the sap of these trees is currently being researched as it contains chemicals that may be useful in AIDS treatment.

Sleeping

Park accommodation can be booked through the Kuching **visitors' information centre** (☎ 082-410-944; www.sarawaktourism.com; Sarawak Tourism Complex, Jln Tun Abang Haji Openg; ☼ 8am-6pm Mon-Fri, 9am-3pm Sat, Sun & holidays).

The Kubah park headquarters offers hostel, resthouse and double-storey chalet accommodation. In the comfortable, clean **hostel** (dm/r RM15/40), rooms are fan-cooled and have shared bathrooms. There's no restaurant, but a kitchen is supplied with all facilities, including a fridge and utensils.

Forest lodges (r RM120-225; ❄) with full facilities sleep eight to 10 people each. Kubah is entirely self-catering; if you have transport, you can get supplies in the local *kampung* or even dine back in Kuching, but otherwise you'll have to bring all your own food.

Getting There & Away

Matang Transport bus 11 leaves Kuching (from the stand near Kuching Mosque) for Red Bridge, near the turn-off for Kubah, at regular intervals (RM2, 40 minutes); there's no set timetable, but services run roughly every 90 minutes in the morning. The bus will drop you off at Red Bridge, near the Jublee Mas Recreation Park, from where it's a 4km walk to the park entrance, quite a lot of it uphill. Follow the signs for Matang Family Park, as the signposts for Kubah at the moment look like they're about to fall off. A taxi from town will cost at least RM70 return; arrange with the driver a time to be picked up. You can also try to get a ride on a private van (RM5 per person or RM35 for the whole van one-way, leaving near Saujana Car Park).

Another option is to drive, but the park is not well signposted. From downtown Kuching go west on Jln Satok, which will take you across Sungai Sarawak. At the first roundabout, take the first exit (Matang) and at the end of the road, take a right at the T-junction (not signposted). Follow the road until the roundabout and take the second exit (the exit itself is not signposted but there is a large sign before you enter the roundabout from this direction indicating the exit). You are now on Jln Matang Baru. Red Bridge is a bridge crossing a stream with metal railings painted red; before reaching it, you will pass Jublee Mas Recreation Park on your right. The junction has the sign for Matang Family Park.

MATANG WILDLIFE CENTRE

A short drive beyond Kubah National Park, the **Matang Wildlife Centre** (☎ 011-225-012; admission RM10; ☽ 8am-5.30pm daily) was set up as a rehabilitation centre for endangered species released from captivity, particularly Borneo's larger mammals. Although it's supposed to recreate natural conditions as closely as possible, there's no denying that it's better described as a zoo located in the jungle.

The centre is popular with locals who come to swim at the **Matang Family Park** on weekends. There's accommodation, a cafeteria and a very good information centre here. There are twice-daily feeding programmes for orangutans, hornbills, sambar deer and crocodiles, as well as rainforest walking trails, including the **Rayu Trail**, which links up with Kubah National Park (three to four hours).

The animals are kept in enclosures, or sometimes even cages, and people who don't like zoos may find it depressing. It is important to remember, however, that the centre is part of an active rehabilitation program and that many of these animals will find themselves being re-released into the wild in the future.

Matang has a **hostel** (dm/r RM15/40) with four-bed rooms, two **forest lodges** (RM150; ☒) sleeping eight, and a **camp site** (per person RM5). Book accommodation at Kuching **visitors' information centre** (☎ 082-410-944; www .sarawaktourism.com; Sarawak Tourism Complex, Jln Tun Abang Haji Openg; ☽ 8am-6pm Mon-Fri, 9am-3pm Sat, Sun & holidays).

The only practical options for getting here from Kuching are by taxi (about RM35 one way) or with a tour (around RM130 for an overnight stay). Walking from Red Bridge is not an option as the entrance is a further 12km from the entrance to Kubah National Park. Try waving down a local private van or hitching.

SEMENGGOH WILDLIFE REHABILITATION CENTRE

Semenggoh Wildlife Rehabilitation Centre (☎ 082-442-180; adult/child RM3/1.50; ☽ 8am-12.45pm & 2-4.15pm) is a good place to see Borneo's famous great ape in fairly natural conditions. There isn't sufficient natural forest in the surrounding area to make actual reintroduction into the wild possible, but it's still a good chance to see orangutans in fairly natural surroundings. Semenggoh is less touristy than the much better known Sepilok Orangutan Rehabilitation Centre in Sabah and it makes an easy day trip out of Kuching. Note that you're not guaranteed any orangutan sightings, because the apes are free to come and go as they please (sightings are least likely when surrounding trees are fruiting, usually between December and May).

The semiwild orangutans are fed from 9am to 10am and again from 3pm to 3.30pm, so it's best to time your visit to coincide with one of these sessions. It's not uncommon for orangutans to turn up at the centre itself rather than the feeding platforms, so don't rush off straight away if everything seems quiet. Even if the orangs are a no-show, other animals such as brightly coloured squirrels often put in an appearance to sneak a nibble at the buckets of fruit.

Semenggoh is 32km south of Kuching. To get there, take STC bus 6 from Kuching (RM2.50, 40 minutes, seven daily). Get off at the Forest Department Nursery, then walk 1.3km down the paved road to the centre. The last return bus passes Semenggoh at 2.20pm, but you should be able to flag down a private van (RM3) or a bus from the main road. A taxi from Kuching to the centre costs around RM40.

Tour companies also operate guided day trips out to the centre for RM50 per person. Note that some tours don't leave sufficient time to explore the gardens and arboretum at the centre (ask before you sign up).

BIDAYUH LONGHOUSES

A visit to a longhouse is a good chance to see how Borneo's indigenous peoples live, but don't expect a scene out of *National Geographic*: these folks are just as keen as the rest of us to enjoy the comforts of modern life and many of the longhouses near Kuching have been on the tour-operators' circuit for years.

Kampung Annah Rais is one of the most commonly visited longhouses. It's an impressive structure with more than 100 doors, and has preserved its traditional look, apart from metal roofs and satellite dishes that is. The villagers also keep the tour operators informed of any special festivities taking place in the village. **Kampung Benuk** is also regularly visited by tour groups, and there are many others in this area. Standard price for admission to these longhouses is RM8/4 per adult/child, which includes a guided tour of the cottage industries in the longhouse. There are quite a few homestay options averaging RM280 for a 2-day 1-night stay per person, including food and activities, and tourists can be accommodated even if they show up unannounced.

To get to Annah Rais, take STC bus 6 or 3A (RM2, one hour) from Kuching to Kota Padawan and try to find a shared van from the parking lot near the hornbill statues at the end of the main street (RM6 and up if there are sufficient passengers to share the ride; it costs RM35 to charter the van).

For Kampung Benuk take STC bus 6 (RM4, 1½ hours, seven daily) and ask the driver to let you off at the village. Travel agencies also have tours starting from around RM80 per person for a day trip, while a taxi will cost RM80 each way.

GUNUNG PENRISSEN

Although it's actually located in Kalimantan, Indonesia, 1329m **Gunung Penrissen** is usually approached from the Sarawak side. Because of its location, it was a military hot spot during the Konfrontasi period, and was the site of a few border skirmishes. Ironically, the military outpost near the peak now serves as a scenic lookout with spectacular views into Kalimantan as well as back into Sarawak. Experienced, well-equipped climbers can climb the mountain, which can be done in a one-day burn or as a two- to three-day overnight trek. It's rough going, and a local guide is essential.

The most practical way to do the trek is to ask a tour operator in Kuching to put together a custom trip for you, as few offer set packages. It's cheaper for a group to attempt the climb to offset the costs of transportation and the hiring of the guide. An alternative arrangement is to ask the tourism office at Kampung Annah Rais to arrange a trek as part of your visit; cost for a guide is around RM50 to RM100 per day, depending on whether you wish to overnight at the summit. The Borneo Highlands Resort runs daily treks to the summit, a six- to seven-hour round trip, from its elevated position on the plateau.

The **Borneo Highlands Resort** (☎ 019-829-0790; www.borneohighlands.com.my; Jln Borneo Heights, Padawan; 3-day 2-night packages from RM688) is a massive development sitting on Gunung Penrissen Plateau, an hour's drive from Kuching. It's practically a village in itself, comprising a golf course, three chalet complexes, spa facilities and gardens. Considerable discounts are usually available through travel agencies. Transport to and from the resort can be arranged with pickups at the airport or hotels in Kuching, costing RM80 per person for a return trip.

WIND CAVE & FAIRY CAVE

About 26km southwest of Kuching, the little town of Bau is the access point to two interesting cave systems, typical of the caves found all across the island of Borneo. There isn't much to detain you in the town itself, but the limestone caves make for an interesting trip out of Kuching, particularly if you won't have the chance to visit the grander caves at Mulu or Niah Caves National Parks. Take a picnic lunch, drinks and a good torch (these can also be hired at the entrance to each cave).

About 3km southwest of Bau, the **Wind Cave** (☎ 082-765490; adult/child RM3/1.50; ⏲ 8.30am-4.30pm) is a network of underground streams on the banks of the Batang Kayan. Slippery, unlit boardwalks run through the caves, allowing you to wander along three main passages with chittering bats swooping over your head. Don't be tempted to leave the boardwalk if you see steps in the rock – this is the entry to a subterranean adventure-caving trail. While the cave system is fairly small, flash floods have been known to occur and you could easily be trapped or worse (there have been two recent deaths in the caves, so please don't take them lightly).

You can take a jungle trail through the surrounding nature reserve as well. About 300m from the entrance to the caves is the river where you can cool off with a refreshing swim. There are also barbecue pits, food stalls and change rooms. Feeble flashlights are available for rent (RM3) at the entrance so do bring your own.

About 5km further south, **Fairy Cave** is an extraordinary elevated chamber 30m above the ground in the side of a cliff. Fanciful mossy rock formations and ferns give the cavern an otherworldly aspect, and many have been designated as fairies with makeshift altars placed in front of them. As with other Chinese shrines, pilgrims will come on the morning of the 1st and the 15th of each lunar month to burn incense and place offerings. A new concrete staircase has been constructed recently to replace the old vertigo-inducing way up. The cavern is quite large and you could spend an hour exploring it.

From Kuching, STC or BTC bus 2 to Bau (RM4, one hour) departs every half-hour between 6.20am and 6pm. You can also take a detour here on your way to or from Gunung Gading National Park; two STC buses 2A, run to Lundu (RM7.80) daily.

To get to Wind Cave, take BTC bus 3 or 3A (RM1, one bus every 90 minutes or so) from Baru and walk the 700m to the entrance. For the Fairy Cave, take BTC bus 3 (RM1.40) and walk the 1.3km from the main road. The last bus back passes through at around 5.30pm. A taxi will cost around RM12 one way.

LUNDU
☎ 082
About 55km west of Kuching, the quiet town of Lundu is the gateway to Gunung Gading

National Park. While most travellers use the town as merely a jumping-off point to the park, it's a pleasant place to get stuck for a day or two.

Lundu has a fish and vegetable market along the riverfront and a hawker centre at the western end of town. The town centre is a square bounded by old Chinese shophouses while brightly painted houses line the quiet country lanes. South of the square behind a row of shops is the bus station, which at this point is nothing more than a ramshackle building with few seats outside while a larger terminal building is being built. Beside it, a compact but very ornate Chinese temple is being constructed. In tribute to the area's main attraction, there's an oversized **rafflesia monument** next to the bus station.

The road north out of town leads to the beaches at **Pandan** (10km) and **Siar** (8.5km), but these beaches are often littered with flotsam and jetsam and you'll do better on the Santubong Peninsula (p176) or Bako National Park (p172).

Sleeping & Eating
Cheng Hak Boarding House (☎ 735-018; 22 Lundu Bazaar; r RM25-35; ✷) This budget place has very plain rooms with a shared squat toilet and shower. Cheaper rooms only have fans. Check-in is at the Goh Joo Hok shop, a few doors down from the Lundu Gading Hotel.

Lundu Gading Hotel (☎ 735-199; 174 Lundu Bazaar, Jln Stunggang; r RM58; ✷) Offering a little more comfort, this central establishment has decent rooms and is a better choice.

Ocean Beach Resort (☎ 082-452254; oceanresort79@ hotmail.com; chalets weekday/weekend RM180/250) Best among the series of bungalow resorts lining the coast north of Lundu, and offering wooden chalets that can sleep up to six, barbecue pits and other amenities.

Chinese *kopitiam* line the town square, and the hawker centre cranks up in the evening. **Happy Seafood Centre** (Jln Blacksmith; dishes from RM2.20), opposite the bus station, serves a variety of Malay and Chinese fare and also sells basic provisions.

Getting There & Away
STC bus EP07 leaves from Jln Penrissen Express Bus Terminal for Lundu (RM10, 75 minutes) four times daily. If you want to stop by the Wind and Fairy Caves on your way

back to Kuching, STC bus 2A goes to Bau (RM7.80) twice daily. STC bus 2B (RM1.60, every hour) from the bus station goes by the beaches at Pandan (30 minutes) and Siar.

GUNUNG GADING NATIONAL PARK

There is some good walking in this pleasant little **park** (☎ 082-735-714; adult/child RM10/5; 🕒 8am-12.30pm & 2-5pm), but most visitors come to see the rare *Rafflesia tuanmudae*. These massive flowers, blessed with a spectacular bouquet of rotting flesh, appear year-round, but at unpredictable times and in varying locations. Check whether any are in bloom before heading to the park by ringing the park headquarters or the Kuching **visitors' information centre** (☎ 082-410-944; www.sarawaktourism.com; Sarawak Tourism Complex, Jln Tun Abang Haji Openg; 🕒 8am-6pm Mon-Fri, 9am-3pm Sat, Sun & holidays); the flowers only last for a few days, so get here as soon as you can if one is in bloom.

The park features a plankwalk built around the area that the flowers are found. If unaccompanied by a ranger, do not step off the plankwalk as the rafflesia flower buds are small, difficult to spot, and can easily be crushed underfoot. If a plant is far away from the main boardwalk, a park ranger may be able to guide you. Do not stray from where he walks and follow his ranger's instructions. Guiding fees are RM20 per hour (per group). November to January are said to be the peak blooming months.

Few visitors take much time to explore beyond the rafflesia, which is a shame as there are some well-marked **walking trails**. Trails to the two viewpoints take about one hour and 1½ hours, passing by some pleasant waterfalls which make for refreshing bathing stops. Trekking up **Gunung Gading** (906m high; three to four hours one way) or **Batu Berkubu** on **Gunung Perigi** (five hours one way) requires a bit more effort. These treks are best as overnight trips, but camping anywhere other than at park headquarters is not allowed, so the only option is to have an early start and make it down by nightfall. A forest hut at the summit of Gunung Gading was being planned at the time of writing. At the top of Gunung Gading are the ruins of a British army camp used during the communist insurgency.

There's a popular **natural swimming pool** a few minutes from the office. The information centre at the park has good photos and displays on the rafflesia, wildlife and local culture. Staff

may offer you a cup of tea if they're not busy, but there's no shop or canteen, so you'll have to bring your own supplies or stroll the 2km to Lundu for an evening meal.

The **hostel** (dm/r RM15/40) has fan rooms with shared bathroom and fully equipped kitchen. Two three-bedroom **lodges** (r RM150; 🖾) with cooking facilities sleep up to six people. Camping, where permitted, costs RM5 per person. Weekdays are the least busy times.

To get to Gunung Gading, first take STC bus EP07 from the Jln Penrissen Express Bus Terminal to Lundu (RM10, 1¼ hours, four daily). The park entrance is 2km north of Lundu, on the road to Pantai Pandan; you can either walk there or take a taxi (RM15) from the Lundu bus station. Vans also operate on this route (RM2), but they only leave when full.

SEMATAN
☎ 082

Sematan, 107km northwest of Kuching by road, is a pleasant fishing village on the coast facing the South China Sea. An attractive promenade lines the waterfront, and a long concrete pier affords wonderful washed-out early morning views as mist shrouds the hills and the surf pounds away in the distance. The northern end of the promenade leads to some colourful stilt houses and a park commemorating the early Malay fishermen of the area. The **beach** here is clean, deserted and lined with coconut palms, but the water is very shallow. In the direction away from town, you can encounter bucolic picture-book *kampung* scenery set against the dramatic Gunung Gading range, perfect for a hike or a bicycle ride.

Sematan is popular with weekending Kuching residents, and its importance for tourists may increase when facilities at Tanjung Datu National Park are improved. The tourist board has also introduced an annual carnival to promote tourism here. At the moment, though, the town is quite undeveloped and offers some good opportunities to experience local life.

Other attractions around the area are a crab farm run by the **Fisheries Development Authority** (☎ 711-358; undpsematan@hotmail.com) and the **Zuhrang Pelangi Silk Farm** (☎ 320-130; www.sematansilk.com; adult/child RM5/2.50), where silk is still produced using manual techniques. It may not always be possible to view silkworms at all times so call ahead.

Sleeping & Eating

Jln Seacom heading west out of town leads to a few beach resorts, usually packed during the weekends, but you'll have the place to yourself on a weekday.

Sematan Hotel (☎ 711-162; 162 Sematan Bazaar; r RM25-50; ⊠) is a friendly place with simple tiled rooms and shared bathrooms. It's on the left-hand side of the road just before entering Sematan.

Sematan Palm Beach Resort (☎ 712-388, 295 Jln Seacom; www.sematanresort.com; weekday/weekend r/chalets for 2 people RM153/180; ⊠) The best of the bunch on Jln Seacom, with cheerfully painted chalets and a restaurant. It also rents out bicycles and sea kayaks. From the beach, you can walk all the way back to town, fording a small stream near its outskirts. Staff at both Sematan Hotel or Palm Beach Resort can help arrange transport to Tanjung Datu and Talang-Satang National Parks.

Kampung Pueh (☎ 013-827-4967; 2-day 1-night stays RM105, 3-days 2-night stays RM180) This Bidayuh Salako village about 9km outside of town has a longhouse homestay program. Activities include a trek up Gunung Gading as well as visits to local industries. Contact Mr Jehim Milos.

Sematan has a couple of Chinese *kopitiam* facing the waterfront and some Malay food stalls near the wharf.

Getting There & Away

To get to Sematan from Kuching, take STC bus EP07 to Lundu (RM10, 1¼ hours, four daily), then try to find a private hired van from the area around the Lundu bus station. A full van will cost around RM5 per person, but if you can't find any other fellow travellers, you'll end up paying between RM20 to RM30 for the whole vehicle.

TELOK MELANO

The Malay village of **Telok Melano** is about 30km down the coast from Sematan (if you're driving, hug the coast in a north westerly direction). It offers pristine beaches and clear blue water against the backdrop of Gunung Melano. Activities such as nature walks, camping, boat trips and fishing are offered, and homestay accommodation (averaging RM230 to RM300 a night, inclusive of meals, national park entrance, boat rental and other activities) with villagers can be arranged Contact Mr Hashim at the **Fisheries Development Authority** (☎ 013-8246785).

Getting to Telok Melano can be tricky. Speedboats for a day trip to Telok Melano can be hired for about RM250. Either the Sematan Hotel or Palm Beach Resort (see left) can arrange for transport. You can also ask independently at the wharf, but be prepared to be turned down if you have not made arrangements in advance, especially on weekends. There is usually a daily boat that runs from Telok Melano to Sematan and back, leaving Sematan wharf at around noon (around RM25 per person, although negotiable; locals will pay less); ask around the wharf or in the market, and with some patience, someone will direct you. Boats operating out of Telok Melano however cannot drop you off for a homestay.

TANJUNG DATU NATIONAL PARK

Located in the far west of the state, abutting the border with Kalimantan, this 14-sq-km park protects rainforest, unpolluted rivers and near-pristine beaches, on which endangered turtles lay their eggs. The park boasts four trails, which include the **Telok Melano Trail** from Telok Melano village and the **Belian Trail,** which makes a steep climb up to the summit of Gunung Melano. The turtle hatchery on the beach is fenced off and strictly off-limits.

For park information and permits, inquire at the Kuching **Visitors' Information Centre** (☎ 082-410-944; www.sarawaktourism.com; Sarawak Tourism Complex, Jln Tun Abang Haji Openg; ⊗ 8am-6pm Mon-Fri, 9am-3pm Sat, Sun & holidays).

Travel here is not recommended between October and March as the sea can get very rough. Snorkelling and scuba diving are allowed in certain areas; divers must be accompanied by an approved guide.

The only accommodation in the park is in the form of a **camp site** (camping per person RM5), for which you can make arrangements at the Kuching Visitors' Information Centre. If tenting is not your cup of tea, the Telok Melano homestays (left) provide a convenient base.

Access for day trips is only possible by boat from Sematan; prices start at around RM450 for up to 10 people. If you visit Gunung Gading on the way, someone at the park office may be able to organise a boat for you, otherwise try the Sematan Hotel or Sematan Palm Beach Resort (see left).

TALANG-SATANG NATIONAL PARK

Talang-Satang National Park consists of two pairs of islands: Pulau Satang Besar and Pulau

Satang Kechil (Big and Small Satang Islands) and Pulau Talang-Talang Besar and Pulau Talang-Talang Kecil (Big and Small Talang-Talang Islands). Together, these islands comprise Sarawak's first marine park, established in 1999 to protect sea turtle egg-laying habitat.

Pulau Satang Besar and Pulau Satang Kecil form the Satang section (9894 hectares), part of which is open to visitors, who must visit under park warden supervision. Permits from Kuching's **Visitors' Information Centre** (☎ 082-410-944; www.sarawaktourism.com; Sarawak Tourism Complex, Jln Tun Abang Haji Openg; ☻ 8am-6pm Mon-Fri, 9am-3pm Sat, Sun & holidays) or the **Forestry Department** (☎ 082-348-001; www.sarawakforestry.com; Hock Lee Center, Jln Datuk Abang Abdul Rahim). On Pulau Satang Besar visitors can watch fragile eggs being moved from the beach to a hatchery and if especially lucky, witness baby turtles being released into the wild. Snorkelling and diving are permitted but only within certain designated areas, and divers must be accompanied by an approved guide.

A Sea Turtle Volunteer Programme has just been launched, where volunteers can help man beach patrols and other programmes over a four-day stay between May and September at the Turtle Conservation Station on Pulau Talang-Talang Besar. Inquire with Sarawak Forestry Department.

The Talang-Talang section (9520 hectares) is off limits to visitors due to the islands' small size and the sensitivity of the marine turtles. Local villagers and fishermen have retained their right to access the park and continue their traditional activities.

The Sematan Hotel or Palm Beach Resort (see p183) can arrange transport to the park; boats cost around RM250. **CPH Tours & Travel** (☎ 082-243-708; www.cphtravel.com.my) run tours to the area. **Mr Ehwan of Buntal** (☎ 019-826-5680), can also run trips here from Buntal for about RM500.

SERIAN
☎ 082

Serian is a tiny town 65km southeast of Kuching, and dominated by Bidayuh and Hakka Chinese. Tour groups often stop here to pick up gifts on the way to the longhouses, such as the Lemanak, located along nearby rivers. Serian boasts a bustling **market**, where people from nearby longhouses come to sell jungle fruits and herbs, snake meat, sago grubs and other unusual produce.

If you are going to Sri Aman, you could stop off at the **Ranchan Recreational Park**, a popular leisure facility with waterfalls, bridges and accommodation. It's just off the main road, and on weekends there's lots of traffic, so hitching is possible; buses 12 and 14 run every half-hour from Serian (RM1). Ask to be let off at the junction for Ranchan, which is about a kilometre outside the park.

STC bus 3A runs between Kuching and Serian (one-way/return, RM6/4, one hour) every half-hour between 6.15am and 6.45pm. The bus station is in the centre of Serian, near the market.

SRI AMAN
☎ 083

Originally known as Simanggang, Sri Aman was renamed in 1974 to commemorate the signing of the peace treaty that signified the end of the communist insurgency in this area. A quiet town on the muddy Batang Lupar, halfway between Kuching and Sarikei, Sri Aman's main claim to fame is the *benak,* a tidal wave that periodically sweeps up the river all the way to Engkilili, scattering all craft in its path. It nearly took the life of writer Somerset Maugham, an event he recorded in a short story called 'The Yellow Streak'. The *benak* actually occurs every day but it's usually too small to be noticed. The really large ones only occur once or twice a year; a schedule for the next few tidal bores is posted at the wharf.

There is an annual festival, called **Pesta Benak,** to help promote Sri Aman as a tourist destination. Currently, there are plans to alternate the site of Pesta Benak to the other tributaries in the future. James Brooke's **Fort Alice**, a large wooden fortress overlooking the river, was built in 1864 and is a prominent although sadly rundown landmark.

The Skrang, Lemanak and Ai rivers flow into the Lupar, and many of the tours organised from Kuching bring groups to the longhouses along these tributaries. There isn't a lot of river traffic at Sri Aman itself, and most boats to the Lemanak and Ai Rivers leave from Engkilili, or outside town where the highway crosses the Batang Lupar.

There are a few hotels in town. **Mega Inn** (☎ 326-998; 1704-06, Jln Durian; r RM55; ❀) has clean, comfortable rooms, while the budget-conscious can look for **Taiwan Hotel** (☎ 322-493; 123 Jln Council; r RM25-35; ❀), which has spartan fan rooms or slightly more expensive air-conditioned ones.

To get to Sri Aman, take STC bus EP09 from the Kuching Regional Bus Terminal (19RM, 3½ hours, five times daily).

BATANG AI REGION

About 170km southeast of Kuching, tucked right up against the border with Kalimantan, Batang Ai is, despite its name (which means River Ai), actually a 240-sq-km reservoir. It's the only nature reserve in Borneo directly managed by indigenous people and it makes an interesting and adventurous, if difficult, trip. The region's rainforest features wildlife such as orangutans, gibbons and hornbills, and there are four walking trails.

The Batang Ai region is one of the few places where one can spot orangutans and hornbills in the wild. It is also possible to join local Ibans on fishing expeditions on the river, or on a hunt, although these days, the real business of hunting is usually carried out using a shotgun instead of a blowpipe. If you don't have the time to make excursions into Kapit or Belaga, Batang Ai makes for more than an adequate Iban longhouse experience.

There's no visitors centre here and no accommodation on the reservoir itself. Transport, lodging and guiding are all provided by a cooperative of local Ibans and most visitors to the park come here through a tour operator from Kuching. Independent access is possible by chartering a boat through the cooperative, but this isn't cheap, and until more facilities are developed, the park is best visited as part of a longhouse tour. Longhouse tours here usually take at least 3 days and 2 nights, and some of the itineraries will offer treks into the park. There are five trails in all, three of them wandering through ancient Iban burial grounds, and the longest of the five summits Bukit Sium Ukap.

The **Hilton Batang Ai Longhouse Resort** (☎ 083-584-338; www.batang.hilton.com; r RM250; ❲ ❳) is remote luxury par excellence. The indigenous-timber 'longhouses' bear little practical resemblance to their local cousins, but score much higher in the comfort stakes. Visits to genuine longhouses, jungle treks and other activities can be arranged. The Batang Ai reservoir is a two-hour boat ride away (the resort can arrange transport). Transfers from Kuching (RM110) take four

to five hours, followed by a short boat ride. Discounts are often available; check with travel agencies or the office at the Kuching **Hilton Hotel** (☎ 082-248-200; www.kuching.hilton.com; Jln Tunku Abdul Rahman).

CENTRAL SARAWAK

SIBU

☎ 084 / pop 229,000

Sibu is the gateway to Batang Rejang, making it a major transit point for travellers and a busy centre for trade between the coast and the upriver hinterland. It's a somewhat chaotic jumble of concrete buildings, with several large markets and a bustling Chinatown on the banks of the Rejang. While it's no rival for Kuching in terms of charm, it's certainly not a bad spot to spend a day before or after a trip upriver.

As well as its hectic waterlife and slightly dodgy nightlife, Sibu is known for a handful of superlatives, boasting Sarawak's tallest building (Wisma Sanyan) and longest bridge (the newly opened 1.22km-long Batang Rejang bridge), as well as the biggest town square in Malaysia.

History

The earliest inhabitants of Sibu were the Melanau people, who were followed by Ibans and Malays. The Brooke administration used the town as an administrative and trading centre in the middle of the 19th century, although nothing remains of the fort they built in 1862. In the late 19th and early 20th century, Chinese immigrants moved to the area from Foochow (Fujian) province in China and the area was briefly known as 'New Foochow'. Batang Rejang reminded these immigrants of the Swan River in Fuzhou, China, and the swan remains the symbol of the city, a fact celebrated with two enormous swan statues – one by the river and one in the middle of town.

Orientation

Sibu lies on the north bank of the Rejang, near the river's confluence with Batang Igan. A graceful seven-storey Chinese pagoda marks the western edge of the waterfront and a small clock tower marks the eastern; between the two, the concrete Pasar Sentral Sibu (PSS; Sibu

SARAWAK

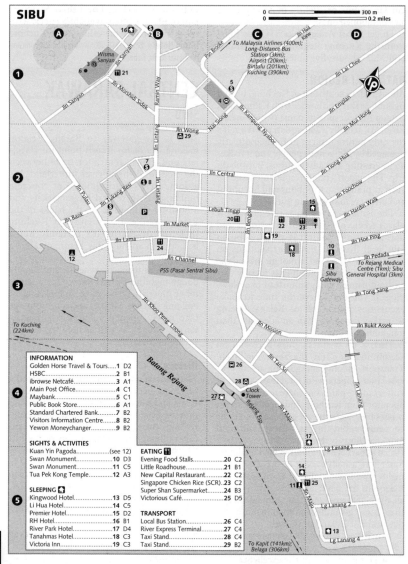

SIBU

0 — 300 m
0 — 0.2 miles

INFORMATION	
Golden Horse Travel & Tours.....**1**	D2
HSBC..**2**	B1
ibrowse Netcafé..........................**3**	A1
Main Post Office.........................**4**	C1
Maybank.....................................**5**	C1
Public Book Store.......................**6**	A1
Standard Chartered Bank............**7**	B2
Visitors Information Centre.........**8**	B2
Yewon Moneychanger..................**9**	B2

SIGHTS & ACTIVITIES	
Kuan Yin Pagoda.....................(see **12**)	
Swan Monument........................**10**	D3
Swan Monument........................**11**	C5
Tua Pek Kong Temple.............**12**	A3

SLEEPING	
Kingwood Hotel.........................**13**	D5
Li Hua Hotel...............................**14**	C5
Premier Hotel.............................**15**	D2
RH Hotel.....................................**16**	B1
River Park Hotel.........................**17**	D4
Tanahmas Hotel.........................**18**	C3
Victoria Inn...............................**19**	C3

EATING	
Evening Food Stalls...................**20**	C2
Little Roadhouse........................**21**	B1
New Capital Restaurant.............**22**	C2
Singapore Chicken Rice (SCR)..**23**	C2
Super Shan Supermarket...........**24**	B3
Victorious Café..........................**25**	D5

TRANSPORT	
Local Bus Station.......................**26**	C4
River Express Terminal...............**27**	C4
Taxi Stand..................................**28**	C4
Taxi Stand..................................**29**	B2

Central Market) building dominates the view over Jln Channel.

The express boat wharf is at the River Express Terminal on the western end of the Rejang Esplanade. Also on the waterfront is the local bus station; the long-distance bus terminal is at Sungai Antu, 3km west of town. The airport is 20km east of the town centre.

Information

Emergency (☎ 999)

Golden Horse Travel & Tours (☎ 323-288; 62 Jln Kampung Nyabor; ☼ 8am-5pm Mon-Sat, 8am-noon Sun) This competent travel agency near Premier Hotel is the place to go for planet tickets etc.

HSBC (☎ 332-177; 131 Jln Kampung Nyabor; ☼ 9am-3pm Mon-Fri) There's an ATM at this bank.

SARAWAK

ibrowse Netcafé (☎ 310-717; 4th fl, Wisma Sanyan, 1 Jln Sanyan; per hr RM3; ◷ 9.30am-9.30pm) Internet access near the western escalator bank on the 4th floor. There are also several other internet cafés on the same floor.

Main post office (☎ 332-312; Jln Kampung Nyabor; ◷ 8am-4.30pm Mon-Fri, 8am-3pm Sat) This is one of the most reliable places in town to get cash.

Public Book Store (4th fl, Wisma Sanyan, 1 Jln Sukan; ◷ 9am-9pm daily) Near ibrowse, this is the best book-store in town, with a small selection of English books.

Rejang Medical Centre (☎ 330-733; www.rejang.com .my; 29 Jln Pedada) A group of private specialist clinics with 24-hour emergency services.

Sibu General Hospital (☎ 343-333; Jln Abdul Tunk Rahman)

Standard Chartered Bank (Jln Tukang Besi) Opposite the visitors information centre; changes travellers cheques and has an ATM. Be prepared to wait for the cheques to go through.

Visitors Information Centre (☎ 340-980; www.sibu .com.my; 32 Jln Tukang Besi; ◷ 8am-5pm Mon-Fri, 8am-12.50pm Sat, closed 1st & 3rd Sat of every month) This office provides information about upriver trips out of Song, Kapit and Belaga.

Yewon moneychanger (☎ 330-577; 8 Jln Tukang Besi; ◷ 8.30am-5.30pm Mon-Sat, noon-3pm Sun) South of the visitors centre; only changes cash.

Sights

Tua Pek Kong Temple (Jln Temple; admission free; ◷ dawn-dusk) An interesting riverside Chinese temple where, if you're lucky, you'll find Mr Tan Teck Chiang in attendance. Mr Tan will give you a tour of the temple and explain (in lavish detail) his interpretation of Taoism and Buddhism. You can also scale the seven-storey pagoda to get a brilliant view over the town and the muddy Batang Rejang as it makes its way seaward.

Sleeping

Most of the budget lodging in Sibu is of a very low standard and this is a city where even budget travellers should opt for a midrange option if at all possible.

MIDRANGE

our pick Li Hua Hotel (☎ 324-000; Lg Lanang 1; r RM45-80; ❄) On the riverfront, about 100m south (upriver) of the Swan Statue, you will find Sibu's best-value hotel, with spotless tile-floor rooms and good views from the upper floors. Highly recommended.

Victoria Inn (☎ 320-099; 80 Jln Market; r RM50-85; ❄) If the River Park and the Li Hua are

full, this centrally located budget hotel is a good choice. It's a tightly packed warren of rooms about a block away from the high-rise Tanahmas Hotel.

River Park Hotel (☎ 316-688; 51-53 Jln Maju; r RM55-80; ❄) The River Park is a fairly typical and well-run midrange hotel with friendly staff and a pleasant riverside location. Some of the rooms are a little old and noisy.

TOP END

Kingwood Hotel (☎ 335-888; kingwood@tm.net.my; 12 Lg Lanang 4; r from RM170; ❄ ▢ ▣) A big hotel on the waterfront, the Kingwood has large, well-appointed rooms, many with good views of the muddy expanse of the Rejang. There is a rooftop pool atop the annexe.

Premier Hotel (☎ 323-222; www.premierh.com.my; Jln Kampung Nyabor; r from 195; ❄ ▢) The Premier has a good location but it's getting a bit long in the tooth. Rooms are about what you'd expect for this price and there's wi-fi in the lobby. A change of carpets would solve a lot of problems here.

Tanahmas Hotel (☎ 333-188; www.tanahmas.com .my; 277 Jln Kampung Nyabor; r from RM190; ❄ ▢ ▣) The square white block isn't the most at-tractive building in town, but the hotel is centrally located, rooms are clean and spa-cious and the staff are competent. There's a café in the lounge. Go for a poolside view rather than a town panorama. Rates include breakfast.

RH Hotel (☎ 365-888; www.rhhotels.com; Jln Kampung Nyabor; r from RM260; ❄ ▣) Easily the best hotel in town, the RH has stylish new rooms with clean lines and good light. The bathrooms are spacious, there's a rooftop pool and it's con-nected to the Wisma Sanyan by a skybridge. Wi-fi is available.

Eating

You'll find the usual selection of Chinese and Malay *kedai kopi* in town, along with a few proper sit-down restaurants and a few markets scattered around for self-caterers.

our pick Victorious Cafe (Jln Maju; meals RM3-8; ◷ breakfast, lunch & early dinner) Dine under the gaze of the Sibu Swan at this popular mostly Chinese *kedai kopi* across the street from the Li Hua Hotel. There's a stall that makes a smoky and wonderful plate of *kway teow*, which you can wash down with a nice iced lemon tea.

Singapore Chicken Rice (SCR) (Jln Kampong Nyabor; meals from RM3; ◷ breakfast, lunch & dinner) The name says it all and this simple dish draws a big lunch and dinner crowd at this popular chain. Not much on ambience, but it's tasty and cheap.

Little Roadhouse (☎ 319-384; Jln Sanyan; dishes RM4-10; ☙ lunch & dinner Tue-Sun) Unlike much of Sibu's nightlife, which leans towards karaoke and underclad young ladies, this balcony restaurant and 'fun pub' is good for a quiet beer, wine or steak.

New Capital Restaurant (☎ 326-066; Jln Kampong Nyabor; meals around RM25 per person; ☙ lunch & dinner) If you feel like a splurge, this brilliant Chinese eatery is sure to satisfy, with excellent fresh fish, meat and vegetable dishes. We recommend the butter prawns and stir-fried *midin* washed down with a fresh fruit juice.

For Chinese and Malay snacks, try the evening food stalls that set up in the late afternoon along Jln Market. You'll also find several stalls on the 1st floor of PSS (Pasar Sentral Sibu).

For self-catering and snacks, browse the markets or head to the **Super Shan supermarket** (Jln Channel).

Getting There & Away

AIR
Malaysia Airlines (☎ 1-300-883-000; www.malaysiaairlines.com.my; 61 Jln Tuanku Osman) Has several flights daily from Sibu to Kuching (RM89), Miri (RM138), Kota Kinabalu (RM210) and Kuala Lumpur (RM319). **Air Asia** (☎ 1-300-889-933; www.airasia.com; Jl Keranji) has dirt-cheap flights between Sibu and both Kuala Lumpur and Johor Bahru.

BOAT
Boats leave from the River Express Terminal at the western end of Jln Bengkel (which is at the southwestern end of town). At least two companies run express boats to Kuching (RM40, 4½ hours, departures 7.30am and 12.45pm daily). Tickets booths are inside the terminal.

Getting to Kapit is the first leg of the journey up Batang Rejang. Several boats motor the 140km from Sibu to Kapit (RM17 to RM30, three hours, departures between 5.30am and 1pm). Some boats continue up to Belaga, but most terminate in Kapit. All boat companies have booths at the terminal and they display their next departure times with large clocks outside their booths, making choosing your boat a snap.

BUS
Bus companies have ticket stalls at the long-distance bus station (Sungai Antu) and around the local bus station on the waterfront. Buses run between the long-distance bus station and Sibu's downtown all day for RM1. A taxi to/from town will cost RM10.

Buses run between Sibu and Kuching (RM40, eight hours, regular departures between 6.30am and 10pm), Miri (RM40, 7½ hours, roughly hourly from 6am to 10pm) and Bintulu (RM20, 3½ hours, roughly hourly from 5.30am to 6pm).

Getting Around
Sibu's airport is 24km east of town. Bus 3A runs to and from town every 1½ hours from 6.30am to 6pm (RM2.50, about 30 minutes). You could also try flagging down any rural bus that passes by. The coupon taxi fare into town is RM28.

The local bus station is on the waterfront. To get to the long-distance bus station, take Lanang Road bus 21 (90 sen) from the local bus station. It leaves roughly hourly between 6.30am and 5.30pm. A taxi costs RM10.

MUKAH
☎ 084
At the mouth of the Sungai Mukah, the small village of Mukah is a quiet coastal town in a sparsely populated part of Sarawak far from the main north–south highway. There's not much to do here, but it's a nice spot to relax for a day or two en route between Miri and Kuching. The main attraction is Kampung Tellian, a quaint *kampung* laced with waterways and plankwalks along the river. It's a short taxi ride from the town of Mukah.

Mukah is accessed by a road that branches off the main north–south highway roughly halfway between Sibu and Bintulu. Once you leave the main highway, the road gets pretty rough. Your backside may complain as you bounce along the potholed road, but the views of the many longhouses en route will take your mind of your sufferings.

Most of the local people are Melanau, and the area's major attraction is the **Kaul Festival**, currently held on the second Sunday in April. *Pesta Kaul*, as it is called locally, is a lively beach celebration that includes enchanting enactments of Melanau rituals and games to honour the spirits of the sea.

Mukah is divided into an old and new section. The bus station is in the new section, while most of the hotels, markets and restaurants are in the old section, along the river, a short walk away.

Sights

In Kampung Tellian, you'll find **Lamin Dana** (☎ 871-543; www.lamindana.com; adult/child RM3/1; 🕙 9am-5pm), a superb cultural enterprise and living museum in a semitraditional Melanau house overlooking a river. Among the activities here are traditional massage by the village midwife, river tours to a sago farm and old-style sago bakehouse, and tastings of Melanau delicacies such as *umai* (raw fish marinated in lime and onions), smoked fish and sago shoots. Cultural shows can also be arranged.

Contact the centre in advance if you intend to visit, and bear in mind that during Chinese New Year, the fourth week of December and the Kaul Festival, accommodation is usually full.

To reach Lamin Dana from Mukah, take a Tellian bus (80 sen) and tell the conductor where you want to go. Lamin Dana can also arrange longboat transport (RM3 per person) to and from the water village – an enjoyable way to reach the town centre. A taxi will cost RM6; walking takes about 45 minutes.

Sleeping & Eating

Lamin Dana (☎ 871-543, 019-849-5962; www.lamindana .com; Kampung Tellian; standard/deluxe r RM75/150) The rooms at the cultural centre in Kampung Tellian are simply furnished and the toilets and showers are clean. A Melanau-style breakfast is included in the price. The house has only nine rooms (eight standard and one family), so booking is a good idea, especially if you want to take part in activities. Lamin Dana can arrange private transport to/from Mukah.

King Ing Hotel (☎ 871-403; 1-2 Jln Boyan; standard/ deluxe r RM50-65; 🖳) The King Ing is the best hotel in town, with simple but neat carpeted rooms. It's not worth paying extra for the deluxe rooms here.

You'll find two other hotels in the centre of the old section of town that aren't quite up to the standards at the King Ing.

Perfectly located right on the river, the small stalls comprising the **riverside hawker centre** (Jln Pasar; dishes RM2-6) are the best spots in town to have lunch or sip a beer and watch life drift, cruise or amble by. The **market** (Jln Pasar) near the Shell station nearby is the best place to buy fruit etc.

Getting There & Away

Mukah's airstrip is just outside town; a van will drop you in the centre for RM5. **MASwings** (www.maswings.com.my; ☎ 1800-88-3000, 03-7843-3000) currently flies from Mukah to Kuching, Miri and Sibu once or twice daily, plus two weekly services to Bintulu. Prices vary.

Mukah is accessible by bus from Sibu (RM15, 3½ hours) and Bintulu (RM20, four hours, four daily).

BATANG REJANG

The 640km Batang Rejang has been called the Amazon of Borneo. Until the advent of 4WD roads and jungle airstrips, the river served as the main highway into the interior of Sarawak. Even now, it sees a daily parade of express boats and barges moving people and goods along its muddy length. Though it's not the jungle-lined wilderness that many travellers imagine, it still retains hints of its wild and romantic nature.

The Rejang drains a huge region of central Borneo, much of which used to be covered with pristine tropical rainforest. Sadly, huge swathes of this forest were felled in the last few decades and replaced by secondary forest, palm-oil plantations or open land. Indeed, a look at recent satellite photos of the upper Rejang show the river and its tributaries surrounded by a network of logging roads that seems to expand with each passing day. Adding to this tragedy was the construction of the Bakun Dam about 40km upriver of Belaga (see p193). If you want to see primary rainforest, you'll do better in Gunung Mulu National Park (see p205), parts of the Kelabit Highlands (see p212), Danum Valley (see p145) or Maliau Basin (see p154).

Many of the indigenous people of the Batang Rejang area still live in communal dwellings known as longhouses. While most longhouses aren't nearly as traditional as most travellers expect, a visit to one scattered along the Rejang's banks and tributaries is a great chance to interact with some of Borneo's indigenous people and to learn something of their culture. For more on longhouses, see the boxed text on p32.

Kapit is the last big settlement on the river, and it's where the longhouse people come for supplies. Further upriver, Belaga is smaller and more laid-back; it's a regular meeting place for friends and relatives from far-flung communities. In either town, the best strategy for finding someone to take you to a longhouse is

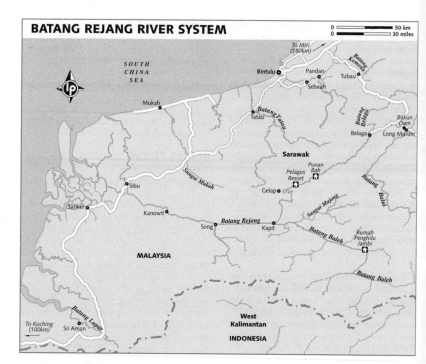

BATANG REJANG RIVER SYSTEM

to make yourself known around town – sit in the cafés and get talking to people. If you don't have a lot of time, it's best to take a tour.

The best time for a trip up the Rejang is in late May/early June. This is the Gawai Dayak harvest festival, when Iban longhouses are busy with feasts and traditional dancing, and visitors are welcome (note that Iban are more prevalent along the lower reaches of the Rejang).

Along the river, the only hotel accommodation available is in Song, Kanowit, Kapit and Belaga.

Kapit
☎ 084 / pop 13,610

The main upriver settlement on the Rejang, Kapit is a bustling trading and transport centre that dates back to the days of the white rajas. The main activity here is wandering the docks and market stalls to see what upriver people are buying and selling. Apart from this, you can visit Fort Sylvia, which dates back to 1880. Although Belaga is further upstream and seems to promise more authentic longhouse experiences, Kapit is in some ways better for this as it offers a wider choice of river

systems and several interesting longhouses within easy reach by river or road.

Fans of Redmond O'Hanlon's *Into the Heart of Borneo* know Kapit as the starting point of the author's jungle adventures, and if you want to head off up the Batang Baleh to emulate them, this is the place to make arrangements.

INFORMATION
Good Time Cyber Centre (☎ 746-303; 354 Jln Yong Chai; per hr RM3) Internet access.
Hua Chiong Travel Service (☎ 796-681; Jln Koh) Airline tickets and local travel services.
Hyper Link Cyber Station (17 Jln Tan Sit; per hr RM3) Internet access.
KL Ling Moneychanger (☎ 796-488; Jln Penghulu Gerinang) Changes cash and travellers cheques.
Lee Cyber Centre (Jln Tan Sit; per hr RM3) Internet access.
Maybank (☎ 790-122; 73C Jln Penghulu Atan)
Public Bank (☎ 790-106; 64 Jln Wharf) Changes cash and travellers cheques.

SIGHTS
A wooden fortification marking the white rajas' progress up the Rejang, **Fort Sylvia** (☎ 799-171;

Kubu; admission free; 10am-noon & 2-5pm Tue-Sun) was built as Fort Kapit in 1880 to keep the peace and gain control of the upper Rejang. In 1925 the fort was renamed to honour Ranee Sylvia, wife of the third raja, Charles Vyner Brooke. The *belian* (ironwood) timbers have lasted well, even after massive flooding in 1934 almost reached the top of the doorway! In 1997 the fort was declared a historical building, and the Tun Jugah Foundation now runs it as a museum and a training centre for artisans, weavers and artists in the Kapit District. At the top of the stairs to the 1st floor is a brilliant mural of a hornbill surrounded by depictions of early Iban life.

The civic centre (Dewan Suarah) houses the **Kapit Museum** (Jln Hospital; admission free; 8am-1pm & 2-5pm Mon-Sat, closed 11.45am-2.15pm Fri). It has a couple of cultural displays and there's a relief map showing all the longhouses in the area, perfect for picking at random if you like a bit of spontaneity. Just opposite the centre is a lake with a network of small pagodas and wooden walkways, good for a stroll or a picnic.

The focus of activity in Kapit is invariably the **waterfront**, which is packed with ferries, barges and longboats, all swarming with people. It's fascinating to watch the activity on the water and to see people shouldering (or sometimes 'heading') impossibly heavy loads up the steep steps from the wharf.

Some of these goods will end up in Kapit's colourful daily **Pasar Teresang** (Wet Market). It's a chatty, noisy hive of grass-roots commerce, and the friendly vendors have a lot of fun trying to explain to tourists how to prepare and eat a galaxy of unfamiliar items.

TOURS

Kapit is a good base from which to explore the Batang Baleh, a river basin that is in many ways more traditional and less deforested than the upper Batang Rejang. **Joshua Muda** (019-467-6004; joshuamuda@hotmail.com), an Iban guide based out of the **New Rejang Inn** (796-600; 104 Jln Teo Chow Beng) leads a variety of trips to traditional Iban longhouses along the Sungai Mujong, a tributary north of the Batang Baleh. Joshua is a knowledgeable and experienced guide, and has even led more ambitious expeditions to the Kalimantan border. Three day, two-night tours start at RM380 per person (minimum of two).

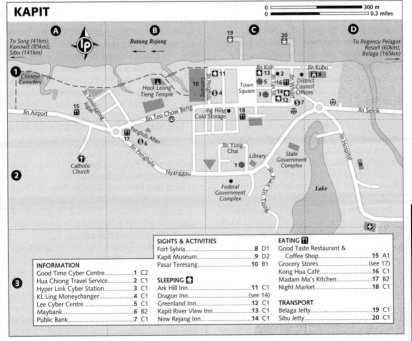

KAPIT

0   300 m
0   0.2 miles

To Song (41km);
Kanowit (85km);
Sibu (141km)

Batang Rejang

To Regency Pelagus
Resort (60km);
Belaga (165km)

Chinese Cemetery

Hock Leong Tieng Temple

Town Square

Jln Koh

Jln Kubu

District Council Offices

Jln Airport

Ing Hing Cold Storage

Jln Teo Chow Beng

Jln Selirik

Catholic Church

Jln Penghulu Attan

Jln Penghulu

Jln Yong Chai

Library

Nyanggau

State Government Complex

Jln Hospital

Federal Government Complex

Lake

SARAWAK

Although in general a visit to a longhouse should be facilitated by a guide, there are a few settlements around Kapit that are quite accustomed to independent visits. Punan Bah, a traditional Iban longhouse, is located two hours north of Kapit along the Batang Rejang, and can be reached by express boat.

Rumah Penghilu Jambi, an Iban longhouse, is located at the final express boat stop along the Batang Baleh; simply ask around at the pier for departure times.

There are also some longhouses that can be reached by road, including Rumah Bundong (10km), an Iban longhouse quite used to day-trippers. **Maaruf Bin Abdullah** (☎ 013-895-5081), a locally based licensed guide, owns a van and can arrange transportation. Alternatively, ask around and negotiate with the van drivers near the morning market.

FESTIVALS & EVENTS
Baleh-Kapit Raft Safari A challenging two-day race recreating the experience of Iban and Orang Ulu people rafting downstream with their jungle produce to Kapit. Teams of eight head 50km down the Balleh and Rejang rivers on homemade rafts, overnighting in Iban longhouses. It's usually held on the last weekend in April. Check with the Kapit Resident's Office (☎ 796-230) or the tourist office in Sibu for dates and entrance fees.
Gawai Dayak Beginning on 1 June, Gawai Dayak celebrates the end of the harvest season in Sarawak. This is the best time to visit the region's longhouses, as the Iban people cut loose in a mania of feasting, dancing and *tuak*-drenched celebrations.

SLEEPING
Ark Hill Inn (☎ 796-168; 451 Jln Penghulu Gerinang; s from RM38, d RM63; ❄) This is about as close as you can get to riverfront accommodation in Kapit, although unfortunately the rooms don't have any riverfront views. Right opposite the market, you trade off a bit of space here for the 'luxury' of two shower heads per bathroom. A bit of noise does seep through but it's bearable.
Dragon Inn (☎ 797-435; 457 Jln Teo Chow Beng; d RM55; ❄) Sharing the same building as the much nicer New Rejang Inn, the Dragon Inn features frighteningly stark fan-cooled, shared-bathroom rooms on its fifth floor, and much pleasanter but bare air-con rooms on the third and fourth floors. Reception takes the form of a desk in the sporting goods store at ground level.
Kapit River View Inn (☎ 796-310; krvinn@tm.net.my; 10 Jln Tan Sit Leong; s & d RM55-60; ❄) Small window-

less, but clean rooms, located directly on the town square and near the boat pier.
New Rejang Inn (☎ 796-600; 457 Jln Teo Chow Beng; r RM65-75; ❄) Clean, tiled rooms with TV, phone and fridge, and a location a mere stone's throw away from the boat wharf make this the best-value accommodation in town. The in-room cable TV is nice, as long as you're happy watching the same program as the hotel staff in the lobby!
Greenland Inn (☎ 796-388; 463-464 Jln Teo Chow Beng; s/d RM80/90; ❄) Kapit has about as much in common with Greenland as Kuching does with Greenwich, but if you can ignore the geographical misnomer, this is a respectable step up from the budget class.
Regency Pelagus Resort (☎ 799-051; www.theregen cyhotel.com.my/Pelagus; full board s RM320-340, d RM400-440; ❄ ☒) Inaccessible by road, Pelagus Resort is a unique longhouse-style resort that's a 45-minute boat ride from Kapit, within earshot of the roaring Pelagus Rapids. The two-tiered wooden design blends beautifully into the jungle, but retains some very nontribal features such as minibars and a helipad. Transport to the resort is arranged by the resort when bookings are made.

EATING
Syarikat Morshidi (Restaurant and Coffee Shop) (cnr Jln Teo Chow Beng and Putena Jaya; dishes RM2-6; ✹ breakfast) If the thought of yet another breakfast of coffee and a sweet snack in a Chinese café makes your teeth hurt, stop by this tiny roadside café that serves a variety of Muslim breakfast specialities, including *nasi lemak* (rice boiled in coconut milk and served with sides) and milky tea.
Kong Hua Café (☎ 796-459; 1B Jln Wharf; dishes RM3-8; ✹ breakfast & lunch) A fine example of the type of old-school Chinese coffee shop that Malaysia does so well. Breakfast here is not much more than sugary snacks though.
Good Taste Restaurant & Coffee Shop (☎ 798-658; Wisma Ngieng Ping Toh, Jln Teo Chow Beng; dishes RM6-12; ✹ breakfast, lunch & dinner) Diner-style mixed cuisine with a loyal following among the office workers in the building above.
Madam Ma's Kitchen (☎ 796-119; Hotel Meligai, 334 Jln Airport; mains RM5-15; ✹ breakfast, lunch & dinner) Ma's is one of the only places in town with air-con, making it a refuge on a hot day (which is every day). The staff are friendly and speak some English, and the chicken curry is pretty tasty. Expect changing menus and special offers.

Kapit is packed with small restaurants and *kedai kopi*, but the best place to eat in the evening has to be the busy **night market** (dishes RM0.50-3.50), which is near the centre of town, roughly behind Ing Hing Cold Storage. In contrast to the rest of Kapit's dining scene, which is overwhelmingly Chinese, this market is almost exclusively Malay-Muslim. As such the emphasis is on *satay* and other halal dishes.

As well as the markets, self-caterers could visit the well-stocked grocery stores located along Penghulu Nyaunggau, opposite the Hotel Meligai.

GETTING THERE & AWAY

Express boats leave for Sibu between 6.30am and 2.30pm (for information on boats from Sibu, see p188). The trip takes 2½ to three hours and tickets are RM17 to RM20 for economy, or RM25 to RM30 first class. Times are not posted on the wharf, and the best bet is simply to ask around, particularly at the hotels.

Boats depart for Belaga (RM30, 4½ hours) at 9am. When the river is low, express boats can't get past the Pelagus Rapids, and smaller speedboats are used instead. Fares for these boats start at RM50. If you want to do a day trip to Pelagus, ask around the wharf or at your hotel, as the express boats don't stop there.

Express boats bound for the Batang Baleh depart before noon and go as far as Rumah Penghilu Jambi (RM30, four to five hours), an Iban longhouse. The last boat from back to Kapit departs Rumah Penghilu Jambi at 12.30pm.

Belaga
☎ 086 / pop 2500

By the time you pull into Belaga after the long journey up the Rejang, you may feel like you've arrived at the very heart of Borneo – in reality you're only about 100km from the coastal city of Bintulu (as the crow flies). Despite this, Belaga certainly feels remote. It's the main bazaar and administrative centre along the upper Rejang.

Belaga is a friendly little town and it's a good place to arrange longhouse visits – there are many Kayan and Kenyah longhouses along the rivers nearby. Otherwise, it shouldn't take long to find someone in Belaga with a suggestion of a longhouse to visit or an offer to guide you. See the boxed text on p32 for more information about longhouses.

Boats will drop you at the bottom of a steep set of concrete steps leading up to the small town centre; all the town's facilities are found here, in the handful of blocks across from the small park. There is no bank here, but the Teck Hua Chan supermarket will change cash.

INFORMATION
Belaga District Office (☎ 461-339) Can arrange permits and guides. Behind Hotel Sing Soon Huat
Hasbee Enterprises (☎ 461-240; 4 Belaga Bazaar) Airline tickets, local travel services and internet.

TOURS
While visiting a longhouse independently can be great, there's a limit to what you can arrange on your own, and the highlight for most visitors in Belaga is taking a longhouse tour. A good package should include jungle trekking, visits to a number of communities, night walks and seasonal activities such as hunting, cooking, land clearing and fruit harvesting.

The most prominent guide operating out of Belaga these days is Daniel Levoh at **Daniel's Corner** (☎ 461-997, 013-848 6351; daniellevoh@hotmail .com; Jln Teh Ah Kiong). A Kayan former teacher, Daniel is friendly and knowledgeable and gets good reviews from travellers. He has good connections with several Kayan-Kenyah longhouses between Belaga and the Bakun Dam, as well as the newly settled area near Asap, and can also arrange other activities such as jungle walks and visits to a waterfall up the Belaga River. Longhouse visits typically last three days and two nights, and start at RM200 (minimum two people).

Mark, a licensed guide based out of **Hasbee Enterprises** (☎ 461-240; 4 Belaga Bazaar), can also arrange longhouse visits, and **Belaga's District Office** (☎ 461-339) behind Hotel Sing Soon Huat can also help arrange guides.

SLEEPING & EATING
Belaga's accommodation is of the cheap and cheerful variety, but if you're doing the longhouse circuit you shouldn't really need to sleep here for more than a night or two.

Hotel Belaga (☎ 461-244; 14 Main Bazaar; r RM30-60; ⊠) A convenient location makes up for less than perfect standards at Belaga's principal dosshouse. The cheap beds here are on the verge of collapse, but the place is clean and the fellow running the place is helpful enough.

SARAWAK

There's a decent Chinese *kopitiam* downstairs that serves mediocre but filling food.

Hotel Sing Soon Huat (☎ 461-307; 26-27 New Bazaar; r RM35-45; 🕸) The bright yellow building behind the Hotel Belaga holds this slightly less appealing establishment.

Jea Corner (off Jln Ului Lian; dishes from RM3; 🕒 dinner) This tiny stall is literally the only place in Belaga still serving food after 6pm. It serves up a small variety of decent Malaysian rice-based dishes. The friendly proprietor, Albert, will probably find you before you find him. He has a wealth of information about the surrounding area and its people and culture – just don't get him started on politics! It's near the District Office.

Kafetaria Mesra Murni (Jln Temengong Mat; dishes RM3-5; 🕒 breakfast, lunch & dinner) This family-run Muslim restaurant can lay claim to having the only real riverfront dining in Belaga. Try the decent *mee goreng* or the exceptionally refreshing *limau ais* (iced lime juice). It's past the park and playground.

GETTING THERE & AWAY
Air
At the time of writing, there were no flights to/from Belaga.

Boat
Boats leave Kapit for Belaga (RM30, 4½ hours) at 9am. When the river is low you'll need to take a speedboat instead; fares start at RM50. Returning to Kapit from Belaga, express boats leave Belaga early (between 6am and 6.30am), from where you can catch onward boats downriver to Sibu. Boats go upriver from Belaga as far as the Bakun Dam area near Rumah Apan (RM10, one hour), from where you can explore the resettled river country north of the Rejang. It's possible to do a loop back to Bintulu this way along a recently paved road.

Land
There is a very good paved road from Bakun to Bintulu/Miri highway (two to three hours to the junction with the coastal highway). The only problem is that there's no public transport, so you'll have to make private arrangements either in Belaga or Miri/Bintulu.

Upriver from Belaga
About 40km upstream from Belaga, the Rejang divides into several rivers, including the mighty Batang Balui, which winds almost all the way to the Kalimantan border. Sadly, just below this junction is the site of the controversial Bakun Dam project, which was started in 1996 and is near completion. In order to build the dam, the surrounding forest was logged and an estimated 11,000 people were forcibly resettled. Once the reservoir above the dam starts to fill, it will flood a huge stretch of the Balui valley and several other tributaries of the Rejang.

Because of the difficulty of getting boats above the dam, it's now very difficult to travel upriver on the Balui, which is a shame, because the upper reaches promise some of the most exciting river trips in Sarawak.

BINTULU
☎ 086 / pop 110,000
Bintulu is a busy little town on the north bank of the Batang Kemena, roughly midway between Sibu and Miri. The town came under James Brooke's sway in 1861, and the simple **Council Negeri Memorial** (Jln Lebuh Raya Abang Galau) north of the town centre commemorates Sarawak's first Council Negeri (State Council), formed in 1867. In the centre of town overlooking the river, you'll find the **Tamu Bintulu** (Bintulu Market; Jln Main Bazaar; 🕒 dawn-late afternoon), as well as **Tua Pek Kong** (Jln Main Bazaar; admission free; 🕒 dawn-dusk), a Chinese temple, about a block away. If you want a break from the city, hire a taxi (about RM10) for the 10km trip to **Tanjung Batu Beach**.

Travellers heading north to Similajau National Park, Niah Caves National Park or Miri, or south to Sibu, the Batang Rejang and Kuching may need to use Bintulu as a staging post or stay overnight for a connection. It's not the most exciting city in Sarawak, but if you are looking for a place to spend the night in this part of the world, it's got an edge over larger and more chaotic Sibu.

Orientation
Bintulu lies along the north bank of Batang Kemena. All the places to stay and eat, banks and other services are situated in the riverside district south of the old airport. The waterfront just north of the shopping area along Jln Masjid has several busy markets. The long-distance bus station is 5km north of town at Medan Jaya, and the airport is 27km west of the centre.

Information
Bintulu Hospital (☎ 331-455; off Jln Lebuh Raya Abang Galau).
Standard Chartered Bank (☎ 334-166; 89 Jln Keppel; 🕒 9am-3pm Mon-Fri) Another useful bank with an ATM.

SARAWAK

HSBC (☎ 315-928; 25 Jln Law Gek Soon; ☼ 9am-3pm Mon-Fri) Best bank in Bintulu. There's an ATM here.

Star Internet (Jln Law Gek Soon; per hr RM3; ☼ 9am-11pm) Internet access. Noisy with slow machines.

Sleeping

BUDGET

Bakun Inn (☎ 311-111; 7 Jln Law Gek Soon; r RM45-60; ☒) This simple hotel on the corner of Jln Law Gek Soon and Jln Keppel is arguably the best budget deal in town. The entrance is in back, near the parking lot.

MIDRANGE

Hoover Hotel (☎ 337-166; 92 Jln Keppel; s/d RM65/86; ☒) Not quite as nice as the Kintown, the acceptable Hoover Hotel has a good down-town location and quite decent, reasonably spacious rooms.

Sunlight Inn (☎ 332-577; 7 Jln Pedada; r RM68-78; ☒) Free wi-fi and a fairly central location make this clean and well-run hotel a good second choice if the Kintown Inn is full.

our pick **Kintown Inn** (☎ 333-666; 93 Jln Keppel; r RM69-80.50; ☒ ▢) The Kintown Inn delivers the best value for money in Bintulu. Rooms are clean and well-appointed, with nice hot showers and good views from the upper floors. And there's one internet terminal in the lobby. It's on the corner of Jln Law Gek Soon and Jln Keppel.

Riverfront Inn (☎ 333-111; riverf@tm.net.my; 256 Taman Sri Dagang; r from RM90; ☒) A long-standing favourite with business and leisure visitors

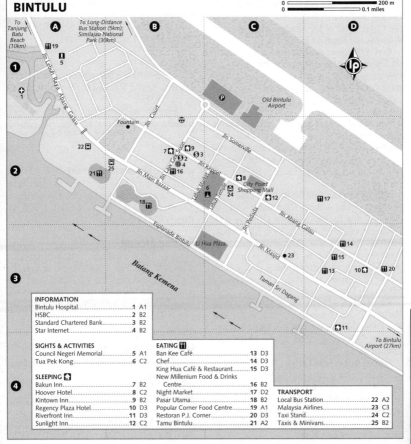

BINTULU

alike, the Riverfront is low-key but still classy. It's well worth paying top whack to get a room overlooking the river – the view is pure Borneo. There's a decent café on the ground floor and wi-fi in the lobby.

TOP END

Regency Plaza Hotel (☎ 335-111; rihbtu@tm.net.my; 116 Jln Abang Galau; r from RM170, ❄ 🖳 ⛊) The service can be a little uneven, but the rooms are spacious and clean, and some have good views at Bintulu's best hotel. The pool was under renovation at the time of writing but should be open again soon. Wi-fi sweetens the deal here.

Eating

Restoran P.J. Corner (Jln Abang Galau; meals from RM3; ❄ breakfast, lunch & dinner) This friendly Malay place serves good fresh fruit juice, rotis, *nasi campur* and a nice plate of *mee goreng*. It's on the eastern end of Jln Abang Galau, roughly opposite the Regency Plaza Hotel.

Chef (92 Jln Abang Galau; cakes from RM0.90; ❄ breakfast, lunch & dinner) No chocolate salty balls here: this drool-inducing bakery-café can satisfy most sweet and savoury cravings, from local cakes and pastries to a good rendition of tiramisu (RM4.50).

New Millenium Food & Drinks Centre (Jln Law Gek Soon; meals from RM3; ❄ breakfast & dinner) This *kedai kopi* is a good spot for breakfast as they serve toast and eggs in addition to the usual Chinese rice and noodle dishes, as well as decent coffee and tea.

our pick **Ban Kee Café** (off Jln Abang Galau; meals from RM10; ❄ lunch & dinner) Run, don't walk, to this brilliant indoor-outdoor Chinese seafood specialist. It doesn't look like much, but the food here is enough to make us want to head back to Bintulu as soon as possible. Try the butter prawns or the baby *kailan* (a Chinese vegetable similar to baby bak choi). The food is fresh as can be.

King Hua Café & Restaurant (Jln Abang Galau; meals from RM10; ❄ lunch & dinner) Next door to the Ban Kee Café, this is a similar, if slightly less appealing Chinese seafood place. There's an English menu.

Popular Corner Food Centre (☎ 334-388; 50 BDA Shahida Commercial Centre; meals from RM20; ❄ lunch & dinner) A gaudy restaurant and seafood centre draped in twinkling lights and neon at the northern end of town. The Hong Kong–style prawns are expensive but tasty. Overall, however, we prefer Ban Kee.

Every evening, a busy **night market** (off Jln Abang Galau; meals from RM1; ❄ nightly from 5.30pm) sets up in a lot off a backstreet between the old airport and Jln Abang Galau. It's a good place to snack track for Malay dishes and fresh fruit.

Finally, there are several food stalls on the upper floor of the **Pasar Utama** (New Market; Jln Main Bazaar; meals RM2-5; ❄ breakfast, lunch & early dinner). The stalls at the neighbouring **Tamu Bintulu** (Bintulu Market; meals RM2-5; ❄ breakfast, lunch & early dinner) sell fresh fruit and jungle produce.

Getting There & Away

AIR

Bintulu airport is 24km west of the centre. A taxi there costs RM25.

Malaysia Airlines (☎ 1-300-883-000, 331-554; www.malaysiaairlines.com.my; Jln Masjid) flies between Bintulu and Kota Kinabalu (RM148), Kuching (RM139), Miri (RM73) and Sibu (RM81), as well as Kuala Lumpur (RM339).

BUS

The long-distance bus station is 5km north of town. Travel between the two by local bus or taxi (RM8).

There are frequent daily services between Bintulu and Kuching (RM60, 10 hours), Miri (RM20, 4½ hours) and Sibu (RM20, 3½ hours).

VAN & LONG-DISTANCE TAXI

Taxis and vans congregate in front of the markets and alongside the Tua Pek Kong temple. The round-trip taxi fare to Simalajau National Park is RM80 per car.

Getting Around

Taxis (official and unofficial) congregate alongside Tua Pek Kong temple and at the big taxi stand near the markets. Most taxi fares around town are RM5. The trip to the long-distance bus station costs RM8; the airport is RM25. If you'd like to arrange a taxi in advance, call **Mr Frankie See** (☎ 016-852-4359).

SIMILAJAU NATIONAL PARK

About 30km northeast of Bintulu, **Similajau National Park** (☎ 086-391-284; admission RM10; ❄ 8am-noon & 2-5pm) is a fine little coastal park with nice white-sand beaches, good walking trails and simple accommodation. While the park does not have the habitat variety of Bako National Park, it's perfect if you want a quiet, relaxing

SARAWAK

natural getaway as you work your way along the coast of Sarawak.

Similajau occupies a narrow 30km coastal strip between the South China Sea and the typical logged-out secondary forest of Sarawak. As such, it's one of the only havens for wildlife in this part of the state and a recent survey recorded 230 bird species, making it one of the most diversely inhabited areas in Sarawak. The forest is also home to 24 species of mammal.

The park headquarters occupies the south bank of the mouth of the Sungai Likau, though most of it lies north of the river, and is accessed by a suspension bridge.

You might be able to arrange a boat up the mangrove-lined Sungai Likau for RM50 per hour (one hour should be enough). If you go in the early morning, you'll see a range of birds, including hornbills, and maybe even some gibbons or macaques. Dolphins can occasionally be spotted out at sea, and marine turtles lay their eggs at certain points along the beach.

Note that saltwater crocodiles are found in the rivers of the park and around river mouths. *Do not* swim or wade in the park's rivers or near river mouths, and be careful when walking near the rivers early or late in the day. Three locals were killed by crocodiles in the area in 2002, so this is not a warning to be taken lightly.

Walking

Other than just relaxing on the beach, the main highlight of Simalajau are its walking trails. All the trails start just north of park headquarters, on the far side of the Likau River. Trails are clear and a guide isn't necessary; a simple trail map is available from park headquarters. Be sure to bring plenty of water as there is no drinking water en route and keep in mind that distances seem much greater in the tropics than they do back home.

As soon as you cross the bridge over the Likau, you'll see a plankwalk off to your right, following the river upstream. This 600m **Education Trail** leads straight through the riverside mangroves and it's brilliant – if you've never been inside a mangrove forest, this is your chance. The mangroves stand atop their branching roots like otherworldly spiders stuck in the Borneo mud.

The main walking trail at Similajau is the **Coastal Trail**, a gently undulating track through mixed dipterocarp and *kerangas* (heath) forest. After crossing the river from headquarters, head left off the boardwalk towards the head-

land. The end point of the trail is **Golden Beach**, a hot and sweaty 9.8km from park headquarters. En route, 7km from headquarters, you'll pass **Turtle Beach 1** and 8km from headquarters you'll pass **Turtle Beach 2**.

The **Selensur Trail** branches off the Coastal Trail at the 5km point and heads inland along the Kenyau River to the **Selunsur Rapids** (the total distance from headquarters is 7.8km).

Another option is **Sebubong Pool**, a natural pool fed by the Sebubong river, which can only be accessed by boat from park headquarters (about RM75 per boat, minimum five people). The trip takes 30 minutes and the pool is a 15-minute walk from the boat drop-off point. If you take the boat, you could also be dropped off at one of the other beaches along the way and walk back.

Sleeping & Eating

Similajau can be visited as a day trip from Bintulu, but if you want to enjoy the beach, go for a nightwalk or do the entire length of the coastal trail, you should stay a night or two. Accommodation for the park can be booked through the park headquarters or the **National Parks & Wildlife Office** (☎ 085-434-184) in Miri.

Comfortable accommodation is provided in the air-conditioned **Drive-In Chalets** (RM75), each with two rooms sleeping up to four people. The two **hostels** (dm/r RM15/40) can accommodate 16 and 72 people respectively, all in four-bed bunk rooms. There's also a **camp site** (per person RM5).

The park **cafeteria** (☷ 9.30am-6pm) has decent food and sundry items for sale. There are no stoves in the chalets or hostels, but there are refrigerators.

Getting There & Away

Bintulu is the gateway to Similajau National Park. There is no regularly scheduled bus or van transport to the park. A taxi or private car will cost RM40 each way from Bintulu – be sure to arrange a pick-up time when you get dropped off.

NORTHERN COASTAL SARAWAK

NIAH CAVES NATIONAL PARK
☎ 085

The vast caverns of **Niah Caves National Park** (☎ 737-454; admission RM10; ☷ park office 8am-5pm) are among Borneo's most incredible natural attractions. Located in some limestone hills about 3km north of Batu Niah town, the caves contain some of the oldest evidence of human habitation in southeast Asia: rock art and small canoe-like coffins (death ships) within the greenish walls of the **Painted Cave** indicate that it was once a burial ground, and carbon dating puts the oldest relics back 40,000 years. Of course, the caves themselves are the real attraction here – a bizarre fantasy world hidden inside the Borneo earth. And the boardwalk through the jungle alone is worth the trip from Miri.

Information

Upon arrival you must register at **park headquarters** (☎ 737-454; ◷ 8am-5pm) to pay the entrance fee, pick up a trail map and book accommodation (if you haven't already).

Advance booking is advisable for accommodation at the park lodges. You can book directly with park headquarters or at the Miri **visitors information centre** (☎ 085-434-181; vic-miri@sarawaktourism.com; 452 Jln Melayu; ◷ 8am-6pm Mon-Fri, 9am-3pm Sat, Sun & holidays) or the Kuching **visitors information centre** (☎ 082-410-944; www.sarawaktourism.com; Sarawak Tourism Complex, Jln Tun Abang Haji Openg; ◷ 8am-6pm Mon-Fri, 9am-3pm Sat, Sun & holidays), but make sure you get a receipt to present if requested at Niah. If you're staying at the hostel you can usually turn up without a booking, especially during the week. If it's busy and there's no accommodation, the worst you'll have to do is head the 3km back to Batu Niah, where there are three hotels.

The Caves

The caves are 3.5km away from park headquarters and you should allow at least four hours for a full exploration of the caves (including the walk there and back). First, walk from the headquarters to the jetty on the Sungai Niah, then cross the river in a small boat (RM1, departs on demand), before climbing to a small **visitors centre andmuseum** (admission free; ◷ 9am-5pm daily), which has some interesting exhibits on the geology and archaeology of the caves. You can (and should) rent a torch (flashlight) here for RM5 (check it before setting out – you'll need it if you want to go any distance into the caves).

From the visitors centre you walk to the caves along a wonderful plankwalk through swampy old-growth rainforest (there are two branches of this plankwalk, take the right branch). Once you get to the limestone outcrop that contains the caves, it's a little unclear which way to go; at the junction just past the place where locals sell souvenirs, go through the gate and climb up to the caves.

You'll pass under a limestone overhang before entering the aptly named **Great Cave**. This impressive cavern measures 250m across at the mouth and 60m at its greatest height. Ascend up to your left here and make your way to the back of the cave. The trail disappears down into the castellated gloom at the back of the cave, and you may find yourself thinking of Jules Verne's *Journey to the Centre of the Earth* or the city of Zion in the *Matrix* films. The stairs and handrails are usually covered with dirt or guano, and can get very slippery in places. The rock formations are spectacular and ominous by turns as you slip in and out of the gloom, and when the sun hits certain overhead vents the cave is perforated by the kind of dramatic light beams that ought to herald the voice of God.

You then make your way through a dark passage known as the **Gan Kira** (Moon Cave). It's not narrow enough to induce claustrophobia (unless you're severely affected), but it will certainly make you wonder what would happen if your torch suddenly died. When you're halfway along, try turning off your flashlight to enjoy the experience of pure, soupy blackness.

After passing through Gan Kira, you then emerge into the forest and traverse another section of boardwalk before arriving at the **Painted Cave**. It's easy to walk straight past the small fenced-off area by the cave entrance that protects the (now empty) death ships and the ancient paintings. A set of small travel binoculars are useful to make out the red hematite figures, as many have faded to little more than indistinct scrawls along a narrow 30m-strip at the back of the cave. To return, retrace your steps (taking the steps up to your left to close the loop in the Great Cave).

Once back on the plank walk, consider taking the other branch of the plank walk on the way back to headquarters, as this will allow you to see another part of the forest.

Sleeping & Eating

Niah Caves can be visited as a day trip from Miri or Bintulu, especially if you go by hire car all the way. If you would like to stay at or near the caves, the best choice is the park accommodation. Otherwise, there are a few simple hotels in Batu Niah town, about 3km away.

Niah Cave Hotel (☎ 737-726; 155 Batu Niah Bazaar; r RM30; 🖵) Over a café in Batu Niah, the simple rooms here with common bathroom are just barely acceptable.

Niah Caves National Park (☎ 737-454; campsites RM5, r from RM45) There are simple and clean hostel rooms and private rooms along with a basic canteen at the park headquarters. Camping is another option.

Niah Cave Inn (☎ 737-333; 621 Batu Niah Bazaar; economy/standard r from RM64/75; 🖵) Despite the unfortunate connotations of its name, this is the best hotel in Batu Niah. The economy rooms aren't worth the price, but the standard rooms are decent.

There are several *kedai kopi* in town, including the **Friendly Café** (Batu Niah Bazaar; meals from RM3; 🕑 breakfast, lunch & dinner), which serves the usual coffee-shop fare. It's opposite the Niah Cave Inn.

Getting There & Away

Batu Niah, the gateway to the park, is 11km west of Niah Junction on the Miri–Bintulu highway. Some express buses travelling between Miri (RM10, 1¾ hours) and Bintulu (RM11, two hours) stop at Niah Junction. When you buy your bus ticket in Miri or Bintulu, check that the bus stops in Niah Junction, as there are two highways between these two towns, and some buses do not go via Niah Junction.

From Niah Junction, you will have to hire a private car to Batu Niah town (RM10) or direct to the park (RM15). The latter is the better option unless you intend to spend the night at Batu Niah. From Batu Niah, you can walk to park headquarters by taking the path that starts behind the town near the Chinese temple and following the river. If you are not staying at the park, make prior arrangements with a car to pick you up and return you to Batu Niah or Niah Junction when you're done visiting the caves.

If you have a group, it can be economical and easy to hire a private car or taxi all the way from Miri.

LAMBIR HILLS NATIONAL PARK

Although **Lambir Hills National Park** (☎ 085-491-030; admission RM10; 🕑 park office 8am-5pm) doesn't have the spectacular scenery of Niah and Mulu, it is the closest primary rainforest to

Miri and it makes a pleasant day or overnight trip out of the city. The park is only 30km from Miri by road and is primarily popular with city residents, who come by the carload to visit the pretty waterfalls, natural swimming pool and riverside picnic shelters. For the more active traveller, the park has a number of pleasant walking trails through its dipterocarp rainforest.

The national park covers 69 sq km and protects a range of low sandstone hills that reach a height of 465m at Bukit Lambir. Much of the forest was logged before the park was declared, but the secondary forest is beautiful in its own right and one 50-hectare plot alone still contains an amazing 1100 tree species. There's also an good range of wildlife present.

Officially, the trails are open 8am to 4pm Monday to Friday and 8am to 5pm on weekends, but if you are seriously interested in wildlife-watching you will have to get an earlier start. Fauna here includes gibbons, tarsiers, pangolins and barking deer, though you are unlikely to see any of these close to the park headquarters. Lambir Hills is also home to many species of birds.

Activities

Lambir Hills has 13 marked walking trails branching off four primary routes. The main trail here follows a small river (Sungai Liam) past two attractive waterfalls to **Latuk Waterfall**, which has a picnic area and is suitable for swimming. It takes no more than 25 minutes to walk the 835m from park headquarters to Latuk Waterfall.

A path branches off just before the second falls and runs to **Tengkorong Waterfall**, which is a somewhat strenuous 2.6km walk (one-way) from park headquarters. Past Tengkorong Waterfall, another trail goes all the way to **Bukit Lambir** (a total of four hours from headquarters), where there are fine views.

Register your name at the trailhead booth before you start out. It is possible to arrive at the park in the morning, do a bit of walking and then be on your way back to Miri or Niah National Park, but this doesn't leave much time to appreciate the forest or its wildlife so try to plan for a longer stay.

Sleeping & Eating

Accommodation at the park is comfortable, but it's only a few hundred metres from the

SARAWAK

main highway so you won't feel like you're in the middle of the jungle. Book at the Miri **visitors information centre** (☎ 085-434-181; vic -miri@sarawaktourism.com; 452 Jln Melayu; ☺ 8am-6pm Mon-Fri, 9am-3pm Sat, Sun & holidays) in advance, particularly on weekends, though you are unlikely to be turned away if you don't have a reservation.

The park's fan-cooled **chalets** (r RM75) have two bedrooms, each with two beds. Air-conditioned **chalets** (r RM100) also have two rooms, equipped with either three single beds or one single and one double bed. There's also **camping** (per person RM5).

There is a simple canteen here as well. There are no cooking facilities at the park, but a canteen sells rice and noodle dishes, drinks and basic provisions. Opening hours depend on demand, but are generally from 8am to about 7pm.

Getting There & Away

The park office, canteen and accommodation are situated beside the highway 30km south of Miri. From Miri, any bus (RM3, 35 minutes) bound for Bekenu or Niah Junction can drop you here. A taxi from Miri costs RM40.

MIRI

☎ 085 / pop 280,000

An oil-rich boomtown at the northern end of Sarawak, Miri is a major transport hub for those heading to/from Brunei, the Kelabit Highlands and three of Sarawak's national parks: Mulu, Niah Caves and Lambir Hills. The town itself is a somewhat poorly laid-out jumble of big hotels, shops, restaurants and a surprising number of bars. While it's not the most prepossessing town in Borneo, it's not a bad place to lay over for a day or two en route to or from the jungle.

Orientation

Miri lies on a narrow plain between the east bank of the Sungai Miri and low hills that were once covered in oil derricks. Most places to stay and eat are within walking distance of each other, spread out between the Centre Point Commercial Centre, local bus station and visitors information centre to the south and the main post office and immigration office to the north. You'll need a bus or taxi to get to the long-distance bus station and airport.

Information

TOURIST INFORMATION

The **visitors information centre** (☎ 434-181; 452 Jln Melayu; ☺ 8am-6pm Mon-Fri, 9am-3pm Sat & Sun) is at the southern end of the town centre. The helpful staff can provide city maps, transport schedules and information on accommodation and tours, and also produces the useful free *Visitors' Guide to Miri*. You can book accommodation with the **National Parks & Wildlife office** (☎ 436-637) here for Gunung Mulu, Niah Caves, Lambir Hills and Similajau National Parks.

Cyber Corner (1st fl, Wisma Pelita, Jln Padang; per hr RM3)

HSBC (Lot 1268, ground fl, Miri Commercial Centre, Jln Melayu) There's an ATM here.

Main post office (☎ 441-222; Jln Post)

Maybank (☎ 412-282; Lot 112, Jln Bendahara; ☺ 9.15am-4.30pm Mon-Thu, 9.15-4pm Fri)

Maybank Bureau de Change (☎ 438-467; 1271 Centre Point Commercial Centre; ☺ 9am-5pm) Dedicated exchange and cash-advance facilities.

Miri City Medical Centre (☎ 426-622; 918 Jln Hokkien) Private medical centre.

Miri General Hospital (☎ 420-033; Jln Cayaha) South of town, off the Miri bypass.

Planet Café (1st fl, Bintang Plaza, 1264 Jln Miri Pujut; per hr RM4) Internet access.

Popular Book Store (☎ 439-052; 2nd fl, Bintang Plaza, 1264 Jln Miri Pujut)

Tally Laundry Services (☎ 430-322; Jln Merbau; per kg RM7; ☺ 8am-6pm)

Sights

The atmospheric old part of town begins around the southern end of Jln Brooke; this is the area most worth exploring. There's plenty of lively commerce around the Chinese shophouse blocks, the **Central Market** and the **Tamu Muhibbah**, where local Dayak come to sell their vegetables. The wide courtyard of the **Tua Pek Kong temple**, near the fish market, is a good spot to watch the river traffic float by. During Chinese New Year, virtually the whole of this area is taken over by a lively street fair and the crowds cram in under red lanterns and gold foil.

Canada Hill, on the low ridge behind the town centre, is the site of Malaysia's first oil well, the Grand Old Lady. Bored in 1910, the well produced around seven barrels a day until it was abandoned in 1972. The new **Petroleum Museum** (☎ 635-516; Jln Canada Hill; admission free; ☺ 9am-5pm, last admission 4.30pm, closed Mon) has a few interesting

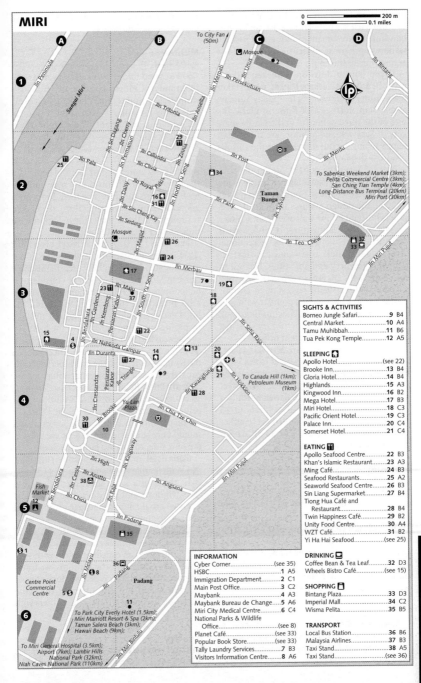

MIRI

0 — 200 m
0 — 0.1 miles

SIGHTS & ACTIVITIES
Borneo Jungle Safari.................**9** B4
Central Market.........................**10** A4
Tamu Muhibbah......................**11** B6
Tua Pek Kong Temple..............**12** A5

SLEEPING
Apollo Hotel.........................(see 22)
Brooke Inn..............................**13** B4
Gloria Hotel............................**14** B4
Highlands...............................**15** A3
Kingwood Inn.........................**16** B2
Mega Hotel.............................**17** B3
Miri Hotel...............................**18** C3
Pacific Orient Hotel.................**19** C3
Palace Inn..............................**20** C4
Somerset Hotel.......................**21** C4

EATING
Apollo Seafood Centre............**22** B3
Khan's Islamic Restaurant........**23** A3
Ming Café...............................**24** B3
Seafood Restaurants................**25** A2
Seaworld Seafood Centre.........**26** B3
Sin Liang Supermarket.............**27** B4
Tiong Hua Café and
  Restaurant...........................**28** B4
Twin Happiness Café................**29** B2
Unity Food Centre...................**30** A4
WZT Café................................**31** B2
Yi Ha Hai Seafood................(see 25)

INFORMATION
Cyber Corner........................(see 35)
HSBC.......................................**1** A5
Immigration Department...........**2** C1
Main Post Office......................**3** C2
Maybank..................................**4** A3
Maybank Bureau de Change.....**5** A6
Miri City Medical Centre...........**6** C4
National Parks & Wildlife
  Office.................................(see 8)
Planet Café..........................(see 33)
Popular Book Store...............(see 33)
Tally Laundry Services..............**7** B3
Visitors Information Centre........**8** A6

DRINKING
Coffee Bean & Tea Leaf...........**32** D3
Wheels Bistro Café................(see 15)

SHOPPING
Bintang Plaza.........................**33** D3
Imperial Mall...........................**34** C2
Wisma Pelita...........................**35** B5

TRANSPORT
Local Bus Station.....................**36** B6
Malaysia Airlines.....................**37** B3
Taxi Stand...............................**38** A5
Taxi Stand............................(see 36)

SARAWAK

displays on the source of the city's wealth. The hill itself is a popular exercise spot with a handful of refreshment kiosks, and it's worth walking up here at sunset just for the views across Miri to the South China Sea.

If you land in Miri on a weekend, don't miss the **Saberkas Weekend Market**, which takes place from Friday evening to midday Sunday, about 3km northeast of Bintang Plaza. It's one of the most colourful and friendly markets in Sarawak and vendors are more than happy to answer questions about the various products displayed.

Not far from the market site, in the suburb of Krokop, the **San Ching Tian temple** is the largest Taoist temple in Southeast Asia. Built in 2000, the design features intricate dragon reliefs brought all the way over from China.

As a self-proclaimed 'resort city', Miri is cultivating a reputation for its recreational areas, and the whole urban landscape is studded with greenery and amenities. Nearest to the centre is the **City Fan**, an expanse of themed gardens that boasts the largest open-air amphitheatre in Malaysia. It's popular with joggers, and also has a public swimming pool, indoor stadium and public library. It's just north of the local government offices.

About 3km south of town, Miri has a passable beach and recreation park at **Taman Selera Beach** (where there's also a food centre). The food centre juts out into the sea for perfect sunset dining. Further on, **Hawaii Beach** is a clean, palm-lined stretch of sand about 15 minutes outside town by bus. To get to either of the beaches, take bus 11 or 13 (RM1.50) from the local bus station.

Sleeping

BUDGET

Highlands (☎ 422-327; www.borneojungles.com; 1271 Jln Sri Dagang; dm RM25, r from RM40; ✳ ☐) The only proper backpacker-style option for miles, Highlands is a clean and popular place with dorms and private rooms. This is a great place to meet other travellers and the staff are informative about travel in Sarawak. It's on the top floor of a block of shops on the west side of town beside the Sungai Miri, above Wheels Bistro Café. Look for the five-storey car park.

Brooke Inn (☎ 412-881; brookeinn@hotmail.com; 14 Jln Brooke; s/d/tr RM43/48/53; ✳) While it stops short of midrange quality, the Brooke Inn is better than most of its competitors. It's a little noisy,

but a decent value. It's on Jln Brooke, smack dab in the middle of town.

MIDRANGE

Apollo Hotel (☎ 433-077; 4 Jln South Yu Seng; r from RM55; ✳) For good midrange value, give us a well-maintained Chinese cheapie any time. It's simple, clean and centrally located. Best of all, you can enjoy some of Miri's best seafood at the adjoining restaurant. The reception is in the back of the building, off the street.

Palace Inn (☎ 421-999; siewpoh@pc.jaring.my; Lot 192 Jln Kwangtung; s/d from RM70/75; ✳) The Palace is significantly more comfortable and better run than most others in this price range and free wi-fi sweetens the deal. The tiled floors are a good move in this swampy Borneo weather. It's roughly in the centre of town, opposite the much larger Somerset Hotel.

Miri Hotel (☎ 421-212; 47 Jln Brooke; r from RM76; ✳) Like the Pacific Orient, this place is not up to the standards of other hotels in this price range in Miri and should only be considered if better options are full. The rooms are perhaps a bit nicer than the Pacific Orient, but the hotel makes one almost unforgivable mistake by piping annoying muzak into the halls.

Kingwood Inn (☎ 415-888; 826 Jln North Yu Seng; r from RM85; ✳) The carpets are a little worn, but otherwise the Kingwood delivers the goods perfectly adequately. It's a decent midrange value.

Pacific Orient Hotel (☎ 413-333; pohotel@streamyx .com; 49 Jln Brooke; r from RM89; ✳ ☐) A little past its prime, the centrally located Pacific Orient is not on par with the Palace or the Somerset and should only be considered if those are full. On the plus side, rooms are fairly spacious.

Gloria Hotel (☎ 416-699; 27 Jln Brooke; r from RM92; ✳) With marble effect and a touch of Chinese style, the Gloria looks great through its big glass windows and provides decent comfort levels where it counts. Cheaper promotional rates often apply.

our pick Somerset Hotel (☎ 422-777; 12 Jln Kwangtung; somerhot@streamyx.com; r from RM99; ✳) The Somerset is an excellent value, with spacious, clean and comfortable rooms, wi-fi and a very central location. When you look at what other hotels in this city offer for the same price, you'll wonder why anyone bothers with them. There's a small bar downstairs.

TOP END

Park City Everly Hotel (☎ 440-288; www.vhhotels.com; Jln Temenggong Datuk Oyong Lawai; r from RM166; ✳ ☐ ☐)

The Park City Everly is a large resort-style hotel on the beach about 2km south of Miri city, very close to the Miri Marriott. The seaview rooms have nice views and the swimming pool is excellent. There's wi-fi on the executive floor and in the lobby. Service can be a bit uneven, but if you can get a good rate here, it's worth considering for those who don't want to stay downtown.

Mega Hotel (☎ 432-432; www.megahotel.com.my; 907 Jln Merbau; r from RM190; 🕃 🖵 🕃) The aptly named Mega Hotel dominates central Miri with its imposing bulk. Things improve once you get past the busy and somewhat confused reception area. Rooms are clean and well maintained and there's 24-hour room service, a convenience store as well as wi-fi on the premises.

Miri Marriott Resort & Spa (☎ 421-121; www .marriotthotels.com/myymc; Jln Temenggong Datuk Oyong Lawai; r from RM327; 🕃 🖵 🕃) Next door to the Park City Everly, the Marriott is the nicest place to stay in Miri. It's a large resort with a spa, a swimming pool, several restaurants and nice common areas. Rooms are spacious with large bathrooms and balconies. Wi-fi is available on premises.

Eating

Central Market (Jln Brooke; meals from RM2; 🕃 breakfast, lunch & dinner) The lively Central Market has a large hawker centre that covers all the bases of Malay, Indian and Chinese food. This is easily the cheapest and best place to eat in Miri. Across the street, you'll find still more choices at the similar Unity Food Centre. It's not far from Yu Lan Plaza, the high building in the centre of town.

Khan's Islamic Restaurant (229 Jln Maju; meals from RM3; 🕃 breakfast, lunch & dinner) This simple canteen is one of Miri's better Indian eateries, whipping up tasty treats such as tandoori chicken and *aloo gobi* (Indian potato-and-cauliflower dish), as well as the usual *roti canai* and a good *nasi biryani*. It's opposite Mega Hotel.

Twin Happiness Cafe (747 Jln Merpati; dishes RM3-7; 🕃 breakfast & lunch) We all take our happiness where we can find it, and the dual joys of good Chinese food and cheap prices make this particular pleasure zone worth seeking out. Besides, how can you not love a place that serves 'drunken prawn'?

WZT Café (Jln Merpati; dishes from RM3; 🕃 breakfast & lunch) This popular coffee shop and eatery is a good spot for breakfast and you can choose from toast served any number of ways. At lunch, the noodle dishes are a good choice.

Ming Café (cnr Jln North Yu Seng & Jln Merbau; dishes from RM3; 🕃 lunch & dinner) Take your pick of Malay, Chinese, Indian and Western food at this corner eating emporium. If you can't face the chaos downtown at the Central Market, this is a kinder, gentler hawker centre. There's a good drink counter that serves fresh juices.

Tiong Hua Café and Restaurant (Jln Kwangtung; meals from RM3; 🕃 breakfast & lunch) If you're just after a quick cuppa or some fried noodles, this standard-issue Chinese *kedai kopi* is a good call. It's unremarkable but very convenient if you're staying at one of the hotels on Jln Kwangtung.

Seaworld Seafood Centre (8 Jln North Yu Seng; meals from RM20; 🕃 lunch & dinner) Not as good as the nearby Apollo Seafood Centre and with somewhat less efficient service, the Seaworld Seafood Centre still draws a crowd. Even if you have no intention of eating seafood, the massed tanks of live aquatic creatures here can make a visit to Seaworld Miri as educational as a visit to Seaworld Florida. If you've never tried frog, this is your chance.

our pick **Apollo Seafood Centre** (4 Jln South Yu Seng; meals from RM30; 🕃 lunch & dinner) This deservedly popular Chinese seafood restaurant is the best place for a great meal in Miri. Just about anything you order will be delicious, and we recommend the crabs and the fried *midin* with *belacan*. If you are a big spender, you could always go for some lobsters straight from the tank.

If you want a little atmosphere with your meal, you might try some of the outdoor Chinese seafood specialists that set up each evening along the Sungai Miri. While they're no better than the excellent Apollo Seafood Centre, they do offer a cool breeze and a bit of a view to go with your food. Options here include Sea Village Seafood Restaurant and Yi Ha Hai Seafood. Meals at either of these places will cost about RM30 per head.

Finally, for self-catering, the **Sin Liang Supermarket** (☎ 413-762; Jln Duranta; 🕃 8.30am-9pm) is centrally located and well stocked.

Drinking

Coffee Bean & Tea Leaf (ground fl, Bintang Plaza, Jln Miri Pujut; drinks from RM3; 🕃 breakfast, lunch & dinner) This international coffee chain out at the mall allows you to recreate the experience of being in suburban America right in the middle of Borneo. The coffee is good here, as are the cakes, and wi-fi clinches the deal for computerised travellers.

Pelita Commercial Centre (cnr Jln Miri Pujut & Jln Sehati) Those keen on a pub crawl might consider catching a taxi to this warren of small bar-lined streets 3km north of the centre (about RM8). Anyone with an aversion to disco glitterballs, karaoke and expats need not apply for the experience.

Wheels Bistro Café (☎ 419-859; 1271 Jln Dagang) Underneath the Highlands hostel, this bistro-pub often has live music and is a favourite hang-out for Miri's expat community.

Shopping

There are two main shopping malls in Miri.

Bintang Plaza (Jln Miri Pujut; ☺ 9am-9pm daily) The modern Bintang Plaza has a few internet cafés, a decent bookshop and several restaurants.

Wisma Pelita (Jln Melayu; ☺ 9am-9pm daily) This downtown shopping mall is a little long in the tooth. There are two internet places here.

Getting There & Away

AIR

Miri is well served by **Malaysia Airlines** (☎ 1-300-883-000; www.malaysiaairlines.com.my; Jln Maju), which has flights to/from Bario (RM70), Bintulu (RM73), Gunung Mulu National Park (RM84), Kota Kinabalu (RM139), Kuching (RM139), Lawas (RM70), Limbang (RM65), Marudi (RM50), Pulau Labuan (RM50), Sibu (RM138). Book flights to/from Bario and Mulu as far in advance as possible.

Air Asia (☎ 1-300-889-933; www.airasia.com) has cheap flights between Miri and both KL and Johor Bahru.

BUS

Most buses operate from the long-distance bus terminal outside of town. Miri Transport Company bus 33 runs there from the downtown bus terminal on Jln Melayu (RM1, 15 minutes). A taxi to the long-distance bus terminal costs around RM20. Note that the long-distance bus terminal is slated to be moved, so ask at your accommodation before setting out.

Main destinations:

Bintulu Buses go daily to Bintulu (RM20, 4½ hours), departing roughly hourly between 6am and 6pm.

Batu Junction Any southbound service can drop you at the Batu Niah turn-off (RM10, 1½ hours).

Kuala Baram The Miri Transport Company bus 1A goes to Kuala Baram (RM4.50, one hour) every two hours between 5.50am and 5.30pm. The bus leaves from the local bus terminal in downtown Miri on Jln Melayu in front of Taman Pelita. From Kuala Baram you can catch an express boat to Marudi.

Kuching The major companies each have a couple of direct buses daily (RM80, 15 to 16 hours), with the morning bus leaving at 8.30am and the night bus at 9pm.

Lambir Hills Frequent north–south buses go past Lambir Hills (RM3, 45 minutes).

Mukah There is one bus from Miri to Mukah (RM40, 12 hours) and Dalat (RM45, 12 hours) at 7.30am.

Sibu There are direct buses from Miri to Sibu (RM40, eight hours) leaving every two hours or so with the earliest at 7am and the last bus at 9pm. All buses to Kuching also stop at Sibu.

If you're headed to Brunei, it's a convoluted bus journey from Miri to Bandar Seri Begawan, Brunei's capital. Four services daily run to Kuala Belait between 7am and 3.30pm (RM13.50, two hours).

At Kuala Belait bus station you can change to a connecting bus to Seria (B$1, 30 minutes), then onto a further service for Bandar Seri Begawan (B$6, two hours). Start your journey early unless you want to spend the night in Kuala Belait or Seria.

Due to the difficulty of getting to Bandar Seri Begawan by public transport, many travellers opt to take private vans organised by guesthouses in Miri. This is a good and usually cheap option, so be sure to ask at the place you're staying at.

Getting Around

At the time of writing, a new long-distance bus terminal was under construction and it's not certain which local bus will make the run between the city and the long-distance bus terminal. Ask on arrival for the local bus.

Taxis from the airport to the city centre run on a coupon system (RM14).

NORTHERN INTERIOR SARAWAK

BATANG BARAM

Like the Rejang to the south, sluggish Sungai Baram is a vital artery for Sarawak's interior; it runs from Miri along the Brunei border before turning south and winding deep into the mountains along the border with Indonesian Kalimantan. It's possible to travel upstream as far as Long Lama on regularly scheduled riverboats. Most travellers, however, take riverboats as far as Marudi, then switch to another riverboat that turns into the Sungai Tutoh and stops at Long Terawan before taking private transport as far as Gunung Mulu National Park. For details on this trip, see p212.

Marudi
☎ 085

Marudi is a quiet town on the banks of the Bantang Baram some 45km inland from Miri. It's of interest to travellers mainly as the place to switch boats en route upriver to Gunung Mulu National Park. The main attraction here is another Brooke outpost, the beige wooden **Fort Hose** (admission free; ☽ 10am-6pm Tue-Sun), built in 1901 and named after Charles Hose, who became administrator of the district in 1891. The site became the Baram District Museum in 1997 and features some interesting historical displays. The surrounding **Taman Tasik** recreation park is a nice hilltop spot with a suspended walkway and river views.

Marudi sits on the north bank of the Batang Baram. It's built around a town square that is about a 100m walk from the jetty. Most places to stay and eat are within a few blocks of the square, as are the restaurants and shops.

There is a reasonable road network around Marudi, giving access to longhouses at Long Selaban and Long Moh. You can also travel much further afield, though you'll have to arrange a lift locally. A road linking Marudi and Miri has been in the pipeline for years, but as yet only a few rough logging tracks exist.

INFORMATION
Public Bank (☎ 756-235; 59 Jln Cinema) It's up the street from the town square, visible from the inland edge of the square.
Skynet Internet (☎ 756-693; 99 Jln Perpaduan; per hr RM2) To get there, walk to the town square from the jetty; take a right on the road leading inland from the town square; take your first left and look for it on your left. It's about 400m from the jetty.

SLEEPING & EATING
Marudi has a few inexpensive hotels but it's unlikely you'll have to spend a night here unless you miss a boat connection.

Grand Hotel (☎ 755-711; Lg Lima; r from RM40; ⌘) The Grand Hotel is a little scruffy but serviceable and friendly. It's roughly behind the Public Bank.

There are plenty of *kedai kopi* around the square and along the main street at the western end of town. The best of these is Shanghai Café, which has good steamed buns, fried noodles and big mugs of tea. You could also try the big **Pasar Rakyat** (Jln Merpati) food centre.

GETTING THERE & AWAY
Air
Marudi is served by **Malaysia Airlines** (☎ 1-300-883-000; Jln Maju; www.malaysiaairlines.com.my), which has flights to/from Miri (RM50) and occasional flights to/from Gunung Mulu National Park and Bario.

Boat
Express boats (RM30, 2½ hours) run between Miri Port (also known as Kuala Baram) and Marudi. To get to Miri Port, you can take a taxi for RM25. The last boat leaves about 3pm daily in both directions. For details on continuing upriver to Gunung Mulu National Park by boat see p212.

GUNUNG MULU NATIONAL PARK
The **Gunung Mulu National Park** (☎ 085-433-561; www.mulupark.com; admission RM10; ☽ park headquarters 8am-5pm) may well be the single most impressive destination in all of Borneo. There are few parks in the world that pack so many natural marvels into such a small space. From some of the world's most incredible (and accessible) caves, to brilliant old-growth tropical rainforest, to some natural oddities such as the Pinnacles formation on Mt Api, this is truly one of the world's great wonders. It belongs at or near the top of any Borneo itinerary.

Among the remarkable features in this 529-sq-km park are its two main mountain peaks: Gunung Mulu (2377m) and Gunung Api (1750m). In between are more rugged mountains, deep gorges with clear rivers, and a unique mosaic of habitats supporting fascinating and diverse species of wildlife. Mulu's most famous attractions, though, are the Pinnacles, a forest of razor-sharp limestone peaks clustered 45m above the rainforest, and the so-called Headhunters' Trail, which follows an old tribal war path. If you're planning on doing any serious trekking in Sarawak, this park should be your first port of call.

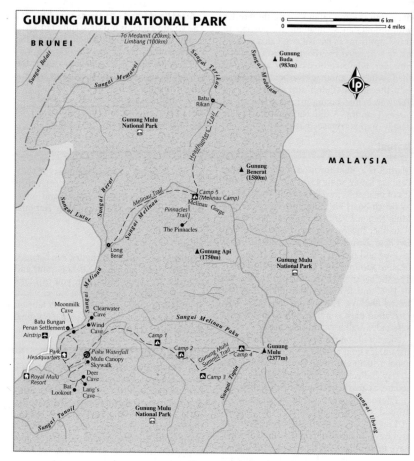

GUNUNG MULU NATIONAL PARK

As if that weren't enough, further charms lie below the surface of Mulu's forested crags; numerous spectacular caves are open to visitors, and a network of underground passages stretches over 300km underneath the park itself. A few years ago cave explorers here discovered the largest chamber in the world, the Sarawak Chamber, reputed to be the size of 16 football fields.

Note that Mulu is only accessible by plane or an all-day river journey. Bring plenty of cash as there are no ATMs or credit-card facilities.

Sights & Activities
SHOW CAVES
Mulu's caves are its most popular attractions, and for good reason: they are awe-some. Four of these are open to all and are easily visited from park headquarters (HQ): Deer Cave, Lang's Cave, Clearwater Cave and Wind Cave.

Deer Cave & Lang's Cave
The star of the lot is **Deer Cave**, which contains the world's largest cave passage – over 2km in length and 174m in height. The cave is reached from park HQ by a fascinating 3km plankwalk. In an unfortunate bit of bureaucratic overkill, the park requires that you join a guided tour to the cave (RM10 per person; tours depart park HQ at 1.45pm and 2.30pm). Once inside the cave, take your time and don't be afraid to hang back and savour the grandeur in the silence. If it's

rained recently, you'll notice a thin waterfall descending from the cave roof – when caught in the sunlight from outside the cave, the effect is magical.

After visiting Deer Cave, your guide will take you to the adjoining **Lang's Cave**, which is smaller but has some fascinating limestone formations.

If you've joined the 2.30pm tour, after visiting Deer and Lang's Caves, your guide may take you to a viewing area where you can observe the giant mouth of Deer Cave, from which millions of bats issue forth in the late afternoon to feed on jungle insects. Problem is, this is not a daily occurrence, and like as not, you'll find yourself spending an hour or more peering hopefully at the cave entrance only for the sun to go down and your guide to have to lead you back to park HQ along the plankwalk in near total darkness (actually, we kind of liked that part).

Wind Cave & Clearwater Cave

Next on the Mulu menu are two more so-called 'show caves': **Wind Cave** and **Clearwater Cave**. Like Deer and Lang's Caves, the park requires that you join a guided tour to visit these caves (RM10 per person; tours depart park HQ at 9.45am and 10.30am). However, in this case it's worth it, and the fee includes a great boat trip up Sungai Melinau. Wind Cave, first on the tour, contains several chambers filled with phantasmagorical forests of stalactites and stalagmites.

Clearwater Cave, another 400m away by river or plankwalk, is said to be the longest cave in Southeast Asia (the tour only visits a tiny segment of the cave near one of its mouths). The real highlight of Clearwater Cave is the underground river that runs through the chambers – it's straight out of *King Solomon's Mines*. Bring a swimsuit, because there's a wonderful swimming hole outside the entrance to Clearwater Cave.

If you like, you can walk back from these caves to park HQ via a concrete path and plankwalk that winds through the narrow passage of **Moonmilk Cave**. This is a highly recommended variation, but be warned that there is a steep climb en route, and you'll need a headlamp for the cave. When you get to the cave, keep an eye out for the jungle creeper that winds its way into the cave – like a giant octopus tentacle exploring the darkness. After a rain, you may encounter clouds of brilliant

black and green Brooke's birdwing butterflies. The total distance from Wind Cave to park HQ is 3km. You can also do the walk in reverse, from park HQ to the cave, which is around 2km. A guide is not necessary for Moonmilk Cave or the walk to/from the cave.

ADVENTURE CAVES

If Mulu's show caves leave you hungry for more, then you might want to consider doing some adventure caving. There are eight well-established adventure caves or cave routes in the park and guides are compulsory and arranged through park HQ.

Caves and routes are graded beginner, intermediate and advanced. If you have no previous spelunking experience, you must first do **Racer Cave** (two hours, RM200 guide fee for groups of one to five people), where your ability will be assessed. If you have no problems there, you can do other beginner or intermediate caves. In order to do an advanced cave, you will have to do an intermediate cave like Racer Cave, have proof of previous caving experience and be able to show current membership of an internationally recognised caving organisation. Minimum ages for adventure caving are eight years for beginner caving, 12 years for intermediate and 16 years for advanced.

Keep in mind that adventure caving is not for everyone, and halfway into a cave passage is not the best time to discover that you suffer from claustrophobia, fear of the dark or simply don't like slithering in the mud with all sorts of unknown creepy crawlies.

HIKING & CLIMBING

Gunung Mulu National Park offers some of the best and most accessible jungle trekking in Borneo. The forest here is in excellent condition and there are trails for every level of fitness and skill, ranging from the easy plankwalks around park HQ to the legendary four-day slog up Gunung Mulu.

Apart from the easy day walks around park HQ and the Mulu Canopy Skywalk, the main trails in the park are the Gunung Mulu Summit Trail, the Pinnacles Route and the Headhunters' Trail. An attempt at any of them will involve some expense and it's best to go with a group to reduce the cost of both transport and guide. Ask around when you get to the park to see if anyone's interested in sharing costs. You should not

THE ADVENTURE CAVES OF MULU

The limestone peaks of Mulu are riddled with some of the world's most incredible caves and the park is one of the best places in the world to try the sport of adventure caving. The park's eight main caves and caving routes are described here. The park produces a brochure called *The Adventure,* which provides additional details on these routes. Contact park headquarters (HQ) for more details or to arrange a guide. Prices here are per person for groups of one to five people unless otherwise indicated.

Turtle Cave (beginner, 45 minutes, RM20, daily at noon) This quick jaunt along the river near the entrance to Clearwater Cave is the perfect introduction to adventure caving. It leaves daily at noon from park HQ.

Lagangs Cave/Beginner Route (beginner, three to four hours, RM200, by arrangement) The beginner route through Lagangs Cave is good for families and groups. The walk to and from the cave takes around three hours, and the cave portion takes about an hour.

Lagangs Cave/Intermediate Route (intermediate, five to six hours, RM200, by arrangement) Similar to the above, but with an extra hour in the cave spent climbing a 150m slope to the cave's exit. Includes a river swim after exiting and a visit to Paku Falls.

Drunken Forest (intermediate, eight hours, RM300, by arrangement) This section of Clearwater Cave is accessed from the Mulu Summit Trail. The entrance is about three hours' walk from park HQ. This section of the cave is famous for a forest of white stalagmites.

Racer Cave (intermediate, four hours, RM200, by arrangement) About 30 minutes' walk from park HQ, this two-hour route requires a bit of upper-body strength.

Stonehorse (advanced, four to five hours, RM200, by arrangement) Start with a 2km walk through the jungle then spend around three hours travelling through large passages with up to 35m ceilings.

Clearwater Connection (advanced, six to eight hours, RM300, by arrangement) A 4.8km trip that starts at Wind Cave and heads into the wild chambers of the famous Clearwater Cave. There is a good bit of scrambling and the route includes a 1.5km river section.

Sarawak Chamber (advanced, 10 to 15 hours, RM500, by arrangement) Considered the largest cave chamber (as opposed to passage) in the world, the Sarawak Chamber is 700m long, 400m wide and 70m high. It is often said that the chamber could hold 10 747s parked nose to tail, but getting them in there would be no mean feat, and just getting yourself in there is no cakewalk: start with a three-hour walk on the Summit Trail, then you enter Good Luck Cave, traverse an 800m river section and perform a 200m traverse before entering the Sarawak Chamber. Ordinary lights are no match for the black ocean of space in the cave, which opens in front of you.

attempt any of these trails without a guide – and you won't be permitted to anyway. Expect rain, leeches, slippery and treacherous conditions, and a very hot workout – carry lots of water. Guides can be arranged at the park HQ. Guides are worth every dollar.

Mulu Canopy Skywalk

One of the real highlights of the park is its brilliant new **Mulu Canopy Skywalk**, easily the best in Southeast Asia. Once again, the park requires that you traverse it as part of a guided walk (RM30 per person; walks depart at 7am, 8.30am, 10.30am, 1pm, 2pm and 2.15pm). Despite the relatively steep cost, we urge you not to skip this attraction – every bit of its 480m length is unforgettable. Climbing to the canopy is really the only way to see what a tropical rainforest is all about, since most of the action happens in the canopy, not on the ground.

The Pinnacles

Best described as the world's worst parachute landing zone (ouch!), the Pinnacles is an incredible formation of 45m stone towers protruding from the forest on the flanks of Gunung Api. Getting to the Pinnacles involves travel by boat and a tough three-day trek.

The trek to the Pinnacles starts with a two- or three-hour boat trip (depending on the level of the river) from park HQ to Long Berar. From here it is an 8km trek to Camp 5 by the Sungai Melinau. Camp 5 has hostel-style accommodation with running water, cold showers, a cooking area, and covered sleeping quarters. You sleep overnight at this picturesque spot before climbing Gunung Api.

The three- to four-hour climb up to the Pinnacles is unrelentingly steep and taxing, and the final section before the Pinnacles involves some serious clambering and a bit of gymnastic ability. You have to start before dawn to have a chance of making it up to the Pinnacles and back in one day, and your guide will turn you back if you haven't reached a specific point in time. You cannot camp at the Pinnacles. The way back down is just as taxing as the way up and once you stagger back into Camp 5, the river will be looking pretty enticing.

Guide and boat fees are RM400 for a three-day two-night trek (one to five people).

Gunung Mulu

If you're very fit and want a real adventure, the climb to the 2376m summit of **Gunung Mulu** is a classic Borneo adventure. The four-day, three-night excursion will test anyone's stamina. You must carry enough food for the entire trip, as well as your own cooking utensils and a sleeping bag (or you can hire porters for RM70 per day). It's not unusual for it to rain every day, in which case you could find yourself wallowing in mud along the way.

There are several camps (basic wooden huts) along the trail; Camps 1, 3 and 4 are the ones usually used for overnight stops. The most common schedule involves an easy first day (about three or four hours' walking) and overnight at Camp 1 beside a beautiful river. On day two you're faced with a long (four or five hours) hard and extremely steep climb to Camp 4. If it hasn't rained, there won't be any water at Camp 4, so carry some up from Camp 3.

On day three leave your pack at Camp 4 and climb to the summit of Gunung Mulu. You can either sleep at Camp 3 for another night and return to the park HQ on day four, or descend the mountain in one day. The latter is quite tough on the legs, but you can cool down in the river along the way.

The guide fee for a group of one to five people is a healthy RM1000.

The Headhunters' Trail

The Headhunters' Trail is a backdoor route from Gunung Mulu National Park to Limbang and can be done in either direction, although most people start at the park. This trail is named after the Kayan war parties that used to make their way up the Sungai Melinau from the Baram area to the Melinau Gorge, then dragged their canoes overland to the Sungai Terikan to raid the peoples of the Limbang

region. A 3m-wide road lined with poles was used to move the canoes, and a canal was dug around Batu Rikan.

Starting from park HQ, you must first take a boat to Long Berar, then walk to Camp 5 (about four hours) and overnight there on the first day. From here, if you're really keen, you can do the climb up to the Pinnacles on the following day (see opposite). The following day involves an 11km walk to the Sungai Terikan (four or five hours), where you could spend the night at the rangers station (Mentawai) or proceed to an Iban longhouse, Rumah Bala Lesong, another three or four hours away. After overnighting in the longhouse, the boat trip continues downriver to Medamit, from where it is possible to travel by minivan to Limbang.

The guide fee for the route is RM200. The boat from the Sungai Terikan to Medamit should cost about RM500. These fees are for one to five people. A suitable payment for food and lodging at the longhouse could be about RM20; and the minivan from Medamit to Limbang costs RM5. Extra costs would include food for the stay at Camp 5, gifts for the longhouse and a tip for your guide if you feel it is warranted.

Other Trails

There are several easy walks around park HQ. The **Moonmilk Cave Trail** leaves from beside park HQ and parallels the river heading upstream to Moonmilk Cave. It's mostly flat for 1.5km until it reaches the steep steps up to the cave. No guide is required and it's paved with concrete, which means easy walking and no leeches – making it a very pleasant way to check out the Borneo rainforest. If you don't feel like the sweaty climb up to the cave, a there-and-back to the base of the steps is a good idea.

About 400m along the **Moonmilk Cave Trail**, a plankwalk branches off on the right and continues through the forest for about 1km, eventually coming out along the main plankwalk to the show caves, near the park accommodation. This is another fun and easy way to experience the jungle.

The plank walk to Deer and Lang's caves leaves from just beyond the park accommodation, past the second longhouse block. It's about 800m to the junction that leads on the left to the Mulu Canopy Skywalk and on the right to Deer and Lang's Caves. If you just

NEW YEAR'S EVE IN BORNEO   Chris Rowthorn

In December of 1996 I travelled with two friends, Anthony and Denise, to Sarawak's Gunung Mulu National Park. After exploring the park, we decided to try the Headhunters' Trail. Our guide for the trip was a young Iban named Mr Larry. After leading us for three days through the jungle, we were met at the river by Mr Larry's father, Mr Siga, who bundled us into a riverboat for the trip down to his longhouse where we planned to stay the night. As we made our way downriver, it dawned on us that it was New Year's Eve.

The first sign of what was to come came in the form of a dull roar emanating from the longhouse, which was as yet invisible beyond the riverbank. Mr Larry and his father ushered us up the steps of the longhouse and into Mr Siga's 'apartment'.

As soon as we sat down, Mr Larry produced a plastic bottle containing a murky white fluid. 'This,' he said proudly, 'is *tuak*, the drink of the Iban people.' Cups were filled and, after a welcoming toast by the chief, we took our first sip. As we drank, the bigwigs of the longhouse filtered in one by one, eager to meet the exotic visitors from abroad. Many of them spoke surprisingly good English, including one man who introduced himself as Alfred. Soon after sitting down, he embarked on a long and somewhat convoluted speech in praise of Bill Clinton. Being a Democrat, I told him that I agreed with everything he had to say. With that, Alfred turned to me and with a great smile on his face announced, 'You and me, we drink together!'

Soon we were ushered into the dining room. Mrs Siga served up a wonderful meal of river fish, rice, local vegetables and, of course, huge pitchers of *tuak*. As we ate, we were repeatedly urged to 'Take rice. Take rice.' I would later come to regret not having taken enough rice. After dinner, as we sat around the table, we were asked to sing a song. We looked at each other in horror – did we know even one complete song between us? After a brief discussion, we settled on the inevitable and launched into dimly remembered Beatles classics' such as 'Yesterday' and 'Yellow Submarine'. Our hosts took this as well as could be expected, given our wretched singing voices and poor grasp of the lyrics.

Meanwhile, the *tuak* kept flowing. While Anthony and Denise begged off for a postdinner nap, Alfred dragged me to another house, which doubled as the longhouse bar. He barked something to the old man who ran the place and moments later a great jug of *tuak* appeared before us. Even though we were literally hurling down glass after glass, Alfred explained that this was just a warm-up. After midnight the real party would begin, and we would traverse the whole length of the longhouse, stopping for a glass of *tuak* at every single door. 'How many doors are there?' I enquired grimly. 'Only forty-five!' Alfred announced with a big smile on his face.

At around 10pm, Anthony and Denise found us. They looked sober and refreshed. I, on the other hand, was extremely drunk. We left the longhouse bar to join the party on the veranda. Up and down its length, knots of people were gathered in furious *tuak*-drinking sessions. Being the only outsiders, we were in great demand at these gatherings and people were literally fighting each other for the honour of our presence. Alfred clearly enjoyed the prestige that came from being the chaperone of these exotic foreign visitors.

By 11pm the party had reached fever pitch. People clustered round us, madly trying to engage us in conversation. One man wanted to talk about durians. Another wanted to introduce us to his dog. Still others simply wanted to offer us tuak. Presiding over this mad talk-fest was Alfred, who was clearly in his element. Caught up in the drinking and talking, I lost all track of time. Suddenly, the revellers struck up a rather alarming chant: 'Get the gun! Get the gun!' Before I knew it, Alfred had dragged me to the railing of the veranda and placed a particularly

walked out to this junction and turned around, you'd probably find the time well spent.

Just before this junction, the Gunung Mulu Summit Branches off (marked Summit Trail) on the left. This is also the **Paku Waterfall Trail**. This flat trail works through the jungle to Paku Waterfalls, an interesting set of three waterfalls

that come right out of a limestone cliff face. There's good swimming here. The total distance from park HQ to the falls is about 1.5km and the return trip takes about three hours at a leisurely pace. Note that the ground can become a swamp after rain. The best advice: don't fight it – just take the plunge and get muddy fearsome-looking shotgun in the hands of the drunkest man in Southeast Asia. After a brief argument about whose watch told the correct time the countdown began, and as the hour struck midnight, I pulled the trigger.

Now that we had properly rung in the New Year, Alfred announced that it was time to start drinking in earnest. I could hardly believe my ears. What did the man think I had been doing up until that point? Renewed supplies of *tuak* were brought forth and two men appeared with a miniature electronic organ and a couple of drums. As soon as they started playing, all but the oldest Iban jumped up to dance.

Before long, I was a sweaty mess. I begged off dancing for a while and wandered down the veranda to join another group of people busily consuming *tuak*. I was soon besieged by offers of 'the local wine', and was growing increasingly drunk by the minute. I was swimming in a sea of *tuak* that seemed to know no end. However, the Iban clearly believed that you could never be too drunk.

The whole longhouse was slowly spinning round me and I felt a horrible nausea coming on. I knew that if I didn't get out of there fast, I was going to make a nasty mess of the veranda floor. I made my way down the longhouse steps and followed a plankwalk that disappeared into a swamp next to the longhouse. Here, I busily set about vomiting up everything I had eaten and drunk in the last six hours. As I was retching, I felt the plankwalk start to shake. I looked up and to my horror there he stood: Alfred. He had found me. The fact that I was being violently ill didn't seem to register with him. 'Come, we go drink *tuak*!' he bellowed. Luckily, Anthony appeared just a few moments later and somehow managed to drag Alfred back to the longhouse. As they disappeared into the darkness, Alfred shouted over his shoulder, 'Chris, I am waiting for you. When you come back, we drink more *tuak*!'

I was not tempted to join Alfred. In a thick drunken haze, I made my way back to the longhouse, peered down the veranda to make sure that no-one was looking, then made a quick dash for the chief's house. I stumbled into the empty house and crawled onto a mattress. The whole longhouse seemed to spiral about me. There was so much alcohol in my bloodstream that unconsciousness quickly took precedence over nausea.

Just as I teetered on the brink of oblivion, something large grabbed my arm and hauled me halfway off the mattress. I opened my eyes to see Alfred staring down at me expectantly. 'Come,' he said. 'Now, we go to forty-five doors!' Even in my wretched drunken state I had to laugh. Was this man serious? Here I was, on the verge of going out like Keith Moon or Jimi Hendrix, and he was suggesting a nightcap of forty-five glasses of tuak! Needless to say, I did not take him up on his offer. As I sank back into unconsciousness, I had a grim vision of the Iban carrying my prostrate form down the length of the longhouse, stopping at each door to pour a glass of *tuak* down my unprotesting throat.

The next morning at 7am, the sound of loud music woke me from a tortured sleep. 'It can't be,' I thought, 'they're not still at it.' But they were. The Iban had partied straight through the night. As for me, I was suffering from an apocalyptic hangover. Even the slightest movement caused rays of pain to shoot through my head. A quick New Year's resolution was in order. I vowed to myself, 'I shall not, as long as I live, consume another drop of alcohol. It is the bane of my existence. It is the root of all evil. It is the ink with which the fool signs his soul over to the devil. GET THEE BEHIND ME SATAN!' Unfortunately, of course, Satan was right in front of me. When I opened the door of the chief's house, an Iban man rushed forward with a glass of *tuak* in his outstretched hand and said, 'The local wine!' I took the cup, and I drank it. In a lifetime of short-lived New Year's resolutions, this was the shortest.

early on. No guide is required for this route, but let the folks at park HQ know before you set out and when you expect to return.

Sleeping & Eating

Due to the park's popularity it's best to pre-book your accommodation in advance with

Mulu Park (☎ 085-792-300; enquiries@mulupark.com; www.mulupark.com). You can also make bookings through National Parks & Wildlife agents in Kuching (p163) or Miri (p200).

Park accommodation is in the form of a 21-bed **hostel** (dm RM25), which has clean, spacious rooms with hot showers and lockers.

Men and women share the same rooms here. In the same building there are **Rainforest Rooms** (d from RM66), which have fans and sleep up to four people. They are comfortable enough, but can be noisy. Finally, there are excellent semidetached **Longhouse Rooms** (d from RM125), which are really cabins. These large, comfortable units have en suite bathrooms with hot showers, air-con and nice porches for sitting out on in the evening. Some of these have four single beds, making them suitable for families or small groups.

There are no cooking facilities in park accommodation. Simple but tasty meals are served at **Café Mulu** (meals RM4-9; ☽ breakfast, lunch & dinner). There's also a pair of café-bars across the suspension bridge from park HQ.

The luxury **Royal Mulu Resort** (☎ 085-790-100; www.royalmuluresort.com; r from RM105, ste from RM299; ☒ ☒), about 3km from the park entrance, is a sprawling resort built around limestone bluffs overlooking the river. Rooms are nicely appointed and the garden is full of flowers, butterflies and birds. There's a pool, a gym, a nice restaurant and a lot of activities. The one strange omission is the lack of mozzie nets on the windows in all the rooms. There is a good spa here and nonguests are welcome – might be just the thing after an ascent of Mulu or a look at the Pinnacles.

Getting There & Away
AIR
Malaysia Airlines (☎ 1-300-883-000; www.malaysiaair lines.com.my) flies to/from Miri (RM84 one way) and Kota Kinabalu (RM179). Book these flights well in advance as they fill up early. The park office is a half-hour walk from the airstrip, or minivans can shuttle you to/from the terminal for RM3/5.

BOAT
It's possible to travel to Mulu from Miri by river, but it's a long, long journey and it actually costs more than flying (if the planes are full, however, this is your only option other than a very expensive 4WD trip). On the plus side, it's an interesting trip and the last section from Long Terawan to the park is thrilling and you'll probably arrive after dark, with your boatmen picking their way upriver with torches. It's one of those great Borneo river trips.

First, you must take a taxi from Miri to Miri Port (also known as Kuala Beram) to

catch the 8am river express to Marudi (RM30, 2½ hours). From Marudi, take the noon boat upriver to Long Terawan (destination plate reads 'Tutoh'; RM20, six hours). Once there, you must charter a boat for the final three-hour journey upriver to the park (RM250). It's best to call ahead to the park to make sure that a boat will be available to take you from Long Terawan to the park.

CAR
The park can arrange 4WD transport to Miri, but it'll cost you several hundred ringgit.

Getting Around
The park headquarters is a 3km walk from the airport, along the road to the Royal Mulu Resort. Minivans run between the airport and headquarters, but there's no regular service – although there's usually one on hand to meet flights. Taxis are usually available (to/from airport RM3/5), or you could try catching a lift with one of the resort vans.

KELABIT HIGHLANDS
☎ 085

A lovely hanging valley in eastern Sarawak, the Kelabit Highlands are tucked up against the Indonesian state of Kalimantan and ringed by jungle-covered mountains on all sides. The main population centre is the languid village of Bario, home to about 800 souls, mostly members of Borneo's indigenous Kelabit people.

The main activity here, other than merely enjoying the clean, cool air, is trekking from longhouse to longhouse on mountain trails. The natural hospitality of the Kelabit people and the relatively unspoiled flora and fauna of the high jungle makes any trip to the highlands a memorable experience, and we highly recommend it for those who have the time and energy.

Unfortunately, logging roads are encroaching on the Highlands and some of the primary forest in the area has already been logged. Much more will be logged in the next few years. Fortunately, some of the logged terrain is now covered with fairly dense secondary forest, which at least approximates the old forests of Borneo.

There are no bank, ATM or credit-card facilities in the whole Kelabit Highlands, and only a few basic shops in Bario and Ba Kelalan. Travellers should bring plenty of small-denomination

KELABIT HIGHLANDS

0 |————————| 15 km
0 |————————| 7.5 miles

To Long Lopeng
1631m
Sungai Trusan
Long Semado
1835m
1396m
1540m
Gunung Murud (2423m)
Sungai Limbang
Ba Kelalan
Pa Rupai
Long Medang
Butu Lawi (2039m)
Long Rapung
Bukit Batu Iran (2020m)
Bukit Batu Buli (2090m)
Pa Lungan
Tang Paya
Long Bawan
1920m
Bario
Pa Ukat
Pa Tik
Kampung Baru
Pa Umor
MALAYSIA
Tama Abu Range
Pa Berang
Pa Main
KALIMANTAN
INDONESIA
Sungai Dapur
Pa Mada (Long Dano)
Pa Dali
SARAWAK
1930m
Ramudu
Batu Patong
Gunung Apad Runan (2110m)
Long Lellang
1980m
Sungai Kelapang
1960m
1940m
Lepo Zink
Logging Roads Not Shown

cash for accommodation, food and guides, plus some extra in case you get stranded. If you plan to go trekking, be sure to bring some leech socks, as the trails of the Highlands are – literally – crawling with leeches.

Bario

The 'capital' of the highlands, Bario is a small settlement spread over a beautiful valley 1500m above sea level, close to the Indonesian border. You wouldn't think it now, but the sleepy village has seen its share of action, during both WWII and the Konfrontasi with Indonesia in the early 1960s.

Bario's appeal lies in its clear mountain air and splendid isolation (access is by air and torturous 4WD road only). The delicious Bario rice is renowned Asia-wide, as are the sweet, juicy local pineapples. The nearby hills are covered in largely untouched forest with abundant wildlife, and in the *kerangas* are pitcher plants, rhododendrons and orchids.

Above all, though, it's the unforced hospitality of the Kelabit people that will quickly win you over, and an amazing number of travellers find themselves extending their stays in Bario

by days, weeks or even years. Do yourself a favour and get stuck here for a while!

ORIENTATION & INFORMATION

Bario is essentially a wide valley dotted with houses, paddies, a church or two and a couple of rough dirt roads. In what might be considered the centre of town, there's a row of tiny blue-roofed shops selling expensive necessities. The immigration office is near the junction of the airport road and the main village road.

The airport is about a 30-minute walk south of the shophouses. You're bound to be offered a lift on arrival, as seemingly everyone in town turns out to meet the daily flights.

There are public telephones by the shophouses; internet access is available at the **Telecentre** (per hr RM10; ☼ 10am-4pm Mon-Sat). As the whole town is solar-powered during the day, these services are not 100% reliable.

SIGHTS & ACTIVITIES

The **Bario Asal longhouse** is one of the oldest in the area, built in the traditional style with a separate fireplace for each family on the wide veranda. You may be able to arrange accommodation here (see below).

Any of the lodges in Bario can organise a wide variety of short walks and longer treks. Of the settlements close to Bario, the easiest to visit are **Pa Umor**, about one hour southeast, and nearby **Pa Ukat**. Keep an eye out for the *dolmen* (stone burial markers) dotted throughout the Highlands; new ones are sometimes found when a trail is blazed through the forest.

You can also trek up to **Bario Gap**, a visible notch that was cut in the rainforest on a ridge above town to celebrate the millennium. Coordinated by local character and guide Peter Matu, this *kawang* (man-made natural monument) follows the Kelabit tradition of changing their surroundings to mark important events.

SLEEPING & EATING

Most Bario accommodation options give you a choice between a bed-only price and a package deal that includes all meals and transport.

Bariew Backpackers Lodge (☎ 791-038; bariew lodge@yahoo.com; bed RM15-20, full board package RM45-55) Perfectly placed in Bario town, a short walk from the shops past the old airstrip, this is an excellent family-run guesthouse frequented

TREKKING IN THE KELABIT HIGHLANDS

The Kelabit Highlands are, arguably, the best place in Borneo for extended treks. Most trails are gently undulating and traverse a variety of primary and secondary forest, as well as cleared areas. While the Highlands are certainly cooler than Borneo's coastal regions, it's still hard work trekking up here and you should be in pretty good shape to consider a multiday trek in the Highlands. You'll also want a good pair of leech socks, comfortable trekking clothes and walking shoes; see the boxed text on p65.

Guided treks range from overnight excursions to five-day slogs as far as distant villages such as Ba Kelalan. Every guesthouse and longhouse in Bario can arrange guides and accommodation, as well as transport to trailheads, if necessary. It's certainly possible to just turn up and make arrangements after you arrive, especially if you don't mind waiting a day or two in Bario before the start of your trek. If you're in a hurry, it makes sense to make arrangements by email or phone before you arrive.

Note that the Highlands are laced with rivers and an increasing number of logging roads. It's possible to combine treks with river trips in the rainy season and following rains, and the experience of travelling through the Highlands by river is pure magic. You can also shorten certain treks by doing one or two legs by 4WD trucks. Boat and road travel increases the cost of a trip, but it may be the only option for those with limited time or those who cannot face the rigors of an all-walking trip. Your lodge owner can consult with you about this and make arrangements.

Going rates for guides (and porters if you need them) start at RM80 per day. To stay overnight in a longhouse, expect to pay RM40 per person (including food). Some treks involve either river trips (highly recommended if the water is high enough) or 4WD trips, which, naturally, significantly increase the cost of the trek.

Finally, keep in mind that it is extremely easy to get lost in the Kelabit Highlands. *Never* attempt to trek for even a short distance without a local guide.

TREKKING ROUTES

The following are the most popular routes in the Kelabit Highlands. These are intended just as a starting point. With some many trails in the area, there is ample scope for custom routes and creative route planning.

Kelapang Loop

Formerly known as the Bario Loop, this three- to five-day trek is the most popular route in the Highlands, taking in three of the main longhouses south of Bario: Pa Dali, Ramadu and Pa Mada (sometimes called Long Dano). The term loop is something of a misnomer: it's more of an out-and-back trek with a small loop at one end. Portions of this can be done by 4WD or river boat.

by sociable locals as well as visitors. The proprietor, Reddish, knows everyone in town and has close ties with the longhouses on the treks around the highlands. As well as basic fan rooms, tasty meals and evening barbecues, the lodge can arrange guides and activities.

De Plateau Lodge (deplateau@gmail.com; bed/full-board package RM20/60) This is another good choice, with comfortable rooms and nice common areas. The owner here can arrange treks, bird-watching and other activities. It's located in a white-timber house surrounded by a lovely garden, 2km east of Bario; stick left when the road forks.

Bario Asal Longhouse (☎ 791-065; paranmaku@yahoo.com; bed/full-board package RM20/RM80) A short walk from 'downtown' Bario, this longhouse is a friendly spot with pictures of the longhouse residents (past and present) hung on the wall. Not too many families live here any more, so it's relatively quiet.

JK View Lodge (rose_sabot@hotmail.com; r per person RM15) Rose's place is a neat little cabin with just four rooms, 500m west of Bario near the shophouses. Meals, treks and tours are available.

Tarawe's Lodge (jtarawe@bario.com; r per person RM20) Simple two- and three-bed accommodation

All three longhouses en route are welcoming, friendly places where you'll get a good glimpse into Kelabit life.

The typical itinerary is as follows: day one – Bario to Pa Mada (eight hours); day two – Pa Mada to Pa Dali (two hours); day three – Pa Dali to Ramadu (three hours); day four – Ramudu to Pa Mada (three hours); day five – Pa Mada to Bario (eight hours). This itinerary can be shortened by taking a boat to Pa Berang and a 4WD to Ramudu (RM100 per person), or by covering multiple stages in one day. Alternatively, you can extend it for as long as you like; the area around Pa Dali is well worth a day or two's exploration, and if you really have a taste for adventure you could attempt to organise an ascent of Gunung Apad Runan (2110m), on the Indonesian border.

Ba Kelalan

The three-day trek from Bario to the village of Ba Kelalan (see p216) is a good route for those who don't want to cover the same ground twice (you can arrange to fly out of Ba Kelalan so that you don't have to return to Bario). It covers a variety of mostly gentle terrain and gives a good overview of the Kelabit Highlands.

The typical itinerary is as follows: day one – Bario to Pa Lungan (four hours); day two – Pa Lungan to Pa Rupai (eight hours); day three – Pa Rupai to Ba Kelalan (three hours). Note that this route takes you through part of Kalimantan, which is officially illegal. Please consult carefully with your guides about whether this is possible at the time you attempt the route. It may be possible to detour around Kalimantan to avoid trouble.

Gunung Murud

Sarawak's highest mountain (2423m) is just begging to be climbed, but very few visitors go to the trouble required to put together a trip. The mountain can be reached from both Ba Kelalan and Bario; from Bario, the more common starting point, a typical return trip takes six days. Needless to say, this is only for the very fit.

The typical itinerary from Bario is as follows: day one – Bario to Pa Lungan (four hours); day two – Pa Lungan to Long Rapung (four hours); day three – Long Rapung to Church Camp (eight hours); day four – Church Camp to summit and back to Church Camp (seven hours); day five – Church Camp to Long Rapung (eight hours); day six – Long Rapung to Bario (eight hours).

Batu Lawi

If you were sitting on the left side of the plane from Miri to Bario, you probably caught a glimpse of the 2046m spire of Batu Lawi. While an ascent of this spire (known as the 'male peak' of the mountain) is only for expert technical rock climbers, an ascent of the lower 'female peak' is possible for fit trekkers without any special technical skills. It's a three-day return trip from Bario.

The typical itinerary is as follows: day one – Bario to Base Camp via Pa Ukat (eight hours); day two – Base Camp to summit to Base Camp (10 hours); day three – Base Camp to Bario (eight hours).

in a small house on the main road. Meals are available if ordered in advance.

Gem's Lodge (☎ 019-815 5779; gems_lodge@yahoo.com; r RM60) Bario itself is hardly a bustling metropolis, but this welcoming guesthouse, just 6km southeast of town near the longhouse village of Pa Umor, is tranquillity incarnate. The owner, Jaman, is one of Bario's nicest, best and most informative guides. He offers a wide array of treks, tours and excursions based on his own formidable local knowledge. There are four pleasant private rooms and a cosy common area. Email ahead to arrange a pick-up.

GETTING THERE & AWAY

The only practical way to Bario is by air and it's easily one of the most exciting flights in Southeast Asia. After crossing the lowlands of western Sarawak, you sweep by the dense rainforest of Brunei, followed by the brilliant peaks of Mulu National Park (you can peer right into the yawning maw of Deer Cave) before flying by the fantastic spire of 2046m Batu Lawi (all of these sights are only visible from the left side of the aircraft as you fly from Miri to Bario).

It takes 30 minutes to walk into Bario from the airport. Turn left at the T-junction.

SARAWAK

Malaysia Airlines (☎ 1-300-883-000; www.malaysia airlines.com.my) has at least one flight daily between Miri and Bario (return RM145, 50 minutes). Communication between the Malaysian Airlines office in Bario and Malaysian Airlines offices elsewhere is haphazard, so reconfirm your flight out of Bario as soon as you arrive. Flights are often booked out well in advance and are dependent on the weather; cancellations aren't uncommon.

Guesthouse operators in Bario can arrange 4WD transport on logging roads down to Miri, but you'll have to pay around RM500 (and your butt cheeks will pay even more dearly as you bounce your way down the hellish roads).

BA KELALAN

Ba Kelalan, known for its apples and organic vegetables, is the other main centre in the highlands, though it's even smaller than Bario.

Trekking to or from Bario is a good option, as you can catch a flight there or back to avoid covering the same stretch twice. The round trip should take three to four days, passing through Pa Lungan and Long Rapung. Walks in this area are difficult – you'll need to have your own food and shelter, and be prepared for some hard slogging.

The best accommodation in Ba Kelalan is the **Apple Lodge**, run by **Borneo Jungle Safari** (☎ 085-435736; www.borneojunglesafari.com; 174A Jln Brooke) in Miri.

MASwings (www.maswings.com.my) currently flies here from Bario twice a week, though flights are often cancelled. Flights and 4WD transport to Lawas are also available.

LIMBANG DIVISION

LIMBANG

☎ 085 / pop 3700

Limbang is the centre of the section of Sarawak that divides Brunei into two parts. It's of limited interest to travellers, but you may find yourself passing through here en route between Brunei and Sabah or after a trip down the Headhunters' Trail from Mulu National Park. Those expecting to find a sleepy backwater will be surprised to find a bustling and relatively prosperous city on the banks of the Sungai Limbang.

Orientation & Information

The main part of Limbang sits along the east bank of the Sungai Limbang, which loops across a forested plain before emptying into Brunei Bay. A range of low hills further east marks the border with Brunei's Temburong district.

The older part of town is only a couple of hundred metres square and is bordered on the riverbank by a two-storey, blue-roofed main market. The massive complex looming over the wharf area is the Purnama Hotel and its attendant shopping mall, Limbang Plaza. The centre is largely comprised of concrete shophouses containing hotels, cafés, karaoke bars and snooker halls.

Boats to Brunei and Labuan leave from the wharf below the blue-roofed market, and taxis park just outside. Boats to Lawas tie up at the jetty a few hundred metres downstream. Buses leave from a stand a couple of blocks east of the river, behind the old part of town. The airport is about 4km south of town.

There are several moneychangers on Jln Kuba and a Maybank on Jln Bank.

Sights

A **tamu** (weekly market) is held on Friday in the car park in front of the main market. Bisayah villagers, many of whom still speak the Brunei Malay dialect, come in from all around the district to attend.

The small but informative **Limbang Regional Museum** (Muzium Wilayah; admission free; ☯ 9am-6pm Tue-Sun) is upstairs in another of Charles Brooke's forts, built in 1897. The collection is well presented and features exhibits on archaeology, culture and crafts of the region. To get here, follow the riverbank upstream (south) past the police station and look for the replica totem pole.

Down the road from the museum and up a steep drive is a pretty **park** with an artificial lake backed by forest. It's a pleasant place to pass some time if you're waiting for a flight.

Sleeping & Eating

Being a port town, most of Limbang's cheaper places are a little sleazy, with hourly rates and grotty rooms. You'll escape the sleaze by paying a bit more for midrange accommodation.

Royal Park Hotel (☎ 212-155; Lot 1089 Jln Buagsiol; r from RM60; ☒) Much better value than the budget fleabags in the centre of town, this clean, well-run hotel is worth the walk to get to. From the town centre, walk north (downstream) along the river. It's about 400m north of Limbang town centre, just in from the river.

Metro Hotel (☎ 211-133; Lot 781 Jln Bangkita; r from RM50; ☒) If you can't be bothered to walk up to the Royal Park, the Metro Hotel is a just barely acceptable option in the middle of town. It's a little smoky and threadbare, but it's within easy walking distance of the jetty and the bus station.

Purnama Hotel (☎ 216-700; Jln Buangsiol; r RM150; ☒) A four-star hotel with friendly staff, the Purnama has large, adequate rooms, a café, a lounge bar, a spa and a fitness centre, as well as all the consumerist delights of Limbang Plaza. Discounts make it particularly good value.

There are food stalls on the 1st floor of the waterfront market, at the bus station and along the river. Basic Malay and Chinese food is served in *kedai kopi* in the town centre.

Getting There & Around

AIR

Malaysia Airlines (☎ 1-300-883-000; www.malaysiaair lines.com.my) has flights to Miri (RM65) and Kota Kinabalu (KK; RM75). The airport is 4km south of the town centre, a RM10 taxi ride.

BOAT

The express boat to Pulau Labuan in Sabah leaves at 8.30am daily (RM25, two hours). Speedboats go to Bandar Seri Begawan in Brunei (RM15, 30 minutes) and Lawas in Sarawak (RM25, one hour) when sufficient passengers turn up (you may find yourself waiting quite a while). Boats leave from the jetty outside the immigration hall on the river, just upstream from the large pink building housing the market (Bengunan Tamu Limbang).

BUS

There are buses to Kuala Lurah, at the border with Brunei, that depart at 9.30am, 1pm and 5pm (RM5.50, one hour). There are buses to Medamit (RM5) but none to the Temburong District of Brunei (you'll have to take a taxi). Buses depart from the stand a few blocks east of the river in the centre of town. There is also a daily bus from Limbang across

Brunei to Miri (RM40, three hours, departs Limbang at 9am).

CAR

A taxi to Kuala Lurah, at the border with Brunei, will cost RM40. Most taxi drivers will refuse to continue over the border to Bandar Seri Begawan (BSB) due to the time it takes to clear immigration. You can walk across the border and catch another taxi onward to BSB for about B$10. A taxi from Limbang to the border with the Temburong District of Brunei will cost RM15, and, once again, taxi drivers will usually refuse to cross. Once across, you'll have to hitch or arrange a private car (which will not be easy). Consider heading to Temburong (Bangar) from BSB or negotiate with a taxi driver from Limbang to take you all the way.

LAWAS

☎ 085 / pop 1080

Lawas is a transit point in the sliver of Sarawak pinched between Sabah and the Temburong district of Brunei. There is of little interest to travellers.

Hotel Perdana (☎ 285-888; Lot 365 Jln Punang; r from 46; ☒) is the best economy hotel in town, although it's a little frayed round the edges. To get there, start with your back to the main market (Pasar Baru Lawas) and go left, following the main road out of town. It will be on your right after about 300m.

There are several **Malaysia Airlines** (☎ 1-300-883-000; www.malaysiaairlines.com.my) flights each week to/from Miri (RM70). The airport is 2km from town. There is a branch of **Maybank** in the centre of town.

A boat to Limbang (RM28, one hour) leaves at 9am every day but Thursday. A boat to Labuan (RM33, two hours) leaves at 7.30am every day except Tuesday and Thursday. Boats leave from the jetty on the west side of town, just downstream from the Shell petrol station. Buses head to Kota Kinabalu in Sabah (RM20) at 7am and 1pm daily.

Brunei Darussalam

The last remnants of an empire that once included all of Borneo and the southwest Philippines, Brunei is now one of the smallest countries on earth – two tiny slivers of land lodged in the northern coast of Sarawak. This tiny country is blessed with some of the largest oil fields in southeast Asia, and, perhaps not surprisingly, one of the wealthiest rulers on earth. Thanks to these underground riches, Brunei has been able to spare most of its above-ground resources, and the country boasts some of the most intact primary rainforest in all of Borneo.

Whatever else you can say about Brunei, this much is certain: it won't be what you expect. Those expecting a mini-Dubai on the shores of the South China Sea will be surprised to find that Brunei is remarkably quiet and undeveloped. Those expecting a stern Islamic theocracy will find a relaxed country and an easy-going people. Those expecting another version of Sarawak or Sabah will find that Brunei feels qualitatively different from its nearest neighbours.

For most people Brunei is merely a stopover on the overland journey between Sabah and Sarawak, or between Europe and Oceania on a Royal Brunei Airlines flight, but there is enough here to make Brunei a destination in its own right. First, there is the capital of Bandar Seri Begawan (BSB) with its soaring mosques and picturesque water-villages. Then, there is the rainforest, which is best experienced in the fine Ulu Temburong National Park. Finally, there are the oddities of the country: the Jerudong Park Playground, a surreal semideserted amusement park, and the Empire Country Club and Hotel, a US$1 billion monument to misguided public spending.

HIGHLIGHTS

- Enjoy the mosques, museums and water villages of Brunei's peaceful capital, **Bandar Seri Begawan** (p221)

- Tear through the marshes between Bandar Seri Begawan and Bangar on one of Brunei's best **boat rides** (p227)

- Climb high above Brunei's intact primary rainforest and swim in a cool jungle river in Brunei's best park, **Ulu Temburong National Park** (p234)

- Trek past the base of giant dipterocarp trees and savour a view that extends all the way to Brunei Bay in **Peradayan Forest Reserve** (p233)

- Marvel at the **Empire Hotel** (p229), a sprawling monument to misguided spending

Empire Hotel ★

Bandar Seri Begawan ★

★ BSB–Bangar Boat Ride

★ Peradayan Forest Reserve

★ Ulu Temburong National Park

| ■ POPULATION: 379,400 | ■ AREA: 5765 SQ KM |

HISTORY

The earliest recorded references to Brunei's presence relate to China's trading connections with 'Puni' in the 6th century, during the Tang dynasty. Prior to the region's embrace of Islam, Brunei was within the boundaries of the Sumatran Srivijaya Empire, then the Majapahit Empire of Java. By the 15th and 16th centuries, the so-called Golden Age of Sultan Bolkiah, Brunei Darussalam had become a considerable power itself in the region, with its rule extending throughout Borneo and into the Philippines.

The Spanish and Portuguese were the first European visitors, arriving in the 16th century, but they failed to make inroads by force. In the early 19th century, the more subtle approach of the British, in the guise of Sarawak's first raja, James Brooke, spelled the end of Brunei's power. A series of 'treaties' was forced upon the sultan as Brooke consolidated his hold over the town of Kuching. In 1888 Brunei became a British protectorate and was gradually whittled away until, with a final dash of absurdity, Limbang was ceded to Sarawak in 1890, dividing the crippled sultanate into two parts.

In 1929, just as Brunei was about to be swallowed up entirely, oil was discovered, turning the tiny state into an economic power overnight. The present sultan's father, Sultan Omar Saifuddien, kept Brunei out of the Malayan confederacy, preferring that the country remain a British protectorate and the oil money remain on home soil. He's credited with laying the foundations for Brunei's solid development.

In 1962, in the lead up to amalgamation with the new state of Malaysia, the British pressured to hold elections. The opposition Ra'ayat Party, which wanted to keep Brunei independent and make the sultan a constitutional monarch within a democracy, won an overwhelming victory. When the sultan refused to allow the new government into power, an armed rebellion broke out, supported by the Indonesian government. The uprising was quickly crushed with British military backing, and the 'Abode of Peace' has been under emergency laws ever since.

Saifuddien abdicated in 1967, leaving the throne to his popular son and heir, Sultan Hassanal Bolkiah. Early in 1984 the new ruler reluctantly led his tightly ruled country into complete independence from Britain. As a former public-school boy and graduate of Royal Military Academy Sandhurst, the sultan rather enjoyed British patronage and the country still has close ties to Britain.

After independence, Brunei veered towards Islamic fundamentalism, adopting a national ideology known as Melayu Islam Beraja (MIB). This institutionalised dogma stresses Malay culture, Islam and monarchy, and is promulgated through the ministries of education, religious affairs and information. In 1991 the sale of alcohol was banned and stricter dress codes were introduced, and in 1992 the study of MIB became compulsory in schools.

In recent years signs have begun to emerge that Brunei is not the model state it once was. The government has recognised a relatively small but growing unemployment problem, and disaffected youths have been blamed for isolated incidents of crime. The most disaffected youth of them all, the sultan's younger brother Prince Jefri, became a byword for extravagance both in his private life and, rather more seriously, in his role as finance minister. Scandals and rumours of financial corruption forced the sultan to sack Jefri in 1997, but the damage had been done, and Brunei found itself with seriously depleted financial reserves.

Perhaps as a result of these factors, the prevailing climate in Brunei today seems to be one of controlled reform as the sultan struggles to keep pace with the modern world. In 2004, the legislative council was finally restored after 20 years of 'emergency' law. So far the 29 incumbents are all royal relatives or cronies, but the constitution has been amended to allow the council to expand to 45 members in the future, with 15 of them elected by the public. In another significant step, former radical leader Muhammad Yasin Abdul Rahman, who was once jailed for his part in the 1962 rebellion, has been allowed to form a new opposition party, the National Development Party.

The mere mention of the words 'election' and 'opposition' must have brought the sultan out in a sweat, as he promptly hedged his bets by adding another clause to the constitution stating that he 'can do no wrong in either his personal or any official capacity'. Perhaps the sultan was worried that his marriage to a 27-year-old Malaysian journalist (technically his third wife – he's still married to the first,

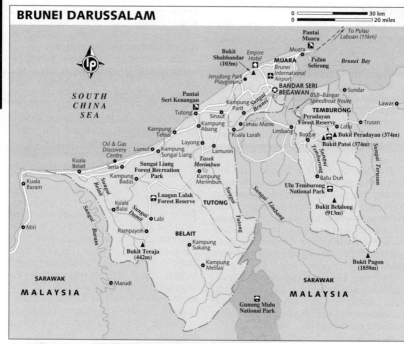

BRUNEI DARUSSALAM

and divorced his second in 2003) might have undermined his popularity. Either way, don't expect to see Bruneians at a polling booth any time soon.

There was a whiff of reform in November 2004 when the sultan amended the constitution to allow for the first parliamentary elections in 40 years. However, only one-third of parliamentarians will be publicly elected and the rest will still be hand-picked by the sultan, when and if the election ever happens (Bruneians are still waiting).

In 1998 the sultan's son, Crown Prince Al-Muhtadee Billah Bolkiah, was proclaimed heir to the throne and began preparing for the role as Brunei's next ruler and 30th sultan. That preparation included the 30-year-old prince's wedding in September 2004 to 17-year-old Sarah Salleh, in a ceremony attended by thousands of guests. While Brunei may not be facing the same promise of prosperity that existed when the current sultan took the throne in 1967, it's clear that the sultan sees the crown prince's careful apprenticeship as crucial for the continuing (and absolute) rule of the monarchy.

Whatever its political waverings, Brunei's wealth still allows its citizens to enjoy an unprecedented standard of living. Literacy stands at 94%, average life expectancy is 77 years, and there are pensions for all, free medical care, free schooling, free sport and leisure centres, cheap loans, subsidies for many purchases (including cars), short working weeks, no income tax and the highest minimum wages in the region. The sultan even marked his 60th birthday in 2006 by awarding civil servants their first pay rise in 20 years. Economic diversification and new deep-sea explorations for oil aim to keep the cash rolling in, and as long as it does, the people of Brunei should stay happy with their lot.

CLIMATE

For information on the climate of Brunei, see p13 and p291.

GETTING THERE & AWAY
Air

There are flights between Brunei and the following cities: Auckland, Bangkok, Brisbane, Darwin, Denpasar (Bali), Dubai, Frankfurt,

Hong Kong, Jakarta, Jeddah, Kuala Lumpur, London, Manila, Perth, Sharjah, Shanghai, Singapore, Surabaya and Sydney, to Bandar Seri Begawan. For details, see p227.

Boat

There are boat connections between Muara (BSB's port) and Pulau Labuan (Sabah), where you can get onward boats to Kota Kinabalu, Limbang and Lawa. There are direct speedboats between BSB and Limbang, in Sarawak's Limbang District. For details, see p227.

Road

There are road connections between Kuala Belait and Miri, in Sarawak (see p232); there are also road connections between BSB and Limbang, in Sarawak (see p227). For details on crossing between Brunei and the Limbang Division of Sarawak (and onward to KK in Sabah) see the Across Temburong By Land boxed text (p234).

GETTING AROUND

Coastal Brunei is laced with excellent roads, and these are well served by taxis and buses. As you head inland, roads peter out almost completely, with only a few paved ones and the occasional dirt track. River travel is possible on a few of the country's rivers, most notably up the Sungai Temburong in the Temburong District. There are no commercial flights around this small country. For details on getting around Brunei, see the Getting There & Away sections in this chapter and the Transport chapter (p302).

VISAS AND OVERLAND TRAVEL

If you are coming overland from Miri in Sarawak to BSB and intend to continue overland up to Sabah, or vice versa (that is, if you want to traverse Brunei in either direction), you should get a multiple-entry visa as you arrive since you'll be entering and leaving Brunei twice, due to the country's unique layout.

Also, note that travelling from Miri to BSB is fiddly, with up to five changes of transport. Several travellers guesthouses in Miri can organise direct minibuses, which cost only a little more. Unfortunately, we haven't seen comparable overland deals between BSB and Kota Kinabalu (Sabah), perhaps because the boat is so easy and fairly direct.

BANDAR SERI BEGAWAN

pop 81,500

Bandar Seri Begawan ('City of the Abdicated Sultan'; BSB) is most notable for the absence of the mayhem that is typical of most southeast Asian cities. In fact, central BSB introduces itself to the traveller as a quiet, pleasant, greenery-dotted city with a low skyline that's decorated with minarets and neat arrangements of buildings. Despite the city's rather sterile atmosphere and almost total lack of nightlife, there is something quite alluring about the city and it is well worth a day or two of lazy exploration.

To start with, you can visit the excellent Royal Regalia Museum and then wander over to the nearby Omar Ali Saifuddien Mosque. After this, you can take a bus down to the Brunei Museum and check out the fine Islamic Art Gallery contained therein. Those with more time might head out to see Jame'Asr Hassanal Bolkiah Mosque or the Istana Nurul Iman, two of the city's better outlying attractions.

However, the real heart and soul of BSB is in its sprawling *kampung ayer* (water villages), and the best time to check them out is in the early evening when another brilliant Borneo sunset starts to set the sky on fire. As you wind your way along Sungai Brunei, you'll be treated to a most pleasing visual composition: otherworldly domed mosques rising out of rickety water villages with the teeming Borneo jungle as a backdrop.

ORIENTATION

Central BSB is a compact grid aligned roughly north–south and bounded on three sides by water: the Brunei and Kedayan Rivers on the south and west respectively, and a tidal canal on the east. Jalan Sultan runs down the middle of the city and forms its main artery. It's also home to the major banks, the post office, airline offices, coffee shops and some good restaurants, as well as the Royal Regalia Museum. The Omar Ali Saifuddien Mosque, on the western edge of the city centre, dominates the landscape. Most sights are within walking distance of, or a short bus ride from, the city centre.

Between Omar Ali Saifuddien Mosque and the riverfront are two massive buildings forming the Yayasan Sultan Haji Hassanal Bolkiah Complex. Usually called the Yayasan Complex, this huge shopping mall leads to Jalan MacArthur, across which are waterfront cafés and the wharf where you can catch boats to nearby destinations.

Stilt villages sprawl along the opposite bank of Sungai Brunei (Brunei River), and along both banks of Sungai Kedayan to the northwest. Long, rickety-looking plankwalks connect them to the shore.

The Brunei Museum is about 6km southeast of the city centre, on Jalan Residency, overlooking the Sungai Brunei and accessible by bus or taxi. With the exception of this museum, most of the sights in the city centre are within easy walking distance of the main hotels.

Maps

Unfortunately, it is impossible to find decent maps of BSB and Brunei. Google Earth has clear and detailed satellite photos of BSB. Otherwise, the *Brunei: Kingdom of Unexpected Treasures* map-brochure is probably your best bet. It's occasionally available at the airport and at businesses around town. There's also a simple map in *Big*, the free what's-on magazine put out by the Brunei Tourism Board. It's available in the same places as the Brunei map.

INFORMATION
Bookshops
Paul & Elizabeth Book Services (☎ 222-0958; 2nd fl, Block B, Yayasan Complex, Jln Pretty) Stock a small range of English-language paperbacks but no city or country maps.

Emergency
Ambulance (☎ 991)
Fire (☎ 995)
Police (☎ 993)

Internet Access
Paul & Elizabeth Cyber Café (☎ 222-0958; 2nd fl, Block B, Yayasan Complex, Jln Pretty; per hr B$1; 8am-9.30pm) On the 2nd floor overlooking the central atrium in the northern building of the complex. Decent connections, bad soundtrack.

Medical Services
Ripas Hospital (☎ 224-2424; Jln Tutong; 24hr) A fully equipped, modern hospital across the Edinburgh Bridge on the western side of Sungai Kedayan.

Money
HSBC (☎ 225-2222; cnr Jln Sultan & Jln Pemancha; 9am-3.30pm Mon-Fri, 9am-11am Sat, closed Sun)

Charges B$15 to change most travellers cheques and has an ATM.
Rupiah Express (ground fl, Britannia House, 1 Jln Cator; 8am-5.30pm Mon-Sat, 8am-3pm Sun) Exchanges cash only.

Post
Main post office (cnr Jln Sultan & Jln Elizabeth Dua; 8.30am to 4.30pm Mon-Thu, Sat, 8.30am-11.30am, 2pm-4pm Fri, closed Sun) Be sure to stop in to the adjoining Stamp Gallery (same hours as post office).

Telephone
Payphones are common in the city centre, and they accept 10c or 20c coins. Phonecards are available from post offices and many retail shops and hotels. SIM cards can only be purchased from the **DST Communications** (☎ 223-2903; ground fl, Yayasan Complex, Jln Pretty; 9am-4pm Mon-Thu, Sat, 9am-11am & 2.30pm-4pm Fri, closed Sun). The standard DST SIM card is B$30 and includes B$5 worth of calls.

Travel Agencies & Tours
Freme Travel Services (☎ 223-4280; www.freme .com; 403B-407B Wisma Jaya, Jln Pemancha) Offers a variety of tours, including the city and Kampung Ayer, and trips to Ulu Temburong and Pulau Selirong.

SIGHTS
Royal Regalia Museum
A celebration of the sultan and all the trappings of Bruneian royalty, the **Royal Regalia Museum** (☎ 222-8358; Jln Sultan; admission free; 8.30am-5pm Sun-Thu, 9-11.30am & 2.30-5pm Fri) belongs at the top of any Brunei itinerary. The first floor is dominated by a recreation of the sultan's coronation day parade, including a huge gilded royal cart, on which the newly crowned sultan was pulled through the streets of BSB.

On the mezzanine floor of the museum you'll find a selection of gifts received by the sultan. Of course, when you are called upon to give a gift to the Sultan of Brunei, you must inevitably confront the question: what do you give the man who has everything? Here you'll see how various heads of state and royalty have answered this question (hint: you'll never go wrong with priceless gold and jewels). We particularly like the mother of all beer mugs, given by Queen Elizabeth, the fine abalone-shell chest given by the Philippines, and the Benjarong porcelain from Thailand.

BANDAR SERI BEGAWAN

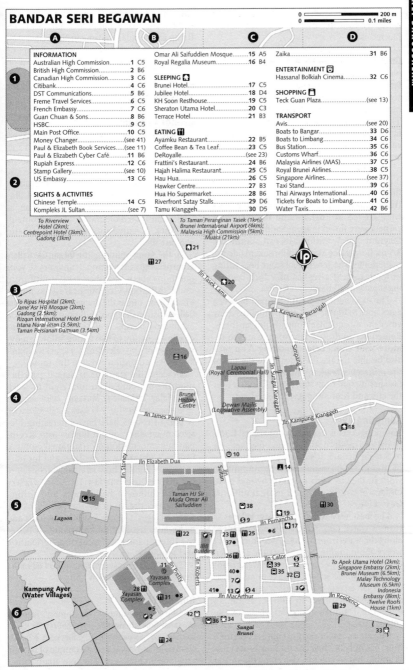

INFORMATION
Australian High Commission	**1** C5
British High Commission	**2** B6
Canadian High Commission	**3** C6
Citibank	**4** C6
DST Communications	**5** B6
Freme Travel Services	**6** C5
French Embassy	**7** C6
Guan Chuan & Sons	**8** B6
HSBC	**9** C5
Main Post Office	**10** C5
Money Changer	(see 41)
Paul & Elizabeth Book Services	(see 11)
Paul & Elizabeth Cyber Café	**11** B6
Rupiah Express	**12** C6
Stamp Gallery	(see 10)
US Embassy	**13** C6

SIGHTS & ACTIVITIES
Chinese Temple	**14** C5
Kompleks JL Sultan	(see 7)

Omar Ali Saifuddien Mosque	**15** A5
Royal Regalia Museum	**16** B4

SLEEPING
Brunei Hotel	**17** C5
Jubilee Hotel	**18** D4
KH Soon Resthouse	**19** C5
Sheraton Utama Hotel	**20** C3
Terrace Hotel	**21** B3

EATING
Ayamku Restaurant	**22** B5
Coffee Bean & Tea Leaf	**23** C5
DeRoyalle	(see 23)
Frattini's Restaurant	**24** B6
Hajah Halima Restaurant	**25** C5
Hau Hua	**26** C5
Hawker Centre	**27** B3
Hua Ho Supermarket	**28** B6
Riverfront Satay Stalls	**29** D6
Tamu Kianggeh	**30** D5

Zaika	**31** B6

ENTERTAINMENT
Hassanal Bolkiah Cinema	**32** C6

SHOPPING
Teck Guan Plaza	(see 13)

TRANSPORT
Avis	(see 20)
Boats to Bangar	**33** D6
Boats to Limbang	**34** C6
Bus Station	**35** C6
Customs Wharf	**36** C6
Malaysia Airlines (MAS)	**37** C5
Royal Brunei Airlines	**38** C5
Singapore Airlines	(see 37)
Taxi Stand	**39** C6
Thai Airways International	**40** C6
Tickets for Boats to Limbang	**41** C6
Water Taxis	**42** B6

On the same level, at the back, you'll find a hall containing medals that the sultan has received.

Omar Ali Saifuddien Mosque

Named after the 28th sultan of Brunei, the **Omar Ali Saifuddien Mosque** (☎ 222-2623; admission free; ☯ 8am-noon, 2-3pm, 5-6pm & 8-9pm Sat-Wed) was built in 1958 at a cost of about US$5 million. The 44m minaret makes it the tallest building in central BSB. Listen for the call to prayer that echoes throughout the city centre, starting before dawn or at dusk.

The interior is simple but tasteful, though it's no match for the stunning exterior. The floor and walls are made from the finest Italian marble, the stained-glass windows were crafted in England and the luxurious carpets were flown in from Saudi Arabia and Belgium. Jigsaw enthusiasts can admire the 3.5 million–piece Venetian mosaic inside the main dome. The ceremonial stone boat sitting in the lagoon is a replica of a 16th-century *mahligai* (royal) barge.

The external compound is open between 8am and 8.30pm, and non-Muslims may enter the mosque itself outside prayer times. Remember to dress appropriately and to remove your shoes before entering. You may also be able to take the elevator to the top of the minaret or walk up the winding staircase (ask permission from staff first). The view over the city and Kampung Ayer is excellent.

Kampung Ayer

Kampung Ayer is a collection of several traditional and modern stilt villages on either side of Sungai Brunei. It's home to a population of around 32,000, some of whom commute to work in the city each morning by taxi boat. Others, of course, pursue a more traditional way of life.

The best way to see the **water villages** is from a water taxi, which can be chartered along the waterfront for B$20 per hour (don't worry about finding one – any time a foreign tourist goes anywhere near the waterfront in BSB, a small school of taxi boats forms with eager drivers offering their services). Be sure to ask the driver to stop off at Taman Persiaran Damuan for great views of the sultan's palace.

Late afternoon or early evening is best for a tour, not only because the midday heat is unbearable, but so you can also enjoy the sunset

over the city. If there's any wind about, you will see kites rising out of the *kampung* (kite-flying is a popular pastime in Brunei).

If you don't feel like exploring the Kampung Ayer by boat, you can also explore them on foot via the plankwalks that connect the settlements to the city (try the ones west of the Yayasan Complex).

Brunei Museum

The **Brunei Museum** (☎ 222-3235; Jln Kota Batu; admission free; ☯ 9.30am-5pm Sun-Thu, 9-11.30am & 2.30-4.30pm Fri) is 4.5km east of central BSB, sitting on a bluff overlooking Sungai Brunei. The main building contains the excellent **Islamic Art Gallery**, which has some wonderful illuminated (decorated) copies of the Koran, as well as an incredible model of the Dome of the Rock executed in mother of pearl and abalone shell.

In the same building, the **Oil and Gas Gallery** is surprisingly interesting. It answers all your questions about how they get the stuff from under the ground to your nearest gas pump. Finally, don't miss the **Brunei Traditional Culture Gallery**, also in the main building. It's got good exhibits on all aspects of Bruneian culture, including a picture of two young fellows enjoying a spot of grass sledding – a sport we didn't know existed until we visited this museum.

Descend the stairs from the car park behind the museum, then turn right to reach the **Malay Technology Museum** (admission free; ☯ 9.30am-5pm Sun-Thu, 9-11.30am & 2.30-4.30pm Fri) A pair of rooms here have interesting life-sized re-creations of stilt houses with accompanying information on traditional cultures. Gallery 1 features water villages and includes reconstructions of how *kampung* architecture has evolved over the last 150 years. Gallery 2 has exhibits of handicrafts and fishing techniques practised by the people of the water villages. Gallery 3 shows the tools and techniques used by the indigenous tribes of the interior for food gathering, agriculture and hunting.

To get to the museum, take bus 39 from the bus station in downtown BSB.

Bolkiah Mosque

The largest mosque in the country, **Jame'Asr Hassanal Bolkiah Mosque** (☎ 223-8741; Jln Hassan Bolkiah, Gadong; admission free; ☯ 8am-noon, 2-3pm, 5-6pm & 8-9pm Sat-Wed), is a fine example of Islamic religious architecture. The four main minarets and two golden domes of the structure are a fantastic sight when illuminated in the evening. The mosque was built in 1992 to celebrate the 25th year of the Sultan's reign. Non-Muslims are forbidden entry on Thursday and Friday. It's located en route to Gadong, about 2.5km northwest of the city centre.

To get to the mosque, take bus 22 or 1 (Circle Line) from the bus station in downtown BSB.

Istana Nurul Iman

The largest palace in the world, according to some calculations, **Istana Nurul Iman** (Jln Tutong), is the official residence of the sultan of Brunei. It's a good thing that the sultan has a large staff, because the upkeep must be daunting – it contains 1788 rooms, 257 bathrooms, and the floor area is around 200,000 sq metres.

Designed by Filipino architect Leandro Locsin, the aesthetics of the palace draw heavily on airport terminal and stadium designs. Nonetheless, it's relatively attractive from a distance or when illuminated in the evening. Those who want to get inside the palace will have to time their visit carefully: the Istana is open to the public only at the end of the fasting month of Ramadan (September).

The best vantage points are from the river and **Taman Persiaran Damuan**, a landscaped park nearby. The Istana is 2.5km out of town. From BSB, take a water taxi there in the early evening and get off at the park.

To get to the museum, take any westbound bus from the bus station in downtown BSB.

Other Attractions

One of BSB's most overlooked sights is the charming **Twelve Roofs House** (Bumbungan Dua Belas; admission free; ☒ 9am-4.30pm Mon-Thu & Sat, 9am-11.30 & 2.30-4.30 Fri), which is the former residence of the British High Commissioners, and now displays photos illustrating British involvement in Brunei and the 'special relationship' between the two countries.

Further out on the north side of town, **Taman Peranginan Tasek** is a more extensive green zone with picnic areas, and peaceful walks to a small waterfall and reservoir. If you're lucky, you may get a glimpse of proboscis monkeys in the early morning or late afternoon. The falls are nicest in the wet season, when the water is deeper. You can swim here but women should remember that the usual rules of modesty apply; T-shirts and shorts are OK. Another

road by the gate leads to a 15-minute uphill walk to a view over the reservoir.

To get here, walk north along Jalan Tasek Lama past the Terrace Hotel and turn right after two sets of traffic lights. It's about 1km to the falls from the entrance gates by the car park – continue past the flowerbeds and picnic tables, then follow the stream. The Sheraton Utama Hotel can provide a map showing the park walks.

SLEEPING

Most of BSB's accommodation options are located in the city centre, with a few outlying options in the Gadong suburb a few kilometres to the northwest. Unlike the rest of Borneo, you'll find few budget options in the city.

Budget

KH Soon Rest House (☎ 222-2052; khsoon_resthouse_brunei@hotmail.com; 2nd fl, 140 Jln Pemancha; s B$30-35, d B$35-39; ☒) This simple guesthouse is a decent budget choice for those seeking a central location. Rooms are spartan but huge and an extra B$5 snags you an attached bathroom. If all you need is a clean place to lay your head in BSB, this should suit.

Apek Utama Hotel (☎ 222-0808; Simpang 229, Jln Kota Batu, Kampung Pintu Malim; r from B$30; ☒) This basic hotel has acceptable rooms with fan or air-con. The management is friendly and a good source of information on travelling around Brunei. The downside is the somewhat inconvenient location: it's 3km east of town, accessed by bus 39 or by water taxi. Note that buses stop running at 6pm, so plan accordingly.

Midrange

Terrace Hotel (☎ 224-3554; www.terracebrunei.com; Jln Tasek Lama; r from B$60; ☒ ☒) Even if you're on a tight budget, consider spending a little more to enjoy the comforts of this excellent midrange hotel. Rooms are clean and well taken care of, and there's a great little swimming pool and wireless internet access. There's also a decent restaurant on the ground floor. Deluxe rooms cost about B$10 more than standard rooms, but are well worth the price. Highly recommended.

Jubilee Hotel (☎ 222-8070; www.jubileehotelbrunei .com; Jln Kg Kianggeh; r from B$70; ☒ ☒) Not quite as appealing as the Terrace, the Jubilee offers simple and clean standard rooms (the deluxe rooms aren't worth the extra price). On-site facilities include a Thai restaurant and billiards. Rates include airport pick-up and breakfast.

Brunei Hotel (☎ 224-2374; www.bruneihotel.com .bn; Jln Pemancha; standard s/d from B$88, deluxe from B$130/150; 🉑) This hotel is like a formerly prosperous oldster going gracefully to seed. The standard rooms are strangely more appealing than the deluxe rooms, the only difference we could see was the size. The place is pervaded by a somewhat musty fug and the industrial air conditioners in the halls don't do much to help this. It's got a great downtown location, but we'll take the Terrace.

Riverview Hotel (☎ 223-8238; riverview_htl@brunet .bn; Jln Gadong; standard s B$60, deluxe s/d from B$88/99; 🉑) Inconveniently located between the city centre and Gadong, the Riverview is a large hotel popular with local and Malaysian guests. The rooms are fairly spacious and well kept. Book well in advance if you want to claim one of the four standard singles.

Top End

Sheraton Utama Hotel (☎ 224-4272; www.starwoodhotels .com/sheraton/utama; Jln Tasek; r from B$158; 🉑 🉐) Located within walking distance of the downtown area, the Sheraton Utama is easily the nicest hotel in town, with no real competition from the two top-end entries in the Gadong area. The standard rooms are fairly spacious and light with adequate but not luxurious bathrooms. The deluxe rooms are a little more spacious and have semiseparate sitting areas. There's also a nice pool, two restaurants (one poolside), a small gym and a spa.

Centrepoint (☎ 243-0430; Abdul Razak Complex, Gadong; r from B$240; 🉑 🉐 🉐) A little long in the tooth, with chaotic and irregular service and a lobby that feels like a shopping mall. Unless you really insist on being in Gadong, you'll do better in a deluxe room at the Terrace or a standard room at the Sheraton. Rooms are spacious and have the typical amenities. However, they can be noisy and if the person in the next room is watching TV, you'll know it.

Rizqun International Hotel (☎ 243-3000; reservation @rizquninternational.com; Abdul Razak Complex, Gadong; r from B$320; 🉑) Under the same ownership as the Centrepoint, this newer spot is more appealing and is worth considering if you can get a great online or travel agency rate, but we'd still rather be in the Sheraton in the city centre. The rooms are new, large and well appointed, but the service appears somewhat inconsistent.

EATING
City Centre

Hajah Halima Restaurant (☎ 223-4803; 54 Jln Sultan; meals from B$2; 🕓 breakfast, lunch & dinner) This popular and friendly Indian Muslim place has just about everything the traveller wants: good coffee, tea, fresh juice and rotis in the morning; and great *nasi biryani* (spiced rice) and set meals for lunch and dinner, not to mention great *mee goreng* (fried noodles) and *murtabaks* (roti stuffed with meat or vegetables). It's the best of the three similar joints on this part of Jalan Sultan. There is no sign – look for the blue paint around the entrance. It's almost directly opposite the Coffee Bean & Tea Leaf.

Riverfront Satay Stalls (Jln Residency; satay from B$2.50; 🕓 midday-early evening) This collection of *satay* and drink vendors right on the riverfront offer one of life's great combinations: *satay* and fresh coconut juice. You can get 10 sticks of chicken or beef *satay* here for about B$2.50. A fresh coconut will add another B$1.50. This is a great place to watch the sunset – when the colours really start working, why not jump into a waiting water taxi and enjoy the view from sea level?

Coffee Bean & Tea Leaf (cnr Jln Sultan & Jln Permancha; coffee drinks from B$3; 🕓 breakfast, lunch & dinner) Travellers and expats alike are drawn like moths to the invisible waves of wi-fi and the aroma of good coffee emanating from this downtown caffeine emporium. Drop by in the afternoon and you'll run into about half of the Western tourists in BSB at any one time.

DeRoyalle Café (Jln Sultan; coffee drinks from B$3; 🕓 breakfast, lunch & dinner) Like its direct neighbour, the Coffee Bean & Tea Leaf, this cosy little coffee shop is a good place to kick back and relax with a magazine. If you're in a hurry, however, we suggest its more famous next-door neighbour, as the staff here is well meaning but service is slow. There's also wi-fi.

Ayamku Restaurant (Jln Permancha; meals from B$3.50; 🕓 lunch & dinner) Brunei's answer to KFC, this is one of the cheapest places in town to get a meal. You can get a big piece of fried chicken, some rice and a drink for about B$3. And, the chicken is surprisingly good. One note: this may be purely coincidental, but many of the diners here seemed remarkably plump for Southeast Asians.

Hau Hua (☎ 222-5396; 48 Jln Sultan; meals around B$10; 🕓 lunch & dinner) This surprisingly good Chinese restaurant does all the standard Chinese dishes and a few lesser-known ones, like broccoli with crab meat. There is an excellent drink menu that includes daily changing specials and good fresh juices.

Zaika (☎ 223-1155; block C, Yayasan Complex; meals from B$15; ⏲ lunch & dinner) This dimly lit northern Indian restaurant is the place to go for a proper sit-down meal in BSB. The kitchen does well with favourites like shish kebab, naan and standard curries, but its attempts at more creative dishes are less successful.

Frattini's Restaurant (☎ 224-2372; Jln MacArthur; meals from B$30; ⏲ lunch & dinner; ♿) Frattini's is one of the few restaurants in BSB to take advantage of the fine riverfront view. It is, without a doubt, the only Italian-Thai restaurant that we've ever come across (yes, we are suspicious of that combination, too). Despite the strange pedigree, it's a good place for a romantic dinner or for when you just can't stand another plate of chicken rice or *mee goreng*. Stick with Italian standards like pasta and salad and you won't go too far wrong.

Self-caterers can walk across the canal to the local produce market, **Tamu Kiangggeh** (Jln Sungai Kiangggeh; ⏲ breakfast, lunch & dinner), where food stalls are sometimes set up. Supplies can also be bought in the basement of the Yayasan Complex at **Hua Ho Supermarket** (☎ 223-1120; basement, Yayasan Complex, Jln Pretty; ⏲ 10am-10pm). Look for shrink-wrapped durian here (just don't try sneaking it into your hotel room).

Finally, there's a small hawker centre in the park opposite the Terrace Hotel. It's something of a hit-or-miss affair, but it's worth a try for a cheap lunch or dinner if you're staying nearby.

Gadong

BSB locals often head to Gadong for a night out (which in Brunei usually amounts to nothing more than dinner and a movie). Based on what you hear from locals, you might start to believe that the place is a seething nightlife zone or at least a fine collection of smart restaurants. Unfortunately, it's neither.

The Mall at Gadong has a good food court on the 3rd floor, with all the usual stalls, including local, Chinese and Thai. The Gadong Centrepoint shopping centre has a branch of Coffee Bean & Tea Leaf (with wi-fi), a branch of Frattini's Restaurant (see above) and a Jaya Hypermarket (really, it's merely a supermarket) for self-catering.

Finally, there is a nightly hawker market in Gadong with stalls selling a great variety of

Malay and Bruneian dishes for rock-bottom prices. Unfortunately, it's geared to car-driving locals who take the food away, and there are no places to sit, so it's of limited interest to travellers.

ENTERTAINMENT

Hassanal Bolkiha Cinema (Jln Sungai Kiangggeh; tickets B$4-8) This small cinema screens a variety of Hollywood action films and Hong Kong kung fu movies. It's about the only game in town as far as 'nightlife' goes in BSB.

GETTING THERE & AWAY

Air

There are flights between BSB and the following cities: Auckland, Bangkok, Brisbane, Darwin, Denpassar (Bali), Dubai, Frankfurt, Hong Kong, Jakarta, Jeddah, Kuala Lumpur, London, Manila, Perth, Sharjah, Shanghai, Singapore, Surabaya and Sydney. Airline offices in Brunei are as follows:

Malaysia Airlines (MAS; ☎ 222-4141; www.malaysia airlines.com; 144 Jln Sultan)

Royal Brunei Airlines (RB; ☎ 221-2222; www .bruneiair.com; RBA Plaza, Jln Sultan)

Singapore Airlines (SI; ☎ 224-4901; www.singapore air.com; 1st fl, Wisma Raya Bldg, 49-50 Jln Sultan)

Thai Airways International (THAI; ☎ 224-2991; www.thaiair.com; 4th fl, 401-403 Kompleks Jln Sultan, 51-55 Jln Sultan)

Boat

Most boats to/from BSB operate from the Muara Ferry Terminal, in Muara, about 25km northeast of the city (B$2 bus ride and a B$40 taxi ride to/from BSB).

There are regular ferries between Muara and Pulau Labuan in Sabah, Malaysia (B$15, 1½ hours, six departures between 7.30am and 4.40pm). From Pulau Labuan, there are two ferries a day onward to Kota Kinabalu, Sabah. Passengers are charged B$1 departure tax at the ferry terminal.

Boats to Limbang in Sarawak, Malaysia (B$10, 30 minutes), make irregular morning departures from the riverfront along Jalan MacArthur. However the service is highly unreliable and departures are often delayed until more passengers turn up so be prepared to wait. Buy your ticket from the moneychanger along the waterfront (Map p223). Another way to get to Limbang or Lawas in Sarawak is to go via Pulau Labuan (see p124).

Boats to/from Bangar (B$6, 45 minutes, about one departure per hour from BSB from 7am to 1pm) operate from the jetty just east of the riverfront satay stalls, along Jalan Residency. Bangar is the starting point for attractions in Brunei's Temburong district. Boats generally don't depart until they've got enough passengers to warrant the trip, so you might have to wait around a while. Even if you do nothing more than grab a quick cup of tea in Bangar and then return to BSB, we highly recommend this journey. In fact, we rank it among the highlights of Brunei. The speedboats tear through nipa-lined waterways at incredible speeds and you wonder how they manage not to get lost in this watery maze.

Bus

If you're heading to Limbang (Sarwak), Bangar (Brunei), Lawas (Sarawak) or Kota Kinabalu (Sabah), you can go overland, but be warned: the overland journey to/from any of these places is more expensive, time-consuming and just plain troublesome than going by boat.

If this doesn't put you off, here's how to do it (starting from BSB). First, catch bus 42, 44 or 48 south to Kuala Lurah (B$1, 30 minutes, last departure 5pm) on the Brunei–Sarawak border (or take a taxi for around B$20). After crossing the border, you can take another bus (RM5.50) or taxi (RM20) to Limbang. From Limbang, it's very difficult and expensive to continue by road to Kota Kinabalu and there is no regular public transport. You'll have to hire a taxi or private car willing to take you across the Temburong district of Brunei and onward to Lawas (around B$200), from where you can catch regularly scheduled buses onward to Kota Kinabalu. For more details see Across Temburong By Land (p234).

To get to Miri in Sarawak, take a bus from BSB to Seria (B$6, two hours), then take another bus onward to Kuala Belait (B$1, one hour). At Kuala Belait, switch to the express bus to Miri (B$15, two hours). Immigration and customs formalities are taken care of on both sides of the Brunei–Sarawak border.

GETTING AROUND
To/From the Airport

BSB's modern airport is 10km northwest of the city. Buses 23, 24 and 38 will get you to and from the airport for B$1. As you leave the terminal, walk diagonally south for 300m to reach the bus stop. Taxis will charge around B$20 for trips between the airport and city centre (the price goes up by at least B$5 after 6pm); taxis are unmetered so agree on the price before getting in. For a cheaper alternative, many hotels offer free or inexpensive pick-up service from the airport, so enquire when you book.

If you travel into BSB by bus, you'll end up at the bus station right in the centre of town, from which you can easily walk to most of the accommodation listed in this book.

Bus

The government bus network covers most sights in and around the city, and the international ferry terminal at Muara. Routes for local buses are displayed at the bus station, beneath the multistorey car park on Jalan Cator, and numbers are displayed on each bus. Apart from the Muara express service (B$2), all fares are B$1. Most buses run every 15 to 20 minutes, and the system operates daily between 6.30am and 6pm.

Some useful routes:

Airport Buses 23, 24, 36 and 38.

Apek Utama Hotel, Brunei Museum and Malay Technology Museum Bus 39.

Gadong Buses 1, 22 and 55.

Hassanal Bolkiah National Stadium and Immigration Department Buses 1 and 34.

Jame'Asr Hassanal Bolkiah Mosque Buses 1 and 22.

Jerudong Park Playground Buses 55 and 57.

Muara Buses 37, 38 and 39.

An express bus (B$2, 40 minutes) departs the bus station about once and hour between 7am and 2pm for the Muara Ferry Terminal.

Car

Hiring a car is a good way to explore the hinterland of Brunei, though you could comfortably see most sights in two days. Prices range from B$80 to B$120 for a sedan; rates for luxury cars such as Mercedes, Volvos and 4WDs are much higher. Mileage and insurance are included, though surcharges may apply if the car is taken into Sarawak. Most rental agencies will bring the car to your hotel and pick it up when you've finished, and drivers can also be arranged, though this could cost B$100 on top of the rental cost. Petrol is cheap and the main roads are in good condition, but some back roads require a 4WD. An international driver's permit is required for driving in Brunei.

Avis (☎ 242-6345; Hj Daud Complex, Jln Gadong; nscsb@brunet.bn; compact cars per day from B$75) will send cars to the airport for those with reservations. There's also a branch office in the Sheraton Utama Hotel, next door to the Terrace Hotel in BSB.

Taxi

Taxis are hard to find in Brunei and you should never count on being able to flag one down on the street. The only place where you can reliably find taxis is outside the bus station on Jalan Caor. Otherwise, arrange a taxi through your hotel.

Taxis in BSB are all unmetered and you need to negotiate the fare with the driver. A trip across town will usually cost B$10, but rates can climb by as much as 30% after 6pm. Other trips include the airport (B$20), Muara (B$30), Sarawak Border near Limbang (B$25), and Miri (Sarawak) (B$160) .

Water Taxi

Water taxis are a good way of getting around if your destination is anywhere near the river. You can find them anywhere on the waterfront at the southern end of town (or, more likely, they'll find you). Fares for short trips shouldn't cost more than B$2 – don't accept higher rates (the locals certainly don't). Hourly rates should be no more than B$20 and you might be able to negotiate a rate as low as B$15 per hour.

AROUND BANDAR SERI BEGAWAN

The area around BSB has some interesting attractions for those who fancy a quick half-day trip outside the city. Less than an hour's drive northwest of the city, Jerudong is home to one of Brunei's most famous attractions: the Jerudong Park Playground, Brunei's famous and now mostly defunct amusement park. Also in Jerudong, the vast Empire Hotel & Country Club is the world's most expensive hotel and an interesting diversion for those with an interest in the grand and the gaudy. Or, if you merely fancy a bit of sunbathing and wading, you

might consider taking a bus out to Pantai Muara (Muara Beach), which is the best beach in the BSB area.

JERUDONG

The two white elephants of Jerudong – the Empire Hotel & Country Club and the Jerudong Park Playground – make a fascinating half-day excursion from the city.

Empire Hotel & Country Club

The **Empire Hotel & Country Club** (☎ 241-8999; www .empire.com.bn; Muara-Tutong Rd) is a prominent reminder of Prince Jefri's scandalous spending habits. The palatial Empire cost US$1.1 billion to build, and it shows – from the soaring height of the monumentally lavish atrium to the Jack Nicklaus–designed golf course. While it's true that the hotel has all the subtlety of a Las Vegas casino, it's definitely a spectacle worth seeing. And, as you wander the grounds, you can't help but wonder how they ever expected this place to pay for itself.

Jerudong Park Playground

The **Jerudong Park Playground**(☎ 261-1894; Jerudong; admission & unlimited rides B$15, or admission B$1 & individual rides B$3; ☷ 5pm-midnight Wed-Fri & Sun, 5pm-2am Sat) is a sprawling amusement park that the sultan built as a gift to his people. Divided into two sections, one for older kids and adults, and one for smaller children, it's now in a semidormant state – over half of the rides are 'closed for maintenance' (read: closed forever, or at least until Michael Jackson comes back to stage another concert). This gives the park a rather surreal air, and you may feel like you're living out a child's fantasy of having an amusement park all to yourself (albeit with most of the rides closed). If you go on a weekend, you'll be less lonely and find a few more rides in operation.

Wandering around the park, especially on a weekday evening, is a truly surreal experience unlike anything else you'll encounter in Southeast Asia – scattered groups of locals and tourists meander around slightly aimlessly, looking at the defunct attractions with a mixture of awe and bewilderment, like inhabitants of the *Planet of the Apes* discovering a postapocalyptic Manhattan.

When the big rides aren't working, admission is discounted to B$5. Sleeveless blouses or shirts are not allowed and proper footwear is required. On Saturdays the park is open until 2am and there are food and drink stalls in the parking lot.

Getting There & Away

It's easy to get to the playground with buses 55 or 57 from the bus station, but the last bus leaves at 5.30pm and getting back to town can be a problem. Major hotels have shuttle services for about B$20 per person. A taxi back to BSB will cost about B$35. You may also meet locals who will offer to drive you to the park, the Empire Hotel, the mosque and the palace; the asking price is around B$48 per car.

Some accommodation in town can arrange group tours to Jerudong, including stops at the Empire Hotel and the Jerudong Park Playground.

PANTAI MUARA

Pantai Muara (Muara Beach) is a popular weekend retreat located 2km from Muara town, which is 25km northeast of BSB. The white sand is clean but like many Bornean beaches it's fairly shallow and littered with flotsam and jetsam. If you want solitude, don't go on the weekend.

To get to Muara, take an express bus (B$2) from the bus station in downtown BSB. Once at Muara, bus 33 will take you from Muara town to either Pantai Muara or Pantai Serasa for B$1.

TUTONG & BELAIT DISTRICTS

The Tutong and Belait district form the bulk of the big western section of Brunei. Most travellers merely pass through this region en route between Miri (Sarawak) and BSB, but there are a few mildly diverting attractions for those who have several days to spend in the country. Buses ply the coastal highway, but if you want to see the sights the best way is to take a tour or rent a car.

TUTONG

About halfway between Seria and BSB, Tutong is the main town in central Brunei. The town itself is unremarkable, but it does have a good beach a couple of kilometres away at Pantai Seri Kenangan, often simply referred to as Pantai Tutong. Set on a spit

of land, with the ocean on one side and the Sungai Tutong on the other, the white-sand, casuarina-lined beach is arguably the best in Brunei. The royal family clearly agrees, as it has a surprisingly modest palace here for discreet getaways. Commoners, sadly, have to make do with picnic tables, a simple restaurant and food hawkers at weekends. The turnoff to the beach is near the Tamu Tutong, where a **market** is held every morning.

After Pantai Seri Kenangan, the beach road continues for another 5km to Kuala Tutong; the beach at the end is quiet and ideal for camping.

TASEK MERIMBUN

About 27km inland from Tutong, Tasek Merimbun is Brunei's largest lake. The marshy blackwater lake is fairly scenic and supports a variety of wildlife. However, like other sites in Brunei, the facilities here haven't been kept up. There used to be a plank walk out to an island in the lake, but it's being reclaimed by nature. Don't even think about swimming or wading here as the lake is inhabited by crocodiles. And a permit is required for boating, so your options are petty much limited to taking a gander for a few minutes or a quick stroll around the lakeshore. All told, it's not worth a special trip out from BSB.

The only way to get there on your own is by car or as part of a tour from BSB (see p222). If you drive, note that the road gets pretty rough between Lammuni and the lake; drive through the *kampong* and stick to the main road.

THE LABI ROAD

As you enter the Belait district, east of Seria, a road branches inland to Labi, taking you past some prime forest areas. This road is the easiest way into the interior of Brunei and it offers the chance to see some Iban longhouses (most of which come complete with parking lots and mod-cons). Nothing on this road is a must see, but if you've got a few days in Brunei and a rental car, it's a good day out of BSB.

The first of these attraction on the road, about 800m from the main highway, is the **Sungai Liang Forest Recreation Park** (Taman Rekreasi Hutan Sungai Liang), a simple little park that makes a good leg stretch on the way to Kuala Belait or into the interior further down the Labi Road. There are paved walking trails, a river, swimming hole and hiking trails. There is also a canopy walkway, but it was closed at the time of writing and looks to remain so indefinitely.

About halfway between the Sungai Liang Forest Recreation Park and Labi is the **Luagan Lalak Forest Reserve** (Taman Rekreasi Hutan Luagan Lalak). This marshy lake is picturesque but like many tourist sites in Brunei it seems that those who started the project have lost interest. There used to be boardwalks around much of the lake but now, almost all that remains open is a rotting stretch leading north from the bottom of the steps down to the lake. It's a nice spot and a good variety of birds call the lake home but due to the state of the facilities, and difficulty and danger of exploring off the plankwalks, it's not worth a specific trip to come here. It's about 24km from the turn-off from the main road.

Another 15km south of Luagan Lake Forest Reserve (or about 40km south of the coastal road), the *kampung* of **Labi** is a small Iban settlement with a few fruit arbours. Note that there is a fork in the road just before Labi (as you head south, away from the main coastal road). Take the left fork to reach Labi and Teraja; don't take the right fork, which is marked Jln Labi Lama (Old Labi Rd).

About 7km south of Labi, you reach **Rumah Panjang Mendaram Besar**, a 'drive-up' longhouse. If you linger outside for a few minutes with a hopeful look on your face, you will probably be invited in and shown some handicrafts.

Another 8km south from Rumah Panjang brings you to the end of the Labi Road, at which you'll find **Rumah Panjang Teraja**, another 'drive-up' Iban longhouse. A guide from the longhouse can take you to a nearby waterfall in around 30 minutes. A trip to the falls should cost about B$15.

SERIA

Seria, a company town spread out along the coast between Tutong and Kuala Belait, is a transit stop on the road to Sarawak. This is where Shell Brunei has its major installations, and the low bungalows accommodate company staff and the Gurkha troops brought in to protect their work.

The coastal plain between here and Kuala Belait is the main centre for oil production in Brunei, and at a beach just outside of town the curvy **Billionth Barrel Monument** commemorates (you guessed it) the billionth barrel of oil produced at the Seria field. From the beach, oil rigs are visible jutting up on the horizon.

If that's just not enough hydrocarbons for you, the flashy new **Oil & Gas Discovery Centre** (☎ 337-7200; www.shell.com.bn/ogdc; off Jln Tengah; adult/child/teenager B$5/1/2; ☾ 9am-5pm Tue-Thu, 10am-noon & 2-6pm Fri, 10am-6pm Sat & Sun) aims to put an 'edutainment' spin on the industry, appealing particularly to young science buffs. The complex includes an exhibition hall, a gallery, a theatre, an education centre and even a playground with skate park to keep any disaffected youths happy. The Discovery Centre is opposite the town centre, on the foreshore. You could walk it from the bus station, but it will be a hot 500m indeed. It's clearly signposted.

Sleeping & Eating

Hotel Koperasi (☎ 322-7589; Jln Sharif Ali Seria; s/d B$55/65; ☒) The only place to stay in Seria is the Hotel Koperasi Seria. It's got acceptable rooms and is not a bad place to spend the night (although you'll find Kuala Belait to be more interesting and attractive). From the bus station, walk northwest 150m past the barbershop.

Muwaffaq Café & Restaurant (ground floor Koperasi Hotel; Jln Sharif Ali Seria; meals from B$5; ☾ breakfast, lunch & dinner) This café is the best spot to eat in town, with a full English picture-menu. A lot of oil workers eat here, so they're used to foreign guests. If this doesn't suit, there are food stalls inside the Kompleks Sri Selera Seria, which is opposite the hotel and near the bus station.

Getting There & Away

About 10 buses a day run between Seria and BSB (B$6, two hours). There are regular local buses between Seria and KB (B$1, every 30 minutes between 6.30am and 7.30pm), where you can catch buses onward to Miri and Kuching.

KUALA BELAIT

The last town before Sarawak, Kuala Belait is the main town in Belait District and the place to get buses to Miri. 'KB' has colonial shophouses in the town centre, the **Silver Jubilee Park** (Jln Maulana) and a reasonable beach, though most travellers just hustle through on their way to or from Sarawak. The **HSBC** bank has an ATM, diagonally opposite the bus station on Jalan McKerron.

You can hire a boat by the market for the 45-minute trip up the river to **Kuala Balai**, a small river village that was once the largest settlement in the district. It's now almost deserted because the residents have left to find work in the oil industry on the coast. The owner of Sentosa Hotel can help arrange transport (about RM100 per boat round-trip), but the trip is not much more than a simple cruise through the *nipah* (mangroves) and there isn't much to see (you're basically just paying for the river trip).

Sleeping

Government Rest House (Rumah Persinggahan Kerajan; ☎ 333-4288; Jln Carey; s/d B$40/60; ✕) As near as you'll get to a budget option in KB, this municipal guesthouse is right on the beach, a 10-minute walk along Jln McKerron from the bus station, then 300m to the right on Jln Carey. It's simple, clean and a good value. We recommend that you phone in advance.

Sentosa Hotel (☎ 333-4341; www.bruneisentosa hotel.com; 92 Jln McKerron; s/d from B$70/88; 🖥 ✕) The Sentosa is easily the best choice in KB. Every room has LAN internet access (if you don't have a cable, they will lend you one). It's clean, well-run and central with competent and helpful management. To get there from the bus station, take a right up the street between the bus station and the taxi station (that is, walk inland or east) and you will see the Sentosa on your left after less than 100m.

Seaview Hotel (☎ 333-2651; Jln Maulana; s/d B$88/104; ✕ 🛒) About 4km out of town along the beach road towards Seria (about a B$10 taxi ride from the bus station), the Seaview is a nice spot to stay if you don't mind the somewhat inconvenient location. It's right on the beach, although the beach here is better for strolling and wading than actual swimming. Some of the rooms offer eponymous sea views. Breakfast is included and there's a well-stocked supermarket frequented by expats. The hotel can also arrange car rental.

Eating

There are several simple restaurants in the shopping area along Jalan Pretty. To get there from the bus station, walk through the adjoining taxi station (keeping the HSBC bank on your left) and you will see it on your right. It's not more than two minutes' walk.

Morning market (☉ 5.30am-11am) Diagonally opposite and slightly up the street from the Sentosa Hotel, this interesting little market is a good place to eat breakfast. It's divided into halal and nonhalal (ie Chinese) sections.

Hing Nam Foong (54 Jln Pretty; meals from B$5; ☉ breakfast, lunch & dinner, closed Tue afternoon) A good little Chinese *kopi tiam* (coffee shop) with an English menu (remember that *mee* means noodles and it will all make sense). We really liked the *char shui po* (steamed buns with pork) here – they're stuffed with more *char sui* (BBQ pork) than usual and they go very well with a steaming cup of tea.

Getting There & Away

The bus and taxi stations are located opposite each other dead in the centre of town, a short walk from the main shopping streets and market.

BUS

There are regular local buses between KB and Seria (B$1, every 30 minutes between 6.30am and 7.30pm).

There are regular buses between KB and Miri in Sarawak (B$10.20 from KB at 7.30am 10.30am, 1.30pm and 3.30pm). If you only want to go as far as the Sarawak border, the fare is B$5.50. Morning departures cross via the new bridge, while afternoon departures use the ferry.

There are also regular buses between KB and Kuching in Sarawak (from KB B$45, departs KB at 10.30am, arrives in Kuching the next day at 5am). This journey involves at least two bus changes: one at the border and one in Miri. For real gluttons for punishment, you can also buy bus tickets all the way to Pontianak here in KB.

TAXI

The taxi fare between KB and BSB is B$80. The taxi fare between KB and Miri in Sarawak is B$80.

TEMBURONG DISTRICT

Separated from the main section of Brunei by a maze of *nipah*-lined waterways, the Temburong District is home to Brunei's best natural attractions. Temburong is wedged like a green dagger in the heart of Sarawak's Limbang Division – a 70km swath of mostly virgin rainforest lining the banks of Sungai Temburong. Once you've seen the mosques, palaces and water villages around BSB, Temburong is the next logical stop in Brunei. And the ride out to Bangar, the district capital, is without a doubt the most fun you can possibly have for B\$6.

Two parks make up the main attractions of Temburong: the Peradayan Forest Reserve, which is good for a quick stroll in the jungle, and the brilliant Ulu Temburong National Park. The former requires no prior arrangements and minimal expenditure, while the latter requires a bit of planning and a fair bit of cash. Of course, as far as we're concerned, if you do nothing more than take the speedboat out to Bangar, quaff a quick cup of tea and then return to BSB, you'd probably think the time well spent.

Note that if you intend to do any hiking at either park, you'll probably want to bring a change of clothes in your day pack, as you'll be pretty rank by the time you rock up at the wharf for the boat trip back to BSB. And for Ulu Temburong National Park, you'll want to bring a swimsuit, as you'll almost certainly be swimming in the river there.

For information on getting to/from Temuburong, see the Bangar Getting There & Away section (right).

BANGAR

Bangar is a small town on the banks of Sungai Temburong that seems perpetually half-asleep, even though it's the administrative centre of (and gateway to) the Temburong district. The **Temburong tourist information centre** (☎ 522-1439; 13 Kedai Rakyat Jati; ☽ 8am-noon & 1.30-4.30pm Mon-Sat, 8am-noon Sun) provides information and books tours. Exiting the boat wharf in Bangar, turn left and you'll find the information centre in the cinnamon-coloured block of offices just before the road-bridge. Behind the information centre is the Youth Hostel, and across the street from the Youth Hostel is the Bangar Resthouse.

Sleeping & Eating

Bangar Resthouse (Rumah Persinggahan Keragaan Daerah Temburong; ☎ 522-1239; Jln Batang Duri; dm B\$15-30; ☒) This is a government-run complex with hospitable staff and lots of six-bed rooms, each with attached bathroom, a small fridge and TV. Families or small groups might also consider renting one of the four-person chalets (B\$80 per night). From the boat wharf, walk to the bridge, turn right and head 200m to the Jalan Batang Duri turn-off; the resthouse is on the corner, signed 'Rumah Persinggahan'.

Youth Hostel (☎ 522-1694, 522-1718; dm B\$10) This basic hostel is part of a youth centre and sits in a fenced compound almost directly behind the information centre. It offers bunk beds in clean fan-cooled rooms.

R.R. Max Cafe (1 Kedai Pekan Bangar; meals B\$2-6; ☽ breakfast, lunch & dinner) The first restaurant in the row of shops on your right as you walk from the boat jetty to the information centre, this simple *kedai kopi* (coffee shop) serves a surprisingly good plate of fried noodles – ask for *mee goreng basah* (fried noodles in sauce with prawns) – and good hot or iced tea to wash it down with.

Getting There & Away

Boats to Bangar (B\$6, 45 minutes, about once per hour from 7am to 1pm) operate from the jetty just east of the riverfront *satay* stalls, along Jln Residency. The last boat back to BSB leaves Bangar at 3.30pm.

PERADAYAN FOREST RESERVE

Fifteen kilometres southeast of Bangar and protected within the **Peradayan Forest Reserve** (admission free) are the peaks of **Bukit Patoi** and **Bukit Peradayan**, which can be reached along walking tracks (bring your own water and trail food). For those who can't be bothered with the trouble or the expense of Ulu Temburong National Park, this is a fine and easy alternative.

The 5km trail up to Bukit Patoi is a steep and sweaty one-hour climb that starts at the entrance to the park. The trail takes you through intact rainforest. At the 1150m point (distance, not altitude – thank God), you reach an interesting cliff, the base of which you skirt as you continue upward. At 1200m you reach a covered shelter. Then it's roughly 15 minutes or 300m to reach a viewpoint, which affords excellent views west over fairly intact forest. Keep an eye out for hornbills; even if you can't spot one, you will likely hear their distinctive calls. There is no water en route, so bring your own.

Most walkers descend back along the same trail, but it's possible to continue over the other side of the summit and around to Bukit Peradayan. The trail eventually rejoins the road some 12km from Bangar near the Labu Km 5 marker. Allow at least three hours for the walk from Bukit Patoi to Bukit Peradayan and back to the road. This trail is harder and indistinct in parts, some of which are impassable.

A park brochure with map is available from the tourist office in Bangar. There are picnic tables and a toilet block at the start of the trail.

ACROSS TEMBURONG BY LAND

Travelling overland from Bandar Seri Begawan (BSB) in Brunei to Kota Kinabalu or the reverse is extremely time-consuming and fiddly. The main problem with this route is that there is no public transport across the Temburong District of Brunei, and no official taxis here either, only private cars. Thus, we strongly recommend going by boat via Pulau Labuan (see p124). However, if you insist on the overland route, here's how you do it from BSB.

First, catch bus 42, 44 or 48 south from BSB to Kuala Lurah (B$1, 30 minutes, last departure 5pm) on the Brunei–Sarawak border, or take a taxi for around B$25. After crossing the border, you can take another bus (RM5.50) or taxi (RM20) to Limbang.

From Limbang, it's very difficult and expensive to continue by road to Bangar (Brunei). A taxi will take you to the border for RM15, but you'll have to find a private car on the other side to continue to Bangar. If you decide to bail on the route at this point, you can take a speedboat from Limbang to Pulau Labuan and continue by boat to Kota Kinabalu (p217).

Once at Bangar, there is no public transport to the eastern border with Sarawak. A private car from Bangar to the eastern Sarawak border costs around B$30, if you can find one, and you'll have to find another private car or taxi on the other side of the border to continue to Lawas. You may be able to persuade the driver to take you all the way to Lawas, but this will cost around B$80.

From Lawas, buses head to Kota Kinabalu in Sabah (RM20) at 7am and 1pm daily.

The Temburong tourist information centre in Bangar can arrange transport to the reserve. A private car (the only means of getting there), will cost about B$10 each way. Hitchhiking is also an option. The road to the Peradayan Forest Reserve – and Lawas (Sarawak) – is across the bridge from Bangar wharf, on the east side of the river.

ULU TEMBURONG NATIONAL PARK

The 500-sq-km **Ulu Temburong National Park** (admission B$5) is surrounded by the Batu Apoi Forest Reserve, which covers most of southern Temburong. One of the many pleasures of visiting this stronghold of primary rainforest is that the only access is by longboat. The park contains an excellent canopy walkway and has simple accommodation in the form of cabins within the park.

Unfortunately, it's difficult and expensive to visit the park on your own. Access to the park is limited by the availability of the longboats that make the journey to the park from the jetty at Batu Duri. These are usually being used by BSB-based tour operators (see p222). If you are on your own and haven't arranged a tour, the best thing to do is to arrive at the information office in Bangar before 9am and ask to join one of the day's tours.

The main attraction at the park is the 60m canopy walkway, which is reached by a 20-minute climb up 1226 steps. The view from the walkway is almost as breathtaking as the climb up and it's one of Brunei's highlights. After

climbing down, the standard route involves a short jungle trek and most visitors take a swim in the cool waters of the Sungai Temburong.

While most people visit the park as a day trip from BSB, it's possible to stay in the simple wooden cabins inside the park. To do so, contact the Bangar tourist information centre (p233) at least three days prior to your visit.

Getting There & Away

The park is accessed by a combination road-river trip from Bangar. First, it is necessary to drive about 20km south from Bangar to the hamlet of Batu Duri where you switch to a river boat for the wonderful river trip to park headquarters. En route to Batu Duri, about 13km south of Bangar, you pass a collection of relatively modern Iban longhouses in the village of Amo.

Unfortunately, there is no public transport down to Batu Duri. Even if you could make it down to Batu Duri under your own steam (say, by rental car or hitching), you'd find it impossible to hire a boat onward to the park: the few longboats that make the trip to park headquarters are controlled by BSB-based tour operators. Thus, for all intents and purposes, it is impossible to visit the park independently – you'll have to sign up for a tour in BSB (see p222). Your only alternative is to catch the first boat out to Bangar from BSB and inquire at the Bangar tourist information centre (p233) if you can join one of the tours scheduled to visit the park that day.

Kalimantan

Kalimantan is one of the world's last, vast wilderness areas, a symphony of natural beauty and indigenous cultures.

Covering two-thirds of Borneo in four provinces, Kalimantan showcases countless natural wonders. It's the last refuge for most of the world's wild orangutans, and home to ancient civilisations, including Dayak tribes that selectively embrace the 21st century, struggling to balance modernity with tradition.

While roads are improving, the best attractions remain tied to Kalimantan's waterways. River boats up the mighty, mysterious Sungai Mahakam lead to rainforests and longhouse villages. Simpler craft with put-put engines reminiscent of cinema's *the African Queen* reveal the great apes and vibrant jungle of Tanjung Puting National Park. Narrow canoes call on Banjarmasin's water villages and floating markets. Off the east coast, amid some of the world's best diving, Pulau Derawan preserves bygone times, where easy smiles remain the openly exchanged currency.

There is a dark side to Kalimantan, too. Ongoing destruction, from logging and intentional forest fires, plus energy extraction, continues to reduce the areas where these natural attractions thrive. This cloud merely underscores that there will never be a better time to visit Kalimantan than right now.

Time is running out: don't miss the boat.

HIGHLIGHTS

- Chugging up Sungai Sekonyer by *klotok* (canoe with water-pump motor) to see orangutans in **Tanjung Puting National Park** (p253), sleeping on deck with cicadas singing lullabies and gibbons' whoops as a morning alarm
- Flying underwater with mantas off **Pulau Derawan** (p284), fishing for dinner on the return trip, returning in time for a sunset volleyball game
- Nailing breakfast at a floating market and trading high-fives at wash time in the waterways of **Banjarmasin** (p260)
- Seeking Dayak longhouse traditions of intricate tattoos and drive-through earlobes above the rapids of **Sungai Mahakam** (p277) or in **Kapuas Hulu** (p244)
- Swinging across bamboo bridges over river valleys in breathtaking **Pegunungan Meratus** (p267), wrapping up with a river raft to hot springs

- POPULATION: 12,223,300
- AREA: 558,266 SQ KM

HISTORY & CULTURE

Kalimantan's riches drew Chinese and Indian traders as far back as AD 400. Hinduism, Chinese settlers, and, a millennium later, Islam all arrived ahead of Europeans. Dutch and English imperialists began sparring over Kalimantan in the early 17th century. Holland won here, while England took Sarawak and Sabah (see p23).

The lurking British, as well as Kalimantan's bounty, spurred Dutch industriousness, particularly during the 1800s. Envoys signed treaties with local sultans, though Banjarmasin fought the imperialists in 1859 and resisted until 1905. Global industrialisation and expanding wealth spurred demand for traditional commodities and new ones: coal and oil.

Petroleum drew Japan's attention during WW II, and the war's end brought independence to Indonesia. But over the past six decades, Kalimantan has struggled to find its place in Indonesia.

Kalimantan is less homogenous than much of Indonesia. It has three major ethnic groups: Malay Indonesians from other islands who tend to follow Islam and live along the coasts and rivers; Chinese, traders in Kalimantan for centuries; and Dayaks, Kalimantan's indigenous inhabitants. Each group holds a majority in parts of Kalimantan.

Population has grown through *transmigrasi* (transmigration), a government policy begun by the Dutch and expanded under Suharto. Clashes between Dayaks and Madurese,

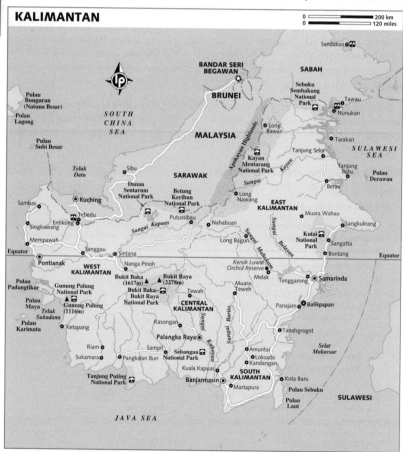

KALIMANTAN

frequent transmigrants, erupt periodically. In many towns, Jln Madura has been renamed.

Beyond *transmigrasi*, economic opportunity and expanding government increasingly bring outsiders to Kalimantan. With a cast now comprising crusading missionaries and imams, loggers, planters and conservationists, government administrators and traditional leaders, the struggle for Kalimantan's soul continues. Joseph Conrad would be busy indeed.

GETTING THERE & AWAY

Balikpapan's Seppingan Airport is Kalimantan's only entry point offering visa on arrival (VOA, see p299). All other entry from outside Indonesia – by land, sea or air – requires a visa in advance. Indonesian consulates in Sabah – Tawau (see p151) and Kota Kinabalu (p91) – issue visas to foreigners.

Air

Silk Air (www.silkair.net) flies between Balikpapan and Singapore. **Batavia Air** (www.batavia-air.co.id) flies between Pontianak and Kuching in Sarawak, plus Batam near Singapore. **Garuda** (www.garuda-indonesia.com) and Batavia fly the most routes to the rest of Indonesia.

Air schedules and carriers constantly change due to rapid growth and, following major accidents in 2007, heightened safety concerns. Now more than ever, rely on travel agents for the best information, service, and prices.

Boat

Boats depart daily (except Sunday) from Tarakan and more frequently from Nunukan in East Kalimantan to Tawau in Sabah.

Pelni (www.pelni.co.id) and other carriers connect to Jakarta, Semarang and Surabaya on Java and Makassar, Pare Pare, Mamuju and Toli Toli on Sulawesi.

Bus

Air-con buses link Pontianak and Kuching (140,000Rp to 200,000Rp, 10 hours).

GETTING AROUND

Roads now connect most major towns, and construction continues. Quality varies dramatically by location and season. Bus routes follow roads but trips often include stops to get out and push or await repairs. Air-con, smoke-free buses remain the exception. Kijangs, a local SUV brand, runs scheduled routes between some cities and

can be chartered everywhere, often through hotels and travel agencies. Where necessary and available, 4WD versions are far more expensive.

For long distances, flights via **Kal-Star** (www.kalstaronline.com), Dirgantara Air Service (DAS) and others may save time and wear, often at surprisingly low fares.

Kapal biasa (river ferries) or *long bots* (narrow wooden boats with covered passenger cabins) are a pleasant alternative to buses and best for exploring the jungle. Scheduled and chartered speedboats and motorised *ces* (canoes) reach many small towns and tributaries.

WEST KALIMANTAN

Blessed with Indonesian Borneo's widest variety of attractions, West Kalimantan (Kalimantan Barat or KalBar) is also blessed – or cursed – with its least-developed tourist infrastructure. A sizable Chinese minority spices the mix. Visitors can find the most traditional villages, wild orangutans, virgin forests and idyllic beaches, but gird for struggle, with success by no means guaranteed.

PONTIANAK

☎ 0561 / pop 520,000

Stoutly astride the equator, Pontianak is Kalimantan's city with big shoulders, processing rubber and timber from the interior and marketing the region's abundant produce. At the confluence of Sungai Landak and Sungai Kapuas, Kalimantan's longest river at 1243km, KalBar's biggest city doubles as gateway to the Dayak settlements and forests of Kapuas Hulu (upper Kapuas). Pontianak's coffee stalls and brisk roadside commerce create an urban buzz rare in Kalimantan.

Orientation

Pontianak's centre of gravity has expanded south across Jln Diponegoro to Jln Gajah Mada. Streets there pulsate far into the night.

Information
INTERNET ACCESS

Centrine Online (per hr 4000Rp; ☖ 7.30am-10pm) Signposted in a short alley off Jln Nusa Indah III.

Mitra Tour & Travel (☎ 733-544; Jln Teuku Umar Komplek; per hr 4000Rp; ☖ 9.30am-midnight) Music, snacks and flight bookings, too.

KALIMANTAN

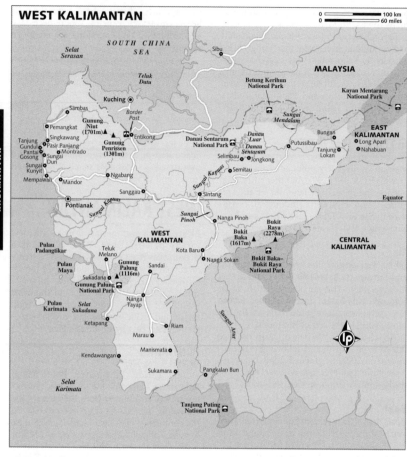

WEST KALIMANTAN

0 — 100 km
0 — 60 miles

SOUTH CHINA SEA

Selat Serasan

Sibu

MALAYSIA

Teluk Datu

Betung Kerihun National Park

Kayan Mentarang National Park

Kuching

Border Post

Sambas
Pemangkat
Gunung Niut (1701m)
Singkawang
Entikong
Gunung Penrissen (1301m)
Sungai Mendalam
Bungan
EAST KALIMANTAN
Long Apari
Nahabuan
Tanjung Gundul
Pasir Panjang
Montrado
Sungai Duri
Danau Sentarum National Park
Danau Luar
Danau Sentarum
Putussibau
Tanjung Lokan
Pantai Gosong
Selimbau
Jongkong
Sungai Kunyit
Mempawah
Mandor
Ngabang
Semitau
Sungai Kapuas
Sintang

Equator

Pontianak
Sungai Kapuas
Sanggau

Sungai Pinoh
Nanga Pinoh
WEST KALIMANTAN
Bukit Raya (2278m)
Bukit Baka (1617m)
CENTRAL KALIMANTAN

Pulau Padangtikar
Teluk Melano
Kota Baru
Nanga Sokan
Bukit Baka–Bukit Raya National Park

Pulau Maya
Gunung Palung (1116m)
Sandai
Gunung Palung National Park
Sukadana
Nanga Tayap

Sungai Arut

Pulau Karimata
Selat Sukadana
Ketapang
Riam
Marau

Kendawangan
Manismata
Sukamara
Pangkalan Bun

Selat Karimata

Tanjung Puting National Park

IMMIGRATION OFFICES

Immigration office (☎ 734-516; Jln Sutoyo)
Malaysian Consulate (☎ 732-986, 736-061; mwptk@ telkom.net; Jln Sultan Syahrir 21, ☽ 8am-4pm Mon-Fri)

MEDICAL SERVICES

Klinik Kharitas Bhakti (☎ 734-373; Jln Siam 153)

MONEY

ATMs abound. For currency exchange:
BII bank (cnr Jln Tanjungpura & Jln Diponegoro)
BNI bank (Jln Tanjungpura)
PT Safari (Jln Tanjungpura 12) Moneychanger with good rates.

POST

Main post office (Jln Sultan Abdur Rahman 49;
☽ 7.30am-9.30pm Mon-Sat, 8am-2pm Sun) Poste restante.

TOURIST INFORMATION

City tourist office (☎ 732-340; Jln Johar 1) City maps (when in stock) and rudimentary information.
Kalimantan Barat tourist office (☎ 736-172; fax 743-104; Jln Sutoyo 17) Ebullient, English-speaking Pak Iwan provides ambitious regional travel tips.

TOUR & TRAVEL AGENCIES

Berjaya Tour & Travel (☎ 737-325; www.berjayatour .com; Jl Pahlawan 224/2) Pontianak agent for Putussibau's ecotourism initiatives (see p243), plus full travel services and a Ketapang branch.
Borneo Access (☎ 081-2576-8066; alexafdal@borneo access.com) Founder and West Borneo Tour Guide Association general secretary Alex Afdhal is a knowledgeable and tireless KalBar booster.

Mentari Tour (☎ 767-196; mentari_tour_ptk@yahoo
.com.sg; Jln Hijas 108)
Panorama Anugrah Pratama Tour & Travel
(☎ 739-483; tour_panorama@yahoo.com; Jln Diponegoro 149) Air, boat and Kuching bus tickets, plus in-town
delivery. Responds to English emails.
Times Tour & Travel (☎ 770-259; timestravell@
yahoo.com; Blok H6, Komplek BTN Jeruju, Jln Yos Sudarso)
English-speaking Iwan aids travellers with ticket delivery
and Sunday service.

Sights
RIVER LIFE
The **taman** (park; Jln Rahadi Usman) between the
ferry crossing and Kartika Hotel showcases
river activity. The **Pinisi Harbour** further south
features these sailing schooners, produced
by South Sulawesi's Bugis seafarers, docked
alongside KalBar's unique *bandung* (floating
general stores).

ISTANA KADRIYAH & MESJID ABDURRAHMAN
The ironwood palace of Syarif Abdurrahman
Alqadrie, Pontianak's sultan from 1770 to 1808,
Istana Kadriyah (admission by donation; ☉ 8.30am-4pm)
is now a museum showing royal relics.

Approximately 100m south, royal mosque
Mesjid Abdurrahman (also known as Mesjid
Jami) has a Sumatran-style square-tiered
roof. Continue across wobbly planks to stilt
houses, best enjoyed at washing times early
or late in the day.

Get here by canoe taxi (3000Rp) or charter
(15,000Rp) from the Kapuas Indah piers.

MUSEUM NEGERI PONTIANAK & DAYAK LONGHOUSE
South of Pontianak's centre, the **museum** (Jln
Ahmad Yani; ☉ 8am-3pm Tue-Sun) features Dayak
tribal artefacts and *tempayan,* ceramics
(mostly water jugs) from Thailand, China
and Borneo dating from the 16th century.

Around the corner, a replica **Dayak longhouse** (Jln Sutoyo) has genuine totems and carved
log steps.

EQUATOR MONUMENT
Grown from a simple marker in 1928 into
a goofy collage of circles and arrows with a
huge replica outside marking *its* spot, the
Equator Monument (Patung Khatulistiwa) makes
much – too much – of Pontianak's geographical draw. It draws crowds every equinox to
experience shadowless sunlight.

Take a *bis kota* (intercity bus; 2000Rp) from
outside Kartika Hotel or an *opelet* (local minivan; 3000Rp) from Siantan terminal heading
northwest. Patung Khatulistiwa is alongside the highway, and, believe us, you can't
miss it.

SAHAM LONGHOUSE
The traditional Dayak dwelling closest to
Pontianak, **Saham longhouse** *(rumah betang)*
in Pahauman is one of KalBar's oldest (more
than 200 years) and longest (180m).

Visit by bus from Batu Layang toward
Ngabang (114km, 7500Rp, 3½ hours) or executive buses toward Sanggau. Get dropped
at the Pahauman turn, then catch a local taxi
or *ojek* (motorcycle taxi; 12km). Kijangs from
Pontianak can cost up to 500,000Rp.

Festivals & Events
Pontianak's geography inspires the twice-
yearly **Equatorial Culture Festival** around the
March and September equinoxes, with Dayak,
Chinese and Malay traditional dancing and
singing, and competitions.

Robok-Robok celebrates the founding of
Pontianak's Mempawah kingdom with a
royal yacht procession, dragon-boat races,
and terrestrial events. Dates follow the Islamic
calendar, falling in mid-January in 2009, and
moving two weeks earlier annually. The **Gawai
Dayak** harvest festival in May is centred on
Pontianak's **Dayak longhouse** (Jln Sutoyo).

Sleeping
BUDGET
Pontianak Raya City Hotel (☎ 732-496; fax 733-781;
Jln Pa'kasih 44; s/d incl breakfast from 77,000/88,0000Rp plus
10% tax; ❄) Open-air corridors and welcoming
staff show the way to cosy economy digs and
huge standard rooms. The harbour end of
town provides abundant traveller services.

Ateng House (☎ 732-683; atenghouse@yahoo.com; Jln
Gadjah Mada 201; s/d incl breakfast 79,000/89,000 plus 15%
tax; ❄) Affiliated with the travel agency underneath it, each bright, cosy room has air-con,
TV, private bathroom, and homely touches
such as bedspread and curtains. Borneo's best
cup of coffee is just outside.

Central Hotel (☎ 737-444, fax 734-993; Jln
Cokroaminoto 232; r incl breakfast 115,000-170,000Rp;
❄) Ignore that ground-floor barber shop:
Central's no clip joint. Large, comfortable, if
weathered, rooms offer Pontianak's cheapest
hot-water showers.

KALIMANTAN

KALIMANTAN

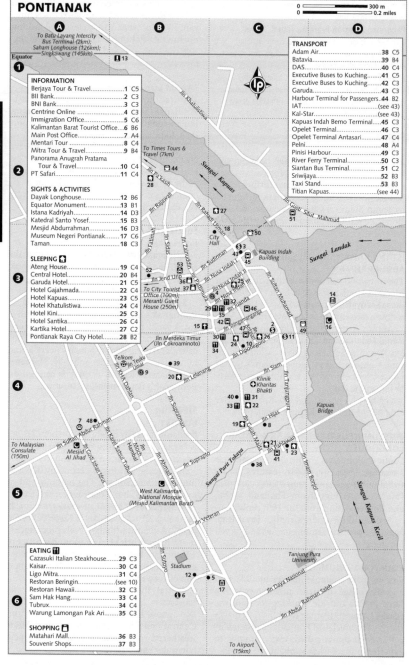

PONTIANAK

More budget options:

Meranti Guest House (☎ 731-783; Jln Meranti 31A; r 50,000-130,000Rp; 🏠) Variety of room types jigsawed into a converted house down a residential street.

Hotel Khatulistiwa (☎ 736-793; fax 734-930; Jln Diponegoro 56; r 77,000-110,000Rp; 🏠) Vast, basic hotel in an alley smack city-centre.

MIDRANGE & TOP END

Kartika Hotel (☎ 734-401; fax 738-457; Jln Rahadi Usman; r incl breakfast 170,000-310,000Rp plus 21% tax; 🏠) Bright yellow décor puts a shine on flagging rooms. The tennis court and river-view restaurant – wipe those windows! – recall Kartika's glory days.

Garuda Hotel (☎ 736-890; fax 739-001; Jln Pahlawan 40; r 199,000-499,000Rp, ste 599,000Rp; 🏠) Renovated in 2005, Garuda's rooms are as tarted up as the visitors to its rooftop disco. Cushy digs score with domestic business travellers.

Hotel Gajahmada (☎ 761-598, 081-2578-9900; hotel -gajahmada@ptk.centrin.net.id; Jln Gajah Mada 177; r including breakfast 230,000-446,000Rp; ste 599,000-788,000Rp; 🏠 🖳) This two-star hotel features fresh, spacious rooms, helpful staff, and a top location. The lobby coffee shop's 24-hour food- and internet-service includes a tantalising Indonesian buffet breakfast.

Hotel Kapuas (☎ 736-122; www.hotelkapuas.com; Jln Gajah Mada 889; r incl breakfast from 261,000Rp, ste incl breakfast from 528,000Rp; 🏠 🖳 🍴) Urban resort amenities such as a fitness centre, tennis court, 100m pool and bar, make Kapuas' posh rooms great value.

Hotel Kini (☎ 732-223; hotelkini_ptk@yahoo.com; Jln Nusa Indah III; r incl breakfast 366,000-420,000Rp, ste incl breakfast 541,000-748,000Rp; 🏠) Newish and garish, 'Hotel Now' indulges guests with semicircular lounge chairs, and a spa and sauna. Call the crooner fronting a jazz combo in its Blue Sapphire Cafe 'high class' or 'high kitsch'. Discounts run big on rooms, but are stingier on suites.

Hotel Santika (☎ 733-777; www.santika.com; Jln Diponegoro 36; r incl breakfast 521,000-558,000Rp, ste incl breakfast 596,000-1,158,000Rp plus 21% tax; 🏠 🖳) Pontianak's freshest three-star entry and part of a national chain, Santika has relaxing rooms, plus a complete business centre.

Eating

Tubrux (☎ 708-1900; Jln Pattimura 211D; drinks from 2,000Rp; 🕑 breakfast, lunch & dinner) The most popular coffee shop downtown. People pack its outdoor and indoor tables to share the local dish. Tubrux also dishes up simple Indonesian food, and solo women will feel comfortable.

Kaisar (☎ 731-554; Jln Pattimura) This bakery-turned-shopping empire's Roman logo nobly roams KalBar. Breads run very sweet or very white.

Restoran Beringin (☎ 732-803; Jln Diponegoro 151; meals 9,000-15,000Rp; 🕑 breakfast, lunch & dinner) Padang restaurant offering enormous variety. With Panorama Tours, it flanks the alley to Hotel Khatulistiwa.

Cazasuki Italian Steakhouse (☎ 733-420; Jln Nusa Indah III; mains 11,000-30,000Rp; 🕑 lunch & dinner) Fusion or confusion? Shabu-shabu, spaghetti, sauerbraten, steaks and burgers, even satay, are all scrumptious.

Restoran Hawaii (☎ 738-038; Jln Nusa Indah III 79-80; mains from 15,000; 🕑 lunch & dinner) This Hawaii is a comfortable place to sample Chinese food, KalBar style, blending traditional and tropical flavours.

Warung Lamongan Pak Ari (Jln Juanda; mains 10,000-18,000Rp; 🕑 lunch & dinner) Giant deep fryers outside draw big crowds for fish or chicken served with special *sambal* (chilli sauce) guaranteed to clear airways.

Food and coffee stalls appear nightly, many along Jln Gajah Mada. For a stellar Chinese street feed and cooking demonstration, try Sam Hak Heng opposite Hotel Gajahmada. Self-caterers, use **Ligo Mitra** (Jln Gajah Mada 77).

Getting There & Away

AIR

Batavia (☎ 734-488; fax 736-604; Jln Cokroaminoto 278A) flies to Kuching (US$50), Batam near Singapore (720,000Rp; continuing to Pekanbaru), Jakarta (365,000Rp), Surabaya via Yogyakarta, and Semarang.

Kal-Star (☎ 739090; Jln Tanjungpura) and **IAT** (Indonesia Air Transport; ☎ 736-603; Pasar Sudirman A16, Jln Tanjungpura) fly to Ketapang (320,000Rp), Pangkalan Bun (650,000Rp) and Semarang (1,170,000Rp) in central Java. IAT and **DAS** (☎ 736-407; Jl Gadjah Mada 67) fly to Putissibau (700,000Rp), with DAS continuing to Samarinda (965,000Rp). **Garuda** (☎ 734-986; Jln Tanjungpura), **Sriwijaya** (☎ 768-777; Jln Jendral Urip 19) and **Adam Air** (☎ 767-999; Jln Veteran 6) also serve Jakarta.

BOAT

Long distance boat services leave from the harbour on Jln Pa'kasih, north of Kartika Hotel. River boats for the 800km journey to Putussibau are virtually extinct.

Pelni (☎ 748-124; fax 748-131; www.pelni.co.id; Jln Sultan Abdur Rahman 12) sails every 14 days to Jakarta (economy 210,000Rp, 36 hours), Semarang (economy 165,000Rp, 38 hours) and Surabaya (economy 197,000Rp, 40 hours).

Titian Kapuas (☎ 731-187; Jln Usin 3) at the harbour entrance is a ticket agent for the twice-weekly *Dharma Kencana* to Semarang (179,000Rp, 32 hours) and *Marisa* to Jakarta (170,000Rp, 32 hours).

Daily jet boats head south along the coast to Ketapang (90,000Rp to 135,000Rp, six to eight hours). In choppy waters, first class is worth it.

BUS

Batu Layang intercity bus terminal is northwest of town. Ferry across the river to Siantan to the white *opelet*, or take a direct *opelet* from Jln Sisingamangaraja. From Batu Layang, daily buses head to Singkawang (15,000Rp, 3½ hours), Sambas (22,000Rp), Sanggau (24,000Rp, four hours) and Sintang (65,000Rp, nine hours).

Chock-a-block on Jln Sisingamangaraja and Jln Pahlawan, several companies run air-con day or night buses to/from Kuching (economy/executive 140,000/200,000Rp, 10 hours). Most also service Singkawang, Sambas, Sanggau, Sintang and Putussibau (200,000Rp, 20 hours). It's more convenient, comfortable, and costly than using Batu Layang.

CAR & MOTORCYCLE

Travel agencies or hotels arrange Kijangs with drivers (per day 750,000Rp plus petrol) for exploring KalBar at your pace. Taxi drivers around town may offer lower prices. For experienced riders only, motorcycles rent for 150,000Rp per day.

Getting Around

Airport taxis cost 60,000Rp to town (15km). Alternatively, hike to the main road to find an *opelet*.

Opelet (minibus; 3000Rp) routes cover most of town with terminals at the Kapus Indah Building, Jln Sisingamangaraja, and Jln Antasari. Taxis wait outside **Matahari Mall** (cnr Jln Jendral Urip & Jln Pattimura), with becaks around **Katedral Santo Yosef**. Hotels have Kijangs standing by; the starting fare for these 'hotel taxis' is Rp20,000.

Motorised canoes depart from piers alongside the Kapuas Indah building. Crossing to Istana Kadriyah or Siantan bus terminal costs 3000Rp. Public ferries, 100m north, to Siantan cost 1000Rp.

SUNGAI KAPUAS

Sungai Kapuas, Kalimantan's longest river, leads to the rich rainforests and indigenous communities of KalBar's eastern highlands. River boats up Sungai Kapuas from Pontianak are a casualty of road building, (poorly) paving the way for brutally bumpy bus rides.

With luck, substantial Bahasa Indonesia, and a lengthy visa, you may be able to travel by *bandung*. An 800km journey from Pontianak to Putussibau on this combination houseboat, freighter and general store can take from four days to four weeks, and itineraries and prices are negotiable.

Beyond Putussibau and along Kapuas Hulu tributaries, travel is still primarily by boat. Similar to local minivan or Kijang travel, that means waiting for enough people to fill a boat, or else chartering one at considerable expense. In general, motorised canoes are less expensive (and slower) than speedboats. Speedboat charter rates average 150,000Rp to 200,000Rp per hour.

Sintang

☎ 0565 / pop 40,000

At the confluence of Sungai Kapuas and Sungai Melawi, and with the grey curtain of Gunung Kelam behind it, Sintang marks the start of Kapuas Hulu, the upper river.

Scattered ATMs around town take international cards. For medical emergencies, consult **Rumah Sakit Ade Mohammad Djoen** (☎ 22805/07/09; Jln Pattimura).

Kobus Centre (Jln Mohammad Saad; ⏰ 9am-2pm) displays a range of local handicrafts, especially the renowned local *ikat* (woven cloth). Father Maessen, a Dutch missionary resident for more than 30 years, founded Kobus to help preserve craft traditions. Kobus and local government support *ikat* production at **Ensaid Panjang** (50km or one hour), one of several Dayak *rumah betang* near Sintang.

Across the river, the former sultan's palace is now **Dara Janti Museum**. The keeper will open it up for a small donation. Boats to cross the river (10,000Rp) congregate beyond the riverfront *warung* (food stalls).

Outside town, **Taman Baning** (2km) is a 215-hectare slice of tropical forest for watching birds and viewing wild orchids. Take an *opelet* (3000Rp) or *ojek* (5000Rp to 10,000Rp).

A more testing trek, **Gunung Kelam** features butterflies, a waterfall *(air terjun)* and panoramic views. The challenging path up the 900m peak has steel ladders on its toughest rock faces. For the 18km trip, take an *opelet* to Pasar Impres (3000Rp) and then a Kelam *opelet* (7000Rp) to the gaudy park entrance.

Eight hours south of Sintang, **Bukit Baka-Bukit Raya National Park**, named for two of Kalimantan's highest peaks, offers extraordinary montane forest vistas, breathtaking waterfalls, meandering rivers, giant rafflesia blooming every March, and barely any tourist facilities. Reach the sprawling 181,000-hectare Schwaner Range reserve by 4WD from Nanga Pinoh or boat from Nanga Popai. From Palangka Raya in central Kalimantan, get there by combining road, river and trekking via Tumbang Jatuh, Tumbang Manggu and Tumbang Gagu. To visit, contact the **park office** (☎ /fax 23521; Jln Dr Wahidin Sudirohusodo).

It's about four hours by 4WD or seven hours by boat to **Danau Sentarum National Park** (see p244).

SLEEPING & EATING

Sakura Hotel (☎ 23418; Jln MT Haryono 58A; r 70,000-128,000Rp; 🔀) The rustic lobby leads to comfortable rooms with refrigerator, Western bathroom, and, in air-con grades, hot water. The spacious parking lot makes Sakura a trucker favourite.

Hotel Setia (☎ 23433; Jln Mahapahit 1-4; r 75,000-85,000Rp; 🔀) In Sintang's centre, Setia snags business travellers. Identical rooms include private *mandi* (a common Indonesian form of bath, consisting of a large water tank from which water is ladled over the body), TV and air-con; walking upstairs saves 10,000Rp.

Sintang Permai Hotel (☎ 22725; Jln MT Haryono 117; r 120,000-140,000Rp; 🔀) Up a hill about 600m outside downtown, Sintang's newest hotel has bright rooms with refrigerator, TV and hot water. Helpful staff arrange chartered cars from 15 minutes upward, and a 24-hour canteen dishes up Indonesian basics (mains 6,000Rp to 14,000Rp).

Warung on stilts blanket the riverfront. Find fruit vendors, food stalls and Padang eateries one block inland on Jln Kol Sugioso. **Sartika Restaurant** (Jln Kol Sugioso; mains 8,000-10,000Rp; 🕑 breakfast, lunch & dinner) offers steamy noodle and vegetable soups that go down well in the mountain air. **Intar** (Jln Kol Sugioso) sells groceries and other essentials, and there's a Kaisar bakery down the street.

GETTING THERE & AWAY

At the time of research there were no flights to Sintang; check in Pontianak for updates.

Buses to Putussibau (125,000Rp, 12 hours), Semitau (50,000Rp, four hours), and Pontianak (90,000 Rp, nine hours) leave from Pasar Durian terminal on Jln Wisapati. The road to Putussibau is partly sealed, but heavy rains still create havoc. When dry, the heavily cratered route is merely hellish.

For buses south to Nanga Pinoh (10,000Rp, one hour) head to Sungai Ukoi bus terminal, 10km southwest of Sintang by *opelet* (10,000Rp).

Putussibau

☎ 0567 / pop 15,000

Putussibau is the last sizable Kapuas Hulu town, and a launch point for excursions to traditional communities and the remaining untouched forests.

Local government, national park authorities, WWF and villagers jointly created **Kompakh** (☎ 085-6500-2101; www.kompakh.org; Kompleks GOR, Jln Pendidikan) to develop ecotourism. Kompakh offers touring options including Danau Sentarum and Betung Kerihun National Parks, longhouse visits, river cruising, and jungle treks from mild to extreme, featuring a trans-Borneo journey by foot and boat. With two weeks' notice, Kompakh can arrange white-water rafting. All tours can be customised, and prices depend on group size and precise itinerary.

Putussibau's centre falls between Sungai Kapuas and Sungai Sibau. Jln Kom Yos Sudarso runs north–south (*angkot* – small minibus – rides 3000Rp), becoming Jln Panjaitan, home to Putussibau's lone ATM, and Jln A Yani to the south near the bus and boat terminals and traditional market. The **Telkom office** (Jln KS Tubun) has internet access. **Rumah Sakit Dr Achmad Diponegoro** (☎ 21129; Jln Kom Yos Sudarso 42) offers medical services.

SLEEPING & EATING

Most hotels can arrange cars, drivers and guides. None include breakfast in their room rates.

Hotel Merpati Indah (☎ 21317; Jln KS Tubun 26; r 40,000-100,000Rp; 🔀) Located 50m from the

Telkom office, this upmarket losmen's economy rooms have fans and shared *mandi*.

Aman Sentosa Hotel (☎ 21691; fax 21357; Jln Diponegoro 14; r 40,000-150,000Rp; ✷) Tour companies still steer foreigners here, once Putussibau's best hotel. Cheapest rooms have fans and shared *mandi*; the best add TV, aircon, refrigerator and private *mandi*.

Permata Bunda Inn (☎ 22249; Jln Kom Yos Sudarso 87; r 50,000-150,000Rp; ✷) This ambitious place boasts phone and photocopy service in the lobby. Luxury-grade rooms feature hot water showers. Its restaurant does filling Indonesian meals (mains 6000Rp to 10,000Rp).

Sanjaya Hotel (☎ 21653; fax 22366; Jln Kom Yos Sudarso 129; r 50,000-200,000Rp; ✷) The newest hotel in town has a lobby wartel, but requires a walk up one or two flights to its rooms. 'VIP' class includes hot-water shower, aircon and refrigerator.

Mess Pemda (☎ 21010; Jln Merdeka 11; r 125,000-150,000Rp; ✷) This government hostel has air-con in every clean, simple room. Its TV lounge broadcasts the local vibe.

Siti Nurbaya (☎ 22082; Jln Kom Yos Sudarso; mains 6000-12,000Rp; ✷ breakfast, lunch & dinner) Combines precooked Padang food and freshly made Indonesian standards.

Famili (☎ 21378; Jln KS Tubun; mains 15,000-20,000Rp; ✷ lunch & dinner) Putussibau's Chinese finest.

Food stalls operate day and night around the market at the south end of town. Try the local speciality *krupuk basah* (5000Rp): ground fish steamed in banana leaf, sprinkled with shrimp crackers and spicy peanut sauce.

GETTING THERE & AWAY

IAT (Indonesia Air Transport; ☎ 22663; Jln Danau Sentarum 21A) and **DAS** (☎ 21046) fly to/from Pontianak (700,000Rp). DAS continues to Samarinda (1,390,000Rp). Taxis from the airport cost 35,000Rp, while taxis to the airport run 20,000Rp.

Several companies downtown operate buses to Pontianak (125,000Rp, 20 hours) and Sintang (90,000Rp, nine hours). A Pontaniak service passes through Sanggau for connections to Kuching in Sarawak. Local buses, *angkot* and *ojek* use the terminal on Jln Rahadi Usman, opposite the market.

Charter boats for Tanjung Lokan in the Kapuas watershed; ask Kompakh or your hotel, or, with Bahasa Indonesia and brass, try it yourself at the pier on Sungai Kapuas

just east of the bridge. The two-day trip costs around 3,000,000Rp.

Around Putussibau

Just upstream from Putussibau, find longhouse villages **Melapi I** and **Sayut** (also called Melapi II). **Semangkok I** and **Semangkok II**, with a much older longhouse, are both up Sungai Mendalam. The trip can take three hours, and charters cost 150,000Rp per hour. *Angkot* (8000Rp) is a cheaper alternative to the Melapi longhouses. Both *rumah betang* accept overnight guests. Etiquette dictates offering cash payment for food and any photographs you snap, plus gifts to show appreciation for the accommodation.

Bangun (1,800,000Rp return, eight hours each way) and **Tanjung Lokan** (3,000,000Rp return, 12 to 16 hours each way) are traditional villages accessible only by longboat. Don't expect longhouses; these are Punan Dayaks, ancestral cave dwellers. Villagers still practise traditional methods of gold mining, incense making, farming, and boat building. Trans-Borneo and Betung Kerihun National Park routes pass Bangun.

DANAU SENTARUM NATIONAL PARK

This 132,000-hectare wetland area regulates the water levels of Sungai Kapuas. In the wet season, lake depths reach 8m. In the dry season, fish huddle in isolated pools.

Danau Sentarum is famous for super red arowana *Scleropages formosus*, an aquarium trophy fish frequently seen leaping out of the lake. Wildlife in peat swamps and lowland rainforest include orangutans, proboscis monkeys, crocodiles, stork and great argus pheasant.

At least four Dayak groups – Iban, Sebaruk, Sontas and Punan – with several longhouses, live in and around the park.

Before visiting, contact the **park office** (☎ 0565-22242; Jln Oesiang Oeray 43) in Sintang for registration (10,000Rp per day). It can also arrange guides (50,000Rp per day) and boats (2,500,000Rp per day). Kompakh in Putussibau (see p243) also arranges tours here.

Local accommodation for visitors is planned. Until then, a basic facility for researchers in Bukit Tekenang, a fishing village with floating houses, has floor mattresses and shared kitchen; you pay what you wish for its use.

KALIMANTAN

BALANCING ECOTOURISM *Katsuki Nose*

As a child, I loved reading stories about animals and became interested in their behaviour, in nature, in forests and even insects. I'd watch ants march for hours.

As I grew older, I collected information about the destruction of nature. I couldn't abandon nature when it came time to get a job; I wanted to promote conservation through my work.

After high school, I couldn't afford university, so I decided to work and study as a volunteer abroad. I contacted WWF Indonesia, and they gave me a job, working to develop ecotourism.

The traditional livelihood of many Dayaks, Borneo's indigenous people, depends on hunting. But with the development of national parks that prohibit hunting, Dayaks need alternative ways to earn a living.

WWF suggested ecotourism as an option for Dayaks. Community members can work as guides, producing and selling crafts, and staging performances. Beside the profits for the Dayaks, tourists also gain enlightenment from the contacts.

Of course, there's a potential downside, too. If overdeveloped or mismanaged, ecotourism can lead to destruction far more serious than hunting. No matter how sensitively it is developed, ecotourism is bound to affect Dayak culture.

Everyday, my WWF colleagues and I work hard to find the right balance.

Katsuki Nose, from Kyoto, Japan, is a volunteer with WWF in Putussibau, West Kalimantan, and helped create the website www.kompakh.org.

Danau Sentarum is reached from Sintang by bus (50,000Rp, four hours) or longboat to Semitau (seven hours). From Putussibau, charter a longboat to Nanga Suhaid (seven hours) or take a minibus to Lanjak (65,000Rp, 3½ hours). Boats for hire and guides can be found in those villages and in settlements within the park.

BETUNG KERIHUN NATIONAL PARK

Sheltering the headwaters of Sungai Kapuas amid a diversity of ecosystems and animals, mountainous **Betung Kerihun National Park** traces the border with Sarawak. WWF's Heart of Borneo initiative aims to unite this park with Malaysia's Lantjak Entimau Wildlife Reserve.

The 800,000 hectare park, named for two Muller Range peaks, has some 1200 tree species accommodating 300-plus species of birds. Eight types of forest, from lowland to montane, shelter orangutan, gibbon, tarsier, various leaf monkeys, sun bear and clouded leopard. Salt springs dotting the park attract wildlife.

Visitors can do trekking, caving, and, with advance arrangement, kayaking, canoeing or white-water rafting, as well as cultural tourism in Tanjung Lokan, Bangun and other settlements scattered around the park. For details, contact Kompakh or **Betung Kerihun National Park office** (☎ /fax 0567-21773; Komodor Yos Sudarso 130, Putussibau).

TRANSBORNEO: PUTUSSIBAU TO LONG APARI

The reasonably fit, ambitious and funded can attempt crossing to East Kalimantan. Trekking experience helps, but even novices are likely to do better than George Muller, the first European to try it. In 1825, Muller crossed the mountain range that now bears his name, then was beheaded.

From Putussibau, trans-Kalimantan travel begins by boat to Tanjung Lokan. Then it's five to seven days walking across the Muller Range and pristine forests to the headwaters of Sungai Mahakam at Long Apari. From there, progressively larger boats carry travellers to Samarinda in three or four days.

Aside from drive and legs, you need dosh for substantial expenses. Figure roughly 3,000,000Rp to Tanjung Lokan. A guide is essential beyond there. Expect to pay 150,000Rp to 250,000Rp per day. Budget at least 3,000,000Rp for boats in East Kalimantan. Food costs around 50,000Rp per person daily and also has to be provided for guides and porters (per day 50,000Rp to 80,000Rp).

Few guides for hire in Tanjung Lokan speak English. Your chances are better in Putussibau: ask at hotels about independent guides. Kompakh (or in Pontianak, its partner Berjaya Tours; p238) can also provide guides or complete tours. Packages start from 12,000,000Rp to 15,000,000Rp per person for two.

Some choose to trek across Kalimantan from Samarinda (see p272) or Balikpapan (see p269).

Aside from where and how (and why), there's the issue of when to trek. In the rainy season, cooler temperatures provide some compensation for the wet. July and August are dry but very hot, and the annual forest fires follow. May and June seem ideal for jungle jaunts. Honeybees agree, and often plague trekkers during those months.

Singkawang
0562 / pop152,000

Known as *Kota Amoy* (City of Young Chinese Women), predominantly Hakka Chinese Singkawang attracts men from Taiwan seeking brides. Even if you're not ready for a lifetime commitment, Singkawang's a pleasant place to get your bearings in KalBar or chill on the beach after trekking.

SLEEPING & EATING

Hotel Sinar Khatulistiwa I (☎ 631-816; Jln Selamat Karman 17; r 45,000-100,000Rp; 🔀) At a busy intersection along Jln Diponegoro, this landmark offers choice. All but top-priced rooms are shabby and noisy.

Hotel Paseban (☎ 631-449; Jln Ismail Tahir 41; r 70,000-120,000Rp; 🔀) Outside the centre (1.5km), this concrete-block truckers' favourite is a solid option. Most basic but comfortable rooms include a Western bathroom. Expect 20% discounts.

ourpick Hotel Prapatan (☎ 636-888; Jln Sejahtera 1; r 150,000-275,000Rp plus 8% tax; 🔀) Shiny and bright Prapatan has modern rooms in Singkawang's centre. It's a favourite with bride-shoppers and business travellers.

Hotel Mahkota (☎ 631-244; Jln Diponegoro 1; hmskal bar@plasa.com; r 315,000-725,000Rp plus 18% tax; 🔀 🖳) This grand dame, the height of luxury a generation ago, still stands proud. Four-star facilities include a swimming pool, a tennis court, a disco, plus blue-and-gold drapery that would do Liberace proud.

Rumah Makan Tio Ciu Selera (☎ 631-226; Jln Diponegoro 106; mains 10,000-16,000Rp; 🕙 lunch & dinner) Chinese food is an obvious local favourite. The speciality here is Chiu Chao–style seafood.

Warung Dangau (☎ 639-000; Jln A Yani; mains 7000-15,000Rp; 🕙 lunch & dinner) Dangau spices its local menu with Malaysian and Singaporean specialities.

GETTING THERE & AWAY

Buses to Pontianak's Batu Layang (15,000Rp, 3½ hours) and Sambas (13,000Rp, three hours) leave frequently until late afternoon from a lot on Jln Sejahtera. Several companies nearby run air-con buses to Sintang (70,000Rp, eight hours), Pontianak's centre (35,000Rp, four hours), and Kuching in Sarawak (80,000Rp, six hours).

Local buses from the Jln Pasar Hulu terminal to Bengkayang stop at Gunung Poteng (5000Rp; see below). Ask to get dropped at the foot of the hill. Kijang leave north to Sambas (13,000Rp, three hours) or south to Mandor (11,000Rp, three hours).

Around Singkawang

Search for the world's largest flower at **Gunung Poteng**, 12km east of town. Each rafflesia plant only blooms once a year, but there are flowerings year-round. Reaching the mountaintop takes two hours.

Ceramic factories 5km south of town produce huge, colourful Chinese jars. The Semanggat Baru factory, 100m from the main road, has an ancient kiln and can ship purchases. Prices start from 250,000Rp. Sinar Terang, 400m further, is another cool kiln.

Pasir Panjang & Tanjung Gundul

Thick coastal forests south of Singkawang shelter some of KalBar's best beaches.

Mobbed on weekends and holidays, **Pasir Panjang** (12km south) has a public pool and other facilities. **Palapa Beach Hotel** (☎ 633-402; fax 633-400; r 195,000-340,000Rp, cottages 250,000-275,000Rp; 🔀) features clean, casual rooms and pokey cottages with carports. Weekday discounts run 33%. Its **Palapa Discotheque** (admission 30,000Rp, 🕙 Friday & Saturday nights) crosses Cinderella's castle with a Chinese temple. The hotel offers snorkelling trips to tiny **Pulau Randayan** (800,000Rp, 40 minutes); overnighting in basic accommodation (100,000Rp) is optional.

Take any *opelet* south from Singkawang's bus terminal (3000Rp, 20 minutes) or *ojek* (15,000Rp) to the **Taman Pasir Panjang** (Long Beach Park; admission 3000Rp) gate, and walk 500m to the beach.

Protected by an unpaved road, **Kura Kura Resort** (☎ 085-8221-81173, 081-5122-637811; www .kurakurabeach.com; charlie@kurakurabeach.com; r incl meals per person 75,000Rp, villas 300,000Rp) is more isolated and relaxed. Owner Charlie Robertson, and

CHARLIE'S EGGSHELLS

To preserve the turtles that lend Kura Kura Resort its name, Charlie Robertson guards their eggs. His beach is a favoured hatchery area, and turtle eggs are a prized delicacy. 'You'll find them on the menu in any Chinese restaurant,' Robertson says. 'Sometimes guests come here with them to cook. I send them away.'

Robertson has tried various strategies to protect turtle eggs. None are perfect.

"I offer to buy the eggs. 'You leave them and I'll pay you for them,'" Robertson says. "But then they tell their friend, 'I know where the eggs are. Charlie will buy them.' I was spending a fortune buying the same turtle eggs three times a day," Robertson laughs.

"People here tell me, 'What's the big deal? My father took turtle eggs, my grandfather did it, and we still have plenty of turtle eggs.' They don't realise, it's the same turtle they've been taking the eggs from all these years, while they've been eating its replacements."

'If I can keep the turtle eggs safe and give the hatchling two months until its shell gets hard, then it's got a chance.' Until then, Charlie's their guardian angel.

wife Siska, strive to preserve this patch of white sand sheltered by unspoiled hills 3km from Tanjung Gundul village. The resort has no electricity or bright lights to avoid disturbing *kura-kura* (turtles) laying eggs ashore (see above). Comfortable, all-wood accommodation includes homestay rooms and a villa sleeping up to seven. The resort commandeers platoon-sized tents for bigger crowds and welcomes individual campers. Snorkelling, trekking, sailing and fishing can be arranged. But a lie-about on the beach to drink in the vista and perhaps a cold beer – resupplies of ice and beer are always welcome here – is about the right speed for most visitors.

To visit Kura Kura, call or email ahead. Because of limited internet access, it's best to SMS an alert after emailing. Access is via Tanjung Gundul (10,000Rp by *opelet*, 23km south of Singkawang).

Another 15km south (or 100km north of Pontianak), well-hidden **Pantai Gosang** overlooks offshore islands. Look for Bapak Dendy, head of the local fisherman's association, for day trips or camping on Palau Pelapis or another idyllic spot.

SAMBAS
☎ 0562 / pop 56,000

Archaeological finds link Sambas to the Srivijaya Kingdom and perhaps 6th-century India. Diamonds and 18th-century gold finds brought Chinese settlers. Sambas is now best known for *kain songket* (cloth with silver or gold thread woven in), but check prices in Pontianak before shopping here.

Keraton Sambas hints at the former prosperity. Now a museum accessible only by

river, the architecture and view are enchanting. Hire a canoe for 10,000Rp and paddle over. Or charter a motorised canoe to tour **stilt homes** along Sungai Sambas. It's similar to canal tours in Banjarmasin (see p262), but Sambas receives far fewer visitors, so you'll get bigger greetings.

Sambas is usually a day-trip destination. For accommodation, try **Hotel Wella** (☎ 392438; Jln Panji Anom; r 40,000-140,000Rp; ✸) or hotels at **Pemangkat Beach**, 25km north of Singkawang, 50km from Sambas:

Hotel Fortuna (☎ 380-123; Jln Wikora; r 50,000-165,000Rp; ✸)
Grand Hotel (☎ 242-558; fax 242-553; Jln Nusantara 69; r 120,000-220,000Rp; ✸)

Transport from Singkawang to Sambas (13,000Rp, three hours) stops at Pemangkat.

Beyond Sambas, long stretches of isolated beach, including Tajung Datok (two hours) at Kalimantan's northwestern tip, offer Robinson Crusoe–type stays.

KETAPANG
0534 / pop 30,000

Gateway to hidden destinations such as Gunung Palung National Park (p249) and KalBar's southwest coast, even Sungai Pawan is hidden as it flows through Ketapang's centre. With effort, travellers can discover river in a soothing park and journey further.

Kendawangan (80km south) has unspoiled, largely undeveloped beaches with quaint fishing settlements and simple losmen (basic accommodation, though not always, and usually cheaper than hotel; often family-run). Reach it by bus or rented car.

ORIENTATION & INFORMATION

Opelets (3000Rp) cover town via Pasar Baru. *Ojek* (from 8000Rp) wait near Hotel Perdana along Jln Merdeka. For cash, ATMs dot Ketapang's centre.

Berjaya Tour & Travel (☎ 770-0907, 081-2562-0680; Jln MT Haryono 142; www.berjayatour.com; ☼ 8am-5pm & 7-9pm) Hard-working wife and husband Mulia Lie and Rudy Salimu are a travellers' English-speaking welcome wagon. This branch of Pontianak's Berjaya Tour (see p238) books flights, ferries, local tours and more.

Karya Tours (☎ /fax 303-6633; Jln A Yani 49) Flights and Gunung Palung National Park arrangements.

Post office (Jln Suprapto) Near Seafood 26 there's also one on Jln Dr Sutomo.

Rumah Sakit Fatima (Jln Jend Sudirman) Hospital.

SLEEPING

Hotel Bersaudara (☎ 32874; Jln Diponegoro 5; r 30,000-60,000Rp; ▨) In an old pink house, this friendly losmen features a 2nd floor balcony shaded by a tree. The cheapest of its clean but tired rooms are bare with shared *mandi* and ceiling fan. A little more money buys much more comfort.

Hotel Anda (☎ 32575; Jln R Suprapto; r 30,000-75,000Rp plus 10% tax; ▨) This simple place draws crowds with scrubbed rooms and low rates. The location has food plus shopping within steps.

Losmen Patra (☎ 32742; Jln Diponegoro 63; r 55,000-75,000Rp; ▨) Exceptionally bright and friendly, Losmen Patra rooms have private *mandi*. There's a *warung kopi* (coffee stall) in the front yard of this quiet, residential setting.

Putra Tanjung Hotel (☎ 32574; Jln Pak Nibung I 12A; r 66,000-104,500Rp, ste 121,000Rp; ▨) This three-storey hotel's small, tidy rooms feature lots of wood. The front desk sports Ketapang's top collection of taxi service name cards, but the staff attitude needs a tune-up.

Hotel Perdana (☎ 33333; fax 32740; Jln Merdeka 112; r 112,500-350,000Rp plus 10% tax; ▨) Ketapang's best hotel has hot-water showers and a crisp, shiny look. The 20% discount from January to March typically extends to other months. The lobby restaurant serves Indonesian food (mains from 8000Rp; open breakfast, lunch and dinner) and cold beer.

EATING

Rumah Makan Anna S (☎ 32751; Jln Diponegoro; mains 7000-12,000Rp; ☼ lunch & dinner) Break from Padang food for West Java home cooking.

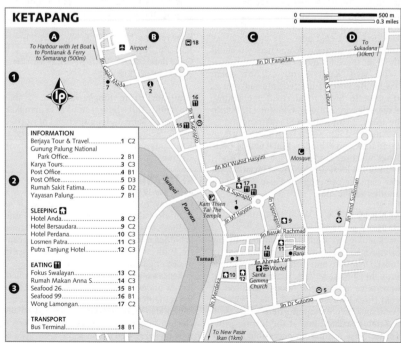

KETAPANG

0 ——— 500 m
0 ——— 0.3 miles

INFORMATION
Berjaya Tour & Travel..................1 C2
Gunung Palung National
　　Park Office..............................2 B1
Karya Tours....................................3 C3
Post Office.....................................4 B1
Post Office.....................................5 D3
Rumah Sakit Fatima.....................6 D2
Yayasan Palung............................7 B1

SLEEPING
Hotel Anda.....................................8 C2
Hotel Bersaudara..........................9 C2
Hotel Perdana..............................10 C3
Losmen Patra...............................11 C3
Putra Tanjung Hotel....................12 C3

EATING
Fokus Swalayan............................13 C2
Rumah Makan Anna S.................14 C3
Seafood 26....................................15 B1
Seafood 99....................................16 B1
Wong Lamongan...........................17 C2

TRANSPORT
Bus Terminal................................18 B1

To Harbour with Jet Boat
to Pontianak & Ferry
to Semarang (500m)

Airport

To
Sukadana
(30km)

Jln Gajah Mada

Jln DI Panjaitan

Jln KS Tubin

Jln R Suprapto

Jln KH Wahid Hasyim

Mosque

Sungai Pawan

Kam Thien
Tai The
Temple

Jln R Suprapto

Jln MT Haryono

Jln Diponegoro

Jln Jend Sudirman

Jln Basuki Rachmad

Taman

Pasar
Baru

Jln Ahmad Yani

Wartel

Santa
Gemma
Church

Jln Merdeka

Jln Dr Sutomo

To New Pasar
Ikan (1km)

KALIMANTAN

BIRDHOUSE BLUES

When banqueters in Taipei and Hong Kong savour birds-nest soup, the key ingredient can hail from Ketapang. The town has dozens of *rumah walet* – tall, dark buildings housing thousands of swiftlets whose spit produces high-priced nests – in a variety of designs. A hexagonal green *rumah walet* in Pasar Baru is the most prominent structure in town.

In Sabah and Sarawak, caves remain the predominant source for swiftlet nests, mainly because villagers jealously guard birds. But throughout Kalimantan, urban *rumah walet* dominate the trade. As town centres lose residents to suburbanisation, these bird houses have become a civic issue.

To suit the birds and maintain security for produce worth hundreds of dollars per kilo, *rumah walet* have no exterior lights or no windows. For some town elders, dark buildings filled with hundreds of noisy birds that occasionally bombard pedestrians during flights equal blight. They contend *rumah walet* encourage urban exodus.

As Indonesia widens its global lead in human bird flu (avian influenza) deaths, complaints, tinged with genuine fear, soar. *Rumah walet* owner associations assure all they are very concerned about avian influenza due to its potential to devastate their business, grimly adding that *rumah walet* tenders would be the people first afflicted.

There could be a satisfying solution to the debate. Despite millions of birds, there's not a bowl of their special soup to be found in Kalimantan. Perhaps an annual birds-nest banquet at Ketapang's ornate **Kam Thien Tai The** (Jln Merdeka Utara 162) temple would soothe local tempers and attract tourists to feather local nests.

Wong Lamongan (Jln R Suprato 22; mains 10,000-13,000Rp; ☉ lunch & dinner) Owner Haji Masuri has a grill on the left, a deep fryer on the right. You choose the fate for fish or chicken.

Seafood 99 (☎ 34222; Jln Suprato 162; mains 10,000-60,000Rp; ☉ lunch & dinner) Locally renowned Chinese seafood served in cosy, air-con comfort.

Seafood 26 (☎ 34575; Jln Suprato 139; mains 8,000-60,000Rp; ☉ lunch & dinner) Open-air Seafood 26 sprawls across a family compound with seating for hundreds. An air-con section in back has karaoke and, thankfully, sound-resistant glass.

Find *warung* and street stalls around Pasar Baru, Jln Suprato and Jln MT Haryono. Self-caterers use **Fokus Swalayan** (Jln Suprato).

GETTING THERE & AWAY
Air
IAT (☎ 303-6736) and **Kal-Star** (☎ 35588) fly to Pontianak (338,000Rp), Pangkalan Bun (378,000Rp) and Semarang (868,000Rp) in central Java. A taxi to/from the airport (6km) costs 40,000Rp; it's 15,000Rp by *ojek*.

Boat
Daily jet boats head to Pontianak (economy/first class 90,000/135,000Rp, six to eight hours) from the harbour north of town on Jln Gajah Mada. Reclining seats in first class give comfort in choppy seas. *Satya Kencana* sails weekly to Semarang (185,000Rp, 30 hours) and Pontianak (85,000Rp, 12 hours).

Bus
Like many bus terminals in Kalimantan, Ketapang's has moved from its former convenient downtown location, and accessible by *opelet* (5km). Northbound buses to Sukadana (17,000Rp, 2½ hours) for Gunung Palung National Park run from 7am. Buses south to Kendawangan (20,000Rp, three hours) depart twice daily – early morning and afternoon.

GUNUNG PALUNG NATIONAL PARK
Perhaps 10% of the world's wild orangutans live in **Gunung Palung National Park** (entrance fee 10,000Rp). Unlike the redheaded apes at some popular sites, orangutans here are completely wild.

Seaside Gunung Palung is among Kalimantan's top biodiversity preserves; the Massenerheburg effect compresses vegetation zones, creating several forest types within this relatively compact 100,000hectare park. The richness extends to wildlife, with three dozen species of mammals and nearly 200 types of birds, representing every avian family, if not every species, in Kalimantan.

Frequented by Harvard and Yale researchers, Gunung Palung has also been a top choice for illegal logging and poaching. Park management has recently cracked down, including patrols by microlight aircraft, and encouraged tourism.

Yayasan Palung (Map p248; ☎/fax 0534-303-6367; yayasanpalung@fastmail.fm; Jln Gajah Mada 97, Ketapang) arranges tours and independent travel. Ketapang independent guide **Lufti Faurusal Hasan** (☎ 081-3450-98018; lfhasan_6677@yahoo.com) also has a good reputation and speaks English.

Orientation & Information

Obtain permits for Gunung Palung at the **park office** (Balai Taman Nasional; Map p248; ☎/fax 0534-770-7345, 0534-32720; Jln Gajah Mada Desa Kali Nilam; ☽ 8am-2pm Mon-Fri, 8am-11am Sat) in Ketapang. Bring a passport copy. The office can arrange transport to Sukadana, guides, tour packages, and supply recommendations for the trip. After shopping, catch the bus north to Sukadana (80km, 20,000Rp, 2½ hours), or charter a Kijang (350,000Rp).

From Sukadana, walk two hours to the new camp at Lubuk Baji. Opportunities for cultural tourism are available en route at Air Pauh and Begasing villages. On a hillside, Lubuk Baji has views of **Gunung Palung** (1116m) and **Gunung Panti** (1050m) plus the distinctive temples of Balinese *transmigrasi* villages.

Opened in 2007 as a community-based ecotourism initiative by Yayasan Palung, Lubuk Baji includes simple sleeping and cooking facilities. Nearby waterfalls include a 30m beauty just below camp, plus swimming holes, all with clear, potable mountain water. Yayasan Palung estimates a two-night stay costs from 400,000Rp to 1,000,000Rp per person, depending on the type of transport used, food choices and excursions.

Batu Barat, in lowland swamp forest, has orangutan, proboscis monkey, sun bear and freshwater crocodile. Black orchids bloom February to April. Accommodation is rough camping or very basic homestays. For Batu Barat, continue past Sukadana to Teluk Melano (7km), then take a motorised canoe along Sungai Matan (50,000Rp). Yayasan Palung estimates 400,000Rp to 800,000Rp for excursions here.

Many Gunung Palung visits end with a splash in the sea at Pulau Datok outside Sukadana.

Park officials hope to open more areas, but Cabang Panti research camp no longer welcomes tourists.

CENTRAL KALIMANTAN

Kalimantan's least-developed province boasts a leading tourist attraction, Tanjung Puting National Park. Beyond that famed orangutan haven, the interior of Central Kalimantan (Kalimantan Tengah, or KalTeng) remains largely unvisited. Indonesia's third-largest province at 153,564 sq km, and with a population of barely two million, KalTeng is mainly flat and poorly drained. Chainsaws have ravaged large swathes of forest, but pockets of jungle and traditional life remain, including longhouses over a century old.

Predominantly Dayak, KalTeng split from South Kalimantan in 1957 to escape Banjarmasin's dominance. Gem and souvenir shops hawking beads and swords reinforce KalTeng's Dayak identity. So does a dearth of vegetables and fruit, since Dayaks focus on protein and rice, with prices double those in KalBar.

PANGKALAN BUN
☎ 0532 / pop 40,000

In 2005, Pangkalan Bun got religion. Since the town went Islamic in a Dayak-dominated province, local authorities banned alcoholic beverages, except for religious ceremonies. However, to date, there's no Church of Bintang (the national beer) conducting services.

Don't call Pangkalan Bun a dry town, though, not with Sungai Arot running through it. (Nor with its copious mud during the rainy season.) Strolling the boardwalk off Jln Antasari yields dozens of photo opportunities, mainly schoolboys vamping during their afternoon swim.

The main drag, Jln P Antasari runs parallel to the river. Beware of confusion Jln Kasumayuda, officially named Jln PRA Kasumayuda is sometimes mistaken for Jln Prakasumayuda.

Most tourists arrive en route to Tanjung Puting National Park. Flight schedules may permit avoiding an overnight stay, but, even without alcohol, Pangkalan Bun can be a pleasure rather than a sentence if you take some time to explore the town.

Information

Many businesses close late afternoons and reopen after dark. Banks around town have ATMs.

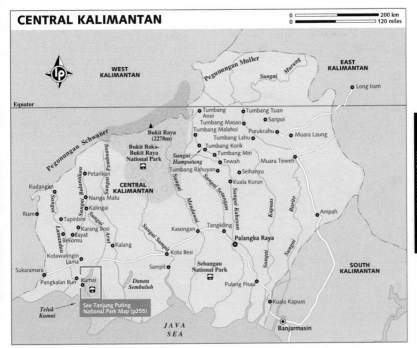

CENTRAL KALIMANTAN

Bayu Angkasa Tour and Travel (☎ 22374; www
.bayuangkasa.co.id; Jln Hasanudin 11/75) KalTeng tours to
Tanjung Puting and beyond.
BNI bank (Jln P Antasari) Exchanges travellers cheques
and cash.
Borneo Holidays (☎ 29673, 081-2500-0508; borneo
holidays@planet-save.com) Owner Harry Purwanto and
guide Danson lead personalised tours of Tanjung Puting
and KalTeng's rivers.
Pahala Internet Café (Jln Kasumayuda; per hr 7000Rp)
Post office (Jln Kasumayuda 29)
Tirta Internet Café (Jln Domba 23; per hr 7000Rp)
Yessoe Travel (☎ 21212) Books air tickets, runs buses,
and suggests guides.

Sleeping

Hotel Bone (☎ 21213; Jln Domba 21; r 35,000-85,000Rp;
🌀) The top feature at the Bone (pronounced
'Bo-nay') is the 2nd floor terrace lounge area
overlooking a quaint side street on the *opelet* route. Fan-cooled economy rooms with
shared *mandi* and large, air-con 'VIP' rooms
are good value.

Hotel Andika (☎ 21218; fax 21923; Jln Hasanudin 20A;
s incl breakfast 40,000Rp; d incl breakfast 50,000-85,000Rp;
🌀) Small porches lend charm to simple

rooms. This helpful hotel arranges cars for a
short time or a full day. Its restaurant (mains
8,000Rp to 15,000Rp; open breakfast, lunch
and dinner) features Indonesian favourites.

Hotel Bahagia (☎ 21226; Jln P Antasari 100; r
50,000-170,000Rp; 🌀) You'll be happy (*bahagia*
is Bahasa Indonesia for happiness) if you beat
domestic travellers to a clean room in this
central spot.

Hotel Mahkota (☎ 21172; Jln P Antasari; r incl breakfast
150,000-270,000Rp; 🌀) Furnishings and afternoon
tea would suit grandma's parlour, but there's
fresh paint, hot water and air-con in every
spacious room.

Hotel Avilla (☎ 27710; fax 27711; Jln Pangeran
Diponegoro 81; r incl breakfast 200,000-250,000Rp; 🌀 🖥)
This bright and stylish place features very
comfortable rooms off its open-air atrium
and accommodating staff. Breakfast is served
in the upstairs dining area before wide
patio doors.

Hotel Blue Kecubung (☎ 21211; fax 21513; Jln
Domba 1; s incl breakfast 186,500-285,500Rp; d incl breakfast
225,500-324,500Rp; 🌀) The choice of overseas
tour groups; the lobby luxury doesn't reach
rooms or service. Beware of the stairs to

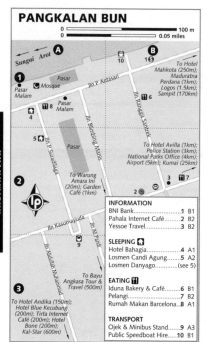

PANGKALAN BUN

INFORMATION	
BNI Bank...................................1	B1
Pahala Internet Café.................2	B2
Yessoe Travel...........................3	B2

SLEEPING	
Hotel Bahagia..........................4	A1
Losmen Candi Agung.................5	A2
Losmen Danyago............(see 5)	

EATING	
Iduna Bakery & Café.................6	B1
Pelangi...................................7	B2
Rumah Makan Barcelona..........8	A1

TRANSPORT	
Ojek & Minibus Stand...............9	A3
Public Speedboat Hire.............10	B1

rooms, the restaurant, and the four flights to the fitness centre.

Losmen Danyago (☎ 22259; Jln P Suradilaga 59; r 35,000Rp), and **Losmen Candi Agung** (☎ 21483; Jln P Suradilaga; r 35,000Rp) above, offer clean, basic rooms with private *mandi* in the centre of town.

Eating

Warung Amara Ini (cnr Gang Addullah Machmud & Jln Kasumayuda; meals 3,000–7,000Rp; ☺ breakfast & lunch) Vegetarians' delight with at least four home-cooked varieties, plus fish and chicken choices dished out cafeteria style. Take away or join the family at a low table around a huge TV.

Rumah Makan Barcelona (Jln P Antasari; meals from 5,000Rp; ☺ breakfast, lunch & dinner) The only thing Castilian in this busy place is the owner's son's favourite football team. Sample local fish, seafood or chicken with a fingerbowl as your lone utensil.

Garden Café (cnr Jln Hasanuddin & Jln Diponegoro; mains 6,000–12,500Rp; ☺ breakfast, lunch & dinner) This open-air corner serves juices and hot drinks, plus basic Indonesian food and snacks. Its shaded

long tables are perfect for catching a breeze and the local buzz.

Iduna Bakery & Café (☎ 24007; Jln Rangga Santrek 5; mains 15,000–32,000Rp; ☺ lunch & dinner) Get your burger fix at this cosmopolitan joint with hip coffees, juices and ice cream. Get your fresh-air fix, too, in smoke-free air-con. The adjacent bakery opens at 7am.

Find more *warung* along Jln Kasumayuda and Jln P Antasari, supplemented by nightly food stalls. The leading supermarket **Pelangi** (Jln Kasumayuda) has ATMs.

Getting There & Away

AIR

Kal-Star (☎ 28765; Jln Hasanuddin 2) and **IAT** (☎ 21224) both offer regular daily flights to/from Pontianak (593,000Rp) via Ketapang and to/from Semarang (717,000Rp).

BOAT

Public speedboats leave from the end of Jln Rangga Santrek for Kotawaringin Lama (50,000Rp, two hours) on Sungai Lamandau.

For ferry services to Java, see opposite.

BUS

Buses to Palangka Raya (70,000Rp to 100,000Rp, 14 hours) are run by Yessoe Travel, **Maduratna Perdana** (☎ 22129; Jln P Antasari 17) and **Logos** (☎ 27275; Jln P Antasari). Most also serve Sampit (50,000Rp, six hours).

Getting Around

Taxis to/from the airport (5km) cost 40,000Rp. *Opelet* around town cost 3,000Rp. Minibuses to Kumai (7500Rp) and *ojek* leave from the roundabout at the end of Jln Kasumayuda.

SUNGAI LAMANDAU & SUNGAI BALANTIKAN

Sungai Lamandau and its tributaries snaking north of Pangkalan Bun sustain Dayak villages with longhouses and traditional lifestyles. If you plan on visiting, patience bear with the irregular, expensive transport is essential, and hiring a guide is heartily recommended.

Two hours from Pangkalan Bun by speedboat (50,000Rp), **Kotawaringin Lama** has a longhouse and frail wooden sultan's palace. From there, 4WDs go to Sukamara (50,000Rp) for speedboats to **Manismata** and **Riam** in West Kalimantan. Hearty travellers can continue from Riam to Ketapang.

Continuing north from Kotawaringin Lama, villages pepper the river to **Bekonsu** (1,000,000Rp, three hours), with longhouses, traditional mausoleums and homestays. From Bekonsu it's about an hour by speedboat (500,000Rp) to **Tapinbini**, where a handful of longhouses defy centuries of weathering and fire. There's a twice-weekly minibus between Tapinbini and Pangkalan Bun (60,000Rp, 10 hours), a less expensive, less comfortable alternative to river travel.

Alternatively, veer off Sungai Lamandau onto more remote **Sungai Balantikan**, where villagers often invite visitors to share *tuak,* the traditional rice wine, that's more potent than palm-sugar *tuak* elsewhere in Indonesia. Hire a speedboat from Pangkalan Bun to **Bayat** (2,000,000Rp, five hours) and stay overnight with a family. From Bayat, rapids require travel by motorised canoe. A feisty rapid at **Nanga Matu** often requires hauling vessels on land for a kilometre or two. From Bayat, in two days, it's possible to explore north to **Petarikan**, staying in **Kalingai** or other villages along the way by motorised canoe (1,500,000Rp).

Though well beyond the beaten path, even by KalTeng standards, tour companies, including **Borneo Holidays** (☎ 0532-29673, 081-2500-0508; borneoholidays@planet-save.com), organise itineraries along both rivers.

KUMAI
☎ 0532 / pop 23,000

Kumai is home port for *klotok* (canoes with water-pump motors) travelling to Tanjung Puting National Park. This small but lively harbour also has passenger ships to Java, freighters, Bugis *pinisi* (schooner) and Maduran schooners bobbing at its docks.

The main street, Jln HM Idris, runs parallel to the river. Hotels are within walking distance here or up Jln Gerliya. There are no money changers, and non-nautical travel is best arranged in Pangkalan Bun.

Sleeping & Eating

Rooms are plentiful in Kumai, *except* the night before a Pelni boat arrives.

Losmen Aloha (☎ 61238; Jln HM Idris 465; s/d 25,000/40,000Rp) Above the commendable restaurant of the same name, Aloha's basic rooms have fans and shared *mandi*.

Losmen Permata Hijau (☎ 61325; Jln HM Idris; r 50,000-60,000Rp) Staff are constantly armed with a broom or mop at this immaculate guesthouse. Even shared *mandi* for budget rooms shine.

Hotel Mentari (☎ 61558; Jln Gerliya 98; r incl breakfast 110,000Rp; ❄) Mentari is fresh and very clean, with rooms bright and well furnished.

At *warung* and food stalls along Jln HM Idris toward the market, try the fresh fish, caught a fly-cast away.

Getting There & Away

Reach Kumai by minibus from Pangkalan Bun (7500Rp, 35 minutes). Taxis from Pangkalan Bun airport to Kumai cost 70,000Rp, including all stops for visiting Tanjung Puting National Park (see p254).

Boats run by Pelni connects Kumai with Semarang (150,000Rp, 24 hours) and Surabaya (170,000Rp, 26 hours) three times weekly. The **Pelni office** (Jln HM Idris) is opposite the market. **Dharma Lautan Utama** (☎ 61008, 081-3483-33444; Jln Gerilya 265) runs boats to Semarang (economy/1st class 140,000/205,000Rp, 19 to 22 hours) weekly and Surabaya (economy/1st class 150,000/200,000Rp, 23 to 26 hours) every four to five days. Send a text message for current schedules.

TANJUNG PUTING NATIONAL PARK

The world's best place to see orangutans in their natural habitat, **Tanjung Puting National Park** is a stellar family vacation destination. Unlike most other outdoor adventures, physical exertions required to enjoy jungle wildlife here are suitable for anyone age four to 84.

Like other orangutan rehabilitation sites, Tanjung Puting guarantees plenty of these irresistible auburn primates close up. What sets Tanjung Puting apart is the journey on Sungai Sekonyer straight out of *The Heart of Darkness* by *klotok*, your private floating losmen.

Motoring gently between walls of pandanus fringing the river like spiky-haired stick-figures, sharp-eyed captains or guides may spot wild orangutans perched on riverside branches or macaques scurrying through the forest canopy shared among 200-plus bird species. Tanjung Puting is also home to sun bears, wild boars, clouded leopards, spotted cats, pythons, gibbons, porcupines and Sambar deer, none of which are likely to turn up along the riverbank.

But absolutely count on seeing proboscis monkeys. Found only in Borneo, these odd creatures with their potbellies, awkward movements (by monkey standards), white

KALIMANTAN

faces highlighted by a tubular nose, and, among the males, obvious, constant sexual readiness – when colonists showed up, natives rechristened the proboscis *monyet belanda* (Dutch monkey) anxiously await *klotok* arrivals. A troop of 30 light-brown monkeys may plunge from branches 10m or higher into the dark river and cross directly in front of the boat. Proboscis monkeys act out Borneo's version of 'Why did the chicken cross the road?' because they know the boat's engine noise and the threat of its propeller scares crocodiles, which find the chubby monkeys delicious.

The only great apes outside Africa, orangutans face a very real threat of extinction this century as their rainforest habitat is converted to furniture from often illegally cut timber and palm-oil plantations; for more information see the boxed texts, p273 and p53. Canadian researcher Dr Biruté Galdikas began research here in 1971. The least known of three female ape-experts mentored by legendary anthropologist Dr Louis Leakey, Dr Galdikas' discoveries included the orangutan's eight-year birth cycle, which makes the species highly vulnerable to extinction. Valuable studies continue at Tanjung Puting.

The 415,040-hectare park was Indonesia's first site for the now-controversial practice of orangutan rehabilitation: training orphaned or former captive orangutans to live in the wild (sometimes known as referalisation). But after prolonged, close contact with human rehabilitators, orangutans never lose their taste for it. Orangutans can also pick up human diseases and spread them to wild populations. Current regulations require reintroduction in areas without native orangutan populations. Tanjung Puting's rehabilitation work is being phased out.

Part of the rehabilitation process that survives is daily feedings to released orangutans at jungle platforms. That's where visitors go to see orangutans. Feedings take place at three camps: **Tanjung Harapan** at 3pm, **Pondok Tangui** at 9am, and **Camp Leakey** at 2pm (but check for schedule changes). Reaching camp feeding-stations requires a short walk through jungle from the dock. Trails can be slippery when wet. Wear boots or enclosed shoes, bring sun (or rain) protection and vats of insect repellent. Camp Leakey and Tanjung Harapan have information centres, and some rangers speak English.

Pasalat is a reforestation camp where saplings of sandalwood, ironwood and other native trees are being reintroduced to combat logging, mining and fires. On Paslat's bulletin board:

Hutan...
Bukan hanya milik kita
Hutan...
Warisan bagi anak cucu kita
Lestarikan Hutan

The Forest...
Not only ours
The Forest...
Our grandchildren's inheritance
Preserve the Forest

Orientation & Information

Visiting Tanjung Puting starts with registration at Pangkalan Bun police station. Bring photocopies of your passport and visa. (Airport taxi-drivers know the steps.)

Next stop is the **PHKA office** (national parks office; Map p252; ☎ /fax 23832; Jln HM Rafi'I Km 1.5; ☷ 7am-2pm Mon-Thu, 7am-11am Fri, 7am-1pm Sat) on the way into Pangkalan Bun from the airport. Registration costs 50,000Rp per day per person, and 5000Rp per day for a *klotok* (15,000Rp for a speedboat). Provide a copy of your police letter from Pangkalan Bun and another photocopy of your passport. Then head to Kumai. When the park office is closed, it may be possible to arrange entry at the park's entry checkpoint. Ask your boat captain or guide.

For additional information about Tanjung Puting's orangutans, conservation efforts, and volunteer opportunities, contact **Friends of the National Parks Foundation** (FNPF; ☎ 0361-977978; www .fnpf.org). Based in Bali, FNPF runs Tanjung Harapan, Pasalat, plus community education and ecofriendly enterprise initiatives; see p258 for more information.

Orangutan Foundation International (OFI; ☎ 1-323-938-6046; www.orangutan.org; 4201 Wilshire Blvd, Ste 407, Los Angeles, CA, USA 90010) runs Camp Leakey and publishes *A Guidebook to Tanjung Puting National Park* by Dr Biruté Galdikas and Dr Gary Shapiro.

The dry season runs May to September when reduced rainfall makes journeys more enjoyable. But higher water during the wet season expands boat access. Tanjung Puting's 200 varieties of wild orchids bloom mainly January to March.

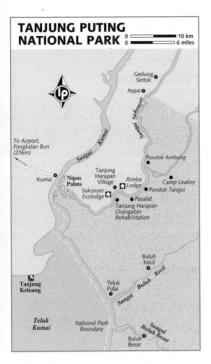

TANJUNG PUTING NATIONAL PARK

0 ——— 10 km
0 ——— 6 miles

KALIMANTAN

Guides

Guides are not required in the park, but are helpful for touring camps and essential for travel beyond them. *Klotok* captains are usually excellent wildlife spotters, but few speak much English.

Guide fees range from 150,000Rp to 250,000Rp per day. In Kumai, freelance guides abound. **Borneo Holidays** (☎ 0532-29673, 081-2500-0508; borneoholidays@planet-save.com) employs former rangers and researchers (from Tanjung Puting and beyond) as guides. Boat operator **Suyono Majit** can also recommend guides. PHKA staff can work as guides; some speak English and know the park. Camp rangers or residents of Tanjung Harapan village, across the river from that camp, are another option.

Rules & Conduct

Follow park regulations to ensure the health of ecosystems and their inhabitants; don't disregard them for the sake of a photo. Never travel park trails without a ranger or guide. Many orangutans are ex-captives and unafraid of humans. No matter what boat crew or rangers do, don't feed orangutans or initiate contact with them. Young ones especially are very hard to resist, but they are highly susceptible to human diseases and you can inflict great harm.

Orangutans are also very strong animals that may grab your camera, bag or anything else hanging off your body. In a tug-of-war, they'll win.

Resist the temptation to swim in rivers. Crocodiles lurk; several years ago a British volunteer was killed swimming just off a dock. Water may also be polluted due to mining activities upstream. Wash safely at the river pool at Camp Leakey dock. Elsewhere, get advice from your boat crew or guide before drawing water.

Klotok Hire

Klotok travel is a windfall pleasure of visiting Tanjung Puting. These 8m-to-10m houseboats serve as transport, accommodation and restaurant, generally for up to four adults. At night, crews moor well away from settlements, so passengers can enjoy sunsets and wildlife peacefully. Sleep on mattresses on deck under mosquito nets, and wake to the haunting cries of gibbons and lilting songs of sunbirds: 'It's like those tapes of the rainforest,' one visitor said.

Three days is a reasonable length of stay, though it's possible to see all three camps and only stay overnight. Some travellers spend a week or more. Three days allows time to survey the rivers unhurriedly and explore around and beyond the camps. Plan river movements for dawn or dusk, when primates come down to the banks.

Boat demand peaks in July and August and around local school holidays, but outside these times hiring a *klotok* independently in Kumai is a simple matter – operators will generally find you. Basic boat designs are similar, but there are differences in size, standard and deck arrangement, so shop around.

Each *klotok* is identified by name: *Harapan Mina III* and *Rosalia* (operated by Pak Muliadi and Pak Housni), *Cahaya Purnama* (Pak Emeng), *Everedy* (Pak Ari), *Garuda I* and *Garuda II* (the Bakso family), *Satria I* and *Satria II* (Suyono Majit), *Omega* (Anung Emen), *Britania* (Jen Joan), *Spirit of the Forest* (Herry Rostaman), *Harapan Mina I* (Anang), *Harapan Mina II* (Maslian), *Gaya Baru* (Andi), *Kalimantan I* (Usup), and *Kalimantan II* (Sukma).

At the time of research, daily rates were 400,000Rp to 450,000Rp for a boat and captain, including fuel. Cooks cost 50,000Rp per day. Food is generally 50,000Rp per person per day. It's optional to provide the crew's food and considered poor form to decline.

Advance book a *klotok* with tour agencies in Pangkalan Bun (see p250) and throughout Kalimantan. Hotels in Kumai can also assist.

Sleeping

Sleeping on a *klotok* is as much a part of the Tanung Puting experience as primates. Only visitors that absolutely must bed down on terra firma should miss it. Some visitors alternate nights on *klotok* and land.

Sekonyer Ecolodge (☎ 021-825-4120; r incl breakfast 350,000-400,000Rp) Across from Tanjung Harapan camp dock and managed by villagers, Sekonyer's all-wood rooms are basic but comfortable, even quaint, with private Western bath and mosquito nets. The hotel cranks up the generator to run fans and recharge camera batteries and helps arrange transport. Its restaurant serves simple fare (mains around 15,000Rp; open breakfast, lunch and dinner).

Rimba Lodge (☎ 0532-671-0589; www.rimbalodge.com; r 450,000-900,000Rp; 🕃) Even by ecolodge standards, Rimba registers charmless and drab. It offers fan-cooled Ruby and Sapphire rooms, the latter with hot water, and Emerald with air-con while the electricity is running. There's a bird-watching platform near the river, a spa, and internet access via radio. The restaurant (mains 20,000Rp to 40,000Rp; set menus 80,000Rp to 95,000Rp; open breakfast, lunch and dinner) serves Chinese and Indonesian food.

In Tanjung Harapan village, behind Sekonyer Ecolounge, a few families offer simple **homestays** (r incl dinner 150,000Rp) in solid, Western-style rooms with private *mandi*. Homestays allow villagers to earn income from tourism and become stakeholders in conservation.

Getting There & Around

Wooden canoes, a quiet alternative to a *klotok* for exploring Sungai Sekonyer's shallow tributaries, rent at some camps for 30,000Rp per day. Bring an umbrella or hat and lots of drinking water.

Speedboats from Kumai cost about 400,000Rp, but they're a last resort. It takes less than two hours to reach Camp Leakey but the trip is uncomfortable, motor noise chases away wildlife, and propellers wreak havoc on river dwellers.

PALANGKA RAYA
☎ 0536 / pop 165,000

Once mooted as a potential capital for all Kalimantan, Palangka Raya means Great and Holy Place. A cantilevered bridge across Sungai Kahayan is among this flat, dusty town's few features living up to its name. Stilt houses and plankwalks recalling the area's original riverside settlement remain off Jln Kalimantan. Action for inhabitants and much of the town's wealth reside in the suburbs. Activity nodes around the core include the market near Rambang pier, and **Bundaran Besar**, a stately traffic circle with a night market.

Information

Several bank ATMs along eastern Jln Ahmad Yani accept international cards.

Bali Indah Photo (Jln Ahmad Yani 77) Prints digital photos or burns them on to CDs. Occasionally stocks maps.

Bank Mandiri (Jln Ahmad Yani; 🕃 7.30am-2.30pm Mon-Fri) Currency exchange.

Bhayangkara Hospital (☎ 322-1520; Jln Ahmad Yani)

Dinas Pariwisata regional tourist office (Jln Tjilik Riwut Km 5; 🕃 7am-2pm Mon-Thu, 7-10.30am Fri) Maps and help for travel into interior. Building's sign reads 'Disparsenibud Propinsini Kalimantan Tenggah'. On taxi route A.

Main post office (Jln Imam Bonjol; 🕃 7.30am-2.15pm) On taxi route D.

Plasa Telkom (Jln Ahmad Yani 45; per hr Rp4500; 🕃 7am-midnight) Fast internet, plus telephone, fax, and groceries next door.

Sights & Activities

Longhouse-style **Mandala Wisata** (Jln Panjaitan) is an arts centre and venue for traditional performances. Shows generally take place on Sunday at 7pm; check the posted schedule for updates.

Museum Balanga (Jln Tjilik Riwut Km 2.5; admission by donation), on taxi route A, has exhibits on Ngaju Dayak ceremonies celebrating birth, marriage and death.

Borneo Orangutan Survival Foundation's **Nyaru Menteng Orangutan Education Centre** (☎ 330-8414; Jln Tjinik Riwut Km 29; admission by donation; 🕃 9am-3pm Sun) opens to visitors on Sundays. Normally, a dozen or so orangutans are visible through floor-to-ceiling windows in this sophisticated facility simulating the forest floor. Nyaru Menteng Arboretum also has a tea-toned peat swamp with monkeys, birds (best viewed early mornings), towering trees, butterflies, and mosquitoes accessible via a patchy boardwalk. Use taxi route A to Jln Tjinik Riwut Km 8 station and take a minibus.

Day-tripping to **Bontoi longhouse** by public transport is much cheaper than by boat. Take taxi E to Milono terminal for a mini-bus to Pulang Pisau (7500Rp, 2½ hours), or book a Kijang (40,000Rp). Sungai Sebangau's black waters lead to **Pagatan**, a picturesque port accessible only by water. Charter a *klotok* (around 300,000Rp) for a sunset cruise into the mangroves to see proboscis monkeys. The wharf showcases Indonesia's cargo vessels, particularly the elegant Bugis *pinisi*. From Palangka Raya, take taxi E 5km south to Kering Bangkirai for the public **boat service** (☎ 081-3490-09176) departing at 7.30am (400,000Rp, four hour). Pagatan's **losmen** (r 40,000Rp) near the pier has clean rooms, private *mandi*, and a balcony overlooking the river.

Reach **Bukit Baka-Bukit Raya National Park** by road, river and trekking from Palangka Raya

via Tumbang Jatuh, Tumbang Manggu and Tumbang Gagu.

Central Kalimantan is renowned for rattan and bamboo crafts. Souvenir shops along Jln Batam (formerly Jln Madura) sell 'export quality' Japanese-style mats with *kanji* labels.

Kalaweit Care Centre (☎ /fax 322-6388; www.kalaweit.org) accepts volunteers for rehabilitation work here with ex-captive gibbons.

Tours

Kalimantan Tourism Development (☎ 0819-5205-6762; www.wowborneo.com; kalimantantours@gmail.com) Offers unique itineraries, including fishing from a *klotok* on Sungai Rungan and cruises on the *Rahai'i Pangun* floating ecohotel, named for a historic Dayak trading vessel that ventured as far as China.

Kevin Maulana (☎ 323-4735; kevinmaulana@telkom.net; Jln Milono Km 1.5) Full-service, full-price tours to the interior. This agency also books flights, Kijangs, and charter cars.

Mulio Angkasa Raya Tour & Travel (☎ 322-1031; www.mulio_angkasa.com; mulio_angkasa@yahoo.com; Jln Ahmad Yani 55) Best bet for all flights, plus tours, car rental and Kijangs.

> **MINER DAMAGE** Kay Howe
>
> When my last child flew the nest, so did I. Indonesia's Friends of the National Parks Foundation (FNPF) drew me to Tanjung Puting National Park. Admiration for FNPF – a plucky NGO creating effective conservation, restoration, and community development programs on tiny budgets – inspired me to volunteer.
>
> I work on issues arising from small-scale gold mining. Rainforest destruction, sedimentation, and methyl mercury infiltration into rivers result from mining practices. Across Indonesia, mercury is used to amalgamate gold, then burned off, often in miners' homes. Foetal exposure causes nerve and brain damage and irreversibly affects children's cognitive development.
>
> I connected FNPF with the Global Mercury Project, and we developed an alternative technology and health awareness campaign. We visit mining villages demonstrating methods to reduce mercury use. We also educate downriver communities about dangers from potential methyl mercury accumulation in fish, a key component of local diets. Awareness throughout Kalimantan remains low, but FNPF is trying to change that
>
> It's a gift for me to work here. The simplicity of life and surroundings are beautiful. The path feels good under my bare feet, the sampan sits like a feather on the river current when I cross. Magically, fireflies announce the night, owa-owa [gibbons] the dawn.
>
> It's a gift to be embraced by this community, wrapped in its culture. I've witnessed joy and heartbreak, attended weddings and funerals, planted trees, fought fires, sweated, laughed and cried with the staff. The experience has humbled me and given me deep respect for these people and their work. They are my heroes, labouring ceaseless in the seemingly impossible task of saving the forest. They feel like my family, and this feels like home.
>
> *Consultant Kay Howe integrates place-based education in solving environmental issues with children.*

Palangka Raya Guide Association – Yusuf Kawaru (☎ 322-3341; Dandang Tingang Hotel, Jln Yos Sudarso 13)

Sleeping

Hotel Melati Serasi (☎ 322-3682; Jln Dr Murjani 54; s 22,000-49,500Rp, d 33,000-66,000Rp, tw 44,000-93,500Rp; 🗶) Very clean and quiet; the cheapest options have shared *mandi* and fan.

Hotel Mahkota (☎ 322-1672; Jln Nias 5; r incl breakfast 44,000-155,000Rp; 🗶) Near the town centre bus-drop and market; choices here range from basic with fan to palatial with air-con, terrace and hot-water shower. A domestic traveller and student favourite.

Hotel Dian Wisata (☎ 322-1241; fax 322-3952; Jln Ahmad Yani 68; r incl breakfast 75,000-125,000Rp; 🗶) Watch your head descending to economy rooms (with shared *mandi*) via the central atrium. Standard and 'VIP' rooms have air-con; all are clean.

Hotel Banama Tingang (☎ 322-8054; fax 322-2438; Jln Ahmad Yani 68; r incl breakfast 80,000-165,000Rp; 🗶) Good value, bridging budget to midrange, and all with air-con and TV.

Hotel Sakura (☎ 322-1680; Jln Ahmad Yani 87; r incl breakfast 160,000-240,000Rp plus 21% tax; 🗶) A friendly place popular with business travellers, Sakura's best feature is its open-air restaurant where a buffet breakfast is served, overlooking a garden with playground swings and a concrete menagerie, including deer and zebra.

Dandang Tingang (☎ 322-1805; www.dandang tingang.com; Jln Yos Sudarso 13; r incl breakfast 126,000-342,000Rp, ste 600,000Rp plus 21% tax; 🗶) In-town resort wannabe cultivates green grounds and rustic air, though it's just beyond Bunderan Besar. Only middle- and upper-range rooms reach resort aspirations.

Eating

Warung Laris 90 (cnr Jln Sumatra & Jln Ahmad Yani; mains 8000-12000Rp; ✆ dinner) Impossible to miss with its screaming pink exterior and nonstop stream of customers, this simple place's speciality is *ayam goreng kalasan* – fried chicken west Java style.

Rumah Makan Melati (Jln Batam; mains 10,000-18,000Rp; ✆ lunch & dinner) Bapak Arila grills up the catch of the day – select it yourself – and local vegetables. This breezy, central corner is a spot to see and be seen.

The food stalls at the *pasar* (market) run day and night around Jln Halmahera and Jln Jawa. For morning coffee, try *warung* on Jln Nias towards Rambang Pier.

For self-catering, **Raja Roti** (Jln Ahmad Yani 8) and **Toko Kue Lirissa** (Jln Ahmad Yani), next to Hotel Dian Wisata sell sweet and savoury breads and cakes. Larissa also has fresh steamed dumplings. **Sendy Supermarket** (cnr Jln Ahmad Yani & Jln Dr Marjani) and **Telaga Biru** (Jln Ahmad Yani) have the best grocery selections.

Getting There & Away

AIR

Garuda (www.garuda-indonesia.com), **Sriwijaya Air** (www.sriwijayaair-online.com) and **Batavia Air** (www.batavia-air.co.id) all fly to Jakarta with fares from 350,000Rp. **DAS** (☎ 322-1550) flights to Purukcahu, Banjarmasin and Muara Teweh were suspended at research time.

Banjarmasin offers more flight options. Kijangs go direct to/from the airport (90,000Rp, five hours).

BOAT

Sungai Kahayan speedboats head to Tewah (300,000Rp, five hours) daily from Gang Flamboyan, off Jln Ahmad Yani.

BUS & KIJANG

Morning and evening buses depart for Pangkalan Bun (95,000Rp, 14 hours) and Banjarmasin (40,000Rp to 60,000Rp, six hours) from Milono bus terminal (5km) on taxi route E. **Yessoe Travel** (☎ 3223466; Jln Banda 7) runs buses from its in-town terminal just north of the market area at comparable fares.

A scheduled Kijang service to Banjarmasin (90,000Rp, five hours) is well organised and comfortable, with a pick-up and drop-off at your designated location.

Getting Around

Minibuses here are called 'taxis' (3000Rp) and ply major thoroughfares. *Ojek* hire costs 20,000Rp per hour. *Becak* (bicycle-rickshaws) congregate on Jln Ahmad Yani around the petrol station near Jln Halmahera.

Taxis to/from the airport (6km, 15 minutes) cost 60,000Rp.

SEBANGAU NATIONAL PARK

Gazetted in 2004, **Sebangau National Park** is a peat swamp forest area between the Katingan and Sebangau Rivers south of Palangka Raya. Researchers estimate the 568,700-hectare park is home to 6900 wild orangutans, among the world's largest populations. Sebangau's biodiversity includes more than 100 bird species, 35 mammal species, and several forest types, most recovered from the 1997–98 fires.

WWF-Indonesia (www.wwf.or.id) campaigned to establish the park and is at the forefront of plans to involve local groups in low-impact logging, home industry, and ecotourism. Its **Palangka Raya office** (☎ 0536-36997; fax 0536-39404; Jln Pangrango 59) has details on those efforts, and travelling independently to Sebangau. Partnering with park researchers, **Kalimantan Tourism Development** (☎ 0819-5205-6762; www.wowborneo.com; kalimantantours@gmail.com) runs day trips tracking wild orangutans. Only the fit need apply, and one-third of the 1,400,000Rp fee directly supports local conservation efforts.

SUNGAI KAHAYAN

Central Kalimantan's interior is so far off the tourist track, there aren't even footprints to follow. Isolation has limited modernisation in Dayak villages above **Tewah** in the headwaters of Sungai Kahayan. Independent travel here is improvised, expensive and sometimes uncomfortable, with excellent Bahasa Indonesia essential. Any route is an adventure. Prices may fluctuate wildly from estimates following.

Take a speedboat from Palangka Raya beyond Tewah, then a *klotok* up Sungai Hamputung to **Tumbang Miri** (200,000Rp, six hours; one-way charter 3,000,000Rp, 5,000,000Rp return) via river rapids. There's also a minibus service from Palangka Raya (200,000Rp; charter 750,000Rp to 1,500,000Rp). Stay at **Losmen Berkat Karunia** (s/d 33,000/44,000Rp) or try the longhouse settlement at **Tumbang Korik**.

Next day, trek to the Dayak village of **Tumbang Malahoi**, with its magnificent old ironwood longhouse. From here, charter a *klotok* to the historic village of **Tumbang Anoi** (500,000Rp, three hours; speedboat 1,000,000Rp, two hours) with a traditional longhouse still in use. Spend the night with a family, and return to Tumbang Miri by *klotok*. Figure at least five days for this route.

A three-day option goes from Tumbang Miri southwest to **Tumbang Rahuyan** or the gold-mining area near **Sungai Antai** (three hours). Continue downriver to **Tumbang Baringei** (three hours), by road via Tumbang Malahoi to **Tumbang Jutuh**, then by *klotok* or speedboat south to **Tangkiling** or by road to Tewah (2½ hours) and on to Palangka Raya. Boats from Tumbang Jutuh leave mornings only and don't run during the dry season.

For a four- to five-day trip, take a speedboat from Palangka Raya to **Kuala Kurun** (200,000Rp, three hours) and travel by *ojek* north to **Seihanyu**. Take a *klotok* on Sungai Kapuas to **Sungai Mendaun** and on to **Jarak Masuparia**. Hike to **Masuparia**, a gold field in the jungle. Continue by *ojek* to **Tumbang Masao** then by *klotok* downstream to **Purukcahu** and **Muara Teweh** or continue from Tumbang Masao to Sungai Barito's headwaters, past a series of rapids north of **Tumbang Tuan**. Given the difficulty, expense and need to negotiate each step, even confirmed independent travellers may want help. Try the **Palangka Raya Guide Association** (☎ 0536-322-3341) or tour agencies in Palangka Raya (see p257).

MUARA TEWEH
☎ 0519 / pop 37,500

In the heart of Sungai Barito logging country, Muara Teweh is the last river-boat stop, unless the water is high enough to reach **Purukcahu**. From Purukcahu you can go further north by boat and hire Dayak guides to trek into the northeastern mountains and forest featuring waterfalls, stone carvings and orchids. Climbing **Gunung Bondang**, a holy peak to some Dayaks, takes a day. Near Gunung Pacungapung, on the border between Central and East Kalimantan, a cement pillar marks the geographic **centre of Borneo**.

You can also trek overland to **Long Iram** in East Kalimantan for boats down Sungai Mahakam to Samarinda. Different routes are possible, via jungle or logging roads on which you can try hitching rides with passing vehicles, for this journey of up to two weeks.

Muara Teweh's main settlement is on the north bank of Sungai Barito. Jln Panglima Batur, parallel to the river, is the main drag. Rooms at the very comfortable **Wisma Pacifik** (☎ 21231; Jln Panglima Batur 87; s/d incl breakfast 170,000/194,000Rp; 🆒) include TV, refrigerator, and hot water, plus English-speaking staff. **Barito Hotel** (☎ 21136; Jln Panglima Batur 43; s/d/tr from 25,000/40,000/55,000Rp) is the alternative.

Find *warung* along Jln Panglima Batur west of Barito Hotel, up the hill on Jln Surapati, and near the market. In Purukcahu there are a couple of **losmen** (r around 35,000Rp), or try the longhouse at Konut (10km).

Muksin Hussein (☎ 22342), who is a teacher in Muara Teweh and speaks English, can help arrange guides. In Purukcahu, ask for Mahrani, a Siang Dayak who also speaks English.

Daily (and nightly) buses travel equally long and uncomfortable routes to Palangka

Raya (50,000Rp, 12 hours) and Banjarmasin (55,000Rp, 12 hours) from the terminal across the bridge (3km). Minibuses to Purukcahu (50,000Rp, three hours) use the terminal on Jln Surapati. Cargo ships still ply Sungai Barito, and it is possible to negotiate a ride.

The airport is 5km north of town, but at the time of research, DAS flights to Palangka Raya were suspended.

SOUTH KALIMANTAN

The seat of Banjar kings that once dominated much of the region, modern South Kalimantan (Kalimantan Selatan, or KalSel) combines Kalimantan's largest and most beguiling city with the scenic Pegunungan Meratus (Meratus Mountains). KalSel packs all that plus three million people and 10,000 sq km of wetland into just 37,660 sq km. So it's relatively easy to combine the urban jungle with treks, rafting and other wilderness activities.

BANJARMASIN
☎ 0511 / pop 810,000

Arriving in Banjarmasin from Central Kalimantan, you should set your watch ahead one hour, but the time difference will seem more significant. While Banjarmasin's back streets and famed waterways still harbour old-time charm, its space-age mosque, towering buildings, and 24-hour internet shops confirm at least one foot firmly in the 21st century.

Orientation

Life in Banjarmasin has migrated toward the suburbs, leaving desolate patches in the centre. But Banjarmasin is large and deeply rooted enough to remain vibrant at its traditional core, around the bend of Sungai Martapura. Most banks are along Jln Lambung Mangkurat. *Angkot* routes run outward into the sprawl. The *belauran* – Banjar for night market – around Jln Katamso is a focus of evening activity and a good place for local cuisine.

MAPS
Gramedia (Jln Veteran 55-61)

Information
INTERNET ACCESS
Daissy Net (Jln Haryono MT 4; per hr 6000Rp; ☼ 24hr)
Air-con Daissy goes smoke-free from 8am to 3pm.

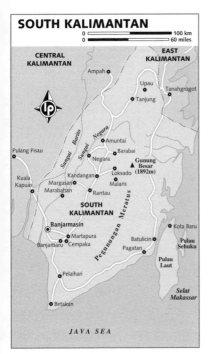

SOUTH KALIMANTAN

Warnet Kyagi (Jln Pangeran Samudera 94-96; upstairs/downstairs per hr 4500/5200Rp; 24hr) Street level has chairs, fans and cigarettes while above has floor cushions, air-con and no butts.

MEDICAL SERVICES
Rumah Sakit Ulin (Jln A Yani Km 2)

MONEY
Major streets and malls have ATMs, plus there's a cluster at Hotel Istana Barito. For foreign exchange:
BNI bank (Bank Negara Indonesia; Jln Lambung Mangkurat)
Lippo Bank (Jln Pangeran Samudera; 8am-3pm Mon-Fri)

POST
Main post office (cnr Jln Pangeran Samudera & Jln Lambung Mangkurat)

TOURIST INFORMATION
South Kalimantan regional tourist office (327-4252; fax 326-4512; Jln Pramuka 4; 7.30am-2.30pm Mon-Thu, 7.30am-11.30am Fri) Even though the staff try hard, tour operators and guides are more helpful.

TRAVEL AGENCIES
See p262 for more guided tours.
Adi Angkasa Travel (436-6100; fax 436-6200; Jln Hasanuddin 27) Flight bookings.
Arjuna Satrya Wisata Putra (335-8150; ground fl, Arjuna Plaza, Jln Lambung Mangkurat) Books domestic flights and regional tours. Operates Amandit River Lodge in Loksado (p265).
Family Tour & Travel (326-8923; familytourtravel@ yahoo.com; Komp Aspol Bina Brata 1E, Jln Y ani Km 4.5) Flights and tours throughout Kalimantan, plus car rental and hotel bookings. The helpful owner Syamsuddinnor speaks English.
Tailah (327-1685; Diamond Homestay, Jln Hasanudin 58) Independent guide.

Sights & Activities
MESJID RAYA SABILAL MUHTADIN
This massive **mosque** (Jln Sudirman) resembles a landed spaceship. During Ramadan, the famous **Pasar Wadai** (Cake Fair) runs along the adjacent riverfront.

FLOATING MARKETS
The 5.30am boarding is worthwhile to join the small, open canoes laden with vivid produce and manoeuvred precisely in tight quarters. For breakfast, supplement your fruit purchases at the floating café, using a bamboo pole with a nail pushed through the end to spike cakes.

Pasar Kuin (30 minutes from Hasanuddin bridge) is the best-known floating market. **Pasar Lokbaintan** (45 minutes) is often busier.

CANAL TRIPS
The water is filthy brown, and those booths behind houses aren't for telephone calls. A trip through people's bathrooms during wash time sounds unappealing. But as water-villagers wash, scrub clothes on wooden plank porches, paddle or swim alongside your boat, or just idle in the late afternoon breeze, their smiles light up these waterways where life dates back at least 350 years. Children are the stars but everyone joins in, trading waves and high fives.

PULAU KEMBANG
Pulau Kembang is home to the long-tailed macaques that greet visitors noisily at the dock. Charter a boat (from 25,000Rp per hour) or elect the optional stop on Pasar Kuin tours. Caution: macaques can be aggressive.

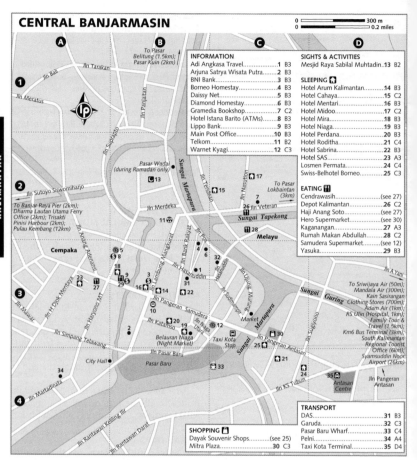

CENTRAL BANJARMASIN

INFORMATION	
Adi Angkasa Travel	1 B3
Arjuna Satrya Wisata Putra	2 B3
BNI Bank	3 B3
Borneo Homestay	4 B3
Daissy Net	5 B3
Diamond Homestay	6 B3
Gramedia Bookshop	7 C2
Hotel Istana Barito (ATMs)	8 B3
Lippo Bank	9 B3
Main Post Office	10 B3
Telkom	11 B2
Warnet Kyagi	12 C3

SIGHTS & ACTIVITIES	
Mesjid Raya Sabilal Muhtadin	13 B2

SLEEPING	
Hotel Arum Kalimantan	14 B3
Hotel Cahaya	15 C2
Hotel Mentari	16 B3
Hotel Midoo	17 C2
Hotel Mira	18 B3
Hotel Niaga	19 B3
Hotel Perdana	20 B3
Hotel Roditha	21 C4
Hotel Sabrina	22 B3
Hotel SAS	23 A3
Losmen Permata	24 C4
Swiss-Belhotel Borneo	25 C3

EATING	
Cendrawasih	(see 27)
Depot Kalimantan	26 C2
Haji Anang Soto	(see 27)
Hero Supermarket	(see 30)
Kaganangan	27 A3
Rumah Makan Abdullah	28 B3
Samudera Supermarket	(see 12)
Yasuka	29 B3

SHOPPING	
Dayak Souvenir Shops	(see 25)
Mitra Plaza	30 C3

TRANSPORT	
DAS	31 B3
Garuda	32 C3
Pasar Baru Wharf	33 C4
Pelni	34 A4
Taxi Kota Terminal	35 D4

Tours

Many travel agents and hotels organise city and Pegunungan Meratus touring with English-speaking guides. **Tailah** (☎ 436-6100, 327-1685), based at **Diamond Homestay**, is the best independent guide in town. Friendly, fluent in English and utterly genuine, he's adept at all itineraries. He lives his motto: 'Enjoy your trip as a family trip.'

Readers give mixed reviews of tours from **Borneo Homestay** (☎ 436-6545; borneo@banjarmasin .wasantara.net.id; Jln Hasanuddin 33) and owner Johan Yasin, head of the South Kalimantan Tour Guide Association.

Going rates run 60,000Rp for canal tours and 75,000Rp for floating markets, including a guide and all transport. Combination

tours with Pulau Kaget (home to proboscis monkeys) cost more.

Guide fees for forest trekking start from 150,000Rp per day, plus food, accommodation and transport.

Sleeping

BUDGET

Losmen Permata (☎ 326-5775; Jln Kol Sugiono 14; s/d 30,000-35,000Rp) The most basic of budget (and above) accommodation between Antasari Centre and Mitra Plaza. The slippery-when-wet outside staircase leads to clean, bare rooms with fan and shared *mandi*.

Hotel Perdana (☎ 335-2376; hotelperdana@plasa.com; Jln Katamso 8; s 60,000Rp, d 75,000-110,000Rp; ❄️) The pick of the *belauran* budget bunch, gracefully ageing Perdana has clean rooms around and above an atrium lounge. Solo female travellers will appreciate management's zero tolerance of prostitutes.

Also available:

Hotel Niaga (☎ 335-2595; Jln Niaga 14; s 30,000-35,000Rp, d 50,000Rp, tr 60,000Rp) Clean and basic, near *belauran* and with fans and shared *mandi*.

Hotel Sabrina (☎ 335-4721; fax 335-4442; Jln Bank Rakyat 5; s 60,000-105,000Rp, d 70,000-125,000Rp, f 145,000Rp; ⊠) Appealing rooms in a prime spot.

MIDRANGE & TOP END

Recent additions offer choices from around 250,000Rp.

ourpick **Hotel SAS** (☎ 335-3054; fax 336-5967; Jln Kacapiring Besar 2; r incl breakfast 72,000-165,000Rp, ste/f 175,000/195,000Rp; ⊠) Dark wood in the open-air lobby looks forbidding, but rooms are comfortable and bright, and staff warm and deceptively efficient. Travel vibes spill from the economy rooms' front porches.

Hotel Midoo (☎ 325-8918; fax 325-0626; Jln Nasution 8; r incl breakfast 135,000-150,000Rp; ⊠) Cross the bridge to this newish hotel off bustling Jln Veteran, Banjarmasin's Chinatown teeming with food options. Large, boxy rooms include air-con, hot water, and 40 TV channels.

Hotel Mira (☎ 336-3955; fax 335-2465; Jln Haryono 49; r incl breakfast 150,000-175,000Rp; ⊠) Centrally located Mira has identical modern, spotless rooms with hot-water showers. Save by climbing to the 3rd floor.

Hotel Roditha (☎ 336-2345; roditthahotel@yahoo.com; Jln Antasari Pasar Pagi 41; r incl breakfast from 230,000Rp, ste incl breakfast from 320,000Rp plus 21% tax; ⊠) The newest and swishest near the Antasari Centre, business-class Roditha features Western bathrooms with glass block accents.

Hotel Arum Kalimantan (☎ 436-6818; arumbjm@ indo.net.id; Jln Lambung Mangkurat; r incl breakfast 450,000-676,000Rp, ste incl breakfast from 1,928,000Rp; ⊠ ⊠) Beyond its cold concrete façade, recently redecorated Arum is classy and cushy. Enjoy buffet breakfast on the open terrace, then work it off at the fitness centre.

More choices:

Hotel Cahaya (☎ 325-3508; fax 326-6748; Jln Tendean 22/64; r incl breakfast 125,000-210,000Rp; ⊠) Clean and cosy, just across Hasanuddin bridge.

Hotel Mentari (☎ 436-8944; fax 335-3350; Jln Lambung Mangkurat 32; r incl breakfast 300,000-500,000Rp; ⊠) Comfortable business hotel, usually offering 30% discounts.

Swiss-Belhotel Borneo (☎ 327-1111; www.swiss -belhotel.com; Jln Pangeran Antasari 86A; s/d incl breakfast from 700,000/760,000Rp; ⊠) Also known as 'Hotel Borneo', luxuries here include frequent 30% discounts.

Eating

Banjar food is one of Indonesia's famed cuisines; for more information see p40. For a taste of street culture, try *belauran* stalls along Jln Niaga Utara.

Depot Kalimantan (☎ 325-8286; Jln Veteran 19; mains 8000-12,000Rp; ☕ breakfast, lunch & dinner) Bright, air-con, no-smoking refuge serves Chinese dishes and fruit juices. Popular with families and couples.

Rumah Makan Abdullah (Jln A Yani Km 1; mains 10,000-16,000Rp; ☕ lunch & dinner) Locals say *nasi kuning* (saffron rice) at this unassuming place, next to Hotel Rahmat is Banjarmasin's best in town.

ourpick **Haji Anang Soto** (☎ 7231549; Jln Pangeran Samudera; mains 12,000-16,000Rp; ☕ lunch & dinner) This hole in the wall between Jln Haryono and Jln Anang Andenansi draws big crowds for *soto banjar*, especially after noon and evening prayers. Broth here is savoury, *lontong* (rice steamed in pandanus leaves) lush, homemade *sambal* scorching.

Cendrawasih (Jln Pangeran Samudera; mains 12,000-44,000Rp; ☕ lunch & dinner) Delve deeper into Banjar cuisine at this renowned spot next to Haji Anang Soto. Pick fish, seafood or chicken for the grill outside and enjoy it inside with a full array of Banjar sauces.

Kaganangan (☎ 436-4203; Jln Pangeran Samudera 8; mains 12,000-45,000Rp; ☕ lunch & dinner) Equally as famous as, and just opposite Cenrawasih, it adds bad attitude toward foreigners.

More food:

Yasuka (☎ 335-8827; Jln Pangeran Samudera 21) Scrumptious homemade ice cream by the dish (4,500Rp) or half-litre (17,500Rp) featuring fruit flavours in season.

Hero Supermarket (Mitra Plaza, Jln Pangeran Antasari)

Samudera Supermarket (Jln Pangeran Samudera 94-96)

Shopping

Banjarmasin residents are fussy about *belauran*. Huge groups of night stalls around Antasari Centre and along Jln Anang Andenansi aren't *belauran*. Outside the city centre, **Pasar Belitung** (Jln Belitung), on the north side of town, is a 2km *belauran*. It's also known as Pasar Tunging, Banjar for 'squat toilet', once the area's commercial staple. Visit during early evening to sample modernised, urbanised traditional life.

Banjarmasin is known for *kain sasirangan* (tie-dyed batik). Market stalls near Antasari bridge sell *sasirangan*, mostly as material. Stores at Jln Ahmad Yani Km 3.7 sell *kain sasirangan* clothes, but large sizes are hard to find.

Shops sell Dayak and other traditional souvenirs along Jln Pangeran Antasari, opposite Mitra Plaza.

Getting There & Away
AIR
Garuda (☎ 335-9065; Jln Hasanudin 31) flies to Jakarta, three times daily (700,000Rp). **Sriwijaya Air** (☎ 327-2377; Jln A Yani Km 2.5), Lion Air, and Wings fly to Jakarta (400,000Rp) and Surabaya (320,000Rp). **Batavia Air** (☎ 335-8996) flies to Surabaya, Jakarta, plus Balikpapan (Rp380,000). **Adam Air** (☎ 326-0999; Jln A Yani Km 4) serves Surabaya. **Mandala Air** (☎ 325-1947; Jln A Yani Km 3) goes to Yogyakarta (350,000Rp).

DAS (☎ 470-5277; Jln Hasanuddin 6) services to Pangkalan Bun, Muara Teweh, Sampit, and Kota Baru was suspended at the time of research; Riau Airlines took over Kota Baru (360,000Rp) flights.

Taxis to/from Syamsuddin Noor Airport (26km) cost 70,000Rp. Alternatively, take an *angkot* to Km 6 terminal, then a Martapura-bound Colt. Get off at the airport approach road, and walk 1.5km to the terminal. From the airport, walk to the Banjarmasin–Martapura highway for a Colt to Km 6.

BOAT
Pelni (☎ 335-3077; Jln Martadinata 10) sails every other day to Semarang (233,500Rp, 24 hours) and twice monthly to Jakarta (359,000Rp, 20 hours) from Trisakti Pinisi Harbour (3km). **Dharma Lautan Utama** (☎ 441-4833; Jln Yos Sudarso 8) ferries depart for Surabaya (165,000Rp, 18 hours) every other day.

River boats from **Pasar Baru wharf** leave five times weekly to Marabahan (15,000Rp, six hours), continuing twice weekly to Negara (20,000Rp, 18 hours).

BUS
The main bus terminal is at Jln A Yani Km 6, southeast of downtown. Colts (minibuses) depart frequently for Banjarbaru (16,000Rp, 25 minutes), Martapura (16,000Rp, 35 minutes), Kandangan (40,000Rp, three hours), Negara (45,000Rp, four hours) and other Penunungan Meratus destinations.

Several companies run day and night buses to Balikpapan (from 75,000Rp, 12 hours), Samarinda (from 115,000Rp, 15 hours), Muara Teweh (60,000Rp, 12 hours), Palangka Raya (35,000Rp, six hours), and Pangkalan Bun (105,000Rp, 20 hours).

One bus leaves daily to Marabahan from Km 6, but it's easier to go to Kayu Tani Ujung in northern Banjarmasin for a Colt (25,000Rp, three hours). There's an extra 500Rp charge for the short ferry crossing. Take an *angkot* to Kayu Tani Ujung (1000Rp) from Antasari terminal.

Getting Around
Angkot routes (3000Rp) fan out from terminals at Jln Pangeran Samudera circle in the city core and Antasari Centre to the east. *Becak* and *ojek* for hire gather around market areas.

Charter boats (from 25,000Rp per hour) near Jln Hasanuddin bridge for canal cruising.

AROUND BANJARMASIN
Three towns southeast of Banjarmasin make interesting day trips, either visited separately or combined.

Banjarbaru
Amid ancient banyan and lontar trees, **Museum Lambung Mangkurat** (☎ 0511-92453; Jln Ahmad Yani 36; admission 750Rp; ◷ 9.30am-2.30pm Tue-Thu, Sat & Sun, 9.30am-11am Fri) exhibits relics from pre-Islamic Hindu temples, Dayak artefacts, and *halat*, Banjar carved-wood walls and doors. The museum is on the Banjarmasin–Martapura Colt route.

Martapura
Just east of Banjarbaru, Martapura has a colourful **market**, rich with regional produce, including precious stones. Purchasing uncut gems – many from local mines – silver jewellery and trading beads requires hard bargaining, with your knowledge and the seller's reputation the only indicators of authenticity.

Area mines close Fridays, so the market swells with workers and families. To avoid crowds, visit another day.

Cempaka
Cempaka's **diamond fields** (◷ closed Fri) illustrate how unglamorous pursuing precious rocks can be. Prospectors work up to their necks in water, hoisting silt to be washed in makeshift

contraptions and sifted for gold specks, diamonds or agate.

From 1846, 20-carat diamonds have been found – and largest of all, the 167.5-carat Tri Sakti (Thrice Sacred) in August 1965. Most diamonds are a fraction as big, but hopes of a huge find keep miners focused.

To reach Cempaka, take a Banjarmasin-Martapura Colt to the huge roundabout just past Banjarbaru. Switch to a green taxi to Alur (2000Rp) and walk 1km from the main road. Touts aplenty show the way. It's customary to tip these 'guides' 2000Rp.

MARABAHAN & MARGASARI

To see river life, take a boat 65km up Sungai Barito from Banjarmasin to Marabahan, a small town with some traditional Banjar-style 'tall roof' wooden houses. Losmen on the river, such as **Hotel Bahtera** (r 30,000Rp), have adequate accommodation with shared *mandi*.

From Marabahan, charter a boat to Margasari, known for rattan and bamboo handicrafts. Colts run daily between Marabahan and Banjarmasin (25,000Rp, three hours). Boats run five times weekly from Banjarmasin's Pasar Baru (15,000Rp, six hours).

KANDANGAN
☎ 0517

Shop here before exploring Penunungan Meratus. The town centre features a crumbling colonial-era market and minibuses can take you deeper into the interior.

Losmen Loksado (☎ 21352; Jln Suprapto 8; r 40,000-60,000Rp), around the corner from the minibus terminal, has comfortable, fan-cooled rooms. Harder to find, **Wisma Duta** (☎ 21073; Jln Permuda 9; r 65,000-150,000Rp; ✺), in a converted family house, has cosy rooms on a quiet street.

Kandangan's speciality is *ketupat,* sticky rice triangles enjoyed across Indonesia, and served with broiled *harawan,* a river fish, with coconut sauce and a squeeze of lime. Try this dish at **Warung Ketupat Kandangan**, 1km northwest of the minibus terminal on the road to Barabai.

Fathurrahman at the government **tourism office** (☎ 21363; Jln Jend Sudirman 26), on the main road, 2km south of the town centre, can suggest trek guides.

Colts run frequently to/from Banjarmasin's Km 6 terminal (40,000Rp, three hours) until midafternoon. Night buses stop en route from Banjarmasin to Balikpapan and Samarinda

around 7pm at a terminal 2km east of town. Catch a Negara-bound minibus (5000Rp) there, or take an *ojek* (15,000Rp).

NEGARA

Northwest of Kandangan, Negara is home to some of world's most spectacular swimmers. A wetland during the rainy season and surrounded by water year-round, Negara's buildings are on stilts. The only land above water is the road, and even that can disappear – in floods of mosquitoes, if not rain.

Negara's incredible swimmers are water-buffalo. Farmers rear buffalo on wooden platforms, releasing them daily for grazing and drinking. Buffalo swim up to 5km until 'canoe cowboys' herd them home late afternoons.

Tour Negara by boat (it may cost 100,000Rp, depending on bargaining skill). The wetlands are also remarkable for prolific fish- and bird-life, and occasional snakes. The town is also noted for forging swords, machetes and *kris* (daggers).

Surprisingly, Negara has no hotel. You might find a homestay, but Kandangan is a better bet. A few *warung* serve *ketupat* and grilled chicken, also known as *ayam panggang.*

Colts from Banjarmasin to Negara (45,000Rp, four hours) leave from Km 6 terminal. From Kandangan to Negara choose among public minibus (7000Rp, one hour), shared Japanese sedan with four people (15,000Rp per person; charter 60,000Rp), or *ojek* (40,000Rp). Twice-weekly boats leave from Pasar Baru pier in Banjarmasin (20,000Rp, 18 hours).

LOKSADO

At the end of the road 40km east of Kandangan, Loksado is the largest of about 20 villages spread around Pegunungan Meratus. Limits of the 2500-sq-km range include Kandangan and Amuntai to the west and KalSel's coast to the east. Thanks to road access, Loksado is an important market village and base for trekking.

Amat (☎ 081-3487-66573), a personable Dayak who speaks good English, is Loksado's tourism source. A new visitor-information kiosk sets standard prices for services.

Reports of accommodation in Loksado, including photos some travel offices display, are greatly exaggerated. Construction of cottages on the small island opposite the village began years ago and remains years from completion. The only current option, three rooms

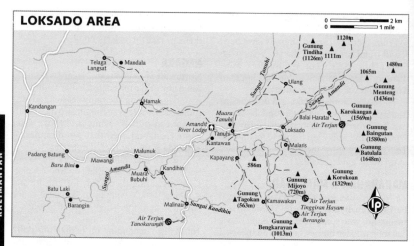

LOKSADO AREA

at **Loksado Guest House** (r 35,000Rp), are virtually unfurnished and absolutely filthy.

Amandit River Lodge (r 125,000Rp), 3km west of Loksado, has simple, comfortable rooms, and guests can arrange for meals. Amandit opens by appointment; give two days' notice to **Arjuna Satrya Wisata Putra** (☎ 0511-335-8150) in Banjarmasin; see p261 for details.

Muara Tanuhi's **hot springs** (admission adult/child 3000/2000Rp), 2km west of Loksado, have **holiday cottages** (☎ 081-2508-6913; r 125,000-150,000Rp) with two pools and a tennis court. The suburban aesthetic targets Banjarmasin weekenders.

Pick-up trucks leave Kandangan terminal for Loksado (12,000Rp, 1½ hours) afternoons, and leave Loksado for Kandangan early mornings.

After treks, many travellers charter bamboo rafts down Sungai Amandit. The usual drop-off point is Muara Tanuhi, two hours downstream (125,000Rp for up to three passengers). Continuing hours further downstream to Muara Bubuhi, crosses some exciting rapids when the river is high and costs a lot more. From the nearby road at Muara Bubuhi, minibuses and *ojek* return to Kandangan. Rafting Loksado to Kandangan takes a full day.

AROUND LOKSADO

Hundreds of mountain paths from Loksado lead over the hills to other villages, many crossing streams via suspension bridges. Villagers negotiate the bridges easily, but newcomers usually set them rocking, amusing onlookers.

Malaris

A 30-minute walk (1.5km) or 10-minute *ojek* ride through bamboo forest southeast of Loksado leads to Malaris. Its aged *balai* (longhouse) once housed 32 families; modernisation means separate houses for families. Ask the *kepala balai* (village head) about **homestays** (30,000Rp).

Upau

One of the smallest Dayak groups, Deah Dayaks have lived at the remote northern edge of Pegunungan Meratus, isolated by centuries of aristocratic intrigue and refusal to embrace Islam. In Upau (meaning 'jackfruit', abundant locally) Deah traditional ceremonies are still performed, including the *balian* (shaman) ceremony to drive evil spirits from the sick, and the *aru* preparing warriors for head-hunting (although they now skip the head-hunting). English is rare, and there's no formal accommodation. But some local families take in guests. Bring food from Tanjung or Upau's Friday market, and offer a modest sum of money.

There's prime trekking in Pegunungan Meratus, 2km away. Villagers Aman and Dudang know the mountains and act as guides. Take a moderate one-day trek into the foothills, or more strenuous two- or three-day adventures. Terrain can be rough, demanding trekking experience.

To reach Upau, go to Tanjung by minibus from Negara (40,000Rp, two hours) or Colt from Banjarmasin's Km 6 (70,000Rp, six hours). From Tanjung, take a red and yellow *angkot* to Upau (6,000Rp, 1½ hours).

Treks

Pegunungan Meratus' combination of lime-stone mountainsides, dense tropical forests, rolling hills and river valleys is breathtaking, more for the scenery's splendour than the difficulty of the journey. Guides are necessary for most treks to find the right paths and best vistas. Enlist one in Loksado, though if you require an English speaker, hire in Banjarmasin. Penunungan Meratus treks are a speciality of **Tailah**: see p262. Guides cost 150,000Rp to 250,000Rp per day, plus transport costs and other expenses. You may also occasionally find villagers willing to show you the way for English practice.

To sample the hills, follow the path from Loksado upstream along Sungai Amandit for three hours (8km) to a series of **air terjun** (waterfalls) past Balai Haratai. Finding the first waterfall is easy, but the middle and top falls and nearby cavern require assistance. Ask for help at Haratai.

Longer treks begin from Loksado or 2km west in **Tanuhi**. The combination of mountains and rivers means plenty of waterfalls and bamboo suspension bridges. The primary forest is a tranquil yet awe-inspiring spectacle. Accommodation is at *balai* along the way, including Haruyan, about four hours from Tanuhi; Kepayang, one to two days; Niwak, two days; and Pangong, three days. Return downstream by bamboo raft.

Barabai, renowned for its scenic views, is another terminus for treks. The **Fusfa Hotel** (☎ 0517-41136; Jln Hasan 144; s/d/tr from 40,000/60,000/90,000Rp; ❄) has clean rooms and a restaurant. Barabai minibuses go to Kandangan (8000Rp, one hour).

It's also possible to trek from Loksado to the coast. Reaching **Kota Baru** on Pulau Laut takes three or four days by foot, minibus and boat, crossing Gunung Besar (1892m), KalSel's highest peak. Return to Banjarmasin by bus (55,000Rp, six hours) or take the coast road north to Balikpapan.

SOUTH COAST

The coast road is an alternative route between Banjarmasin and Balikpapan, via **Pagatan**, a beach area, and **Batulicin**, a port.

Bugis from South Sulawesi build elegant *pinisi* schooners here. Every 17 April, they perform **Mapan Retasi**, literally 'giving the sea food', culminating week-long celebrations.

From Banjarmasin's Km 6 terminal, Colts run to Pagatan (40,000Rp, five hours) and buses to Batulicin (45,000Rp, six hours). From Batulicin, Pelni boats serve Makassar. Minibuses continue north toward Balikapapan.

EAST KALIMANTAN

East Kalimantan (Kalimantan Timur or KalTim) has Borneo's richest and most diverse natural resources. Its oil, coal and timber fuel coastal development while extraction wounds ecosystems and traditional cultures. But not all of KalTim has been reduced to denuded grassland and urban sprawl. Measuring 202,000 sq km, East Kalimantan has space for effective preservation and areas where distance and natural obstacles make exploitation excessively difficult, at least for now. With time, planning, patience and budget, travellers can reach even these out of the way places. But not every worthy KalTim destination requires an enormous ordeal or outlay. River boats make it relatively easy and inexpensive to explore Dayak communities along Sungai Mahakam.

BALIKPAPAN

☎ 0542 / pop 510,000

Catering to oil men on expense accounts, this gateway city rarely gets its due from other travellers. Balikpapan is Indonesia's urban frontier: everyone seems to have come from someplace else to work hard and make a new life. These newcomers enhance Balikpapan's cosmopolitan, welcoming air. Sungai Mahakam journeys can originate here, and you may find Balikpapan more pleasant than Samarinda.

Oil fields made Balikpapan a target for Japanese forces in 1941 and for advancing Allies in 1944–45. A memorial near Pertamina Hospital honours 229 Australians who died here, with a Japanese memorial near the beach at Lamaru, east of the airport.

Orientation

Shopping mall **Balikpapan Plaza** (cnr Jln Sudirman & Jln Ahmad Yani) anchors the town centre. East along Jln Sudirman leads to produce at Pasar Baru and eventually the airport, west to government offices, plus Pasar Klandasan, which specialises in clothing. Jln Sudirman

KALIMANTAN

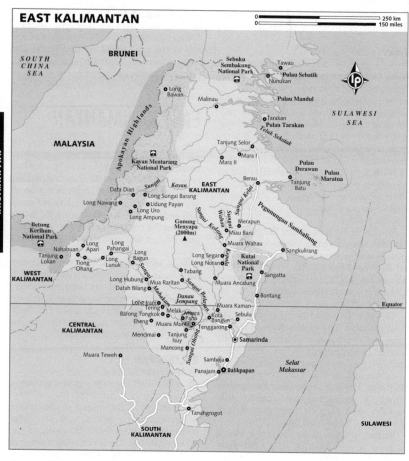

EAST KALIMANTAN

0 ——— 250 km
0 ——— 150 miles

SOUTH
CHINA
SEA

BRUNEI

Long
Bawan

Sebuku
Sembakung
National Park

Tawau

Pulau Sebatik

Nunukan

MALAYSIA

Malinau

Pulau Mandul

SULAWESI
SEA

Apokayan Highlands

Tarakan
Pulau Tarakan
Teluk Sekatak

Tanjung Selor

Kayan Mentarang
National Park

Mara II

Mara I

Pulau
Derawan
Pulau
Maratua

Data Dian

Sungai Kayan

EAST
KALIMANTAN

Berau

Tanjung
Batu

Long Sungai Barang

Long Nawang

Lidung Payan
Long Uro
Long Ampung

Sungai Kelai

Pegunungan Sambaliung

Betung
Kerihun
National Park

Gunung
Menyapa
(2000m)
▲

Sungai Kedang

Merapun

Miau Baru

Sangkulirang

Nahabuan

Long
Apari

Long
Pahangai

Muara Wahau

Tanjung
Lokan

Tiong
Ohang

Long
Lunuk

Long
Bagun

Long Segar

Long Noran

Sungai Wahau

Sungai Kelai

Kutai
National
Park

WEST
KALIMANTAN

Long Hubung

Datah Bilang

Mua Raritan

Tabang

Muara Ancalung

Sangatta

Bontang

Equator

CENTRAL
KALIMANTAN

Long Iram

Barong Tongkok

Eheng

Tering

Mencimai

Melak

Muara Muntai

Tanjung
Isuy

Mancong

Danau
Jempang

Muara
Pahu

Sungai Belayan

Sungai Mahakam

Sungai Ohang

Muara Kaman

Kota
Bangun

Sebulu

Tenggarong

Samarinda

Selat
Makassar

Muara Teweh

Samboja

Panajam

Balikpapan

SULAWESI

Tanahgrogot

SOUTH
KALIMANTAN

---

also parallels the reviving waterfront with restaurants, clubs and hotels, all pleasantly low-key. A shopping and hotel complex, opening mid-2008, promises to raise the volume substantially.

MAPS
Gramedia (2nd fl, Balikpapan Plaza)

Information
COURSES
Suprioso (☎ 081-5455-28484; per hr 135,000Rp) Bahasa Indonesia lessons.

INTERNET ACCESS
Bcom (Jln Ahmad Yani; per hr 6000Rp) Next to Hotel Budiman.

Family Net (ground flr, BRI Bank Bldg, Jln Sudirman 37; per hr 7000Rp)

MONEY
Banks along Jln Sudirman have ATMs. Many handle foreign exchange:
BNI (cnr Jln Ahmad Yani & Jln Sudirman)
BRI (Jln Sudirman 37)
Haji La Tunrung Star Group (Jln Ahmad Yani 51; ⏱ 7.30am-9pm) Moneychanger with several branches.

MEDICAL SERVICES
Pertamina Hospital (☎ 734020; www.rspb.co.id; Jln Sudirman 1)
Rumah Sakit Ibu Restu (☎ 422304; Jln Ahmad Yani 85) Opposite Bondy's.
Rumah Sakit Umum (☎ 734181; Jln Ahmad Yani)

TRAVEL AGENCIES

Agung Sedayu (☎ 420-601; fax 420-447; Jln Sudirman 28) Best source for Pelni schedule and all boat tickets. Also books domestic flights.

Bayu Buana Travel (☎ 422-751; www.bayubuana travel.com; Jln Ahmad Yani) Very helpful English-speaking staff for flights, Sungai Mahakam tours.

Golden Nusa Travel (☎ 417-321; ticket-bpn@golden nusa.com; Hotel Benakutai, Jln Ahmad Yani) Staff speak English and try hard to please.

Kaltim Adventure (☎ 732-563; kaltim_adven turebpn@yahoo.com; Complex Balikpapan Permai, Jln Sudirman) Boats, domestic flights plus Sungai Mahakam tours.

Totogasono Travel (☎ 413-535; tgs_lestari@hotmail .com; Jln Ahmad Yani 40) All flights.

Tours

Rivertours (☎ 422-269; fax 422-211; rivertours@bor neokalimantan.com) Established specialist with first-class tours and connections throughout Kalimantan.

Transborneo Adventure (☎ 762-671; tborneo@ indo.net.id; Jln Sudirman 21) Wide menu includes dolphin ecotours with Yayasan Konservasi RASI (see p279).

Sleeping

Find budget options near the fork of Jln Ahmad Yani and Jln Pangeran Antasari, also called Gunung Kawi, 2km from Balikpapan Plaza via *angkot* route 3 or 5.

BUDGET

Hotel Murni (☎ 738-692; Jln P Antasari No 2; s/d incl breakfast from 55,000/75,000Rp; ☒) This family-run losmen has immaculate rooms, all with private *mandi*, on three floors. Indonesian solo travellers are mainstays: meet over tea on the enormous red leather sofa.

Hotel Ayu (☎ 425-290; Jln P Antasari, Gunung Kawi 18; r 100,000-160,000Rp; ☒) Hidden delight with spotless, bright rooms up a flight of stairs. The cheapest rooms require climbing more stairs.

Hotel Gajah Mada (☎ 734-634; fax 734-636; Jln Sudirman 328; s 95,000-235,000Rp, d 135,000-285,000Rp plus 10% tax; ☒) Good luck beating domestic travellers to these glistening and lovely rooms – some with water views – right next to Balikpapan Plaza.

Hotel Citra Nusantara (☎ 425-366; fax 410-311; Jln Gajahmada 76; s incl breakfast 110,000-175,000Rp, d incl breakfast 130,000-200,000Rp; ☒) Just off the main road, this guesthouse's shared *mandi* budget rooms are basic – the higher ranks surprisingly modern – all with a fresh scent.

MIDRANGE

Several new options cost around 250,000Rp.

Hotel Buana Lestari (☎ 737-175; blh_bpp@indo.net.id; Jln Sudirman 418; r incl breakfast from 193,000Rp; ☒) This local chain's economy-class hotel's luxury touches include buffet breakfast in its 24-hour coffee shop, big rooms and comfortable beds. Popular with domestic businesspeople.

City Hotel (☎ 427-500; www.cityhotel.co.id; Jln Sudirman 45; r incl breakfast 215,000-245,000Rp, ste 275,000Rp; ☒) Fraying around the edges, City Hotel's good value rooms have hot-water shower and TV. Huge suites include kitchen table, refrigerator and bathtub.

Hotel Grand Tiga Mustika (☎ 733-788; fax 733-288; Jln ARS Muhammad 51; r incl breakfast from 363,000Rp, ste from 665,000Rp, plus 21% tax; ☒ ☒) From emerald-green dragons poolside to cherry-wood sofas, new Grand Tiga Mustika ('three magical stones') runs to Chinese kitsch. But it's serious three-star value.

Hotel Pacific (☎ 750-888, 750-345; www.hotel pacificbalikpapan.com; Jln Ahmad Yani 33; r incl breakfast US$55-75, ste US$90-100; ☒) Pacific's game is 'Let's Make a Deal': ignore posted rates and negotiate for standard rooms around 350,000Rp. Comfortable, tasteful Southeast Asian furnishings and first-class service are worth the bother.

More midrange:

Bintang Hotel (☎ 735-908; bintangh@indosat.net .id; Jln Sudirman Blok B, 31-34; r incl breakfast 215,000-245,000Rp, f/ste 345,000/495,000Rp plus 10% tax; ☒ ☒) Comfortable waterfront favourite.

Mirama Hotel (☎ 412-442; mirama@indonet.net.id; Jln Pranoto 16; r incl breakfast 265,000-315,000Rp, ste 530,000-580,000Rp plus 21% tax; ☒) Freshly renovated value with 35% discounts.

TOP END

Le Grandeur (☎ 420-155; www.legrandeurhotels.com; bppres@legrandeurhotels.com; Jln Sudirman; r incl breakfast 640,000-890,000Rp; ☒ ☒ ☒) Formerly the Dusit, seafront Le Grandeur caters to expense-account travellers with indulgent rooms, a fitness centre, tennis courts, and a lounge bar. Outside Balikpapan's centre, but a nearby bustling shopping area lends an urban buzz.

Hotel Gran Senyiur (☎ 080-0122-6677, 820-211; hgs@ senyiurhotels.com; Jln ARS Mohammad 7; r/ste incl breakfast from 1,100,000/1,700,000Rp; ☒ ☒ ☒) Balikpapan's classiest choice mixes Kalimantan style – wooden floors, Dayak *doyo* bark cloth on walls – with five-star luxury. There are several good restaurant choices on the premises..

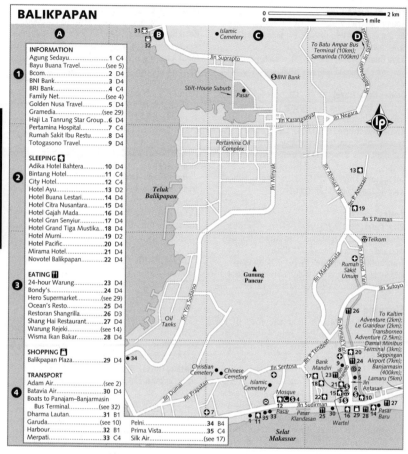

BALIKPAPAN

INFORMATION
Agung Sedayu.....................1 C4
Bayu Buana Travel..............(see 5)
Bcom................................2 D4
BNI Bank............................3 D4
BRI Bank............................4 C4
Family Net.........................(see 4)
Golden Nusa Travel.............5 D4
Gramedia..........................(see 29)
Haji La Tanrung Star Group...6 D4
Pertamina Hospital..............7 C4
Rumah Sakit Ibu Restu........8 D4
Totogasono Travel...............9 D4

SLEEPING
Adika Hotel Bahtera............10 D4
Bintang Hotel....................11 C4
City Hotel.........................12 C4
Hotel Ayu.........................13 D2
Hotel Buana Lestari.............14 D4
Hotel Citra Nusantara..........15 D4
Hotel Gajah Mada...............16 D4
Hotel Gran Senyiur..............17 D4
Hotel Grand Tiga Mustika.....18 D4
Hotel Murni.......................19 D2
Hotel Pacific......................20 D4
Mirama Hotel.....................21 D4
Novotel Balikpapan.............22 D4

EATING
24-hour Warung..................23 D4
Bondy's.............................24 D4
Hero Supermarket...............(see 29)
Ocean's Resto....................25 D4
Restoran Shangrilla..............26 D3
Shang Hai Restaurant..........27 D4
Warung Rejeki....................(see 14)
Wisma Ikan Bakar...............28 D4

SHOPPING
Balikpapan Plaza.................29 D4

TRANSPORT
Adam Air...........................(see 2)
Batavia Air........................30 D4
Boats to Panajam–Banjarmasin
Bus Terminal....................(see 32)
Dharma Lautan...................31 B1
Garuda..............................(see 10)
Harbour............................32 B1
Merpati.............................33 C4
Pelni.................................34 B4
Prima Vista........................35 C4
Silk Air..............................(see 17)

More luxury options:

Adika Hotel Bahtera (☎ 418-000; www.bahtera
hotel.com; Jln Sudirman 2; r incl breakfast US$60-95, ste
incl breakfast US$120-200 plus 21% tax; ▨) Bargain
for a moderate room below 400,000Rp at this behemoth
opposite Balikpapan Plaza.

Novotel Balikpapan (☎ 080-7177-7777, 733-111; www
.novotel.com/asia; Jln Brigjen Ery Suparjan 2; r incl breakfast
from 765,000Rp; ▨ ⚏) Lush international sterility.

Eating & Drinking

Find cheap eats around Gunung Kawi, along
the waterfront, particularly around Pasar
Klandasan; there's a trio of all-night *warung*
on Jln Pranoto.

Wisma Ikan Bakar (Jln Sudirman 16; meals 11,000-
28,000Rp; ☽ lunch & dinner) The 'Grilled Fish Inn'

ain't just another *warung*. Select fish or seafood for the fire and enjoy it with *lalapan* style:
served with sambal and aromatic leaves.

Restoran Shangrilla (Jln Ahmad Yani 29; mains
14,000-25,000Rp; ☽ lunch & dinner) This popular,
family-run restaurant serves meek and dar-
ing Indonesian-Chinese versions of seafood
(pages of it!), duck, beef, frog and chicken.

Ocean's Resto (☎ 739-439; Ruko Bandar waterfront,
Jln Sudirman; mains from 18,000Rp; ☽ lunch & dinner) In
the fledgling waterfront district, choose fish
or seafood, sold by weight, plus burgers, fish
and chips, and Indonesian food. Sit inside
with air-con or go rustic in the garden with
the sea breeze and casual vibe.

Shang Hai Restaurant (☎ 422-951; Jln Sudirman;
mains 22,000-40,000Rp; ☽ lunch & dinner) Water views

are a bonus at this cool and classy home of superb Chinese seafood. Shellfish cooked in various styles and claypots are the order.

Bondy's (☎ 424-285; Jln Ahmad Yani; mains 30,000-50,000Rp; ☺ lunch & dinner) An institution among expats and local *riche*, this boozy garden restaurant features fish on ice, steaks and Indonesian favourites. Bread and desserts featuring homemade ice cream, come from the bakery in front.

Most large hotels have restaurants serving Western and tame Indonesian cuisine, plus pubs, live music and dancing. *Ruko*, near the waterfront east of Pasar Klandasan, conceal dance clubs.

Cheap eats:

Warung Rejeki (Jln Sudirman 15; mains 8000-10,000Rp; ☺ breakfast, lunch & dinner) Late-night option for Indonesian mainstays.

Hero Supermarket (Balikpapan Plaza, Jln Sudirman) Commendable food court here, too.

Getting There & Away

AIR

SilkAir (☎ 730-800; Hotel Gran Senyiur, Jln ARS Muhammad 7) flies daily to Singapore (US$291). **Merpati** (☎ 424-452; Jln Sudirman 32) flies daily to Makassar (796,000Rp). **Garuda** (☎ 422301; Adika Hotel Bahtera, Jln Sudirman 2) flies to Manado, Surabaya (310,000Rp), Denpasar (663,000Rp) and Tarakan (327,000Rp). **Riau Airlines** (☎ 761-855-333; www.riau-airlines.com) flies daily to Balikpapan (500,000Rp). **Kal-Star** (☎ 737-473; Jln Sudirman 80) and Riau Airlines fly to Berau (500,000Rp), with Kal-Star connecting to Tarakan (761,000Rp), Nunukan (893,000Rp) and Tanjung Selor (761,000Rp).

Batavia (☎ 739-225, 766-886; www.batavia-air .co.id/; Jln Sudirman 15C) flies to Banjarmasin (395,000Rp), Tarakan, Jakarta, Surabaya, Yogyakarta (545,000Rp), Palu (415,000Rp) and Manado (565,000Rp). **Adam Air** (☎ 743999; www.adamair.co.id; Jln Ahmad Yani 40) and **Lion Air** (☎ 0804-177-8899, 707-3761; www.lionair.co.id) fly to Jakarta and Surabaya. Mandala also flies to Tarakan. Air Asia (350,000Rp) and Sriwijaya Air also serve Jakarta.

BOAT

Agung Sedayu (☎ 420-601) is the best source for all nautical transport information and tickets. See p269.

Pelni (☎ 424-171; Jln Yos Sudarso 76) sails to Makassar (economy/1st class 122,000/377,000Rp, 36 hours), Pare Pare, Surabaya, and beyond.

Dharma Lautan (☎ 422-194; Kampung Baru dock) runs daily ferries to Mamuju (96,000Rp, 14 hours). **Prima Vista** (☎ 732-607; Jln Sudirman 138) sells tickets for Pare Pare (120,000Rp, 20 hours), Makassar (125,000Rp, 24 hours), and Surabaya (160,000, 36 hours).

BUS

Buses to Samarinda (19,500Rp, two hours) leave from Batu Ampar bus terminal at the north end of town. Buses to Banjarmasin (from 75,000Rp, 12 hours) leave from the terminal across the harbour. Take a route 6 *angkot* to Jln Monginsidi and hop on a speedboat (6000Rp, 10 minutes) to the other side.

Getting Around

Taxis to/from Seppingan Airport cost 35,000Rp. Or catch a route 7 *angkot* on the highway outside the airport to Damai minibus terminal. Transfer to a route 1 or 3 *angkot* downtown.

Balikpapan Plaza is a focal point for *angkot* (3000Rp). Drivers frequently equip their rides with vast speakers, cranked to ear-splitting levels.

Ojek drivers congregate near Balikpapan Plaza, Gunung Kawi and other strategic spots. Bargaining begins at around 10,000Rp.

SAMBOJA LODGE

It's not surprising that **Borneo Orangutan Survival Foundation** (BOS; www.orangutan.or.id) has a low profile. It follows modern orangutan rehabilitation theory, minimising contact between humans and orangutans. The resident primatologist at the BOS Samboja Lestari reintroduction project warns, 'Those wishing to hug orangutans will need to go elsewhere.' (In fact, no orangutan rehabilitation program endorses hugging.)

Despite the antisocial agenda, BOS opened **Samboja Lodge** (☎ 081-153-7630; www.sambojalodge .com; r with meals US$100, ste with meals US$150-200; ☒) for day-trippers, overnighters and long-term volunteers. Visitors can observe, from a suitable distance, BOS projects, perhaps assist, and savour 1850 splendid hectares of regenerating forest.

Samboja Lestari is open on Saturday mornings by appointment – other times by special arrangement – for **day visits** (☎ 0542-702-3600; fax 0542-413069; admission by donation US$50 Saturdays, other time US$70). Samboja Lestari is located 90 minutes from Balikpapan and the

KALIMANTAN

unpaved approach road requires 4WD during the rainy season.

The site houses three BOS projects: Samboja Lestari Land Rehabilitation Program; Samboja Lestari Wanariset Orangutan and Sun Bear Project; and Samboja Lodge. Two lookout towers and self-guided nature trails facilitate observing three species of eagle, deer, butterflies and occasional wild primates. Every visitor plants a native species tree as part of the BOS reforestation program.

Overnight visitors can assist projects through the **Helping Hands program** (US$20 per day). Tasks include enclosure cleaning, organic farming, and wildlife behaviour observation.

BOS also arranges limited visits to orangutan release areas. At **Meratus Forest Camp** (per person per day US$50), about five hours from Samboja, humans are caged to prevent interaction with released orangutans. Guides lead forest treks to spot orangutans in trees. The price includes meals and accommodation, but not 4WD transport, which is approximately US$100 per day.

During the 1990s, BOS released 75 orangutans into **Sungai Wain**, less than an hour from Samboja. Day-trekking there costs US$37, excluding transport. Plans include a camp for overnight stays there, too.

Samboja staff can facilitate trips to other KalTim sights. BOS doesn't want anyone touching the apes, but it will lend visitors a hand.

SAMARINDA
☎ 0541 / pop 600,000

Samarinda's reputation as a travellers' haven is greatly exaggerated. East Kalimantan's largest city is a prime example of exodus from urban centres. Places where travellers most easily find services don't attract leading elements of Samarinda's citizenry. Travellers come here as a launch point to unspoiled forests and Dayak villages on Sungai Mahakam; avoid lingering and just hit the road.

Orientation

The town centres around **Pasar Pagi** (morning market; Jln Sudirman) and **Mesra Indah Mall** just opposite. *Angkot* (3000Rp) congregate here. Hotels also cluster here, running north toward Tumendung Airport. The town centre spreads east through **Citra Niaga** traditional market and west to Jln Awang Long. The striking main mosque, **Mesjid Raya Darussalam**

(Jln Niaga Selatan), with its missile-like minarets, is between the markets. River boats leave from docks 3km west. Long-distance bus terminals are dispersed inconveniently around town.

MAPS
Gramedia (Mesra Indah, Jln KH Khalid)

Information
INTERNET ACCESS
Internet Cafe (Hotel MJ, Jln KH Khalid 1; per hr 10,000Rp; ☺ 24hr)
Sumangkat Internet (Jln Agus Salim 35; per hr 6000Rp; ☺ 8am-midnight) Plus postal services and *wartel*.
Warnet Mesra Indah (Mesra Indah Mall, 2nd floor; per hr 6000Rp; ☺ 9am-9pm) Pornography ads start sessions and persist; also postal services and *wartel*.

MEDICAL SERVICES
Rumah Sakit Haji Darjad (☎ 732-698; Jln Dahlia) Modern, massive hospital. Off Jln Basuki Rahmat.
RS Bhakti Nguraha (☎ 741-363; Jln Basuki Rahmat 150) Clinic.

MONEY
There are plenty of ATMs in town. For foreign exchange:
Bank Central Asia (BCA; Jln Sudirman)
Bank Negara Indoneasia (BNI; cnr Jln P Sebatik & Jln Panglima Batur)

POST
Main post office (cnr Jln Gajah Mada & Jln Awang Long)

TOURIST INFORMATION
Tourist office (☎ 736-850; cnr Jln Sudirman & Jln Awang Long) Kalimantan's best tourism office with knowledgeable, friendly staff (some English-speaking), helpful maps and accurate information.

TRAVEL AGENCIES
Many Samarinda travel agencies offer tours upriver. For air tickets:
Angkasa Express (☎ 200-281; aexsri@telkom.net; Plaza Lembuswana)
Prima Tour & Travel (☎ 737-777; prima_sriol@yahoo .co.id; Hotel MJ, Jln Khalid 1)

Tours
Independent guides have made Samarinda the main starting point for touring the mighty Mahakam and beyond. **Junaid Nawawi** (☎ 085-2502-49370; junaid.nawawi@plasa.com; Hotel Pirus;

ORANGUTAN FACTS

Three per cent: that's all that separates human DNA from orangutan, which means 'person of the forest' in Malay. Looking into their soulful brown eyes or seeing one use a banana leaf as an umbrella seemingly confirms the intelligence of humans' third-closest relative, casting it as a distant redheaded cousin rather than a powerful, wild animal.

The only great apes outside Africa, orangutans once ranged throughout Southeast Asia but species survive only on Sumatra *(Pongo abelii)* and Borneo *(Pongo pygmaeus)*. As few as 15,000 wild orangutans survive, compared with 250,000 a century ago.

Males of this gingery, long-haired species grow to 80kg and 1.5m, with an arm span of more than 2m. They sport black cheek pads and throat pouches for their booming long calls, heard for up to 2km, warning off rivals. Females are smaller and grow beards. Their eight-year birth cycle, the longest among mammals, exposes the species to extinction.

Nature's largest arboreal animal, orangutans rarely come to the ground, building up to a half-dozen nests daily for sleeping. They are crucial to the rainforest as seed dispersers, and the forest is crucial to them. They forage over large ranges, eating more than 200 varieties of fruit, bark and leaves, plus occasional insects and meat.

According to 'The Last Stand of the Orangutan', a 2007 United Nations Environmental Program (UNEP) report, humans are destroying orangutans' rainforest habitat at a rapidly accelerating rate. By 2022 – 10 years earlier than a 2002 UNEP projection – researchers estimate 98 percent of Borneo's rainforest will be gone, thanks to human destruction.

What's in that 3% difference that's making it so difficult for us and our redheaded cousins to get along?

2-5pm), **Suryadi** (☎ 081-6459-8263) and **Rustam** (☎ 735-641; 081-2585-4915) get good reviews.

Mesra Tours (☎ 738-787; fax 741-017; www.mesra .com/tour; Hotel Mesra, Jln Pahlawan 1) runs full service Sungai Mahakam tours, treks to West Kalimantan, Apokayan Highlands and beyond, and books flights.

Sights

On the south side of Sungai Mahakam, Samarinda-style sarongs are woven in **Samarinda Seberang**. Take a yellow *angkot* from Pasar Pagi.

Every Sunday at 2pm, **Pampang**, 26km west of Samarinda, has Kenyah Dayak ceremonies at its longhouse. These are not made-for-tourist performances, and rituals are relatively unadulterated. Do offer a small donation for snapping photographs. Public minibuses to Pampang leave from Segiri terminal (7000Rp, one hour). Chartering a taxi or Kijang with other travellers for 100,000Rp is an alternative.

Sleeping

Hotels in Samarinda, particularly budget choices, trend towards old and tired. Nostalgic backpackers can probably have the same room, maybe the same mattress, their parents enjoyed.

BUDGET

Hanyani Hotel (☎ 742-653; Jln Pirus 31; r 70,000-140,000Rp; 🟥) Large rooms in this cavernous place include *mandi* and a choice of one or two beds. Fan-cooled economy rooms are often cleaner on the 3rd floor. Request discounts.

Hotel Gelora (☎ 742-024; gelora@smd.mega.net.id; Jln Niaga Selatan 62; r 75,000-200,000Rp; 🟥) Overlooking Citra Niaga market and routinely overlooked by foreigners, Gelora is a well-kept secret. All rooms include *mandi*; rooms with air-con start from 99,000Rp.

More choices:

Aida (☎ 742-572; Jln KH Mas Tumenggung; r incl breakfast from 75,000Rp; 🟥) Variety of rooms, marginally cleaner than neighbours.

Hotel Hidayah I (☎ 731-210, 731-261; Jln KH Mas Temenggung; s incl breakfast 100,000-155,000Rp, d 125,000-190,000Rp; 🟥) Skidding downhill. Guides still frequent its balcony (coffee) bar.

Hotel Hidayah II (☎ 741-712; Jln Khalid 25; s from 75,000Rp, d 125,000-175,000Rp; 🟥) Clean but worn.

MIDRANGE

Hotel Mega Sentosa (☎ 749-218; fax 749219; Jln Veteran 88; r incl breakfast 150,000-225,000Rp, ste incl breakfast 300,000-375,000Rp; 🟥) On a quiet street near Pasir Pagi and with helpful staff, its generous rooms are worth hiking the flight or two of steps. The restaurant (mains 12,000Rp to

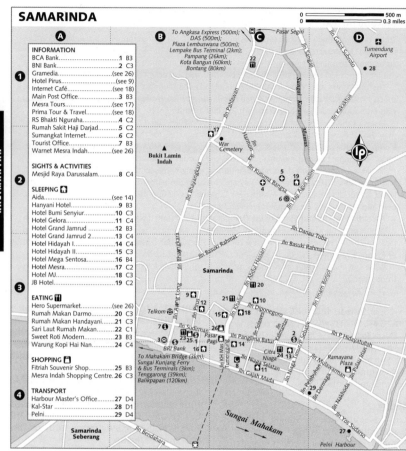

SAMARINDA

0 ——————— 500 m
0 ——————— 0.3 miles

INFORMATION
BCA Bank.......................................**1** B3
BNI Bank..**2** C3
Gramedia....................................(see 26)
Hotel Pirus.................................(see 9)
Internet Café..............................(see 18)
Main Post Office............................**3** B3
Mesra Tours...............................(see 17)
Prima Tour & Travel....................(see 18)
RS Bhakti Nguraha.........................**4** C2
Rumah Sakit Haji Darjad................**5** C2
Sumangkat Internet......................**6** C2
Tourist Office................................**7** B3
Warnet Mesra Indah....................(see 26)

SIGHTS & ACTIVITIES
Mesjid Raya Darussalam.................**8** C4

SLEEPING
Aida...(see 14)
Hanyani Hotel...............................**9** B3
Hotel Bumi Senyiur.......................**10** C3
Hotel Gelora.................................**11** C4
Hotel Grand Jamrud......................**12** B3
Hotel Grand Jamrud 2...................**13** C3
Hotel Hidayah I.............................**14** C4
Hotel Hidayah II............................**15** C3
Hotel Mega Sentosa......................**16** B4
Hotel Mesra..................................**17** C2
Hotel MJ......................................**18** C3
JB Hotel..**19** C2

EATING
Hero Supermarket.......................(see 26)
Rumah Makan Darmo.....................**20** C3
Rumah Makan Handayani...............**21** C3
Sari Laut Rumah Makan..................**22** C1
Sweet Roti Modern........................**23** B3
Warung Kopi Hai Nan.....................**24** C4

SHOPPING
Fitriah Souvenir Shop.....................**25** B3
Mesra Indah Shopping Centre........**26** C3

TRANSPORT
Harbour Master's Office.................**27** D4
Kal-Star.......................................**28** D1
Pelni..**29** D4

To Angkasa Express (500m);
DAS (500m);
Plaza Lembuswana (500m);
Lempake Bus Terminal (2km);
Pampang (26km);
Kota Bangun (60km);
Bontang (80km)

Pasar Segiri

Tumendung
Airport

Bukit Lamin
Indah

War
Cemetery

Samarinda

Telkom

Pasar
Pagi

BRI Bank

To Mahakam Bridge (3km);
Sungai Kunjang Ferry
& Bus Terminals (3km);
Tenggarong (39km);
Balikpapan (120km)

Samarinda
Seberang

Ramayana
Plaza

Citra
Niaga

Sungai Mahakam

Pelni Harbour

30,000Rp) offers buffet breakfast and 24-hour room service.

JB Hotel (☎ 737-688; jbhotel_samarinda@yahoo.com; Jln Agus Salim 16; r 150,000-240,000Rp; ✷) New and bright, JB caters to domestic business-travellers with smart rooms. Add 30,000Rp for buffet breakfast for two, or skip it and try nearby *warung*.

Hotel Grand Jamrud (☎ 743-828; fax 743-837; Jln Jamrud 34; r incl breakfast 160,000-315,000Rp; ✷) Immaculately maintained in a quiet location, Grand Jamrud attracts government travellers and business meetings. Economy rooms run boxy but comfortable.

Hotel Grand Jamrud 2 (☎ 731-233; fax 736-096; Jln Panglima Batur 45; r incl breakfast 200,000-389,000Rp; ✷) Has simple and spotless rooms in a nightlife node.

Hotel MJ (☎ 747-689, www.mjhotel.com; Jln Khalid 1; r incl breakfast 240,000-349,000Rp, ste incl breakfast 465,000-575,000Rp plus 21% tax; ✷ ☐) Catering to business travellers, MJ has sunlit rooms with inoffensive décor. There's a restaurant, a travel agent, an internet café and a boutique on the ground floor, and a free computer terminal in the lobby. Suites are discounted 20% on weekends.

TOP END
Hotel Mesra (☎ 732-772; www.mesra.com/hotel; Jln Pahlawan 1; r incl breakfast 320,000-630,000Rp, cottages 850,000Rp, ste 1,648,000Rp; ✷ ☒) On a green hill overlooking downtown, Hotel Mesra has a rustic resort-feel in comfortable rooms and oversized cottages with KalTim touches. Outsiders can use the pool (15,000Rp).

Hotel Bumi Senyiur (☎ 741-443; www.senyiurhotels .com; Jln Diponegoro 17-19; r incl breakfast 615,000-880,000Rp, ste incl breakfast from 1,348,000Rp plus 21% tax; 🌐 🖳 🎇) Indonesia's president stays here when visiting Samarinda, and so would you if someone else paid. Rooms are tastefully indulgent with local accents including *meranti* (red hardwood) floors and rattan or wooden furniture.

Eating

For trendy dining after dark–food stalls with everything from sizzling *udang galah* (giant river prawns) to chic fusion – try Jln Juanda on *angkot* route A.

Rumah Makan Handayani (☎ 732-452; Jln Abdul Hassan 7; mains 7,000-15,000Rp; 🕑 breakfast, lunch & dinner) Cheerful and cheap central Java entry in culinary *tour de Indonesia* running north from Mesra Indah Mall. Find Banjar, Padang, Bugis and more along the route, with most open until late at night.

our pick **Rumah Makan Darmo** (☎ 737-287; Jln Abdul Hassan 38; mains 12,000-20,000Rp; 🕑 lunch & dinner) Quality far exceeds prices at this rare Chinese restaurant attuned to individual diners and couples. Fresh seafood is the speciality, and there's smoke-free air-con upstairs.

Sari Laut Rumah Makan (☎ 735-848; Jln Pahlawan; mains 25,000-40,000Rp; 🕑 dinner) The name 'Seafood' is its claim to fame. *Udang galah* served fragrant, spicy or Padang-style nets Samarindans and Javanese tourists.

Citra Niaga's many *warung* serve local specialities and Indonesian standards.

Self-catering and snacks:

Warung Kopi Hai Nan (Jln Niaga Utara 50) Chinese-Indonesian-Western bakery and coffee shop.

Sweet Roti Modern (Jln Sudirman 8) This bakery's aroma perfumes the street.

Hero supermarket (Mesra Indah Mall)

Shopping

Mesra Indah Shopping Centre has a mix of local and chain stores, plus a food court. Citra Niaga shops sell Dayak rattan, *doyo*, carvings and other souvenirs. **Fitriah Souvenir Shop** (Jln Sudirman 10) offers high-quality items with price tags to match.

Getting There & Away

AIR

Kal-Star (☎ 742-110; Jln Gatot Subroto 80) flies to Tarakan (660,000Rp), Berau and Nunukan (796,000Rp). **DAS** (☎ 736-989; Blk D, No 8, Jln Komplek Lembuswana) has twice weekly services to Data

Dawai (184,000Rp). DAS also flies to Long Ampung (206,000Rp) five times weekly, and Balikpapan (193,000Rp), Putussibau (690,000Rp) and Pontianak (965,000Rp).

BOAT

Pelni (☎ 741-402; Jln Yos Sudarso 76) routes visit Pare Pare (127,500Rp, 21 hours), Surabaya (258,000Rp, 24 hours), Toli Toli (134,000Rp, 24 hours), Tarakan (259,000Rp, 24 hours) and Nunukan (225,000Rp, 24 hours).

In addition, there's a twice-weekly private service to Pare Pare (125,000Rp, 24 hours). Just ask the **harbour master** (Jln Yos Sudarso 2) for details.

Mahakam river ferries (*kapal biasa*) leave at 7am from Sungai Kunjang terminal (3km via *angkot*) for Tenggarong (20,000Rp, two hours), Melak (100,000Rp, 16 hours), Long Iram (120,000Rp, 18 hours) and – sometimes – Long Bagun (350,000Rp, 36 hours).

BUS

Samarinda has multiple bus terminals. Sungai Kunjang terminal serves Kota Bagun (20,000Rp, three hours) and Balikpapan (19,500Rp, two hours). Use Lempake terminal at the north end of town for Bontang (20,000Rp, three hours), Sangatta (25,000Rp, four hours), and Berau (135,000Rp, 16 hours). Buses leave as filled from 7am until early afternoon. Minibuses to Tenggarong (10,000Rp, one hour) depart Harapan Baru terminal on the south bank of Sungai Makaham, reached via *angkot* route G. Minibuses for Sunday afternoon Dayak rituals at Pampang (7000Rp, one hour) leave from Segiri terminal at the north end of Jln Pahlawan.

Getting Around

Minibuses, called *angkot* or taxis (3000Rp, watch for overcharging), converge at Pasar Pagi.

Taxis from **Tumendung Airport** (3km) cost 35,000Rp. Alternatively, walk 100m to Jln Gatot Subroto, turn left and catch *angkot* B into town.

KUTAI NATIONAL PARK

Lauded by wild orangutan buffs, Kutai National Park's 198,000 hectares include coastal mangroves, Indonesia's largest, relatively untouched ironwood forest, plus a wide variety of wild orchids. The park was hit hard by the fires of 1997–98, but has recovered

KALIMANTAN

to face renewed threat from illegal loggers and wildcat miners. Kutai is surrounded by energy extraction – coal, oil, gas – and park authorities have enlisted companies in preservation efforts.

Besides orangutans, Kutai has at least a half-dozen primate species from leaf to proboscis monkeys to slow loris, mainly in the coastal areas. Sun bear, deer, flat-headed cat and other mammals are found throughout the park. Abundant bird-life includes sea eagle, stork, and myna. Treks feature encounters with golf ball–size, tiger-striped beetles straight out of Alice's Wonderland. It's also possible to spot wildlife by motorised canoe along the park's numerous waterways.

Kutai has visitor facilities at **Sangkimah**. Take a bus from Samarinda's Lempake terminal to Bontang (20,000Rp, three hours) to register at the **National Park office** (PHKA; ☎ 0548-27218; Jln Mularman 236; ☷ 7.30am-4pm Mon-Thu, 8am-noon Fri). Registration is free, but a passport photocopy is required. Call ahead for weekend arrivals.

Guides are not required inside Kutai but finding orangutans without one is difficult. PHKA charges 50,000Rp per day (or 100,000Rp for trekking), plus transport costs. It's possible to charter a boat from the PHKA office into the park for 200,000Rp.

Overnight accommodation is at **basic guesthouses** (dm 100,000Rp) at Sangkimah or Camp Kakap near Sangatta, one hour further north along the main highway. Facilities are rudimentary; bring your own food.

Exploring Kutai from **Sangatta** was a more attractive option when Papa Charlie, a beloved boatman on Sungai Sangatta, ran gameviewing day trips. He's no longer on the scene, and no-one has adequately replaced him. Without that attractive choice, there's not much reason to come to Sangatta, a booming coal town. **Pak Willis** (☎ 081-3474-23297) supervises University of Kyoto research facilities at Camp Kakap and can arrange visits. The 20-minute boat ride from Kabo Jaya, a fishing village east of town, to Camp Kakak costs 300,000Rp (return), or about 500,000Rp from Sangatta's riverside market.

In Sangatta, **Golden Hotel** (☎ 0549-25000; Jln Dipnegoro; r incl breakfast 125,000-250,000Rp; ☷) is the best value for accommodation. **Warung Akrab** (Jln IA Muis II 20; mains from 7000Rp; ☷ breakfast, lunch & dinner) dishes up great and cheap local fish. Swim upmarket for fish and seafood at **Warung Diponegoro** (Jln APT Pranoto; mains from 15,000Rp; ☷ lunch & dinner) – look for the young coconuts and barbecue grill outside. **Dayak Coffee Shop and Restaurant** (☎ 0549-21333; Hotel Kutai Permai; Jln Yos Sudarso I; mains from 20,000Rp; ☷ breakfast, lunch & dinner) exudes country class within wood-panelled walls.

TENGGARONG
☎ 0541 / pop 75,000

Once capital of the mighty Kutai sultanate, Tenggarong is first stop on many Mahakam river boats. The main attractions are a museum in the former palace and the Erau Festival that brings thousands of Dayaks to town. Some travellers adopt Tenggarong as a laid-back alternative to Samarinda, most skip it altogether.

Orientation & Information
Bank Danamon (Jln Ahmad Yani) ATM.
Kumala Net Cafe (Komplek Pertokaan Pasar Tangga Arung, Kios 5, Jln Maduningrat; per hr 10,000Rp; ☷ 9am-10pm)
Lippo Bank (Jln Sudirman) ATM.
Tourist office (☎ 661-042; fax 661-093; Jln Ahmad Yani 12) Information on Erau Festival and other attractions.

Sights
Guarded by ceramic dragons and snakes, **Mulawarman Museum** (Jln Diponegoro; admission 2500Rp; ☷ 9am-4pm, closed Mon & Friday) honours the Kutai sultanate that ruled for 19 generations and continues to occupy local pride of place. Royal remnants in this stolid former palace include an elaborate puppet theatre with gamelan, a gift from Yogyakarta's sultan. The basement holds royal porcelain, including Yuan, Han, Ming and Qing dynasty water-jars. Topping it off is an (unintentionally) amusing exhibit of traditional headwear from every Indonesian province.

Behind the museum, the royal cemetery, souvenir shops and *warung* lead to the latest **Kedaton Kertanegara** (Sultan's Palace). The ornate building with finely crafted wooden balconies and stained-glass windows is vacant, except during Erau Festival, when the sultan takes up temporary residence.

Festivals & Events
Once a year, Dayaks travel to Tenggarong from throughout Kalimantan for the **Erau Festival**. Though touristy, it's a chance to see traditional dances and ritual ceremonies and join a vast intertribal party. Events take

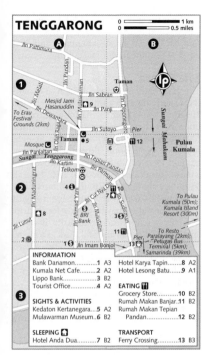

TENGGARONG

INFORMATION
Bank Danamon............1 A3	Hotel Karya Tapin........8 A2
Kumala Net Cafe.........2 A2	Hotel Lesong Batu.......9 A1
Lippo Bank..................3 B2	
Tourist Office..............4 A2	**EATING**
	Grocery Store...........10 B2
SIGHTS & ACTIVITIES	Rumah Makan Banjar..11 B2
Kedaton Kertanegara...5 A2	Rumah Makan Tepian
Mulawarman Museum..6 B2	Pandan.................12 B2
SLEEPING	**TRANSPORT**
Hotel Anda Dua.........7 B2	Ferry Crossing...........13 B3

place at the *kedaton* (walled city palace) and around town.

The festival is usually held in late September for one to two weeks. Tourist offices in Tenggarong or Samarinda can provide upcoming dates.

Sleeping

Hotel Anda Dua (☎ 661409; Jln Sudirman 65; r 60,000-150,000Rp; ﹛) Basic, fan-cooled rooms with shared *mandi* occupy the rustic front section of this friendly hotel behind a **grocery store**. Further back, 'Anda Dua Plus' has comfortable air-con rooms with private bathroom and breakfast included.

Hotel Karya Tapin (☎ 661-258; Jln Maduningrat 29; r incl breakfast 175,000-200,000Rp plus 10% tax; ﹛) Spotless rooms at this small hotel include high ceilings, TV, showers and homely touches. The location on a bustling side street has many *warung*.

Kumala Island Resort (☎ 708-2401; Pulau Kumala; r from 500,000Rp; ﹛ ﹜) On the southern tip of Pulau Kamala – home to a kitsch amusement park – this hotel has comfortable, generic rooms with private balconies and fancier cottages.

Hotel Lesong Batu (☎ 663-499; www.kutaikartanegara .com/lesongbatu; Jln Panji 1; r incl breakfast 532,000-602,000Rp, ste 2,108,000Rp; ﹛) Rooms are appropriately enormous and opulent for a hotel that boasts a sultan's suite. Less explicably, there's a 1940s red Plymouth parked in the lobby.

Eating

Rumah Makan Tepian Pandan (Jln Diponegoro 23; mains 10,000-20,000Rp; ﹛ breakfast, lunch & dinner) A relaxed, open-air *warung* serving Kutai cuisine, a local spin on Indonesian standards, with a side dish of river views.

Rumah Makan Banjar (☎ 661-782; Jln Sudirman 62; meals 15,000Rp-25,000Rp; ﹛ lunch & dinner) Family-run place has high and low tables and a cheerful atmosphere for savouring grilled fish and chicken.

Resto Paralayang (☎ 665-005; Jln Pahawan, Bukit Biru; mains from 20,000Rp; ﹛ lunch & dinner) Décor and food are both special at Tenggarong's classiest restaurant, in a house with woven rattan walls and an open courtyard. Choose cushions on the floor or booths with embroidered *doyo* lampshades. Menu features Indonesian-style seafood.

Find *warung* along Jln Maduningrat and Jln Cut Nya Din, near Jln Sudirman.

Getting There & Away

Kijangs to/from Samarinda (10,000Rp, 1¼ hours) wait at Petugas bus terminal, 5km south of Tenggarong's centre. From here, take an *angkot* into town (2500Rp). *Ojek* cost 5000Rp. Kijangs from Petugas terminal also serve Kota Bangun (15,000Rp, two hours). In Samarinda, Tenggaraong Kijangs terminate at the end of *angkot* route G, on Sungai Mahakam's south bank.

Mahakam *kapal biasa* from Samarinda (20,000Rp, two hours) stop 2km north of town, with *angkot* (2,500Rp) to the town centre. Next stop upriver is Kota Bangun (40,000Rp, five to six hours).

SUNGAI MAHAKAM

The 920km-long Sungai Mahakam provides easy access – by Kalimantan standards – to the natural wonders and traditional communities of southeast Borneo and beyond. Much of the riverbank, especially near Samarinda, bears scars of industrialisation and resource exploitation. Veering onto tributaries and small lakes transports travellers back into jungle and societies that resist the 21st century.

KALIMANTAN

Passenger boats leave Samarinda daily at 7am. These *kapal biasa* are 4m wide and at least four times as long, comfortable, with an open lower deck for sitting. Sarongs or newspapers can mark out territory. A canteen serves mainly instant noodle variations. On the upper level, simple mattresses are laid across the floor for sleeping. If you're making an overnight journey, head directly upstairs to stake a claim. Bedding is surprisingly clean (usually), the atmosphere laid-back and friendly. In recent years, upgraded boat engines have slashed travel times.

Much of the year, *kapal biasa* terminate at Long Iram (120,000Rp, 18 hours), 409km from Samarinda. When the river is right, boats continue to Long Bagun, 523km upstream (350,000Rp, 36 hours) where rapids stop them. These volatile waters and the rough terrain around them shelter this section of the river from exploitation.

To explore further, charter a motorised canoe, usually called a *ces* (pronounced 'chess'). It's an 18-hour trip from Long Bagun to **Long Pahangai** through some of the most volatile portions of the river. Only attempt this stretch with seasoned local boaters. Running with the current back to Long Bagun takes six or seven hours.

Ces continue upriver to Long Apari, a focal point for cross-Borneo trips. From there it's about a three-day walk to the West Kalimantan headwaters of Sungai Kapuas at Tanjung Lokan.

On the lower Mahakam, it's easy to travel by *kapal biasa*. In the upper reaches, Bahasa Indonesia and/or guides are essential. Some travellers hire guides along the river, others take them from the start. (See p269 and p272 for information about guides and tour operators.) Expect to pay guides at least 150,000Rp daily (plus food, transport and accommodation). Even without a guide, Mahakam travel gets expensive beyond the *kapal biasa*, with charter rates from 100,000Rp per hour for a *ces* and 1,000,000Rp per hour for a speedboat. The cost of a guide may be offset by his ability to negotiate better deals on boat hires and other transport.

Some travellers complain of disappointing trips with cheap guides, but high prices don't guarantee quality. Discuss the trip and expectations with the guide – and see if they're someone you'd like at your side under sometimes fantastic, often difficult conditions.

Along the way, ask about village festivals and celebrations. In the face of modernisation, such events are the best opportunities to observe genuine traditional culture.

Kota Bangun

The dusty entry point to Mahakam lake country, Kota Bangun is a transport interchange. Heading to or from Samarinda, travellers often elect the bus ride to/from Samarinda (20,000Rp, three hours) over seven to eight hours via *kapal biasa*. From Kota Bangun, bargain for a *ces* to ride the 'backroads' via Muara Muntai (250,000Rp, 1½ hours), Tanjung Isuy (450,000Rp, three hours), and Mancong (650,000Rp; six hours). From August to October waters may be too low for the trip. Maskur, a schoolteacher in Kota Bangun, speaks good English and will work as a guide.

To try spotting the critically endangered Irrawaddy dolphin (*Ocaella brevirostris*; *pesut* in Bahasa Indonesia), take a *ces* – never a speedboat for dolphins – to Muara Muntai via Danau Semayang and Sungai Pela. Dolphins are sometimes seen in these waters, but better dolphin-watching lies ahead at Maura Pahu (opposite).

Alternatively, charter a *ces* for about 450,000Rp and bring lunch for an excursion north. Motor about 1½ hours to Muara Kaman, the site of Kalimantan's first Hindu kingdom, with renowned fishing to the north. It's about 30 minutes through Kedang Kepala to Danau Siran. Enjoy abundant birdlife, monkeys and spectacular sunsets, but be warned: the losmen in Muara Kaman is dismal.

In Kota Bangun, **Losmen Muzirat** (☎ 081-2553-2287; Jln Mesjid Raya 46; s/d 20,000/40,000Rp), opposite the main mosque, has clean, basic rooms with shared *mandi* and brusque staff.

Muara Muntai

Built on mud flats, Muara Muntai is a colourful market town in the heart of Mahakam lake country, with sturdy boardwalks for streets and many fine wooden buildings, such as the Bappeda (Agency for Regional Development) office straight ahead from the dock. Muara Muntai goes quiet during afternoon prayers but the boardwalks fill up after dark. That's especially true when the weekly night market takes place; appropriately, the day market also floats.

Penginapan Adi Guna (☎ 0541-205871, 081-5451-46578; r 50,000Rp) Has basic fan-cooled rooms and large shared *mandi*. There's free flowing coffee and tea, best enjoyed on the balcony. To find it, follow the boardwalk from the dock and turn right.

To the left of the docks, the smaller **Penginapan Tiara** (☎ 081-3473-76794; s/d 30,000/50,000Rp) also offers simple fan-cooled rooms, shared *mandi* and balcony. It's less breezy than Adi Guna.

Reach Muara Muntai from Samarinda by *kapal biasa* (70,000Rp, 10 hours) or bus to Kota Bangun (20,000Rp, three hours) and *ces* from there (200,000Rp, two hours). Chartering a *ces* here for lake cruising costs about 500,000Rp per day.

Tanjung Isuy

On the southwest shore of Danau Jempang, Tanjung Isuy is the Mahakam's first Dayak village. Don't expect traditional dress and tattoos, but mobile phones and motorcycles. The embracing of modern conveniences in this Banuaq Dayak territory remains largely skin deep, though, with community identity intact. Local life still means rising with the roosters, watching the river flow, and chatting on the front porch, catching the night breeze.

Tour groups arrive by speedboat in Tanjung Isuy for an 'authentic' Dayak experience. Most mob the longhouse souvenir stalls, watch a pay-by-the-hour mix of Dayak dancing, and zoom away. Activity focuses on **Louu Taman Jamrout**, a longhouse vacated in the 1970s, and rebuilt by provincial authorities as a craft centre and tourist hostel.

Performances in Louu Taman Jamrout are certainly commercial, but they are also lively, rhythmic and fun for all. Aficionados and social anthropologists may find the combination of Kenyah, Kayan and Banuaq dance disconcerting, but it's unmistakeably entertaining. Independent travellers can commission a dance for 350,000Rp.

The cruise between Muara Muntai and Tanjung Isuy crosses lush wetlands, shallow lakes and **Jantur**, a Banjar village built on a flooded mud flat. Jantur's **mesjid** (mosque), on a bend in the river, is accessible only by boat. The cemetery next door is the highest point in town, a proud 20cm above water level at the end of wet season. Bodies buried here must be anchored in their graves to prevent bobbing to the surface.

Tanjung Isuy has two good losmen. About 500m from the jetty, **Losmen Wisata** (Jln Indonesia Australia; s/d 35,000/50,000Rp) offers rooms with double beds off a central dining area. The airy common space has wall-to-wall windows for superior views, and a long, conversation-inducing table. Just next door is **Louu Taman Jamrout** (Jln Indonesia Australia; per person 60,000Rp), where the Dayak performances are held. Both have shared *mandi*, mosquito nets, a roughly equal number of boosters, and can suggest the best of nearby *warung*.

Doyo weavings and *mandau* with carved handles (as well as a lot of junk) are available at reasonable prices at the craft centre next to Louu Taman Jamrout. Down the road toward the dock, a house across from the first intersection sells carvings and weavings.

Tanjung Isuy is not on the *kapal biasa* route from Samarinda. Chartering a *ces* from Muara Muntai (200,000Rp, 1½ to two hours) is the easiest way to get here. A public *ces* to Muara Muntai leaves daily in the early evening (from 60,000Rp, depending on the number of passengers). You can charter a *ces* direct to Kota Bangun (450,000Rp, three hours), then catch a bus and be in Samarinda or Balikpapan that night. In dry season, Tanjung Isuy is 30 minutes by Kijang or *ojek* from Mancong.

Muara Pahu

The Mahakam's confluence with Sungai Kedang Pahu is the top spot along the river to view *pesut*, the Irrawaddy dolphin species without the bottle nose of its saltwater cousins. An estimated 55 to 75 of these critically endangered species remain, mainly in this small section of wetland from Danau Semayang through the various tributaries to Muara Pahu.

Into the 1980s, *pesut* were common all along the Mahakam to Samarinda. They have been a completely protected species under Indonesian law since 1990 and are a provincial symbol for KalTim. But they suffer high mortality rates due to gill-net entanglement and, to a lesser extent, boat collisions. More long term, their habitat is threatened by pollution from speedboats and coal-carrying tugboats, chemical waste from mining, depletion of their prey through unsustainable fishing techniques, and sedimentation in lakes.

Yayasan Konservasi RASI (YK-RASI; Conservation Foundation for Rare Aquatic Species of Indonesia; www.geocities .com/yayasan_konservasi_rasi) fights to save the *pesut* see p281. It hopes to create a 70km conservation-area along the Mahakam and tributaries, centred on Muara Pahu, where YK-RASI has opened the **Mahakam Information Centre** with a riverside veranda for dolphin-watching.

The centre arrange *ces* charters around Muara Pahu lasting from one hour to all day (100,000Rp to 450,000Rp), starting with Sungai Bolowan to the Kedang Pahu. Alternatively, Jintan is a black-water river leading into peat swamp. For long trips, bring lunch and plenty of water.

It's also possible to combine dolphin-watching with transport to Maura Muntai or Tanjung Isuy (300,000Rp) via Sungai Baroh, rich with birds and monkeys; to Melak (400,000Rp); and south to Dayak villages Damai or Lambing (500,000Rp). Trained boatmen go slow for wildlife viewing, so travel times vary.

Kapal biasa to/from Samarinda (80,000Rp, 12 hours) pass Muara Pahu in the early evening. **Pension Anna** (r 60,000Rp) has decent rooms.

Mancong

Riverside jungle teeming with birdlife makes journeying to Mancong, a scenic highlight of Mahakam lake country, worth the time and money required. Trees along Sungai Ohong host proboscis monkeys, majestic hornbills soar above, dazzling kingfishers skim the water for prey, and ibis laze around docks hoping for handouts.

A village of about 500, Mancong resembles life on the Mahakam before logging, oil and coal became dominant. The forest still surrounds the village almost entirely. A two-storey **longhouse** is the grandest structure, rebuilt with government assistance in 1987 on the ruins of the 1930s original. The longhouse was abandoned as families built separate houses and is now reserved for folk dances and ceremonies. The dozen totems in front each signifies a buffalo slaughtered. Just one family lives in the longhouse, so it's among the cleanest, most orderly in Borneo. Overnight guests are welcome (60,000Rp per person; no bedding, food or electricity). Ask the family for permission to stay, or if no-one is inside, inquire at the souvenir shack by the jetty.

To visit Mancong, charter a *ces* from Tanjung Isuy (250,000Rp return) early in the morning. Ask the boater to go slowly to enjoy the scenery, lengthening the trip to about three hours each way. In the dry season, it's possible to travel to/from Tanjung Isuy by *ojek* (100,000Rp, 30 minutes).

UPPER MAHAKAM
Melak & Around

The early morning wail of 4WDs and slosh of mixing concrete drown out bird songs in Melak, far different from fishing villages along the route from Samarinda. Hosting a colourful market on Tuesdays, Melak is a good supply stop for trips further north. Areas surrounding Melak are the real reason to stop here.

The **orchid reserve** at Kersik Luway (16km southwest), particularly noted for black orchids, was badly damaged in the fires of 1997–98. Recovery remains slow. Prime season is around February, with scattered blooms year-round.

Tiny **Eheng** (30km southwest) remains a bastion of traditional tattoos and elongated ear lobes. It has a patched longhouse built in 1960 and housing 30 families, although they spend most of their time away, farming rice or collecting rattan and other forest products. They return Monday nights to gossip, gamble and get set for Tuesday's weekly market. Residents welcome visitors to join the fun or even spend the night, but Bahasa Indonesia is required. You'll need to pay for your stay (rates vary) provide your own bedding and food, plus gifts (see p35). Reach Eheng from Melak by minibus (12,000Rp, one hour) via Barong Tongkok. Chartering an *ojek* in Melak costs about 75,000Rp a day, a 4WD costs 300,000Rp.

Near Eheng, **Mencimai** has an excellent **museum** (admission by donation; ☉ 8am-2pm Mon-Fri) with explanations in English and Bahasa Indonesia of Banuaq methods of shifting cultivation, collecting wild honey, trapping pigs (and monkeys), and producing *doyo*. It also displays antique *mandau*, rattan and other relics.

From Barong Tongkok, minibuses run south to Damai and Muara Lawa (22,000Rp, two to three hours) with an old rattan longhouse. Both villages have losmen.

In Melak, **Penginapan Setiawan** (☎ 0545-41437; Jln Dr Sutomo; r 50,000Rp) is the newest losmen with spacious rooms off a bright, open corridor. Tea, coffee and boiled drinking water flow freely. Rooms are older at **Penginapan Blue Safir** (☎ 0545-41098; Jln Dr Sutomo; r 50,000Rp) next door. About 100m nearer the jetty, **Warung Banjar** (Jln Dr Sutomo; mains 10,000Rp; ☉ lunch & dinner) serves great barbecued catfish with soup and rice.

PRESERVING THE PESUT *Budiono*

As a child, I played in Balikpapan Bay's mangroves, always looking for colourful fish. Alarmed by forest destruction through timber companies' failure to practice selective logging and reforestation, plus illegal logging and lack of law enforcement, I chose to study Forestry Management, focused on conservation, at Mulawarman University in Samarinda.

Assisting with coastal dolphin research, I was fascinated by their intelligence and social behaviour. I got interested in Sungai Mahakam dolphins, too. After participating in *pesut Mahakam* research in 2000, I founded a local NGO with my wife, Danielle Kreb, who took her PhD on these dolphins. Through research and awareness campaigns, we try to help preserve the *pesut*.

I hope that responsible, sustainable ecotourism will increase local community and government awareness about dolphin conservation. Area residents welcome additional tourists; some try selling their handicrafts. We've trained local boatmen how to behave when dolphins approach; so far tourists approve of the way boatmen manoeuvre slowly after spotting wildlife.

I've also done bird surveys in Sungai Mahakam, lakes and wetlands since 2001. Birds appeal to me as dynamic, beautiful creatures. Unfortunately, many people like to capture birds. Our job is to explain that birds are legally protected and should be left in peace.

Another big problem we confront is river degradation from excessive logging, mining and plantations. Erosion and floods increase yearly. Poverty also grows due to land loss and decreasing natural resources such as fish.

Despite the problems, I'm optimistic. The government has started investing in alternative resource use for small communities and reforestation projects. These processes take time, and law enforcement remains sporadic. Meanwhile we may have more years of heavy flooding ahead, not so bad for dolphins…

Budiono, founder of Yayasan Konservasi for Rare Aquatic Species of Indonesia (YK-RASI), lives in Samarinda.

Souvenir shops around town sell rattan and *doyo* bags, hats, baskets and more for 25,000Rp to 50,000Rp, depending on size and quality, plus occasional *mandau* and other relics.

Boats leave daily to Samarinda between 11am and 2pm (120,000Rp, 15 hours, 325km). To/ from Tanjung Isuy, charter a *ces* (500,000Rp, four hours).

The daily bus to Samarinda (100,000Rp, nine hours) is an exceedingly uncomfortable ride, much of it on unsealed roads. Minibuses operate between Melak and Tering (9,000Rp, one hour).

Tering & Long Iram

In Sungai Mahakam's gold-mining country, **Long Iram** (120,000Rp, 24 hours from Samarinda) is often the last stop for river boats and travellers. It's a pleasant little village, with a handful of colonial buildings on a bend in the river, below rapids rendered impassable when water gets too high or too low.

From the village centre it's a stroll through market gardens or a short *ces* (60,000Rp, 40 minutes) to **Tering**, three settlements straddling the Mahakam. Walk north along Jln

Soewondo, turn right at the path to the police station and cross scenic bridges to **Danau Gap** (3km). Some residents of **Tering Lama**, a Bahau Dayak village on the northern bank, still sport traditional tattoos and elongated earlobes. The village also has four traditional wooden statues and a magnificent church at its eastern end.

To stay overnight in Long Iram, get dropped at the floating café on the east bank, climb to the main road, turn right and look for the tiny sign (opposite the two-storey shops) for **Penginapan Wahyu** (Jln Soewondo 57; r per person incl breakfast 70,000Rp).

Down the road, **Warung Lestari** has the best food on the Mahakam. Order whatever's on the stove.

Datah Bilang

Datah Bilang is a Protestant community of Kenyah and Bahau Dayaks, who moved from the Apokayan Highlands in the 1970s. Some older women have traditional elongated ear lobes and will charge 15,000Rp to 20,000Rp per photograph. **Long Hubung** (100,000Rp, 45 minutes) is another Bahau Dayak village with a basic **losmen** (r 50,000Rp).

Travellers with a thirst for back roads and good knowledge of Bahasa Indonesia can tackle Sungai Merah northeast into the highlands then cross to Tabang, a rare route that takes around six days. Trekking experience, equipment, food and a Kenyah or Punan guide are essential; ask around in Datah Bilang and expect to pay at least 250,000Rp per day. From Tabang, continue to Kota Bangun via Sungai Belayan (see right).

Long Bagun to Long Apari

When conditions allow, *kapal biasa* from Samarinda reach **Long Bagun** (350,000Rp, 36 hours), a small settlement with an abandoned longhouse, a decent shop for supplies, and quite basic **Penginapan Artomorow** (r 40,000Rp). Rapids and shallows that restrict access for large vessels have also protected forests to the east and dampened the impact of modernisation.

From Long Bagun, travellers can charter boats or trek through the forests. River rapids between Long Bagun and the next major settlement, **Long Pahangai**, are treacherous, and sometimes boating is not possible. When conditions allow, it's a four-hour longboat trip from Long Bagun to Long Pahangai, then another day to Long Apari. **Long Lunuk**, between Long Pahangai and Long Apari, is a good base to visit Kenyah villages. Alternatively, stay at **Tiong Ohang**, two hours upstream from Long Lunuk. **Long Apari**, the uppermost longhouse village on the Mahakam is spectacularly scenic. A boat from Long Lunuk takes five to six hours. From here, cross-Borneo trekkers veer toward West Kalimantan.

To see Sungai Mahakam from the top, fly to Data Dawai, an airstrip near Long Lunuk, with **DAS** (☎ 0541-736989; Block D, No 8, Jln Komplek Lembuswana, Samarinda) from Samarinda (184,000Rp). Check with DAS or travel agents for more options. From Data Dawai, work downriver to Samarinda, or trek overland to the Apokayan Highlands; see p285 for more information.

SUNGAI KEDANG KEPALA

Sungai Kedang Kepala branches north from the Mahakam near **Muara Kaman** and has regular boat service. The trip from Samarinda to **Muara Wahau** takes three days and two nights, via Kenyah and Bahau villages: **Tanjung Manis**, **Long Noran** and **Long Segar**. The main attraction is seeing what few tourists see. Villages are isolated, and many inhabitants have moved

to more convenient locations. Nearby caves held 5th-century Sanskrit finds, now in Tenggarong's museum. To explore independently, charter a motorised canoe for 150,000Rp daily or a speedboat for 1,000,000Rp.

An alternative route from Samarinda to Berau goes north by boat from Muara Wahau to **Miau Baru**. Then try hitching rides to the Dayak village of **Merapun** (two hours). From Merapun, it's 12 hours on Sungai Kelai to Berau.

SUNGAI BELAYAN

An adventurous yet cultural route follows Sungai Belayan, branching northwest from the Mahakam at Kota Bangun, to **Tabang**. Chartered longboats from Samarinda to Tabang (250,000Rp) take three days and two nights. A chartered *ces* from Kota Bangun to Tabang only takes about a day, but the convenience costs more than 1,000,000Rp.

Tabang can also be reached from the upper Mahakam (see p281). Find a guide at either end to trek through traditional rainforests of nomadic Punan Dayaks.

BERAU

☎ 0554 / pop 52,000

So nice they named it twice, Berau is also called Tanjung Redep. At the confluence of Sungai Kelai and Segah forming Sungai Berau, it's visited by tourists solely as a transit point to Pulau Derawan. That requires an overnight stay coming and going, and Berau's relaxed, low-key character lets travellers enjoy the sentence.

Technically, Tanjung Redep is the spit of land between Sungai Kelai and Segah, and that's where the action is. During the day, you won't find many surprises aside from clean streets and accommodating *angkot* drivers. At night, Jln A Yani comes alive with coffee and snack stalls lining the riverfront. Turning the corner onto Jln Antasari, fruit vendors and food stalls offer more substantial fare, leading to the night market on Jln Soetomo. Berau's who's who can tell visitors what's what.

Information

Find ATMs along Jln P Antasari and Jln Maulana.

BNI bank (Jln Maulana) Foreign exchange.

Lia Tours (☎ 2707879; fax 2707283; Hotel Sederhana, Jln P Antasari) Dive resort and flight bookings.

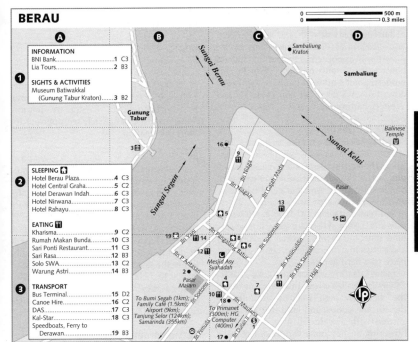

BERAU

INFORMATION
BNI Bank....................................1 C3
Lia Tours..................................2 B3

SIGHTS & ACTIVITIES
Museum Batiwakkal
(Gunung Tabur Kraton)......3 B2

SLEEPING
Hotel Berau Plaza....................4 C3
Hotel Central Graha................5 C2
Hotel Derawan Indah..............6 C3
Hotel Nirwana.........................7 C3
Hotel Rahayu...........................8 C3

EATING
Kharisma...................................9 C2
Rumah Makan Bunda............10 C3
Sari Ponti Restaurant.............11 C3
Sari Rasa.................................12 B3
Solo SWA................................13 C2
Warung Astri...........................14 B3

TRANSPORT
Bus Terminal..........................15 D2
Canoe Hire.............................16 C2
DAS...17 C3
Kal-Star..................................18 C3
Speedboats, Ferry to
Derawan..............................19 B3

KALIMANTAN

Primanet (Jln Mangga II; per hr 6500Rp; 24hr)
Internet access with comfy pillows on the floor and air-con.
Tell the *angkot* driver 'Jln Mangaa Dua'.

HG Computer (Jln Mangga II; per hr 7,000Rp; 24hr)
About 100m from Primanet, HG offers both chairs or
floor booths, air-con and a midnight to 6am discount to
6000Rp.

Sights & Activities

Across Sungai Segah, **Museum Batiwakkal** (admission by donation; 8am-1pm Mon-Thur & Sat, 8-11am Fri)
recounts the local sultanate's complex history
with rival Sambaliung.

Sleeping

Rooms usually include morning tea or coffee
and cake; bearers will bang on the door until
you take it.

Hotel Central Graha (22580; Jln A Yani; r 30,000-
135,000Rp;) Tidiest of Berau's cheap digs,
Central Graha has spartan fan-cooled rooms
with shared *mandi*, very comfortable air-
con rooms, plus friendly staff and a riverfront location. Travellers wait for Kijangs to
Tanjung Batu in its lobby, a good spot to swap
road tales.

Hotel Nirwana (21893; fax 22506 Jln Aminuddin 715;
s 40,000-100,000Rp, d 45,000-110,000Rp;) 'The hotel
with the Muslim atmosphere' (management's
slogan despite the Buddhist name) has worn
but clean rooms. Choose between fan and
shared *mandi* upstairs, and fan or air-con with
private *mandi* downstairs.

Hotel Rahayu (21142; cnr Jln Panglima Batur & Jln
Gajah Mada; r 70,000-130,000Rp;) Relatively new,
blindingly efficient and absolutely spotless,
Hotel Rahayu offers great value in a central
but quiet spot. Cosy rooms include private
mandi or Western bath.

Hotel Berau Plaza (23111; Jln P Antasari; r 150,000-
190,000Rp;) See beyond the inconsistent
rooms and relish the funky charm, prime
location, and staff that's warm and casual yet
efficient. All rooms have air-con and private
bathroom. Ask to see the pretty-in-pink VIP
suite with chandelier.

Bumi Segah (24041; fax 21534; Jln Pulau Sampit
747; r incl breakfast 220,000-300,000Rp;) Just outside of town via *angkot*, Berau's newest hotel
has huge, fully featured rooms complete
with amenities. A favourite with travellers
for Berau Coal and the Nature Conservancy,

Bumi Segah represents a new milestone in carbon offsetting.

Hotel Derawan Indah (☎ 24255; Jln Panglima Batur 396; r incl breakfast 250,000–350,000Rp plus 21% tax; ❄ ☎) A swimming pool across the parking lot and lighted tennis court on the roof make this modern hotel a hit with families. Richly endowed rooms include air-con, cable TV and Western bathrooms.

Eating & Drinking

Rumah Makan Bunda (☎ 21305; Jln Antasari 5; mains 12,000–25,000Rp; ☻ lunch & dinner) The menu includes the usual suspects plus Javanese favourites, but focus on fresh fish *lalapan* style with bonus side dishes. Ambience and tableware are miles beyond standard *warung*.

Sari Ponti Restaurant (☎ 23616; Jln Akb Sanipah; mains from 12,000Rp; ☻ lunch & dinner) Chinese seafood stars, but there's chicken, pigeon, beef and a vegetarian menu, too. A family-run that place tries hard to please.

Family Cafe (Jln Pulau Sampit; mains 15,000–30,000Rp; ☻ breakfast, lunch & dinner) Take the *angkot* to the big yellow sign, walk up the hill past the chicken coops, and land in a lily pond garden with a waterfall over fake rocks, flowering bushes and a variety of trees. It's the place to go for a leisurely afternoon or big night out in Berau, as long as you don't need beer: alcohol's not on the menu. Chicken, fish and vegetables are, Indonesian or Western style.

Warung along Jln A Yani and Jln Niaga serve economical Indonesian standards from early morning until late night. **Warung Astri** (Jln A Yani; meals 8000–17,0000Rp) serves them with river views. **Sari Rasa** (Jln Niaga; meals 11,000–14,000Rp) offers breakfast favourite *nasi kuning* with chicken, egg, tempeh, and zesty tomato *sambal* all day.

Among night stalls along Jln Antasari, **Cafe Antasari** (mains 8000–13,000Rp; ☻ dinner), opposite Hotel Berau Plaza, stands out for restaurant-quality fish and seafood done Chinese or Indonesian style. For self-catering, use **Solo SWA** (Jln Sudirman) or **Kharisma** (Jln A Yani).

Getting There & Away
AIR

Kal-Star (☎ 21007; fax 20279; Jln Maulana 45) offers daily flights (except Sunday) to Tarakan (317,500Rp), Tanjung Selor (180,000Rp), Nunukan (380,000Rp), Balikpapan and Samarinda. **Riau Airlines** (☎ 761-855-333; www.riau-airlines.com) flies daily to Balikpapan (500,000Rp).

DAS (☎ /fax 21260; Jln Durian I 26) also flies to Samarinda (498,000Rp).

BOAT

Speedboats (*sepit*) to Pulau Derawan (three hours) wait off Jln A Yani. Negotiations start at 2,000,000Rp one way; anything under 1,000,000Rp is a bargain. Cheaper Derawan transport goes via Kijang to Tanjung Batu, or KM Tasmania I; see opposite for more information.

BUS

The convenient **bus terminal** (Jln Hari Isa) is just south of the market on *angkot* routes. Buses over good roads to Tanjung Selor (50,000Rp, 3½ hours) are scheduled hourly from 7.30am to 10.30am but won't roll with fewer than 15 passengers. Buses to Samarinda (135,000Rp, 16 hours), over atrocious roads, are scheduled 14 times daily, from 10am to 5pm, subject to the same rule. Kijangs (Tanjung Selor 60,000 to 75,000Rp; Samarinda 175,000Rp) gather across from the terminal and demand a minimum of four passengers. Buy multiple seats to leave faster.

Getting Around

Taxis to the airport (9km) cost 40,000Rp. Berau *angkot* (3,000Rp) drivers are Kalimantan's most compliant, breaking routes to reach your destination. River crossings by fan-tail canoe cost 3,000Rp; charters cost 50,000Rp per hour.

PULAU DERAWAN & SANGALAKI ARCHIPELAGO
☎ 0551

Diving in the Sangalaki Archipelago richly deserves its world renown. But fabulous marine life – from majestic mantas winging through the brine to turtles and sea horses playing tag amid pier pilings – is not the best reason to visit Pulau Derawan. At least as much as places where people dress in beads and paint their faces, Derawan's island village recalls a bygone culture.

Sangalaki's inhabited island nearest the Borneo 'mainland', Derawan is a teardrop-shaped oasis of 125 households, mainly of Bajau people. It can be circled on foot in less than an hour. There are no cars, just a handful of motorcycles, and electricity only runs fro, dusk to dawn. Without TV and air-con to pull people inside during afternoons, they sit outside, catching and shooting the breeze. This practice at being neighbours makes Derawan downright neighbourly for visitors.

Among the 30-odd other islands in the archipelago, **Nabucco** and **Matarua** also have accommodation. **Sangalaki** is home to rays, green turtles and a **Turtle Foundation** (www.turtle-foundation.org) monitoring outpost. **Kakaban** has an ecologically intriguing lake where jellyfish have lost their sting.

Activities

Pulau Derawan's underwater activities are conducted from Derawan Dive Resort and Losmen Danakan. Individual local dives cost around US$30, including tank and equipment hire; snorkelling gear costs US$6 to hire per day. Dive trips to Pulau Sangalaki and other islands cost more. Village boats to dive sites cost around 500,000Rp, if transport isn't part of your package. They fish for dinner on the trip back.

Sleeping & Eating

Losmen offer cakes with coffee, or tea with a sweet cake or bread in the morning, rather than full breakfast. Unfortunately, at the time of writing, **Sangalaki Dive Resort** (www.sangalaki.net) was closed.

Losmen Ilham (Pulau Derawan; r 40,000-45,000Rp) Small losmen has clean rooms with fans (when the electricity is on) and shared *mandi*. The attached *warung* serves Indonesian food (meals 8000Rp to 16,000Rp).

our pick **Losmen Danakan** (☎ 086-8121-6143; Pulau Derawan; r per person incl meals 75,000Rp) In the sea patois among Bajau, Bugis, Chinese and Indian traders in these waters, *danakan* means 'family'. Ibu Ridahi, Pak Kasino and welcoming staff make the name fit. Built over the water, this immaculate homestay features comfortable fan-cooled, all-wood rooms and shared *mandi*, some with Western toilets. Meals are simply lovely.

Derawan Dive Resort (☎ 0542-707-2615; www.divederawan.com; Pulau Derawan; 5-night package per person from US$970; ✹) Timber cottages have rustic charm. Packages include transfer from Berau and three dives daily.

More accommodation options:

Penginapan Derawan Lestari I (Pulau Derawan; r 50,000Rp) Haji Ismail's simple losmen on stilts over the water resembles Danakan but falls short.

Penginapan Derawan Lestari II (☎ 081-3476-15894; Pulau Derawan; r 50,000-100,000Rp; ✹) Clean, family-home option with air-con nightly.

Maratua Paradise Resort (www.borneo.org; Pulau Maratua; 4-night package per person from US$855; ✹) Packages include beach chalet accommodation (US$15 extra for stilt cottages), island transfers and four dives daily.

Nabucco Island Resort (☎ 0542-593635; www.nabucco island.com; Pulau Nabucco; d incl meals per person €60; ✹) The rate covers cottages over the surf only, without dives or transfers to this isolated, indulgent resort. The manager has a soft spot for backpackers and may give discounts.

A handful of *warung* on Pulau Derawan offer simple meals and snacks; a few sell warm beer out the back door. Bring fruit from Berau or Tarakan for variety. Tanjung Batu, a fishing village, has a couple of *warung* and **Losmen Famili** (r 30,000Rp) for rooms with shared *mandi* (no fan), in case you're stuck waiting for a boat. We don't recommend Derawan Beach Cafe & Cottage. When we visited, there was a noisy, smelly generator, and we experienced less than courteous treatment.

Getting There & Away

From Berau, the economy route to Derawan is a Kijang (50,000Rp, at least two hours) to Tanjung Batu, and a boat from there. Kijangs wait along the riverfront from 9am, but won't leave with fewer than five passengers, which often means departing midafternoon. Book in advance at Central Graha Hotel (p283) and get picked up at your hotel when the Kijang is ready to go. At Tanjung Batu, hire a speedboat (*sepit*; 200,000Rp, one hour) to Pulau Derawan or try to negotiate a ride with a fishing boat. Stay close to Indonesians arriving with you and you may get lucky; at the very least, you can share the boat cost.

A direct speedboat from Berau can cost up to 2,000,000Rp (three hours). The owner of Derawan Beach Cafe and Cottage runs **KM Tasmania I** (☎ 081-2531-6153, 081-3465-62765), scheduled from Berau Saturdays at 10am, and from Derawan Sundays from the pier at Beach Café (80,000Rp, five hours). But it often doesn't leave Berau at all, due to insufficient passenger numbers.

From Derawan, losmen can arrange a village boat to Tanjung Batu (100,000Rp, 2½ hours). Leave early: Kijangs depart for Berau at 8am sharp.

SUNGAI KAYAN & APOKAYAN HIGHLANDS

Between Berau and Tarakan, **Tanjung Selor** guards the mouth of Sungai Kayan. Regular longboats travel the Kayan to Long Bia or follow the fork west along Sungai Pujungan as the Kayan branches south. A long section of rapids – Kalimantan's wildest white water – shelters the Kayan's Apokayan Highlands' headwaters from boats, and most loggers, too.

Kayan Mentarang National Park follows the border with Sarawak from the Kayan's headwaters to KalTim's northwest corner. This 1.36 million–hectare park is the largest forest area in Southeast Asia, a storehouse of global biodiversity – new species of plants and even animals are discovered regularly – and the centrepiece of WWF's Heart of Borneo initiative to protect contiguous forests in Indonesia, Malaysia and Brunei.

There's fabulous trekking in the Apokayan Highlands. You can cross overland with a guide from Long Ampung to the Mahakam headwaters in about a week. Guides based in Samarinda or Balikpapan lead easy or vigorous treks of various lengths to Dayak longhouses and pristine forests. The landscape and the culture are linked, and each worth exploring. Despite poor soil quality, Dayak farmers have raised rice here for centuries, using traditional techniques and varieties adapted to local conditions.

WWF helped organise the Hulu Pujungan Ecotourism Committee, branded **Borneo Ecotourism** (www.borneo-ecotourism.com). This community initiative gives local (mainly Kenyah) communities in the upper Pujungan a stake in preservation efforts while nurturing traditional culture and sustainable tourism. The enterprise offers homestays, boat transport from Long Pujungan, and tours. From **Long Jelet**, it runs day trips to Batu Ului and U'ung Melu'ung waterfall, a moderate two-day trek to 70m Sungai Bum waterfall and ancient burial caves, and a rugged five day climb into Apokayan through the Apo Napu high pass to Datu Dian, returning via Sungai Kat. For details, check www.borneo-ecotourism.com or contact the **WWF office in Malinau** (☎ 0551-43144; km@indo.net.id).

Kal-Star (www.kalstaronline.com) flies to Tanjung Selor daily except Sunday from Balikpapan (761,000Rp) via Berau (220,000Rp). **DAS** (☎ 736989; Block D, No 8, Jln Komplek Lembusuana, Samarinda) flies to Long Ampung (206,000Rp, five times weekly) and Data Dawai (184,000Rp, twice weekly) from Samarinda. Check with DAS in Samarinda for updates. **Missionary Air Fellowship** (MAF; ☎ 0551-22904; fax 0551-23590)

flies from Tarakan; contact well in advance for arrangements.

LONG BAWAN

In KalTim's northwest corner, Long Bawan is the launch point to explore the Hulu Krayan (not Kayan) end of **Kayan Mentarang National Park**, near the Sabah border. To ensure confusion for travellers, there's a different Sungai Kayan up here, unrelated to the Kayan further south. Get the landscape sorted at **Penginapan Agung Raya** (☎ 086-8121-05064; 60,000Rp), a small, clean losmen.

A guide (100,000Rp per day) is essential for trekking here; porters (80,000Rp per day) are helpful. Ask Penginapan Agung Raya to contact Alex Balang, who speaks English. Village homestays run 60,000Rp to 90,000Rp including meals. Motorised canoe hire (200,000Rp per hour) is the biggest expense.

The Krayan Hulu Ecotourism Committee organises treks from Long Bawan south to Long Layu and Long Rungan, a heath forest with many orchid species. The trek takes about five days. For details and to find the committee's representative in Long Bawan, contact **Borneo Ecotourism** (www.borneo-ecotourism.com), or the **WWF office in Malinau** (☎ 0551-43144; km@indo.net.id).

Elevation makes it difficult to penetrate this area by river, so the best access is by air. **DAS** (☎ 0551-21248) flies from Tarakan via Nunukan to Long Bawan (342,000Rp). **Missionary Air Fellowship** (MAF; ☎ 0551-22904; fax 0551-23590) flies from Tarakan. Book as far ahead as possible for either.

SEBUKU SEMBAKUNG NATIONAL PARK

Indonesia's newest national park, Sebuku Sembakung is Kalimantan's only elephant habitat. The 400,000-hectare protected area along KalTim's north border with Sabah is also in WWF's Heart of Borneo initiative.

Sebuku Sembakung has six types of forests, from tidal swamp to green hills with limestone outcrops. Elephants favour plains in the reserve's central lowland forest.

The park has no facilities for visitors. **Borneo Ecotourism** (www.borneo-ecotourism.com) or the **WWF office in Malinau** (☎ 0551 43144; km@indo .net.id) can arrange visits. Access to the park is via Sungai Sembuku from Nunukan by *ces* (4,000,000Rp, one day). Pachydermophiles note that elephants are more easily sought (and more often seen) along Sabah's Sungai Kinabatangan (see p143).

TARAKAN
☎ 0551 / pop 165,000

This clean island town on the Celebes Sea, the crossing point to and from Tawau in East Sabah, is a pleasant way to greet Indonesia or make a retreat. **THM Plaza**, a mix of traditional shops, *warung* and national chains at Jln Yos Sudarso and Jln Sudirman, marks Tarakan's centre, flanked by newer **Grand Tarakan Mall**. Down Jln Gajah Mada, popular **Gusher Plaza** (pronounced 'guesser') has Tarakan's only department store amid more shops, stalls and *warung*.

Information

Travellers will find ATMs along Jln Yos Sudarso, Jln Sudirman, and at Gusher. Many businesses close on Sunday.

Angkasa Express (☎ 30288; fax 24848; Hotel Tarakan Plaza, Jln Yos Sudarso) Air and Pelni tickets; branches in Balikpapan, Samarinda and Surabaya.

BNI bank (Bank Negara Indonesia; Jln Yos Sudarso) Foreign exchange.

Derawan Travel (☎ 35599/fax 35799; Hotel Paradise, Jln Mulawarman 21) Ibu Mei is Tarakan's master of domestic flight connections.

Haji La Tunrung Star Group (☎ 21405; Jln Yos Sudarso 32; ☯ 7.30am-8pm) Moneychanging daily.

Immigration office (☎ 21242; Jln Sumatra) Information on visas and crossings to/from Malaysia.

Perta Medika Hospital (☎ 31403; Jln Mulawarman)

Post office (Jln Yos Sudarso)

Tourist office (☎ 32100; Jln Sudirman 76, 4th fl; ☯ 8am-4pm Mon-Thu, 8-11am Fri) Good maps. The WWF representative in the government environmental department one floor above knows more about Sebuku Sembakung and Kayan Mentarang National Parks and surrounds.

Utama Computer (Jln Sudirman 155; per hr 5000Rp; ☯ 9.30am-10.30pm) Internet access.

Warnet Jaya (Jln Kl Hajar Dewantara; per hr 5000Rp; ☯ 8am-11pm) Internet access.

Sights

See two Borneo exclusives, proboscis monkeys and *ikan tempankul* – a fish that walks out of the water – at the **mangrove forest** (Jln Gajah Mada; ☯ 8am-5pm), 300m from the town centre. Spread over 9 hectares, with shaded boardwalks and benches, the mangroves also shelter macaques and many bird species.

Japanese and Australian forces clashed bloodily over Tarakan late in WWII. There's an **Australian memorial** (*kuburan Australia*) at the Indonesian military barracks. A **Japanese**

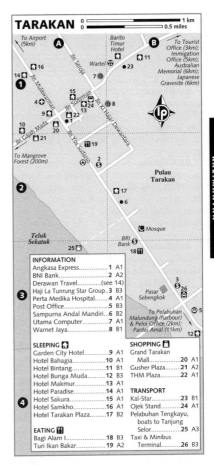

TARAKAN

gravesite (*kuburan Jepang*) is in nearby hills, amid old bunkers.

Pantai Amal (11km) is a swimming beach that can be reached by minibus (3000Rp) or taxi (10,000Rp).

Sleeping

Tarakan's budget options are limited but there's good midrange choice.

Hotel Bunga Muda (☎ 21349; Jln Yos Sudarso 7; r 55,000-132,000Rp; ☒) Ibu Ida runs this clean place between the harbours, featuring *wartel*, travel bookings and plenty of smiles. VIP rooms, the only ones with air-con, sleep up to four.

Hotel Bahagia (☎ 37141; fax 24778; Jln Gajah Mada; r 60,000-150,000Rp; ☒) Opposite Gusher Plaza, the 3rd-floor economy rooms at 'Hotel

Happiness' – watch your head climbing up – are worth the hike. The big, bright digs have shared bathrooms in Asian and Western styles. Higher-priced rooms include private Western bathrooms, breakfast and air-con, but some lack windows.

Hotel Paradise (☎ 22999; fax 32668; Jln Mulawarman 21; r incl breakfast from 100,000-155,000Rp, ste 275,000Rp; ⊠) Weathered on the outside, rooms inside these five levels of Paradise are well kept, all with air-con and Western bath. Oddly, there's an upper-floor discount despite the lobby lift.

Hotel Makmur (☎ 31988, 085-2465-70888; fax 23565; Jln Sudirman 18; s incl breakfast 140,000Rp, d incl breakfast 160,000-225,000Rp; ⊠) Snug, ultramodern standard rooms have hot-water showers, air-con, refrigerator, kettle, cable TV, but no window. Deluxe accommodations add windows and cushiony chairs.

Hotel Sakura (☎ 22730; s 80,000-120,000Rp; d 120,000-160,000Rp; ⊠)You can save across the street, at Makmur's budget cousin.

Hotel Bintang (☎ 33533; fax 35068; Jln Sudirman 20; r incl breakfast 150,000-205,000Rp plus 10% tax; ⊠) It looks small from outside, but Bintang ('star' in Bahasa Indonesia) shines with spacious rooms fitted out like higher-priced hotels. Haggle for high-floor discounts at this four -storey walk-up.

Hotel Tarakan Plaza (☎ 21870; fax 21029; Jln Yos Sudarso 1; r incl breakfast 225,000-300,000Rp; ⊠) Rooms at this newly renovated classic are all the same ample size with added features at higher prices. The Angkasa Express (see p287) travel office is here.

For high-rollers:

Hotel Samkho (☎ 35100; fax 35882; Jln Mulawarman 10; r from 237,000Rp plus 10% tax; ⊠) Plush business-class hotel with frequent 15% discounts.

Garden City Hotel (☎ 21133; fax 36633; Jln Mualwarman 15; r from 500,000Rp plus 10% tax; ⊠ ⌨) Top-shelf business hotel. Pricey even with deep discounts.

Eating

Fish is the dish in Tarakan. Stalls mushroom nightly, particularly on Jln Sudirman, many serving excellent *ikan* (or *ayam*) *lalapan*, grilled or fried, 10,000Rp to 15,000Rp, depending on fish size and variety. One of the best is about 500m north of THM Plaza, just beyond the Barito Timur Hotel. For fish more formally at twice the price, try **Turi Ikan Bakar**

or **Bagi Alam I** on Jln Yos Sudarso. *Warung* abound on Jln Seroja, and at THM Plaza and Gusher.

Getting There & Away

AIR

Batavia Air (770,000Rp), Mandala Airlines (589,000Rp) and Sriwijaya Air (678,000Rp) fly to Balikpapan, connecting to Jakarta, Surabaya and beyond. **Kal-Star** (☎ 51578, 25840; Jln Sudirman 9) flies twice daily except Sunday to Nunukan (230,000Rp), Berau (320,000Rp), and Samarinda (761,000Rp). **DAS** (☎ 21248) flies to Malinau (250,000Rp), Long Ampung (400,000Rp), Nunukan (200,000Rp) and Long Bawan (342,000Rp), Berau and Balikpapan. **Mission Aviation Fellowship** (MAF; ☎ 22904) offers limited scheduled and charter flights into the interior.

BOAT

Pelni (☎ 51169; Jln Yos Sudarso) ships steam to Makassar (250,000Rp), Pantaloan (110,000Rp), Pare Pare (221,500Rp), Surabaya (365,000Rp) and beyond from Pelabuhan Malundung, the main harbour at the south end of Jln Yos Sudarso. Travel agents are generally more helpful than Pelni's office.

Morning ferries to Tawau in Sabah (180,000Rp, 3½ hours) depart daily except Sunday from Pelabuhan Malundung. *Indomaya* and *Tawindo Express* run on alternate days and are very similar; choose the day, not the boat. Immigration formalities are at the ferry terminal. Officials take your passport and return it, stamped for Malaysian entry, upon arrival in Tawau. It's also possible to cross into Sabah daily via Nunukan (150,000Rp, 2½ hours, Nunukan–Tawau 75,000Rp, 1¼ hours).

Eight boats run daily to Tanjung Selor (70,000Rp, 1½ hours) from Pelabuhan Tengkayu on Jln Yos Sudarso, opposite the post office.

Getting Around

A taxi to/from Juwata Airport (6km) costs 35,000Rp. Alternatively, walk about 200m to the highway and catch an *angkot* (3000Rp). *Angkot* routes follow Jln Yos Sudarso, Jln Sudirman and Jln Gajah Mada. *Ojeks* gather on Jln Sudirman above THM Plaza and across from Gusher.

Directory

CONTENTS

ACCOMMODATION

Accommodation in Borneo runs the gamut from international-standard hotels to rickety longhouses deep in the jungle. Naturally, in the bigger cities of the coasts, you'll have a wide range of choices. In smaller towns, on outlying islands, and in the hinterlands, you may be limited to very simple lodgings

---

BOOK YOUR STAY ONLINE

For more accommodation reviews and recommendations by Lonely Planet authors, check out the online booking service at www.lonelyplanet.com/hotels. You'll find the true, insider lowdown on the best places to stay. Reviews are thorough and independent. Best of all, you can book online.

---

indeed. Sabah and Sarawak have the best range of accommodation, particularly in the upper brackets. Kalimantan has fewer international-standard hotels and resorts. Brunei has the world's most expensive hotel, but beyond that, the range of accommodation is fairly limited.

In terms of cost, Borneo is good value. If you really want to stretch your money and don't mind simple accommodation, you can spend as little as US$5 per night on accommodation in most places in Borneo, with the exception of Brunei, where you'll have to double that. Upper budget accommodation is also good value, at least compared to many other parts of the world, especially if you book online.

International-Standard Hotels

There are international-standard hotels in Kota Kinabalu, Labuan, Kuching and Bandar Seri Begawan, and hotels of near international standard in most of the other big cities of Borneo. These have all the mod-cons and amenities you'd expect. Booking online is the way to go at most of these places and you'll often get rates half or less than the rack rates – you can often get excellent rooms for less than US$100 per night, sometimes half that.

Local Hotels

Small local hotels are the mainstay of budget travellers and backpackers across Borneo, and you can generally find a room in one of these places for between US$10 and US$15 per night. These simple places are usually run by locals of Chinese ancestry, but Muslim places also exist.

These hotels are generally fairly spartan: bare floors and just a bed, chair and table, wardrobe and sink. The showers and toilets are usually en suite, but may occasionally be down the hall. Your usual choices with these rooms are fan versus air-con and standard versus deluxe. It's often worth paying extra for a deluxe room, as these have often been refurbished recently and are sometimes *much* nicer than standard rooms for only a bit more money – it never hurts to ask if you can see a room.

DIRECTORY

PRACTICALITIES

■ Electrical sockets are 220V AC; 50 Hz. Sarawak and Sabah (Malaysia) and Brunei use UK-style plugs with three square pins. Kalimantan (Indonesia) uses European-style plugs with two round prongs.

■ Video recorders use the PAL system, also used in Australia, New Zealand, the UK and most of Europe.

■ Brunei, Indonesia and Malaysia use the metric system.

One thing to look for in these local hotels is tile floors. Carpets do very poorly in the tropics and after only a year or two, they take on a dank fug that makes any room unpleasant.

Resorts

There are island and beach resorts of various classes along Borneo's coast and on its offshore islands. Sabah has several excellent seaside resorts right in Kota Kinabalu, as well as two more a short drive up the coast. In addition to these, there are resorts on several of Sabah's offshore islands like Pulau Mantanani, Pulau Manukan, Pulau Tiga, Layang Layang and off of Semporna. Sarawak's most famous resort area is the Santubong Peninsula, just north of Kuching, as well as a few beach resorts in Miri. Kalimantan has several seaside and island resorts along its coast, including the quaint island of Derawan.

Guesthouses & Backpackers

In the major tourist cities of Borneo you will find accommodation specifically designed for foreign travellers on a budget. These places are usually pretty similar, offering a choice of dorm beds or simple private rooms (usually with common bathrooms), a common area, an internet terminal or two, a basic kitchen and, if you're lucky, a rooftop garden for hanging out in the evening. Some of these places rent bicycles and conduct tours of local sights. Dorm rooms in places like these average about US$5 per night and private rooms run around US$12. Dorms are the better value here, since you can often get a much better private room in a cheap hotel for about the same price.

Longhouses

Longhouses are the traditional dwellings of the indigenous peoples of Borneo. These communal dwellings may contain up to 100 individual family 'apartments' built under one long roof. The most important area of a longhouse is the common veranda, which serves as a social area. These days there are two main types of longhouse: 'tourist longhouses' and 'authentic longhouses'. While a visit to a tourist longhouse is easily enough arranged it is unlikely to be of much interest. A visit to an authentic, living longhouse is likely to be of more interest. The best place to visit a longhouse is Sarawak or Kalimantan. For details, see boxed text, p32.

Camping

Camping is another good, cheap option in Borneo. Many of the national parks have official campgrounds and a few will permit camping in nondesignated sites you are into the back country. There are also many lonely stretches of beach along the coast and on islands that are ideal for camping. If you do decide to camp in Borneo, a two-season tent with mosquito netting is ideal. As for sleeping bags, a summer-weight bag or just a bag liner will usually suffice, unless you intend to do some climbing (the mountains of Borneo get colder than you'd imagine).

ACTIVITIES

The name of the game in Borneo is adventure sports: trekking, mountain climbing, diving, snorkelling, river rafting, mountain biking and caving. For information on these sports, see the Borneo Outdoors chapter (p54). Apart from outdoor sports, you can also study the culture of Borneo's indigenous people at various longhouses in Kalimantan, Sabah and Sarawak. You can also study Malay cooking in cities like Kuching (p166).

BUSINESS HOURS

Government offices are usually open Monday to Friday from 8am to 4.15pm. Most close for lunch from 12.45 to 2pm, and on Friday the lunch break is from 12.15pm to 2.45pm for Friday prayers at the mosque. On Saturday the offices are open from 8am to 12.45pm.

Bank hours are generally 10am to 3pm on weekdays and 9.30am to 11.30am on Saturday. Shop hours are variable, although a good rule of thumb for small shops is that they're open

Monday to Saturday from 9am to 6pm. Major department stores, shopping malls, Chinese emporiums and some large stores are open from around 10am until 9pm or 10pm seven days a week.

Kopitiam or *kedai kopi* (Borneo's ubiquitous coffee-shop restaurants) that cater to the breakfast crowd will open very early, well before dawn, but close before lunch. Others (generally the newer ones) will only open later in the morning and stay open until 9pm or 10pm.

In smaller villages, opening hours are rarely set, and you may find a shop unexpectedly closed for a few hours in the afternoon. Don't worry, it'll reopen soon enough.

Bars usually open around dinnertime and close at around 2am.

CHILDREN

Children receive discounts for most attractions and transport at most places in Borneo. Chinese hotels are also a good bargain as they charge by the room rather than the number of people. However cots are not widely available in cheap accommodation. Public transport is comfortable and relatively well organised.

Baby formula and diapers are widely available in Borneo, as is baby food. However, it makes sense to stock up on these items before heading to remote destinations or islands.

Most of the activities in Sarawak are of the outdoors-adventure kind, so if you have a child who prefers shopping malls or television games, they might get bored very quickly. Of course, children who love the outdoors or are inquisitive about their environment and different cultures will have an absolute blast.

CLIMATE CHARTS

For more information on when to visit Borneo, see Getting Started (p13).

COURSES

Sarawak cooking courses are available in Kuching (p166). In addition, when you stay at a longhouse in Sarawak or Kalimantan, you may have a chance to study local crafts in an informal way.

DANGERS & ANNOYANCES

Borneo is a safe and relatively easy place in which to travel. Brunei is on par with Japan in terms of safety, and Sabah is not far behind, with little to worry about beyond the occasional

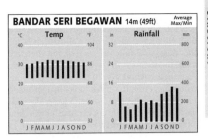

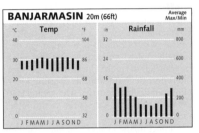

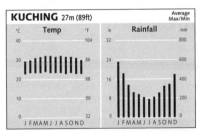

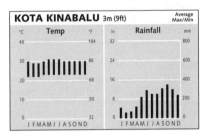

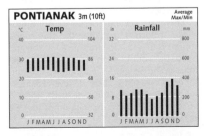

opportunistic crime. Most of Sarawak is also very safe for travellers, although towns like Sibu do have a few dodgy areas. Kalimantan is, for the most part, quite safe as well, but there are a few unsafe areas in parts of the bigger cities. As with anywhere else in the world, use your common sense: if a place looks dangerous, it probably is. Never let Borneo's generally laid-back attitude and safe appearance lull you into a false sense of security.

Theft
Purse snatching is relatively common in Kalimantan, Sarawak and Sabah. Usually, a couple of guys ride up to a pedestrian on a (usually stolen) motorcycle and the pillion rider makes the grab. The crime occurs more often on ostentatious locals sporting lots of bling rather than tourists. The greater danger is that the grab causes the victim to fall, causing injury.

Opportunistic crimes can also occur on beaches, in guesthouses and in restaurants and bars. As usual, it pays to take good care of your valuables and to put them in hotel safety deposit boxes when possible.

Violence
While Borneo is generally very safe for travellers of both sexes, physical attacks have been known to occur, particularly after hours and in dangerous neighbourhoods. In small logging camps and villages across Borneo, things can get dodgy when alcohol enters the picture.

The Natural World
Redmond O'Hanlon observed in his book *Into the Heart of Borneo* that, given all the nasty creatures to be found in Borneo, the ideal outfit would be a rubber suit with a pair of steel waders. Fortunately, Mr O'Hanlon was being dramatic. Sure, there are plenty of things that can kill you in Borneo, but if you use a little common sense and take the normal precautions, there is not much to worry about.

There are several species of poisonous snake in Borneo, including the king cobra, so it pays to watch the trail ahead of you and not to put your hand in places you can't see. Malaria and dengue fever are known to occur; for details see p313. There are several dangers on coral reefs, including cone shells, which is another reason never to walk on or touch a coral reef.

Crocodiles are a very real danger in Borneo, and you should exercise caution swimming in rivers even very far inland, and never swim near river mouths. Also, take great care (or simply avoid) walking in marshy areas near the coast or along estuaries. If you swim in the ocean, do it far from river mouths and in clear water.

And, no discussion of dangers and annoyances in Borneo would be complete without a mention of leeches. Fortunately, these fall squarely into the category of annoyances rather than dangers. Yes, leeches are horrible, unpleasant and can make your life hell, but they can't really hurt you beyond drawing a little blood. For more on leeches, see the boxed text p67.

EMBASSIES & CONSULATES
Embassies & Consulates in Borneo
EMBASSIES IN BRUNEI
Australia (☎ 222-9435; www.bruneidarussalam.embassy .gov.au; Level 6, DAR Takaful IBB Utama, Jln Pemancha)
France (☎ 222-0960; www.ambafrance-bn.org; Complex Jl Sultan, Units 301-306, 51-55 Jln Sultan)
Germany (☎ 222-5547; www.bandar-seri-begawan .diplo.de/Vertretung/bandarseribegawan/en/Startseite. html; 2nd fl, Unit 2.01, Block A, Yayasan Sultan Haji Hassanal Bolkiah Complex, Jln Pretty)
Malaysia (☎ 238-1095; www.kln.gov.my/perwakilan /seribegawan; 61 Simpang 336, Jln Kebangsaan)
New Zealand (☎ 03 2078-2533; www.nzembassy .com/home.cfm?c=23; Level 21, Menara IMC, 8 Jl Sultan Ismail, Kuala Lumpur 50250, Malaysia)
Philippines (☎ 224-1465; www.philippineembassy brunei.net; 17 Simpang 126, Km 2, Jln Tutong)
Singapore (☎ 226-2741; www.mfa.gov.sg/brunei; 8 Simpang 74, Jln Subok)
UK (☎ 222-2231; www.britishhighcommission.gov .uk/brunei; Unit 2.01, 2nd fl, Block D, Yayasan Sultan Haji Hassanal Bolkiah Complex, Jln Pretty)
USA (☎ 222-0384; bandar.usembassy.gov/index.html; 3rd fl, Teck Guan Plaza, Jln Sultan)

CONSULATES IN KALIMANTAN
Malaysia (☎ 03-732986, 736061; www.kln.gov .my/perwakilan/pontianak; Jln Sultan Syahrir 21, Pontianak; ☱ 8am-4pm Mon-Fri)

CONSULATES IN SABAH
Australia (☎ 088-267-151; www.malaysia.embassy .au; Suite 10.1, Level 10, Wisma Great Eastern Life, 65 Jln Gaya, Kota Kimbalu)
Indonesia Kota Kinabalu ☎ 88-218-600; indocon@indo con.po.my; Lorong Kemajuan, Karamunsing, Kota Kimbalu; Tawau ☎ 089-772-052, 752-969; Jln Tanjong Batu, Tawau

CONSULATES IN SARAWAK

Indonesia (☎ 082-421-734; 6th fl, Bangunan Binamas, Jln Padungan, Kuching)
New Zealand (☎ 082-482-177; shazwi69@tm.net.my; Lot 8679, Section 64, Pending Commercial Centre, Kuching)

Embassies & Consulates in Kuala Lumpur

Australia (☎ 03-2146 5555; www.malaysia.embassy .gov.au; 6 Jln Yap Kwan Sweng)
Brunei (☎ 03-21612800; kualalumpur.malaysia@mfa .gov.bn; No 19-01 Tingkat 19, Menara Tan & Tan, Jln Tun Razak)
France (☎ 03-2053 5500; www.ambafrance-my.org; 192 Jln Ampang)
Indonesia (☎ 03-2116 4000; www.kbrikl.org.my; 233 Jln Tun Razak)
New Zealand (☎ 03-2078 2533; www.nzembassy.com /home.cfm?c=23; Level 21, Menara IMC, Jln Sultan Ismail)
Philippines (☎ 03-2148 9989; www.philembassykl.org .my; 1 Changkat Kia Peng)
Singapore (☎ 03-2161 6277; www.mfa.gov.sg/kl/; 209 Jln Tun Razak)
Thailand (☎ 03-2148 8222; www.mfa.go.th/web/1830 .php?depcode=23000100; 206 Jln Ampang)
UK (☎ 03-2170 2200; www.britain.org.my; 185 Jln Ampang)
USA (☎ 03-2168 5000; malaysia.usembassy.gov; 376 Jln Tun Razak)

Embassies & Consulates in Jakarta

Australia (☎ 021-2550 5555; www.indonesia.embassy .gov.au; Jln HR Rasuna Said Kav C 15-16)
Brunei (☎ 021-3190-6080; www.mfa.gov.bn/overseas _missions/indonesia.htm; Jln Teuku Umar No 9 Menteng)
France (☎ 021-2355 7600; www.ambafrance-id.org; Jln MH Thamrin No 20)
Germany (☎ 021-3985 5000; www.jakarta.diplo.de /Vertretung/jakarta/en/Startseite.html; Jln MH Thamrin 1)
New Zealand (☎ 021-570 9460; www.nzembassy.com /home.cfm?c=41; BRI II Bldg, 23rd fl, Jln Jend Sudirman Kav 44-46)
UK (☎ 021-315 6264; www.britain.or.id; Jln M H Thamrin 75)
USA (☎ 021-3435 9000; www.usembassyjakarta.org; Jln Merdeka Selatan 4-5)

Borneo Embassies Abroad

BRUNEI EMBASSIES ABROAD

Australia (☎ 02-6285 4500; bruneihc@netspeed.com .au; 10 Beale Cres, Deakin, ACT 2600)
France (☎ 01 53 64 67 60; paris.france@mfa.gov.bn; 7 Rue de Presbourg, Paris 75116017)
Germany (☎ 030-206 07 600; berlin@brunei-embassy .de; Kronenstrasse 55-58, Berlin 10117)

UK (☎ 020-7581-0521; london.uk@mfa.gov.bn; 19 Belgrave Sq, London SW1X 8PG)
USA (☎ 202-237 1838; www.bruneiembassy.org; 3520 International Court, Washington DC 20008)

INDONESIAN EMBASSIES ABROAD

Australia (☎ 0-6250 8600; www.kbri-canberra.org .au; 8 Darwin Ave, Yarralumla, Canberra ACT 2600)
France (☎ 01 45 03 07 60; www.amb-indonesie.fr; 47-49 Rue Cortambert, Paris 75116)
Germany (☎ 030-478070; www.indonesian-embassy .de; Lehrter St 16-17, Berlin 10577)
New Zealand (☎ 04-4758 697; www.indonesianem bassy.org.nz; 70 Glen Rd, Kelburn, Wellington)
Philippines (☎ 02-892 5061; www.kbrimanila.org.ph; 185 Salcedo St, Legaspi Village, Makati, Manila 1200)
Singapore (☎ 6737 7422; www.kbrisingapura.com; 7 Chatsworth Rd, Singapore 249761)
Thailand (☎ 02-252 3135; www.kbri-bangkok.com; 600-602 Petchburi Rd, Ratchatewi, Bangkok 10400)
UK (☎ 020-7499 7661; www.indonesianembassy.org.uk; 38 Grosvenor Sq, London W1K2HW)
USA (☎ 202-775 5365; www.embassyofindonesia.org; 2020 Massachusetts Ave NW, Washington, DC 20036)

MALAYSIAN EMBASSIES ABROAD

Australia (☎ 02-6273 1543; malcanberra@netspeed .com.au; 7 Perth Ave, Yarralumla, Canberra ACT 2600)
France (☎ 01 45 53 11 85; malparis@kln.gov.my; 2, bis rue Benouville, Paris 75116)
Germany (☎ 030-88 57 49 0; mwberlin@malemb.de; Klingelhoeferstr. 6, Berlin 10785)
New Zealand (☎ 04-385 2439; mwwelton@xtra.co.nz; 10 Washington Ave, Brooklyn, Wellington)
Philippines (☎ 02-864 0761; malmanila@kln.gov .my; 10th &11th Floor, World Center Bldg, No 330, Sen. Gil Puyat Ave, Makati City 1200, Manila)
Singapore (☎ 6235 0111; mwspore@singnet.com .sg; 301 Jervois Rd, Singapore 249077)
Thailand (☎ 02-679 2190; malbangkok@kln.gov.my; 35 South Sathorn Rd, Bangkok 10120)
UK (☎ 020-7235 8033; mwlon@btconnect.com; 45 Belgrave Sq, London SW1X 8QT)
USA (☎ 202-572 9700; malwashdc@kln.gov.my; 3516 International Court, NW, Washington, DC 20008)

FESTIVALS & EVENTS

This section lists major festivals and events that take place annually in Borneo. Needless to say, this list is not exhaustive; ask at local tourist offices or at your accommodation for details on small local festivals and events happening when you're in town. For details on national holidays in Brunei, Indonesia and Malaysia, see p295.

Borneo-Wide Festivals

JANUARY/FEBRUARY

Chinese New Year Held in January or February depending on the Chinese lunar calendar. In the days leading up to the event, cities will usually have cultural events, but on the day itself, and a few days thereafter, Chinese-run businesses will close up shop for a few days. Chinese New Year's Eve is the occasion of the reunion dinner, and Chinese families will wait until midnight to greet the New Year with a raucous (and illegal) display of firecrackers and fireworks in front of their homes and businesses. Expect lots of food and sweets to be on sale too.

MARCH/APRIL

Easter Held on the first full moon after the vernal equinox. Easter is an important feast for Borneo's many practising Christians, including upriver longhouse communities. Services are held at Christian churches wherever there are sizable Christian communities.

VARIABLE

The Feast of Ramadan (Hari Raya Puasa) Held after the fasting month of Ramadan. On the morning of the feast day, Muslims will pray at the mosque and then visit the graves of departed loved ones. The next few days are spent visiting and receiving family and friends. During the month of Ramadan, special markets are set up selling special food for Muslims for the breaking of their fast at sunset. Since the Islamic calendar is 11 days shorter than the Gregorian calendar, the feast of Ramadan occurs progressively earlier every year. In 2008, it will be held in early October.

DECEMBER

Christmas Christmas, on 25 December, is celebrated by Borneo's Christians in a similar fashion to Christians elsewhere, although there's less emphasis on Santa and his reindeer.

Brunei

Brunei's Muslim majority celebrates the Muslim festivals mentioned above, while the Iban minority observes the same festivals as their counterparts in Sarawak.

Kalimantan

VARIABLE

Robok-Robok To be held mid-January in 2009, moving two weeks earlier annually. This festival celebrates the founding of Pontianak's Mempawah kingdom with a royal yacht procession, dragon-boat races and terrestrial events.

VARIABLE

Equatorial Culture Festival Held around the vernal and autumnal equinoxes. With participation by Dayak, Chinese and Indonesian communities, this festival involves traditional dancing, singing and competitions.

SEPTEMBER

Erau Festival Held in Tenggarong in late September. This Dayak festival, though touristy, is a chance to see traditional dances and ritual ceremonies and join a vast intertribal party. The festival is usually held in late September for one to two weeks. Tourist offices in Tenggarong or Samarinda can provide upcoming dates.

Sabah & Sarawak

Malaysia has an interesting holiday and festival schedule owing to the heterogeneous nature of its population. Because of the roving nature of Ramadan according to the other calendars, sometimes, the feast of Ramadan can coincide with feast days of the other major ethnic groups, leading to extended holidays for everyone. Recently, when Hari Raya Puasa coincided with Deepavali, the local wits dubbed it Deepa Raya, while the last time it coincided with Chinese New Year, it was called Kongsi Raya (*kongsi* is Hokkien for 'to share'). Information on public events during these festivals can be gotten from the local tourist board.

JUNE

Gawai Dayak (Harvest Festival, 1 June) This is the annual harvest festival for the indigenous peoples of Sarawak (known collectively as Dayaks). It occurs on 1 June to coincide with the rice harvest. The actual date of 1 June was only agreed upon as a consensus date between the different Dayak tribes in the 1950s. During Gawai, members of the Dayak community visit each other in their homes and a lot of eating and *tuak* (rice wine) drinking is done. Many Dayak village communities will also hold community events such as village dances and beauty contests. Because the majority of Dayaks in Sarawak are now Christian, the old animist harvest traditions are fading into obscurity.

AUGUST

Hari Merdeka (National Day) This festival, held on 31 August, commemorates Malaysia's independence from Britain (the word *merdeka* means 'freedom'). There are usually parades and fireworks in major cities.

FOOD & DRINK

There are three main ethnic groups in Borneo: Indonesian-Malays, ethnic Chinese and indigenous peoples. In addition, there is a significant population of people of Indian descent. The food of Borneo perfectly reflects this ethnic mix. Outside the big cities, where you can find a fair bit of Western food, you'll usually be choosing between Malay/Indonesian food and Chinese food when you travel in Borneo.

Malay-Indonesian food typically involves rice dishes with a variety of vegetable and meat, fish, or vegetable dishes for accompaniment, often prepared like a curry. As you head out into the country, your choices will sometimes narrow to two dishes you will come to know very well if you spend any time in Borneo: *nasi goreng* (fried rice) and *mee goreng* (fried noodles).

Chinese dishes are centred on noodles and rice, with steamed buns and simple dim sum making occasional appearances. Chicken rice is a typical dish and it's usually very cheap and reasonably filling. Noodle dishes predominate at breakfast, and you can usually choose dry or in soup. Big cities have excellent Chinese seafood places where you can enjoy locally-caught seafood prepared in the Chinese way.

As you head into the interior and stay with indigenous peoples, you might get to sample some Borneo jungle foods, including deer, monkey, wild boar, river fish and jungle ferns. Needless to say, it will be a culinary adventure and a great story to tell to the folks back home.

While travelling in Borneo, you will probably eat at least half of your meals in Borneo's ubiquitous *kopitiam* or *kedai kopi* (coffee shop restaurants, the former being the Chinese rendering, the latter being the Bahasa rendering). For details on these places, see p41 and the boxed text, p39.

GAY & LESBIAN TRAVELLERS

Homosexuality is a crime in Malaysia, and there's a 'Morality Police Force' going around supposedly investigating incidents of homosexuality in the populace. Apparently they target gay men much more than lesbians. Malaysia is still by and large a socially conservative society and 'out' behaviour is looked upon disapprovingly; we strongly suggest some discretion. Brunei, being an even more devoutly Muslim country, has a much sterner outlook. Homosexuality is not a crime in Indonesia (Kalimantan), but the state is fairly conservative in these matters, so obviously 'out' behaviour is also not a good idea.

HOLIDAYS

Brunei

Brunei National Day 23 February
Hari Raya Aidiladha February/March
Muslim New Year (Hizrah) Variable

Royal Brunei Armed Forces Day 31 May
Prophet's Birthday Variable.
Sultan of Brunei's Birthday 15 July
Hari Raya Aidilfitri Variable.

Kalimantan

New Year's Day Celebrated on 1 January.
Muharram (Islamic New Year) Usually late January.
Imlek (Chinese New Year) National holiday from late January to early February.
Good Friday Late March or early April
Paskah (Easter) Late March or early April
Maulud Nabi Muhammed (Birthday of the Prophet Muhammed) Celebrated on one day between late March and early May.
Hari Proklamasi Kemerdekaan (Independence Day) 17 August
Isra Miraj Nabi Muhammed (Celebration of the Ascension of the Prophet Muhammed) Held on one day between late August and mid-September.
Idui Adha Muslim Festival held between December and January.
Hari Natal (Christmas Day) Celebrated on 25 December.

Sabah & Sarawak

New Year's Day 1 January
Awal Muharram Varies but currently in January.
Chinese New Year Varies between January and February.
Federal Territory Day (only in Labuan) 1 February
Prophet's Birthday Varies but currently in March.
Good Friday Varies between March and May.
Labour Day 1 May
Wesak Day Around May
Harvest Festival (Sabah only) 30 and 31 May
Gawai Dayak (Sarawak only) 1 and 2 June
Birthday of SPB Yang di-Pertuan Agong 3 June
National Day 31 August
Birthday of the Sarawak Chief Minister (Sarawak only) 9 September
Birthday of the Sabah Chief Minister (Sabah only) 16 September
Deepavali (Not in Sarawak and Labuan) Around October
Hari Raya Puasa Varies but currently in October.
Christmas 25 December

INSURANCE

Do not travel without travel insurance. Check the fine print of a policy to see if it excludes dangerous activities like diving, mountain climbing, caving etc. If you plan on doing these things in Borneo, you'll want a policy that covers these things. Note that if you want to visit Sabah's Maliau Basin Conservation Area (p154), your plan will have to cover helicopter evacuation.

INTERNET ACCESS

Borneo, despite its image as a wild and remote place, is pretty well wired these days. Internet cafés can be found in the main towns and cities of the coast and, increasingly, even in the smaller towns of the interior. Access is usually quite cheap, averaging around US$1.50 per hour.

Many Western-style coffee shops (such as Coffee Bean & Tea Leaf and Starbucks) offer free wi-fi access to customers, as do most top-end hotels and a few midrange ones. Backpackers and guesthouses usually have at least one terminal for the use of guests, sometimes for a nominal charge.

Keep in mind that there are plenty of places in Borneo where you can't get internet access of any sort, including several of the offshore islands and huge sections of the interior. If you've got urgent online activity, you'll have to get it done before heading off the map.

LEGAL MATTERS

Drug possession, smuggling or dealing is punishable by death in Brunei and Malaysia, and by harsh penalties in Kalimantan. Illegal gambling and possession of pornography are also punishable by severe penalties in these countries. It is illegal to work without a proper working visa in these countries. Finally, the sale of alcohol is illegal in Brunei and you can only import 12 cans of beer or two bottles of spirits.

MAPS

Getting a hold of accurate and up-to-date maps of Borneo is a real problem, since they often don't exist or are not available to the public. Malaysia still keeps most of their maps classified as a holdover from the Konfrontasi with Indonesia, which happened in the 1960s! Brunei doesn't officially release any of its maps to non-Bruneians and accurate maps of Kalimantan are simply impossible to get.

Periplus publishes *Sabah & Kota Kinabalu* (1:800,000), which is the best map available of Sabah and Kota Kinabalu and should be sufficient to give you the general lay of the land. They also publish *Sarawak* (1:1,000,000), which is the best available map of Sarawak and Kuching. Periplus does not publish a Kalimantan map, so you'll have to do with their Indonesia map if you want something beyond the maps in this book. Likewise, there is no commercially produced map of Brunei.

Drivers may find the lack of detailed maps frustrating, but you can usually make your way around at least Sabah and Sarawak using the Periplus maps mentioned above.

Google Earth is a very useful resource for planning travel in Borneo and it's particularly useful for showing extents of jungle cover, for those planning a trek into the sticks. It also shows river networks and road networks fairly well, particularly in coastal Sabah. Google Earth has very accurate and clear images of Kuching, Kota Kinabalu, Labuan, Pontianak and Bandar Seri Begawan. Indeed, for Brunei, Google Earth is easily the best supplement to the maps in this book.

MEDIA

There are English-language newspapers of varying quality in Brunei, Kalimantan, Sabah and Sarawak. International papers and magazines are available in the bigger cities like Kota Kinabalu, Kuching and Pontianak. Around Kota Kinabalu and Kuching, you can get English-language radio stations, beamed over from Peninsular Malaysia. Once you head into the hinterlands, you probably won't pick up anything of any language without a shortwave radio. Television stations from Jakarta or Kuala Lumpur, with occasional English-language content, can be seen on televisions in hotels around Borneo. Finally, in the first-class hotels around Borneo you can usually get CNN, BBC, Star and other satellite programming.

MONEY
Brunei

The official currency is the Brunei dollar (B$), but Singapore dollars are exchanged at an equal rate and can be used (so don't be surprised if you get Singapore dollars as change – there is no need to raise a fuss).

Banks in the region are efficient and there are plenty of moneychangers. For cashing travellers cheques, banks usually charge around 3% and will only change a maximum of US$200, whereas moneychangers have no charges (theoretically there should be no limit for moneychangers but travellers may have problems with larger amounts).

Kalimantan

The unit of currency used in Indonesia is the rupiah (Rp). Denominations of 25, 50, 100 and 500 rupiah are in circulation in both the old silver-coloured coins and the newer bronze-coloured coins. A 1000Rp coin is also minted but rarely seen, and the 25Rp coin has almost vanished. Notes come in 500, 1000, 5000, 10,000, 20,000, 50,000 and 100,000 rupiah denominations.

Sabah & Sarawak

Malaysia's currency is the ringgit (RM or MYR), which is subdivided into 100 sen. Denominations of notes are RM1, RM5, RM10, RM50 and RM100. Coins are denominated into 1 sen, 5 sen, 10 sen, 20 sen and 50 sen pieces.

Malaysians sometimes refer to the ringgit as a dollar, which can be confusing. You can be sure that, unless they are specifically talking about a foreign currency, when they say 'dollar', they mean 'ringgit'.

POST
Brunei

Post offices open from 8am to 4.30pm Monday to Thursday and Saturday (8am to 11am and 2pm to 4pm Friday; closed Sunday).

Letters (up to 10g) cost 75c to send to Australia and New Zealand, 90c to the UK, and B$1.20 to the USA and Canada. An airmail postcard to Malaysia and Singapore is 20c; to most other places in Southeast Asia it's 35c; to the Pacific, Europe, Africa and Australia it's 50c; and to the Americas it's 60c. Aerograms are 45c regardless of destination.

Kalimantan

Post restante is reasonably efficient in Indonesia. Expected mail always seems to arrive at its destination – eventually. Have your letters addressed to you with your surname in underlined capitals, but check for your mail under both your first and family names.

Mail delivered to Australia or the USA usually takes around 10 to 15 days; to Europe it takes up to three weeks. A postcard/letter to the USA costs 5000/10,000Rp; to Australia 7500/15,000Rp; and to the UK 8000/18,000Rp. For anything over 20g, the charge is based on weight. Sending large parcels can be quite expensive. Those weighing a maximum of 7kg can be sent by airmail, or by cheaper sea mail if they weigh up to 10kg.

Sabah & Sarawak

POS Malaysia Berhad (www.pos.com.my) runs an efficient postal system. Post offices are open Monday to Saturday from 8am to 5pm, and are closed on Sundays and public holidays.

Aerograms and postcards cost 50 sen to send to any destination. Letters weighing 20g and under cost 90 sen to nearby Asian countries, RM1.40 to more distant Asian countries, Australia and NZ, RM1.50 to the UK and Europe and RM1.80 to North and South America. Parcel rates vary between RM20 and RM60 per kilo, depending on the destination.

Main post offices in larger cities like Kota Kinabalu and Kuching stock packaging materials and stationery.

SHOPPING

Most large cities will have everything you need, from toiletries and other necessities, to consumer electronics, although the choice may not be as wide as in the large metropolises in Southeast Asia. Bargaining should only be attempted at outdoor markets and in some family-run shops.

Most tourists to Borneo will be looking for bargains in batiks and handicrafts. There should be a wide variety to choose from. Most large cities will have a 'tourist' district with a concentration of shops catering to those interested in the craft market, and there are even items on sale in the longhouses that are part of the homestay circuit. More adventurous travellers might want to venture to weekend markets in search of something off the beaten track, although the chance of finding something truly unique is quite low.

The standard repertoire of handicrafts from Borneo are batik (most batik found in Malaysian Borneo actually originates from Indonesia), *puak kumbu* (traditional Dayak weaving), *songket* (traditional Malay weaving with gold thread), wooden sculpture, your usual collection of tourist-quality blowpipes and, in Kuching, chintzy cat paraphernalia.

The local arts scene has started to come into its own in recent years, with artists fusing local design and a modern sensibility. Ramsay Ong is well known in the Kuching arts scene, and there are charming new art galleries opening up, featuring other lesser names who have been waiting in the wings.

TELEPHONE

You'll be surprised how easy it is to make phone calls in Borneo. These days, due to the prevalence of mobile (cell) phone networks, many travellers opt to bring their own mobile phone to Borneo and buy a local prepaid SIM card (this is only possible if your phone is

DIRECTORY

BORNEO MOBILE-PHONE FREQUENCIES

- **Brunei** GSM900
- **Indonesia (Kalimantan)** GSM900/ GSM1800
- **Malaysia (Sabah & Sarawak)** GSM900/ GSM1800

---

not 'locked' – check before arrival). Another option is to buy a cheap mobile phone upon arrival. If you plan on spending a few weeks in the country and making a lot of reservations or social calls, this is probably the easiest way to go. For information on mobile-phone frequencies, see the boxed text above.

Brunei

DST (www.dst-group.com), Brunei's telephone company, runs a fairly efficient telephone service. Unlike Indonesia or Malaysia, SIM cards are not commonly available. The only place to buy one is at the main DST office in BSB (see p222).

Brunei's country code is ☎ 673. From inside Brunei, the international access code is ☎ 00. Within Brunei, there are no area codes.

Due to the prevalence of foreign workers in Brunei, there are many shops in downtown BSB where you can make cheap international phone calls. These places are the easiest and cheapest ways to call overseas. Otherwise, Hallo Kad and JTB are the most common types of phonecards. They're available from some retail shops in BSB. These can be used in phone booths to make international calls.

Kalimantan

The country code for Indonesia is ☎ 62. When calling Indonesia from overseas, dial ☎ 62, then the area code (minus the first zero), then the number you want to reach.

Telkom, the government telecommunications agency *(wartel)*, is the cheapest place to make international and long-distance *(interlokal)* phone calls. They are usually open 24 hours, provide Home Country Direct phones and permit collect calls. Private *wartel* are more convenient but slightly more expensive and may not offer a collect call service. When calling home, dial ☎ 001 plus the country code and the area code, minus the initial

zero if it has one, followed by the rest of the number. Midrange and top-end hotels have International Direct Dialing on room phones but are more expensive than the *wartels*. Long distance calls within Indonesia are priced according to zones and charges rise with distance. Include the area code when dialling out of a province.

Public phones or mobile phones are both convenient for travellers. Most public phones use magnetic *kartu telepon* (phonecards), while newer phones require *kartu chip* with embedded computer chips. Card denominations range from 5000Rp to 100,000Rp and are available widely. International calls cost about the same as from *wartel* phones.

While some travellers may opt to use international roaming with their own mobile phones in Indonesia, buying a local SIM card from one of the big GSM (global) networks and calling with a local number is much cheaper for local calls. Telkomsel and Excelcomindo have the most extensive networks and Telkomsel's simPATI cards are readily available (many Fuji photoshops stock them).

Sabah & Sarawak

The country code for Malaysia is ☎ 60. When calling Malaysia from overseas, dial ☎ 60, then the area code (minus the first zero), then the number you want to reach.

International direct dial (IDD) calls and operator-assisted calls can be made from any private phone. The access code for making international calls is ☎ 00. Call ☎ 108 for the international operator and ☎ 103 for directory inquiries.

The easiest way to call overseas is to buy an international phone card from a convenience store like 7-11, or newsagents. Otherwise, you can make calls from travel agents, guesthouses, hotels, internet cafés and some small businesses that advertise the service.

TIME

Sabah, Sarawak and Brunei are all UTC +8. Thus, Sabah, Sarawak and Brunei are all eight hours ahead of London, 16 hours ahead of US Pacific Standard Time, 13 hours ahead of US Eastern Standard Time and two hours behind Australian Eastern Standard Time.

Kalimantan is divided into two times zones: Indonesian Western Standard Time (UTC +7), which is observed in West and Central

Kalimantan; and Indonesian Central Standard Time (UTC+8), which is observed in East and South Kalimantan.

TOILETS

You'll find a lot of squat style ('Turkish') toilets in Borneo, particularly in public places, while Western-style seated toilets are more common in hotels and guesthouses. Public toilets can be a bit of an adventure. The floors are usually inexplicably flooded with water and the lighting poor, while some spectacular odours lurk in the dark. It is common to find broken cisterns; in this case, there will usually be a large tub of water and a plastic bucket with which you are expected to use as a flushing mechanism by pouring water into the toilet yourself.

Toilet paper will usually not be available so keep a small stash handy in your pocket. In major malls, expect to fork over a 20 sen fee to use the facilities, although don't expect much more in cleanliness for what you pay for. You can pay extra to buy some tissues. In urban areas, it is generally safe to discard used toilet paper into the bowl without causing a disaster unless otherwise stated. This is not so in rural bogs; if there is a wastepaper basket, discard your toilet paper there.

TOURIST INFORMATION
Brunei

Brunei's national tourist body, **Brunei Tourism** (www.tourismbrunei.com), has a useful website, with a host of useful pages under the Visitor Info section of the site. Unfortunately, it doesn't maintain a tourist information office in downtown BSB or at the airport. In fact, there is no tourist information office in BSB, which means that you will have to use hotel desks, travel agencies and anyone else you can collar for a chat as a de facto tourist information office.

Kalimantan

Indonesia's national tourist organisation, the **Directorate General of Tourism** (www.budpar.go.id), maintains a relatively unhelpful website on tourism in Indonesia. This organisation is not the place to have specific questions answered or to plan your trip.

There are local tourist offices in many of Kalimantan's bigger cities, ranging from very helpful to well meaning but hopeless. Where these offices exist, we list them under

the Information heading in each destination chapter. As in other parts of Borneo, your best source of information is often accommodation owners, travel agents and other travellers.

Sabah & Sarawak

Malaysia's national tourist body, **Tourism Malaysia** (http://travel.tourism.gov.my), is of limited use to travellers. Its offices both inside and outside Malaysia are long on brochures and short on hard, practical information. Tourism Malaysia and state tourism offices are listed in the destination chapters where there are representatives.

Most cities in Sabah and Sarawak have local tourist information offices where you can often get better, more reliable and up-to-date information. Where these exist, we list them under the Information headings in the destination chapters.

TRAVELLERS WITH DISABILITIES

Borneo has have a long way to go in this regard. Most buildings, public transport, and tourist destinations are not wheelchair accessible, and, in fact, navigating Malaysian cities in a wheelchair can be a very trying experience, due to varying pavement heights and other infrastructure shortcomings. Most tour companies that operate tours into the interior also do not accommodate people with physical disabilities.

VISAS
Brunei

Visitors must have a valid passport, or an internationally recognised travel document valid for at least six months beyond the date of entry into Brunei.

For those travellers wishing to visit for up to 14 days, visas are not necessary for citizens of Belgium, Canada, Denmark, France, Indonesia, Italy, Japan, Luxembourg, the Netherlands, Norway, the Philippines, Poland, Spain, Sweden, Switzerland, Thailand and the Republic of the Maldives. Austrian, British, German, Malaysian, New Zealand, Singaporean and South Korean nationals do not require a visa for visits of 30 days or less. US citizens do not need a visa for visits of up to 90 days. Australian citizens entering by air can get 30-day visas on arrival for B$30.

Israeli citizens are not permitted to enter Brunei. People of all other nationalities should obtain a visa before visiting Brunei.

Bruneian embassies overseas have been known to give incorrect advice, so you should double check information if in doubt. Visas can be renewed when in Brunei.

Transit passengers are issued a 72-hour visa at the airport, which is enough to see most of the sights, but ties you to travelling by air.

Kalimantan

Indonesia has three visa categories: visa free; visa on arrival (VOA); and visa in advance. Citizens of Brunei Darussalam, Chile, Hong Kong SAR, Macao SAR, Malaysia, Morocco, Peru, the Philipines, Singapore, Thailand and Vietnam do not require a visa for visits of up to 30 days.

Visas on arrival are available from recognised ports of entry in Indonesia. These include ferry ports to/from Sumatra: Penang–Medan, Penang–Belawan, Melaka–Dumai and Singapore–Batam/Bintan. Visas on arrival are not available at land border-crossings. There are two types: a seven-day (US$10) and a 30-day (US$25). These are nonextendable and travellers wishing to stay longer must apply for a visa before departure. At present, citizens of 34 nations are eligible for a VOA, including most developed Western countries. Indonesian visa requirements, however, are prone to wild fluctuations, so it is best to contact the Indonesian embassy in your home country for further information. See p292 for embassy and consulate contact information.

If you are not eligible for visa-free or VOA status, or you plan to arrive at a nonapproved port, you need to apply for a 30-day or 60-day visa in advance. Prices vary: check with your local embassy. The main crossings that require an advance visa include the road crossing at Entikong between Pontianak (Kalimantan) and Kuching (Sarawak), between Tarakan (Kalimantan) and Tawau (Sabah). Visas are not extendable and you may not be permitted to board a departure flight with an expired visa without resolving the issue at immigration first.

Proof of onward travel, such as a return or through ticket, is officially required when you arrive, but immigration officials often won't ask. If you don't have one, however, you may be forced to buy one on the spot. You may also be asked to show evidence of sufficient funds (US$1000). Travellers cheques are best and credit cards, while not guaranteed, work sometimes.

Sabah & Sarawak

Commonwealth citizens (except those from India, Bangladesh, Sri Lanka and Pakistan), and citizens of the Republic of Ireland, Switzerland, the Netherlands, San Marino and Liechtenstein do not require a visa to visit Malaysia.

Citizens of Austria, Belgium, Czech Republic, Denmark, Finland, Germany, Hungary, Iceland, Italy, Japan, Luxembourg, Norway, Slovak Republic, South Korea, Sweden, the USA and most Arab countries do not require a visa for a visit not exceeding three months.

Citizens of France, Greece, Poland, South Africa and many South American and African countries do not require a visa for a visit not exceeding one month. Most other nationalities are given a shorter stay period or require a visa. Citizens of Israel cannot enter Malaysia.

Nationalities of most countries are given a 30- or 60-day visa on arrival, depending on the expected length of stay. As a general rule, if you arrive by air you will be given 60 days automatically, though coming overland you may be given 30 days unless you specifically ask for a 60-day permit. It's then possible to get an extension at an immigration office in the country for a total stay of up to three months. This is a straightforward procedure which can easily be done in major Malaysian cities (immigration offices are listed in the text).

SARAWAK VISAS

Sarawak is semiautonomous and treated in some ways like a separate country. If you travel from Peninsular Malaysia or Sabah into Sarawak, your passport will be checked on arrival in Sarawak and a new stay permit issued, either for 30 days or for the same period as your original Malaysia entry visa. If you are travelling directly to Sarawak, you will usually be given a 30-day entry stamp on arrival. When you leave Sarawak, your passport will be checked and a departure stamp put in your passport. When you travel from Sarawak to Peninsular Malaysia or into Sabah, you do not start a new entry period, so your 30-day (or longer) permit from Sarawak remains valid.

WOMEN TRAVELLERS

Borneo is a relatively easy and pleasant place for women travellers. You might worry that, due to the fact that Indonesia, Malaysia and Brunei are Muslim countries, it might be necessary to wear headscarves and the like, or that you will suffer from a lot of harassment. Neither of these is case, although you should dress fairly conservatively and do cover up when visiting a mosque (robes and scarves are sometimes provided).

You will generally find that things feel and are much more open and liberal here in Borneo than in, say, northeast Peninsular Malaysia.

Some women have reported being the object of catcalls and come-ons in Brunei, especially from passing motorists.

As with anywhere else, it pays to use common sense and caution. Do not get lulled into a false sense of security just because everyone seems so relaxed and easygoing. Solo hitchhiking is a bad idea anywhere, and Borneo is no exception. Do not walk alone at night if possible, lock the door to your hotel room and do not accept drinks or food from strangers.

Transport

CONTENTS

GETTING THERE & AWAY

The vast majority of travellers arrive in Borneo by air. Most fly from nearby Asian cities like Bangkok, Hong Kong, Kuala Lumpur or Singapore, but there are also flights to Borneo from Oceania, Europe and the Middle East. You can also reach Borneo by boat from Java (Indonesia) and the island of Mindanao, in the southern Philippines. See the airfares map on pp308-9.

BRUNEI

You can fly to Brunei from cities in Asia, the Middle East, Europe and Oceania. You can also arrive by boat from Sabah or bus/taxi from Sarawak.

Air

ASIA
Royal Brunei Airlines (www.bruneiair.com) Flights from Bangkok, Denpasar, Hong Kong, Jakarta, Kuala Lumpur, Manila, Shanghai and Surabaya to Bandar Seri Begawan (BSB).
Thai Airways international (www.thaiair.com) Has flights from Bangkok to BSB.

EUROPE
Royal Brunei Airlines (www.bruneiair.com) Has flights from Frankfurt and London to BSB.

OCEANIA
Royal Brunei Airlines (www.bruneiair.com) Has flights from Auckland, Brisbane, Darwin, Perth and Sydney to Bandar Seri Begawan.

PENINSULAR MALAYSIA/SINGAPORE
Malaysia Airlines (www.malaysiaairlines.com) Has flights from Kuala Lumpur to Bandar Seri Begawan.
Royal Brunei Airlines (www.bruneiair.com) Has flights from Kuala Lumpur and Singapore to Bandar Seri Begawan.

OTHER PARTS OF BORNEO
Royal Brunei Airlines (www.bruneiair.com) Has flights from Kota Kinabalu (Sabah) and Kuching (Sarawak) to Bandar Seri Begawan.

For more details see p227.

Boat

There are daily ferries from Kota Kinabalu (Sabah) to Pulau Labuan (Sabah), where you can catch onward ferries to Muara, the port of Bandar Seri Begawan. This trip, which can be done in one day, is an easy way to travel between Sabah and Brunei. For details, see p124.

Bus

There are road connections between Kuala Belait and Miri, in Sarawak (see p232). There are also road connections between Bandar Seri Begawan and Limbang, in Sarawak (see p227). For details on crossing between Brunei and the Limbang Division of Sarawak (and onward to Kota Kinabalu in

---

THINGS CHANGE...

The information in this chapter is particularly vulnerable to change. Check directly with the airline or a travel agent to make sure you understand how a fare (and ticket you may buy) works and be aware of the security requirements for international travel. Shop carefully. The details given in this chapter should be regarded as pointers and are not a substitute for your own careful, up-to-date research.

TRANSPORT

CLIMATE CHANGE & TRAVEL

Climate change is a serious threat to the ecosystems that humans rely upon, and air travel is the fastest-growing contributor to the problem. Lonely Planet regards travel, overall, as a global benefit, but believes we all have a responsibility to limit our personal impact on global warming.

Flying & Climate Change

Pretty much every form of motor travel generates CO_2 (the main cause of human-induced climate change) but planes are far and away the worst offenders, not just because of the sheer distances they allow us to travel, but because they release greenhouse gases high into the atmosphere. The statistics are frightening: two people taking a return flight between Europe and the US will contribute as much to climate change as an average household's gas and electricity consumption over a whole year.

Carbon Offset Schemes

Climatecare.org and other websites use 'carbon calculators' that allow jetsetters to offset the greenhouse gases they are responsible for with contributions to energy-saving projects and other climate-friendly initiatives in the developing world – including projects in India, Honduras, Kazakhstan and Uganda.

Lonely Planet, together with Rough Guides and other concerned partners in the travel industry, supports the carbon offset scheme run by climatecare.org. Lonely Planet offsets all of its staff and author travel.

For more information check out our website: lonelyplanet.com.

Sabah) see the Across Temburong by Land box text, p234.

KALIMANTAN

Kalimantan has fewer transport connections than Brunei or Sabah/Sarawak. Apart from one flight from neighbouring Sarawak, the only flights to Kalimantan originate from other parts of Indonesia (Java or Sulawesi). You can also reach Kalimantan by boat from Java, Sulawesi and Sabah, or by road from Sarawak.

Air
TO/FROM OTHER PARTS OF INDONESIA
To/From Java
Adam Air (www.adamair.co.id) Has flights from Batam, Jakarta, Jogyakarta and Surabaya to Pontianak. They also fly from Batam, Jakarta, Jogyakarta, Semerang and Surabaya to Balikpapan.
Batavia (www.batavia-air.co.id/English) Flies from Jakarta, Surabaya, Yogyakarta and Semarang to Pontianak. They also fly from Jakarta, Surabaya and Yogyakarta to Balikpapan.
Garuda (www.garuda-indonesia/com) Has flights from Jakarta and Surabaya to Pontianak.
Sriwijaya (www.sriwijayaair-online.com) Has flights from Jakarta to Pontianak and Balikpapan.

To/From Sulawesi
Batavia (www.batavia-air.co.id/English) has flights from Makassar, Manado and Palu to Balikpapan.

For more details on air connections, see the Pontianak Getting There & Away section (p241) and the Balikpapan Getting There & Away section (p271).

TO/FROM OTHER PARTS OF BORNEO
Batavia (www.batavia-air.co.id/English) Has flights from Kuching (Sarawak) to Pontianak.

Boat
TO/FROM INDONESIA
Java
Pelni (www.pelni.co.id) Has routes that include: Tanjung Priok (Jakarta) to Pontianak; Semarang (Java) to Pontianak and Balikpapan; Surabaya (Java) to Pontianak and Balikpapan; Makassar (Sulawesi) to Balikpapan.
Titian Kapuas (☎ 731187; Jln Usin 3, Pontianak) Has ferries from Semarang and Jakarta to Pontianak.

To/From Sulawesi
Pelni (www.pelni.co.id) Has a route between Makassar (Sulawesi) and Balikpapan.
Prima Vista (☎ 732607; Jln Sudirman 138, Balikpapan) Has ferries between Balikpapan and Pare Pare (Sulawesi), Makassar and Surabaya.

For more details on boat connections, see the Pontianak Getting There & Away section (p241) and the Balikpapan Getting There & Away section (p271).

TO/FROM SABAH

There are boats from Tawau, in east Sabah, to Tarakan in northeast Kalimantan. For details, see p153.

Bus

FROM SARAWAK

There are several daily buses from Kuching (Sarawak) to Pontianak. For details, see p171.

SABAH

Air

TO/FROM ASIA

There are flights to Kota Kinabalu from the following Asian cities: Cebu and Manila (Philippines); Guangzhou, Hong Kong and Macau (China); Kaohsiung and Taipei (Taiwan); Seoul/Incheon (Korea); Singapore; and Tokyo (Japan).

TO/FROM PENINSULAR MALAYSIA & SINGAPORE

There are flights to Kota Kinabalu from the following cities in West Malaysia: Kuala Lumpur, Kuala Terengganu, Kuantan, Penang and Johor Bahru (note that it's usually much cheaper to fly to/from Johor Bahru than Kuala Lumpur, so consider taking a bus to/from Johor Bahru). There are also flights from Singapore.

TO/FROM OTHER PARTS OF BORNEO

There are also flights to/from the following cities in Borneo: Bandar Seri Begawan, Bintulu, Kuching, Miri, and Sibu (all in Sarawak).

For details, see p100.

Boat

BRUNEI

There are boats from Muara (the port of Bandar Seri Begawan) to Pulau Labuan (Sabah), where you can catch a boat to Kota Kinabalu. Due to the difficulty of the overland route from Brunei to Sabah, this is the best way to move from Brunei to Kota Kinabalu (unless you prefer to fly). For details, see p124.

SARAWAK

There are boats from Limbang and Lawas, both in northern Sarawak, to Pulau Labuan (Sabah), where you can catch a boat to Kota Kinabalu. Due to the difficulty of the overland route across the Limbang Division of Sarawak to Sabah, this is the best way to move from Brunei or Limbang to Kota Kinabalu (unless you fly). For details, see p124.

KALIMANTAN

There are boats from Nunukan/Tarakan in Kalimantan to Tawau, in east Sabah. For details, see p153.

THE PHILIPPINES

There are boats from Zamboanga, on the island of Mindanao in the southern Philippines, to Sandakan, in east Sabah. For details, see p138.

Bus

There are road connections between Lawas, in Sarawak's northern Limbang Division and Sipitang, in far southwest Sabah (with daily buses going the whole way north to Kota Kinabalu from Lawas). For details, see p121.

SARAWAK

Many travellers enter Kuching by air from either Peninsular Malaysia or Singapore or Kota Kinabalu, in Sabah, but you can also come overland from Bandar Seri Begawan in Brunei, or from Kota Kinabalu or Sipitang (Sabah) to Lawas.

Air

TO/FROM ASIA

There are flights from Guangzhou and Hong to Kuching.

TO/FROM PENINSULAR MALAYSIA & SINGAPORE

There are flights from Johor Bahru, Kuala Lumpur, Penang and Singapore to Kuching. There are also flights from Kuala Lumpur to Bintulu, Miri and Sibu.

TO/FROM OTHER PARTS OF BORNEO

There are flights from Bandar Seri Begawan and Kota Kinabalu to Kuching. There are also flights from Kota Kinabalu to Bintulu, Miri and Sibu.

For details, see the Getting There & Away sections of Kuching (p171), Bintulu (p196), Miri (p204) and Sibu (p185).

Boat

There are speedboats from Bandar Seri Begawan, in Brunei to Limbang, in far northern Sarawak; for details, see p227. There are also speedboats from Pulau Labuan (Sabah) to Limbang and Lawas (both in far northern Sarawak); for further details see p124.

BORNEO BORDER CROSSINGS

Travelling between the three countries of Borneo is relatively easy, but you may be surprised to find that there are no legal border crossings in the middle of the island. Instead, all the land crossings are located near the coast. In addition to these, it's possible to travel between the three countries of Borneo by boat along the coast of the island.

Note that some travellers have reported successfully crossing from Sarawak (Malaysia) into Kalimantan (Indonesia) and back in at the Kelabit Highlands, but this is not an official crossing and you risk trouble by attempting this crossing without prior permission from the relevant authorities. Note the following abbreviations: B (Brunei), M (Malaysia), I (Indonesia).

Sabah–Sarawak

There are boats between Pulau Labuan (M), in Sabah, and Limbang (M) and Lawas (M), both in the Limbang District of northern Sarawak. For details, see p124.

Sabah–Brunei

There are boats between Pulau Labuan (M), in Sabah, and Muara (B), the port of Bandar Seri Begawan. Due to the difficulty of the overland route between Sabah and Brunei, this is the best way to travel between Sabah and Brunei (unless you prefer to fly). For details, see p124.

Sabah–Kalimantan

There are boats between Tawau (M), in east Sabah, and Tarakan (I), in northeast Kalimantan. For details, see p153.

Brunei–Sarawak

There are road connections between Kuala Belait (B), in southwest Brunei, and Miri (M), in northeast Sarawak (see p232). There are road connections between Bandar Seri Begawan and Limbang (M), in the Limbang Division of Sarawak (see p227). There are also road connections between Bangar (B), in the Temburong District of Brunei, and Lawas (M), in the Limbang Division of Sarawak (and onward to Kota Kinabalu in Sabah: see the Across Temburong by Land box, p234.

Sarawak–Kalimantan

There are several daily buses between Kuching (M), in southwest Sarawak, and Pontianak (I), in far western Kalimantan, crossing at the Tebedu–Entikong crossing. For details, see p171.

Bus

There are daily express buses from Pontianak (Kalimantan) to Kuching; see p171. There are buses from Kuala Belait (Brunei) to Miri (see p232). There are buses from Kota Kinabalu (Sabah) to Lawas, in far northern Sarawak. For details, see p217.

GETTING AROUND

AIR

Borneo is covered by a surprisingly extensive network of flights and it's often remarkably cheap to fly around the island. Sometimes, flying is the only practical way to reach a particular destination, as is the case with isolated communities in Sarawak's Kelabit Highlands and the mountainous regions of northwest Kalimantan.

Jet plane, such as Boeing 737s, are usually used for longer flights, say between Kota Kinabalu (Sabah) and Kuching (Sarawak), while shorter flights usually involve smaller propeller planes such as DeHavilland Twin Otters.

Needless to say, there is something incredibly romantic and exciting about buzzing over the Borneo jungle in a light plane. Aerial sightseeing is one of the great highlights of flying around Borneo and few plane journeys will equal the thrill of the Miri (Sarawak) to Gunung Mulu National Park (Sarawak) route, which takes you right past the peak of Gunung Mulu and Batu Lawi.

In most cases, you can buy tickets on relatively short notice, but for a few destinations, including Gunung Mulu National Park, Bario and Ba Kelalan (all in Sarawak), you should buy tickets well in advance. A few of the airlines flying in Borneo have websites where you can

BORDER CROSSINGS

make online reservations, but, in most cases the best way to buy tickets is to go directly to a local travel agency after you arrive. Prices don't vary much between agents, so there's little to be gained by marching from one to another. See the airfares map on pp308-9.

Malaysian Borneo

Air travel within Malaysian Borneo (Sabah and Sarawak) is handled by **Malaysia Airlines** (MAS; ☎ inside Malaysia 1-300-883-000, outside Malaysia 03-515-555; www.malaysiaairlines.com) and **Air Asia** (☎ within Malaysia 03-8775-4000, outside Malaysia 03-8660-4343; www.airasia.com), with rural routes now being operated by **MASwings** (☎ within Malaysia 1-300-88-3000, outside Malaysia 03-7843-3000; www.maswings .com.my), an MAS subsidiary.

Kalimantan

Air travel within Kalimantan is handled by **IAT** (Indonesia Air Transport; ☎ inside Kalimantan 0561-736603, outside Indonesia 62-21-808-70666; www.iat .co.id), **DAS** (Dirgantara Air Service ☎ inside Kalimantan 0561-736407, outside Indonesia 62-0561-736407) and **Kal-Star** (☎ inside Kalimantan 0561-737473, outside Indonesia 62-0561-73747).

Intra Borneo

Batavia (www.batavia-air.co.id/English) has flights between Kuching, in Sarawak, and Pontianak, in Kalimantan.

Royal Brunei Airlines (www.bruneiair.com) flies between Bandar Seri Begawan, in Brunei, and Kuching, in Sarawak, and Kota Kinabalu, in Sabah.

Brunei

There are no commercial flights within Brunei.

BICYCLE

Borneo has a fairly extensive network of paved roads and a variety of roadside terrain, but it's unlikely that Borneo will take off as one of the world's great bike-touring destinations. Several factors contribute to making the island hard going for bike tourers. Few roads have shoulders and roads are crowded with logging trucks and other trucks, some of which drive very fast and rather erratically. Roads are in various states of disrepair, with long sections reverting to dirt or potholes, or under construction. Finally, of course, there's the tropical heat – Borneo lies right on the equator and the heat, humidity and sun can be merciless.

That said, there is limited scope for bicycle touring in parts of Sabah, especially in the Pegalan Valley (p124). Wherever you bicycle in Borneo, keep in mind that you're in the tropics and the sun can burn exposed skin in a matter of minutes. Likewise, bring plenty of water and take extreme caution with traffic: drivers are not used to seeing bicycles and will give you precious little leeway.

For details on mountain biking in Borneo, see the Mountain Biking section in the Borneo Outdoors chapter (p68).

BOAT

Until the advent of airplanes and 4WD vehicles, boats were the only practical way of covering long distances in Borneo, whether moving up and down the coast or heading into the interior. Boats still play a major role in Borneo transport and you'll almost certainly take a few journeys by boat as you explore the island. Craft run the gamut from large ocean-going ferries, complete with first-class sections and Hong Kong kung fu movies, to leaky dugout canoes propelled by handmade paddles.

Coastal Travel

Ferries and speedboats link various coastal cities and towns in Borneo and they're often the best way to cover a particular leg, sparing you from Borneo's sometimes bumpy or nonexistent roads. The Kota Kinabalu–Pulau Labuan–Muara (Bandar Seri Begawan) route is the best way to move between Sabah and Brunei. Likewise, the Kuching–Sibu ferry takes about half the time of the corresponding bus route. In Kalimantan, boats are the only practical way to get between certain points, like Berau and Tarakan.

Ferries usually cost between a third and a half of the corresponding flight fare. A good example is the Kuching–Sibu route, where the boat costs RM36, while the flight costs RM89. Ferries used on these routes tend to be fairly comfortable, although arctic air-con and the aforementioned kung fu movies can make you wish for an early arrival. Consider bringing a fleece to Borneo for such journeys; a pair of ear plugs may also come in handy.

River Travel

The quintessential Borneo experience is a trip upriver into the island's interior. Despite the recent increase in 4WD logging roads and rural airstrips, rivers still serve as the main means of access to the interior. Sarawak's Batang Rejang is sometimes called 'The Amazon of Borneo' and a journey upriver is still romantic, despite the lack of intact forest en route. To the north, Sungai Baram is another highway into Sarawak's interior. Kalimantan also has two fantastic river routes into the interior: Sungai Kaupuas, which heads inland from Pontianak; and the might Sungai Makaham, which heads all the way inland to near the mountainous border with Sarawak.

On the wider downstream stretches of these rivers, cigar-shaped speedboats are the norm (often mistakenly believed to have been made from used airplane fuselages). These seat up to 60 people, with two cramped seats on either side of a long aisle. It's sometimes possible to sit on the roof of these things, but be warned: the wind will make you forget about the intensity of the sun and you can get a second-degree sunburn in no time.

As you head upriver, you may transfer to smaller boats that seat 10 or fewer and move at a snail's pace. These little craft call to mind the film *The African Queen*, and, despite their slow pace, are a very pleasant way to travel.

Further upstream, in the narrow tributaries, the only craft that can make any headway over the occasional rapids and around the snags are long dugout or plank canoes, powered either by outboard motors or paddles or poles.

Travel on regularly scheduled river boats is quite cheap. Travelling upriver from Sibu to Kapit along the Batang Rejang, for instance, costs around US$8 for a second-class seat. Hiring boats and boatmen to take you up a distant tributary, à la Redmond O'Hanlon, can cost upwards of US$100 per day, with fuel being the biggest expense.

BUS

Borneo's coastal cities are connected by a network of cheap, relatively comfortable and relatively safe buses. On longer runs between larger cities, buses are typical modern air-con coaches, while buses to villages around a city are sometimes closer to old-style school buses. Even on the proper coaches, maintenance on amenities such as seat cushions is usually overlooked, the focus being on keeping the aging hulks sputtering and on the road.

TRANSPORT

TRANSPORT

BORNEO AIRFARES

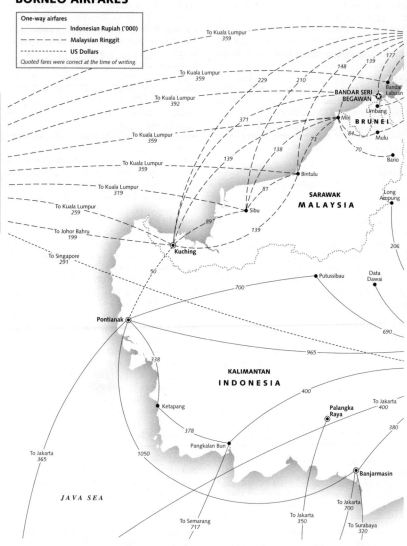

One-way airfares
— Indonesian Rupiah ('000)
— — Malaysian Ringgit
·········· US Dollars
Quoted fares were correct at the time of writing.

To Kuala Lumpur 359
To Kuala Lumpur 359
To Kuala Lumpur 392
To Kuala Lumpur 359
To Kuala Lumpur 359
To Kuala Lumpur 319
To Kuala Lumpur 259
To Johor Bahru 199
To Singapore 291

177
139
148
229
210
371
73
84
70
138
139
81
89
139
50
700
690
965
400
338
378
1050
365
717
380
350
700
320
206

BANDAR SERI BEGAWAN
Bandar Labuan
Limbang
BRUNEI
Miri
Mulu
Bario
Bintulu
Long Ampung
SARAWAK
MALAYSIA
Sibu
Kuching
Putussibau
Data Dawai
Pontianak
KALIMANTAN
INDONESIA
Ketapang
Palangka Raya
To Jakarta 400
Pangkalan Bun
Banjarmasin
To Jakarta 700
To Jakarta 350
To Surabaya 320
JAVA SEA
To Jakarta 365
To Semarang 717

Most bus companies are operated as private enterprises with no central oversight, so there may be more than one company operating in a city, with overlapping routes and confusing route numbers. Some cities are taking steps to remedy this situation; the city of Kuching has just recently merged all six of their major bus companies into one,

and is slowly moving towards a modernised bus system.

In most cities, public bus services have been hit hard by the proliferation of *van sapu*, privately operated minivans that ply certain routes in the city (see p312). In recent years, many intracity bus routes have had their services reduced or cancelled. Most large cit-

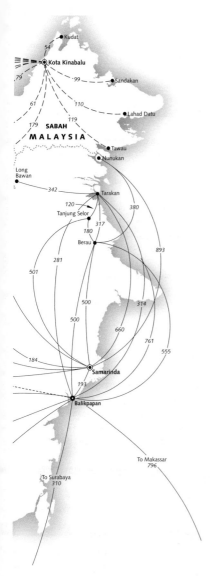

TRANSPORT

downtown area, while long-distance buses usually depart from a special long-distance bus terminal on the outskirts of town. It can sometimes be rather confusing trying to figure out where to catch a bus to a specific destination. The sure-fire solution, if you're unsure, is to ask at the place where you're staying.

There will always be a local bus that does the route between downtown and the long-distance bus terminal. A taxi is always a good option for getting to the terminal as well, and they are usually close enough to the city so the fare won't break the bank.

There is usually no need to purchase bus tickets in advance. The usual drill when travelling between cities is to just show up at the long-distance bus terminal in the morning and shop around for the next departure. Bus companies usually make this very easy for you, displaying large clocks showing the time of the next departure or employing touts to inform you when they're going.

Note that there are more departures in the mornings, and it pays to show up early, especially if you are crossing a border, where there may be no onward transport late in the day.

Costs

Bus travel is usually the cheapest way to travel between two cities in Borneo. A good example would be the Kuching-to-Miri run along the coast of Sarawak: the plane trip costs a minimum of RM139 while a bus will only set you back RM80. Of course, after 14 hours on the bus, you may wish that you had splashed out on the plane ticket.

CAR & MOTORCYCLE

There are roads of varying quality along most of Borneo's coast and a few roads leading into the interior. Brunei boasts the most advanced roads of Borneo's three countries, with a proper highway running up and down the west coast. Sabah takes second place, with a good network of reasonable roads up and down its west coast and a decent highway heading over to the east coast. Sarawak's road network, while fairly extensive, is rougher, with a fair share of sections either under construction or in need of it. Kalimantan's road network is perhaps the roughest and least extensive of the bunch, with lots of sections yet to be paved.

Driving is not particularly challenging or hair-raising in most parts of Borneo and it's

ies still have regular bus services to major destinations, however.

Bus Stations

Spend any time travelling around Borneo and you'll quickly get used to a peculiar feature of Borneo bus travel: buses to nearby destinations usually depart from stops in the

DRIVING IN BORNEO

Renting a car and driving yourself around Borneo is an excellent way to see the island, particularly in Sabah and Sarawak. It's easier to drive in Borneo than you might expect, but there are some peculiar features and dangers to look out for. These include:

- Sudden bumps with no warning sign: If you're carrying too much speed, you can suddenly find yourself airborne.
- Sudden end to pavement with no warning sign: Feel like a spot of unplanned off-road driving?
- Getting stuck behind logging trucks and other lumbering vehicles: This may be your most lasting memory of driving in Borneo. Passing these things on hills in a dilapidated old rental is at least as thrilling as climbing Mt Kinabalu.
- Dogs: You'll find them sleeping in the road or loitering beside the road; some are remarkably blasé about cars or they plainly have a death wish.
- Few divided highways: Most roads in Borneo are just two lanes, so you're almost always jockeying to pass.
- Rental cars with tiny engines: Many of the rental cars in Borneo seem to be outfitted with lawnmower engines; take them for a test drive and keep in mind that if you're driving across, say, Sabah, you'll need power to get you over the hills.
- Headlights? Why bother? Most drivers don't use headlights in the rain and seem surprised if you do, often flashing you.
- AWAS: Borneo's most popular road sign, this means 'warning', but you'll often be unable to figure out what the danger is.
- Roundabouts: If you're from a country like the USA, where they don't have such things, you may find these tricky.
- Devilish one-way systems in towns: We thought we'd never escape the town of Kota Belud, in Sabah, and pictured a grim future living out of the car and driving round that town forever.
- Parking in Kota Kinabalu on a holiday: Don't even think of finding a parking place.
- Huge hazards unmarked: How about a nice sinkhole right in the middle of the road? How about one with no warning signs? Welcome to driving in Borneo. This is the reason we strongly advise against driving at night. Where are the AWAS signs when you need them?
- Cows: Behave like Borneo's dogs, which means they consider cars to be intruders on their roads.
- Signs petering out: They'll get you started in the direction of a some place, then they'll magically peter out, leaving you scratching your head.
- Oncoming truck warning: When you approach a large vehicle coming toward you on a two-lane road, assume that there is a car behind it about to dart out and try to pass. Drive with extra caution.

quite easy to explore much of the island by car. However, there are some hazards and peculiarities to keep in mind. For details on these, see the Driving in Borneo box, above.

City driving is generally safe and orderly. In general, traffic is quite sedate compared to the chaos that rules most of Southeast Asia's roads. Motorcycles and scooters tend to forgo the concept of traffic lanes and will squeeze into the space between cars, so keep an extra eye out when changing lanes. None of the major cities in Borneo are large enough to cause that much congestion, although tailbacks are starting to be a problem in Kuching.

Rules of the Road

Driving is on the left in all three countries that share Borneo. Seat belts are compulsory for the driver and front-seat passenger (there usually are no seat belts in the back seat). Roundabouts are a common feature on Borneo roads and these can be a little daunting if you're unused to them. The simple rule is this: always yield to those already in the roundabout. And, of course, always look to the right when entering a roundabout, as this is where the traffic will be coming from. Otherwise, traffic signals and signs are all pretty obvious and the rules are similar to those of most Western countries.

Rental

Renting a car to explore Borneo is a good option for those who can afford it, especially in Sabah, where the roads are quite good and the drives quite scenic. You'll appreciate having a car to travel easily from Kota Kinabalu up to Mt Kinabalu or out to Poring Hot Springs, and the trip around the Crocker Range is rewarding. Exploring the east coast of Sabah is also quite easy by car.

You will find car rental companies in the arrivals halls of the larger airports in Borneo. Despite the fact that several companies are usually represented at these counters, you'll often find that they are all just fronts for one large local car rental agency, which makes it very difficult to try to play one of against another. You'll also find car rental agencies in the downtown areas of Borneo's larger cities. If you can't find a car rental agency, you can usually arrange car rental at a local travel agency.

Car rental averages around RM150 per day and RM600 per week in Sabah and Sarawak, although you can often get significantly cheaper prices if you bargain hard or go through a local Chinese businessperson. Rates in Brunei are more expensive, averaging B$75 per day. Rates in Kalimantan are quite cheap, averaging around 100,000Rp per day, although you'll sometimes find it's cheaper and easier to simply hire a taxi for the whole day.

The most common rental cars in Sabah, Sarawak and Brunei are Protons, which are Malaysia automobiles based on Mitsubishi designs. The humble Proton Wira is often the default (ie cheapest) model. It's usually sufficient for driving around Borneo, but be sure to test the car – you'll want sufficient power to be able to overtake logging trucks and to make it over mountain passes (like the one over the shoulder of Mt Kinabalu). There is nothing quite like the feeling of trying to overtake a

> **BORNEO DRIVING WORDS**
>
> - *Awas*: warning or attention
> - *Zon had laju*: speed limit zone
> - *Hadapan*: ahead
> - *Pekan*: town or city
> - *Pusat Bandaraya/Pusat Banda*: city centre
> - *Simpang ke*: exit to
> - *Selemat datant ke*: welcome to

lumbering logging truck on a hill and realising that the old engine isn't up to the task.

A valid overseas licence is needed to rent a car. An International Driving Permit is usually not required by local car-hire companies but it is recommended that you bring one. Age limits apply, and most companies require that drivers be at least 23 years old.

HITCHING

Hitching is certainly possible in most parts of Borneo. It's usually quite safe for male travellers to hitch, but we don't recommend it for female travellers. Keep in mind that some drivers will expect a small 'tip' or contribution to gas for driving you. At the very least, if they stop for food, you should offer to pay for their meal.

Keep in mind that hitching is never entirely safe in any country in the world, and we don't recommend it. Travellers who decide to hitch should understand that they are taking a small but potentially serious risk. People who do choose to hitch will be safer if they travel in pairs and let someone know where they are planning to go. Women travellers considering hitching in Malaysia should have a look at p301.

LONG-DISTANCE TAXI

In addition to the taxis that serve destinations within a city, some cities also have ranks of long-distance taxis that will do intercity routes and travel to outlying destinations. These taxis are ideal for groups of four, and are also available on a share basis. As soon as a full complement of four passengers turns up, off you go.

Between major towns you have a reasonable chance of finding other passengers to share without having to wait too long, but otherwise you will have to charter a whole taxi, which is four times the single fare rate (in this book we generally quote the rate for the whole car). As Malaysia becomes increasingly wealthy, and people can afford to hire a whole taxi, the share system is becoming less reliable. Early in the morning is the best time to find other people to share a taxi, or you can inquire at the taxi stand the day before to see when is the best time.

Taxi drivers often drive at frighteningly high speeds. They don't have as many head-on collisions as you might expect, but closing your eyes at times of high stress certainly helps! You also have the option of demanding that the driver slow down, but this is met with varying degrees of hostility. Another tactic is to look for aging taxis and taxi drivers – they must be doing something right to have made it this far!

Full-day charter rates for taxis will run close to US$100, including gas, in Borneo. Keep in mind that the rate will go up the further you intend to travel. You may be able to negotiate a better rate through the owner of your accommodation or a travel agency. Make sure that all terms are fully agreed upon up front and don't pay anything until the end of the day.

TOURS

Many international tour operators offer tours to Borneo. One international operator with a good reputation and a wide variety of Borneo tours is Peninsular Malaysia based **Ping Anchorage** (www.pinganchorage.com.my). Other tour operators in Borneo:

Berjaya Tour & Travel (www.berjayatour.com) This Kalimantan operator offers tours throughout the state.

Borneo Eco Tours (www.borneoecotours.com) This Sabah-based operator handles a wide range of Borneo tours with an eco angle.

Freme Travel Services (www.freme.com) This Brunei tour operator offers tours to all of Brunei's attractions, both natural and cultural.

Special Interest Tours (www.sitoursborneo.com) This operator, based in Sandakan (Sabah), specialises in wildlife tours in eastern Sabah.

In addition to these, you will find smaller tour operators of all levels of competence and reliability in most of Borneo's main cities. Most guesthouses and hotels have relationships with at least one local tour operator and some run their own in-house travel agencies. It's best to ask other travellers about their experiences with these before plunking down any money.

TRAIN

There is only one railway on Borneo, the Sabah State Railway, which runs from Tanjung Aru, near Kota Kinabalu, to Tenom. It's currently closed for overhaul, and will not reopen until at least the beginning of 2008. There is very little information on the operation of the line but we would imagine that it will continue to be slow (averaging about 30 km/h) and the carriages will continue to have no air-con. The overhaul is supposed to be for stabilising the track against environmental dangers such as mud slides. We hear the route is very scenic, though.

LOCAL TRANSPORT
Bicycle

Within cities, bicycles are becoming a very rare sight, as increased prosperity has brought the creature comforts of gas guzzling to Malaysia. However, some guesthouses rent or lend bicycles to their guests. Out in the country, locals still use bicycles to get around small *kampung* (villages) and, if you can get a hold of a bicycle, this is often a very pleasant way to spend a day.

For details on mountain biking in Borneo, see the Mountain Biking section in the Borneo Outdoors chapter (p68).

Boat

Small motorised and paddle boats are used for short river, bay and ocean journeys in various parts of Borneo. Examples include the trip across the Sungai Sarawak in Kuching; journeys around the Kampung Ayer (Water Village) in Bandar Seri Begawan; trips out to the islands of Tunku Abdul Rahman National Park from Kota Kinabalul and the journey across the Sungai Kapuas in Pontianak. Rates vary tremendously for these journeys – the difference being whether locals use the boats for transport or if the boat is mostly for tourists. Prices are listed in the relevant sections.

Taxis

Taxis are common in Borneo's bigger cities; meters, drivers who use them, and fixed rates, are not. Luckily, you'll find that most drivers in Borneo are quite honest. Just be sure to set the price before starting out and only pay upon arrival. As a rule of thumb, you can count on spending about US$2 for a typical taxi ride across a typical town in Borneo. We list prices for particular journeys in the various sections of this book.

Health Dr Trish Batchelor

There are good medical facilities in the larger cities of Borneo, particularly in Sabah, Sarawak and Brunei. You will have no problem communicating with doctors in Borneo and nurses tend to speak a smattering of English. Pharmacists also tend to speak reasonable English. Of course, as you head into the hinterlands, you will find few if any medical facilities and you will encounter more potential hazards and health risks than in the city.

Travellers tend to worry about contracting infectious diseases when travelling in Borneo, but infections are not nearly as common as you might fear and rarely cause serious illness or death in travellers. Malaria does exist, but outbreaks are usually limited to small upland areas around logging camps. Pre-existing medical conditions, such as heart disease, and accidental injury (especially traffic accidents) account for most life-threatening situations. Of course, there is always a chance that you will fall ill in some way. Fortunately, most common illnesses can either be prevented with some common-sense behaviour or be treated easily with a well-stocked traveller's medical kit.

The following advice is a general guide only and does not replace the advice of a doctor trained in travel medicine.

BEFORE YOU GO

Pack medications in their original, clearly labelled containers. A signed and dated letter from your physician describing your medical conditions and medications, including generic names, is also a good idea. If carrying syringes or needles, be sure to have a physician's letter documenting their medical necessity. If you have a heart condition, bring a copy of your ECG taken just prior to travelling.

If you take any regular medication, bring double your needs in case of loss or theft, and carry these extra supplies separately. You may be able to buy some medications over the counter in Borneo without a doctor's prescription, but it can be difficult to find some of the newer drugs, particularly the latest antidepressants, blood-pressure medications and contraceptive pills.

INSURANCE

Even if you are fit and healthy, don't travel without health insurance – accidents do happen. Declare any existing medical conditions you have – the insurance company will check if your problem is pre-existing and will not cover you if it is undeclared. You may require extra cover for adventure activities such as rock climbing. If your health insurance doesn't cover you for medical expenses abroad, consider getting extra insurance. If you're uninsured, emergency evacuation is expensive: bills of over US$100,000 are not uncommon.

Find out in advance if your insurance plan will make payments directly to providers or reimburse you later for overseas health expenses (Doctors may expect payment in cash).

RECOMMENDED VACCINATIONS

Specialised travel-medicine clinics are your best source of information; they stock all available vaccines and will be able to give specific recommendations for you and your trip. The doctors will take into account factors such as past vaccination history, the length of your trip, activities

HEALTH

HEALTH

MEDICAL KIT CHECK LIST

Consider including the following in your medical kit:

- **Antibiotics** – consider including these if you're travelling well off the beaten track; see your doctor, as they must be prescribed, and carry the prescription with you
- **Antifungal cream or powder** – for fungal skin infections and thrush
- **Antihistamine** – for allergies such as hay fever; to ease the itch from insect bites or stings; and to prevent motion sickness
- **Antiseptic (such as povidone-iodine or betadine)** – for cuts and grazes
- **Antispasmodic** – for stomach cramps, eg Buscopan
- **Aspirin or paracetamol (acetaminophen in the USA)** – for pain or fever
- **Bandages, Band-Aids (plasters) and other wound dressings**
- **Calamine lotion, sting relief spray or aloe vera** – to ease irritation from sunburn and insect bites or stings
- **Cold and flu tablets, throat lozenges and nasal decongestant** – general medicine
- **Contraceptives**
- **DEET-based insect repellent**
- **Ibuprofen** – or another anti-inflammatory
- **Iodine tablets** (unless you are pregnant or have a thyroid problem) – to purify water
- **Loperamide or diphenoxylate** – 'blockers' for diarrhoea
- **Multivitamins** – consider for long trips, when dietary vitamin intake may be inadequate
- **Permethrin** – to impregnate clothing and mosquito nets
- **Prochlorperazine or metaclopramide** – for nausea and vomiting
- **Rehydration mixture** – to prevent dehydration, which may occur, for example, during bouts of diarrhoea; particularly important when travelling with children
- **Scissors, tweezers and a thermometer** – note that mercury thermometers are prohibited by airlines
- **Sterile kit** – in case you need injections in a country with medical-hygiene problems; discuss with your doctor
- **Sunscreen, lip balm and eye drops**
- **Water purification tablets**

---

you may be undertaking and underlying medical conditions including allergies.

Most vaccines don't produce immunity until at least two weeks after they're given, so visit a doctor four to eight weeks before departure. Ask your doctor for an International Certificate of Vaccination (otherwise known as the yellow booklet), which will list all the vaccinations you've received.

Proof of vaccination against yellow fever will be required only if you have visited a country in the yellow-fever zone (parts of Africa and South America) within six days prior to entering Malaysia, Brunei or Indonesia. If you're coming from Africa or South America, check to see if you require proof of vaccination.

The World Health Organization recommends the following vaccinations for travellers to Borneo:

Adult diphtheria and tetanus Single booster recommended if none in the previous 10 years. Side effects include sore arm and fever.

Hepatitis A Provides almost 100% protection for up to a year, a booster after 12 months provides at least another 20 years protection. Mild side effects such as headache and sore arm occur in 5% to 10% of people.

Hepatitis B Now considered routine for most travellers. Given as three shots over six months. Lifetime protection occurs in 95% of people.

Measles, mumps and rubella Two doses of MMR required unless you have had the diseases. Many young adults require a booster.

Polio Only one booster required as an adult for lifetime protection. Inactivated polio vaccine is safe during pregnancy.

Typhoid Recommended unless your trip is less than a week and only to developed cities. The vaccine offers around 70% protection, lasts for two to three years and comes as a single shot.

Varicella If you haven't had chickenpox, discuss this vaccination with your doctor.

These immunisations are recommended for longer-term travellers (more than one month) or those at special risk:

Japanese B Encephalitis Three injections in all. Booster recommended after two years. Sore arm and headache are the most common side effects.

Meningitis Single injection. Recommended for long-term backpackers aged under 25.

Rabies Three injections in all. A booster after one year will then provide 10 years protection. Side effects are rare – occasionally headache and sore arm.

Tuberculosis A complex issue. Adult long-term travellers are usually recommended to have a TB skin test before and after travel, rather than vaccination. Only one vaccine given in a lifetime.

ONLINE RESOURCES

There's a wealth of travel health advice on the internet. For further information:

CDC (www.cdc.gov) Has good general information.

Lonely Planet (www.lonelyplanet.com) A good place to start.

MD Travel Health (www.mdtravelhealth.com) Provides complete travel-health recommendations for every country and is updated daily.

World Health Organization (www.who.int/ith) Publishes a superb book called *International Travel and Health*, which is revised annually and is available online at no cost.

HEALTH ADVISORIES

It's usually a good idea to consult your government's travel health website before departure, if one is available:

Australia www.dfat.gov.au/travel
Canada www.travelhealth.gc.ca
New Zealand www.mfat.govt.nz/travel
South Africa www.dfa.gov.za/travelling
United Kingdom www.doh.gov.uk/traveladvice
United States www.cdc.gov/travel

FURTHER READING

Lonely Planet's pocket size *Healthy Travel Asia & India* is packed with useful information including pretrip planning, emergency first aid, immunisation and disease information and what to do if you get sick on the road. *Travel with Children* from Lonely Planet includes advice on travel health for young children. Other recommended references include *Traveller's Health* by Dr Richard Dawood (Oxford University Press), and *Travelling Well* by Dr Deborah Mills, available at www.travellingwell.com.au.

IN TRANSIT

DEEP VEIN THROMBOSIS (DVT)

Blood clots forming in the legs during plane flights, chiefly because of prolonged immobility, is known as deep vein thrombosis (DVT). The longer the flight, the greater the risk. Though most blood clots are reabsorbed uneventfully, some may break off and travel through the blood vessels to the lungs, where they may cause life-threatening complications.

The chief symptom of DVT is swelling or pain of the foot, ankle or calf, usually but not always on just one side. When a blood clot travels to the lungs, it may cause chest pain and difficulty breathing. Travellers with any of these symptoms should immediately seek medical attention.

To prevent the development of DVT on long flights you should walk about the cabin, perform isometric compressions of the leg muscles (ie contract the leg muscles while sitting), drink plenty of fluids, and avoid alcohol and tobacco.

JET LAG & MOTION SICKNESS

Jet lag is common when crossing more than five time zones; it results in insomnia, fatigue, malaise or nausea. To avoid jet lag try drinking plenty of fluids (nonalcoholic) and eating light meals. Upon arrival, seek exposure to natural sunlight and readjust your schedule (for meals, sleep etc) as soon as possible.

Antihistamines such as dimenhydrinate (Dramamine) and meclizine (Antivert, Bonine) are usually the first choice for treating motion sickness. Their main side effect is drowsiness. A herbal alternative is ginger, which works like a charm for some people.

HEALTH

IN BORNEO

AVAILABILITY & COST OF HEALTH CARE

There are good hospitals in the major cities of Sabah, Sarawak, Brunei and Kalimantan. You will also find clinics catering specifically to travellers and expats in these cities. These clinics are usually more expensive than local medical facilities, but are worth utilising, as they will offer a superior standard of care. Additionally they understand the local system, and are aware of the safest local hospitals and best specialists. They can also liaise with insurance companies should you require evacuation.

Away from the big cities, you will find very little in terms of medical facilities. There may be local doctors in villages, but you will usually have to travel to the nearest city to get proper medical care.

In terms of cost, you will find medical care to be extremely reasonable in Borneo, particularly if you come from the United States. Costs are similar to other Southeast Asian countries. Needless to say, private clinics cost more than public hospitals, but even then, costs for most simple procedures and tests won't break the bank.

Self-treatment may be appropriate if your problem is only minor (eg traveller's diarrhoea), you are carrying the appropriate medication and you cannot attend a recommended clinic. If you think you may have a serious disease, especially malaria, do not waste time – travel to the nearest quality facility to receive attention. It's always better to be assessed by a doctor than to rely on self-treatment.

Clinics catering specifically to travellers are listed under Information in the capital city sections in this book. Your embassy and insurance company will also have contacts for medical facilities.

INFECTIOUS DISEASES

Cutaneous Larva Migrans

Found in Borneo, and caused by the dog hookworm, the rash symptomatic of cutaneous larva migrans starts as a small lump, then slowly spreads in a linear fashion. It's intensely itchy, especially at night, but it's easily treated with medications; it should not be cut out or frozen.

Dengue Fever

This mosquito-borne disease is present in Borneo. As there's no vaccine available, it can only be prevented by avoiding mosquito bites. The mosquito that carries dengue fever bites during both day and night, so use insect-avoidance measures at all times. Symptoms include high fever, severe headache and body ache (dengue was previously known as 'breakbone fever'). Some people develop a rash and experience diarrhoea. The southern islands of Thailand are particularly high risk. There's no specific treatment, just rest and paracetamol – don't take aspirin as it increases the likelihood of haemorrhaging. See a doctor to be diagnosed and monitored.

Filariasis

Filariasis is a mosquito-borne disease, very common in local populations, yet very rare in travellers. Mosquito-avoidance measures are the best way to prevent this disease.

Hepatitis A

This food- and water-borne virus infects the liver, causing jaundice (yellow skin and eyes), nausea and lethargy. There's no specific treatment for hepatitis A, you just need to allow time for the liver to heal. All travellers to Borneo should be vaccinated against hepatitis A.

Hepatitis B

The only sexually transmitted disease that can be prevented by vaccination, hepatitis B is spread by body fluids, including sexual contact. In some parts of Asia up to 20% of the population are carriers of hepatitis B, and usually are unaware of this. The long-term consequences can include liver cancer and cirrhosis.

Hepatitis E

Hepatitis E is transmitted through contaminated food and water, has similar symptoms to hepatitis A, but is far less common. It's a severe problem in pregnant women and can result in the death of both mother and baby. There is currently no vaccine, and prevention is by following safe eating and drinking guidelines while you're travelling in Borneo.

LEPTOSPIROSIS WARNING

In 2000, dozens of participants in an Eco-Challenge event held at Borneo Rainforest Lodge in Danum Valley (Sabah) came down with leptospirosis, apparently from swimming in the Sungai Segama (Segama River) near the lodge. We also have heard reports of more recent cases linked to swimming in this river. At this time, we recommend that you completely avoid swimming, wading in or drinking from that river, regardless of what you're told by the lodge operators.

HIV

HIV is rapidly increasing through much of Southeast Asia, including Borneo, with heterosexual sex now the main method of transmission.

Japanese B Encephalitis

Rare in travellers, this viral disease transmitted by mosquitoes is found in Borneo. Most cases of Japanese B encephalitis occur in rural areas and vaccination is recommended for travellers spending more than one month outside cities. There is no treatment, and a third of infected people will die while another third will suffer permanent brain damage.

Leptospirosis

Leptospirosis is most commonly contracted after river rafting or canyoning. Early symptoms are very similar to the flu and include headache and fever. It can vary from a very mild to a fatal disease. Diagnosis is through blood tests and it is easily treated with Doxycycline.

Malaria

For such a serious and potentially deadly disease, there is an enormous amount of misinformation concerning malaria. You must get expert advice as to whether your trip actually puts you at risk. Many areas, particularly city and resort areas, have minimal to no risk of malaria, and the risk of side effects from the tablets may outweigh the risk of getting the disease. For some rural areas, however, the risk of contracting the disease far outweighs the risk of any tablet side-effects. Remember that malaria can be fatal. Before you travel, seek medical advice on the right medication and dosage for you.

Malaria is not common but present in Borneo, particularly in parts of Kalimantan. In most of Brunei, Sabah and Sarawak, it is not common, and is usually only found in or around lumber camps with significant numbers of migrant workers. One reason for the relative rarity of malaria is the relatively low mosquito population in much of Borneo (if only we could say the same for leeches!). Nonetheless, if you are going to be travelling in the hinterlands of any of the three countries of Borneo, you should consider taking antimalarials. Also, you should get the most up-to-date information on dangerous areas before your trip and as soon as you arrive in country.

Malaria is caused by a parasite transmitted through the bite of an infected mosquito. The most important symptom of malaria is fever, but general symptoms such as headache, diarrhoea, cough or chills may also occur. Diagnosis can be made only by taking a blood sample.

Two strategies should be combined to prevent malaria – mosquito avoidance and antimalarial medications. Most people who catch malaria are taking inadequate or no antimalarial medication.

Travellers are advised to prevent mosquito bites by taking these steps:

- Use a DEET-containing insect repellent on exposed skin. Wash this off at night, as long as you are sleeping under a mosquito net treated with permethrin. Natural repellents such as citronella can be effective, but must be applied more frequently than products containing DEET.
- Sleep under a mosquito net impregnated with permethrin.
- Choose accommodation with screens and fans (if not air-con).
- Impregnate clothing with permethrin in high-risk areas.
- Wear long sleeves and trousers in light colours.
- Use mosquito coils.
- Spray your room with insect repellent before going out for your evening meal.

There are a variety of antimalarial medications available:

Artesunate Artesunate derivatives are not suitable as a preventive medication. They are useful treatments under medical supervision.

HEALTH

Chloroquine & Paludrine The effectiveness of this combination is now limited in most of Southeast Asia. Common side effects include nausea (40% of people) and mouth ulcers. Generally not recommended.

Doxycycline This daily tablet is a broad-spectrum antibiotic that has the added benefit of helping to prevent a variety of tropical diseases, including leptospirosis, tick-borne diseases, typhus and melioidosis. The potential side effects include photosensitivity (a tendency to sunburn), thrush in women, indigestion, heartburn, nausea and interference with the contraceptive pill. More serious side effects include ulceration of the oesophagus – you can help prevent this by taking your tablet with a meal and a large glass of water, and never lying down within half an hour of taking it. Must be taken for four weeks after leaving the risk area.

Lariam (Mefloquine) Lariam has received much bad press, some of it justified, some not. This weekly tablet suits many people. Serious side effects are rare but include depression, anxiety, psychosis and having fits. Anyone with a history of depression, anxiety, other psychological disorders or epilepsy should not take Lariam. It's considered safe in the second and third trimesters of pregnancy. It's around 90% effective in most parts of Asia, but there's significant resistance in parts of northern Thailand, Laos and Cambodia. Tablets must be taken for four weeks after leaving the risk area.

Malarone This new drug is a combination of Atovaquone and Proguanil. Side effects are uncommon and mild, most commonly nausea and headache. It is the best tablet for scuba divers and for those on short trips to high-risk areas. It must be taken for one week after leaving the risk area.

A final option is to take no preventive medication but to have a supply of emergency medication should you develop the symptoms of malaria. This is less than ideal, and you'll need to get to a good medical facility within 24 hours of developing a fever. If you choose this option the most effective and safest treatment is Malarone (four tablets once daily for three days). Other options include Mefloquine and quinine but the side effects of these drugs at treatment doses make them less desirable. Fansidar is no longer recommended.

Measles

Occurring in Borneo, this highly contagious bacterial infection is spread via coughing and sneezing. Most people born before 1966 are immune, as they had the disease in childhood. Measles starts with a high fever and rash and can be complicated by pneumonia and brain disease. There is no specific treatment.

Rabies

Rabies is present in Kalimantan but not in Sabah, Sarawak and Brunei (although new cases are always possible in any part of the island). This fatal disease is spread by the bite or lick of an infected animal – most commonly a dog or monkey. You should seek medical advice immediately after any animal bite and commence postexposure treatment.

Having pretravel vaccination means the postbite treatment is greatly simplified. If an animal bites you, gently wash the wound with soap and water, and apply an iodine-based antiseptic. If you are not prevaccinated you will need to receive rabies immunoglobulin as soon as possible.

STDs

Among the most common sexually transmitted diseases in Southeast Asia, including Borneo, are herpes, warts, syphilis, gonorrhoea and chlamydia. People carrying these diseases often have no signs of infection. Condoms will prevent gonorrhoea and chlamydia but not warts or herpes. If after a sexual encounter you develop any rash, lumps, discharge or pain when passing urine, seek immediate medical attention. If you've been sexually active during your travels, have an STD check on your return home.

Tuberculosis

While tuberculosis (TB) is rare in travellers in Borneo, medical and aid workers and long-term travellers who have significant contact with the local population should take precautions. Vaccination is usually given only to children under the age of five, but adults at risk are recommended to have TB testing both before and after travelling. The main symptoms are fever, cough, weight loss, night sweats and tiredness.

Typhoid

This serious bacterial infection is spread via food and water and is found in Borneo. It causes a high, slowly progressive fever, a headache, and may be accompanied by a dry cough and stomach pain. It's diagnosed by blood tests and treated with antibiotics. Vaccination is recommended for travellers spending more than a week in the region, or travelling outside

---

DRINKING WATER

- Never drink tap water.
- Bottled water is generally safe – check that the seal is intact at purchase.
- Avoid ice.
- Avoid fresh juices – they may have been watered down.
- Boiling water is the most efficient method of purifying it.
- The best chemical purifier is iodine. It should not be used by pregnant women or those with thyroid problems.
- Water filters should also filter out viruses. Ensure your filter has a chemical barrier such as iodine and a small pore size, ie less than 4 microns.

---

the major cities. Be aware that vaccination is not 100% effective so you must still be careful with what you eat and drink.

Typhus

Murine typhus is spread by the bite of a flea, whereas scrub typhus is spread via a mite. Although present in Borneo, these diseases are rare in travellers. Symptoms include fever, muscle pains and a rash. You can prevent typhus by following general insect-avoidance measures. Doxycycline will also prevent it.

TRAVELLER'S DIARRHOEA

Traveller's diarrhoea is by far the most common problem affecting travellers – between 30% to 50% of people will suffer from it within two weeks of starting their trip. In over 80% of cases, traveller's diarrhoea is caused by a bacteria (there are numerous potential culprits), and therefore responds promptly to treatment with antibiotics. Treatment with antibiotics will depend on your situation – how sick you are, how quickly you need to get better, where you are etc. Traveller's diarrhoea is defined as the passage of more than three watery bowel-actions within 24 hours, plus at least one other symptom such as fever, cramps, nausea, vomiting or feeling generally unwell. Treatment consists of staying well-hydrated; rehydration solutions such as Gastrolyte are the best for this. Antibiotics such as Norfloxacin, Ciprofloxacin or Azithromycin will kill the bacteria quickly.

Loperamide is just a 'stopper' and doesn't get to the cause of the problem. It can be helpful, for example if you have to go on a long bus ride. Don't take Loperamide if you have a fever, or blood in your stools. Seek medical attention quickly if you do not respond to an appropriate antibiotic.

Amoebic Dysentery

Amoebic dysentery is very rare in travellers but is often misdiagnosed by poor quality labs in Asia. Symptoms are similar to bacterial diarrhoea, ie fever, bloody diarrhoea and generally feeling unwell. You should always seek reliable medical care if you have blood in your diarrhoea. Treatment involves two drugs – Tinidazole or Metroniadzole to kill the parasite in your gut and then a second drug to kill the cysts. If left untreated complications such as liver abscess and abscess in the gut can occur.

Giardiasis

Giardia is a parasite that is relatively common in travellers. Symptoms include nausea, bloating, excess gas, fatigue and intermittent diarrhoea. 'Eggy' burps are often attributed solely to Giardia, but work in Nepal has shown that they are not specific to Giardia. The parasite will eventually go away if left untreated but this can take months. The treatment of choice is Tinidazole, with Metronidazole being a second line option.

ENVIRONMENTAL HAZARDS
Diving

Divers and surfers should seek specialised advice before they travel, to ensure their medical kit contains treatment for coral cuts and tropical ear infections, as well as the standard problems. Divers should ensure their insurance covers them for decompression illness – get specialised dive insurance through an organisation such as **DAN** (Divers Alert Network; www .danseap.org). Have a dive medical before you leave your home country.

Food

Hygiene standards are relatively high in most of Borneo. However, there is always the risk of contracting traveller's diarrhoea. Ways to avoid it include eating only freshly cooked food and avoiding shellfish and food that has been sitting around in buffets. Peel all fruit, cook vegetables, and soak salads in iodine water for at least 20 minutes. Eat in busy restaurants with a high turnover of customers.

Heat

Borneo is hot and humid throughout the year. Most people take at least two weeks to adapt to the hot climate. Swelling of the feet and ankles is common, as are muscle cramps caused by excessive sweating. Prevent these by avoiding dehydration and too much activity in the heat. Take it easy when you first arrive. Don't eat salt tablets (they aggravate the gut) but drinking rehydration solution or eating salty food helps. Treat cramps by stopping activity, resting, rehydrating with double-strength rehydration solution and gently stretching.

Dehydration is the main contributor to heat exhaustion. Symptoms include feeling weak, headache, irritability, nausea or vomiting, sweaty skin, a fast, weak pulse and a slightly increased body temperature. Treatment involves getting the victim out of the heat and/or sun, fanning them and applying cool wet cloths to the skin, laying the victim flat with their legs raised and rehydrating with water containing a quarter of a teaspoon of salt per litre. Recovery is usually rapid although it's common to feel weak for some days afterwards.

Heatstroke is a serious medical emergency. Symptoms come on suddenly and include weakness, nausea, a hot dry body with a body temperature of over 41°C, dizziness, confusion, loss of coordination, fits, and eventual collapse and loss of consciousness. Seek medical help and commence cooling by getting the sufferer out of the heat, removing their clothes, fanning them and applying cool, wet cloths or ice to their body, especially to the groin and armpits.

Prickly heat is a common skin rash in the tropics, caused by sweat being trapped under the skin. The result is an itchy rash of tiny lumps. If you develop prickly heat, treat it by moving out of the heat and into an air-conditioned area for a few hours and by having cool showers. Creams and ointments clog the skin so they should be avoided. Locally bought prickly-heat powder can be helpful for relief.

Tropical fatigue is common in long-term expatriates based in the tropics. It's rarely due to disease but is caused by the climate, inadequate mental rest, excessive alcohol intake and the demands of daily work in a different culture.

Insect Bites & Stings

Bedbugs don't carry disease but their bites are very itchy. They live in the cracks of furniture and walls and then migrate to the bed at night to feed on you. You can treat the itch with an antihistamine. Lice inhabit various parts of your body but most commonly your head and pubic area. They can be difficult to treat and you may need numerous applications of an antilice shampoo such as permethrin. Transmission is via close contact with an infected person. Pubic lice are usually contracted from sexual contact.

Ticks are contracted after walking in the bush. Ticks are commonly found behind the ears, on the belly and in armpits. If you have had a tick bite and experience symptoms such as a rash at the site of the bite or elsewhere, a fever or muscle aches you should see a doctor. Doxycycline prevents tick-borne diseases.

Leeches are found in humid rainforest areas. They do not transmit any disease but their bites are often intensely itchy for weeks afterwards and can easily become infected. Apply iodine-based antiseptic to any leech bite to help prevent infection (see also the boxed text on p67).

Bee and wasp stings mainly cause problems for people who are allergic to them. Anyone with a serious bee or wasp allergy should carry an injection of adrenaline (eg an EpiPen) for emergency treatment. For others, pain is the main problem – apply ice to the sting and take painkillers.

Most jellyfish in Southeast Asian waters are not dangerous, just irritating. First aid for jellyfish stings involves pouring vinegar onto the affected area to neutralise the poison. Don't rub sand or water onto the stings. Take painkillers, and anyone who feels ill in any way after being stung should seek medical advice. Take local advice if there are dangerous jellyfish around and keep out of the water.

Parasites

Numerous parasites are common in local populations in Borneo; however, most of these are rare in travellers. The two rules to follow if you wish to avoid parasitic infections are to wear shoes and to avoid eating raw food, especially fish, pork and vegetables. A number of parasites including strongyloides, hookworm and cutaneous larva migrans are transmitted via the skin by walking barefoot.

Skin Problems

Fungal rashes are common in humid climates. There are two common fungal rashes that affect travellers. The first occurs in moist areas that get less air such as the groin, armpits and between the toes. It starts as a red patch that slowly spreads and is usually itchy. Treatment involves keeping the skin dry, avoiding chafing and using an antifungal cream such as Clotrimazole or Lamisil. Tinea versicolour is also common – this fungus causes small, light-coloured patches, most commonly on the back, chest and shoulders. Consult a doctor.

Cuts and scratches become easily infected in humid climates. Take meticulous care of any cuts and scratches to prevent complications such as abscesses. Immediately wash all wounds in clean water and apply antiseptic. If you develop signs of infection (increasing pain and redness) see a doctor. Divers and surfers should be particularly careful with coral cuts as they become easily infected.

Snakes

Borneo is home to many species of poisonous and harmless snakes. Assume all snakes are poisonous and never try to catch one. Always wear boots and long pants if walking in an area that may have snakes. First aid in the event of a snake bite involves pressure immobilisation via an elastic bandage firmly wrapped around the affected limb, starting at the bite site and working up towards the chest. The bandage should not be so tight that the circulation is cut off; the fingers or toes should be kept free so the circulation can be checked. Immobilise the limb with a splint and carry the victim to medical attention. Don't use tourniquets or try to suck the venom out. Antivenin is available for most species.

Sunburn

Even on a cloudy day, sunburn can occur rapidly. Always use a strong sunscreen (at least factor 15 if not more), making sure to reapply it after a swim, and always wear a wide-brimmed hat and sunglasses outdoors. Avoid lying in the sun during the hottest part of the day (10am to 2pm). If you become sunburnt, stay out of the sun until you have recovered, apply cool compresses and take painkillers for the discomfort. One-percent hydrocortisone cream applied twice daily is also helpful.

TRAVELLING WITH CHILDREN

Borneo is a great place to travel with children. However, there are specific issues you should consider before travelling with your child.

All your children's routine vaccinations should be up to date, as many of the common childhood diseases that have been eliminated in the West are still present in parts of Borneo. A travel health clinic can advise you on specific vaccines, but think seriously about rabies vaccination if you're visiting rural areas or travelling for more than a month, as children are more vulnerable to severe animal bites.

Children are more prone to getting serious forms of mosquito-borne diseases such as malaria, Japanese B encephalitis and dengue fever. In particular, malaria is very serious in children and can rapidly lead to death – you should think seriously before taking your child into a malaria-risk area. Permethrin-impregnated clothing is safe to use, and insect repellents should contain between 10% and 20% DEET.

Diarrhoea can cause rapid dehydration and you should pay particular attention to keeping your child well hydrated. The best antibiotic for children with diarrhoea is Azithromycin.

Children can get very sick very quickly so locate good medical facilities at your destination and make contact if you are worried – it's always better to get a medical opinion than to try and treat your own children.

WOMEN'S HEALTH

Pregnant women should receive specialised advice before travelling. The ideal time to travel is in the second trimester (between 16 and 28 weeks), when the risk of pregnancy-related problems is at its lowest and pregnant women generally feel at their best. During the first trimester there's a risk of miscarriage and in the third trimester complications such as premature labour and high blood pressure are possible. It's wise to travel with a companion. Always carry a list of quality medical facilities available at your destination and ensure you continue your standard antenatal care at these facilities. Avoid travel in rural areas

HEALTH

with poor transport and medical facilities. Most of all, ensure travel insurance covers all pregnancy-related possibilities, including premature labour.

Malaria is a high-risk disease in pregnancy. The World Health Organization recommends that pregnant women do not travel to areas with malaria resistant to Chloroquine. None of the more effective antimalarial drugs are completely safe in pregnancy.

Traveller's diarrhoea can quickly lead to dehydration and result in inadequate blood flow to the placenta. Many of the drugs used to treat various diarrhoea bugs are not rec-ommended in pregnancy. Azithromycin is considered safe.

In urban areas, supplies of sanitary prod-ucts are readily available. Birth-control options may be limited so bring adequate supplies of your own form of contraception. Heat, humidity and antibiotics can all con-tribute to thrush. Treatment is with antifungal creams and pessaries such as Clotrimazole. A practical alternative is a single tablet of Fluconazole (Diflucan). Urinary-tract infec-tions can be precipitated by dehydration or long bus journeys without toilet stops; bring suitable antibiotics.

Language

WHO SPEAKS WHAT WHERE?

Bahasa Malaysia (also known as Bahasa Melayu, literally 'Malay language') is the official language of Malaysian Borneo (Sabah and Sarawak) and Brunei. It is the native tongue of those of Malay descent in Malaysian Borneo and Brunei. Bahasa Indonesia is the official language of Kalimantan and is the mother tongue of most of the non-Chinese living there. Bahasa Indonesia and Bahasa Malaysia are very similar and if you can speak a little of either, you'll be able to use it across the island.

While almost everyone in Malaysian Borneo will understand Bahasa Malaysia, several dialects of it are spoken in various regions in Borneo, especially in Sarawak and Brunei. Younger speakers will reply to you in standard Bahasa, but older individuals may only speak their particular dialect, which can be quite different from standard Bahasa.

Various dialects of Chinese are spoken by those of Chinese ancestry in Borneo, with one or other dialect serving as the main lingua franca for the Chinese communities in each city. Because Mandarin is the main medium of instruction in Chinese-language schools in Borneo, which most ethnic Chinese attend until at least the end of their elementary schooling, Mandarin is fairly widely spoken and understood. Most ethnic Chinese, particularly young people, also speak some English.

Each of Borneo's indigenous groups has its own language, most of which are infused with Bahasa words. Except for a few very old people in isolated upriver communities, members of Borneo's indigenous groups all speak Bahasa Malaysia (in Malaysian Borneo or Brunei) or Bahasa Indonesia (in Kalimantan). Quite a few also speak surprisingly good English, which is taught even in very small communities.

You'll find it easy to get by with only English in Borneo, particularly in Sabah, Sarawak and Brunei. English is the most common second language for all of Borneo's ethnic groups and is often used by people of different backgrounds, like ethnic Chinese and ethnic Malays, to communicate with one another.

If you have a knack for languages and want to learn a little of the local lingo to use on your travels, you'll find Bahasa (either Indonesian or Malaysian) to be the most useful and the easiest to pick up. For a comprehensive guide to either language, get a copy of Lonely Planet's compact *Indonesian* or *Malay Phrasebook*.

THE TWO BAHASAS

There are obvious similarities between Bahasa Indonesia and Bahasa Malaysia, to the extent that the two are often identical. We've avoided duplication in this language guide by providing translations in both languages only where the differences are significant enough to cause confusion, indicated by (I) and (M).

PRONUNCIATION

Most letters are pronounced more or less the same as their English counterparts. Nearly all syllables carry equal emphasis, but a good approximation is to lightly stress the second-last syllable. The main exception to the rule is the unstressed **e** in words such as *besar* (big), pronounced 'be-sarr'.

a	as in 'father'
ai	as in 'aisle'
au	a drawn out 'ow', as in 'cow'
c	the one most likely to trip up English speakers; always as the 'ch' in 'chair'
e	a neutral vowel like the 'a' in 'ago' when unstressed, eg *besar* (big); when it's stressed it's more like the 'a' in 'may', eg *meja* (table). There's no single rule to determine whether **e** is stressed or unstressed.
g	always hard, as in 'go'
h	a little stronger than the 'h' in 'her'; almost silent at the end of a word
i	as in 'unique'
j	as in 'jet'
k	as English 'k', except at the end of the word, when it's more like a glottal stop (ie the 'nonsound' created by the short closing of the throat in the expression 'oh-oh!')
ng	as the 'ng' in 'singer'
ngg	as 'ng' + 'g' (as in 'anger')
ny	as in 'canyon'
o	as in 'for' (with no 'r' sound)
r	pronounced clearly and distinctly
u	as in 'put'
ua	as 'w' when at the start of a word

ACCOMMODATION

I'm looking for a ...	*Saya cari ...*
campground	*tempat kemah/kemping* (I)
	tempat perkhemahan (M)
guesthouse	*rumah yang disewakan* (I)
	rumah tetamu (M)
hotel	*hotel*
youth hostel	*losmen pemuda* (I)
	asrama belia (M)

Where is there a cheap hotel?
Hotel yang murah di mana? (I)
Di mana ada hotel yang murah? (M)
What is the address?
Alamatnya di mana? (I)
Apakah alamatnya? (M)
Do you have any rooms available?
Ada kamar/bilik kosongkah? (I/M)

I'd like a ...
Saya cari ... (I)
Saya hendak ... (M)
   single room
   (kamar/bilik) untuk seorang (I/M)
   double-bed room
   tempat tidur besar satu kamar (I)
   bilik untuk dua orang (M)

room with two beds
kamar dengan dua tempat tidur (I)
bilik yang ada dua katil (M)
room with a bathroom
kamar dengan kama mandi (I)
bilik dengan bilik mandi (M)

How much is it (per day/per person)?
Berapa harga satu (malam/orang)?
Could you write it down, please?
Anda bisa tolong tuliskan? (I)
Tolong tuliskan alamat itu? (M)
Is breakfast included?
Makan pagi termasukkah?
May I see it?
Boleh saya lihat?
Where is the bathroom?
(Kamar/Bilik) mandi di mana? (I/M)

CONVERSATION & ESSENTIALS
Be Polite!
Pronouns, particularly 'you', are rarely used in Bahasa. A variety of terms relating to a person's age and gender are generally used, and most have a familial tone. Titles and polite forms of address are crucial as they acknowledge the age and status of those participating in the conversation. Using the incorrect form of address can be seen as a sign of disrespect and result in poor communication, especially with officials.

Bahasa Indonesia
Anda is the egalitarian form designed to overcome the plethora of words for the second person. The term *bapak* (father) or simply *pak* is used for an older man, or anyone old enough to be a father; *ibu* (mother) or simply *bu* is the equivalent for an older woman.

To show respect to elders or 'superiors', you should use the words *Bapak* (father) or *Ibu* (mother). If you know the person's name (eg Anungseto or Ninik), you can address them as *Bapak Anungseto* (lit: father Anungseto) or *Ibu Ninik* (lit: mother Ninik). Those of similar age and status to you can politely be addressed as *Saudara/Saudari* (brother/sister). If you're a young woman, expect to be called *Nona* (Miss) by your elders.

Bahasa Malaysia
Kamu is an egalitarian second-person pronoun, corresponding to 'you' in English. The polite pronoun corresponding to English 'I/we' is *kami*. In polite speech, you

wouldn't normally use first-person pronouns, but would refer to yourself by name or form of address, eg *Makcik nak pergi ke pasar* (Auntie wants to go to the market).

When addressing a man or a woman old enough to be your parent, use *pakcik* (uncle) or *makcik* (aunt). For someone only slightly older, use *abang* or *bang* (older brother) and *kakak* or *kak* (older sister). For people old enough to be your grandparents, *datuk* and *nenek* (grandfather and grandmother) are used. For a man or woman you meet on the street you can also use *encik* or *cik* respectively.

SIGNS	
Masuk	Entrance
Keluar	Exit
Buka	Open
Tutup	Closed
Dilarang	Prohibited
Ada Kamar Kosong/	Rooms Available
Bilik Kosong (I/M)	
Polisi	Police
Kamar Kecil/Toilet (I)	Toilets/WC
Tandas (M)	
Pria/Lelaki (I/M)	Men
Wanita/Perempuan (I/M)	Women

Welcome.	*Selamat datang.*
Hi.	*Helo.*
Good morning.	*Selamat pagi.* (before 11am)
Hello.	*Selamat siang.* (noon to 2pm)
	Selamat tengahari. (M)
	Selamat sore. (3pm to 6pm)
	Selamat petang. (M)
Good evening.	*Selamat malam.* (after dark)
Good night.	*Selamat tidur.* (to someone going to bed)
Goodbye.	*Selamat tinggal.* (to one staying)
	Selamat jalan. (to one leaving)
Yes.	*Ya.*

To indicate negation, *tidak* is used with verbs, adjectives and adverbs; *bukan* with nouns and pronouns.

No. (not)	*Tidak.*
No. (negative)	*Bukan.*
Maybe.	*Mungkin.*
Please.	*Tolong.* (asking for help)
	Silahkan. (giving permission)
Thank you (very much).	*Terima kasih (banyak-banyak).*
You're welcome.	*Kembali.* (I)
	Sama-sama. (M)
Sorry/Pardon.	*Maaf.*
Excuse me, ...	*Maaf, ...*
Just a minute.	*Tunggu sebentar.*
How are you?	*Apa kabar?*
I'm fine.	*Kabar baik.*
What's your name?	*Siapa nama anda?* (I)
	Siapa nama kamu? (M)
My name is ...	*Nama saya ...*
Where are you from?	*Anda dari mana?* (I)
	Kamu datang dari mana? (M)
I'm from ...	*Saya dari ...*
How old are you?	*Berapa umur anda?* (I)
	Berapa umur kamu? (M)
I'm ... years old.	*Umur saya ... tahun.*

I (don't) like ...	*Saya (tidak) suka ...*
Good, fine, OK.	*Baik.*
No good.	*Tidak baik.*

DIRECTIONS

Where is ...?	*Di mana ...?*
Which way?	*Ke mana?*
Go straight ahead.	*Jalan terus.*
Turn left/right.	*Belok kiri/kanan.*
Stop!	*Berhenti!*
at the corner	*di sudut* (I)
	di simpang (M)
at the traffic lights	*di lampu lalu-lintas* (I)
	di tempat lampu isyarat (M)
here/there/over there	*di sini/di situ/di sana*
behind	*di belakang*
opposite	*di seberang* (I)
	berhadapan dengan (M)
near (to)	*dekat (dengan)*
far (from)	*jauh (dari)*
north	*utara*
south	*selatan*
east	*timur*
west	*barat*
beach	*pantai*
island	*pulau*
lake	*danau/tasik* (I/M)
sea	*laut*

HEALTH

Where is a ...	*Di mana ada ...*
chemist/pharmacy	*apotik/farmasi*
dentist	*doktor gigi*
doctor	*doktor*
hospital	*rumah sakit* (I)
	hospital (M)
I'm ...	*Saya sakit ...*
asthmatic	*asma/lelah* (I/M)
diabetic	*kencing manis*
epileptic	*epilepsi/gila babi* (I/M)

EMERGENCIES

Help!	*Tolong saya!*
There's been an accident!	*Ada kecelakaan!*
I'm lost.	*Saya sesat.*
Leave me alone!	*Jangan ganggu saya!*
Call ...!	*Panggil ...!*
an ambulance	*ambulans*
a doctor	*doktor*
the police	*polis*

I'm allergic to ...	*Saya alergi ...* (I)
	Saya alergik kepada ... (M)
antibiotics	*antibiotik*
aspirin	*aspirin*
nuts	*kacang*
penicillin	*penisilin*

I'm ill.	*Saya sakit.*
It hurts here.	*Sakitnya di sini.* (I)
	Sini sakit. (M)
antiseptic	*penangkal infeksi/antiseptik*
condoms	*kondom*
diarrhoea	*mencret/cirit-birit* (I/M)
fever	*demam panas*
headache	*sakit kepala*
medicine	*obat*
nausea	*mual*
sanitary napkins	*(tuala/pembalut) wanita* (I/M)
sunblock cream	*sunscreen/tabir surya/sunblock* (I)
	krim pelindung cahaya matahari (M)
tampons	*tampon*

LANGUAGE DIFFICULTIES

Do you speak English?
Bisa berbicara Bahasa Inggris? (I)
Bolehkah anda berbicara Bahasa Inggeris? (I)
Does anyone here speak English?
Ada yang bisa berbicara Bahasa Inggris di sini? (I)
Ada orang yang berbicara Bahasa Inggeris di sini? (M)
What does ... mean?
Apa artinya/maksudnya ...? (I/M)
I (don't) understand.
Saya (tidak) mengerti. (I)
Saya (tidak) faham. (M)
Please write that word down.
Tolong tuliskan kata itu.
Can you show me (on the map)?
Anda bisa tolong tunjukkan pada saya (di peta)? (I)
Tolong tunjukkan (di peta)? (M)

NUMBERS

0	*nol* (I)
	kosong/sifar (M)
1	*satu*
2	*dua*
3	*tiga*
4	*empat*
5	*lima*
6	*enam*
7	*tujuh*
8	*delapan/lapan* (I/M)
9	*sembilan*
10	*sepuluh*

A half is *setengah*, pronounced 'steng-ah', eg *setengah kilo* (half a kilo). 'Approximately' is *kira-kira* in Bahasa Indonesia and *lebih-kurang* in Bahasa Malaysia. After the numbers one to 10, the 'teens' are *belas*, the 'tens' *puluh*, the 'hundreds' *ratus*, the 'thousands' *ribu* and 'millions' *juta,* but as a prefix *satu* (one) becomes *se-*, eg *seratus* (one hundred).

11	*sebelas*
12	*dua belas*
13	*tiga belas*
14	*empat belas*
15	*lima belas*
16	*enam belas*
17	*tujuh belas*
18	*lapan belas*
19	*sembilan belas*
20	*dua puluh*
21	*dua puluh satu*
22	*dua puluh dua*
25	*dua puluh lima*
30	*tiga puluh*
40	*empat puluh*
50	*lima puluh*
60	*enam puluh*
70	*tujuh puluh*
80	*delapan/lapan puluh* (I/M)
90	*sembilan puluh*
99	*sembilan puluh sembilan*
100	*seratus*
150	*seratus lima puluh*
200	*dua ratus*
777	*tujuh ratus tujuh puluh tujuh*
1000	*seribu*

PAPERWORK

name	*nama*
nationality	*kebangsaan/bangsa* (I/M)

LANGUAGE

date of birth	*tanggal kelahiran* (I)
	tarikh lahir (M)
place of birth	*tempat kelahiran*
sex/gender	*jenis kelamin* (I)
	jantina (M)
passport	*paspot*
visa	*visa*

QUESTION WORDS

Who?	*Siapa/Siapakah?* (I/M)
What is it?	*Apa itu?*
When?	*Kapan/Bilakah?* (I/M)
Where?	*Di mana?*
Which?	*Yang mana?*
Why?	*Kenapa?*
How/How many?	*Bagaimana/Berapa?*

SHOPPING & SERVICES

What is this?	*Apa ini?*
How much is it?	*Berapa (harganya)?*
I'd like to buy ...	*Saya (mau/nak) beli ...* (I/M)
I don't like it.	*Saya tidak suka.*
May I look at it?	*Boleh saya lihat?* (I)
	Boleh saya tengok barang itu? (M)
I'm just looking.	*Saya lihat-lihat saja.* (I)
	Saya nak tengok saja. (M)
Can you lower the price?	*Boleh kurangkah?*
No more than ...	*Tak lebih dari ...*
I'll take it.	*Saya beli.* (I)
	Saya nak beli ini. (M)
I'd like to change (money).	*Saya (mau/nak) tukar uang* (I/M)
What time does it open/close?	*Jam berapa buka/tutup?*
I want to call ...	*Saya mau menelepon ...*
this/that	*ini/itu*
big/small	*besar/kecil*
bigger/smaller	*lebih besar/lebih kecil*
more/less	*lebih/kurang*
expensive	*mahal*
Do you accept ...?	*Bisa bayar pakai ...?* (I)
	Boleh bayar dengan ...? (M)
credit cards	*(kartu/kad) kredit* (I/M)
travellers cheques	*cek (perjalanan/kembara)* (I/M)
I'm looking for a/the ...	*Saya cari ...*
bank	*bank*
city centre	*pusat kota/pusat bandar* (I/M)
... embassy	*kedutaan ...*

food stall	*warung*
market	*pasar*
museum	*museum*
police station	*(kantor/stesen) polis* (I/M)
post office	*(kantor/pejabat) pos* (I/M)
public phone	*telepon umum*
public toilet	*WC ('way say') umum* (I)
	tandas awam (M)
restaurant	*rumah makan* (I)
	restoran (M)
telephone centre	*wartel* (I)
	pusat telefon (M)
tourist office	*kantor pariwisata* (I)
	pejabat pelancong (M)

TIME & DATES

What time is it?	*Jam berapa sekarang?* (I)
	Pukul berapa? (M)
When?	*Kapan/Bila?* (I/M)
(It's) 7 o'clock.	*Jam/Pukul tujuh.* (I/M)
How many hours?	*Berapa jam?*
five hours	*lima jam*
in the morning	*pagi*
in the afternoon	*siang/tengahari* (I/M)
in the evening	*malam/petang* (I/M)
at night	*malam*
today	*hari ini*
tomorrow	*esok/besok*
hour	*jam*
day	*hari*
week	*minggu*
month	*bulan*
year	*tahun*
Monday	*hari Senin/Isnin* (I/M)
Tuesday	*hari Selasa*
Wednesday	*hari Rabu*
Thursday	*hari Kamis*
Friday	*hari Jumat/Jumaat* (I/M)
Saturday	*hari Sabtu*
Sunday	*hari Minggu*
January	*Januari*
February	*Februari*
March	*Maret/Mac* (I/M)
April	*April*
May	*Mei*
June	*Juni/Jun* (I/M)
July	*Juli/Julai* (I/M)
August	*Agustus/Ogos* (I/M)
September	*September*
October	*Oktober*
November	*November*
December	*Desember*

TRANSPORT
Public Transport

What time does the ... leave?	*Jam berapa ... berangkat?* (I) *Pukul berapa ... berangkat?* (M)
ship/boat	*kapal/bot*
bus	*bis/bas* (M)
plane	*kapal terbang*

I'd like a ... ticket.	*Saya (mau/nak) tiket ...* (I/M)
one-way	*sekali jalan/sehala* (I/M)
return	*pulang pergi/pergi-balik* (I/M)

I want to go to ...	*Saya (mau/nak) ke ...* (I/M)
the first	*pertama*
the last	*terakhir*
ticket	*tiket*
ticket office	*(loket/pejabat) tiket* (I/M)
timetable	*jadual*
airport	*bandara* (I) *lapangan terbang* (M)
bus station	*terminal bis/stesen bas* (I/M)
bus stop	*halte bis/perhentian bas* (I/M)

Private Transport

I'd like to hire a ...	*Saya mau sewa ...* (I) *Saya nak menyewa ...* (M)
bicycle	*sepeda/basikal* (I/M)
car	*mobil/kereta* (I/M)
4WD	*gardan ganda/4WD* (I/M)
motorbike	*sepeda motor/motosikal* (I/M)

Is this the road to ...?	*Apakah jalan ini ke ...?* (I) *Adakah jalan ini ke ...?* *Inikah jalan ke ...?* (M)
Where's a service station?	*Di mana pompa bensin?* (I) *Stesen minyak di mana?* (M)
Please fill it up.	*Tolong isi sampai penuh.* (I) *Tolong penuhkan tangki.* (M)
I'd like ... litres.	*Minta ... liter bensin.* (I) *Saya nak ... liter.* (M)
diesel	*disel*
petrol	*bensin/petrol* (I/M)

ROAD SIGNS

Beri Jalan	Give Way
Bahaya	Danger
Dilarang Parkir (I)/ **Dilarang Letak Kereta** (I/M)	No Parking
Jalan Memutar/ **Lencongan** (I/M)	Detour
Masuk	Entry
Dilarang Mendahului	No Overtaking
Kurangi Kecepatan (I) **Kurang Laju** (M)	Slow Down
Dilarang Masuk	No Entry
Satu Arah/ **Jalan Sehala** (I/M)	One Way
Keluar	Exit
Kosongkan	Keep Clear

I need a mechanic.	*Saya perlu montir.* (I) *Kami memerlukan mekanik.* (M)
The car has broken down at ...	*Mobil mogok di ...* (I) *Kereta saya telah rosak di ...* (M)
The motorbike won't start.	*Motor tidak bisa jalan.* (I) *Motosikal saya tidak dapat dihidupkan.* (M)
I have a flat tyre.	*Ban saya kempes.* (I) *Tayarnya kempis.* (M)
I've run out of petrol.	*Saya kehabisan bensin.* (I) *Minyak sudah habis.* (M)
I had an accident.	*Saya mengalami kecelakaan.* (I) *Saya terlibat dalam kemalangan.* (M)
(How long) Can I park here?	*(Berapa lama) Saya boleh parkir di sini?* (I) *(Beberapa lama) Boleh saya letak kereta di sini?* (M)
Where do I pay?	*Saya membayar di mana?* (I) *Di mana tempat membayar?* (M)

Also available from Lonely Planet:
Indonesian and *Malay Phrasebooks*

Glossary

For terms used in *kedai kopi* and *kopitiams* (Malay and Chinese coffee shops) see the Kedai Kopi section on p41.

ABC – ais kacang, a Malay/Indonesia shaved ice treat
adat – Malay customary law
agama – religion
air – water
air terjun – waterfall
alor – groove; furrow; main channel of a river
ampang – dam
ang pow – red packets of money used as offerings, payment or gifts
APEC – Asia-Pacific Economic Cooperation
arak – Malay local alcohol
arrack – see *arak*
Asean – Association of Southeast Asian Nations
atap – roof thatching
ayam – chicken

Bahasa Malaysia – Malay language; also known as Bahasa Melayu
balai – house or longhouse (Kalimantan)
balian – shaman (Kalimantan)
bandar – seaport; town
batang – stem; tree trunk; the main branch of a river
batik – technique of imprinting cloth with dye to produce multicoloured patterns
batu – stone; rock; milepost
belacan – fermented shrimp paste
belauran – night markets (Kalimantan)
bandung – floating general stores (Kalimantan)
bis kota – intercity bus (Kalimantan)
bobihizan – female priestess in Dayak communities
bomoh – spiritual healer
bukit – hill
bumboat – motorised *sampan* (small boat)
bumiputra – literally, sons of the soil; indigenous Malays
bunga raya – hibiscus flower (national flower of Malaysia)

ces – motorised canoes

dadah – drugs
dagang/daging – beef
dato', datuk – literally, grandfather; general male nonroyal title of distinction
dayak – indigenous peoples of Borneo, used mostly in Kalimantan and Sarawak
dipterocarp – family of trees, native to Malaysia, that have two-winged fruits

dolmen – stone burial markers found in Kelabit areas
dusun – small town; orchard; fruit grove

genting – mountain pass
godown – river warehouse
goreng – fried, as in *nasi goreng* (fried rice)
gua – cave
gunung – mountain

hilir – lower reaches of a river
hutan – jungle; forest

imam – keeper of Islamic knowledge and leader of prayer
ikan – fish
ikat – woven cloth
istana – palace

jalan – road

kain sasirangan – tied-dyed batik
kain songket – traditional Malay handwoven fabric with gold threads
kampung – village; also spelt kampong
kangkar – Chinese village
kapal biasa – river boats (Kalimantan term)
karst – characteristic scenery of a limestone region, including features such as underground streams and caverns
kedai kopi – coffee shop (Bahasa term)
kerangas – distinctive vegetation zone of Borneo, usually found on sandstone, containing pitcher plants and other unusual flora
khalwat – literally, close proximity; exhibition of public affection between the sexes which is prohibited for unmarried Muslim couples
klotok – Kalimantan houseboat
kongsi – Chinese clan organisations, also known as ritual brotherhoods, heaven-man-earth societies, triads or secret societies; meeting house for Chinese of the same clan
kopitiam – coffee shop (Chinese term)
kota – fort; city
kramat – Malay shrine
KTM – Keretapi Tanah Melayu; Malaysian Railways System
kuala – river mouth; place where a tributary joins a larger river
kueh – Malay/Indonesian cakes, often made with coconut (also spelled 'kuih')
kway teow – thick white Chinese noodles

laksamana – admiral
lalapan – raw vegetables (Kalimantan)

langur – small, usually tree-dwelling monkey
laut – sea
lebuh – street
Lebuhraya – expressway or freeway; usually refers to the North-South Highway, which runs from Johor Bahru to Bukit Kayu Hitam at the Thai border
lorong – narrow street; alley
LRT – Light Rail Transit (Kuala Lumpur)
lubuk – deep pool

macaque – any of several small species of monkey
mandau – machete (Kalimantan)
mandi – bathe; Southeast Asian wash basin
masjid – mosque
MCP – Malayan Communist Party
mee – noodles
Melayu Islam Beraja – MIB; Brunei's national ideology
merdeka – independence
midin – Borneo edible jungle fern
Molong – Penang hunter/gatherer lifestyle
muara – river mouth
muezzin – mosque official who calls the faithful to prayer

nasi – rice
nasi campur – rice buffet served in Malay/Indonesian restaurants (pronounced 'nah see cham poor')
negara – country
negeri – state

ojek – motorcycle taxi (Kalimantan)
opelet – mininbus (Kalimantan)
orang asing – foreigner
Orang Asli – literally, Original People; Malaysian aborigines
Orang Laut – literally, Coastal People
Orang Ulu – literally, Upriver People

padang – grassy area; field; also the city square
pantai – beach
pao – Chinese steamed buns (sometimes filled with meat or sweet bean paste)
parang – long jungle knife
pasar – market
pasar malam – night market
Pejabat Residen – Resident's Office
pekan – market place; town
pelabuhan – port
penghulu – chief or village head
pengkalan – quay
permuda – youth militias active in the WWII period in Indonesia
pondok – hut or shelter

pua kumbu – traditional finely woven cloth
pulau – island
puteri – princess

raja – prince; ruler
rakyat – common people
rantau – straight coastline
rattan – stems from climbing palms used for wickerwork and canes
rimba – jungle
roti – bread
rumah – house
rumah betang – longhouse (Kalimantan)
rumah panjai/rumah panjang – longhouse
rumah walet – Kalimantan birdhouse

sambal – curry sauce or paste
sampan – small boat
sarung – all-purpose cloth, often sewn into a tube, and worn by women, men and children; also spelt sarong
seberang – opposite side of road; far bank of a river
selat – strait
semenanjung – peninsula
simpang – crossing; junction
songkok – traditional Malay headdress worn by males
sungai – river
syariah – Islamic system of law

tambang – river ferry; fare
tamu – weekly market
tanah – land
tanjung – headland
tasik – lake
teluk – bay; sometimes spelt *telok*
temenggong – Malay administrator
towkang – Chinese junk
transmigrasi – transmigration (Indonesian government policy)
tuai rumah – longhouse chief (Sarawak)
tuak – rice wine drunk in indigenous communities
tudong – headscarf
tunku – prince

ujung – cape
UMNO – United Malays National Organisation

wartel – public phone office (Kalimantan)
warung – small eating stalls
warung kopi – coffee stall (Kalimantan)
wayang – Chinese opera
wayang kulit – shadow-puppet theatre
wisma – office block or shopping centre

The Authors

CHRIS ROWTHORN **Coordinating Author, Borneo Outdoors, Sabah, Sarawak & Brunei**

Chris is an English/American journalist based in Kyoto, Japan. On his first trip to Borneo in 1997, he almost died from hypothermia on the summit of Mt Kinabalu and spent new year's eve in a Sarawak longhouse (later the subject of a story that appeared in *Lonely Planet Unpacked*). This trip, he trekked into Maliau Basin, hung out with orangutans in Danum Valley and dived on the reefs of Layang Layang. When he's not deep in the Borneo rainforest, he's up to his neck in Japanese hot springs or exploring the islands of Thailand and the Philippines. Chris's photographs of Borneo can be found online at www.intoborneo.com.

MUHAMMAD COHEN **History, the Culture, Food & Drink, East Sabah, Kalimantan**

Native New Yorker Muhammad Cohen made his first Asian landfall in Malaysia in 1992, returned as a backpacking reporter in 1994, and moved to Hong Kong a year later. His first Hong Kong vacation began in Sabah; he kept coming to dive Pulau Sipadan and climb Kinabalu. Once a diplomat in Tanzania, Cohen initially discovered Indonesia by visiting an ex-neighbour from Dar es Salaam. Since then, he's picked up the language and a taste for *ikan bakar lalapan*. An author for *Southeast Asia on a Shoestring*, Cohen also wrote *Hong Kong On Air* (www.hongkongonair.com), a novel about the 1997 handover, TV news, love, betrayal, high finance and cheap lingerie.

CHINA WILLIAMS **Gateway Kuala Lumpur, Gateway Singapore, Gateway Jakarta**

China has travelled across Southeast Asia as a backpacker and as a Lonely Planet author, having worked on guides to Thailand, Malaysia and Indonesia. She grew up in South Carolina, where the hot summers and casual chit-chat prepared her well for this region of the world. Her first encounter with Asia was as an English teacher in rural Thailand, arriving just a few months before the Asian currency crash. Since then, she's claimed partial residence in Bangkok but now keeps closer to home, which is outside of Washington, DC, to take care of her son, Felix, and husband, Matt.

LONELY PLANET AUTHORS

Why is our travel information the best in the world? It's simple: our authors are independent, dedicated travellers. They don't research using just the internet or phone, and they don't take freebies in exchange for positive coverage. They travel widely, to all the popular spots and off the beaten track. They personally visit thousands of hotels, restaurants, cafés, bars, galleries, palaces, museums and more – and they take pride in getting all the details right, and telling it how it is. Think you can do it? Find out how at lonelyplanet.com.

CONTRIBUTING AUTHORS

Dr Trish Batchelor wrote the Health chapter. She is a general practitioner and travel medicine specialist who is currently the Medical Director of the Travel Doctor clinic in Canberra, as well as being a Medical Advisor to the Travel Doctor New Zealand clinics. She previously worked at the CIWEC Clinic in Nepal and has a special interest in the impact of tourism on host countries. She has travelled extensively throughout Southeast and East Asia

David Lukas wrote the Environment chapter. He is a professional naturalist who lives on the border of Yosemite National Park, where he conducts research and writes about the natural world. His many travels include spending a year in western Borneo studying rainforest ecology. He is the author of environment chapters for about 20 Lonely Planet guides ranging from *Nova Scotia* to *Costa Rica*.

Behind the Scenes

THIS BOOK

This 1st edition of Borneo was coordinated by Chris Rowthorn, who researched Sarawak, the west of Sabah, and Brunei. Muhammad Cohen researched Kalimantan, the east of Sabah and wrote the History and Culture chapters. The gateway chapters were compiled by China Williams, David Lukas wrote the Environment chapter, and Dr Trish Batchelor wrote the Health chapter. Special thanks to the late Tom Parkinson, LP author, who was a passionate advocate for Borneo and integral in the development and planning of this book.

Commissioning Editors Errol Hunt, Tasmin McNaughtan, Suzannah Shwer
Coordinating Editors Shawn Low, Justin Flynn
Coordinating Cartographer Erin McManus
Coordinating Layout Designer Jacqueline McLeod
Managing Editor Melanie Dankel
Managing Cartographer David Connolly
Managing Layout Designer Adam McCrow
Assisting Editors Gennifer Ciavarra, Victoria Harrison
Assisting Cartographers Anna Clarkson
Cover Designer Wendy Wright
Project Manager Eoin Dunlevy
Language Content Coordinator Quentin Frayne
Talk2Us Coordinator Nicole Hansen

Thanks to Dave Burnett, Lisa Knights, John Mazzocchi, Kate Morgan, Naomi Parker, Raphael Richards, Wibowo Rusli, Celia Wood

THANKS
CHRIS ROWTHORN

Chris Rowthorn would like to thank the following people: Dr Stephen Sutton, Karen Chin, Jeremy Tan, Celeste Brash, Ah Ming, Mike and Judy Steel, Lawrence Lee, Julie and Steve Wickham, Nobutaka Iwase and family, Gavin Sham, George Hong, Perrin Lindelauf, George and Rosalyn from Kuching, Frankie See of Bintulu, Bian from Mulu, Peter and Fiona Ninnes, Reddish Aren, Sanna Raisanen, Junaidi Payne, David Lukas, Suzannah Shwer, Errol Hunt, David Connolly, Shawn Low, Robert Grani, David Bignell, Tomoko Kanamori and the whole crew from the Holiday: Mohd Asran Ahchiri, Ms Wong, Puan Rose, Samsudin, Fadzli, Ervina, Razwan, Nesly, Musnie, Jane, Martha and Belli.

MUHAMMAD COHEN

First, a salute to the strangers who pretended my Bahasa Indonesia was better than their English, and offered other kindnesses, small and large. Special thanks to my Indonesian 'family': Adelaide Worcester, Rapinah Worcester, plus Heri, Dan and

---

THE LONELY PLANET STORY

Fresh from an epic journey across Europe, Asia and Australia in 1972, Tony and Maureen Wheeler sat at their kitchen table stapling together notes. The first Lonely Planet guidebook, *Across Asia on the Cheap*, was born.

Travellers snapped up the guides. Inspired by their success, the Wheelers began publishing books to Southeast Asia, India and beyond. Demand was prodigious, and the Wheelers expanded the business rapidly to keep up. Over the years, Lonely Planet extended its coverage to every country and into the virtual world via lonelyplanet.com and the Thorn Tree message board.

As Lonely Planet became a globally loved brand, Tony and Maureen received several offers for the company. But it wasn't until 2007 that they found a partner whom they trusted to remain true to the company's principles of travelling widely, treading lightly and giving sustainably. In October of that year, BBC Worldwide acquired a 75% share in the company, pledging to uphold Lonely Planet's commitment to independent travel, trustworthy advice and editorial independence.

Today, Lonely Planet has offices in Melbourne, London and Oakland, with over 500 staff members and 300 authors. Tony and Maureen are still actively involved with Lonely Planet. They're travelling more often than ever, and they're devoting their spare time to charitable projects. And the company is still driven by the philosophy of *Across Asia on the Cheap*: 'All you've got to do is decide to go and the hardest part is over. So go!'

SEND US YOUR FEEDBACK

We love to hear from travellers – your comments keep us on our toes and help make our books better. Our well-travelled team reads every word on what you loved or loathed about this book. Although we cannot reply individually to postal submissions, we always guarantee that your feedback goes straight to the appropriate authors, in time for the next edition. Each person who sends us information is thanked in the next edition – and the most useful submissions are rewarded with a free book.

To send us your updates – and find out about Lonely Planet events, newsletters and travel news – visit our award-winning website: **www.lonelyplanet.com/contact**.

Note: we may edit, reproduce and incorporate your comments in Lonely Planet products such as guidebooks, websites and digital products, so let us know if you don't want your comments reproduced or your name acknowledged. For a copy of our privacy policy visit www.lonelyplanet.com/privacy.

friends in Tarakan; fellow travellers Campbell Bridge, Amy Marta and Liang-Ruey Tu; Marinda in Banjarmasin; Ika in Pontianak; Borneo Bob Kendall in Bali and his brother-in-law Pak Husni in Banjarmasin; and Sari of Tirian. For East Sabah, salaam to Dr Stephen Sutton, Gary Theseira, and Ioannis Gatsiounis. Most all, to my wife, who held our daughter's birth until I came home.

ACKNOWLEDGMENTS

Many thanks to the following for the use of their content:

Globe on title page ©Mountain High Maps 1993 Digital Wisdom, Inc.

Internal photographs p7 (#4) Peter Guttman/Corbis; p57 Frans Lanting/Corbis; p59 Dave Marsden/Alamy; p61 (bottom) Jay Sturdevant/Alamy; p62 Chris Fredriksson/Alamy; p64 Jeremy Horner/Alamy. All other photographs by Lonely Planet Images, and by John Banagan p5; Holger Leue p6 (#3); Jean-Bernard Carillet p6 (#2), p58; Tom Cockrem p7 (#6); Glenn Beanland p7 (#5); Christer Fredriksson p8 (#8), p61; Michael Aw p8 (#9), p59 (#6); Peter Solness p8 (#7); Mark Daffey p60; Andrew Brownbill p62 (#1); Peter Ptschelinzew p63.

All images are the copyright of the photographers unless otherwise indicated. Many of the images in this guide are available for licensing from Lonely Planet Images: www.lonelyplanetimages.com.

Index

INDEX

000 Map pages
000 Photograph pages

INDEX

INDEX

000 Map pages
000 Photograph pages

INDEX

000 Map pages
000 Photograph pages

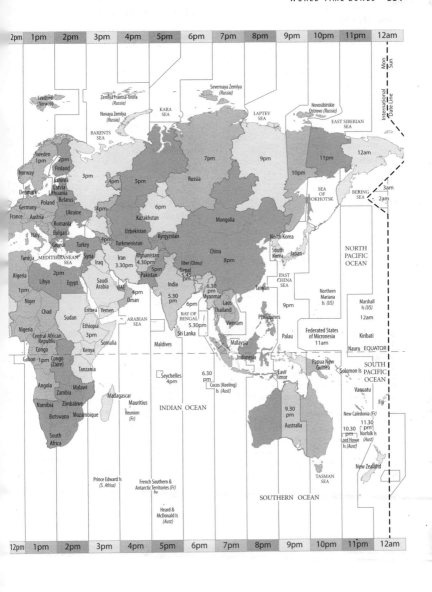

MAP LEGEND
ROUTES

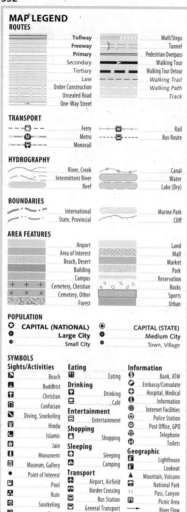

Tollway	Mall/Steps
Freeway	Tunnel
Primary	Pedestrian Overpass
Secondary	Walking Tour
Tertiary	Walking Tour Detour
Lane	Walking Trail
Under Construction	Walking Path
Unsealed Road	Track
One-Way Street	

TRANSPORT

Ferry	Rail
Metro	Bus Route
Monorail	

HYDROGRAPHY

River, Creek	Canal
Intermittent River	Water
Reef	Lake (Dry)

BOUNDARIES

International	Marine Park
State, Provincial	Cliff

AREA FEATURES

Airport	Land
Area of Interest	Mall
Beach, Desert	Market
Building	Park
Campus	Reservation
Cemetery, Christian	Rocks
Cemetery, Other	Sports
Forest	Urban

POPULATION

✪ CAPITAL (NATIONAL)	◉ CAPITAL (STATE)
● Large City	● Medium City
● Small City	● Town, Village

SYMBOLS

Sights/Activities
- Beach
- Buddhist
- Christian
- Confucian
- Diving, Snorkeling
- Hindu
- Islamic
- Jain
- Monument
- Museum, Gallery
- Point of Interest
- Pool
- Ruin
- Snorkeling
- Taoist
- Trail Head
- Zoo, Bird Sanctuary

Eating
- Eating

Drinking
- Drinking
- Café

Entertainment
- Entertainment

Shopping
- Shopping

Sleeping
- Sleeping
- Camping

Transport
- Airport, Airfield
- Border Crossing
- Bus Station
- General Transport
- Parking Area
- Petrol Station
- Taxi Rank

Information
- Bank, ATM
- Embassy/Consulate
- Hospital, Medical
- Information
- Internet Facilities
- Police Station
- Post Office, GPO
- Telephone
- Toilets

Geographic
- Lighthouse
- Lookout
- Mountain, Volcano
- National Park
- Pass, Canyon
- Picnic Area
- River Flow
- Shelter, Hut
- Spot Height
- Waterfall

LONELY PLANET OFFICES

Australia
Head Office
Locked Bag 1, Footscray, Victoria 3011
☎ 03 8379 8000, fax 03 8379 8111
talk2us@lonelyplanet.com.au

USA
150 Linden St, Oakland, CA 94607
☎ 510 250 6400, toll free 800 275 8555
fax 510 893 8572
info@lonelyplanet.com

UK
2nd fl, 186 City Rd,
London EC1V 2NT
☎ 020 7106 2100, fax 020 7106 2101
go@lonelyplanet.co.uk

Published by Lonely Planet Publications Pty Ltd
ABN 36 005 607 983

© Lonely Planet Publications Pty Ltd 2008

© photographers as indicated 2008

Cover photograph: Tarsier clinging to tree vine, Frans Lanting/Corbis.
Many of the images in this guide are available for licensing from
Lonely Planet Images: www.lonelyplanetimages.com.

All rights reserved. No part of this publication may be copied, stored
in a retrieval system, or transmitted in any form by any means,
electronic, mechanical, recording or otherwise, except brief extracts
for the purpose of review, and no part of this publication may be sold
or hired, without the written permission of the publisher.

Printed through Colorcraft Ltd, Hong Kong.
Printed in China.

Lonely Planet and the Lonely Planet logo are trademarks of Lonely
Planet and are registered in the US Patent and Trademark Office and
in other countries.

Lonely Planet does not allow its name or logo to be appropriated by
commercial establishments, such as retailers, restaurants or hotels.
Please let us know of any misuses: www.lonelyplanet.com/ip.

BIBLIO RPL Ltée

G – SEP. 2008

Although the authors and Lonely Planet have taken
all reasonable care in preparing this book, we make
no warranty about the accuracy or completeness of
its content and, to the maximum extent permitted,
disclaim all liability arising from its use.